Ireland

M Guillot/MICHELIN

"Were such scenery lying upon English shores it would
be a world's wonder. If it were on the Mediterranean or
the Baltic, English travellers would flock to it. Why not
come to see it in Ireland?"

William Makepeace Thackeray

Ireland lies at the western edge of Europe, warmed by the Gulf Stream but also liberally watered by rain from the Atlantic, which produces some of the best grassland in Europe and the title of the Emerald Isle. The scenery is dramatic – soaring mountains, towering cliffs and great sandy beaches, quiet lakes and peat bogs, forest parks and luxuriant gardens.

Despite many waves of immigration – Vikings, Normans, English and Scots, French Huguenots and other religious dissenters – Ireland has preserved a stronger Celtic tradition than other European countries; slim round towers and ancient Christian crosses recall early Irish piety and scholarship. The many ruined castles and tower houses bear witness to Ireland's turbulent history, when tribe fought against tribe or against the foreign invader. The relatively peaceful years of the 18C saw a great flowering of Irish craftsmanship which is displayed in the museums and graces the elegant Georgian buildings. Beautiful articles are still produced by men and women practising traditional skills.

The unhurried pace of life and the predominantly rural environment fosters the enjoyment of gentle country pursuits. The Irish talent for music and lively talk – known as crack *(craic)* – livens up any public gathering; whether in Dublin or in a country village no visitor is far from a convivial local bar.

While conserving its best traditions and its natural environment, Ireland offers its visitors not only a warm welcome but the benefits of a modern fast-growing economy, which exploits to the full its membership of the European Union and provides employment for its well-educated young workforce.

Contents

Key

★★★ Worth a journey

★★ Worth a detour

★ Interesting

Tourism

⊘	Admission Times and Charges listed at the end of the guide		►►	Visit if time permits
◉	Sightseeing route with departure point indicated		AZ B	Map co-ordinates locating sights
♠♣♥♦	Ecclesiastical building		🛈	Tourist information
✡ ☾	Synagogue – Mosque		⊷ ∴	Historic house, castle – Ruins
⌂	Building (with main entrance)		∪ ☼	Dam – Factory or power station
■	Statue, small building		☆ ∩	Fort – Cave
✝	Wayside cross		⊤⊤	Prehistoric site
◎	Fountain		▼ Ѱ	Viewing table – View
━●━■━►	Fortified walls – Tower – Gate		▲	Miscellaneous sight

Recreation

🏇	Racecourse		🏃	Waymarked footpath
⛸	Skating rink		◊	Outdoor leisure park/centre
⩟ ⩞	Outdoor, indoor swimming pool		🎢	Theme/Amusement park
⎊	Marina, moorings		⚘	Wildlife/Safari park, zoo
⌂	Mountain refuge hut		❋	Gardens, park, arboretum
▫━▫━▫	Overhead cable-car		⊘	Aviary, bird sanctuary
🚂	Tourist or steam railway			

Additional symbols

══ ══	Motorway (unclassified)		⊠ ⊛	Post office – Telephone centre
❶ ❶	Junction: complete, limited		✉	Covered market
▭▭ ══	Pedestrian street		⋅✗⋅	Barracks
ɪ═════ɪ	Unsuitable for traffic, street subject to restrictions		△	Swing bridge
▭▭ ‑‑‑‑	Steps – Footpath		∪ ✗	Quarry – Mine
🚆 🚌	Railway – Coach station		Ⓑ Ⓕ	Ferry (river and lake crossings)
▯+++++▯	Funicular – Rack-railway		⛴	Ferry services: Passengers and cars
━●━ ⊙	Tram – Metro, Underground		⛴	Foot passengers only
Bert (R.)...	Main shopping street		③	Access route number common to MICHELIN maps and town plans

Abbreviations and special symbols

C	County council offices		U	University
H	Town hall		M3	Motorway
M	Museum		A2	Primary route
POL.	Police		❸	Hotel
T	Theatre		🌳	Forest or Country Park

Using this guide

- The summary maps on pages 6–11 are designed to assist at the planning stage: the **Map of Principal Sights** identifies the major attractions; the **Map of Touring Programmes** outlines regional motoring itineraries; the **Map of Activities** shows a range of leisure and sporting activities and places to stay. It is worth reading the **Introduction** before setting out as it gives background information on history, the arts and traditional culture.

- The main natural and cultural attractions are presented in alphabetical order in the **Sights** section; excursions to places in the surrounding district are attached to many of the town chapters. Place names often have two versions – the English and the Irish; the official version has been adopted in this guide. There is a glossary of Irish place names in the chapter about language in the Introduction.

- The clock symbol ⊙ placed after the name of a sight refers to the Admission times and charges chapter in the **Practical Information** section, which also includes useful travel advice, addresses, information on recreational facilities and a calendar of events.

- This guide is designed to be used in conjunction with the Michelin road **Map 923** (Ireland) and **Map 986** (Great Britain and Ireland) and the Michelin Tourist and Motoring **Atlas Great Britain and Ireland**. Cross references to these maps appear in blue print under the chapter headings in the Sights section. For a selection of hotels and restaurants, consult the **Northern Ireland and Republic of Ireland** sections in the **Michelin Red Guide Great Britain and Ireland**, which also contains town plans.

- To find a particular place or historic figure or event or practical information, consult the **Index**.

- We greatly appreciate comments and suggestions from our readers. Write to us at the address shown on the inside front cover or at our website: www.michelin-travel.com

W Webster/National Trust Photographic

Principal sights

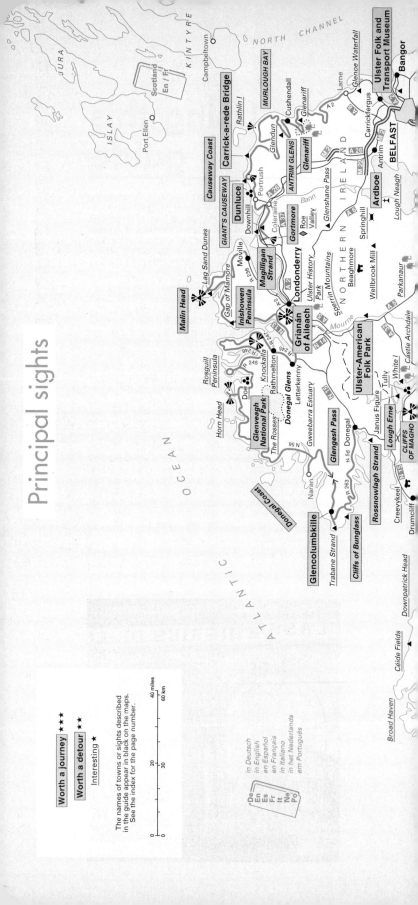

Worth a journey ★★★
Worth a detour ★★
Interesting ★

The names of towns or sights described
in the guide appear in black on the maps.
See the index for the page number.

De	in Deutsch
En	in English
Es	en Español
Fr	en Français
It	in Italiano
Ne	in het Nederlands
Po	em Português

0   20   40 miles
0   30   60 km

ATLANTIC OCEAN

NORTH CHANNEL

JURA
ISLAY
KINTYRE
Campbeltown
Port Ellen

Scotland
En / Fr

Rathlin I
Murlough Bay
Carrick-a-rede Bridge
Causeway Coast
Giant's Causeway
Dunluce
Portrush
Downhill
Coleraine
Portstewart
Glenoe Waterfall
Cushendall
Cushendun
Glendun
Antrim Glens
Glenariff
Glenariff
Larne
A 2
Glenshane Pass
Glenshane Pass
Roe Valley
Gortmore
Ulster History Park
Londonderry
Magilligan Strand
Lag Sand Dunes
Moville
Gap of Mamore
Inishowen Peninsula
Malin Head
Grianán of Aileach
Sperrin Mountains
Beaghmore
Springhill
Wellbrook Mill
Ardboe
Lough Neagh
Antrim
BELFAST
Ulster Folk and Transport Museum
Bangor
Carrickfergus
M 2
A 26
A 6
Bann
NORTHERN IRELAND
Mourne
Horn Head
Rosguill Peninsula
Doe
Knockalla
Rathmelton
Letterkenny
Gweebarra Estuary
The Rosses
Glenveagh National Park
Donegal Glens
Glengesh Pass
Naran
Donegal Coast
Glencolumbkille
Trabane Strand
Cliffs of Bunglass
Rossnowlagh Strand
Donegal
Janus Figure
Tully
White I
Lough Erne
Cliffs of Magho
Ulster-American Folk Park
Castle Archdale
Parkanaur
Creevykeel
Drumcliff
Céide Fields
Downpatrick Head
Broad Haven

N 56
N 13
N 14
N 15
R 238
R 245
R 246
A 5
A 4
A 32
A 2
A 37

Touring Programmes

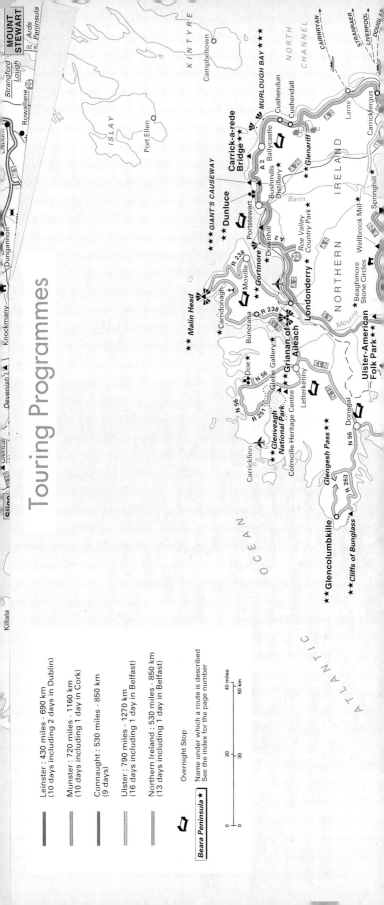

Leinster : 430 miles - 690 km
(10 days including 2 days in Dublin)

Munster : 720 miles - 1160 km
(10 days including 1 day in Cork)

Connaught : 530 miles - 850 km
(9 days)

Ulster : 790 miles - 1270 km
(16 days including 1 day in Belfast)

Northern Ireland : 530 miles - 850 km
(13 days including 1 day in Belfast)

Overnight Stop

Beara Peninsula ★ — Name under which a route is described
See the index for the page number

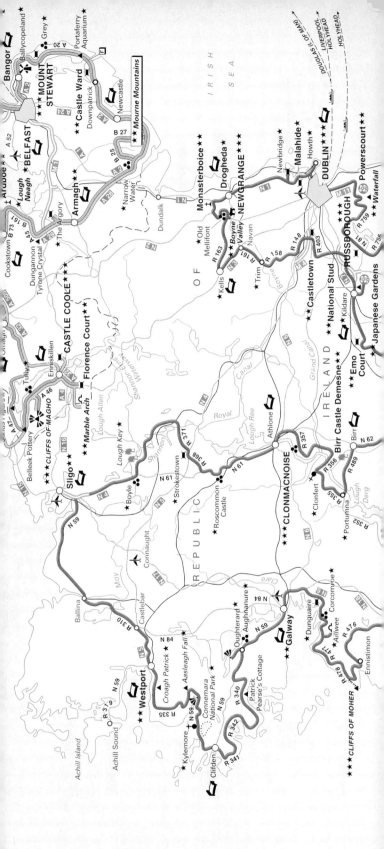

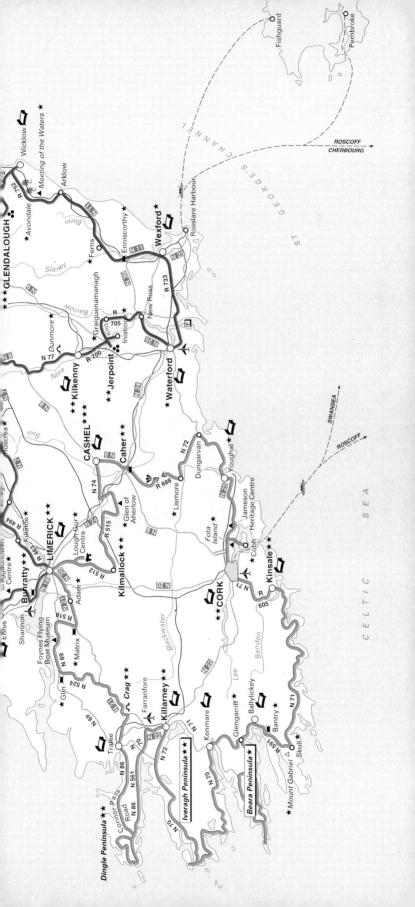

Activities

Legend:
- Overnight stop
- Sightseeing centre
- Resort
- Seaside resort
- Spa
- Marina
- Beach
- Surf
- Nature reserve
- Garden
- Golf
- Racecourse
- Greyhound track
- Waymarked footpath
- Wildlife/Safari park, Zoo
- Country park
- Forest, Forest park
- Airfield
- Airport
- Tourist or steam railway
- Fishing

OCEAN

Aranmore I

Portnoo

ATLANTIC

Killybegs

Bundora

Rosses Point

Strandhill

SLIG

Belmullet

Killala

Achill I

Ballina

Inishcrone

L Conn

R Moy

Boyle

Newport

Castlebar

WESPORT

REPUBLIC

Lough Mask

Clifden

Lough Corrib

Tuam

Cashel

IRELAND

Galway

BALLINASLOE

SALTHILL

Aran I

Loughrea

Lisdoonvarna

Ballyvaughan

Lahinch

Lough Derg

Killee

Kilrush

Killaloe

Nenagh

R Shannon

Limerick

Ballybunnion

Adare

Listowel

N 21

Tralee

N 20

Tipperary

N 8

Dingle

Cahe

KILLARNEY

Mallow

Waterville

Kenmare

Macroom

R Lee

CORK

Youghal

Castletownbere

Glengarriff

Cobh

Bantry

R Bandon

KINSALE

Bere I

Skibbereen

Clonakilty

Clear I

CELTIC

ROSCOFF   SWANSEA

0   50 km
0   30 miles

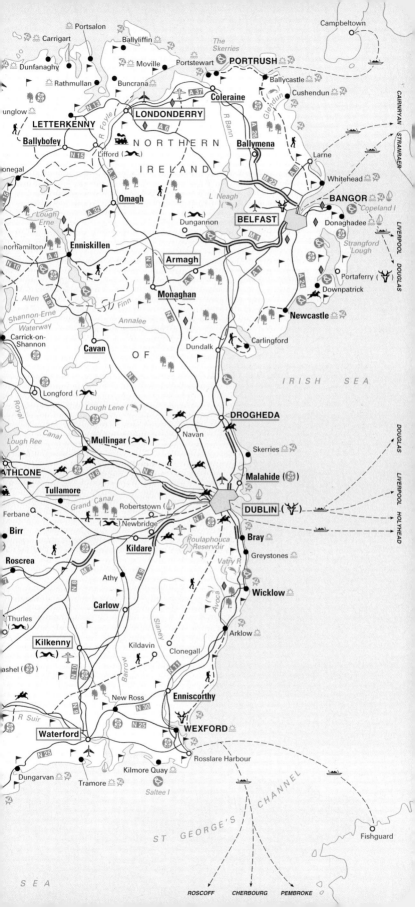

Mannin Bay, Co Galway

Introduction

Landscape

Ireland has a mild damp climate, owing to the presence of the Gulf Stream, and a high incidence of rainfall, particularly on the west coast, owing to its exposed position facing the Atlantic Ocean. The high humidity produces the vivid green landscape which prompts the title "the Emerald Isle" and favours the formation of extensive bogs which cover 15 per cent of the land mass.

Ireland is a predominantly agricultural country with few mineral deposits and little heavy industry. The peripheral highland is unbreached except by the major river estuaries and between Dublin and Dundalk where the large central lowland, a limestone area of low relief and minimal gradients, extends to the east coast.

Pre-Ice Age Formation – The oldest rocks in Ireland date from the Pre-Cambrian and the lower Paleozoic era (600–400 million years ago) when layers of marine sediments were forced upwards in great folds running northeast to southwest and domes of granite magma were intruded into the earth's crust. These granites form the Leinster Chain (Wicklow Mountains and Blackstairs Mountains) and also parts of west Donegal; much eroded, granite also surrounds Lough Conn in Co Mayo and underlies the bog in South Galway.

During the Devonian Period (395 million years ago) the highland was gradually eroded to sealevel; a new ocean flooded in causing the existing layer of sediment to harden into "Old Red Sandstone" (370 million years ago). During the next 20 million years further layers of sediment accumulated and hardened into the lower Carboniferous Limestone, the commonest rock in Ireland, which underlies the central lowland and appears as upland in South Donegal, Sligo, Leitrim and the Burren. Above it rare seams of coal were formed from layers of plant remains compressed during the upper Carboniferous period (320 million years ago).

Continental collisions (Armorican folding) in the Permian Period (280 million years ago) caused the Carboniferous rocks and the "Old Red Sandstone" to fold along an east-west axis in Southern Ireland. This movement created the highest mountains in Ireland, those in Munster which are composed of "Old Red Sandstone".

Volcanic activity early in the Tertiary era (65-54 million years ago) produced the highlands flanking Carlingford Lough (Mourne Mountains, Slieve Gullion and Carlingford Mountain). It also created the many-sided rock columns of the Giant's Causeway

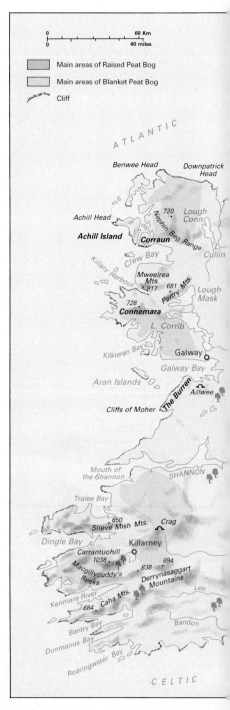

carved from thick layers of lava which hardened to form sheets of igneous rock, known as basalt, overlying the older Chalk. The area covered by the basalt has been reduced by erosion to leave the Antrim Plateau as a bog-covered tableland in Ulster.

Glacial Features – During the Ice Age (1.5 million to 10 000 years ago) the upper layers of sediments were largely eroded and the action of the glaciers created many troughs, corries and lakes, some impounded by moraines. Ice sheets also left unconsolidated deposits of clay, sand and gravel.

Long winding ridges of sandy gravel deposited by retreating glaciers are known as **eskers**; their steep sides are usually uncultivated. Eskers generally occur in chains running east-west and provide the firm ground on either bank at the major Shannon crossings – Athlone, Shannonbridge and Banagher.

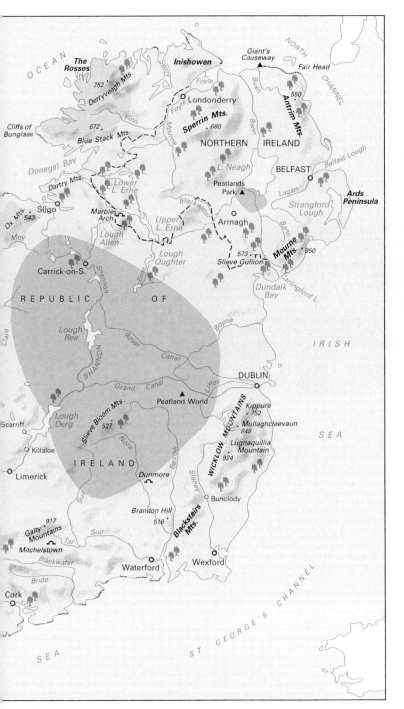

Ice sheets also moulded swarms of **drumlins**, low egg-shaped mounds with or without a core of solid rock. They are most clearly visible where they are partially submerged in Clew Bay, Lough Erne and Strangford Lough. In the drumlin country which extends from the Ards Peninsula to Donegal Bay the crests are often capped by a church or a farm; the villages and pasture descend their slopes to the reedy undrained pastures in the intervening depressions.

Sea Cliffs – In many places the mountains meet the sea in impressive cliffs. The most famous are the **Cliffs of Moher** which are especially spectacular in a westerly gale. Less extensive but equally awesome are the **Cliffs of Bunglass**. The cliffs at **Achill Head** are higher but visible only from the sea. The north coast of Mayo from **Benwee Head** (over 800ft/244m) to **Downpatrick Head** presents a variety of superb cliff scenery. At **Fair Head** the Antrim Plateau ends in a fine escarpment, in which the horizontal solidified lava flows are clearly visible.

Caves – The edges of the limestone country often favour the formation of caves. Rainwater, which is slightly acid, together with peaty streams, slowly dissolves the porous limestone, forming underground chambers and passages which are gradually enlarged by complex underground river courses. The five caves open to visitors present impressive and beautiful examples of stalactites, stalagmites and other concretions.

Rivers and Lakes – The rivers (16530mi/26600km) are of two types. Those that rise on the seaward side of the mountains and drain straight into the sea are short and steep. Those that drain inland form slow-moving lowland streams, lined by water meadows *(callows)* and punctuated by lakes where their course meets a depression, such as Lough Neagh on the **Bann** and Lough Allen, Lough Ree and Lough Derg on the **Shannon**.

Several Irish rivers have eroded their courses through rocky upland rather than flowing round it. The reason may be that the surface which originally determined the course of the river has been eroded or that the obstructing upland has been raised by earth movements so slowly that the river has not needed to alter its course. Instead of flowing west out of Lough Derg at Scarriff the Shannon makes its way south through the Killaloe Gap. Both the **Barrow** and the **Nore** describe a lazy meander through fertile farmlands and water meadows in their upper reaches, but then force a passage through the granite of the Leinster Chain at Graiguenamanagh and Inistioge where they descend into steep-sided wooded valleys. The **Slaney** does not veer southwest to join the Barrow but flows southeast through a gap in the mountains at Bunclody. The rivers of south Cork – **Blackwater, Lee** and **Bandon** – flow on parallel west-east courses before turning sharply south through several rock ridges to the sea.

In other places glacial deposits have forced rivers to change course; the Liffey adopted its northerly course when the sand and gravel of The Curragh, deposited at the end of the Ice Age, obstructed its original western course to the Barrow. The Bush in Co Antrim was similarly diverted west at Armoy.

Many Irish rivers, particularly in the south, end in drowned river valleys, where the sea water penetrates several miles inland. Waterford Harbour, a drowned river estuary, is shared by the Suir, the Barrow and the Nore, which are known as the Three Sisters. Three river estuaries are true ice-eroded **fjords** – Killary Harbour, Lough Swilly and Carlingford Lough.

Ireland's most famous and longest river, the **Shannon**, which is navigable between Carrick-on-Shannon and Killaloe, is most unusual. Owing to its lack of significant gradient and the gentle character of the flanking terrain, its slow course south has not created a well-defined valley and it frequently widens out into lakes as if in flood.

The many lakes in Ireland (357000 acres/144585ha) vary in size from a reedy pool to an inland sea. They are mostly concentrated in the west and north, particularly in the belt of drumlin country. A unique Irish feature is the **turlough** *(turlach)*, a dry lake which floods intermittently according to fluctuations in the water table.

Reservoirs have been created in the Wicklow and Mourne Mountains to supply water to Dublin and Belfast respectively.

Peat Bogs – The ecology, conservation and exploitation of peat bogs is explained at the Peatland World at Lullymore and at Peatlands Park in Co Armagh. Some raised bogland (eg Clara Bog northwest of Tullamore) is being conserved so that botanists can study the habitat. Peatlands can be dangerous; it is unwise to visit them alone or to walk on a bog as some of the pools are very deep.

Peat is an excellent preservative medium and has yielded some interesting archeological material, particularly sections of bog road which were formed by laying cut branches in the surface of the bog *(see p 219)*. Butter packed in wooden churns, **bog butter**, keeps well in peat for a few hundred years, eventually turning into a sort of cream cheese. **Bogwood** is the trunks or stumps of pine trees which grew on the bogs between 2500 BC and 2000 BC, during a decrease in rainfall, and died when the rainfall increased.

Peat is formed in water-logged basins by the accumulation of dead plants incompletely decomposed. The growth of micro-organisms which break down plant material is inhibited by the acidity of the water which is due to the presence of bog mosses (sphagnum species). **Blanket bog** occurs where the average rainfall is over 47in/

Turf cutting in Connemara

1 200mm pa (at least 235 days); it is dependent on high rainfall and humidity and is usually found in mountainous areas, particularly on the western seaboard. The bog is composed of dead grasses and sedges (depth from 6ft/2m to 20ft/6m) but very little bog moss. **Raised bog**, which is more suitable for industrial exploitation, occurs where average rainfall is 31in/800mm–35in/900mm pa; it grows above the local ground water and covers most of the central plain. The bog is mostly composed of bog moss (up to 39ft/12m in depth) which forms a dome; the surface is covered by bog plants. Owing to the shortage of timber, **hand-cut peat** has been the chief source of fuel for many centuries; most people have turbary rights on a local bog where they cut the sods by hand. First an area is drained, then the top layer containing live plants is deposited on a previously cut surface to encourage regeneration. The turfs are cut with a slane *(sleán)*, a narrow spade with a side blade set at a right angle, and laid on a spreadground to dry. The sods are turned as each side dries and then loosely stacked into footings. When thoroughly dry the sods are stacked into clamps near the house. In a fine summer a family can harvest enough fuel for several years.

Since 1946 Bord na Móna (Peat Development Authority) has developed the machinery and techniques for **mechanical peat harvesting**. The raised bogs of Ireland are expected to produce 300 million tonnes of peat before they are exhausted. After the type and extent of turf has been assessed, the bog is drained for five to seven years, levelled with a slight slope to the nearest drain, and then a light railway is laid on the surface to carry away the harvested peat. **Moss peat**, which is suitable for **horticulture** as it is less dense and retains both air and water, comes from just under the surface. It is harvested between June and December. **Sod peat**, used for **fuel**, is harvested by a machine which mixes together the peat from different levels to produce a consistent texture. **Milled peat** is scraped off the surface of the bog in fine weather and made into **briquettes** for the domestic hearth or burned in power stations.

Woodland – Originally Ireland was densely covered in trees, particularly forests of sessile oak. Clearance for agriculture began in the Stone Age. In the 17C and 18C much of what remained was cut down for building and smelting and by the British army to deny refuge to the rebellious Irish. Remnants of the native Irish oakwoods are to be found by the Upper Lake in Killarney, at Abbeyleix and at Coolattin at the southern end of the Wicklow Mountains.

The native species of tree in Ireland, which spread from southern Europe after the Ice Age, include the hawthorn, considered sacred, and the ash which is used for making hurley sticks.

The **Irish Yew**, its branches pointing upwards, is a deviation from the bushy common yew. All Irish yews are cuttings from the original tree which was found and propagated at Florence Court in 1767. They are most commonly found in graveyards but are also used to good effect in formal gardens.

In the 18C many landowners planted their demesnes with both native and exotic species; in 1735 the Dublin Society began to offer premiums for artificial planting. Among the species introduced at this time are the eucalyptus, magnolia, tree rhododendron and eucryphia, horse and sweet chestnut, beech and copper beech, Scots pine, Chilean pine (monkey puzzle tree) and Cedar of Lebanon, which was planted singly near the house so that its silhouette could be admired.

Many of the former private estates are now **Forest Parks** in public ownership. As estate incomes dwindled in the late 19C and early 20C many woods were felled for timber; by 1920 only 0.5 per cent of the land was forested. The present policy

19

Gardens

When protected from the wind in Ireland, plants will grow quickly and to a considerable height owing to the Gulf Stream and the high annual rainfall. Most are designed to take advantage of natural features but a few formal 17C gardens have survived *(see p 266)*. The Palladian mansions of the 18C were designed to be surrounded by greensward; flowers and vegetables were grown in walled gardens at some distance from the house. Shrubs and flowerbeds close to the house were introduced by the Victorians, who also created tennis courts and bowling greens; many of the 19C alterations were paid for with the proceeds from the compulsory sale of land under the Land Acts.

Pitcher plant *(Sarracena purpurea)*

Strawberry *(Arbutus unedo)*

A Giannami / Y Gladu / G Hofer / R Konig / G Laurent / C Nardin / P Petit / I Tamaud / IACANA

Bog cotton *(Eriophorum angustifolium)*

Bog heather *(Calluna vulgaris)*

of reafforestation, promoted by the forestry training centre *(see p 268)*, aims to increase the area of land covered by forest from about 8 per cent to 24 per cent, to make Ireland self-sufficient in timber and use poor land profitably; trees are suitable for drumlin soils. The best species have proved to be conifers but the planting of broad-leaf deciduous trees, particularly on cut-away bog land, is increasing.

Flora – The mild climate and heavy rainfall encourage lush plant growth. Palm trees are an unexpected sight. On the shores of the Upper Lake in Killarney the strawberry tree grows up to 30ft/9m. The Mediterranean Heath, an erica which grows to over 6ft/2m, is found in the sheltered valley east of Corraun in Co Mayo. In spring the yellow flowers of the gorse (also known as whin and furze) brighten the landscape. Later in the year fuchsias and rhododendrons grow wild in the hedgerows.

In the Burren a profusion of calcium-loving plants attracts the botanists; Arctic, Alpine and Mediterranean plants thrive in Connemara. The **shamrock** *(seamróg)*, a plant with trifoliate leaves *(trifolium minus)*, which, according to tradition, was used by St Patrick to illustrate the doctrine of the Trinity, is now the national emblem and worn on St Patrick's Day.

Irish Yew *(Taxus baccata)*

Gorse *(Ulex europaeus)*

Sessile oak *(Quercus petraea)*

Fuchsia *(Fuchsia)*

Water lily *(Nymphea alba)*

National Trust Photographic Library

Mount Stewart Garden

Fauna – There are no snakes in Ireland; according to tradition they were annihilated by St Patrick.

Skeletons of the Giant Irish Deer are on display in the Dublin and Belfast Museums but the animal itself is now extinct. The fallow deer *(see pp 223 and 312)* was introduced by the Normans; some of the present herds are confined in parks but most are wild. The only remaining native red deer are in Killarney; those elsewhere are re-introductions and in Co Wicklow they are mostly hybridized with the local Sika, a type introduced in the 19C.

Badgers are common and stoats (sometimes called weasels in Ireland) are widespread. The rarest mammal is the pine marten, which is found predominantly in Co Sligo and Co Clare. Red squirrels are found in coniferous forests; the grey has now spread from Co Longford where it was introduced in 1911.

The waterways provide a habitat for numerous otters and for the mink which has thrived in the wild since the 1960s. Both the common seal and the grey, which is more numerous, are found along the coasts.

Potatoes

The tuber, which for many years was the staple product of Irish families, was introduced, together with tobacco, in the 16C by Sir Walter Raleigh. He presented some Virginia tubers to Lord Southwell, who was responsible for the first open field cultivation of the potato in Ireland c 1580.

An obelisk commemorating this event stands in the grounds of Killua Castle, beside the road between Kells and Mullingar (N 52).

The traditional form of cultivation is known as the lazy-bed. Rows of ridges betray the site of old potato fields; in the past, pressure of population meant that the higher less productive land was cultivated.

Potatoes figure widely in Irish cooking; many menus still include colcannon and potato cakes, which often accompany a cooked Irish breakfast.

Agriculture – Since prehistoric times Ireland has raised cattle and sheep. Exports of dairy products (including a variety of cheeses), bacon, stout and whiskeys make a significant contribution to the economy. Ireland has 95 per cent of the best grassland in the European Union. As early as 1894 the Irish Agricultural Organisation Society was established by Horace Plunkett to raise dairy produce to compete with New Zealand and Denmark. Subsidies under the Common Agricultural Policy of the European Union have raised farming incomes since 1972 but may be reduced when funds are redirected to eastern European countries.

The **Golden Vale** in Co Tipperary contains prime farmland used for raising beef and dairy cattle and for growing barley, wheat and sugar beet, much of which is for cattle feed. The best grazing and fattening **pasture** in Ireland is found in the lowland along the east coast. Good **sheep pasture** is found on the bare limestone of the Plains of Galway and in Donegal, where the wool is turned into tweed and carpets. Owing to high sunshine

Flax and Linen

The pale blue fields of flax in flower are no longer a regular feature of the summer landscape but Ireland still manufactures **linen** products with linen imported mainly from Belgium.

A sandy soil is best for the cultivation of flax to produce a good linen thread; if the plant is grown for linseed, a heavy soil is better.

The process of turning flax into linen cloth uses a number of specialized terms. **Retting** means steeping bundles of cut flax upright in water for two to three weeks until the hard outer sheath has rotted; the bundles are then removed from the flax dam (also known as a lint dam), a stinking smelly job, and dried. The bundles are then passed between rollers, also known as breakers, to break up the outer sheath, and twisted into a **strick** by the **strickerman** and placed in a **strick box**. **Scutching** means holding a **strick** over a bar in the path of a wheel with five wooden blades revolving at speed to remove the outer sheath; this process was then repeated by a more experienced worker, a **bufferman**. **Beetling** is the process by which balks of woven linen cloth are passed under a row of heavy wooden hammers which flatten the threads to close up the weave and give the cloth a smooth sheen.

The many processes involved in the production of linen cloth can be traced in various museums *(see pp 136, 325 and 345)*.

duration and a light well-drained soil with a high calcareous content, central Wexford provides good **arable land**, particularly for malting barley. The best **grain-growing land** is situated in the Ards Peninsula where the farms are comparatively large.

Two-thirds of Ireland's **fruit trees** grow in the Garden of Ulster in Co Armagh (25sq mi/65m^2); strawberries are the speciality of Enniscorthy in Co Wexford.

Horse breeding – Until early this century Ireland supplied the best cavalry and carriage horses in the British Isles; horse breeding, particularly blood stock, is still an important activity, in which 12 000 (5 per cent) of the agricultural labour force is employed. The headquarters of the business is The Curragh near Kildare.

Subsistence farming – This form of farming is still practised in the Gaeltacht *(see p 38)* in such places as Connemara and the Rosses in Co Donegal, where the hay is turned by hand and the cottages are built in clusters *(clachans)* in the traditional Irish way. Transhumance, known in Ireland as **booleying** (from *buaile* meaning a milking pasture), whereby the cattle were taken up to summer pasture in the mountains, persisted in some regions until the 19C. The system of land holding known as **rundale** or **runrig** survived in the western parts of the country until the Great Famine (1845–49). Land held in common was portioned out among tenants so that all received a share of both good and poorer land; as there were no fences and one man could have strips of land scattered over up to 40 different fields, the system led to frequent disputes and the holdings were subdivided in families until each division was too small to support a man, wife and children.

Fishing – Ireland has always relied on fishing for some of its livelihood; in the Middle Ages there was considerable trade in salt fish with the Continent. In the 20 years from 1963 to 1983 Irish commercial fish-landings increased seven-fold. There are five main fishing ports in the Republic – Killybegs, Rossaveel, Castletownbere, Dunmore East and Arklow – and three in Northern Ireland – Portavogie, Ardglass and Kilkeel. Fish farming of shellfish and fin-fish such as salmon is also a growing industry in the bays and estuaries.

The mostly unpolluted lakes and rivers provide many miles of **freshwater angling**. The habitat of the salmon and the trout is found in the coastal estuaries and mountain streams. The extensive coastline provides many opportunities for **sea angling** both from the shore and by boat.

Slea Head, Dingle

Slide File, Dublin

Mining – Mining activity fluctuates from year to year as mineral deposits are exhausted or cease to be profitable. The Tara Mine in Co Meath is the largest lead and zinc mine in Europe. Coal and barytes are mined in Tipperary and slate is extracted at Portroe near Nenagh and from an underground quarry on Valencia Island.

Power – In the past in most areas **mills** and other machinery were turned by water power, except in drumlin country and Co Wexford where such power was unavailable and windmills were built.

In the 20C various hydro-electric schemes were built to produce power: in 1929 at Ardnacrushna, on the steep fall on the **Shannon** between Limerick and Killaloe, which until 1949 supplied electricity to the whole country; from 1948 to 1952 on the **Erne** at Assaroe upstream from Ballyshannon, on the **Liffey** forming the Poulaphouca Reservoir and in the **Lee** valley west of Cork. The Turlough Hill Electricity Generating Station in the Wicklow Gap, which is the only installation of its kind in Ireland, works on the pumped storage principle; to generate electricity water is pumped between two adjacent interconnecting lakes.

Since 1993, 14 per cent of the country's electricity has been provided by eight peat-burning power stations – five burn milled peat and three burn sod peat.

The wind farm at Bellacorrick in Co Mayo is to be supplemented by one in Co Kerry but another 20 are required.

Transport – Before railways and modern roads the easiest method of transport was by water. The earliest boats were cots, fashioned from hollowed-out tree trunks and used on inland waters, or curraghs like the *Brendan (see p 170)* which will ride a rough sea; St Patrick and the Celtic monks travelled great distances in such craft.

Formerly in the country districts goods were carried in shoulder creels, in donkey panniers, in sledges with wooden runners (slipes) or in carts drawn by donkeys or horses. Donkeys are still used in the west of Ireland. In an outside cart the passengers sit back to back facing the roadside; in an inside cart they sit face to face. Horse-drawn **jaunting cars** can be hired in some tourist resorts, particularly Killarney and Dublin.

Slide File, Dublin

Traditional Curraghs

Canals – Early attempts to improve the waterways concentrated on regulating the flow of rivers and cutting **canals** to by-pass shallows. The canals which began to cover Ireland from the 1750s were built with Government funds in the hope that they would promote trade. As well as heavy goods and agricultural produce they carried passengers who travelled in flyboats, towed by teams of galloping horses at an average of 8mph/13kph, and stayed overnight in the canal hotels. Anthony Trollope *(see p 61 et 102)* travelled by canal boat during his early years in Ireland; his novel *The Kellys and the O'Kellys* contains a good description of travelling by flyboat. With the arrival of the railways the canals went into decline but have since been restored for leisure use with several companies offering cruising holidays on canal barges on the Grand Canal and the Barrow Navigation.

Railways – The first **railway** was built in 1838 from Dublin to Dún Laoghaire (then Kingstown). The network soon spread with narrow-gauge (3ft/1m) lines in the rural areas (Cork, Clare, Leitrim, Cavan, Donegal and Antrim). In 1922 there were 3 454mi/5 555km of line of which 2 896mi/4 660km were built to Irish standard gauge (5ft 3ins/1.06m). By 1961 all the narrow-gauge lines had closed. The standard gauge network now consists of lines from Dublin to the larger provincial towns.

Road network – The latter part of the 20C has produced great improvements in the **road system** with the construction of by-passes and motorways. There were few roads in Ireland until the 18C when Alexander Nimmo constructed the roads from Killarney via Kenmare to Glengarriff, and from Galway to Clifden; in 1832 William Bald built the road on the Antrim Coast. Several road projects were carried out during the Famine and under the Congested Districts Board to provide work in the western counties. Modern road improvements are financed in part with EU funds.

Airports – There are three international **airports** in Ireland – Dublin, Shannon, Belfast – and several domestic airports – Carrickfin in Donegal, Connaught, Cork, Bantry, Belfast City, Farranfore near Killarney, Galway, Londonderry and Sligo.

Post-war economic development – Although Ireland itself escaped the blight of heavy industry the country profited from the 19C industrial revolution through being part of the United Kingdom. The shipyards of Belfast and car construction developed beside textiles and agriculture (food and drink). In the years immediately following independence Ireland concentrated on being self-sufficient. During the Second World War (known in the Republic as the Emergency) Ireland served the Allies as a supply base and several companies converted to the manufacture of arms. After 1945 the government of the Republic adopted a policy of attracting foreign investment.

Although Ireland has specialized in electronics and biotechnology, its major economic strength is in the chemical industry (fertilizers and pharmaceutical products) and in information technology (software, computers and semi-conductors). These "modern" activities constitute 75% of the total industrial output. Economic development has been assisted by various factors – the work of the Industrial Development Authority; investment in research and development and in education; the highly qualified Irish workforce which is among the best-educated in Europe, receives relatively low salaries and is not extensively unionized; state intervention in various forms – European subsidies granted to the Irish government; grants made to companies which set up plants in Ireland (tax relief, repatriation of profits, installation grants, tax-free zones). Progress was well advanced in 1972 when Ireland joined the European Union and the only adverse factors were the increase in the cost of oil and the competition of the countries of South-East Asia.

Since 1993 the country has experienced another period of expansion which has enabled it to join the single European currency project in the first phase; it is one of the few countries to comply with the criteria for convergence set by the Maastricht Treaty (February 1992).

The only weak points are a heavy dependence on the United Kingdom and a high rate of unemployment (between 17% and 25%). The falling birth rate will reduce the rate of unemployment and the need for emigration but the proportion of elderly people is rising. Government policy tries to foster economic activity in the rural areas, particularly on the western seaboard but 35% of the population lives in Great Dublin.

Tourism – The development of **tourism** has stimulated the development of service industries and both have made great advances together. The foreign currency earned through tourism since 1989 has covered half the deficit on the balance of payments. The rural tranquillity of the country, which is so attractive to the residents of the large conurbations of Europe, is being conserved and exploited. Fishing and golf continue to attract large numbers of visitors. The renovation of the canals has been put in hand as canal cruising is joining river cruising in popularity among tourists; in the late 1990s there were over 1 000 cruisers on the River Shannon. All-weather sites – an important consideration in a rainy climate – have been developed by roofing over some of the ruined buildings of historic significance and installing a sympathetic interpretation centre. All-weather leisure facilities – swimming baths etc – are a good investment both for tourism and for the local population.

Historical table

6000- 1750 BC	Stone Age; c 3000 BC men turned to farming from hunting and gathering.
1750-500 BC	Bronze Age.
500 BC AD 450	Iron Age; Celtic tribes arrived from Europe; inter-tribal strife for supremacy and the title of High King *(Ard Rí)*.
55 BC	Roman invasion of Britain. Roman coins and jewellery, found at Drumanagh near Dublin.
4C-5C	Irish Celts (known as Scots) colonized the west of England and Scotland.
432-61	**St Patrick's mission** to convert Ireland to Christianity.
6C-11C	Monastic age; Irish missionaries travelled to the European mainland.
795	**Viking Invasions** – Vikings from Norway and Denmark made raids on the monasteries near the coasts and waterways; in 841 they began to settle, founding Viking towns on river estuaries; they taught the Irish how to make seaworthy vessels and introduced overseas trade and coinage.
1014	**Battle of Clontarf – Brian Ború**, king of Munster, gained a Pyrrhic victory against the combined forces of the Danish Vikings and the king of Leinster. His death was followed by a decline in the power of the church and the High King.
1156	Death of Turlough O'Connor, last powerful native ruler.
1159	Henry II (1154–89) received the title "Lord of Ireland" from Pope Adrian IV and the Pope's blessing to invade Ireland.
1168	Henry II invited by Dermot, King of Leinster, to mount an expedition against Dermot's enemies; the Anglo-Normans landed in Co Wexford the following year.
1177	**Anglo-Norman** invasion of Ulster under John de Courcy.
1185	**Prince John** visited Ireland, accompanied by Gerald of Wales *(see p 228)*.
1210	**King John** again in Ireland.
1297	First **Irish Parliament** convened.
1315-18	**Bruce Invasion** – Edward Bruce, brother to King Robert of Scotland, landed at Carrickfergus with 6 000 Scottish mercenaries (gallowglasses) to prevent aid reaching Edward II of England who had been defeated at the **Battle of Bannockburn** (1314) by Robert Bruce; he was crowned king in 1316 but died at the Battle of Faughart near Dundalk in 1318.
1348-50	**Black Death** – About one-third of the population died.
1366	**The Statutes of Kilkenny** prohibited fosterage, bareback riding, hurling, the Irish language and Irish dress and patronage of Irish story tellers and poets; in 1465 the laws against Irish culture were strengthened but the attempt to maintain the distinction between the Anglo-Normans and the native Irish proved vain.

Charters

In medieval Europe, when monarchs issued charters to towns and cities, they guaranteed certain immunities from the authority of the shire and sheriff and established a borough with various rights and privileges:

- to own and dispose of property by sale or hereditary bequest;
- to commute tolls and dues and replace them with a fixed payment;
- to be a member of a guild;
- to establish a local law court;
- to enjoy a degree of self-government by appointing local officers;
- to have a seal;
- to hold a market and collect the market tolls.

An incorporated borough was a legal entity which could sue and be sued, own property and employ salaried officials to administer such public property; various towns were granted the status of county boroughs, ie equal with counties.

1394-1399	**Richard II** landed in Ireland with an army to re-establish control.
1446	First mention of **The Pale** to describe the area of English influence in the Middle Ages; by the 15C it was only a narrow coastal strip from Dundalk to south of Dublin.
1471	The Earl of Kildare first appointed **Lord Deputy**.
1487	Lambert Simnel crowned Edward V of England in Dublin by the Earl of Kildare.

1491	Perkin Warbeck, pretender to the English throne, landed in Cork without the opposition of the Earl of Kildare.
1494	Sir Edward Poynings appointed Lord Deputy: under **Poynings' Law** the Irish parliament could neither meet nor propose legislation without royal consent.
1534-40	**Kildare (Geraldine) Revolt** which brought down the house of Kildare.
1539	**Reformation** and **Dissolution of the Monasteries**.
1541	Henry VIII declared **King of Ireland** by the Irish Parliament.
1556	Colonization of Co Laois (Queen's County) and Offaly (King's County).
1579	**Desmond (Munster) Rebellion** severely crushed by Elizabeth I; confiscation and colonization.

Spanish Armada

Some 30 ships of the Spanish Armada were wrecked off the Irish coast between Antrim and Kerry. It has been estimated that they contained 8 000 sailors and gunners, 2 100 rowers, 19 000 soldiers and 2 431 pieces of ordnance. Those survivors who were not killed by the Irish were hunted by the English.

Port na Spaniagh on the Giant's Causeway marks the place where the *Gerona*, a galleass, was wrecked without survivors; some of its treasures recovered by diving on the wreck in 1968 are on display in the Ulster Museum.

On the Inishowen Peninsula at Kinnagoe Bay many interesting military relics were found in the wrecks of *La Duquesa St Anna* and *La Trinidad Valencia*. A map on the clifftop *(at the road junction)* plots the sites of the many ships of the Spanish Armada which were wrecked on the Irish coast.

Three ships *Juliana*, *La Levia* and *La Santa Maria de Vision* were wrecked at Streedagh Point, north of Sligo; over 1 300 men are thought to have died.

One of the survivors who came ashore at Streedagh, Captain Francisco de Cuellar, wrote an account of the shipwreck and of his journey from Sligo through Leitrim, Donegal and Derry to Antrim; from there he sailed to Scotland and returned via Antwerp to Spain.

1585	Ireland mapped and divided into counties; 27 sent members to Parliament.
1588	**Spanish Armada** – After its defeat in the English Channel, the Spanish Armada, driven by the wind, sailed up the east coast of Great Britain and round the north coast of Scotland. Off the Irish coast stormy weather further depleted its ranks.
1598	**Battle of Yellow Ford** – Irish victory *(see p 311)*.
1601	**Siege of Kinsale** – 4 000 Spanish troops landed in Kinsale to assist Hugh O'Neill but withdrew when besieged.
1603	Submission of Hugh O'Neill, Earl of Tyrone, and Rory O'Donnell, Earl of Tyrconnell, at Mellifont to **Lord Mountjoy**, Queen Elizabeth's Deputy.
1607	**Flight of the Earls** – The Earls of Tyrconnell and Tyrone sailed from Rathmullan *(see p 135)* into exile on the continent.
1607-41	**Plantation of Ulster** under James I in which Protestants from the Scottish lowlands settled in the northern counties of Ireland.
1641	**Confederate Rebellion** provoked by the policies of the King's Deputy and the desire of the dispossessed Irish to regain their land.
1642	**Confederation of Kilkenny** – The Irish and Old English Catholics formed an alliance to defend their religion, land and political rights.
1646	**Battle of Benburb** – Irish victory *(see p 311)*.
1649	**Oliver Cromwell** landed in Dublin to avenge the Ulster Protestants; he stormed Drogheda and Wexford and sent many of the people as slaves to the West Indies.
1657	First **Quaker settlement** established at Mountmellick in Co Offaly by William Edmundson, founder of the Irish Quaker movement; his Will was witnessed by Thomas Winsloe of Birr who played host to William Penn in 1698. Quakers were known for their industry and integrity and were the most active in providing relief during the Great Famine *(see below)*.
1653	Under the **Cromwellian Settlement** most Roman Catholic landowners judged unsympathetic to the Commonwealth were dispossessed and ordered to retreat west of the Shannon; the proportion of Irish land owned by Roman Catholics dropped to one-tenth whereas 30 years earlier it had been nearly two-thirds; by 1685 only 22% of Ireland belonged to Roman Catholics.
1658	Completion of the **Down Survey** in which the re-distribution of land under the Commonwealth was noted down *(see p 175)*.

1660	**Restoration** of Charles II who returned some land to Roman Catholic owners.
1678	**Oates Conspiracy**, which alleged the existence of a Jesuit plot to procure the death of Charles II and the succession of his brother; it was in fact invented by Titus Oates but led to the arrest and imprisonment and even the death of various Roman Catholics, among them Oliver Plunkett, Archbishop of Armagh *(see p 140)*.
1685	Revocation of the Edict of Nantes in France caused many **Huguenots** (Protestants) to flee to England and Ireland.
1688	**Glorious Revolution** – James II deposed; William of Orange accepted the English throne.
1690	**Battle of the Boyne** – King William III of England and his allies representing the Protestant interest defeated King James II of England, supported by Louis XIV of France. The Irish Army retreated west to Athlone.
1691	**Siege of Limerick** – Following the battles of Athlone and Aughrim *(see p 222)*, the Irish army again retreated to Limerick where it was besieged and surrendered. Under the military terms of the **Treaty of Limerick** the Irish defenders were allowed to surrender with honour. Eleven thousand later joined the French army; at their head was Patrick Sarsfield and they were known as the **Wild Geese**. The civil terms, guaranteeing the religious and property rights pertaining to Roman Catholics under Charles II, were not upheld by the English parliament.
1695	**Penal Laws** *(see p 36)* curtailing the power of Roman Catholics.
1765	**Edmund Burke** (1729–97), the great orator, entered Parliament as a Whig; he defined the role of an MP as a representative not a delegate; he advocated Irish free trade and Catholic relief; in his last years he was particularly concerned by Irish political questions.
1778	**Volunteers** formed to defend Ireland against the French, as English troops were withdrawn to fight in the American War of Independence; they supported the demand for an independent Irish parliament.
1782	**Repeal of Poynings' Law** and the establishment of an independent Irish Parliament, known as Grattan's Parliament after Henry Grattan who had led the campaign for independence.

Huguenots

The first Huguenots came to Ireland at the invitation of the Duke of Ormond to work in textiles in Chapelizod but the greater number came after 1685, in all about 5000. The Huguenots were Calvinists, who recognized only two sacraments, baptism and communion. In Dublin they used the Lady Chapel in St Patrick's Cathedral from 1666 to 1816; they had two burial grounds in Cathedral Lane (1668-1858) and in Merrion Row (fl 1693). They settled in Dublin, in the southeast of Ireland and in Cork.

The army of William of Orange contained about 3000 Huguenots, who played a leading role both at the Battle of the Boyne, where their leader Schomberg was killed, and at Aughrim under Ruvigny. When the Huguenot regiments were demobbed, many settled on the estate at Portarlington which had been granted to Ruvigny.

Huguenot names figure prominently in many fields of activity. In Dublin they introduced the weaving of silk and also of poplin, a mixture of wool and silk. Louis Crommelin, who came to Ireland from Picardy via Holland, was appointed to develop the Irish linen industry. In 1698 he settled in Lisburn, already home to many Huguenots, and introduced improved methods of flax cultivation and the use of water power to drive the looms.

Sir Francis Beaufort, who originated the Beaufort Scale of wind velocity, and William Dargan, who built most of the Irish railway system, were both of Huguenot descent. So too were James Gandon and Richard Cassells, who designed some of Ireland's finest buildings.

Several Huguenots were talented artists – James Tabary, designer and woodcarver, who worked with his brothers at Kilmainham Hospital; George du Noyer, a miniaturist, who worked for the Ordnance Survey and sketched archeological sites; Gabriel Béranger, who was employed by the Royal Antiquarian Society to make drawings of historical ruins.

Many performed in the theatre and concert world as composers, organists, violinists and violin makers, or as singers and dancers.

From their role as gold- and silver-smiths, a field in which they excelled, they moved into banking. The chain of the Chief Magistrate of Dublin was made by Jeremiah D'Olier in 1796; his sons and grandsons were governors of the Bank of Ireland. David La Touche III, whose grandfather arrived with William of Orange in 1690, was a merchant and banker and a founder member of the Bank of Ireland.

1791-93	**Catholic Relief Acts** *(see p 36).*
1795	Foundation of the **Orange Order** *(see p 284)* in September 1795 in a farm-house near the Diamond Hill in Co Armagh after a fight between two armed bands of tenant farmers in which the Peep O'Day Boys (Protestants) beat the Defenders (Roman Catholics). Owing to the increase in population and the competition for tenancies, the Protestants feared they would be underbid by the Roman Catholics and tried to frighten them into leaving the district.
1796	Abortive French invasion in Bantry Bay *(see p 81).*
1798	**Rebellion of the United Irishmen** launched by Wolfe Tone; the main engagements were in Antrim, Wexford and Mayo; the rising was severely suppressed and 30 000 rebels died. The movement, which was founded in 1791 in Belfast, became a secret society dedicated to the establishment of a republic when suppressed by the government in 1794.
1800	**Act of Union** – Suppression of the Irish Parliament. Ireland was represented at Westminster by 100 seats in the House of Commons and 28 temporal and four spiritual lords in the Upper House: £1 250 000 was spent in compensation (£15 000 per seat) and Union peerages were conferred to secure compliance.
1803	**Emmet Rebellion** – An abortive rising led by Robert Emmet (1778–1803), who had been a political exile in France; he counted on the invasion of England by Napoleon and support from Thomas Russell in Ulster and Michael Dwyer in Wicklow. Emmet was hanged but his speech from the dock was an inspiration for future generations of nationalists.
1823	**Daniel O'Connell** (1775–1847), a Roman Catholic lawyer, known as the Counsellor and the Liberator, campaigned for the recognition of the rights of Catholics; he was elected MP for Clare in 1828; he denounced violence and organized mass meetings to rally support for repeal of the Act of Union.
1829	**Roman Catholic Emancipation Act** enabling Roman Catholics to enter Parliament.
1848	Abortive **Young Ireland Uprising** led by William Smith O'Brien (1803–64).
1858	Founding of the **Irish Republican Brotherhood (IRB)** to overthrow British rule in Ireland; it dissolved itself in 1924.

National Gallery of Ireland, Dublin

Daniel O'Connell (1775–1847)
by George Mulvany (1809–69)

Great Famine (1845-49)

Potato blight *(phytophthora infestans)* destroyed the potato crop on which the bulk of the population depended for food; 800 000 people died of hunger, typhus and cholera; hundreds of coffinless bodies were buried in mass famine graves; thousands of starving people overwhelmed the workhouses and the depot towns from which the Indian corn imported by the government was distributed; the workhouse capacity was 100 000 but five times that number qualified for relief; the Quakers did most to bring relief to the hungry; soup kitchens were set up by compassionate landlords and by Protestant groups seeking converts; 50 large cauldrons were imported in 1847 from the Darby works in Coalbrookdale in England; public works were instituted to provide employment and relief; some landlords evicted their penniless tenants (in 1847 16 landlords were murdered), others arranged for their emigration; so many died during the voyage or in quarantine that the vessels were known as coffin ships; one million Irish men and women emigrated to England, Canada and the USA.

1867	**Manchester Martyrs** – The 'martyrs' were three Fenians who were executed for the murder of a policeman during an attack on a police van in Manchester to release two Fenian prisoners. The doubtful nature of some of the evidence led to a lack of confidence in British justice among the Irish.
1870-1933	**Land Acts** – A series of 17 acts which transferred the ownership of the large estates from the landlords to their former tenants.

29

1875-91	**Charles Stewart Parnell** (1846–91), elected MP for Meath in 1875, became President of the Land League and leader of the party campaigning for Home Rule.
1886	First **Home Rule** Bill, granting Ireland various degrees of independence in domestic matters, introduced by Gladstone but rejected by Parliament.
1869	Disestablishment of the **Church of Ireland** (Anglican).
1879-82	**Land League** formed by Michael Davitt to campaign for the reform of the tenancy laws and land purchase by passive resistance. It proposed the extension of the Ulster Custom (fair rent, free sale, fixity of tenure) to the whole country. Parnell advocated that those who opposed the Land League be ostracized; the most well-known victim of this treatment, Captain Boycott, involuntarily gave a new word to the English language.
1891-1923	**Congested Districts' Board** – Funds from the disestablished Church of Ireland were used in the poorer, mainly western, districts of Ireland to construct harbours and promote fishing, fish curing and modern farming methods; after 1903 the Board was empowered to re-distribute large estates to smallholders.
1893	Second **Home Rule** Bill introduced and rejected by Parliament.
1905-08	**Sinn Féin** (Ourselves) founded to promote the idea of a dual monarchy.

Royal Visits

In the Middle Ages royal visits were rare. King John, whose name is attached to several ruined castles, visited Ireland in 1185 and again in 1210. In 1394 and 1399 Richard II arrived with an army to re-establish control.

Although the 10th Earl of Ormond, known as Black Tom, built Ormond Castle *c*1568 to receive Queen Elizabeth, she never visited Ireland.

In 1821 George IV landed at Dún Laoghaire, renamed Kingstown in his honour. The state bedroom at Castle Coole was refurbished to receive him but he spent most of his visit at Slane Castle, as the guest of the 1st Marquess Conyngham, whose wife, Elizabeth Dennison, was his mistress. The 3rd Earl of Kingston rebuilt Mitchelstown Castle with a Royal Tower containing a bedroom for the king, but His Majesty never returned to Ireland.

The next royal visitor was his niece, Queen Victoria, who made her first tour in 1849 to Dublin, Cork and Belfast. In 1853 she returned to open the Dublin exhibition and in August 1861 she visited Killarney.

The state visit of King Edward VII and Queen Alexandra in 1907 was marred by the theft of the Crown Jewels from Dublin Castle four days before their arrival.

1912	Third **Home Rule** Bill introduced by Asquith, delayed by the veto of the House of Lords but finally signed by George V in September 1914; it was suspended for the duration of the war.
1913	**Tramway Strike** in Dublin organized by James Larkin and James Connolly .
1914-18	**First World War** in which many Irishmen fought as volunteers as there was no conscription in Ireland.
1916	**Easter Rising** – On the outbreak of war in 1914 both nationalists and unionists agreed to the postponement of Home Rule but the Military Council of the Irish Republican Brotherhood, the more militant nationalists, secretly organized an uprising. Despite the capture of Sir Roger Casement and a cargo of arms from Germany and despite a last-minute confusion in orders, the rising was not cancelled. On Easter Monday columns of Volunteers marched into Dublin and took possession of various strongpoints including the General Post Office, where they set up their headquarters; from its steps Patrick Pearse announced the establishment of a republic. The insurgents were hopelessly outnumbered and outgunned and on Saturday they surrendered. Although intended to be a national rebellion, it was confined to Dublin and failed. The insurrection had not enjoyed public support but attitudes changed when the ringleaders were tried by court martial and executed.
1917	**Sinn Féin** reorganized under Eamon de Valera as a nation-wide movement for the independence of Ireland and withdrawal from Westminster.
1918	**General Election** at which Sinn Féin candidates won 73 seats.
1919	**Declaration of Independence** drafted on 8 January and read in Irish, English and French on 21 January at the meeting of the first Irish Assembly *(Dáil Éireann)* in Dublin.
1919-21	**Irish Republican Army (IRA)** launched a campaign to make British administration in Ireland impossible; martial law was proclaimed; the Royal Irish Constabulary was reinforced by British ex-servicemen known as the Black and Tans.

1920	**Government of Ireland Act** provided for partition; the six counties of Northern Ireland remained within the UK, in accordance with the wishes of the Loyalists led by Edward Carson , with a separate parliament; dominion status was granted to the remaining 26 counties.
1922-23	**Civil War** between the Free State Army and the Republicans who were defeated; Michael Collins, who was pro-Treaty and a potential political leader, was assassinated.
1922	Constitution of the **Irish Free State** , which comprised the 26 counties; the two-tier legislature consisted of the Senate and *Dáil Éireann*.
1937	New Constitution which changed the official name of the country to **Éire** .
1939-45	**Second World War** (known in Éire as the Emergency).
1949	Éire changed its name to the **Republic of Ireland**.
1955	Republic of Ireland joined the United Nations; Irish troops involved in peace-keeping missions.
1967	Northern Ireland Civil Rights Association formed to demand reform in local government.
1969	**People's Democracy** March from Belfast to Derry. British troops sent to Northern Ireland in peace-keeping role to assist the police in maintaining law and order.
1971	**Provisional IRA** began a campaign of bombing and shooting to force the British to withdraw from Northern Ireland. Internment without trial introduced.
1972	Parliament of Northern Ireland at Stormont prorogued in March; direct rule from Westminster introduced.

1 FINGAL   2 SOUTH DUBLIN   3 DÚN LAOGHAIRE-RATHDOWN

1973	Republic of Ireland and Northern Ireland became members of the European Union (EU), then the EEC, leading to a period of agricultural prosperity and access to Community funds for development projects.
1974	Power-sharing Executive in Northern Ireland brought down by a Unionist strike.
1975	Northern Ireland Convention held; internment suspended.
1976	Collapse of the Convention; British Ambassador to Ireland killed in Dublin.
1979	Murder of Earl Mountbatten in Co Sligo and of eight soldiers in Warrenpoint.
1981	Death of hunger-strikers in H blocks protest.
1983	Failure of the All-Ireland Forum; confirmation of ban on abortion in the Republic.
1985	**Anglo-Irish Agreement** accorded the government in Dublin a limited consultative role in the administration of Northern Ireland.
1986	Confirmation of the ban on divorce in the Republic.
1991	Series of tri-partite talks set in motion by Peter Brooke, Secretary of State for Northern Ireland, involving the political parties in Northern Ireland, the British Government and the Dublin Government.
1993	**Downing Street Declaration** made jointly by the Prime Minister of the United Kingdom and the Taoiseach of the Republic of Ireland in which it was stated that the British Government had no selfish, strategic or economic interest in Northern Ireland and that the Irish government accepted that the democratic right of self-determination by the people of Ireland as a whole must be achieved and exercised with and subject to the agreement and consent of a majority of the people of Northern Ireland.
1994	Declaration by the IRA of a complete **cessation of violence** on 31 August followed by an announcement by the Combined Loyalist Military Command that they would universally cease all operational hostilities as from midnight on Thursday 13 October.
1996	**Cancellation of the ceasefire** by the IRA in February.
1997	Declaration of **second ceasefire** by the IRA; start of talks at Stormont attended by representatives of all political parties to negotiate an agreement.
1998	**Stormont Agreement** approved by referendum. Elections held for the new Assembly in Northern Ireland.

Prehistoric Ireland

The first traces of human habitation in Ireland date from c 7000 BC. Mesolithic hunter-gatherers from Britain crossed the North Channel and spread west and south. They were followed c 4000 BC by Neolithic farmers. Traces of their huts have been found at Lough Gur *(see p 206)*. They kept cattle, sheep and goats and made clearings in the forests to plant wheat and barley. A site where these Stone Age people made flint tools has been found in Glenaan *(see p 278)*.

Burial Mounds – The most visible and enduring monuments of the Neolithic people who lived in Ireland between 4000 and 2000 BC are their elaborate **Megalithic tombs**. The most impressive are the **passage tombs** at Newgrange, Knowth and Dowth in the Boyne Valley *(see p 92)*, on Bricklieve Mountain, at Loughcrew, at Fourknocks, and Knockmany. Each grave consisted of a passage leading to a chamber roofed with a flat stone or a corbelled structure, sometimes with smaller chambers off the other three sides and sometimes containing stone basins. It was covered by a circular mound of earth or stones retained by a ring of upright stones. Passage graves date from 3000-2500 BC.

The earliest Megalithic structures, **court tombs**, consisted of a long chamber divided into compartments and covered by a long mound of stones retained by a kerb of upright stones. Before the entrance was a semicircular open court flanked by standing stones as at Creevykeel *(see p 246)* and Ossian's Grave *(see p 278)*.

A third style of Megalithic tomb is known as the **portal tomb**; like Proleek *(see p 165)*, they are found mostly near the east coast of Ireland. The tomb consisted of two standing stones in front with others behind supporting a massive capstone, which was hauled into place up an earth ramp long since removed. They date from c 2000 BC. Burial chambers which are wider at one end than the other are known as **wedge tombs**; they too were covered by mounds of stones or earth retained by standing stones near the entrance. They date from c 2000 BC.

Stone Circles – Stone circles, which date from the Bronze Age (1750–500 BC), are mostly found in the southwest of the country and are usually composed of an uneven number of stones *(see pp 138, 190, 210 and 344)*. The stone circle at Drombeg *(see p 210)* seems to have been used to determine the shortest day of the year.

Standing Stones – Single standing stones also date from the Bronze Age; their purpose seems to have been to mark boundaries or the site of graves. Later generations sometimes converted them into Christian monuments by inscribing them with a cross or an Ogam inscription *(see p 34)*.

Celtic tradition

Archeological evidence suggests that the first Celts (Gaels) arrived in Ireland from the continent of Europe in the early Iron Age (3C BC), although they may have begun to arrive as early as 1500 BC, and their influence endured well into the historical period.

Farmers and Herdsmen – The Celts did not congregate in towns but established isolated settled communities in a country much covered by forest. They lived in circular homesteads, where their animals were sheltered at night. They cultivated crops in fields round the homestead but their chief wealth lay in their herds of cattle which they moved in summer up to high pastures where they built light dwellings (booleys). The Celts brought with them various culinary techniques – ale brewing, butter churning, the making of leavened bread, the use of salt, vinegar and honey to preserve food, and iron cauldrons for cooking.

Celtic Craftsmanship – Celtic craftsmen made personal ornaments, such as brooches for fastening clothes, horse harness, and sword sheaths, decorated with S- and C-shaped curves, spirals and zigzags, with basketry-work in the interstices.
Similar designs, identified by archeologists as **La Tène** after the continental Celtic centre found at La Tène which flourished during the last five centuries BC, are found on two granite monuments – at Turoe *(see p 221)* and Castlestrange *(see p 239)* – which date from the 3C BC. They are the only two such monuments to have survived in Ireland and were probably used in religious ceremonies. They resemble the Greek *omphalos* at Delphi, a site raided by the Celts in 290 BC.

Religion – The Celts seem to have acknowledged many gods, one of whom was the tribal god and varied from tribe to tribe, and they regarded certain trees, wells, springs and rivers – particularly the River Boyne – as sacred. Their priests, the druids, who took precedence in society, trained for many years (12–20) and learned all their lore by heart. They read omens in animal entrails or the flight of birds. They also performed sacrifices of animals after a victory and sometimes of human beings, when a criminal was the preferred victim. There were four great feasts in the year: Imbolg (1 February), Bealtaine (1 May), Lughnasa (1 August) and Samhain (1 November). Assemblies, at which games and races took place, were held at ancient royal or assembly sites such as Tara and Tullaghoge. The Celts buried their dead, sometimes cremated, with offerings of food and ornaments; they believed that after death they went to join their ancestors, the gods of the Otherworld, who were thought to live in sacred mounds, now known to be prehistoric burial mounds such as at Newgrange and Tara.

National Museum of Ireland, Dublin

Tara Brooch (8C)

Celtic Society – In addition to their priestly office the druids had two others. As judges *(brithem)* they interpreted the Brehon law which provided a scale of compensation for wrongdoing, even murder, payable by the kin of the malefactor; the code also recognized fasting with witnesses in front of the house of a malefactor as a means of redress. As genealogists, historians and poets *(filid)*, they recorded the history of the clan; the training for this role was conducted by Bardic schools. The Celts were grouped in clans *(túath)* which were divided into families *(derbfine)*. There was no primogeniture; members of three generations – uncles, brothers, nephews as well as sons of the king – were eligible to succeed to the kingship of the clan. It was the custom for sons to be fostered out with other families during their youth; this practice created another strand in the complex pattern of loyalties.

Heroic Exploits – The Celts were great warriors; their weapons, spearheads or swords, were made of iron or bronze. In the 4C and 5C the Irish Celts (known as Scots) combined with the Picts from north of the Antonine Wall in Britain to raid Roman Britain; Irish colonies were established in the Isle of Man, Cornwall and Wales. Late in the 5C the sons of Erc from the kingdom of Dál Riada in Antrim established a second Dál Riada in Argyll, which by the mid 9C had expanded to cover the whole of Scotland. The Celts' exploits in battle – family feuds over succession, inter-tribal cattle raids or foreign invasions – were celebrated by the bards in verse and song. There are four cycles of ancient Irish sagas.

The **Mythological Cycle** tells of the heroes or gods who inhabited Ireland before the arrival of the Celts and contains the stories of the Battle of Moytura, the Children of Lir and the Wooing of Etain.

The **Ulster Cycle** recounts the deeds of the **Red Branch Knights** of Navan Fort; it includes the **Cattle Raid of Cooley** (Táin Bó Cuailgne), an epic poem which describes how Queen Maeve of Connaught set out to capture the famous Brown Bull of Cooley and how Ferdia, the Connaught champion, was defeated by **Cúchulain**, the Ulster champion. The **Ossianic Cycle** (also known as the Fenian Cycle) is set in the reign of Cormac mac Airt, who is said to have reigned at Tara in the 3C, and tells about Fionn mac Cumhaill and the Fianna whose capital was on the Hill of Allen.

The **Historical Cycle**, which is also known as the Cycle of Kings, is probably a mixture of history and fiction.

Ogam Stones – Ogam script based on the Latin alphabet began to be used in Ireland about the 4C (Ogmios was the Celtic god of eloquence). It consists of 20 characters written as groups of a maximum of five straight lines on either side of or horizontally or diagonally through a central line which was usually the vertical edge of a standing stone.

Most Ogam inscriptions are commemorative inscriptions of the 4C to 7C but the script continued in use until the 8C or later. Ogam stones have been found not only in Ireland (300) but also in the west of Great Britain.

Slide File, Dublin

Turoe Stone

Christianity in Ireland

Although the majority of the population of Ireland (75%) is Roman Catholic, most of their churches are of recent date and are built in the new centres of population or next to a ruined monastery, where the faithful heard mass in the Penal Days and where they often continue to be buried. As a result of the Reformation *(see below)* the traditional religious sites are usually occupied by the Church of Ireland, a member of the Anglican Communion. In the north the Presbyterian Church predominates. Methodism has a limited following. Huguenots, Protestants from France, settled in the south and east after the Revocation of the Edict of Nantes in 1683. In the past the Quakers, who first settled at Rosenallis in Co Laois in the 17C, played a significant social role.

Christianity was probably introduced to Ireland from Roman Britain or Gaul in the 4C. Palladius, the first bishop, was appointed in 431 by Pope Celestine I but his mission met with little success; the sites of three of his churches have been identified in Wicklow.

St Patrick – The patron saint of Ireland was born on the west coast of Roman Britain where he was captured as a young man by Irish raiders. After six years of slavery near Slemish, he escaped to France and then returned to his birthplace. Inspired by a vision that the people of Ireland were calling him, he went to France to study, possibly at the monasteries of Lérins, Tours and Auxerre. In 432 in middle age he returned to Ireland to convert the people to Christianity. He is thought to have founded his first church at Saul and then travelled to Slane to challenge the High King and the druids of Tara. He worked widely in Leinster, Meath and Connaught. In 444, after a visit to Rome, he founded the cathedral church of Armagh, which is still the ecclesiastical capital of Ireland. St Patrick founded many churches and created numerous bishoprics; when he died, probably at Saul in 461, the country was organized into dioceses, which coincided with the petty Irish kingdoms, each ruled by a bishop.

Celtic Church – As continental Europe was overrun by barbarians, the church in Ireland developed a distinctive form of organization based on monasticism. In the mid 6C and 7C a great many monasteries were founded and by the 8C the administration of the church had been taken over by the abbots. Bishops continued to perform the sacramental duties but new bishops were consecrated but not appointed to particular sees.

Some **monasteries** grew up round a hermit's retreat but many were founded by the head of a clan; members of the family entered the religious life and filled the various

Ardagh Chalice (8C)

National Museum of Irelande

offices, as abbot, bishop, priest, teacher or ascetic. The manual work was done either by the monks or by the original tenants of the land, married men with families, whose elder sons usually received a clerical education in the monastery school. Most monasteries were self-sufficent communities providing their own food, clothing, books, tools and horses. Some monasteries seem to have been founded on sites which had pagan religious associations; others were set up by the main highways, often on the boundaries of a kingdom.

There were few nunneries, possibly because **women** had less access to independent land or funds. Kildare was the most famous; at Clonmacnoise there was a separate church for women built outside the precinct.

The monastic **libraries** contained copies of the Scriptures, the early Fathers, some classical authors and some history; much early Christian scholarship was preserved in Ireland after the fall of the Roman Empire. In the scriptorium the monks made copies of existing texts or wrote their own learned works. They prepared their own materials – vellum, pens, ink and coloured pigments; their techniques are well described and illustrated at the Colmcille Heritage Centre *(see p 136)*. Important books such as

Irish Missionary Monks

In the period known as the Dark Ages, the early years of the second millenium, the monks of the Irish Celtic church travelled great distances overseas in the service of God; some were driven out by the Viking invasions. The one who went furthest was probably **Brendan** *(see p 170)* who may have reached America. **Patrick**, the patron saint of Ireland, went to study in the south of France. Bangor Abbey sent out many missionary monks – **Columbanus**, who travelled from Bangor in 590 to Luxeuil in northern France and then on to Bobbio in Italy where he died in 615; **Gall**, a disciple and companion of Columbanus, founded a church in Bregenz on Lake Constanz and gave his name to St Gall – the monastery contains a fine collection of early Irish manuscripts; **Rubha** sailed to Britain in 671 and founded Applecross in Scotland. There was a strong link with Iona in Scotland; **Columba** (Colmcille in Irish), who was born in Donegal *(see p 136)* left his native country to found a monastery in Iona. In c 635 **Aidan**, an Irish clerk from Iona, moved to Lindisfarne, in the north of England. Another monk of Iona was **Adomnán**, who became 9th Abbot of Iona in 679 and died there in 704; he was born in Ireland c 628 and he wrote a life of Columba, from whose grandfather he was descended; he pursuaded the church in Northern Ireland, but not Iona, to reject the Celtic calendar and customs; in 697 his law was enacted at Birr for the protection of women, children and clergy, especially in time of war. **Dicuil** went first to Iona and thence in 800 to the court of Charlemagne in France; he wrote about grammar, astronomy and geography. **Fursey** (Fursa) went from Ireland to East Anglia but ultimately he settled in northern France, where he founded a monastery at Lagny near Paris and, after his death in 648, he became patron of the monastery of Péronne, which was founded near his tomb; another who settled in France was **Johanne Eriugena**, who lived in Laon in the second half of 9C; he was called the most important philosopher in the west between Augustine and Thomas Aquinas; **Sedulius Scottus** settled in Liège in the mid 9C but was also associated with Cologne. Several went to Germany and beyond – **Kilian** to Wurzburg in Germany *(see p 191)*; **Mariannus Scottus** in the 11C to Cologne, Fulda and Mainz. Another of the same name **Mariannus Scottus** (Muiredach MacaRobertaig), a member of an important Donegal family, founded the Irish monastery of St Peter in Ratisbon, where he died 1088. **Virgil** (Fergal) left Ireland in 742 and travelled via France and Bavaria to Austria, where he became patron of Salzburg. **Donatus** fled from the Vikings in the 9C and travelled as far as Fiesole in Italy.

the Gospels were beautifully illuminated; such **illuminated work** is on display in the Library of Trinity College in Dublin. Leather satchels were made, in which the books could be hung from hooks to protect them from mice and damp. In their **schools** the monks taught church Latin and the study of religious texts.

Irish monks developed a strong tradition of **asceticism** with a threefold classification of martyrdom. White martyrdom meant parting from all they loved, withdrawing from society or going into exile to serve God; green was to endure labour in penitence and repentance, and red involved submission to the cross or tribulation. Ascetics seeking to contemplate the presence of God would form small monastic communities in remote places, particularly on islands. The monastic community on Great Skellig eminently fulfils this need; there was little here for the monks to do except gardening and fishing, and the island is accessible only in fine weather.

Romanization – Following four synods held in the first half of the 12C the Irish church was gradually reorganized on the Roman pattern. Four provinces and 33 new dioceses were created, each with a bishop. Some monastic churches became cathedrals, others were used as parish churches.

Monastic orders from the continent were introduced. The Augustinians took over earlier monastic centres to be near the people. The Cistercians chose new and remote sites in accordance with their ascetic rule which attracted many Irish monks; by 1272 there were 38 Cistercian houses in Ireland. The Franciscans settled in the towns in the 13C; in the 15C the Observants spread to the west and north.

The Irish church was further diminished by the Normans with the encouragement of King Henry II and Popes Adrian IV and Alexander III so as "to extend the bounds of the Roman Church". Under the Statute of Kilkenny (1366) Irishmen were forbidden to enter English-run monasteries, and English-speaking clergy were to be appointed to English-speaking parishes.

Reformation – In the 16C the churches in England and Ireland were declared independent of Rome; the monasteries were suppressed. Trinity College in Dublin was founded in 1591 to provide Irish priests for the established church; although Roman Catholics were admitted to degrees in 1793, membership was confined to Anglicans until 1873. The 16C reforms were only intermittently enforced in Ireland; the majority of the people remained faithful to the Roman church and many monasteries continued until suppressed by Cromwell. Early in the 17C the Plantation of Ulster with lowland Scots introduced fervent Presbyterianism.

Penal Laws – Under the repressive measures introduced after the Battle of the Boyne (1690), Roman Catholics were barred from the armed forces, law, commerce, from civic office or office under the crown, from land purchase; Roman Catholic estates could pass in toto to an eldest son if he converted to the established church but otherwise had to be divided among all the sons. No Roman Catholic could attend school, keep a school or go abroad to school. All Roman Catholic bishops and regular clergy were banished from Ireland, and Roman Catholic worship was forbidden. Roman Catholic priests travelled the country in disguise and said mass out of doors in remote places or in ruined monastery churches; they used sacramental vessels which could be dismantled to avoid detection. Education was conducted in **hedge schools** which taught Latin, Greek, arithmetic, Irish, English, history and geography; the masters, who were paid in money or kind, were respected members of the Irish community; several were poets.

Denominational Freedom – Under the Catholic Relief Acts of 1791 and 1793, freedom of worship and education were granted. In 1795 **Maynooth Seminary** was established for training Roman Catholic clergy. In 1820 Edmund Rice (1762–1844), a former pupil of a hedge school, obtained papal recognition of the **Christian Brothers** (see p 198), an order which established many boys' schools in Ireland. In 1831 the 18C hedge schools were replaced by the National Schools. In 1869 the Church of Ireland, a member of the Anglican Communion, was disestablished. Apart from Trinity College and two short-lived 16C colleges at Maynooth and Galway, Ireland had no medieval universities. In 1845 charters were issued to incorporate three colleges in Belfast, Cork and Galway but, owing to Roman Catholic opposition, only Queen's College in Belfast thrived. The Catholic University, founded in Dublin in 1854 with Cardinal Newman as Rector, was incorporated as University College when the National University of Ireland was founded in 1908; two years later Maynooth was also recognized as a college of the National University.

Pilgrimages and Patterns – Many old religious sites are still visited by pilgrims on saints' feast days: in Glencolumbkille on St Columba's Day (9 June); at Clonmacnoise on St Kieran's Day (9 September); at Croagh Patrick in July. The most rigorous pilgrimage takes place at St Patrick's Purgatory, an island in Lough Derg (southeast of Donegal) where St Patrick spent 40 days in prayer and fasting; during the season (1 June to 15 August) pilgrims spend three days barefoot, take part in an all-night vigil and exist on one meal a day of bread and hot black tea or coffee.

A **pattern** (the word is a corruption of patron) is a communal visit to a holy well under the protection of the local patron saint. Prayers are said; coins, flowers and pieces of cloth are left as tokens of gratitude or hope. In the past these holidays were celebrated with drinking and often ended in fighting and disorder.

Gaelic heritage

17C Decline – Until the 16C the population of Ireland spoke Gaelic, a development of Goidelic, the language of the Ogam inscriptions, which was introduced by Celts from the Continent. The first documents in Irish in Latin writing date from the 7C, although a list of Irish names appeared in Ptolemy's Geography in AD 150. The decline in the use of the Gaelic language was caused by the gradual imposition of English law and administration in the 16C and the repressive clauses of the Penal Laws *(see p 36)* in the 17C. Many Irish people turned to English to achieve a position in society. This trend was accelerated by the teaching of English in the National Schools which were set up in 1831. During and after the famine (1845–47) many Gaelic speakers died or emigrated; in 1835 half the population was estimated to speak Gaelic; in 1851 one-quarter of the population was recorded as Gaelic-speaking; by 1911 the number had fallen to one-eighth.

19C Revival – The 19C saw a revival of interest in Ireland's Gaelic heritage, which was closely linked with nationalist politics. Various societies were set up to promote the Gaelic language and culture.

SLIDE FILE

Hurling

One of the earliest was the **Gaelic Athletic Association** *(Cumann Lúthchleas Gael)*, a largely rural movement, founded in 1884 in Thurles; the principal games fostered are hurling *(iománaíocht)*, Gaelic football *(peil)* and handball *(liathróid láimhe)*. The national GAA stadium, Croke Park in Dublin, is named after the association's first patron, Archbishop Croke (1824–1902).

Hurling

Hurling has been played in Ireland for over 2 000 years. It features in Irish myth, as an aristocratic, even royal, game and is mentioned favourably in early legal documents. It was banned by the Statute of Kilkenny (1367) and again by the Galway Statute (1537) but it remained popular despite fines and imprisonment. By 1600 it was again in favour with the authorities and greatly patronized by the landlords until the Rebellion in 1798. It then fell into decline until the establishment of the GAA.

Hurling is played with a curved stick, a hurl *(camán)* made from ash, and a ball *(sliothar)* made of animal hair covered in leather, on a rectangular pitch (150 x 90 yd – 137m x 82m) by two teams, each consisting of 15 men – six backs, two midfield players, six forwards and a goalkeeper. The game lasts an hour, ie 30min each half, and is supervised by a referee, two linesmen and four umpires. There are two goals, one at each end, consisting of two uprights held apart by a crossbar to form an H; one point is gained when the ball passes over the bar; three points when the ball goes under the bar. The ball may be lifted or struck with the *camán* on the ground or in the air; it may be juggled or carried on the *camán* or kicked or caught in the hand.

In 1892 the **Irish Literary Society** was founded in London at Yeats' father's house. WB Yeats was joined by Edward Martyn and Lady Gregory and in 1899 the society became the **Irish Literary Theatre** (later the Irish National Theatre at the Abbey Theatre); George Moore returned to Dublin especially to take part in the new movement. In 1893 the **Gaelic League** *(Conradh na Gaeilge)*, a non-sectarian and non-political organization was founded by Douglas Hyde *(see p 90)* for the "de-Anglicisation of Ireland" through the revival of Gaelic as a spoken language and a return to Irish cultural roots. It was largely an urban organization which instituted an annual festival of native culture and campaigned for St Patrick's Day (17 March) to be a national holiday.

The **Gaelic Summer Schools,** which were started then, have become a permanent feature of the Gaelic-speaking districts, inspiring and entertaining each new generation. In 1909 Gaelic became a compulsory subject for matriculation to the National University.

Gaeltacht – This is the name given to the parts of the country where people still speak Gaelic. Most of them are in the most sparsely populated and beautiful regions of Ireland, on the west coast – Donegal, Mayo, Galway and Kerry – and in pockets in the south – near Cork, in Co Waterford and Co Meath.

In 1922 the Constitution stated that Gaelic was an official language and its study was made compulsory in primary schools. In 1923 it became an obligatory qualification for entry into the Civil Service of the Irish Free State.

In 1925 in order to foster the use of Gaelic the new Irish government set up a Commission to investigate conditions in the Gaeltacht; as a result of its report **Gaeltarra Éireann** (1935) and **Údarás na Gaeltachta** (1980) were established to develop the resources of the Gaelic-speaking regions.

With the help of Government sponsorship the **Folklore of Ireland Society,** still in existence, was founded by Douglas Hyde and other folklore scholars and enthusiasts. The **Irish Folklore Commission** was founded in 1935 for the collection, preservation and publication of Irish folklore; it became the Department of Irish Folklore, when its staff and holdings were transferred to University College Dublin in 1971.

In 1928 further state sponsorship enabled the **Irish Theatre** *(Taibhearc na Gaillimhe)* to be launched by Micheál Mac Liammóir and Hilton Edwards, joint founders of the Gate Theatre in Dublin. The following year Queen's College Galway became a bilingual institution and a Gaelic Faculty was established. Under the Constitution of 1937 Gaelic was named as the first offical language before English.

In 1972 *Siamsa Tíre,* which had been set up in Tralee in 1968, became the **National Folk Theatre of Ireland;** its name derives from *siamsa,* an Irish word which describes the old Irish custom of visiting one's neighbours in the evening for entertainment. Also in 1972 the **Gaelic Radio Service** *(Radió na Gaeltachta)* was started; the Irish language television station *(Telefís na Gaeilge)* was started in October 1996. Irish literature has been translated into many languages. Some of the best-known authors include the Connemara-born Máirtín Cadhain, former professor of Irish at Trinity College, whose novel *Cré na Cille* (1949) *(The Clay of the Graveyard)* is the best-known prose writing in recent times. The authors of the Great Blasket Island, off the coast of Co Kerry, have produced numerous works describing island life before the island became uninhabited in the early 1950s. Modern Irish poetry, composed by Seán O Ríordéin, Máirtín O Direáin and Nuala ní Dhomhnaill among others, has appeared in a number of languages.

PLACE NAMES

Certain elements occur very frequently in Irish place names and most have a clear meaning.

Alt − cliff

Ard − high, height, hillock

Áth − ford

Bád − boat

Baile − town, townland, homestead

Bán − white, fair; grassland

Beag − little

Béal − opening, entrance, river mouth

Bealtaine − 1 May, month of May

Beann − peak, pointed hill, horn, gable

Beannchair − abounding in peaks or gables

Bearna − gap

Beith − birch tree

Bile − venerated tree

Bó − cow

Boireann − large rock, rocky district

Both − hut, tent

Bóthar − road

Buí − yellow

Bun − end, bottom

Cabhán − hollow

Caiseal − castle, circular stone fort

Caisleán − castle

Caladh − harbour, landing place, marshy

Capall − horse

Carraig − rock

Cath − battle

Cathair − circular stone fort, city

Cealtrach − old burial ground

Céide − hillock

Cill − church

Cillín − little church, children's burial ground

Cliath − a hurdle

Cloch − stone

Cluain − meadow

Cnap − knob, round little hill

Cno − hill

Coinicéar − rabbit warren

Com − mountain recess

Dairbhre − oak-grove

Dearg − red

Díseart − desert, hermitage

Doire − wooded area

Droichead − bridge

Droim − ridge, hillock

Dubh − black

Dún − fort

Eaglais − church

Eas − waterfall

Eiscir − ridge of high land

Eochaill − yew wood

Fear − man

Fearbán − strip of land

Fionn − white, fair-haired person

Fir − men

Gall − foreigner

Gorm − blue

Gort − field

Inbhear − river mouth

Inis − island

Iúr − yew tree

Lár − centre

Leithinis − peninsula

Lios − circular earthen fort, ring fort

Mór − large

Móta − moat, high mound

Muc − pig

Muirbheach − level stretch of sandy land along the seashore

Muireasc − seaside marsh meadow

Óg − young

Oileán − island

Omhna − tree, tree-trunk

Poll − hole, cave

Ráth − earthen rampart

Rinn − point of land

Sagart − priest

Sceir − sharp rock

Sean − old

Sí − bewitching, enchanting; fairy mound

Slí − route, way

Sliabh − mountain

Sruth − stream

Teach − house

Teampall − church

Tobar − well

Tóchar − causeway

Trá − beach, strand

Túr − tower

Turlach − winter lake

Uachtar − top, upper part

Irish diaspora

Forty million people of Irish descent live in the USA, 5 million in Canada, 5 million in Australia, unnumbered millions in Great Britain. There are numerous organizations in Ireland involved in tracing ancestors.

The first transatlantic emigrants were mostly Presbyterians, the Ulster-Scots (known in the USA as Scotch-Irish), descendants of lowland Scots who had settled in Ulster in the 17C. They emigrated early in the 18C owing to religious disability.

Ulster-Scots – Scotch-Irish

Theodore Roosevelt's mother, speaking of her family who came from Co Antrim, described them as "a grim stern people, strong and simple, powerful for good and evil, swayed by gusts of stormy passion, the love of freedom rooted in their very hearts' core ... relentless, revengeful, suspicious, knowing neither ruth nor pity; they were also upright, resolute and fearless, loyal to their friends and devoted to their country".

The Scotch-Irish had an influence in America out of all proportion to their numbers, particularly in the War of Independence and in education. Over a quarter of the Presidents of the USA are descended from Scotch-Irish settlers. This Irish-American connection is traced in detail at the Ulster-American Folk Park *(see p 346)* and Andrew Jackson Centre *(see p 300)* as well as several other family homesteads. Several allied military leaders in the Second World War were of Ulster stock: Alanbrooke, Alexander, Auchinleck, Dill and Montgomery.

The much greater wave of emigrants in the 19C was largely composed of Roman Catholics from Donegal, Connaught, Munster and Leinster fleeing from the famine in the 1840s. Many landed first in Canada but later crossed the frontier into the USA to escape from British rule. Their descendants include John F Kennedy, Ronald Reagan and Bill Clinton.

The numbers who emigrated to Australia and New Zealand were smaller and included some who were transported to the penal colonies.

The flow of immigrants into Great Britain has waxed and waned since the Irish established colonies in Wales and Scotland in the 5C. Many, particularly those who left Ireland during the Famine in the hope of reaching America but were too weak or penniless to continue, settled in Liverpool and Glasgow. London has a flourishing Irish community, particularly north of the river. Margaret Thatcher, Prime Minister of the United Kingdom (1978–91), is descended from Catherine Sullivan who emigrated in 1811 from Kenmare and became a washerwoman in England.

In the 18C and 19C many Irishmen, who went to work in Britain on the canals or in agriculture and the building trade, returned home for the winter. Irish emigrants in the late 20C are highly qualified young men and women seeking employment not only in English-speaking countries such as Great Britain and the USA but also throughout the countries of the European Union. In recent years emigration has declined and immigration has increased. In 1997 there was a net inflow of 15 000 people, the highest such figure since the 1970s. Many of these people are the same highly qualified former emigrants, returning to the higher standards of living and new culturally revitalised society of modern Ireland.

A project is in progress throughout the country to collect all information available from parish records, tombstones and other sources. Access to these computer records and assistance in tracing ancestors can be obtained through the many regional Genealogical Centres (see p 365).

There are 243 Irish clans which hold annual clan gatherings on ancestral sites.

Architecture

Prehistoric

The earliest surviving Irish buildings were composed of courses of **dry stones** laid without mortar. To form a roof, as in a round **beehive hut** *(clochán)*, the stones were laid to overlap each other in diminishing circular courses until they met in the centre; this **corbelling** technique was later also used in rectangular buildings to form gable roofs. The early inhabitants built **stone forts** *(cashels)* to protect their cattle from raiders; these stone precincts were sometimes occupied by early Christian monastic communities, who built stone churches and huts within the enclosure.

NEWGRANGE PASSAGE GRAVE – Interior of roof – 3000 BC

BEEHIVE STONE HUT – Pre-Christian and later

STONE FORT – Pre-Christian and later

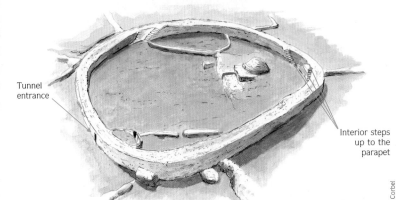

Tunnel entrance

Interior steps up to the parapet

R. Corbel

ECCLESIASTICAL BUILDINGS
6C to 12C

KILMACDUAGH ROUND TOWER – 7C

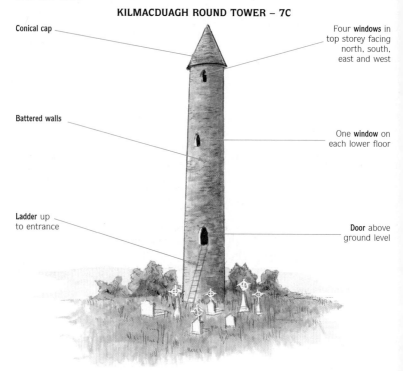

Conical cap

Four **windows** in top storey facing north, south, east and west

Battered walls

One **window** on each lower floor

Ladder up to entrance

Door above ground level

Romanesque (Norman)

CLONFERT CATHEDRAL, Co Galway – West door – 12C

The inner arch immediately surrounding the door is 300 years later than rest of doorway, which consists of five rows of columns and five rows of round-headed arches framing the door, surmounted by a hood moulding containing a triangular pediment, the whole capped by a finial.

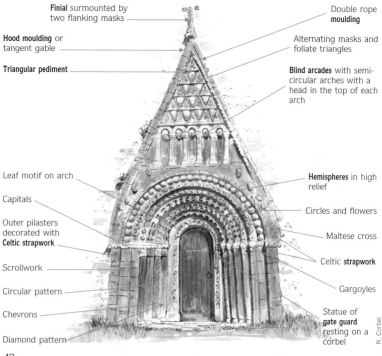

Finial surmounted by two flanking masks

Double rope **moulding**

Hood moulding or tangent gable

Alternating masks and foliate triangles

Triangular pediment

Blind arcades with semi-circular arches with a head in the top of each arch

Leaf motif on arch

Hemispheres in high relief

Capitals

Circles and flowers

Outer pilasters decorated with **Celtic strapwork**

Maltese cross

Scrollwork

Celtic **strapwork**

Circular pattern

Gargoyles

Chevrons

Diamond pattern

Statue of **gate guard** resting on a corbel

R. Corbel

Medieval

JERPOINT ABBEY, Co Kilkenny – 12C with 15C tower

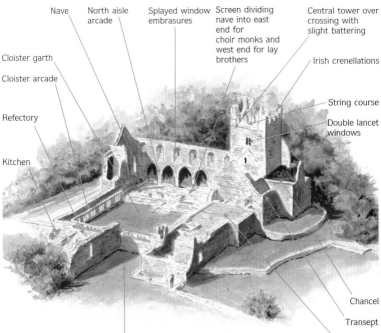

Nave

North aisle arcade

Splayed window embrasures

Screen dividing nave into east end for choir monks and west end for lay brothers

Central tower over crossing with slight battering

Cloister garth

Cloister arcade

Irish crenellations

Refectory

String course

Double lancet windows

Kitchen

Chancel

Transept

Calefactory (warming room)

Chapter House

Gothic

ST PATRICK'S CATHEDRAL, Dublin – 13C

Construction begun in the Early English style but extensively restored in the 19C.

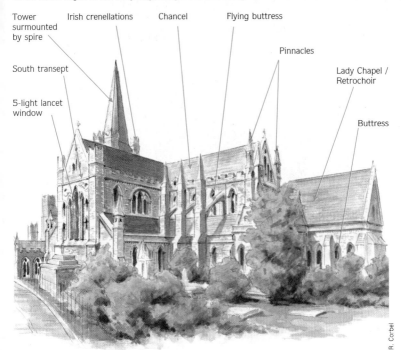

Tower surmounted by spire

Irish crenellations

Chancel

Flying buttress

Pinnacles

South transept

Lady Chapel / Retrochoir

5-light lancet window

Buttress

R. Corbel

Neo-Classical

CHRIST CHURCH CATHEDRAL, Waterford – 18C

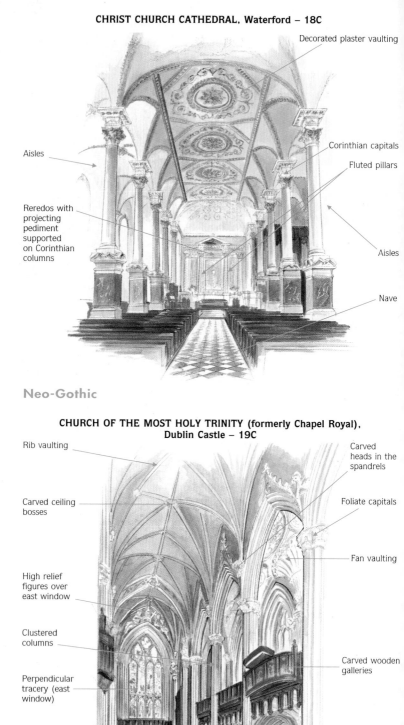

Decorated plaster vaulting

Aisles

Corinthian capitals

Fluted pillars

Reredos with projecting pediment supported on Corinthian columns

Aisles

Nave

Neo-Gothic

CHURCH OF THE MOST HOLY TRINITY (formerly Chapel Royal), Dublin Castle – 19C

Rib vaulting

Carved heads in the spandrels

Carved ceiling bosses

Foliate capitals

High relief figures over east window

Fan vaulting

Clustered columns

Carved wooden galleries

Perpendicular tracery (east window)

R. Corbel

44

MILITARY STRUCTURES

Norman

Motte and bailey

In the immediate post-invasion years, the Normans built timber castles, surmounting a natural or artificial earthern mound *(motte)*. A outer stockaded enclosure *(bailey)* contained stables, store-houses etc. Later castles were built of stone.

Tower

Timber stockade

Motte

Drawbridge

Bailey

Ditch and rampart

TRIM CASTLE, Co Meath – Late 12C – early 13C

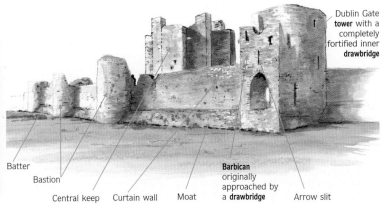

Dublin Gate **tower** with a completely fortified inner **drawbridge**

Batter

Bastion

Central keep

Curtain wall

Moat

Barbican originally approached by a **drawbridge**

Arrow slit

15C-17C

DUNGUAIRE CASTLE, Co Galway – 1520 restored in the 19C

Fortified dwelling, consisting of a **tower house** surrounded by a courtyard, known as a **bawn**, enclosed by defensive wall; the main living accommodation with windows was on the upper floors.

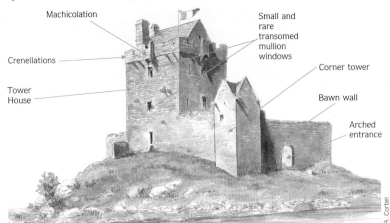

Machicolation

Small and rare transomed mullion windows

Crenellations

Corner tower

Tower House

Bawn wall

Arched entrance

R. Corbel

CHARLES FORT, Co Cork – c 1670

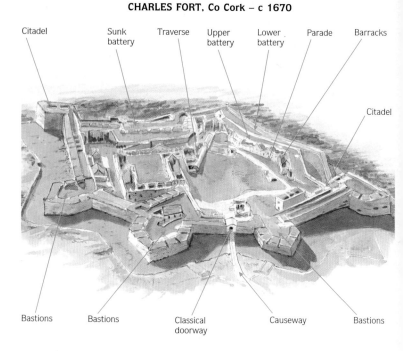

Citadel Sunk battery Traverse Upper battery Lower battery Parade Barracks Citadel

Bastions Bastions Classical doorway Causeway Bastions

DOMESTIC BUILDINGS

Traditional vernacular

COUNTRY COTTAGE

Single storey thatched dwelling with a few small windows. The simplest form of dwelling with only one hearth could be extended, by the addition of supplementary rooms, with or without a hearth, either at ground level, in the roof space or by creating an upper floor.

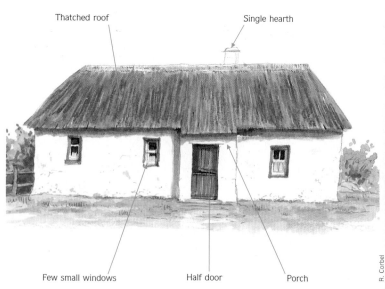

Thatched roof Single hearth

Few small windows Half door Porch

R. Corbel

PORTUMNA CASTLE, Co Galway – 1518

Semi-fortified house, with symmetrical fenestration, approached through formal walled gardens.

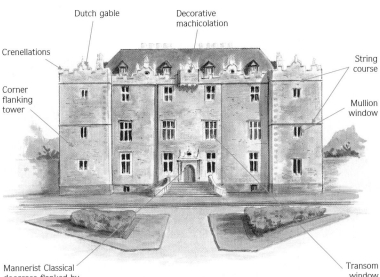

Dutch gable

Decorative
machicolation

Crenellations

String
course

Corner
flanking
tower

Mullion
window

Mannerist Classical
doorcase flanked by
gun loops

Transom
window

SPRINGHILL, Co Tyrone – c 1680 with 18C additions

Unfortified house with symmetrical facade and large and regular fenestration.

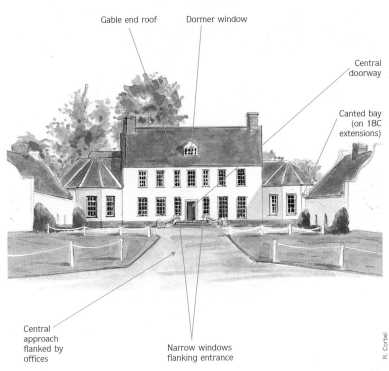

Gable end roof

Dormer window

Central
doorway

Canted bay
(on 18C
extensions)

Central
approach
flanked by
offices

Narrow windows
flanking entrance

R. Corbel

RUSSBOROUGH, Co Wicklow – 1743-56

House in the **Palladian style** consisting of a main **residential block** linked by curved or straight colonnades to two **flanking service blocks** containing the kitchens and stables.

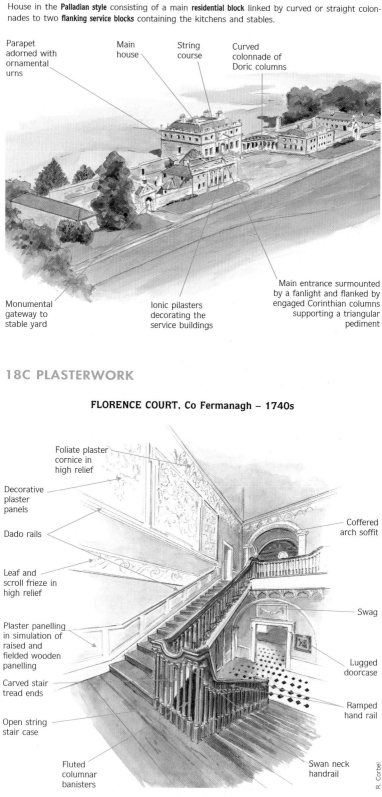

Parapet adorned with ornamental urns

Main house

String course

Curved colonnade of Doric columns

Monumental gateway to stable yard

Ionic pilasters decorating the service buildings

Main entrance surmounted by a fanlight and flanked by engaged Corinthian columns supporting a triangular pediment

18C PLASTERWORK

FLORENCE COURT, Co Fermanagh – 1740s

Foliate plaster cornice in high relief

Decorative plaster panels

Dado rails

Leaf and scroll frieze in high relief

Plaster panelling in simulation of raised and fielded wooden panelling

Carved stair tread ends

Open string stair case

Fluted columnar banisters

Coffered arch soffit

Swag

Lugged doorcase

Ramped hand rail

Swan neck handrail

R. Corbel

48

GEORGIAN URBAN HOUSING

Urban terrace houses built of red brick, with 4 storeys over basement, three bays wide, with regular fenestration, composed of sash windows with wooden glazing bars. The tall windows emphasized the importance of the first floor reception rooms.

Wrought-iron decorative balconies

Simulated stone work

Doorcase with pillars and fanlight

Doorcases and fanlights (1740s)

Door case capped by a lantern fan light and flanked by pillars with Ionic capitals

Door case capped by a decorated fan light and flanked by pillars with Ionic capitals

Door case capped by a decorative fan light and flanked by pillars with Ionic capitals and by side lights and door scrapers

Door case capped by a decorated fan light and flanked by pillars with Ionic capitals

R. Corbel

49

Suburban housing in Dublin, one storey over basement, built detached or in terraces with the front doors in pairs and sometimes slightly recessed.

Decorated fan light

Door case with consoles

Sash window with glazing bars

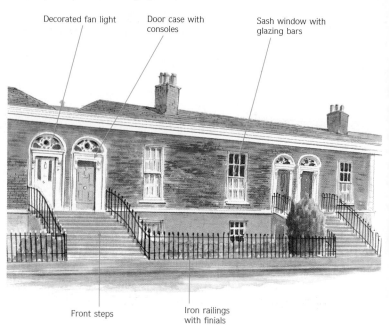

Front steps

Iron railings with finials

Revival styles

Medieval styles such as Gothic and Norman were revived featuring asymmetric façades and fenestration and varied rooflines.

LISMORE CASTLE, Co Waterford – 19C Neo-Gothic

Look-out turret

Hood moulding

Corbelling

String course

Crenellated and corbelled parapet

Canted bay

String course

Canted bay

Window tracery

R. Corbel

CIVIC BUILDINGS
Neo-Classical

MONAGHAN MARKET HOUSE, Co Monaghan – 1791

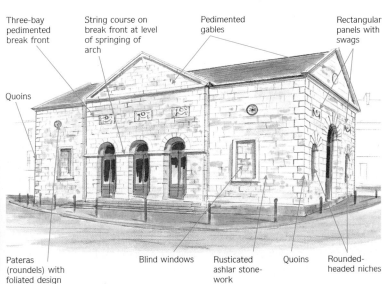

Three-bay pedimented break front

String course on break front at level of springing of arch

Pedimented gables

Rectangular panels with swags

Quoins

Pateras (roundels) with foliated design

Blind windows

Rusticated ashlar stone-work

Quoins

Rounded-headed niches

Arts and Crafts

CAVAN TOWN HALL, Co Cavan – 1908-10

Irish contribution to a series of provincial town halls in the remoter parts of Europe. Lofty fenestration for the offices and smaller windows for ancillary accommodation.

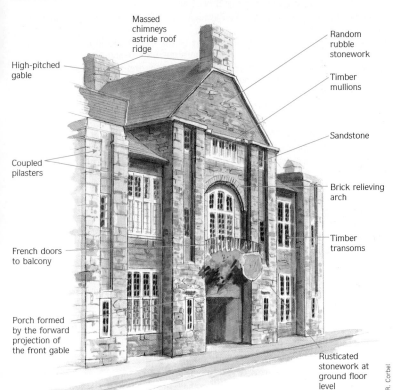

Massed chimneys astride roof ridge

Random rubble stonework

High-pitched gable

Timber mullions

Sandstone

Coupled pilasters

Brick relieving arch

Timber transoms

French doors to balcony

Porch formed by the forward projection of the front gable

Rusticated stonework at ground floor level

R. Corbel

51

GLOSSARY OF ARCHITECTURAL TERMS

Aisle: lateral divisions running parallel with the nave in medieval and other buildings, usually churches.

Ambulatory: passage giving access between the choir and apse of a church.

Apse: rounded or polygonal end of a church or chapel.

Arcade: a series of arches, resting on piers or columns.

Architrave: the beam, or lowest portion of the entablature *(see below)*, extending from column to column. Also used of the moulded frame around the head and side of a window or door opening.

Archivolt: concentric mouldings on the face of an arch resting on the impost.

Baldaquin: canopy supported by pillars set over an altar, throne or tomb.

Baptistery: building, separate from the church, containing the font.

Barbican: outwork of a medieval castle, often with a tower, defending a gate or bridge.

Barrel vaulting: continuous arched vault of semicircular section.

Battering: a slight inward inclination of a wall from its base upwards.

Battlements: parapet of medieval fortifications, with a walkway for archers or cross-bowmen, protected by merlons *(see below)*, with embrasures *(see below)* between them.

Broach spire: octagonal spire rising from a square tower without a parapet, having pyramidal broaches at the angles.

Buttress: vertical mass of masonry built against a wall, so strengthening it and resisting the outward pressure of a vaulted roof *(see Flying buttress)*.

Capital: crowning feature of a column or pillar.

Chancel: part of the church set aside for clergy and choir, to the east of the nave.

Chantry chapel: chapel endowed for religious services for the soul of the founder.

Chapter-house: place of assembly for the governing body of a monastery or cathedral. In medieval England, often multi-sided, with vaulting supported on a central pillar.

Chevron: Norman decoration of zigzag mouldings used around windows and doorways.

Choir: western part of the chancel, used by the choir, immediately east of the screen separating nave and chancel.

Clerestory: upper storey of the nave *(see below)* of a church, generally pierced by a row of windows.

Corbel: stone bracket, often richly carved, projecting from a wall to support roof beams, the ribs of a vault, a statue or an oriel window.

Corbelling: courses of brick or stone projecting from those below to carry a super structure or form a roof.

Cornice: crowning projection, the upper part of the entablature in Classical architecture. Also used for the projecting decoration around the ceiling of a room.

Crossing: central area of a cruciform church, where the transepts cross the nave and choir. A tower is often set above this space.

Crypt: underground chamber beneath a church, used as place of burial or charnel-houses. They often also housed the bones or relics of a saint or martyr.

Cupola: hemispherical roof.

Donjon: keep or central fortress of a castle.

Drum: vertical walling supporting a dome, sometimes with windows.

Embrasure: the space between two merlons *(see below)*, on a battlement, through which archers could fire, while protected by the merlons.

Entablature: in Classical architecture, the entire portion above the columns, comprising architrave, frieze *(see below)* and cornice *(see above)*.

Fan vaulting: system of vaulting peculiar to English Perpendicular architecture, all ribs having the same curve, resembling the framework of a fan.

Finial: top or finishing portion of a pinnacle, gable, bench end or other feature.

Fluting: narrow concave channelling cut vertically on a shaft or column.

Flying buttress: external arch springing over the roof of an aisle and supporting the clerestory wall, counteracting the thrust of the nave vault *(see Buttress)*.

Frieze: central division of the entablature – horizontal decorative design at high level.

Gable: triangular end section of a wall of a building, enclosed by the line of the roof.

Hammerbeam roof: late Gothic form of roof construction with no tie-beam. Wooden arches rest on corbels and beams bracketed to the walls and eaves.

Harling: wall plastered with roughcast. Often painted or with colour incorporated.

Impost: upper course of brickwork or masonry upon which an arch rests.

Jamb: upright side of a window or door opening.

Keep: inner tower and strongest part of a medieval fortress *(see Donjon)*.

Keystone: central, wedge-shaped stone which locks an arch together *(see Voussoir)*.

Lancet: Early English (13C) sharp-pointed arch.

Lantern: glazed construction, for ventilation and light, often surmounting a dome.

Lierne: short intermediate rib in Gothic vaulting.

Loggia: open-sided gallery or arcade.

Machicolation: in medieval military architecture, a row of openings below a projecting parapet through which missiles could be rained down on the enemy.

Merlon: upstanding portion between two embrasures on a battlement.

Misericord: tip-up seat in choir stalls, with a small projection on the underside, to support a person having to stand through a long service. Often fancifully and grotesquely carved.

Mullions: vertical ribs dividing a window into a number of lights.

Narthex: western portico at the entrance to early Christian churches.

Nave: central main body of a church, west of the choir, into which lay persons were admitted, chancel and choir being reserved for the priests.

Ogee: arch used in late Gothic period, combining convex and concave curve, ending in a point.

Oriel: window projecting from a wall on corbels.

Pediment: triangular termination above the entablature, in Classical architecture some-times "broken" in Renaissance designs.

Pilaster: rectangular pillar, projecting from the wall.

Rose window: circular window with mullions converging like the spokes of a wheel.

Screen: partition, often richly carved, separating nave from choir and chancel.

Skewputt: gable's corner stone.

Spandrel: triangular space between the curves of arches and the frame in which they are set.

Squinch: arch placed diagonally across the internal corner angles of a square tower, converting the square into an octagonal form.

Tierceron: secondary rib in Gothic vaulting.

Transept: arms of a cruciform church set at right angles to nave and choir.

Transom: horizontal cross-bar or division of a window *(see Mullions)*.

Tympanum: space between the flat lintel and the arch of a doorway.

Undercroft: vaulted chamber partly or wholly below ground, in a medieval building.

Volute: spiral scroll used at the corners of Ionic, Corinthian and Composite capitals.

Voussoir: wedge-shaped stones of an arch, their sides tapering towards the imaginary centre of the circle of the arch.

Ecclesiastical Architecture

Little remains of most early Christian settlements as the buildings were made of perish-able material – wood or wattle and daub. The records describe beautiful wooden churches, made of smooth planks constructed with great craft and skill, but none has survived. The Irish seem to have preferred to build in wood until the 9C when the monasteries were pillaged and set on fire by Vikings.

Early monasteries consisted of an area enclosed by a circular wall or bank and divided into concentric rings, as at Nendrum *(see p 350)*, or into sectors assigned to diffe-rent uses. The most important sector was the graveyard, since it was seen as the gateway to heaven; a saint's grave brought a monastery fame and increased wealth as it was thought desirable to be buried near the grave of a saint. The drystone beehive huts at Nendrum were constructed on the corbel principle also seen at Dunquin (Dun Chaoin). The boundaries of monastic enclosures were often marked by stone pillars or high crosses. The times of worship were reckoned by means of a sundial.

Round Towers – The slender tapering round towers which are almost unique to Ireland mark the site of early monasteries. They were built between about AD 950 and 12C as bell-towers – the Irish name is bell house – where hand bells, the only kind available, were rung from the top floor to announce the services. There were usually four windows on the top floor and one on each of the lower floors, which were linked by wooden ladders as at Devenish and Kilkenny. The towers were also used to store treasures and possibly as places of refuge; in almost every case the entrance was several feet (10ft/3m) above ground level, facing roughly towards the major church of the site.

Intact towers vary in height (from 50ft/17m to over 100ft/30m). All were surmounted by a conical cap, created on the corbel principle, which has sometimes been replaced by later battlements. About 65 survive in varying condition, with 12 intact. Most were constructed without foundations and all are tapered. Kilmacduagh is a very fine in-stance of a well-preserved 11C or 12C tower (about 100ft/30m tall).

Tomb Shrines – Some saints' graves are marked by a stone **mortuary house** which resembles a miniature church. These structures, such as St Ciaran's at Clonmacnoise, are among the earliest identifiable stone buildings in Ireland. There was usually a hand hole at one end through which the faithful could touch the relics.

Churches – Most early **stone churches** consisted of a single chamber with a west door and an east window; churches with a nave and chancel date from the 12C. In some buildings the north and south walls project beyond the west wall to form antae, probably a copy in stone of a feature required to support the barge-boards of a wooden structure. None of the surviving churches is very large but there are often several churches on one site. The very large stones employed accentuate the smallness of the churches. The roofs would have been made of thatch or shingles.

The rare **stone-roofed** churches, an Irish peculiarity, employ the corbelling technique. The simplest is Gallarus Oratory; St Doulagh's near Malahide is a 13C church still roofed with stone slabs; St Columba's House, St Mochta's House, St Flannan's Oratory and Cormac's Chapel have a small room between the vaulted ceiling and the roof. The earliest examples are devoid of ornament; an exception to this rule is found on White Island in Co Fermanagh, where seven figurative slabs are attached to the walls (which may be later insertions). Doorways were sometimes trabeated, that is the jambs incline somewhat and are covered by a massive flat lintel as at Reefert Church in Glendalough.

Romanesque – The first church in the Romanesque style, which was introduced from the Continent in the 12C, was Cormac's Chapel at Cashel finished in 1139. In Ireland Romanesque churches are always small; their typical features, to which carved decoration is limited, are round-headed doorways, windows and arches. Ornament includes fantastic animals, human masks and geometric designs such as bosses, zigzags and "teeth". There were no free-standing pillar capitals to carve. Cormac's Chapel has fine carvings, several series of blind arcades, painted rib vaults (the earliest in Ireland) and the earliest extant frescoes, now conserved.

Profusely ornamented west doorways are perhaps unique to Ireland, exemplified by Clonfert (after 1167), Ardfert and St Cronan's in Roscrea. At Clonfert the stylized foliage is of classical derivation – the inner arch is later than the main doorcase.

Gothic – Gothic architecture, introduced to Ireland in the late 12C, is on a much smaller scale than elsewhere. Most cathedrals show English and Welsh influences, whereas monasteries, founded by Continental monastic orders, are built according to their usual plan of a quadrangle enclosed by cloisters bordered by the church on the north side, the sacristy and chapter-house on the east, the refectory and kitchens on the south and the store on the west, with dormitories above the east and south ranges. At Jerpoint the church is in the form of a cross with a large vaulted chancel, nave and side aisles divided by arcades; the fine battlemented crossing tower is 15C. Holy Cross, in its present form predominantly 15C, retains its earlier layout with the convent buildings to the south of the church. The distinctive features are the narrow lancet windows. There was a distinctive tendency in the late 13C to light the choir with as many lancets as possible, as at Ennis, Sligo and Ardfert. Vaulting is unusual but Holy Cross Abbey has a very good vaulted east end.

Early in the 13C many cathedrals were remodelled; the two Anglican cathedrals in Dublin contain building from this period, although they have been much altered. St Patrick's Cathedral in Dublin, completed in 1254, to which a tower was added in 1372, is very English in its form and decoration. The flying buttresses to the Lady Chapel (reconstructed mid 19C) are relatively unusual.

A second period of building occurred in the 15C and coincided with the construction of many Franciscan houses in the west. Most existing churches were altered to conform to the new fashion. Broad traceried windows were inserted which let in more light and provided the stonemasons with opportunities for decoration. There is an Irish character to the capitals in the cloisters at Jerpoint (15C) and high-relief carving on the webs between the pillars.

Few medieval churches have survived but among those which have been in constant use for worship or have been restored in this century are the cathedrals in Dublin, Ballintubber Abbey in Co Mayo, Holy Cross Abbey north of Cashel, Black Abbey in Kilkenny and Duiske Abbey in Graiguenamanagh north of New Ross.

Planter's Gothic – This style was introduced in the early 17C by settlers from England and Scotland who built many parish churches throughout Ireland, a few of which survive unaltered; one of the best examples is St Columb's Cathedral in Londonderry. A parish church of the period is Waringstown in Co Down.

18C-19C Classical – Classical details began to be used in the 17C. St Michan's in Dublin (c 1685) and Lismore (1680) by William Robinson retain some details of 17C work. The early Georgian St Anne's in Shandon in Cork has an imposing west tower with an eastern flavour. The neo-Classical rectangular building with a pillared portico, inspired by the Greek temple, was popular with all the major denominations: St Werburgh's (1754–59), St George's (1812), St Stephen's (1825) and the Pro-Cathedral (finished after 1840) in Dublin, St John the Evangelist (1781–85) at Coolbanagher by Gandon and St George's (1816) in Belfast. Christ Church Cathedral (1790s) by John Roberts in Waterford has a good Classical interior although the galleries have been removed.

Gothic Revival – Many early 19C Gothic churches, such as the Church of the Most Holy Trinity (formerly the Chapel Royal) in Dublin Castle are filled with ornament, with decorative galleries, plaster vaulting and rich oak carvings. Later the influence of Augustus Welby Pugin, who practised widely in Ireland, and JJ McCarthy promoted antiquarian correctness, as at St Fin Barre's in Cork (1862) by William Burges. The spate of building which followed the Emancipation Act was hampered by the Famine and limited funds. Nevertheless many Roman Catholic cathedrals and parish churches were constructed in eclectic Gothic variations, whereas those for dissenting congregations were quite pared down in style.

20C Churches – Despite widespread eclecticism, as with the correct Classicism of Cavan Cathedral (finished 1942) by Ralph Byrne, some modern influences emerged. The earliest example, Christ the King (1927) at Turner's Cross in Cork by Barry Byrne of Chicago, is rigorously modern for its date. The changes in practice introduced by Vatican II, which favour the concept of churches in the round, have inspired many exciting modern designs, some of which reflect local physical features – St Conal's Church, Glenties, Co Donegal; St Michael's Church, Creeslough, Co Donegal; Dominican Church, Athy; Prince of Peace Church, Fossa, near Killarney; Holy Trinity, Bunclody.

Stained Glass – No medieval stained glass survives in situ in Ireland. The revival of stained glass began in the 1770s with the enamelling work of Thomas Jervais and Richard Hand, much of which was secular. Both worked extensively in England. Several foreign and Irish firms competed during the 19C for church commissions. The fashion for the neo-Gothic style of architecture in the 19C for both churches and houses created such a demand for stained glass that it declined in artistic quality towards the end of the century; good examples from this period are St Patrick's Roman Catholic Church in Dundalk, which has glass by Early of Dublin, Hardman of Birmingham and Meyer of Munich, the east window of St Patrick's Anglican Church in Monaghan by the German FS Barff, and the altar window of the Cathedral of the Assumption in Tuam by Michael O'Connor (1801–67).

A revival in Irish stained glass occurred early in the 20C with the foundation of **An Túr Gloine** (the Tower of Glass) (1903–63) at the instigation of Edward Martyn and Sarah Purser. The manager was AE Childe who also ran the stained glass section in the Dublin Metropolitan School of Art and had been trained by the William Morris studio. Sarah Purser, who was a portrait painter, did designs for several windows including *Cormac of Cashel* in St Patrick's Cathedral. Another founder member was Michael Healy (d 1941) whose work can be seen in Loughrea Cathedral.

Two works by Wilhelmina Margaret Geddes from Belfast, who worked for An Túr Gloine from 1912 to 1925, can be seen in the Municipal Gallery of Modern Art in Dublin – *Episodes from the Life of St Colman* (strong black line used) and in the Ulster Museum – *The Fate of the Children of Lir* (1930).

Evie Hone, who was trained in abstract painting, discovered the fascination of stained glass during a trip to France and joined An Túr Gloine in 1934. Her work, which was often inspired by Irish medieval sculpture, includes *The Ascension* (1948) for the Roman Catholic church in Kingscourt, Co Cavan, and *The Beatitudes* (1946) for a chapel in the Jesuit Retreat House at Tullabeg near Tullamore.

Harry Clarke (1889–1931), who trained under Childe at the Metropolitan School of Art, developed a distinctive personal style as early as 1915, drawing from iconography and legends in a symbolist manner. His first public commission, 12 windows for the Honan Chapel in University College Cork, is one of his greatest works. His "Geneva Window" (1928) is in the Municipal Gallery of Modern Art in Dublin. Just before his death he executed his most important ecclesiastical commission *The Last Judgement with the Blessed Virgin Mary and St Paul* for St Patrick's Church in Newport.

A current revival is headed by James Scanlon and Maud Cotter, both based in Cork.

Secular Architecture

Prehistoric Dwellings – The earliest human dwellings known in Ireland are the huts of Stone Age men found at Lough Gur.

By the Iron Age, men were living in **homesteads**, approached by a causeway. The ringfort was enclosed by an earth bank *(ráth* or *dún)* or by a stone wall *(caiseal)* and was surrounded by a ditch. An artificial island *(crannóg)* was formed by heaping up stones in a marsh or lake. Many such dwellings were in use from the Iron Age until the 17C. There is a replica at Craggaunowen *(see p 170)*. Stone forts *(cashels)* like Dún Aengus *(see p 75)* and Grianán of Aileach *(see p 186)*, although restored at various periods, illustrate the type, built on a hill with massive walls and mural chambers.

Within the homestead individual huts were built of wattle and daub or of stone with a thatched roof. In the west, beehive huts *(clocháin)* were built entirely of stone using the same technique of **corbelling** inwards to form a roof that was used in the passage graves, such as Newgrange *(see p 92)*. Similar stone huts are also found in the monastery on Great Skellig and at Clochan na Carraige. They demonstrate the use of drystone construction in a treeless land.

At the centre of the homestead there was often an underground stone passage, called a souterrain, used for storage or refuge.

Norman Castles – The first castles built by Normans were of the **motte and bailey** type. The motte was a natural or artificial mound of earth surrounded by a ditch and usually surmounted by a wooden tower as at Clough in Co Down; the bailey was an area attached to the motte and enclosed by a paling fence. From the start of the 13C, they built more solid stone donjons (keeps) which were square with corner buttresses, as at Trim, Carrickfergus and Greencastle, polygonal as at Dundrum and Athlone or round as at Nenagh; battering (a sloping face) was later added to the base; the donjon was surrounded by a stone wall of enclosure or incorporated in it. Trim, completed in 1220, has several surviving gates and barbicans and a massive keep. During the 13C entrance towers became more important and barbicans were added for additional defence. In the latter half of the 13C a new symmetrical design was developed consisting of an inner ward with four round corner towers and a combined gatehouse/donjon in the middle of one wall, as at Roscommon, which is an early example of this type called the "keepless" castle.

Tower Houses – After the Black Death (1348–50) building resumed on a more modest scale. In 1429 a £10 subsidy was offered by Edward VI for the construction of a castle or tower; the original minimum dimensions (20ft/6m x 16ft/5m x 40ft/12m high) were later reduced to 15ft/4.5m x 12ft/3.5m x 40ft/12m high. Over 70% of tower houses, which were erected by native and settler alike, are south of the Dublin–Galway axis. The most distinctive feature is their verticality, one room on each of four to five storeys.

The ground floor, used as a store, was roofed with cradle vaulting formed on wicker centering; the living room, also vaulted, was often on the fourth floor where it was safer to have large windows. There was sometimes a hidden room between the vaulting and the floor above. In the 16C and 17C large windows were often opened on the top floors. The winding or straight stair, of stone, is set either within the thickness of the walls or in a turret.

The tower defences consisted of corner loop holes, battering at the base, double-stepped merlons, known as **Irish crenellations**, and external machicolations over the corners and the entrance; the door was also defended internally by a **murder hole** in the ceiling above it. Most such towers, which were built between 1450 and 1650, were surrounded by a **bawn**, an area enclosed by a defensive wall as can still be seen at Aughnanure and Dunguaire; the largest such castles are Bunratty and Blarney. Only in the later and larger castles is decoration evident. Thoor Ballylee was converted into a summer house by William Butler Yeats. The tower houses built in the north exhibit Scottish building styles with crow-stepped gables and corbelled turrets as at Monea.

Plantation Castles – As the country came more firmly under English control in the late 16C, more luxurious rectangular houses were built with square corner towers, as at Kanturk (c 1603), Portumna (c 1618) and Ballygally (1625). Portumna, reroofed recently, has intact bawn (garden) walls, corner towers and later gatehouse. Often an existing tower house was extended by the addition of a more modern house, as at Leamaneh, Donegal and Carrick-on-Suir. These buildings show a Renaissance influence in plain and regular fenestration with large mullioned windows.

Towns and Cities – Celts lived not in towns but in isolated farmsteads. Early villages *(clachans)* were formed of clusters of wattle-and-daub cottages arranged in a haphazard manner. The Vikings founded a number of towns on estuaries, including Drogheda, Dublin, Waterford and Wexford. Norman foundations were mostly confined to the south and east of the country. Towns were often fortified but few stretches of town walls have survived apart from late 13C walls at Fethard *(see p 114)* and Youghal *(see p 270)*.

The first widespread foundation of towns occurred in the late 16C and 17C during the plantations of Ulster, Munster and some parts of Leinster; they consisted of poor-quality timber-framed houses, which have not survived, set out round a green or lining a street. The green was often known as "The Diamond" although rarely a true diamond shape. The name "Diamond" mostly survives in Ulster, in particular in the city of Derry, itself fortified in the 17C with walls which are still intact.

Most towns of Norse origin in Ireland had a **Tholsel** (toll stall), where payment for rights of privilege or passage was made; the building was often an arch or gateway several storeys high. Almshouses and similar charitable foundations were established in prosperous settlements; early survivors include Shee's Alms House (1582) in Kilkenny and the Earl of Cork's Almshouses (1613; recently restored) in Youghal. Kinsale Courthouse is an early surviving civic buiding; the main block is 17C with added brick front on arches (1706). Monaghan Market House is a small but fine neo-Classical structure, the arches originally open for trade.

In the 18C and 19C many country landlords indulged in town planning, setting out wide streets as in Strokestown and Moy, tree-lined malls as in Westport, Birr and Castlebar, unusual formal street plans, such as the X-shape in Kenmare, rows of cottages built of local stone as at Glassan, northeast of Athlone, and Shillelagh in Co Wicklow or the picturesque thatched houses of Adare.

In the major towns elegant terraces of houses of Classically-inspired design were built of local stone or red brick, some of which was imported from Somerset via Bristol. In 19C Dublin the materials used were grey brick from local glacial clays, local limestone and grey Wicklow granite. Although most terraces were erected piecemeal and lack a unified aesthetic, the influence of the Wide Streets Commissioners (in Dublin from 1758) led to distinctly Irish Georgian doorways – usually flanked by columns – and ordered fenestration. The tallest windows are on the principal floor, decreasing in size towards the parapet. Some later terraces by the Wide Streets Commissioners and others, were more standardized – Fitzwilliam Street and Square (south side) in Dublin, and Pery Square in Limerick. In early 19C Dublin a particular type of house, of one, two or three storeys, with basement raised up to ground level and sweeping steps to the main entrance, became very popular. Internal decoration was often of a very high standard, with Classical motifs common in chimneypieces, plasterwork and timberwork. The Gothic style was often used for detached houses and mansions or civic buildings in the second half of the 19C; Trinity College Museum (completed 1857) by Deane and Woodward is a classic of the Venetian Gothic revival. The Arts and Crafts movement did not find much architectural expression in Ireland; Cavan Town Hall (1908) by William Scott is a notable exception with expressive use of planes and textures. University College Dublin in Earlsfort Terrace (1912) by RM Butler and the College of Sciences in Upper Merrion Street in Dublin (1904–13) by Sir Aston Webb exemplify the Classical revival. The young Free State restored with admirable promptness the bombed General Post Office, the Four Courts and the Custom House but the record of new design is relatively poor. The Department of Industry and Commerce in Dublin (1935–39) by Basil Boyd Barrett is an exception, steadfastly of the Monumental Style.

Coastal Fortifications – In the Restoration period several important towns were provided with star forts; the most complete surviving fortification is Charles Fort in Kinsale (from 1671) by William Robinson; the buildings within are mostly of 18C date. After the French invasion of Bantry Bay in 1796 and Killala in 1798, signal towers were built on the Irish coast. The building of Martello towers began in 1804 (a year earlier than in England) when the threat of a French invasion was very real; about 50 of these squat towers with very thick walls punctuate the coast near Dublin and Cork and along the Shannon estuary. The so-called Joyce Tower in Sandycove, built of ashlar granite, is typical. Many towers had a battery attached.

Vernacular Houses – The 1841 Census identified four grades of housing, of which the lowest was a windowless one-room mud cabin with a thatched roof *(bothán)*, a type of dwelling which predominated west of a line from Londonderry to Cork. Among the rural population nearly 50% lived in one-room cabins and the percentage was higher in the poorest parts of the West. Such cabins contained little or no furniture; more windows or rooms meant higher rents.

The half door, which is to be found all over Ireland, allowed in light while keeping animals out of the house. Such simple dwellings were often destroyed during evictions or fell into decay but examples have been reconstructed or recreated in Bunratty Folk Park, Glencolmcille Folk Village, the Ulster-American Folk Park and the Ulster Folk Park near Bangor. The middle grades of house, single- and two-storey farmhouses, have survived in greater numbers, with glazed windows, hearths and a hierarchy of rooms for distinct social uses.

The Irish **long house**, in which all the rooms were interconnecting with the stairs at one end, was a style which lasted from the Middle Ages to the 18C; the one at Cratloe *(see p 216)* is one of the few to survive.

The box-style Georgian house, often a rectory or agent's house, with symmetrical elevation, some Classical detailing such as Venetian or Wyatt windows and a fanlit and columnated doorcase, was very popular with people of more substantial means.

Country Houses – Between the Battle of the Boyne (1690) and the Rebellion (1798) there was a period of relative peace and prosperity for the Anglo-Irish Ascendancy during which most of the important country houses were built. While Dutch gables and red brick are attributed to the influence of William of Orange, in general English and French inspiration predominated in the late 17C. In the 18C the influence was mainly Italian sources, often distilled through England and latterly Greek-inspired architects, while in the 19C the English Gothic and Tudor revivalists were influential. In general, country houses were built of local stone.

Springhill *(see p 344)* is of Restoration date, with later flanking additions; it illustrates the effect of understated Classical symmetry and fenestration. The gabled roof is typical of early houses.

The most popular style in the 18C was the **Palladian villa** which consisted of a central residence – two or three storeys high – flanked by curved or straight colonnades ending in pavilions (usually one storey lower) which housed the kitchens or stables and farm buildings.

The major architect of the first half of the 18C was **Richard Castle** (originally Cassels) (1690–1751), a Huguenot from Hesse-Kassel, who arrived in Ireland in 1728; he knew Richard Boyle, 3rd Earl of Burlington and 4th Earl of Cork, who inherited large estates in Ireland and Yorkshire, acted as patron to William Kent and popularized the work of Palladio in England. Castle's many houses – Powerscourt, Westport, Russborough, Newbridge – tend to be very solid. He took over the practice of **Sir Edward Lovett Pearce**, who died at the age of 34 in 1733. Pearce had the major role in designing Castletown *(see p 164)*; his House of Parliament (from 1729), now the Bank of Ireland in Dublin, was the earliest Burlingtonian public building in the British Isles.

No principal architect took over Castle's mantle before the arrival of James Gandon. The influence of **Robert Adam** (1728–92) arrived in Ireland in 1770, the date of the mausoleum he designed at Templepatrick. Sir William Chambers' work in Ireland is exemplified by The Casino, Marino (1769–80), a vastly expensive neo-Classical gentleman's retreat cum folly.

James Gandon (1742–1823) was brought to Ireland in 1781 by Lord Portarlington to design Emo Court *(see p 79)*. His Classical style is well illustrated by the Customs House and the Four Courts in Dublin.

Many grand houses such as Florence Court, Castle Ward and Bantry House with their grand interiors, have never been attributed to a known architect. The chief work of **James Wyatt** (1746–1813) was at Castle Coole but he also contributed to Slane Castle.

One of the best known of Irish architects is **Francis Johnston** (1761–1829), an exponent of both the Classical and the Gothic styles, who designed several public buildings in Armagh from 1786 to 1793 and was then sent by Richard Robinson to work under Thomas Cooley in Dublin. He was employed by the Office of Public Works, where he was responsible for Civil Buildings. His contemporary, Richard Morrison, with his son William Vitruvius Morrison, designed grand Classical interiors at Kilruddery *(see p 266)* which have survived.

Many of the **interiors** were decorated with exuberant stuccowork executed by the Swiss-Italian **Lafranchini** brothers, one of whom executed the stairwell plasterwork at Castletown. Contemporary work of similar quality was carried out by Robert West, a Dublin stuccadore. Powerscourt House in Dublin has first-floor rooms by Michael **Stapleton**, one of the most skilled craftsmen in plaster in Dublin in the 18C and the principal exponent of Adam decor.

The **Gothic style**, which made its debut in England at Strawberry Hill (1748–1792), first appeared in Ireland in the 1760s at Castle Ward and at Malahide Castle where two tall Gothic towers were added to the medieval core during restoration after a fire. At first Gothic features were added to buildings that were basically Classical and symmetrical such as Castle Ward and Slane Castle which was begun in 1785 by James Wyatt and completed by Francis Johnston; both contain intricate stuccowork vaulted ceilings. In addition to the crenellations, machicolations and pointed arches, one of the key features of the Gothic style was asymmetry. In 1815 it appeared in the gate lodges built at Glin; at about the same time Tullynally Castle was converted into a vast irregular Gothic pile by – among others – Johnston and Morrison. Existing medieval castles or tower houses or Classical mansions, such as Kilkenny Castle (c 1826) by William Robertson and Dromoland Castle (1826) by George and James Pain, were enlarged and reworked in Gothic or Tudor style. Johnstown Castle and Ashford Castle are later examples of such Gothicizing which was romantic in flavour but distinctly Victorian in convenience. At Birr the surviving gatehouse was extended; Sir Joseph Paxton was responsible for the 19C additions to Lismore for the Duke of Devonshire. Some new houses were built entirely in the antiquated style; Gosford Castle is neo-Norman; Adare Manor (1832), by the noted English Gothicist Augustus Pugin, is an unusually early example of a neo-Gothic building; Glenveagh was designed in the Irish Baronial style; for Belfast Castle, Lanyon and Lynn chose the Scottish Baronial style, which was also used for Blarney Castle House. In later years genuine defensive features were introduced in response to the Fenian threat.

Two grand exercises in landscape building – the Italianate sunken garden at Heywood (1906–10) *(see p 80)* and the National War Memorial in Dublin (1930–40) – are by Sir Edwin Lutyens. The trimphal arch, in the northeast corner of St Stephen's Green in Dublin, was designed by John Howard Pentland and erected in 1906–07 to commemorate the Boer War.

Sculpture

Cross-slabs – The earliest stone monuments are the slabs laid flat over an individual grave but they cannot be categorized definitively as grave markers. The designs evolved from early (8C) irregularly-shaped stones marked with small crosses, through crosses inscribed in squares (8C and 9C), ringed crosses with a circle at the intersection (9C) to crosses with a circle at the intersection and semcircles at the ends of the arms (10C, 11C and 12C). Many bear the inscription OR or OROIT DO (meaning A prayer for...) followed by the name of the deceased, some of whom can be identified from the **Annals of the Four Masters** *(see p 130)*. Clonmacnoise has the largest collection of cross-slabs in the country. Some of the smaller slabs are standing monuments. Standing pillars probably followed from cross-slabs as both types have in common simple cross carvings. Coffin-shaped slabs were introduced by the Normans. Most early inscriptions are in Latin; after the 16C English was used.

High Crosses – The free-standing highly-decorated crosses are most numerous in the east of Ireland but they are also found in western and northern Britain. It is thought that high crosses are the successors to small painted or bronze-covered wooden crosses, possibly carved in stone to prevent theft by raiders, and used as a focus for kneeling congregations. They vary in height (from 6ft/2m to 20ft/6m) and most stand on a pyramidal base; the head of the cross is usually ringed and surmounted by a finial often in the shape of a small shrine. The ring probably has a symbolic purpose. The early carving on late 8C crosses, including some at Clonmacnoise, is mostly decorative consisting of spirals and interlacing. In the 9C and 10C, panels of figures appear illustrating stories at first from the New and then from the Old Testament; such biblical figures or scenes are rare in early Christian art. Animal scenes are often executed on the base. The Cross of Moone *(see p 79)* includes animal and biblical iconography. The 12C crosses are a fresh batch, not a direct continuation, often lacking a ring *(see CASHEL, GLENDALOUGH)*. By this date the figure of a bishop or abbot in the Continental style predominates. The best groups of crosses are at Monasterboice, Clonmacnoise, Kells and Ahenny.

Medieval sculpture – Funeral monuments provide the largest evidence for schools or periods of sculpture, as few movable sculptures have survived. There are some exceptions – the wooden Kilcorban Madonna in Loughrea Diocesan Museum and the fine alabaster statue of the Trinity displayed in the Black Abbey in Kilkenny. The carved bestiary misericords (c 1489) in St Mary's Cathedral in Limerick are unique survivors as are the figurative stone carvings (15C; re-erected in the 20C) in the cloisters at Jerpoint.

A distinctive feature of this period is the medieval box tomb found in the chancel of many churches. The lid usually bears a carved effigy of the dead man and sometimes of his wife too. The sides are decorated with figures of the Apostles and saints *(see p 197)*. In the 15C and 16C, figures and scenes from the crucifixion were carved in high relief, as on the tomb of Bishop Wellesley (c 1539) in Kildare Cathedral and the Butler effigies in St Canice's Cathedral in Kilkenny. Although predominantly religious, 17C sculpture, such as the Jacobean Segrave or Cosgrave stucco tableaux in St Audeon's Church in Dublin, widened in scope to include stone and timber carved chimneypieces; there are two fine examples of the former in the castles in Donegal and Carrick-on-Suir. On a grand scale are the Renaissance-inspired 17C tombs such as the O'Brien Monument (1600) in St Mary's Cathedral in Limerick, the Chichester Monument (c 1614) in St Nicholas' Church in Carrickfergus and the Earl of Cork's Monument (1620) in Youghal. Carvings from the Restoration period – fine wood relief and stone – survive, especially at the Kilmainham Hospital.

From the early 18C both literal and allegorical funerary monuments were popular; an early example is the monument to Sir Donat O'Brian (d 1717) by William Kidwell in Christ Church Cathedral in Dublin. Church monuments on a large scale by John Van Nost the younger (c 1712–80) can be seen in Tullamore Cathedral and Waterford Cathedral. The monumental tomb (over 23ft/7m tall) to David la Touche at Delgany in Co Wicklow by John Hickey has fine neo-Classical elements.

The spate of building in the 18C provided much work for sculptors in the secular field. The figures of **Justice** and **Mars** above the gates of Dublin Castle are the work of **Van Nost** as is a statue of George III, now in the Mansion House. **Edward Smyth** (1749–1812), who was a pupil of the Dublin Society's Schools, created the riverine heads on the keystones of the arches and the arms of Ireland on the Custom House and also worked on the Four Courts under James Gandon and on the Bank of Ireland; he had been apprenticed to Simon Vierpyl (c 1725–1810) who worked on the Marino Casino. Vierpyl's work at the Casino includes the urns flanking the external steps; the lions adjacent are the work of the English sculptor Joseph Wilton. Smyth's son John, also a fine sculptor, crafted funerary monuments at Ferns in Co Wexford and Goresbridge in Co Kilkenny.

The 19C saw the dominance of Greek Revival detailing; in St Patrick's Church in Monaghan there is a good collection of monuments, especially the monument to Lady Rossmore (c 807) by Thomas Kirk (1781–1845). John Hogan (1800–58) is acknowledged as a most distinguished sculptor; see his fine plaster The Drunken Faun in the Crawford Art Galley in Cork. Two of his

Irish Picture Library

Barrow – Riverine head from the Custom House, Dublin

59

contemporaries, who worked on the Albert Memorial in London, were Patrick Mac-Dowell (1799–1870), who carved the group of Europe on the base of the monument, and John Henry Foley (1818–74) who sculpted the bronze figure of Prince Albert; Foley's best work in Dublin is the O'Connell Monument and the statues of Burke, Goldsmith and Grattan on College Green outside Trinity College in Dublin. The best work of Thomas Farrell (1827–1900) is the Cullen Memorial (1881) in the Pro-Cathedral in Dublin.

On a monumental scale is the Wellington Testimonial (c 1817) in Phoenix Park in Dublin by English architect Sir Robert Smirke; it has bronze reliefs on the base by the sculptors Joseph Robinson Kirk, Farrell and Hogan. The work of Oliver Sheppard (1864–1941) is strongly influenced by the Art Nouveau style.

The Parnell Monument in O'Connell Street in Dublin was designed by Augustus St Gaudens in 1911.

The portrait sculptor, **Albert Power** (1883–1945), a resident of Dublin, was elected Associate of RHA in 1911; there are examples of his work in Cavan Cathedral, Mullingar Cathedral and in Eyre Square in Galway.

More recent work of note includes the *Children of Lir* by Oisin Kelly (1916–81) in the Garden of Remembrance in Dublin. The Belfast sculptor FE McWilliam (1909–92) is well represented by a series of bronze figurative sculptures in the Ulster Museum.

Painting

When Gaelic culture waned in the 17C the chief influences on art in Ireland were English and European. A guild of painters was founded in Dublin in 1670 but there was little development until the Dublin Society's Schools were set up in 1746 to promote design in art and manufacture. The first master Robert West (d 1770) and his assistant, James Mannin (d 1779), had trained in France. The School's most outstanding pupil was pro-

The Board of Trinity college, Dublin

Portrait of John in the Book of Kells

bably **Hugh Douglas Hamilton** (1739–1808) who excelled at pastel portraits; in 1778 he visited Italy and while in Rome developed as a painter in oils.

Susanna Drury (fl 1733–70), whose paintings of the Giant's Causeway are in the Ulster Museum, was a member of the Irish school of landscape painting which emerged in the 18C. **George Barret** (c 1732–84), who moved to England in 1763, introduced the Romantic element into his landscapes. Several Irish artists travelled to Italy. Thomas Roberts (1748–78), a pupil of the Dublin Society's Schools and a brilliant landscape artist, was familiar with Dutch and French painting and exhibited several works in the style of Claude Vernet. The dominant figure of the 18C is **James Barry** (1741–1806) who produced large-scale works in the neo-Classical tradition. He travelled widely, including in Italy, studying painting and sculpture. Joseph Peacock (c 1783–1837) from Dublin was famous for his outdoor fair scenes.

Among 18C visitors to Dublin were Vincent Valdré (1742–1814), who painted three panels for the ceiling of St Patrick's Hall in Dublin Castle, and Angelica Kauffmann (1741–1807) who spent seven months in Ireland in 1771 as the guest of the Viceroy, Lord Townshend.

In 1823 the **Royal Hibernian Academy** was incorporated by charter to encourage Irish artists by offering them an annual opportunity of exhibiting their works.

After the Act of Union in 1800 many Irish artists moved to London: Martin Archer Shee (1769–1850), who became President of the Royal Academy in 1830, and Daniel Maclise (1806–70), a popular historical painter. Nathaniel Hone (1831–1917) spent 17 years in France painting out of doors like the painters of the Barbizon school. Roderic O'Conor (1860–1940) from Co Roscommon studied in Antwerp and in France where he met Gauguin, whose influence, together with that of Van Gogh, is obvious in his work. **Sir John Lavery** (1856–1948) from Belfast studied in Paris and is known for his portraits, although he also painted scenes from the French countryside. Another artist who studied abroad is **Sarah Purser** (1848–1943) who was a prolific portrait painter and a founder of An Túr Gloine.

The 20C has produced several artists of note. **Jack B Yeats** (1871–1957), brother of William Butler Yeats the poet, painted his views of Irish life with bold brushstrokes in brilliant colours. **Paul Henry** (1876–1958) is known for his ability to represent the luminous quality of the light in the west of Ireland. **William Orpen** (1878–1931), who trained at the Metropolitan School of Art in Dublin and the Slade in London, became a fashionable portrait painter and an official war artist; among his Irish pupils were **Seán Keating** (1889–1977) and **Patrick Tuohy** (1894–1930). Cubism was introduced to Ireland by **Mainie Jellett** (1897–1944) and **Evie Hone** (1894–1955) who is better known for her work in stained glass.

In 1991 the National Gallery and the Hugh Lane Gallery were joined by the Irish Museum of Modern Art at Kilmainham, which is to commission works for its permanent collection and provide a stimulus for future generations.

Letters

Irish men and women of letters have made a significant contribution to English literature through poetry, novels and drama. Poetry was an art form practised by the Celtic bard and medieval monk but theatrical performances were unknown to Gaelic society. To the English language the Irish brought a talent for fantasy, wit and satire and Gaelic speech patterns. Four Irish writers have been awarded the Nobel Prize for Literature: William Butler Yeats in 1923, George Bernard Shaw in 1925, Samuel Beckett in 1969 and Seamus Heaney in 1995.

18C-19C LITERATURE

The first flowering of Anglo-Irish literature came in the late 17C and 18C when **Jonathan Swift** (1667–1745) published his satires of 18C Irish society in Dublin, William Congreve (1670–1729) produced his witty comedies, George Farquhar (1678–1707) wrote his stage works, **Oliver Goldsmith** (1728–74) composed poetry, novels and plays and **Richard Brinsley Sheridan** (1751–1816) his satirical comedies.

Most Irish writers who achieved success and fame moved to London. Three writers in exile who made a significant contribution to English literature and theatre in the 19C were George Moore (1852–1933), who described high society in Dublin *(Drama in Muslin)* and introduced the realism of Zola into the novel *(Esther Waters)*, **Oscar Wilde** (1854–1900), whose plays *(Lady Windermere's Fan, The Importance of Being Earnest)* were hugely successful in the London theatre, and **George Bernard Shaw** (1856–1950), who commented on the Anglo-Irish dilemma in his journalism and his play *John Bull's Other Island* and explored the contradictions of English society *(Pygmalion)*.

George Russell (1867–1935), known as AE, was a mystic, poet and painter, economist and journalist and an influential figure in the **Gaelic Revival**. The dominant writer of the period, however, whose writing was greatly influenced by the old Irish myths and legends, was **William Butler Yeats** (1856–1939), who established his name as a poet and playwright and was a founder member of the Abbey Theatre.

Some of the greatest successes written for the **Abbey Theatre** were the plays of **John Millington Synge** (1871–1909), *Riders to the Sea* and *Playboy of the Western World*, inspired by the Aran Islands, and *The Shadow of the Glen*, inspired by the Wicklow Mountains, where language dominates in the bleak landscape; and the pacifist plays of **Sean O'Casey** (1880–1964), *The Shadow of a Gunman, Juno and the Paycock* and *The Plough and the Stars*, written in the aftermath of the First World War.

Irish Themes

Several successful authors chose Irish themes for their work. Maria Edgeworth (1767–1849) achieved international fame and the admiration of Sir Walter Scott with her novels *Castle Rackrent* and *The Absentee;* William Carleton (1794–1869) wrote about rural life in County Tyrone. The theme of the novel *The Collegians* by Gerald Griffin (1803–40) was reworked by Dion Boucicault for the stage as *The Colleen Bawn* and by Benedict as an opera *The Lily of Killarney*. **Anthony Trollope** (1815–82), who began his literary career while working for the Post Office in Ireland, wrote several novels on Irish themes. Canon Sheehan (1852–1913) was admired in Russia by Tolstoy and in the USA for his novels about rural life. Somerville and Ross, a literary partnership composed of **Edith Somerville** (1858–1949) and her cousin, Violet Florence Martin (1862–1915), whose pen-name was **Martin Ross**, produced novels about Anglo-Irish society, *The Real Charlotte* and the highly humorous *Experiences of an Irish RM*.

Literary Exiles

The narrow-mindedness of Irish society, expressed by George Moore, is also criticized in the work of **James Joyce** (1882–1941), who wrote his famous work *Ulysses* abroad, of Frank O'Connor (1903–66), who emigrated to America, and of **Samuel Beckett** (1906–89), who emigrated to Paris and wrote in French and English; with *Waiting for Godot* he was recognized as a leading figure in the Theatre of the Absurd.

20C

The early 20C produced the bleak realistic poetry of **Patrick Kavanagh** from Monaghan (1904–67 *Ploughman and Other Poems*) – whose influence can be seen in the work of John Montague (b 1929 *The Rough Field)* and Northern poet Seamus Heaney (b 1939 *The Death of a Naturalist*) – and of **Louis MacNeice** (1907–63), who was a member of Auden's circle and an early influence on Derek Mahon (b 1941 *The Hudson Letter*). Novelists included Flann O'Brien (1911–66, real name **Brian O'Nolan**, who wrote a famous newspaper column as Myles na Gopaleen.

The theme of the Big House survives in the work of Elizabeth Bowen (1899–1973 *The Last September)*, **Molly Keane**, writing as MJ Farrell (1905–97 *The Last Puppetstown)*, Aidan Higgins (b 1927 *Langrishe, Go Down)* and Jennifer Johnston (b 1930 *The Illusionist)*. Influential novelists include **Edna O'Brien** (b 1932 *The Country Girls)*, whose frank accounts of female

James Joyce (1882–1941)
painted in 1934
by Jacques Blanche (1861–1942)

National Gallery of Ireland, Dublin

sexuality in the 1950s were banned in Ireland on first publication and publicly burned in her home village in Co Clare, and the highly-acclaimed John MacGahern (b 1934 *Amongst Women)*, now living in Co Leitrim. In 1997 *Angela's Ashes* by Frank McCourt won the Pulitzer Prize. Northern Irish writers Brian Moore (b 1921 *The Lonely Passion of Judith Hearne)*, Patrick McCabe (b 1955 *Butcher Boy)* and Eoin MacNamee (b 1960 *Resurrection Man)* have all seen their work quickly turned into films, as have many writers from the south, including **Roddy Doyle** (b 1958 *The Commitments* and *Paddy Clarke Ha Ha Ha*, which won the Booker prize) and Colin Bateman (b 1962 *Cycle of Violence)*. Alongside the established pillars of Irish drama – such as **Brian Friel** (b 1929 *Dancing at Lughnasa*, adapted as a film in 1998), Thomas Kilroy (b 1934 *The Secret Fall of Constance Wilde)*, Thomas Murphy (b 1935 *Bailegangaire)* and Frank McGuinness (b 1956 *Observe the Sons of Ulster Marching towards the Somme)* – a new wave of young Irish writers is making an international impact. Encouraged by the Abbey and the Gate Theatres in Dublin, the Royal Court in London and independent theatre companies, such as Rough Magic in Dublin, the Druid Theatre Company in Galway and Red Kettle in Waterford, this new wave includes Martin McDonagh (*The Leenane Trilogy)*, Conor McPherson (b 1971 *The* Weir), Marina Carr (b 1964 *The Mai)* and Enda Walsh *(Disco Pigs)*.

Music

Ireland is the only country with a musical instrument – the harp – as its national emblem. Traditional music, song and dance are among the most vibrant aspects of Irish culture. The oldest-known form of Irish music, generally called *sean-nós* (old style) singing, is a highly ornate, unaccompanied, individual style associated for the most part with songs in Irish. Many of these are sung to slow airs without any regular rhythm and others are sung to faster tunes. Traditional songs in English include international ballads and native Hiberno-English songs.

The harp dominated the musical scene from the Middle Ages until it was proscribed by the English because of its nationalist allure. Irish harpists, who trained for many years, were admired for their rapid fingerwork and their quick and lively technique. The harp was used to accompany the singing or recitation of poetry. Turlough O'Carolan (Carolan) (1670–1738) started too late in life to reach the highest standard of skill but he left over 200 tunes which show remarkable melodic invention and are still played.

The first documented mention of mouth-blown pipes in Ireland occurs in an 11C text and the earliest depiction dates from the 15C; these pipes appear to have been primarily for entertainment purposes. The particularly Irish form of pipes, the *uilleann* (elbow) pipes, which have regulators and drones operated by the fingers, emerged in the 18C. These pipes are closely identified with Irish traditional music and are renowned for the unique sound produced by highly skilled musicians.

Other instruments played by traditional musicians include the violin, called the fiddle by traditional musicians, the flute and the free-reed instruments such as the accordion, melodeon and concertina. In more recent years the guitar, banjo and **bodhrán** (goatskin drum) have become very popular at music sessions. The most popular form of dance is "set dancing" which dates from the 18C and is, for the most part, an adaptation of military dances to existing tunes such as jigs, reels, hornpipes and polkas. Individual *sean-nós* (old style) dancing is also a feature of Irish traditional music. In recent years traditional music has become an important industry.

The highly musical life of Dublin in the 18C produced two firsts: the first performance of Handel's *Messiah*, conducted by the composer himself, and the birth of John Field (1782–1837), an outstanding pianist who invented the Nocturne. In 1792 a great harp festival was held in Belfast. Many of the traditional tunes were written down by Edward Bunting, one of the earliest collectors of traditional tunes. Some of these were sung to words written by Thomas Moore *(The Last Rose of Summer)*. These tunes enjoyed great popularity in elegant drawing rooms as Moore's Melodies. In the 19C many Irish musicians made their name in England or abroad. Sir Charles Villiers Stanford (1852–1924) taught Vaughan Williams and Holst as well as making his name as a composer. Sir Hamilton Harty (1879–1941) was best known as the conductor of the Hallé Orchestra. John McCormack (1884–1945) spent most of his career as a tenor singer in the USA. Margaret Sheridan (1889–1957) was in Puccini's opinion one of the best interpreters of his work. Three 19C Irish operas – *The Bohemian Girl* by William Balfe, *Maritana* by Vincent Wallace and *The Lily of Killarney* by Benedict – achieved considerable popularity.

The Wexford Opera Festival was inspired by a long-established love of opera in Ireland and provides many young singers with an opportunity to start a career. The Radio Telefis Eireann Symphony Orchestra sets a standard for trained musicians. There are many Irish musicians of international stature of which **James Galway**, the flautist, is probably the best known.

Two significant names among modern composers are **Seán Ó'Riada** (1931–71), who wrote two settings for the Mass in Irish, and **Seoirse Bodley** (b 1933) who has evolved a system of notation for Irish slow airs and has written a setting of the Mass in English and compositions for the Irish harp.

Since independence in 1922 the native tradition of singing, piping, fiddling and dancing has come into its own, revitalised by the popularity of Irish-American folk songs written by nostalgic emigrants. Traditional informal music, now a regular part of Irish pub sesssions and of dances (known as a *céiles*, pronounced with a hard c to rhyme with daily), was first brought to a world-wide audience by the highly influential group **The Chieftains**, and the traditional melodies of **Enya** and **Clannad** (singing in both English and Irish) penetrated the realm of popular music.

Irish rock musicians, including **Thin Lizzy, Van Morrison** and **U2** have also found huge international success. Today "Irish" music incorporates many strands, from musicians such as **The Cranberries, Sinéad O'Connor, Shane MacGowan** with **The Pogues** and now **The Popes**, and **The Corrs**, whose music is influenced by a traditional Celtic poetic vision, to the commercial success of pure pop practised by **Boyzone** and **B*Witched**, and the more "Indie" sound of groups such as **Ash**. The phenomenon of **Riverdance**, now seen on five continents, has done for Irish dance what the Chieftains and the Dubliners did for Irish music.

Folk Musicians in a pub

Cinema

Cinema first appeared in Ireland on 20 April 1896 with a projection of a film by the Lumiére brothers in Dublin and by 1909 the *Volta* in Dublin had been opened by James Joyce himself; the seventh art began to play a major role in Irish life. In 1904 JT Jameson, a newsreel cameraman, founded the Irish Animated Company (IAC); together with the American cinema, which was anxious to please the many Irish immigrants in the States, it made cinema acceptable in Ireland and launched the local industry. In 1916 and 1917 two more companies were set up — Film Company of Ireland (FCOI) and General Film Supply (GFS).

It was not until the founding of the Free State in 1922 that Irish cinema truly flourished in Ireland. Political events supplied the first themes — the Easter Rising of 1916 in *Irish Destiny* (1926) by Isaac Eppel; other incidents in the War of Independence in *Guest of the Nation* (1935) by Denis Johnston and *The Dawn* (1936) by Tom Cooper. From the post-war era the following titles stand out — *The Rocky Road to Dublin* (1968) by Peter Lennon, *Mise Eire* (1959) by George Morrisson, *Maeve* (1981) by Pat Murphy and *The Year of the French* (1981) from the novel by Thomas Flanagan. The **Irish Film Board**, created in 1982 and relaunched in 1993, has fostered a new flowering of talent by providing funds and has enhanced the reputation of Irish films in the international field.

In the last decades of the 20C several talented directors, such as **Neil Jordan** and **Jim Sheridan**, have dealt with serious subjects — the events in Northern Ireland — as well as turning a critical eye on Irish society, a popular theme with the new generation of film-makers. Among the most successful titles are *Angel* (1982) by Neil Jordan, *Reefer and the Model* (1987) by Joe Comerford, *My Left Foot* (1989), *The Field* (1990), *In the Name of the Father* (1993) and *The Boxer* (1998) by Jim Sheridan (who often worked in collaboration with Daniel Day-Lewis, his favourite actor), *The Crying Game* (1992) by Neil Jordan and *The Butcher Boy* (1998) and *Michael Collins* (1996). Although **Ken Loach** left Ireland and worked abroad, his work must be mentioned — *Hidden Agenda* (1990), *Land and Freedom* (1995) and *Carla's Song* (1997).

The category of films produced in Ireland or by film-makers of Irish descent working abroad includes *The Informer* (1935) and *The Quiet Man* (1952) by **John Ford**; the latter, the second film by the famous American director about the return to his native land of a boxer, played by John Wayne, acquired a great following. In recent years the use of Irish themes has proved successful — *The Dead* (1987) from a short story by James Joyce, *The Commitments* (1991) about the story of soul musicians in Dublin, directed by **Alan Parker**, *The Snapper* (1993) and *The Van* (1996) by **Stephen Frears**, and *Michael Collins* (1996) by Neil Jordan about the career of the man who played a leading role in the struggle for independence in the 1920s.

Three recent Irish TV series have earned great popularity in the UK — *Father Ted*, *The Ambassador* starring Pauline Collins and partly filmed in Ely Place in Dublin, and *Ballykissangel* (filmed in Avoca in the Wicklow Mountains).

Cinema

The Irish Film Board provides loans and equity investment to independent Irish film-makers. The films listed below were produced under this policy or were filmed in Ireland or deal with Irish themes:

The Dawn (1933–34) — filmed in Killarney with a cast of 250 mainly local amateurs, who performed on Thursdays, early closing day.

Ulysses (1967) — filmed in Dublin.

Ryan's Daughter (1968) — filmed on Banna Strand and the Dingle Peninsula.

The Year of the French (1981) — filmed in and around Killala in Co Mayo.

The Lonely Passion of Judith Hearne (1987) — filmed in Blessington Street, Dublin.

My Left Foot (1989) — filmed in Bray, at Killruddery and on Killiney Hill.

The Field (1990) — filmed near Leenane in Connemara.

December Bride (1990) — filmed in Dublin and near Strangford Lough.

The Commitments (1991) — based on a novel by Roddy Doyle.

Into the West (1992) — about children being led on an adventure by a horse.

Circle of Friends (1993) — based on a novel by Maeve Binchy.

The Snapper (1993) — based on a novel by Roddy Doyle and filmed in Dublin.

Braveheart (1996) — filmed in Trim.

Michael Collins (1996) — filmed in Dublin and elsewhere in Ireland.

Crafts

Ireland produces not only certain articles which have an international reputation but also many less well-known hand-made articles created by small enterprises; some are grouped together in special craft villages such as Roundstone in Connemara, Dingle or Donegal town; others congregate in certain regions such as weavers in Donegal. The **Kilkenny Design Centre**, set up in the early 1960s, has infused new life into domestic and industrial design in Ireland. Many of their attractive articles of clothing and domestic items are on sale in the Kilkenny shop in Nassau Street in Dublin.

Tweed – The term was first recognized late in the 19C to describe the hand-woven woollen cloth produced in Co Donegal. Donegal tweed is still the most well-known and is now produced, mostly on power looms, by four firms, in Ardara, Donegal Town, Downies and Kilcar. Three of these companies also employ out-workers using hand-looms and most have diversified into the production of knitwear and ready-made garments or into weaving other natural fibres – linen, cotton and silk. The original tweeds were made from natural undyed wool – grey, brown or cream; as coloured wool was produced only in small quantities it was introduced as speckles when the wool was carded. The dyes used were obtained from plants, lichens, turf, soot and minerals.

Avoca Weavers *(see WICKLOW MOUNTAINS)* were founded in 1723 and the Kerry Woollen Mills *(see KILLARNEY)* also date from the 18C. Foxford *(see CASTLEBAR)* and Blarney were started in the 19C.

Knitwear – The thick cream-coloured (undyed) knitwear associated with the Aran Islands is the best known of Irish knitwear and is on sale throughout the country. Ireland produces a great variety of other knitted garments in a variety of textures and colours, particularly thick sweaters to keep out the wind and rain, using the traditional stitches – basket, blackberry, blanket, cable, diamond, moss, plait, trellis and zigzag.

Lace – In the 19C there were many lace-making centres in Ireland but few have survived. In most the skill was fostered by the nuns; the lacemakers of Clones and Carrickmacross have now formed themselves into cooperatives. Kenmare needlepoint lace is the most difficult to make; Clones is a crochet lace but the other centres produce "mixed lace" on a base of machine-made cotton net.

Linen – The demand for bed linen, table linen and tea towels keeps some 20 Irish linen houses in business. The popularity of linen as an apparel fabric has revived in recent years, since blending with synthetic or other natural fibres has reduced its ten-

Irish Linen Centre

Linen hand-loom

dency to crease. It is now used by top fashion designers all over the world who appreciate its sheen and interesting texture, its durability and versatility – it is cool in summer and a good insulator in winter; it dyes well in bright clear colours.

Porcelain and Pottery – The largest porcelain factory is the one at **Belleek** which produces fine translucent Parian ware and specializes in woven basket pieces and naturalistic flower decoration. Similar wares are produced by Donegal Irish Parian china. The Irish Dresden factory *(see KILMALLOCK)* preserves and develops the tradition of delicate ornamental porcelain figures which originated in Germany. There are many studio potteries in Ireland producing hand-turned articles, such as those in Connemara and the Stephen Pearce Pottery in Shanagarry.

Glass – The most famous and oldest glass factory in Ireland is in **Waterford**, but since its revival in 1951 several smaller enterprises have started to produce hand-blown lead crystal which is cut, engraved or undecorated – Cavan Crystal, Galway Crystal, Grange Crystal, Kerry Glass Studio, Sligo Crystal, Tipperary Crystal, Tyrone Crystal. Most have factory shops where first- and second-quality pieces can be bought and many offer a guided tour of the workshops.

Woodwork – There are a number of craftsmen producing hand-turned articles such as bowls, lamp stands and ornaments; the unique pieces are the graceful and delightful carvings produced by artists from skeletal pieces of **bogwood**. Some wood-turners produce musical instruments such as pipes and drums *(bodhráns)*.

Metalwork – Throughout the country, and especially in the craft villages, artists are working in gold, silver, bronze, pewter and enamel to produce dishes and plaques, necklaces, pendants and earrings; the traditional Claddagh rings *(see GALWAY)* worked in gold show a heart with two clasped hands.

Bogwood

The extensive peat bogs of the Midlands – on the banks of the Shannon south and west of Longford and Athlone, as well as those in the north of Co Mayo – are being exploited by **Bord na Mona**, principally to generate electricity; narrow-gauge railway tracks carry wagons loaded with peat to the processing plant.
The tree roots uncovered by the great peat-harvesting machines are turned into beautiful and fascinating bogwood sculptures by Michael Casey, whose studio is at Barley Harbour on the east bank of Lough Ree. Several of his works stand in the attractive village of **Newtown Cashel**, which clusters round its green beside the church (1833).

Food and drink

Ireland is a sociable and hospitable country where people readily gather in a bar or round a table. There are two culinary traditions: the elaborate meals served in town and country mansions, and the simple dishes of the rural and urban poor.
Although history has identified the potato (introduced at the end of the 16C) as the staple food of Ireland, the country has always produced a good range of vegetables and fruit, meat and dairy products and a wide variety of fresh- and salt-water fish; The Dublin Bay prawn and the Galway oyster have a more than local reputation. Each year in October a **gourmet festival** is organized by the many excellent restaurants in Kinsale; their high standard of *haute cuisine* can be found throughout the country, as well as the traditional fried breakfast and high tea.

Breakfast – The traditional **Irish Fry**, known in the north as an "Ulster Fry", consists of fried egg, sausage, bacon, black pudding, potato cakes, mushrooms and tomatoes; it is usually eaten at breakfast but is also served as the evening meal. Other breakfast dishes are kippers and kedgeree.

Fish – The king of the freshwater fish is the **salmon**, wild or farmed; as a main dish it is usually poached or grilled. Irish smoked salmon is traditionally cured with oakwood. Archeologists have found evidence by the River Bann of a salmon weir and traces of salmon-smoking dating from 2000 BC.
The other most frequently-served freshwater fish is **trout**, farmed or wild. **Shellfish**, such as crab, lobster, scallops, mussels and Dublin Bay prawns (also known as langoustines or scampi) are usually available near the coast, particularly in the southwest. Galway Bay oysters are plump and succulent.
The Irish fishing grounds produce Dover sole (known locally as Black sole), lemon sole, plaice, monkfish, turbot, brill, John Dory, cod, hake, haddock, mackerel and herring.

Farmhouse Cakes

Meat – Prime **beef** is raised on the lush pastures in the east and south of Ireland; **lamb** comes from the uplands. **Pork** is presented in many ways: as joints and chops; as ham or bacon; as pigs' trotters *(crúibíní)*, known in English as crubeens; in white puddings; in black puddings *(drisheen)* flavoured with tansy and eaten for breakfast. The most popular game is rabbit but hare and pheasant are also served.

Traditional Dishes – These tend to be the simple dishes prepared by the poor people. There is no official recipe for **Irish stew** which consists of neck of mutton layered in a pot with potatoes, onions and herbs. **Colcannon** is a Harvest or Hallowe'en dish of mashed potatoes, onions, parsnips and white cabbage, mixed with butter and cream. **Champ** is a simpler dish of potatoes mashed with butter to which are added chopped chives or other green vegetables such as parsley, spring onions (scallions), chopped shallots, nettles, peas, cabbage or even carrots (cooked in milk which is added to the purée). Nettles are also made into soup. To make **coddle** a forehock of bacon, pork sausages, potatoes and onions are stewed in layers. **Collar and cabbage** is composed of a collar of bacon, which has been boiled, coated in breadcrumbs and brown sugar and baked, served with cabbage cooked in the bacon stock.

Seaweed – Various sorts of seaweed, a highly nutritious source of vitamins and minerals, were traditionally used to thicken soups and stews. **Carrageen** is still used to make a dessert with a delicate flavour. **Dulse** is made into a sweet.

Dairy Products – Irish cookery makes liberal use of butter and cream. Ice-cream is particularly popular as a dessert. In recent years many hand-made **cheeses** have appeared on the market: **Cashel Blue** (a soft, creamy, blue-veined cheese made from cow's

Whiskey or Whisky

Irish whiskey is usually but not invariably spelled with an "e" and Scottish whisky without. No certain place – Scotland or Ireland – or date is known for the invention of this spirit but it was being distilled and drunk throughout Ireland by the 16C. It flourished in the reign of Elizabeth I, who seems to have had a taste for it. Illicit whiskey *(potheen)* appeared in the 17C when the government introduced a tax on distilling (1661) and set up a department of Excisemen (Gaugers) to police the distilleries. By the end of the 17C, 2 000 stills were in operation. The most successful brands were made by the larger companies in Dublin – John Power, John Jameson, George Roe and William Jameson. They and other brands were exported all over the British Empire. Sales increased in 1872 when French brandy became scarce owing to a disease in the Cognac district of France but other factors led to a severe decline. Father Mathew, a Capuchin friar, toured Ireland in the 1840s and 1850s preaching against the evil of drink; temperance societies were set up and the consumption of alcohol dropped by over 35%. Blended whiskey, produced in Scotland, entered the market and proved very popular but the Irish distillers preferred to maintain the lightness and fuller flavour of their traditional product. When prohibition was introduced in the USA in the 1920s, the American export market was lost; the British Empire was closed off by the War of Independence. In 1966 the few surviving distilleries combined forces as the Irish Distillers Company and founded a new distillery in Midleton; in the early 1970s they took over Bushmills but were themselves taken over by Pernod-Ricard in 1989.

Bushmills Distillery

milk in Tipperary; milder than Stilton), **Cooleeny** (a Camembert-type soft cheese from Thurles in Co Tipperary), **Milleens** (a distinctive spicy cheese from West Cork; as it matures the rind is washed with salt water), **Gubbeen** (soft surface-ripening cheese from Skull in Co Cork).

Bread – A great variety of breads and cakes is baked for breakfast and tea. The most well-known is **soda bread** made of white or brown flour and buttermilk. **Barm Brack** is a rich fruit cake made with yeast (*báirín breac* = speckled cake).

Beverages – Stout made by **Guinness** or Murphys is the traditional thirst-quencher in Ireland but beer drinking is not uncommon. Black Velvet is a mixture of stout and champagne.

Although there are now only three **whiskey** distilleries in Ireland – Bushmills in Co Antrim, which produces the only malt, and Midleton in Co Cork, both owned by the same company, and Cooley in Dundalk – there are many different brands of whiskey. Their distinctive flavours arise from subtle variations in the production process.

Irish Coffee, a delicious creation, consists of a measure of whiskey, brown sugar and very hot black coffee mixed in a heated glass and topped with a layer of fresh cream; it is said to have been served first to passengers landing at Shannon Airport, Foynes, in the early days of transatlantic flying.

Triple distillation

The main distinction of Irish whiskey is that it is distilled three times. Since the beginning of the 20C, only barley or wheat have been used. The grain, including the husks, is milled to produce 'grist' which is mixed with hot water (60°C at Midleton and 63°C at Bushmills) and stirred in a large vessel (mash tun) to release the sugars, and the liquid is then drawn off. This process is repeated twice; the liquid from the third mashing is added to the first mashing of new grist. The spent solids are known as draff. The liquid from the first and second mashing (wort) is pumped into vessels called washbacks; yeast is added which reacts with the sugars to produce a light brown liquid. When fermentation is complete the liquid is pumped to the stills, where it is distilled three times (at Cooley as at most Scottish distilleries it is distilled only twice). The spirit is matured in old sherry or Bourbon casks and then blended (vatted) for two or three days.

World
Heritage List

In 1972 the United Nations Educational, Scientific and Cultural Organization (UNESCO) adopted a Convention for the preservation of cultural and natural sites. To date, more than 150 States Parties have signed this international agreement, which has listed over 500 sites "of outstanding universal value" on the World Heritage List. Each year a committee of representatives from 21 countries, assisted by technical organizations (ICOMOS – International Council on Monuments and Sites; IUCN – International Union for Conservation of Nature and Natural Resources; ICCROM – International Centre for the Study of the Preservation and Restoration of Cultural Property, the Rome Centre), evaluates the proposals for new sites to be included on the list, which grows longer as new nominations are accepted and more countries sign the Convention. To be considered, a site must be nominated by the country in which it is located.

The protected cultural heritage may be monuments (buildings, sculptures, archeological structures etc) with unique historical, artistic or scientific features; groups of buildings (such as religious communities, ancient cities); or sites (human settlements, examples of exceptional landscapes, cultural landscapes) which are the combined works of man and nature of exceptional beauty. Natural sites may be a testimony to the stages of the earth's geo logical history or to the development of human cultures and creative genius or represent significant ongoing ecological processes, contain superlative natural phenomena or provide a habitat for threatened species.

Signatories of the Convention pledge to co-operate to preserve and protect these sites around the world as a common heritage to be shared by all humanity.

Some of the most well-known places which the World Heritage Committee has inscribed include: Australia's Great Barrier Reef (1981), the Canadian Rocky Mountain Parks (1984), The Great Wall of China (1987), the Statue of Liberty (1984), the Kremlin (1990), Mont-Saint-Michel and its Bay (Great Britain and Ireland, 1979), Durham Castle and Cathedral (1986).

UNESCO World Heritage sites included in this guide are:
Boyne Valley
Skellig Michael
Giant's Causeway

Custom House, Dublin

Republic
of Ireland

ACHILL ISLAND ★
Co Mayo
Michelin Atlas p 94 and Map 923 – BC 6

Achill Island (36223 acres/14659ha) is approached by a bridge across Achill Sound from Corraun Hill (1715ft/521m), itself a peninsula joined to the mainland by a narrow isthmus at Mulrany. The magnificent cliff scenery, the sandy bays, the surfing and boating and the sea angling attract many summer visitors.

The island is dominated by two peaks – Slievemore (2204ft/671m) and Croaghaun (2192ft/667m); the latter ends in the dramatic sea cliffs of Achill Head, accessible only by boat.

Doogort is a small resort with sandy beaches on the north coast. There are longer sandy beaches at **Trawmore Strand** and **Keem Strand** on the west coast.

The **Atlantic Drive** runs parallel with the rocky shore between Dooega Head and the mouth of Achill Sound.

On the shore of the Sound south of the bridge to the mainland stand the ruins (restored) of **Kildavnet** (Kildownet) **Church** (c1700), which contains Stations of the Cross in Gaelic. The name means the church of Dympna, an Irish saint who sought shelter on Achill in the 7C.

Kildavnet (Kildownet) **Castle**, a square four-storey 15C **tower house**, commanding the southern entrance to Achill Sound, is chiefly associated with Grace O'Malley *(see p 260)*; there are traces of a boat slip and the original bawn.

For adjacent sights see CASTLEBAR, KILLALA, WESTPORT.

ADARE ★
ÁTHA DARA – Co Limerick – Population 1042
Michelin Atlas p 84 and Map 923 – F10

Adare is set on the west bank of the River Maigue, in the fertile wooded lands of west Limerick. The broad Main Street is lined with thatched cottages, mostly at least two centuries old. Adare has changed little since most of the other buildings were erected in the late 19C.

Nothing remains of the original settlement, built 1000 years ago near the castle. During the 12C the Anglo-Normans settled in Adare; a century later the Fitzgeralds, Earls of Kildare, acquired the land. There is no trace of the town walls that were built when Adare was incorporated in the 14C.

SIGHTS

Adare Heritage Centre ⊘ – There is more to Adare than picturesque thatched cottages. The historical exhibition tells of Norman invaders, medieval abbeys and the influential Dunraven family. Its highlight is a model which brings to life the town in 1500; there is also an audio-visual presentation *(15min)*.

★**Adare Friary** – *Access via Adare Golf Course; ask at the Club House.* Beside the River Maigue are the ruins of the Franciscan friary founded by the Earl of Kildare in 1464; extensions were built in the 15C and 16C. The nave, choir, south transept and **cloisters** are reasonably well preserved. The **Kilmallock Gate** was once the main entrance.

Desmond Castle – *Access via Adare Golf Course; ask at the Club House; restoration in progress.* The castle had already ceased to be of strategic importance when much of it was demolished by Cromwell's forces. A large square tower stands in the inner ward of the early 14C castle surrounded by a moat. The upper storey of the building in the southwest corner of the outer ward was the **great hall**. Nearby are the remains of **St Nicholas Church** (11C) and the **Desmond Chapel** (14C).

Adare Manor – The neo-Gothic limestone mansion, now a hotel open to non-residents, was begun in 1832; among the architects involved were James Pain and Augustus Welby Pugin. The carved inscriptions state that it was built by the Earl of Dunraven. The interior contains an elaborately panelled staircase and a long gallery (132ft/40m). The grounds, which include a maze and a lake, border the River Maigue.

Church of the Most Holy Trinity (Roman Catholic) – *Main Street facing the town park.* The square tower and the south wall of the present church were part of a monastery, constructed about 1230 by Maurice Fitzgerald, second Baron of Offaly; it was the only house in Ireland of the Trinitarian Order. The 50 monks were put to death in 1539 at the Dissolution of the Monasteries. The ruins were restored by the 1st Earl of Dunraven and enlarged in 1852. At the rear stands a completely restored 14C **dovecot**.

★**Adare Parish Church (Anglican)** – The church consists of the nave and part of the choir of the church of the Augustinian priory founded in 1315. The cloisters (north side) were converted into a mausoleum for the family of Quin, the Earls of Dunraven.

EXCURSIONS

Croom Mills ⊘ – *5mi/8km south of Adare by N 20.* The exhibition and audio-visual film trace the history of the mill built by Denis Lyons in 1788 on the River Maigue. The exhibits on the top floor give hands-on experience of how the machinery worked. The windows of the restaurant overlook the mill race which drives the nearby waterwheel.

★**Castle Matrix** ⊘ – *Rath-keale; 7.5mi/13km west of Adare by N 21; concealed entrance on north side of busy main road.* The Norman tower was built in 1440 by the 7th Earl of Desmond; he and his father, the 4th Earl, are

> **"Crom Abu"**
> The battle cry of the Earls of Kildare derives from their estates and castle at Croom on the River Maigue in Co Limerick.

the earliest-recorded Norman poets in the Irish language. The Great Hall houses a fine **library** and objets d'art. The castle also houses an **international arts centre** and the **Heraldry Society of Ireland**. It was at Castle Matrix that Edmund Spenser, the poet, and Walter Raleigh, then a captain, met for the first time in 1580 and began a lifelong friendship.

★**Irish Palatine Heritage Centre** ⊘ – *Rathkeale; 7.5mi/13km west of Adare by N 21.* The centre, housed in an old station-master's house re-erected on a new site, presents an exhibition of photographs, documents, arms, domestic articles and larger artefacts, recalling the settlement of South German Protestants in the area of Rathkeale in the early 18C, their innovative farming methods, their contribution to Methodism and their dispersion throughout the English-speaking world. There is also a genealogical service for tracing Palatine ancestors.

> **Irish Palatines**
>
> In 1709, following two invasions and a winter of extreme cold, the Irish Palatines emigrated from their native land, the Rhineland–Palatinate in South Germany (hence their name), and travelled to England in response to the provision of funds by the English Government to enable them to travel to Carolina in the USA. When the government funds ran out, many were stranded in London until the Dublin government offered to take 500 families; 821 families arrived in Ireland. Landlords were offered subsidies to accept the immigrants; some went to Counties Kerry, Tipperary and Wexford but the majority settled on the estate of Lord Southwell in Rathkeale, where their names – Bovenizer, Corneille, Delmege, Miller, Rynard, Piper, Sparling, Stark, Switzer, Teskey – sounded a foreign note. They were an industrious people, who introduced new farming techniques, and a pious, God-fearing people, mostly Lutherans or Calvinists. They responded with great enthusiasm to the preaching of John Wesleyl, who returned to visit them on several occasions after his first visit in 1756.
>
> One of Wesley's preachers, Philip Embury, and his cousin Barbara Heck emigrated to America in 1760. The sermon preached by Philip in his house in New York in 1766 led to the founding of the Methodist Episcopal Church in America.

★**Newcastle West** – *16mi/26km west of Adare by N 21.* Population 3 287. This thriving market town, known for its spring water, takes its name from the **castle** (recently restored) in the town square. Originally the castle belonged to the Knights Templar but later passed into the ownership of the Earls of Desmond. The banqueting hall, now known as **Desmond Hall** ⊘, contains an oak minstrels' gallery (restored) and a hooded fireplace (reconstruction); it stands over a 13C vaulted stone chamber, originally an ecclesiastical building with lancet windows. From the external staircase other remains of the castle can be seen, including the Great Hall *(Halla Mór)* which once housed the local cinema.

Askeaton – *13mi/20km northwest of Adare by N 21 and R 518.* Population 893. On a small island in the River Deel stand the ruins of **Desmond Castle** (15C). The tower and walls are largely intact; the Desmond Hall (90ft/27m x 30ft/-9m x 27ft/8m) was one of the largest of its kind in Ireland.

North of the town centre on the east bank of the river are the ruins of **Askeaton Franciscan Friary**, a 15C foundation. A representation of St Francis is to be found in the northeast corner of the cloisters which are on the south side.

Foynes Flying Boat Museum ⊙ – *21mi/34km west of Adare by N 21, R 518 and N 69.* Before and during the Second World War the small seaport of Foynes (population 650), which faces Foynes Island in the Shannon Estuary, was the operational base for flying boats, the original Shannon Airport. The old terminal building now houses a **museum** displaying many models, photographs and log books. The film Atlantic Conquest contains original footage linked by a modern commentary. The radio and weather room houses the original equipment, which is still in operation and provided the first information used by the Irish Meteorological Service.

Entrance Hall, Glin Castle

Irish Picture Library

★**Glin Castle** ⊙ – *29mi/47km west of Adare by N 21, R 518 and N 69.* In the village of Glin (population 569) by the stream stands the ruined **keep** of the castle of the Knights of Glin, destroyed in 1600 by Queen Elizabeth's forces. The **modern castle** was built about 1780–85 west of the village; the battlements and tower were added about 1820 when the three Gothic turreted lodges were built at the entrances to the estate. The property has been owned by the unusually-titled hereditary Knights of Glin since about 1300. The mild climate enables palm trees to grow in the **formal gardens** behind the house.

The **interior** is notable for its very fine neo-Classical plasterwork, particularly in the front hall which leads to the most unusual double flying **staircase** with a Venetian window overlooking the formal gardens. The main reception rooms have a notable collection of mahogany mid-18C Irish furniture. Inset into one of the library walls is a mahogany pedimented bookcase which conceals a hidden door leading to the staircase. Other rarities are paintings on chicken skin and a room warmer consisting of a wooden surround containing an open bronze pan holding charcoal. The rooms are hung with an interesting collection of family portraits and other Irish paintings.

For adjacent sights see KILMALLOCK, LIMERICK, TRALEE.

ARAN ISLANDS ★

OILEÁIN ÁRAINN – Co Galway – Population 2 000
Michelin Atlas p 88 and Map 923 – CD 8

The three Aran Islands extend in an oblique line across the mouth of Galway Bay. The smallest, Inisheer, is not far (5mi/8km) from the mainland; the middle island, Inishmaan, is slightly larger (6sq mi/7.77km²); the largest island, Inishmore, is about 7mi/11.3km from the coast of Connemara.

Although included for administrative purposes in Co Galway, the islands are geologically and historically linked to The Burren on the mainland. The land rises in natural terraces from a flat sandy shore facing Galway Bay to high cliffs (300ft/91m) confronting the Atlantic; constant sea erosion forms ledges used by fishermen. There are over

400 different wild flowers including fuchsias. Rainfall is lower than on the mainland and the islands are never touched by frost. Trees are rare and the tiny fields, created laboriously over the years out of layers of sand and seaweed, are divided by open-work drystone walls through which the wind can pass. Traditionally the white cottages were thatched with straw tied down against the wind. Fishing and farming are the main activities.

Literary Tradition

Gaelic is still spoken on the islands and the people are great story tellers and music makers. Local stories were the inspiration of JM Synge's play *Riders to the Sea*, which is set on Inishmaan, and of *The Playboy of the Western World*. His book *The Aran Islands* (1907) and the film *Man of Aran* (1934) by Robert Flaherty, an American, illustrate the traditional island way of life.

Cows spent the summer grazing in Connemara but returned to Aran where it was dry for the winter; ponies however wintered in Connemara and worked on Aran during the summer months. Illicit whiskey and also peat for fuel were imported by boat from Connemara in exchange for potatoes and limestone.

Despite or because of their remote situation the Aran Islands have been inhabited for centuries. The earliest surviving ruins are the great stone forts which date from the prehistoric era. The later more abundant ruins date from the early and medieval Christian period (5C–16C) when the Aran monasteries were important cultural centres.

Traditional crafts are still practised, particularly the production of the distinctive cream-coloured Aran knitwear using the symbolic stitches which represent elements in nature and the Aran way of life; originally the women spun the wool and the men did the knitting using goose quills for needles.

Access ⊘

By air from Inverin *(20mi/32km west of Galway by R 336)*.
By sea from Galway, from Rossaveel *(23mi/37km west of Galway by R 336)* and from Doolin in the Burren (Inisheer only).

INISHMORE (ARAINN)

The island (population 1 000) (9mi/14.5km x 2.5mi/4km) is served by one road which runs from the airstrip along the shore of Killeany Bay *(Cuan Chill Éinne)*, through Kilronan *(Cill Rónáin)* to the remote hamlet of Bun Gabhla overlooking Brannock Island *(Oileán Dá Bhranóg)* and the lighthouse. The old tracks and walls (7 000mi/11 265km) run from northeast to southwest following the natural rifts and the traditional pattern of movement carting seaweed from the shore to fertilize the fields. At the roadside stand square pillars topped by crosses erected in memory of islanders who died abroad or at sea.

Aran Heritage Centre (Ionad Arann) ⊘ – *In Kilronin*. The centre provides an introduction to the landscape, traditions and culture of the islands, particularly Inishmore.

★★★ **Dún Aenghus (Dún Aonghasa)** – *4.5mi/7.2km west of Kilronan; 20min there and back on foot from Kilmurvy (Cill Mhuirbhigh)*. A path leads uphill to a great drystone fort

Inishmore

set on the very edge of the cliffs (200ft/61m above sea-level). It is one of the finest prehistoric monuments in Europe and consists of three lines of defence. The ground between the outer and the middle wall is spiked with stone stakes set at an angle to impede attack. A square tunnel in the thickness of the wall leads into the inner compound. The inner wall, which has steps up to wall walks, describes a semicircle beginning and ending on the cliff edge; it is not known whether the fort was originally this shape or whether some of it has collapsed into the sea.

St Brecan's Church (Teampall Bhreacáin) – *5.5mi/8.8km west of Kilronan.* In a hollow on the north coast overlooking a small bay is an ancient monastic site including an early church, greatly altered in the late Middle Ages, and dedicated to St Brecan whose grave is opposite the west door. In the southeast corner of the graveyard is a stone inscribed to seven Roman saints.

St Kieran's Church (Teampall Chiaráin) – *1mi/1.7km northwest of Kilronan; bear right in Mainistir.* Half way down the slope to the shore stands a small ruined church dedicated to St Kieran of Clonmacnoise. Surrounding the church are four cross-inscribed stones and St Kieran's Well.

Arkin's Castle (Caisleán Aircín) – *1mi/1.6km south of Kilronan in Killeany.* On the south shore of Killeany Bay stand the ruins of a tower house which was probably built by John Rawson, to whom the islands were granted by Elizabeth I in 1588. It was fortified by Lord Clanrickard against the Cromwellians who captured it in 1652, lost it and recaptured it in 1653.

St Benen's Church (Teampall Bheanáin) – *1mi/1.6km south of Kilronan; in Killeany bear right; 10min there and back on foot.* A path climbs the hill past St Eany's oratory (6C or 7C) with a narrow north door and a slim east window. There is a good **view** of Killeany Bay and of the mainland: the Burren *(south)* and the mountains of Connemara *(north).*

St Eany's Church (Teaghlach Éinne) – *1.5mi/2.4km south of Kilronan.* On the coast south of the airstrip, almost submerged by the surrounding graves, are the ruins of an early church with antae and a round-headed window. St Enda is said to be buried here on the site of the monastery, which he founded in about 490. His reputation as a teacher attracted so many famous men to study under him – St Kieran of Clonmacnoise, St Finnian of Moville on Inishowen, St Jarlath of Tuam, St Colman of Kilmacduagh near Loughrea – that the island, where 227 saints are buried, became known as Aran of the Saints.

INISHMAAN (INIS MEÁIN)

The island (3mi/5km x 1mi/2km) slopes from a bare rocky plateau northeast to a sandy shore. The houses are strung out in the lee of the high ground. JM Synge is said to have favoured a sheltered spot called Synge's Chair *(Cathaoir Synge)* on the western cliffs overlooking Gregory's Sound *(Sunda Ghrióra).*

Dún Conor (Dún Chonchúir) – The huge prehistoric fort (restored) stands on high ground in the centre of the island on the edge of a narrow valley; it consists of a thick stone wall (17.5ft/5.65m), stepped on the inside, round an oval enclosure (227ft/69m x 115ft/35m), which is flanked to the east by an outer court; the entrance is protected by a stone bastion.

Dún Moher or Dún Fearbhaigh – This smaller stone fort (103ft/31m x 90ft/27m) stands on the edge of the high ground overlooking the landing jetty at Cora Point.

INISHEER (INIS OÍRR)

On the smallest island the houses cluster along the north coast.
Near the airstrip are the ruins of **St Cavan's Church** *(Teampall Chaomháin),* threatened by the sand; the chancel with its round-headed east window dates from the early 10C; the chancel arch and south door are medieval, probably 14C. The grave of St Cavan, the brother of St Kevin of Glendalough, lies nearby *(northeast).*
In the centre of the settlements stands **Dún Formna**, a stone fort (170ft/52m x 123ft/37m), which contains the ruins of a tower house, probably built by the O'Briens in the 14C and destroyed by the Cromwellians in 1652.
Northwest of the houses are the ruins of **St Gobnet's Church** *(Kilgobnet);* the small medieval oratory has an altar, a round-headed east window and a flat-headed doorway narrowing towards the top.

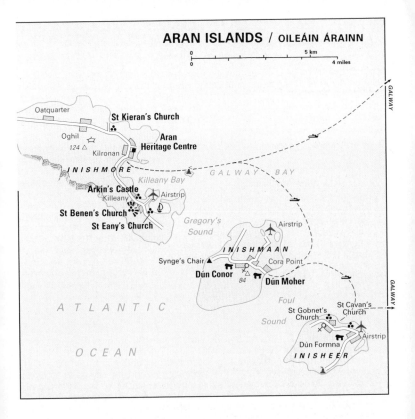

ARAN ISLANDS / OILEÁIN ÁRAINN

ARDMORE ★

AIRD MHÓR – Co Waterford – Population 436
Michelin Atlas p 79 and Map 923 – I 12

Ardmore is renowned as a holiday resort with a small pier, a large amusement park and an extensive sandy beach which is safe for bathing. From the hotel in the village there is a steep climb to the well-defined footpath that leads past Dysert church to Ram Head (2mi/3km) for a view of the coast. It is also noted for its ecclesiastical remains which date from the time of St Declan.

★ **Round Tower** – The round tower, which probably dates from the 12C, stands four storeys high (97ft/29m) and is crowned by its conical cap. It is built of regular masonry and has roll moulding round the doorway, projecting string courses marking each storey and projecting corbels carved with human and other ornaments.

★ **Church** – *Next to the round tower.* The "cathedral", which dates from the 10C to 14C, has an interior arcade and a pointed arch dividing the nave and chancel. The outstanding feature is the exterior **arcade★** of sunken panels placed on the west gable, probably during 12C restoration work; there are 13 recesses above and two larger ones below. All but three of the upper panels are filled with sculptures similar in style to those found on high crosses dating from the 10C; this suggests that they were brought to Ardmore from elsewhere; the best-known panel (*n° 10*) depicts the Weighing of Souls. The original building, also known as **St Declan's Oratory**, probably dates from the 5C settlement of Ardmore by St Declan; the eastern part of the church appears to be 14C.

Dysert Church – *Footpath to Ram Head.* Near the cliff edge are the ruins of the west gable and south wall of a church. Nearby is **St Declan's Holy Well**.
On the beach below is St Declan's Stone, a glacial boulder said to have carried the saint's bell across St George's Channel from Wales.

EXCURSIONS

★ **Whiting Bay** – *2mi/3.2km west of Ardmore by the coast road.* The bay, which is flanked by Cabin Point and Ardoginna Head, is very isolated but offers fine **views** *(southwest)* across Youghal Bay to Knockadoon Head.
For adjacent sights see DUNGARVAN, LISMORE, YOUGHAL.

ATHLONE

Athlone, the "Ford of Luan", occupies a strategic position commanding a crossing point on the River Shannon south of Lough Ree. It is the county town of Westmeath. Early in the 20C, owing to its central position on the map, it was proposed as the capital of the new Republic. There is a **fine view**★ of Lough Ree from Ballykeeran Viewpoint *(4mi/6.4km northeast by N 55)* and there are excursions on Lough Ree from the marina at Coosan Point.

Siege of Athlone – Following the Battle of the Boyne *(see p 91)* the Jacobite forces retreated to Athlone. In June 1691 the Williamite army under Ginkel made a determined assault on the bridge; Sergeant Custume, who died in its defence, is commemorated in the name of the local barracks. After 10 days of bombardment the town and the castle fell. Ginkel was made Earl of Athlone. The Jacobites withdrew southwest to Aughrim *(see p 222)*.

John McCormack

The famous tenor singer, John McCormack (1884–1945), was born in The Bawn, a narrow street in the centre of Athlone. He had a beautiful tenor voice and sang in the Palestrina Choir of the Pro-Cathedral in Dublin. He spent most of his career in the USA and was made a Count of the Papal Court for his charity work.

SIGHTS

Athlone Castle ⊙ – *Market Square.* Early in the 13C John de Grey, Justiciar of Ireland, built a stone castle on the west bank. The curtain wall and its three fortified towers date from the late 13C. The oldest part of the structure is the central polygonal **keep;** early in the 19C the upper part was greatly altered to accommodate heavy artillery supplemented by new defences, known as the Batteries, west of the town. From the battlements there is a good **view** of the river and the town. The **Exhibition Centre** provides an audio-visual presentation of the Siege of Athlone and the life story of the world-famous tenor, **John McCormack**.
The **Castle Museum**, housed in the keep, covers local history and folk life and displays souvenirs (gramophone and silver cups) of John McCormack.

Church of St Peter and St Paul – *Market Square.* The church with its twin towers and cathedral-like proportions was designed by Ralph Byrne and consecrated in 1937. Most of the stained-glass windows were designed by the Harry Clarke studios but the one in the priest's sacristy is by Sarah Purser.

Town Centre – From the bridge the main street curves east towards the site of the Dublin Gate. In a side turning *(left)* stand the ruins of Court Devenish *(private)*, a Jacobean house (1620) ruined in 1622. The Bawn, a narrow street *(left)*, contains the **birthplace of John McCormack**. The **Franciscan Church** (1931), south of the main street, was built in the Hiberno-Romanesque style inspired by old Irish designs. The **Strand** along the river bank to Burgess Park provides a fine view of the weir, the eel fisheries and the old port on the west bank.
For adjacent sights see BIRR, CLONMACNOISE, LONGFORD, LOUGHREA, MULLINGAR, ROSCOMMON, TULLAMORE.

ATHY

Athy is a pleasant small town on the River Barrow, for many years the property of the Fitzgeralds, Dukes of Leinster. At the beginning of the Middle Ages it was the largest town in Co Kildare, clustered round a fortified crossing of the river. Athy marks the confluence of the River Barrow and the Barrow Line, a southern branch of the Grand Canal; it provides pleasant riverside walks and good fishing for coarse and trout anglers.
In 1944 **Macra na Feirme**, a cultural and social organization for young farming people, was founded in the Town Hall.

Town Centre – The present bridge, known as Crom-a-Boo Bridge, from the war cry of the Geraldine family, dates from 1796. Beside it stands White's Castle *(private)* which was built in the 16C.
The main square beside the river is graced by the **Courthouse**, which was built in 1856 as the Corn Exchange. On the opposite side of the square stands the **Town Hall**, which dates from the mid 18C and has housed a market, council chambers and law courts.

The brick-vaulted ground floor now houses the **Heritage Centre** ⊙ ; its displays evoke the history of the town and of the personalities and events associated with it, such as the Antarctic explorer Ernest Shackleton and the famous Gordon Bennett motor race.

Dominican Church – The fan-shaped modern church is furnished with stained-glass windows and Stations of the Cross by George Campbell, a noted North of Ireland artist of the earlier 20C.

EXCURSIONS

East of Barrow Valley

Ballitore – *7mi/11km east by minor road.* Population 293. The 18C **Quaker meeting house** ⊙ has been converted into a small library and museum describing Quaker settlements in the area; there is a Quaker graveyard on the far side of the village. **Crookstown Mill and Heritage Centre** ⊙ housed in a converted 1840 cornmill, contains material on the baking and milling industries, items of local historical interest, a graphic/photographic gallery and furniture workshops.

Irish Pewter Mill, Museum and Crafts Centre ⊙ – *Timolin; 11mi/16km east by minor road to Ballitore and south by N 9.* The museum displays moulds, tools and dies used for making pewter as long ago as the Middle Ages. There are demonstrations of pewter vessels being cast and a video of the spinning, smithing and polishing. The building, which is about 1 000 years old, was originally a mill or part of a nunnery.

★**Moone High Cross** – *12mi/19km east by minor road to Ballitore and south by N 9.* The scanty ruins of a 6C monastery founded by St Columba enclose a high cross (17.5ft/5.3m high) which was elaborately restored in the 19C. The 51 carved panels show scenes from the Bible; the 12 Apostles grouped in three tiers appear on the west face.

Baltinglass Abbey – *15mi/24km east by minor road to Ballitore, south by N 9 and a minor road east via Graney.* Beside the 19C Anglican church are the ruins of Baltinglass Abbey, which was founded by Dermot MacMurrough, King of Leinster, in 1148 and suppressed in 1536. Six Gothic arches flank the nave; the 19C tower and parts of the original cloisters (restored) still stand. Baltinglass, which was started by monks from Mellifont *(see p 93)*, sent out monks in its turn to found Jerpoint *(see p 197)*.

The town (population 1 066) lies at the foot of steep Baltinglass Hill; the main square is dominated by the 1798 memorial, commemorating Michael Dwyer, who was enabled to escape by his faithful comrade Sam MacAllister drawing the fire of the British soldiers on himself.

★**Castledermot High Crosses** – *9.5mi/16km southeast by R 418.* The site of a monastery founded by St Dermot is marked by two **high crosses** made of granite carved with biblical scenes and a 10C **round tower**, topped by medieval battlements. Of the Franciscan friary founded by Lord Ossory in 1302 only the chancel walls survive.

West of Barrow Valley

★★**Emo Court** ⊙ – *20mi/32km north by R 417, west by N 7 and north by R 422.* The **house** was designed in the Classical style by James Gandon in 1792 for Lord Portarlington, formerly John Dawson, a banker and an architect; the interior decor (1835–40) was completed by Louis Vulliamy. The tour of the house *(30min)* includes the entrance hall, the rotunda, the dining room, library and drawing room, all restored to their early glory and furnished with some fine pieces and varied examples of Wedgwood pottery.

An avenue of Wellingtonias, the first in Ireland, links the house to the Dublin Road. Extensive **gardens** spread from the house to the lake. The Clucker Garden is planted with azaleas, rhododendrons and Japanese maples; four statues of the Seasons and a ring garden adorn the lawns; the Grapery, which is planted with trees and shrubs, descends to the lakeside walk.

St John the Evangelist ⊙ – *Coolbanagher; from the gates of Emo Court take the road opposite through the village; turn left into R 419 (Portarlington-Portlaoise road).* James Gandon also designed this church, his only one, in 1785 for Lord Carlow. The interior is decorated with plaster swags and garlands.

★**Stradbally** – *9mi/15km northwest by R 428.* Population 1 046. The steeply-sloping flower-lined Main Street climbs towards a range of low hills. An unusual pagoda-like structure with a red roof in the Market Place commemorates Dr William Perceval, a local doctor who died in 1899 after 54 years of local practice.

The **Steam Museum** ⊙ displays a collection of old steam-powered rollers and threshing machines. A narrow-gauge steam railway (1mi/1.6km) runs through the woods. A rally of steam machines is held in the village in August.

★**Rock of Dunamase** – *12mi/20km northwest by R 428 and N 80.* The rock rising straight from the plain is crowned by the extensive and impressive ruins of the O'More clan fortress, destroyed by Cromwell's army in the mid 17C.

From the summit (200ft/60m high) there are excellent **views**★ of the surrounding plain and woods.

★**Timahoe Round Tower** – *10mi/16km west by minor road.* The round tower (96ft/29m high) was probably built in the 12C; the top leans from the vertical (2ft/0.6m); the Romanesque double doorway has steps to the interior.

The ruins of a 15C church *(east)* were converted into a castle in the 17C.

A **memorial** on the broad village green marks the visit of Erskine Childers, former President of Ireland, on 31 May 1974. Richard Nixon, President of the USA (1969–74), whose ancestors came from the village, visited Timahoe in 1970.

Abbeyleix – *24mi/39km west of Athy by N 78 south to Newtown and R 430 west.* Abbeyleix, originally the site of a 12C abbey, seems unchanged since the period when it was dominated by the de Vesci family, who laid it out in the mid 18C at the gates of their mansion. It is an excellent example of a planned estate settlement and has been designated a Heritage Town. The **Abbeyleix Heritage House** ⊘, in the old school, traces the history of Abbeyleix and its role in the evolution of the region, in which the actions of the de Vescis feature prominently. There is a fine model of the town in its setting as well as one of the Rock of Dunamase.

The old walled garden of a former Brigidine convent has been redesigned as the **Abbey Sense Garden** ⊘, with elaborate planting and other features intended to appeal to touch, taste, smell and sound as well as sight.

Heywood Gardens ⊘ – *Near Ballinakill; 3.5mi/6km southeast of Abbeyleix.* Although the mansion which they once graced has long since been replaced by a modern college building, these gardens are a fine example of the partnership between the architect Edwin Lutyens (1869–1944) and the garden designer Gertrude Jekyll (1843–1932). Architectural influences predominate, with terraces, massive retaining walls, gateways, flights of steps, pleached lime walk and hedges of clipped yew. A sunken garden has at its centre a pool overlooked by a pavilion, paths and lawns have a prospect of church towers and distant mountains, and a pergola is set high above a pond and wooded dell.

For adjacent sights see CARLOW, GLENDALOUGH, KILDARE, KILKENNY, POWERSCOURT, RUSSBOROUGH, TULLAMORE, WICKLOW MOUNTAINS.

BANTRY BAY ★

Co Cork

Michelin Atlas p 77 and Map 923 – D 12

The narrow deep-water bay in the lee of the Beara Peninsula has long been known to mariners as a safe anchorage. It takes its name from Bantry *(Beanntraí)*, a market and fishing town (population 2 777), which has changed little since the 19C; it is situated on the south shore, opposite Whiddy Island. On the north shore at the head of a natural harbour is Glengarriff *(An Gleann Garbh)*, which has been a tourist resort since the mid 19C when it acquired a certain popularity among early Victorian travellers; as early as the 1830s visitors to the area were publishing their impressions of the exotic flora which flourish in the mild climate of southwest Cork.

In about 1839 work started on blasting the tunnels that carry the road between Glengarriff and Kenmare, thus connecting the resort with Killarney. In the late 19C, when the railway was extended to Bantry, a paddle steamer service was established between Bantry and Glengarriff.

★★ILNACULLIN ⊘

Garinish Island (37 acres/ 15ha), also known as **Ilnacullin**, lies in Glengarriff Harbour. Early this century it was turned into a meticulously planned Italianate garden, featuring Classical pavilions and an extensive variety of exotic floral species; flowers are in bloom all year because of the mild weather and the garden's protected position. A path leads to the **Martello Tower** (135ft/41m above sea-level), the highest point on the island.

Out and about in Bantry Bay

There is a **ferry** ⊘ from Bantry Pier to **Whiddy Island** and there are scenic cruises of Bantry Bay.

The indoor swimming pool, children's pool and toddlers' pool and leisure centre at the Westlodge Hotel in Bantry are open to the public throughout the year.

The **Bantry Mussel Fair** is held in May *(second weekend)* each year and the **International Chamber Music Week** in July *(second week)*.

1796 French Armada

In the winter of this year a French fleet commanded by General Hoche and inspired and accompanied by Wolfe Tone, an Irishman, set sail from Brest intending to invade Ireland and expel the British. The fleet, which carried 15 000 troops and consisted of 19 ships of the line, 13 frigates, six corvettes and luggers, and nine transport vessels, was dispersed by fog, and a contrary wind prevented some ships from entering Bantry Bay. Their appearance and the threat of invasion by 6–7 000 foreign troops caused great alarm. A storm blew up forcing the ships to retire. Some cut anchor and one of the anchors (17cwt/863kg), brought up by a local trawler in 1964, now stands beside the road south of Bantry (N 71). Ten French warships were destroyed, including the frigate *La Surveillante*, which was scuttled by its crew on 2 January 1797. By the time Hoche arrived in the second group of ships, the first had returned to France and he was obliged to retreat. One of the French longboats, which was captured, is now displayed in the National Maritime Museum in Dún Laoghaire

★ GLENGARRIFF

The town consists of little more than a main street with shops and pubs, hotels and guesthouses. Queen Victoria stayed at the **Eccles Hotel**, which was built in 1833 as a coaching stage and has retained its original façade and some interior features. George Bernard Shaw wrote part of his play *St Joan* in the dining room and the remainder on Garinish island.

The Church of the Holy Trinity (Anglican), built in 1866 in the Gothic style, has memorials and **stained-glass** windows of interest; the Church of the Sacred Heart (Roman Catholic) is early 20C, faced with locally quarried stone.

There are pleasant walks along the wooded shore of the Blue Pool (*poll gorm* in Irish) in the northwest corner of Glengarriff Harbour. The best views of Glengarriff are from the top of **Shrone Hill** (919ft/280m – *southwest*) and from the mountain road to Kenmare.

★ BANTRY HOUSE ⊙

Ten years after its construction in 1740, Bantry House was purchased by the White family, which had settled on Whiddy Island in the late 17C. In recognition of his loyal service against the French threat in 1796, Richard White (1767–1851) was raised to the peerage. His son, Viscount Berehaven (1800–68), enlarged the house and laid out the **terraced Italianate gardens** (*109 steps*) which rise behind the house on the south side. The north front overlooking Bantry Bay and Whiddy Island was added in 1820 and the house was further enlarged in 1840.

B Lynch /Bord Fáilte, Dublin

Bantry House Gardens

1796 Bantry French Armada – *East stables*. The converted buildings now house a detailed exhibition on the French Armada *(see above)*. It describes the historical context of the expedition and the composition of the fleet and traces the sequence of events, using a cut-away model of *La Surveillante*, which was scuttled in Bantry Bay, exhibits rescued from the sea and extracts from the journal of Wolfe Tone, who is shown in his cabin on board one of the frigates.

House – There are family portraits throughout the house. Many items among the furniture and furnishings were bought by Viscount Berehaven who travelled widely in Europe. Set into the hall floor are four coloured panels from Pompeii. In the **inner hall** hangs the original standard of the Bantry Yeoman Cavalry formed in 1776; beside the huge fireplace stands an impressive Russian travelling household shrine containing many 15C and 16C icons, brought from Russia in the 19C.

The **Rose and Gobelin Drawing Rooms** are furnished with late-18C Savonnerie carpets, a Gobelin tapestry and Aubusson tapestries; one was made for Marie-Antoinette, the other covering the settee and chairs depicts the fables of La Fontaine. The **dining room**, a spectacular room with royal blue walls, is dominated by **portraits** of King George III and Queen Charlotte, which were presented by the king at the time of the ennoblement; between them hangs a Gobelin tapestry. The fireplace is 18C, with ironwork made in Bandon; the Spanish chandelier is decorated with Meissen porcelain flowers. The long **library**, heated by two fireplaces, contains many old and rare **books** and an 1897 Blüthner grand piano.

17C Spanish leather decorates the panelling on the walls of the main **stairs**.

The **old kitchen**, with its range, now serves as a tea room next to the craft shop.

WHIDDY ISLAND

The island has had a varied history as the many ruins testify: Kilmore church and graveyard; Reenavanig Castle, the first residence of the White family; fortifications, including three gun batteries, erected by O'Sullivan Bere in 1801. An American Sea Plane Base was in operation on the island for a few months at the end of the First World War. The oil refinery, built in 1968, ceased operations in 1979 following the explosion of the tanker *Betelgeuse*.

EXCURSIONS

★**Gougane Barra Forest Park** – *23mi/38km – half a day. From Ballylickey take R 584 east inland.*
The approach road climbs inland between the vertical rock walls of the **Pass of Keimaneigh** (2mi/3.2km).
West of the lake which is the source of the River Lee a **forest drive** (3mi/4.8km) makes a loop through the extensive forest park (walks and nature trails) which rises up the steep mountain slopes beside the tumbling mountain stream. St Finbar, the 6C founder of Cork, had a hermitage on the island in the lake. A small causeway leads to the modern island chapel, a popular place of pilgrimage, built in the Irish Romanesque style.

Kilnaruane Inscribed Stone – *2mi/3km south of Bantry by N 71; turn left at the Westlodge Hotel (sign). After 0.25mi/0.4km park by the signpost; walk across the field (right).* On the hilltop marking the site of a now-vanished ecclesiastical establishment stands a 9C stone pillar, which may have been the shaft of a high cross. The stone bears panels of interlacing as well as *(northeast face)* a boat with four oarsmen, possibly a curragh, navigating through a sea of crosses, and *(southwest face)* a cross, a figure at prayer and St Paul and St Anthony in the Desert.
For adjacent sights see BEARA PENINSULA, KILLARNEY, SKIBBEREEN.

BEARA PENINSULA ★
Co Cork & Co Kerry
Michelin Atlas p 76 and Map 923 – BC 12,13

The wealth of the 19C copper mines has gone leaving only disused workings but the magnificent scenery of sandy beaches backed by the Caha and Slieve Miskish Mountains remains.

COAST AND MOUNTAIN ROAD
Round tour of 85mi/137km – 1 day

From Glengarriff (see p 81) take R 572 west; in Adrigole turn right (sign) to the Healy Pass.

★★**Healy Pass** – *The road is particularly steep near Glanmore Lake.* The road, which was opened in 1931, climbs through a series of tortuous hairpin bends *(7mi/11km)* to the summit; on a clear day the **views**★★ are very impressive.

At the crossroads turn left to Derreen Gardens (sign).

The **Healy Pass** was named after Tim Healy, who was born in Bantry in 1855. He was a Nationalist MP at Westminster from 1880 until 1916 and in 1922 he was appointed the first Governor-General of the Irish Free State. At a presentation in the Anchor Bar, Bantry, on his retirement as Lord Chief Justice of Ireland, he was invited to choose a leaving present; he asked for improvements to be made to the bridle pass from Adrigole to Lauragh on the Beara Peninsula.

★**Derreen Gardens** ⊘ – The gardens were planted 100 years ago by the 5th Lord Lansdowne beside Kilmakilloge Harbour, an inlet on the south shore of the Kenmare River. The woodland gardens contain many azaleas and rhododendrons; the most notable attraction is the grove of New Zealand tree ferns.

Take R 571 west for 8mi/12.9km to the Ballycrovane junction.

Ballycrovane Ogam Pillar Stone – In a field stands the tallest pillar stone in Ireland (15ft/5m high); the Ogam inscription – MAQI-DECCEDDAS AVI TURANIAS – of the son of Deich descendant of Torainn – was probably added later.

Continue west to Eyeries.

Eyeries – This tiny village, the home of Milleens cheese, looks like the film set of an Irish mountain settlement with four pubs, a couple of shops and scattered cottages. There is a beach *(1mi/1.6km west).*

Take R 575 west along the coast to Allihies.

Allihies – In the 19C Allihies was a prosperous mining community; above the straggling village *(sign)* are the extensive remains of the **copper mines★**. Old engine houses and spoil heaps still stand sentinel on the mountainside. The mine buildings and outcrops may be explored but with great care as there are many abandoned mineshafts in the immediate area. The mines were started in 1812 and enjoyed their greatest prosperity until 1842, although working continued intermittently until 1962. Many Cornish miners were brought to Allihies but of that "invasion" no trace is left today.

Slide File, Dublin

Allihies

Ballydonegan Strand – *1mi/1.6km south.* The magnificent beach is composed of crushed stone from the mines.

Continue south on R 575; after 2.5mi/4.2km turn right onto R 572.

Garnish Bay – At low tide one can walk from the tiny hamlet of six houses and a post office to **Garnish Island**, a good vantage-point for **views★** *(north)* of the Iveragh Peninsula and *(northwest)* of the Skellig Islands.

Continue west to Dursey Island.

Dursey Island ⊙ – *Access by cable-car. Limited tourist accommodation.* There is one village, Kilmichael (population 50), and one road; from the western end one can see the old and new Bull Rock lighthouses.

Return east; after 1.5mi/2.4km turn right to Crow Head.

Crow Head – The bleak headland is a good vantage-point for Mizen Head *(south)* and the Skellig Islands *(north)*. On 23 July 1943 a Luftwaffe Junkers plane crashed in fog killing all four crew *(plaque).*

Continue east on R 572; after 6mi/9.7km turn left.

Slieve Miskish Mountains – *After 2mi/3km the road becomes a track suitable only for climbers.* The high climb into the mountains is rewarded with splendid **views★**; the summit commands the entire length of Bantry Bay.

Return to R 572 and continue east; after 1mi/1.6km turn right (sign) to Dunboy Castle (0.5mi/0.8km).

Dunboy Castle – Surrounded by Dunboy woods *(walks and picnic areas)* are the remains of O'Sullivan Bere Castle, which was destroyed during a siege in 1602, and the vast shell of the 19C Dunboy Castle, part French château, part Italian villa, which was burned down in 1921 during the War of Independence. It was built by the Puxley family, the local landlords, with the huge royalties produced by the Beara copper mines. The history of the family and the mines inspired Daphne du Maurier to write *Hungry Hill.*

Continue east on R 572 to Castletownbere.

Castletownbere – Population 921. This fishing town was developed in the early 19C when rich copper deposits were discovered at Allihies. The area was particularly badly hit by the 19C potato famine. Later in the century Castletownbere became an important fishing port; fish processing is now a substantial industry.

Bere Island ⊘ – *No tourist accommodation.* The island, which is inhabited by a dozen families, is the headquarters of a sailing school. Once an important base for the Royal Navy, Bere Island was handed over by the British Government in 1938, together with Spike Island and Crosshaven fort in Cork Harbour and Lough Swilly in Donegal.

Take R 572 east to return to Glengarriff.

For adjacent sights see BANTRY BAY, IVERAGH PENINSULA, KILLARNEY.

BIRR ★

BIORRA – Co Offaly – Population 3 355
Michelin Atlas p 90 and Map 923 – I 8

Birr lies at the confluence of the Little Brosna and Camcor Rivers in the south mid-lands. Owing to its central position, it was referred to as Umbilicus Hiberniae in the Down Survey *(see p 175)*. It is an attractive Georgian town dominated by Birr castle and demesne.

Parsonstown – Until the establishment of the Irish Free State Birr was known as Parsonstown in King's County. In 1620 the small village was granted to Sir Lawrence Parsons, who started weekly markets, set up a glass factory and built most of the castle. In 1642 much of the new town was destroyed by fire during a siege by local clans; in 1690 Birr was garrisoned by the Williamites and besieged by the Duke of Berwick. During the more peaceful 18C and 19C the town and the castle and demesne were much extended.

Out and about in Birr

Birr Vintage Week is an annual event *(second half of August)*, during which there is a Georgian Cricket Match played by men in period costume according to the 1744 rules, and the Irish Independent Carriage Driving championships are held in the Castle demesne. An astronomy weekend takes place in September. Concerts are given in the Castle and the park; exhibitions are held in the **Castle gallery**.

The Parsons, later ennobled as the **Earls of Rosse**, constantly improved their property and inaugurated some notable "firsts". **Sir William Parsons**, a patron of Handel, enabled the composer to stage the first performance of *Messiah* in Dublin in 1742. His grandson, another Sir William, the 4th baronet, devoted much time to the late-18C Volunteers. **Sir Lawrence**, the 5th baronet, was more nationalist in political sentiment and a friend of **Wolfe Tone** but he retired from politics after the Act of Union in 1800. In the 19C the family genius made **scientific discoveries** and in the 20C was directed towards the collection and propagation of the **rare botanical species** to be found in the gardens.

★★ BIRR CASTLE DEMESNE *2–3hr*

Gardens – The pleasure grounds (100 acres/40ha) have over 1 000 species of trees and shrubs. The 4th baronet started to landscape the park, creating the lake out of a bog and planting many trees. The 6th Earl, who collected seeds from the Americas and the Far East earlier this century, gave the demesne one of the world's finest collections of trees and shrubs, particularly strong on Chinese and Himalayan species. Some of the trees are so rare that seeds have been taken from them for the Royal Botanical Gardens at Kew in London.

The spring-flowering varieties include magnolias, crab apples and cherries while the chestnuts, maples and weeping beech provide strong autumnal colours. The **formal gardens** are subdivided by pleached hornbeam alleys and box hedges which appear in the Guinness Book of Records as the tallest in the world.

Extensive herbaceous displays adorn the terraces below the crenellated 17C **castle** *(private)*.

There are many attractive **walks**: the high and low walks near the castle, the lilac walk, the lagoon walk, the lake walk and the river walk with bridges over the Camcor and Little Brosna Rivers which bisect the gardens and form waterfalls.

★★**Great Telescope** – In the 1840s the 3rd Earl of Rosse built a telescope, the **Leviathan of Parsonstown**, which enabled him to see further into space than anyone before; its mirror (72in/183cm) was cast in a furnace built at the bottom of the castle moat and fired with turf from nearby bogs. Astronomers came from as far as Australia, Russia and the USA to see the telescope, which was in use for 60 years until 1908. Lord Rosse used it to explore the nebulae and, as photography was not sufficiently advanced to record the results, he drew them. The restoration of the telescope to full working order was completed in 1997.

Great Telescope, Birr

Birr Scientific and Heritage Foundation

Galleries of Discovery – The exhibition set in part of the stable yard celebrates the brilliant activities of the Parsons family – the building of the first-known example of a wrought-iron Suspension Bridge by the 2nd Earl of Rosse; the construction of the great telescope and the discovery of distant galaxies by the 3rd Earl of Rosse; the invention of the Steam Turbine Engine by Charles Parsons in the 1890s; the pioneering work in photography by Mary Countess of Rosse in the 1850s; the world-wide plant-collecting expeditions conducted by the 5th and 6th Earls of Rosse.

★BIRR TOWN

Oxmantown Mall leads from Birr Castle gates between a row of elegant Georgian houses and a line of mature trees to **St Brendan's** 19C Anglican church. **Oxmantown Hall** (1899), which has been restored and is used as a small theatre for the Birr Stage Guild, is decorated with carved wooden gables and heraldic beasts.
The town centre is formed by **Emmet Square**, formerly Cumberland Square after the Duke of Cumberland, whose statue (1747) once crowned the central column; among the Georgian houses is Dooley's Hotel (1740).
In **John's Mall** stands a statue of the 3rd Earl of Rosse, the astronomer.
There is a riverside walk on the south bank of the Camcor.

Birr Heritage Centre – *John's Mall*. The centre, which traces the history of Birr, occupies John's Hall, an old schoolhouse built in 1833 in the style of a Greek temple to designs by Bernard Mullins.
It is flanked by the **Birr Stone**, a large limestone rock, which was probably part of a megalithic monument near Seffin, the supposed meeting place of the mythical Fianna warriors; in 1828 it was removed to a mansion in Co Clare to be used as the Mass rock but returned to Birr in 1974.
The Russian cannon dates from the Crimean War (1854–56).

One of the signatories of the American Declaration of Independence in 1776, Charles Carroll of Carrollton, was the grandson of Charles Carroll, who emigrated in 1688 from Letterluna in the Slieve Bloom mountains to the USA, where he was granted land in Maryland.

EXCURSIONS

★Slieve Bloom Mountains – *Round tour of 46mi/73km – half or whole day. From Birr take R 440 east.* **Kinnitty** (population 265), a small unspoiled village with a wide main street, is the western gateway to the Slieve Bloom Mountains, which have been designated an environmental park. Maps and relevant information on exploring the uplands are available from the **Slieve Bloom Display Centre** ⊙ . In the graveyard of the local Anglican church *(minor road south to Roscrea)* is the **Kinnitty Pyramid** (1830), inspired by the pyramid of Cheops in Egypt, as the burial place of the Bernard family from Kinnitty Castle.

The **Slieve Bloom Way** (44mi/70km), a long-distance footpath, provides those with energy with a fine view of the heights (1 728ft/527m), which are covered in mountain blanket bog and several pine and spruce plantations; there are scenic routes, riverside and forest walks, picnic areas and hilltop **viewing points.**

A less adventurous tour may be accomplished by taking the road east from Kinnitty to Drimmo, which passes **Forelacka Glen** *(right)* in a fold of the hills and runs parallel with the Camcor river before veering south towards the Delour River. The minor road north to Clonaslee passes through **The Cut** before descending the Gorragh River valley.

Banagher (Beannchar) – *8mi/13km north by R 439.* Population 1 423. The town is situated on the south bank of the Shannon at an important crossing point. The plaque on the bridge, built in 1843, bears the name King's County, the former name of Co Offaly.

On the west bank of the Shannon stands Cromwell's Castle; its name derives from the fact that bastions were added to the original tower house in about 1650; in the Napoleonic period a cannon was mounted on the top.

Charlotte Brontë *(see p 333)* spent her honeymoon nearby and her husband, the Revd Arthur Nicholls, whose family owned Hill House and whose brother was Manager of the Dublin–Banagher stretch of the Grand Canal, resided in Banagher after her death.

Another literary resident was Anthony Trollope *(see p 102)*.

Shannon Harbour – *11mi/18km north by R 439 and minor roads from Banagher.* The junction of the Grand Canal and the Shannon is now a popular mooring for river cruisers. In its commercial heyday a dry dock, warehousing, a customs post and a hotel (now in ruins) were available beside the lock and canal basin; the local population numbered 1 000, up to 300 000 tons of produce were transhipped annually and over 250 000 people used the passenger barges, many of them emigrants on their way via Limerick and Cobh to Australia, Canada and America. The locality provides excellent coarse fishing and a paradise for birdwatchers to see the rare birds, including the corncrake, which visit the wet grasslands known as the Shannon Callows.

Clonmacnoise and West Offaly Railway ⊙ – *16mi/25km north of Birr by N 52, N 62 and R 357.* The narrow-gauge railway takes passengers on a guided tour (45min–5.5mi/8km) of the **Blackwater Bog**, which is part of the Bog of Allen (20 000 acres/8 090ha), one of the largest unbroken raised bogs in Ireland. The tour includes a view of the various stages in the process of harvesting the peat to fuel the electricity power station at Shannonbridge, and a half-way halt where visitors may step out onto the bog to see and try turf cutting with a *slane*, to study the bog plants and handle a piece of bog wood, 4 000 to 7 000 years old. The railway runs past two trial conifer plantations, established on worked-out bog, and an island farm, which occupies a patch of agricultural land completely surrounded by bog.

Cloghan Castle ⊙ – *12mi/20km north by R 439; in Banagher turn left; at Lusmagh Church keep straight on.* Cloghan Castle, a tower house built in 1336 by Eoghan O'Madden and extended by the Cromwellians, stands on the site of a 7C monastery founded by St Cronan on the north bank of the Little Brosna River. The tour, conducted by the owners, starts in the Great Hall and passes up spiral stairs and through passages in the thickness of the walls to end on the roof with a fine view of the site. On display are pieces of armour and weapons, old furniture and china, silk pictures, four-poster and tester beds, and the family tree from the 3C AD to the 20C of the present owner, O'Donovan.

Gallen Grave Slabs – *14mi/22km north by N 52 and N 62. Turn right into the drive (0.5mi/0.8km) to Gallen Priory.* The ruins of a 13C church, on the site of a monastery founded in the 5C beside the River Brosna, contain a collection of early Christian grave slabs (8C to 11C); most are attached to the rebuilt west gable.

For adjacent sights see ATHLONE, CLONMACNOISE, NENAGH, PORTUMNA, ROSCREA, TULLAMORE.

BLARNEY CASTLE ★★

Co Cork

Michelin Atlas p 78 and Map 923 – G 12

The gift of eloquent speech is said to be bestowed on all those who kiss the **Blarney Stone.** This is harder than it sounds since the famous piece of rock is set inside the parapet at the top of the castle and can be reached only by lying upside-down with a guide holding one's legs. The stone is believed to have been brought to Ireland during the Crusades.

In the 16C Queen Elizabeth I commanded the Earl of Leicester to take the castle from the head of the McCarthy clan. The Earl was frustrated in his mission but he sent back numerous progress reports which so irritated the Queen that she referred to them as "all Blarney".

Blarney Castle ◷ – Much of the present castle, which is a tower house, dates from 1446; it includes the Great Hall, the Banqueting Hall, the Earl's Room and the Young Ladies' Room. It surmounts a series of passages leading to the dungeons.

Blarney Castle

B Lynch /Bord Fáilte, Dublin

★**Blarney Castle House** – The house *(private)* was built in the 1870s in the Scottish baronial style with fine corner turrets and conical-roofed bartizans; it is surrounded by formal gardens and walks giving extensive views of Blarney lake.

Rock Close – The 19C gardens, which are built on a druidic site beside the Blarney River, contain wishing steps, which should be negotiated up and down with one's eyes closed. Two dolmens are sited in the close, which has a Fairy Glade with a sacrificial rock, also said to have druidic connotations.

Agricultural Museum – The museum displays a variety of 19C agricultural implements which have become obsolete owing to the application of modern technology to farm machinery.

Blarney Woollen Mills – The 19C woollen factory (restored) is operated as a commercial enterprise; visitors may make purchases in the enormous ground-floor shop.

For adjacent sights see COBH, CORK, KINSALE, MALLOW.

BOYLE

MAINISTIR NA BÚILLE – Co Roscommon – Population 1 695
Michelin Atlas p 96 and Map 923 – H 6

Boyle lies at the southern foot of the Curlew Mountains (867ft/264m) on the River Boyle. It is a good centre for trout and coarse fishing and the main town in the northern half of Co Roscommon, a region formerly known as Moylurg.

In 1617 the lands of the MacDermots, Lords of Moylurg, were granted to Sir John King; his fourth son, Edward, who drowned in 1636 while travelling from England to Ireland, was the subject of Milton's *Lycidas.*

SIGHTS

★**Boyle Abbey** ◷ – *2mi/3.2km east of Boyle by N 4.* The ruins belong to a Cistercian house founded in 1161 by monks from Mellifont *(see p 93).* The church is an impressive example of Cistercian architecture, showing the transition from Romanesque to Gothic style; the buildings were damaged by the Cromwellians and used as a military barrack from the 16C to 18C.

The **gatehouse,** which houses a model of the abbey and information on the monastic life *(upstairs),* opens into the cloister garth. Little remains of the cloister buildings. The chancel and transepts (12C) are the oldest part of the **church;** the barrel vault and the pointed arches derive from Burgundy, the home of the Cistercian Order. The east window is 13C. Contrary to the usual Cistercian practice the tower seems to have been part of the original design although its windows are probably 14C.

The five eastern arches on the south side of the nave date from about 1180, those on the north side from about 1190–1200; the capitals of the western pillars show West of England influence in the trumpet scallops and West of Ireland influence in the animal carving. The west window is Gothic and similar to Christ Church Cathedral in Dublin.

★King House ⊙ – At the east end of the main street stands the King mansion. It was probably designed for Sir Henry King c 1730 by William Halfpenny, an assistant of Sir Edward Lovett Pearce. It has a long narrow central hall terminating in Venetian windows, an 11-bay garden front facing the river and vaulted ceilings on all four floors; it was probably intended to have a fourth side enclosing the courtyard.

It now houses a detailed exhibition on the O'Connors, Kings of Connaught, on the MacDermots of Moylurg, on the house and its restoration after years of neglect, and on the King family (later Earls of Kingston) and their subsequent house at Rockingham *(see below)*, and on the house as a military barracks occupied by the Connaught Rangers and the Irish Army. Visitors can try their hand at writing with a quill pen and listen to recordings – a Gaelic love poem, the words and even voices of members of the King family.

Frybrook House ⊙ – *Parking in front of the house.* This is a modest Georgian house (c 1750) built for Henry Fry, who was invited to Boyle by the Earl of Kingston *(see above)* and became Chief Magistrate of the area. The tour includes the reception rooms, the principal bedroom and the staircase. Among the furnishings, some of which are original, is a postbox designed by John Nash as a model of the gatehouse at Castle Leslie. The gardens are being restored.

EXCURSIONS

★Mountain Drive *Round tour of 50mi/80km north of Boyle – half a day*

From Boyle take N 4 north.

As it climbs over the Curlew Mountains (867ft/264m) the road provides splendid **views★** of the lakes *(east).*

In Ballinafad turn left.

Ballinafad Castle – The castle, now in ruins, was built in 1590 to a 13C design with four round corner towers which are square within. It was known as the Castle of the Curlews, as it protected the Curlew Mountain pass.

Battle of the Curlews

In 1599 the last Irish victory in the Elizabethan campaign to control the country was fought in the Curlew Mountains; the English under Sir Conyers Clifford *(see below)*, President of Connaught, who was killed, were defeated by the forces of Hugh Roe O'Donnell.

Continue north on N 4. In Castlebaldwin turn left (sign) to Carrowkeel Cemetery; at the fork bear left. Park at the gate if it is locked; 1hr on foot there and back.

Carrowkeel Megalithic Cemetery – The bleak hilltop in the Bricklieve Mountains (1 057ft/321m), which provides a fine **view★★** of the surrounding country, is the site of a megalithic cemetery. The stone mounds, mostly round, contain passage graves dating from the Late Stone Age (2500 to 2000 BC). On a lower ridge (east) are about 50 round huts, probably the dwellings of the people who built the tombs.

From Castlebaldwin take the road along the shore of Lough Arrow. At the end of the lake turn left to Ballyfarnan. Make a detour east on R 284 towards Keadew (Keadue).

O'Carolan's Grave – The tombstones *(left)* mark the site of Kilronan Abbey, founded in the 6C between Lough Meelagh and the Arigna Mountains. The doorway of the ruined church is 12C–13C. In the transept is the tombstone of **Turlough O'Carolan**.

Turlough O'Carolan (1670–1738)

The blind harpist (also known as Turlough Carolan) who wrote poetry and music, including the melody of *The Star-Spangled Banner*, was born in Nobber in Co Meath. In 1684 his family moved to Carrick-on-Shannon, where Mrs MacDermot Roe became his patron, providing for his education and musical studies. She gave him a horse which enabled him to perform his compositions at the big houses. After his marriage in 1720 he lived for several years in Mohill, where he is commemorated by a statue in the town centre. He died in 1738 in Keadew (Keadue) where an annual harp Festival *(see p 371)* is held in his honour; his funeral lasted four days.

Holy Well – The well on the lake shore is named after St Lasair, the daughter of St Ronan who founded the monastery.

Return to Ballyfarnan; turn right into a steep minor road (narrow entry between two houses) to Altgowlan.

★**Arigna Scenic Drive (Slí)** – From the **viewpoint** *(right)* there is a superb view of Lough Skean and Lough Meelagh. As the road crosses the watershed another fine view opens up of the steep Arigna Valley and the southern end of Lough Allen. The spoil heaps are the result of iron-ore mining. The charcoal required for smelting was obtained by felling rather than coppicing the local oakwoods.

At the T-junction turn right; after 2.5mi/4km turn left into Arigna.

Arigna – Arigna lies in a narrow river valley between steep mountains which contain some of the rare coal seams in Ireland. The coal, which was first mined to fuel the iron furnaces, later supplied the local power station until it closed in 1990.

In Arigna cross the river and turn left uphill; after 1.5mi/2.4km turn right (sign) onto a very steep and narrow road. At the next junction turn right.

★**View** – As the road descends from the bare and rugged heights there is an extensive view of Lough Allen, the most northerly of the great Shannon lakes. The river rises in a bog at Shannon Pot *(9mi/14.5km north)*. On the east shore stands Slieve Anierin (1927ft/586m), the highest point in the Iron Mountains.

At the bottom of the hill turn right onto R 280 to Drumshanbo.

Drumshanbo (Droim Seanbho) – Population 588. The town at the southern end of Lough Allen is a major coarse fishing centre offering anglers not only the waters of the Shannon but also a string of lakes in the drumlin country extending east beyond Ballinamore, which are linked by the Ballinamore and Ballyconnell Canal.

The **Sliabh an Iarainn Visitor Centre** ⊘ presents an exhibition and an audio-visual presentation on the history of the area – iron and coal mines, the narrow-gauge Cavan and Leitrim Railway, sweathouses (an ancient form of sauna bath).

From Drumshanbo take R 280 south to Leitrim.

Leitrim – The village which gave its name to the county is set at the western end of the **Shannon–Erne Waterway** *(see p 315)*.

Shannon-Erne Waterway

This canal was built (1847–58) as the Ballinamore–Ballyconnell Navigation by the engineer John McMahon to join the River Shannon with Lough Erne, the final link in a waterway system which enabled barges to travel between Dublin, Belfast, Limerick and Waterford. Because of railway competition and the lack of industry the hoped-for traffic failed to develop and the canal was abandoned in 1869; by 1880 it was derelict. In 1994 it was reopened for leisure use. The waterway (40mi/65km – 13hr) passes through 16 locks and under 34 stone bridges, traverses a chain of lakes – Lough Scur, St John's Lough, Garadice Lough – and follows the course of the Woodford River.

From Leitrim take R 284 and a minor road west to Cootehall; in Cootehall turn right and then left; continue northwest via Knockvicar to Corrigeenroe; in Corrigeenroe turn left to return to Boyle.

The road provides views of the lake and the mountains as it runs parallel with the Boyle River and skirts the north and west shores of Lough Key.

★**Lough Key Forest Park** ⊘

2mi/3.2km east of Boyle by N 4

Until 1959 the park (865 acres/350ha) was part of the Rockingham estate, which had been confiscated from the MacDermots under Cromwell (17C) and granted to the King family, later Stafford-King-Harman, Earls of Kingston.

The **Moylurg Tower**, a modern structure *(132 steps)*, provides an excellent view of the ancient region of Moylurg: Lough Key and its islands *(north)*, the Curlew Mountains *(northwest)* and the Plains of Boyle *(south)*. It stands on the site once occupied by a 16C MacDermot castle and the two mansions built by the King family. The second mansion, which burned down in 1957, was designed by John Nash in 1810 to look the same from all sides; it was serviced by tunnels, one of which runs from the foot of the tower to the restaurant.

Castle Island, Lough Key

The grounds were designed by Humphry Repton. The **woodlands** include many of the ornamental trees planted in the 18C. A **nature trail** leads past the Wishing Chair and over the Fairy Bridge, built of local limestone in 1836, to the **Bog Garden** which contains a wide range of rhododendrons and azaleas and other peat-loving plants; the paths are paved with cross-sections of oak trunks. Another bridge leads to Drumman's Island.

There are **boat trips** on the lake among its many islands: Castle Island, where a 19C folly incorporates traces of a MacDermot castle; Church Island which was occupied by a monastery from the 6C to 16C; Trinity Island *(private)*, where Sir Conyers Clifford *(see above)* was buried in a monastery of Premonstratensian canons.

Tibohine

12mi/19km southwest of Boyle by N 61, R 361 and N 5

Dr Douglas Hyde Centre ⊙ – Tibohine Anglican Church, where his father was Rector, is now devoted to the life of Douglas Hyde (1860–1949), first President of the Irish Republic (1938–45), who lived at Ratra House *(northwest)* and is buried at Tibohine. Unusually for one of Anglo-Irish origin, Douglas Hyde was an Irish scholar and collected Irish poetry and folk tales. His aim was the preservation of Gaelic as the national language of Ireland, the study and publication of existing Irish literature and the cultivation of a modern Irish literature.

For adjacent sights see CARRICK-ON-SHANNON, CASTLEBAR, KILLALA, KNOCK, SLIGO, STROKESTOWN.

BOYNE VALLEY ★★

Co Meath

Michelin Atlas p 93 and Map 923 – M 6

The fertile and well-wooded Boyne Valley holds a significant place in Irish and European history. The prehistoric inhabitants built huge grave mounds on the banks of the river and on hilltop sites such as Loughcrew *(see p 191)*.

In the pre-Christian era the High Kings of Ireland held court at Tara and the Celtic Feast of Samhain (November) was celebrated by the druids on the Hill of Ward near Athboy west of Navan.

Christianity was brought to the region by St Patrick himself. The early monastic sites at Kells and Monasterboice, which are typical of the early Irish church before its Romanization in the 12C, contrast with the European style of monastery at Mellifont, Slane and Bective.

The Norman settlers from Wales and England built castles such as Navan motte and Trim to defend the territory under their control against the native Irish; the area, known as the Pale, fluctuated in size throughout the Middle Ages. Some castles were later converted into stately homes.

Battle of the Boyne

The battle fought on 12 July 1690 was the decisive engagement in the War of the Two Kings *(Cogadh an Dá Rí)* between King James II of England, supported by Louis XIV of France, and King William III of England (William of Orange) and his allies, who were engaged in a struggle for the domination of Europe. The soldiers involved – 36 000 in William's army and 25 000 in James's – were of many nationalities: British, Danes, Dutch, Finns, French, Germans, Irish, Poles, Prussians and Swiss.

Whereas the French troops supporting James were under orders to delay William, the latter wished to achieve a speedy victory. As he was making observations on the morning of the battle, he narrowly escaped death from a bullet which tore his coat and grazed his shoulder. He sent some of his force upstream to attack the French left flank and his main force crossed the Boyne at the ford at Oldbridge and attacked the Jacobite army drawn up on the south bank; five crossings were made between 10am and 2pm. There are a viewing platform *(78 steps)* and diagram on the north bank of the river overlooking the crossing point.

During the battle the Duke of Schomberg, once a Marshal of France in Louis XIV's army, who had left France because he was a Protestant and become a soldier of fortune, was killed. William lost 500 men; James lost about 1 000. When he heard that William had crossed the river, he left for Dublin. The following day he rode to Duncannon near Waterford and took ship to Kinsale; from there he sailed to France. In the hope of reversing the Cromwellian land settlement, the Irish fought on until the following year when they suffered a series of defeats at Athlone, Aughrim and Limerick.

The Williamite victory meant the defeat of the Stuart cause in the United Kingdom and determined the balance of power in Europe. Its outcome is still a factor in Irish politics.

PREHISTORIC BURIAL SITES

The prehistoric burial sites at Knowth, Dowth and Newgrange are the oldest in the British Isles; they are 500 years older than the pyramids in Egypt and 1 000 years earlier than Stonehenge.

The burial mounds contain passage graves, built by a farming and stock-raising community in the Neolithic Era (3000–2000 BC) on the south-facing slope overlooking the River Boyne, which was then the main artery of communication. There are some 40 graves, consisting of three major graves and many satellites.

Present knowledge suggests that Dowth was built first to align with the setting sun. It was followed by Newgrange where the rising sun penetrates the inner chamber at the winter solstice. Knowth was built later facing east–west to align with the rising sun in March and the setting sun in September.

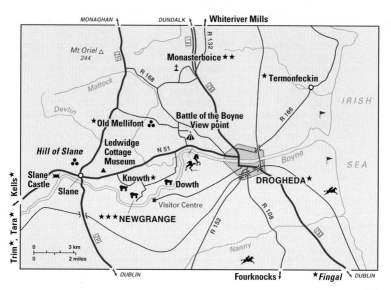

Brú na Bóinne Visitor Centre ⊘ – *South bank; footbridge over the river and bus shuttle to graves from north bank; no other access.* The display shows the site by the river as a dwelling place, and describes the clothing, food and housing of the Neolithic people, their technical knowledge, how the stones were moved on rollers and the different phases of construction and decoration.

★★★**Newgrange** ⊘ – Newgrange is one of the best examples of a passage grave in western Europe.

The **mound** (1.25 acres/0.5ha, 260ft/79m–280ft/85m in diameter and 37ft/11m high) consists of a cairn of medium-sized stones enclosed within a circle of 97 kerb stones, some of which are decorated, set on their long edges, ends touching, surmounted by a facing of round granite boulders.

Excavations in 1963 made it possible to reconstruct the original south front **revetment** of white quartz stones, except where the entrance has been enlarged to accommodate visitors.

Above the entrance, which was originally closed by an upright slab *(right)*, is the **roof box**, a unique structure with a finely-decorated lintel, through which the rays of the rising sun penetrate to the inner chamber for 17 minutes at the winter solstice (21 December).

The passage, which is lined with large standing stones, some decorated and all dressed, leads into a corbelled **chamber** a third of the way into the mound. The three de-

corated recesses contain stone **basins**, which held the bones of the dead together with funeral offerings of stone and bone beads and pendants, bone pins and small stone balls resembling marbles. The corbelled vaulted roof, completed by a central capstone (4 tonnes), is quite water-proof as the outer face of the stones is grooved to drain off water.

The mound was surrounded at a distance (39ft/12m-49ft/15m) by a **great circle** of standing stones. The four opposite the entrance are among the largest; most have been broken off near ground level.

South of the mound are traces of a late-Neolithic – early-Bronze Age **pit circle** which was uncovered in 1982.

Christopher Hill, Belfast

Newgrange

★**Knowth** ⊘ – *Excavations in progress.* The mound (40ft/12m high, 220ft/67m in diameter) probably dates from 2500 to 2000 BC. It contains two decorated passage graves discovered in 1967 and 1968; one is simply an enlargement of the passageway but the other is circular and corbelled with side chambers. It is aligned east–west and is surrounded by smaller tombs facing the large central mound. In the early centuries AD the central mound was surrounded by deep defensive ditches. In about 8C AD the settlement expanded and several souterrains and rectangular houses were built. From the 12C to 14C the site was occupied by the Normans who constructed a rectangular stone structure on the top of the mound.

Excavations conducted since 1962 have made it possible to reconstruct the smaller tombs which had collapsed owing to the passage of time and conversion of the material to other uses.

Dowth – *Closed for excavation.* The mound, which was raised by man in 3000 BC (1 acre/0.4ha, 280ft/85m in diameter, 50ft/15.24m high), contains two tombs and a souterrain connecting with the north tomb. The base of the mound was enclosed by about 100 kerb stones, many ornamented, although most are covered by landslip.

Fourknocks – *11mi/18km south of Drogheda by R 108; after 10mi/16km turn right; park in the road. Key available from the last house on the right before the stile.*
The passage grave, which dates from c 1500 BC, is unusually large compared with the size of the mound. The interior contains stones decorated with zigzags and other prehistoric designs and a human face. It contained over 60 burials.

MONASTIC SITES

★★ Monasterboice – *8mi/13km north of Drogheda by N 1.* Three **high crosses** mark the site of the monastery founded by St Buithe (Boethius), who died in 521. It was a dual foundation for men and women and an important centre of learning closely connected with Armagh.

The **South Cross** was erected by Muiredach in the 9C. The west face shows the Crucifixion, Christ with Peter and Paul, the raised Christ flanked by Apostles and the Mocking of Jesus; on the east face are the Last Judgement, the Adoration of the Magi, Moses striking the Rock, David and Goliath, the Fall of Man, and Cain slaying Abel.

The **West Cross** *(between the two ruined churches)* is unusually tall (23ft/7m) and the subjects of some of the carvings are rare. The west face shows the Crucifixion; on the shaft are the Arrest of Christ, Christ surrounded by Apostles, the Resurrection of the Dead, the Soldiers at the Tomb. The east face shows Christ Militans with *(above)* Christ walking on the water, *(right)* Simon Magus and *(below)* the Fiery Furnace; on the shaft are Goliath, Samuel anointing David, the Golden Calf, the Sacrifice of Isaac, David killing a lion.

The **North Cross** *(northeast corner of the graveyard)* also shows the Crucifixion on the west face. The original shaft is contained in the same enclosure as well as a monastic sundial indicating the hours of the Divine Office.

Behind the north church lies an early **grave slab** bearing the name Ruarcan.

The **round tower** and its treasures were burned in 1097.

★ Mellifont Old Abbey ⊘ – *6mi/10km west of Drogheda by N 51, R 168 and a minor road west of Tullyallen.* Mellifont, the honey fountain, was founded on the banks of the River Mattock, was founded by St Malachy in 1142 with four Irish and nine French monks. It was the first Cistercian house in Ireland. Modern Mellifont Abbey (1938) is at Collon *(3mi/4.8km north).*

Still standing are the ruined **gatehouse** *(right)* beside the approach road, the vaulted **Chapter House** (14C) and four faces of the two-storey **octagonal lavabo** (12C), where the monks washed their hands before eating in the refectory opposite. Excavation has revealed the outline of the monastic buildings.

Slide File, Dublin

South Cross (east face), Monasterboice

The 12C church, which was consecrated in 1157, was designed by one of the Frenchmen; it had a crypt at the west end and three chapels in the transepts – two apsidal chapels flanking a central rectangular one. In 1225 the chancel and transepts were extended. In 1556 the abbey became a private house which was abandoned in 1727.

Hill of Slane – The hilltop site has been associated with Christianity since the 5C. In 433 St Patrick travelled from Saul by sea and on foot to Slane, where he lit a fire on the hilltop on Easter Eve to challenge the druids who were holding a festival at Tara. As anyone who kindled a fire within sight of Tara did so on pain of death, Patrick was brought before Laoghaire, the High King, to whom he preached the Gospel.

Although the king remained a pagan, he allowed his subjects freedom of conscience. Erc converted and founded a monastery at Slane; he is said to be buried in the ruined mortuary house in the graveyard.

The church, which was in use until 1723, was part of **Slane Friary**, a Franciscan house, founded in 1512 by Sir Christopher Flemyng; the Flemyng arms are on the west wall of the courtyard. The friary, which housed four priests, four lay-brothers and four choristers, was suppressed in 1540, occupied by Capuchins in 1631 and abandoned under Cromwell.

On the west face of the hill is a motte raised by Richard le Flemyng of Flanders, who arrived in Ireland in 1175.

★ Termonfeckin – *6mi/10km from Drogheda by R 167 east and R 166 north.* Population 589. Close to the shore stands a 15C or 16C three-storey **tower house** ⊘ which has an unusual corbelled roof *(45 steps)*: **view** of the coast from Drogheda *(south)* to Clogher Head *(north).*

In the graveyard of St Fechin's Church stands a 10C **high cross** depicting *(east face)* the Crucifixion and *(west face)* Christ in Glory; it marks the site of a monastery founded by St Fechin of Fore *(see p 231).*

SLANE

The centre of Slane (population 699), known as the "square", was laid out by Viscount Conyngham in the late 18C; it is lit by oil lamps and bordered by four detached houses, each flanked by two smaller houses.

The Gothic Gate *(south of the crossroads)* was designed by Francis Johnston c 1795 as an entrance to Slane Castle. From the bridge over the Boyne there is a **view** of Slane Castle, Slane Mill (1766), the weir and the canal; there is a towpath walk upstream to Navan and downstream to Drogheda.

Slane Castle ⊘ – *0.25mi/0.5km west of Slane by N 51*. The impressive raised **site** overlooking the River Boyne is surmounted by an elegant assembly of square turrets, crenellations and artificial machicolations. The present house was built between 1785 and 1821 on the site of a confiscated Fleming fortress purchased by the Conynghams in 1641. It is the work of James Gandon, James Wyatt, Francis Johnston and Thomas Hopper. Capability Brown designed the stables and grounds although he did not visit Slane.

Ledwidge Cottage Museum ⊘ – *0.5mi/0.8km east of Slane by N 51*. The cottage displays some of the manuscripts of the poet, Francis Ledwidge (1887–1917), whose work, first published through the patronage of Lord Dunsany, reflects his love of the Meath countryside. His childhood home, this four-roomed semi-detached cottage, built under the Labourers' Dwellings Act (1886), has been restored to its original appearance.

For adjacent sights see DROGHEDA, FINGAL, KELLS, TARA, TRIM.

BUNRATTY ★★

Co Clare
Michelin Atlas p 84 and Map 923 – F 9

On the banks of the Bunratty River where it flows into the Shannon Estuary stands Bunratty Castle guarding the main road from Limerick to Ennis.

TOUR ⊘

★★**Castle** – The tower house, built in 1460, was restored in the 1950s to its 16C state and now displays the Gort collection of furniture and tapestries dating from the 14C to the 17C. In the evenings medieval-style banquets are held in the Great Hall which has a fine **oak roof**.

Folk Park – The park illustrates country life in Ireland at the turn of the century when the old agricultural practices were giving way to the modern era. Some of the buildings in the park were transferred from their original sites and some are replicas: the blacksmith's forge, complete with bellows and iron-working tools; the

Bunratty Castle

Slide File, Dublin

flour mill with its river-driven horizontal wheel; the houses of many regional types including the mountain farmhouse, with its settle bed and flagstone floor, and the more elaborate thatched Golden Vale farmhouse.

The **village** contains typical 19C shops, such as a pawnshop, with its three balls symbol, a pub, a post office, a hardware shop, a grocery store, a draper's shop and a printer's workshop complete with hand-set type and a hand-operated printing press.

Bunratty House – The house, built in 1804, is a local adaptation of the Georgian box house so common in Ireland. The **Talbot Collection of agricultural machinery** is displayed in the farmyard.

For adjacent sights see ADARE, ENNIS, LIMERICK.

The BURREN ★★
BOIREANN – Co Clare
Michelin Atlas pp 88–89 and Map 923 – E 8

The vast limestone plateau which covers much of Co Clare is gradually being established as a national park. The limestone is deeply fissured and most of the rivers have gone underground creating an extensive cave system and many swallow holes. When the water table rises sufficiently high, a hollow with a porous bed may fill with water and become a *turlach*.

The Burren is noted for the "opposite" contrasts of its flower population with Mediterranean and Alpine species flourishing side by side, on the dry horizontal surfaces (clints) or in the fissures (grykes).

Four thousand years of farming has largely denuded the country of trees and vegetation and the old Celtic practice of booleying *(see p 33)* is practised in reverse: in winter the cattle are kept on the higher ground, which remains relatively dry and warm owing to the Gulf Stream, and in summer, when the uplands may suffer from drought, they are kept near the homesteads, where they can be tended and watered.

Out and about in the Burren

Doolin, on the coast, is a national shrine to Irish traditional music of international stature both for the audience and for the quality of the musicianship.

There are seaside resorts to the south at **Liscannor, Lahinch** (population 550) and **Milltown Malbay** (population 615).

Slide File, Dublin

Cliffs of Moher

The BURREN

SIGHTS

In rough clockwise order starting in the north

★**Corcomroe Abbey** – The ruins of this Cistercian abbey are almost indistinguishable from the stone of the surrounding Burren. The abbey of St Mary of the Fertile Rock was founded in about 1180 by Donal Mor O'Brien or more likely his son Donat. There are carved capitals and fine vaulting in the choir and transept chapels. It was here that William Butler Yeats set his verse play *The Dreaming of the Bones*. On the north slope of Turlough Hill (925ft/282m) are the ruins of three 12C churches.

Burren exposure ⊘ – *Ballyvaughan ; just east of the village centre by N 67*. This interpretation centre occupies a splendid setting overlooking the harbour; it uses a series of audio-visual presentations to describe the geology, flora and human history which have combined in the unique landscape of the Burren.

Newtown Castle and Trail – *2mi/3km southwest of Ballyvaughan by N 67*. The stone spiral staircase of this fine 16C defensive tower house leads to a series of exhibits illustrating the recent restoration of the building and the importance of the region in medieval times as a centre for the study of law. The gallery of the Great Hall beneath the new domed roof leads to a balcony with extensive views over the Burren. A trail on the hillside behind the tower leads to a variety of natural and historic man-made features including an early lime kiln and a Victorian gazebo.

Corkscrew Hill – There is a good **view** of the limestone terraces from Corkscrew Hill on the road between Ballyvaughan and Lisdoonvarna *(N 67)*.

Aillwee Cave ⊘ – *Park in the upper car park*. The single tunnel stretching deep into the Burren (0.75mi/1km) presents stalactites and stalagmites and a **waterfall**★ which is impressively floodlit from below. The bones of a brown bear were found in one of the hibernation pits near the entrance. At the back of the Highway, the largest chamber, there is a vertical drop; even in dry weather the sound of flowing water can be heard.

The **visitor centre**, built in the style of a stone fort in harmony with its surroundings, explains the formation of the cave and its discovery in 1940 by a local herdsman, Jack McCann. Adjacent is the tiny entrance to the extensive cave systems discovered in 1987.

Megalithic tombs – Some of the many **megalithic tombs** in the Burren, in particular **Poulnabrone** ★, lie on the east side of the road between Aillwee and Leamaneh Castle *(R 480)*.

Burren Perfumery ⊘ – *Carron (signed)*. In this seemingly inhospitable limestone landscape an astonishing diversity of Mediterranean and Alpine flowers live side by side; they are the floral inspiration for a range of perfumes made here by traditional methods of distilling and blending. An audio-visual *(9min)* and photographic display give a close-up view of some of the many species of flowers growing nearby.

Leamaneh Castle ⊘ – Only the shell remains of a four-storey Elizabethan-style fortified house with mullioned windows which was built in the 17C by Conor O'Brien, who was killed in 1651 during the Cromwellian wars. From the top *(88 steps)* of the adjoining 15C **tower house** there is a fine **view**.

★**Kilfenora High Crosses** – The site of a monastery founded by St Fachtna in the 6C is marked by the remains of three 12C high crosses; a fourth cross *(100yd/90m west in a field)* shows the Crucifixion. The cathedral was built about 1190 and altered in the 15C.

96

The chancel is noted for its finely-carved triple-light east window and two effigies of bishops, thought to be 14C. The roofed nave is used for Anglican services. In the past Kilfenora (population 200) was an important episcopal see.

Burren Centre ⊘ – *Kilfenora*. The centre provides information on the district through an audio-visual presentation *(20min)* and static displays. The large-scale model of the Burren, replicas of the rare flora and fauna and reproductions of local treasures help visitors to appreciate the unique qualities of the Burren region.

Ennistimon (Inis Díomáin) – Population 917. The **waterfalls** on the River Cullenagh are visible from the seven-arch bridge that spans the river, from the river bank *(through arched entry in the Main Street)* and from the grounds of the Falls Hotel. The town is noted for its fine shop façades, many in Irish and preserving their traditional character.

Birchfield House – The ruins of the vast house, built by Cornelius O'Brien, local MP for over 20 years, are dominated by a tall column erected in his honour in 1853.

***Cliffs of Moher** ⊘ – *As the cliff edge is extremely dangerous the clifftop path is fenced. The site attracts large numbers of tourist coaches.* Great dark sandstone cliffs (600ft/182m high – nearly 5mi/8km long) rise sheer from the Atlantic; screaming sea birds throng the ledges or wheel and swoop above the waves. The best view is from **O'Brien's Tower**, built in 1853 by Cornelius O'Brien. The **Visitor Centre** provides much information on the flora and fauna of the area, including examples of local bird life.

Lisdoonvarna (Lios Dúin Bhearna) – Population 842. The village is Ireland's only spa : the sulphur spring at the Spa Wells health centre is used for medicinal purposes.

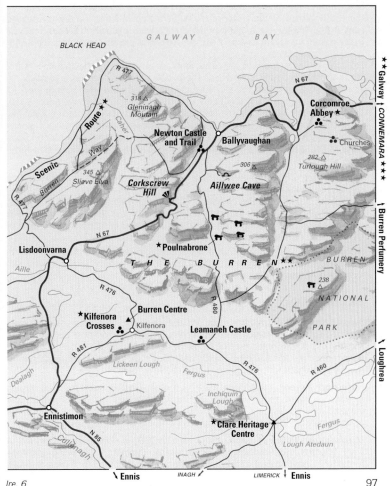

A 17C crucifix adorns the Roman Catholic Church of Our Lady of Lourdes (1878). Every September bachelors from Ireland and beyond arrive in the town to seek a wife at the Lisdoonvarna Fair.

★★Scenic Route – The coast road *(R 477)* south of Black Head provides a fine view of the huge boulders, deposited at the end of the Ice Age, which rest on the bare limestone pavement; in fine weather the Aran Islands, of similar geological formation, are visible offshore.

For adjacent sights see ARAN ISLANDS, CONNEMARA, ENNIS, GALWAY, LOUGHREA.

CAHER

AN CATHAIR – Co Tipperary – Population 2 236
Michelin Atlas p 85 and Map 923 – I 11

Caher (or **CAHIR**, pronounced Care) is an attractive historic town in south Tipperary beside the River Suir which provides attractive walks.

The town, which is dominated by its 13C castle, was largely developed by the Butler family in the 18C; from this period date the mills, the Market House, now the library, and Caher House, now a hotel, which was used by Lord Caher as the family seat after the castle had fallen into disrepair.

In spite of two 19C bankruptcies, which brought the town near to ruin, Caher developed a milling industry, owing to the diligence of six local Quaker families. The Great War Memorial, which commemorates the many local men who died in the First World War, mostly in Irish regiments, is a rarity in an Irish town.

SIGHTS

★★Caher Castle ⊘ – The castle (restored) stands on a strategic riverside site where Brian Ború, High King of Ireland (926–1014), had a residence. It was begun in the 13C by either the Worcester or the de Bermingham families and was extended early in the 15C by the Anglo-Norman Butlers who retained possession until the castle passed into State care in 1961. An **audio-visual presentation** surveys the neighbouring historic sites.

The high enclosing walls of the castle embrace an outer, middle and inner ward; there are three towers and a keep. The middle gate incorporates a **portcullis**, restored to working order. The battlements in the inner ward were built in the 19C. The **keep** was originally a 13C gate tower with a spiral stairway to the upper levels. The next largest building is the **northwest tower**, which dates from the 13C. The large room on the first floor has a 15C double-light window, while a similar window is to be found in the main room of the second floor. The roof and two walls of the **great hall** date from the 1840s. Both buildings display period furniture.

Town Centre – The split-level square is surrounded by shops and houses little changed since the 1950s.

The ruined church *(Old Church Street, N 24 to Clonmel)*, last used in the 1820s, had a curtain wall, which allowed Roman Catholics and Protestants to worship simultaneously; in the 19C, when Caher was an important garrison town, part of the adjoining cemetery was reserved for military burials.

St Paul's Church *(Church Street, N 8 north towards Cashel)*, the Anglican church, was designed in 1820 by John Nash, the famous Regency architect who also worked in Antrim and Cookstown.

EXCURSIONS

★Swiss Cottage ⊘ – *1mi/2km south of Caher by R 670.* The ornate two-storeyed thatched cottage (restored) was designed by John Nash and built between 1812 and 1814 as a fishing and hunting lodge for Lord Caher. In one of the two ground-floor rooms, the hand-painted French wallpaper shows views of the Bosporus. Nearby an elegant cast-iron bridge spans the River Suir.

Burncourt House – *8mi/13km west by N 8; in Boolakennedy turn left. Access through farmyard and across a field.* The ruined house, with its 26 gables and many chimneys, was built in 1640. Ten years later it was set on fire by the wife of its owner, Sir Richard Everard, to deny it to the Cromwellian army.

Mitchelstown Cave ⊘ – *9mi/14.5km west by N 8; in Boolakennedy turn left.* A flight of steps leads into three massive caverns (1mi/2km) containing dripstone formations – stalactites and stalagmites. The most impressive is the Tower of Babel,

Dúchas, Dublin

Swiss Cottage, Caher

a huge calcite column, in the very straight Kingston Gallery (250ft/76m long). The cave system was discovered by a quarryman in 1833. The nearby Old Caves are open only to experienced potholers.

Ronald Reagan Centre ⓥ – *Ballyporeen; 11mi/18km southwest by R 668 and R 665.* The centre shows videos, photographs and other souvenirs of the visit made in 1984 by Ronald Reagan, former US President, whose great-grandfather was born in 1829 in the vicinity of Ballyporeen (population 319).

For adjacent sights see CASHEL, CLONMEL, LISMORE, TIPPERARY.

CARLOW

CEATHARLACH – Co Carlow – Population 11 271
Michelin Atlas p 86 and Map 923 – L 9

The administrative centre of Ireland's second-smallest county, Carlow is situated on the east bank of the River Barrow where it is joined by its tributary the Burren. Below the bridge (1815) old warehouses line the quays; upstream there is a riverside walk. Carlow's most important traditional industry is sugar beet refining; in recent years the town has attracted a number of international manufacturing firms.

Frontier Town – Set on the southern frontier of the Pale, Carlow saw many battles for its possession between its Anglo-Norman rulers and the displaced native Irish. Except for the west wall and two towers (in the grounds of Corcoran's mineral water factory), the Norman **castle** (1207–13) was demolished in 1814 when a local Dr Middleton, who wanted to turn the building into an asylum, placed explosives round the walls to reduce their thickness.

The town walls, built in 1361, came under bombardment in 1650 from Ireton, Cromwell's general and son-in-law.

The last battle between the English and the Irish took place on 25 May 1798 when an army of insurgents was confronted by Crown forces in Tullow Street. Six hundred and forty United Irishmen were killed; some 400 were buried in gravel pits in Craiguecullen, a suburb of Carlow on the west bank of the river. The dead are commemorated by a memorial of Celtic design at Governey Park.

SIGHTS

Carlow Museum ⓥ – A reconstructed dairy, forge and kitchen show what farm life was like in the 19C; the printing press (1856) was used by the *Nationalist and Leinster Times*, Carlow's weekly newspaper.

Other curiosities include an Irish deer's head, lacking only its teeth, which dates from about 10 000 BC.

Cathedral – The Roman Catholic cathedral, started in 1829, the year of the Emancipation Act, and completed four years later, is a cruciform structure in the late English Gothic style surmounted by a striking slender tower, terminating in a lantern.

River Barrow

After photo B. Lynch /BORD FAILTE, Dublin

A **marble monument** by John Hogan commemorates Bishop Doyle (1786–1834), otherwise known as JKL (James of Kildare and Leighlin), a prolific writer on current affairs and politics; the allegorical female figure represents Ireland raised to one knee as a result of the bishop's efforts.

Courthouse – According to tradition, the neo-Classical courthouse (1830), designed by William Vitruvius Morrison, should have been erected in Cork but the plans were sent to Carlow by mistake.

Surrounded by impressive railings, the polygonal building has an extended porch and an Ionic portico overlooking a broad flight of steps, interrupted halfway by a plaza.

Cigar Divan – *50 Dublin Street*. The name of this shop, which has an authentic Victorian shopfront with advertisements engraved on the glass, derives from the late 19C, when Turkish cigarettes were fashionable.

EXCURSIONS

Browneshill Portal Tomb – *2mi/3km east of Carlow; from lay-by on the eastern by-pass (sign) 500yd/0.5km on foot.* Just below the brow of the low range of hills east of Carlow is this massive Megalithic dolmen, erected at some point between 3000 and 4000 BC. Its tilted capstone may weigh as much as 150 tons, making it the heaviest in Europe.

Altamont Gardens ⊘ – *12mi/19km east by R 725 to Tullow; turn right onto N 81 and left (sign)*. Designed in both formal and informal styles, the gardens have many specimen trees, an arboretum and a small garden with species of flowers normally found growing in Ireland's marshy bogs. The lake was dug out by hand to provide employment during the Famine.

On the horizon rise Mount Leinster *(south)* in the Blackstairs Mountains, and the Wicklow Mountains *(northeast)* across the River Slaney.

Leighlinbridge – *7.5mi/13km south either by N 9 down the east bank of the Barrow or by the minor road down the west bank*. Population 510. This attractive small village is set on the banks of the River Barrow, spanned by a bridge built in 1320.

The mound of Dinn Righ *(south of the village)* is the site of the ancient palace of the kings of Leinster.

At Old Leighlin *(2mi/3km west)* is the 12C Anglican cathedral, largely rebuilt in the 16C.

Killeshin Church – *2.5mi/4km west by R 430*. This idyllically located little ruin, its nave long since used as a graveyard, has a Romanesque west door with superb carving featuring animal heads and an inscription reading "A Prayer for Diarmit King of Leinster".

For adjacent sights see ATHY, GLENDALOUGH, KILKENNY, WICKLOW MOUNTAINS.

Help us in our constant task of keeping up-to-date.
Send your comments and suggestions to

Michelin Tyre PLC
Tourism Department
38 Clarendon Road
WATFORD, Herts
WD1 1SX
Tel: 01923 415000
Fax: 01923 415250
Web site: www.michelin-travel.com

CARRICK-ON-SHANNON ★

CORA DROMA RÚISC – Co Leitrim – Population 1 868
Michelin Atlas p 96 and Map 923 – H 6

Carrick-on-Shannon, now the county town of Co Leitrim, is an important crossing point on the River Shannon. Until the 16C the district, known as West Breifne, was held by the O'Rourkes, who ruled from their main stronghold at Leitrim. The town was fortified at the time of the Plantation when it was granted a charter by James I. It benefited from the improvements to the Shannon Navigation in 1846 and from the arrival of the Midland Great Western Railway in 1862. The town marks the upper limit of navigation on the Shannon and is a centre for cruising and angling.

SIGHTS

Costello Chapel ⊙ – *Bridge Street*. At the top of the street *(right)* stands a tiny mortuary chapel (16ft/5m x 12ft/4m), which was built by Edward Costello as a memorial to his wife who died in 1877. She was buried in April 1879 under a thick glass slab (left) and her husband was interred in 1891; during the intervening 12 years mass was celebrated in the chapel on the first Friday of the month.

St George's Terrace – At the east end of the street stands the **Town Clock**, erected in 1905. The **Market house** and yard *(south side)* were built in 1839 by the local landlord, CM St George, whose elegant house, **Hatley Manor** *(north side)*, was built in the 1830s and named after his ancestral home in Cambridgeshire. Next to it stands the Courthouse, designed in 1821 by William Farrell but now without its entrance portico which was supported on four Doric columns. An underground passage linked it to the neighbouring County Gaol (1822–1968). The gaol site, ideally placed in a bend of the River Shannon, is now occupied by a modern **marina**.

SHANNON VALLEY *Drive of 25mi/40km*

From Carrick-on-Shannon take N 4 southeast.

Jamestown – The stone arch through which the road enters from the north was part of the defensive wall enclosing the village which was established in 1622 to guard the river crossing.

Drumsna – Population 160. It was here that Anthony Trollope was inspired by the ruins of the Jones family mansion and the history of their downfall to write his first novel.

South of Drumnsa turn left onto R 201 to Mohill.

Mohill – Population 796. At the centre of the town there is a statue of Turlough O'Carolan (Carolan) *(see BOYLE)* seated at his harp; he lived in Mohill for several years.

Leave Mohill by R 201 which bears right at the end of the main street; at the fork bear right onto L 112; at the next fork bear right; after 0.75mi/1.2km turn left onto a narrow road (sign).

★**Lough Rynn Demesne** – Three **walled gardens** (3 acres/1.2ha), created in 1859 and now planted in the manner of a Victorian pleasure garden, ascend in three terraces from a turreted gazebo (1867) on the lake shore.
The **Blue Gate** leads to the **arboretum** which contains some rare trees (labelled); Californian redwoods, palm trees, a tulip tree, a Japanese cedar which is 140 years old and a Chilean pine (monkey puzzle) which is said to be the oldest in Ireland. The **dairy yard** (1830) has retained the original tiles and marble slabs; the **coach yard** (1850) is fitted with sliding doors; the farmyard (1840) was greatly extended in 1858; the former estate office, now a restaurant, has a small **rent window** and unusual shutters raised by leather straps.
The estate was acquired by the Clements family in 1750 and the estate buildings were erected by the 3rd Earl of Leitrim after 1854; his hasty temper, aggravated by a painful war wound, led to his assassination in 1878 for harsh treatment of his tenants.

On leaving the demesne turn right. At the T-junction turn right; after two side turnings and two crossroads bear right to Dromod.

Dromod and Roosky (population 249) are two attractive Shannonside villages where river cruisers can moor and replenish their supplies.

From Roosky continue south on N 4; after 3mi/4.8km turn left (sign) to Cloonmorris Abbey (1mi/1.6km).

Cloonmorris Ogam Stone – Beside the entrance to the graveyard of the ruined 12C church stands an Ogam stone bearing the name Qenuven.

Anthony Trollope (1815–82) in Ireland

In 1841, having been in the employ of the Post Office since 1834, Trollope was appointed a Surveyor's Clerk in Ireland, where he lived in various locations for the following 17 years before returning permanently to England. He travelled from Dublin by canal boat to his first appointment in **Banagher**, where he took up hunting, a sport he pursued with great enthusiasm for the next 35 years. He was acquainted with Sir William Gregory of Coole Park *(see LOUGHREA)*, a contemporary of his at Harrow. In 1843 during a visit to Drumsna *(see above)* he was inspired to begin his first novel, *The Macdermots of Ballycloran*, published in 1847. On 11 June 1844 he married Rose Heseltine, whom he had met in 1842 while on business in Dún Laoghaire (then known as Kingstown).

Later that year they moved to **Clonmel**, where they live in rented rooms on the first floor of a house in O'Connell Street (then High Street) and there two sons were born – Henry Merivale in March 1846 and Frederic James in September 1847. In 1845 Anthony began his second novel, also on an Irish theme, *The Kellys and the O'Kellys*, which was published in 1848.

Their next move took the family to **Mallow**, where they leased a house in the High Street from 1848 to 1851 and Anthony was able to indulge his passion for hunting with the Duhallow, the oldest hunt in Ireland,, the Limerick, the Muskerry and the United.

While on secondment in the Channel Islands in 1853, Trollope took up an existing idea and introduced the first **post boxes**, which were painted sage green.

In 1854, after a year in Belfast as Acting Surveyor, he was appointed Surveyor of the Northern District of Ireland but obtained permission to administer his duties from Dublin, where he lived at 5 Seaview Terrace, Donnybrook. As his work involved a good deal of travelling, he created a portable desk *(see p 293)* so that he could write on the train.

His third Irish novel, *Castle Richmond*, in which the action takes place during the Great Famine, was begun in 1859, the year in which he was transferred permanently to England. At the end of his life he began a fourth Irish novel about agrarian reform, *The Landleaguers*, but died in December 1882 before it was finished.

Return to N 4 and continue south; in Newtown Forbes bear right onto a minor road (direction Killashee); turn right onto N 4 and then bear left to Cloondara.

At **Cloondara** the junction of the Royal Canal, the Camlin River and the Shannon is marked by two locks, a picturesque cluster of houses beside the canal basin, a hump-backed bridge, old watermill and ruined church.

Rejoin N 5 west of the village and continue to Termonbarry.

The bridge at **Termonbarry** has a lifting section to allow boats to pass and provides a fine view of the lock and weir on the Shannon.

For adjacent sights see BOYLE, CAVAN, KNOCK, LONGFORD, ROSCOMMON, STROKESTOWN.

CASHEL ★★★

CAISEAL – Co Tipperary – Population 2 346
Michelin Atlas p 85 and Map 923 – I 10

The Rock of Cashel, an outcrop of limestone (200ft/61m) rising from the Tipperary plain, is the focal point of the town and the surrounding district. Topped by one of the most striking ecclesiastical ruins in Ireland, St Patrick's Rock has outstanding architectural remnants of the early Christian era.

Royal Seat – From about 370 until 1101 the rock was the seat of the kings of Munster, and therefore the provincial capital, and comparable in regal stature to Tara *(see p 248)*, home of the High Kings of Ireland. St Patrick visited Cashel in 450 when he baptized King Aengus; there is a legend that during the ceremony, St Patrick accidentally pierced the king's foot with the point of his staff but the king, believing it to be part of the ritual, remained composed. Cashel was a place of much importance during the 10C when the holy Cormac MacCullinan was king of Munster; he was also a bishop but not of Cashel.

Ecclesiastical Site – In 1101 the site was given to the ecclesiastical authorities whose first building, Cormac's chapel, was consecrated in 1134. The first cathedral was founded in 1169.
The arrival of Henry II in Ireland three years later marked the start of a prolonged period of unrest for Cashel. In 1494 the cathedral was burned down by Gerald Mor, the Great Earl of Kildare. The greatest act of desecration came in 1647, when Lord Inchiquin, seeking the presidency of Munster under the Cromwellian regime, attacked the town of Cashel. Hundreds of people fled to the rock. Lord Inchiquin ordered turf to be piled against the walls of the cathedral and in the subsequent fire many were roasted to death. By the end of that terrible day, most of the population of 3 000 had been killed.

In 1749 the Anglican Archbishop of Cashel decided to move the cathedral into town. The great storm of 1847 did much damage to the abandoned building. In 1874 the Rock became a National Monument and was subsequently restored.

> ### Around Cashel
> There is a **tram** which runs between the Heritage Centre in the town and the Rock of Cashel. There is a footpath up to the Rock from the gardens of the Cashel Palace Hotel.

★★★ROCK OF CASHEL ⊘

Public car park beside the Rock. Access to the Rock via the Hall of the Vicars Choral (see below).

★★Cormac's Chapel – The highly-ornate Romanesque building, which is flanked by twin towers, is divided into a nave and a chancel. It is decorated with some of the earliest frescoes in Ireland. Almost every stone of the interior is adorned with carvings. The south tower gives access to the chamber contained between the barrel vault and the stone roof. The chapel was started by Cormac MacCarthy, king and bishop of Cashel, in 1127 and consecrated in 1134. Legend says that it was built of local sandstone and every block was passed from hand to hand from the quarry to Cashel *(12mi/19km).*

Rock of Cashel

Christophe Boisvieux

103

★**Round Tower** – In perfect condition, the round tower is built from irregularly-coursed sandstone (92ft/28m high). The round-headed doorway (12ft/3.5m above ground-level) has an architrave and the four top-storey windows are pointed.

Cathedral – Most of the ruin, including the high-set lancet windows, dates from the 13C. The cathedral was built to a cruciform plan without aisles; the central tower probably dates from the 14C. The transepts have two east chapels each.
In the south wall of the choir is the tomb (**1**) of Archbishop Miler MacGrath who changed his religious beliefs several times during the course of his 100-year life; he died in 1621.
The west tower (91ft/28m), also called the **castle**, was built as a fortified residence by Archbishop O'Hedigan in 1450. The first three storeys are covered by a pointed vault supporting the principal room.

★**Museum** – The museum, which is housed in the undercroft of the Hall of the Vicars Choral, displays articles associated with the Rock – the stone cross of St Patrick (12C) which has lost one arm, an evil eye stone and replicas of the 9C Cashel bell and brooch (originals in the Hunt Museum in Limerick), and of a 17C wine cup and jug (originals in the GPA Bolton Library – *see below*).

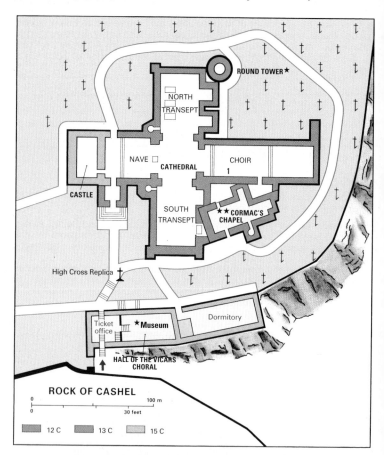

Hall of the Vicars Choral – The building (extensively renovated in the 1970s) was the clergy residence. The main hall *(upstairs)* contains a huge 17C stone fireplace and fine items of medieval-style furniture made by modern craftsmen. The kitchen has been restored to its original state: butter churns and three-legged stools. A video presentation in the Dormitory sets Cashel in the context of Irish history.

Brú Ború ⊘ – *At the foot of the Rock.* A modern village green is a fitting focal point for this cultural centre, which presents performances of native Irish music, song and dance, story-telling and folk theatre; it also houses Celtic Studies and a genealogy centre.

TOWN CENTRE

Cashel Heritage Centre ⊘ – The display traces the history of Cashel with a model of Cashel and commentary – display of royal heirlooms and relics of the house of McCarthy Mor.

★**Cashel Palace Gardens** ⊘ – The gardens, which lead to the Rock of Cashel, contain a 1702 mulberry tree and hop plants, descendants of those used in 1759 to brew the first Guinness dark beer which was invented by Richard Guinis, agent to the Archbishop of Cashel; his son Arthur founded the world-famous brewery in Dublin. The Palladian mansion, now a luxury hotel, was built in 1730 as the archbishop's palace, designed by Edward Lovett Pearce for Archbishop Theophilus Bolton. The original panelling and plasterwork in the hall is complemented by the red pine staircase, as impressive as that in the Damer House *(see ROSCREA)*.

★**GPA Bolton Library** ⊘ – This small building, standing in the grounds of the Anglican cathedral, dates from 1836 (renovated in 1986).
The oldest of its 12 000 books is a monk's encyclopedia dating from 1168; it also contains two leaves from Chaucer's *The Book of Fame*, printed by William Caxton at Westminster in London in 1483, a note signed by Jonathan Swift *(see p 148)* and a collection of ecclesiastical silver.

Cathedral ⊘ – The austere Anglican cathedral was built, with little ornamentation, between 1749 and 1784; it occupies the site of the old parish church of St John the Baptist and is dedicated jointly to St John and to St Patrick of the Rock. The five gates and two towers of the town defences (14C) were demolished in the 18C but substantial remains of the walls still enclose the graveyard; a number of 13C carved stone coffin lids have been placed against the walls.

Hore Abbey – *0.5mi/0.8km west of the Rock of Cashel*. The last Cistercian house to be founded in medieval Ireland, Hore Abbey was established by monks from Mellifont *(see BOYNE VALLEY)* in 1272. Most of the present extensive ruins date from the late 13C. The church was built in cruciform shape, with a chancel, two eastern chapels to each transept and an aisled nave.

Dominican Friary – The friary was founded by Archbishop David MacKelly *(Dáibhí Mac Ceallaigh)*, a Cork Dominican, in 1243 and suppressed in 1540. The church, which was rebuilt after a fire in 1480, has a long narrow nave and choir; the chancel walls and tower are in a good state of preservation.

Parish Church – The Roman Catholic church of St John the Baptist, the oldest RC church in use in Ireland, was opened in 1795, screened by a row of cottages. The mosaics on the façade were added to commemorate the Eucharistic Congress held in Ireland in 1932; another mosaic of Christ the King decorates the baptistery. The interior is unusual in that two galleries run the full length of the building and the ceiling resembles the upturned hull of a ship.

Folk Village ⊘ – The folk village is a small reconstruction of 18C Irish rural life.

Bothán Scoir ⊘ – *Clonmel Road*. The smoky interior of the 17C thatched stone cottage has been restored with period furniture and fittings.

EXCURSIONS

★★**Holy Cross Abbey** ⊘ – *9mi/16km north of Cashel by R 660*. The abbey was founded for the Benedictines by Donal O'Brien, King of Munster, in 1168. Fourteen years later it was transferred to the Cistercians and became a major place of pilgrimage, as it was reputed to contain a relic of the True Cross. It was suppressed in 1536 and given to the Earl of Ormond in 1563. Through the intercession of the Butler family the monks stayed at Holy Cross until the 17C. After falling into considerable disrepair the roofless abbey was abandoned for 200 years but is now used as a parish church.
The church consists of a nave with aisles, transepts with side chapels and chancel with square tower; the floor slopes upwards from east to west; three windows – east, west and south transept – contain **stained glass.** There is fine 15C stonework and an early-15C **wall painting**, one of the few from this era surviving in Ireland; it is a secular work, showing two hunters and a stag resting beneath an oak tree.
The west range of the restored **cloisters** contains an exhibition and audio-visual presentation and a tourist information office. The original monks' **dormitory** in the east range provides accommodation for resident priests. There is a mill wheel in the adjacent outbuildings.
The **grounds** contain a replica of the Vatican gardens, including the Stations of the Cross and an altar, commemorating the Italian stigmatist Padre Pio.
The eight-arch **bridge** spanning the River Suir, a copy of the original, was constructed in 1626 by James Butler, Baron of Dunboyne, and his wife Margaret O'Brien; it is ornamented with their arms and carries a short prayer; "May the two who built it escape the pit of hell".

★**Athassel Abbey** – *5mi/8km west by N 74 and minor road south from Golden; across two fields*. The extensive ruins of a 12C Augustinian priory stretch over a wide area. The abbey was destroyed in 1447 but the central tower of the main

P O'Dea (Bord Fáilte) Dublin

Holy Cross Abbey

church, the nave and chancel walls are reasonably preserved. In the church is a tomb, believed to be that of the Norman, William de Burgh, who established the priory. Many of the outbuildings are badly decayed and overgrown. The town which once surrounded the priory was destroyed twice, first in 1319 and finally in 1329.

Lár na Páirce ⊙ – *14mi/23km north by N 8 and N 62 to Thurles; Slievenamon Road.* An elegant 19C building now houses a detailed display tracing the history of the Gaelic Games. The GAA *(see p 37)* was formed, at a meeting held on 1 November 1884 in Miss Hayes' Commercial Hotel in Liberty Square in Thurles, not only to revive Gaelic games but also to give active support to the Irish languages, traditional dancing, music and song. Here one can learn that hurling (the men's game) and camogie (the women's game) are played with a hurley, study the rules of Gaelic football and handball, gaze at souvenirs of former champions or use the computer to look up information on current players and teams.

For adjacent sights see CAHER, CLONMEL, KILKENNY, ROSCREA, TIPPERARY.

CASTLEBAR

CAISLEÁN AN BHARRAIGH – Co Mayo – Population 6073
Michelin Atlas pp 94–95 and Map 923 – E 6

Castlebar, the county town and commercial centre of Mayo, is pleasantly sited on the Castlebar River. To the north it is dominated by the dark heather-clad slopes of the **Nephin Beg** range of mountains, which is flanked to the east by **Lough Conn** and Lough Cullin and the River Moy Valley. To the south extend the **Plains of Mayo**, flatter agricultural land, where a handful of towns is situated. Castlebar is a good centre from which to explore the region.

In **The Mall**, which was once Lord Lucan's cricket pitch, stands a monument commemorating the 1798 rebellion of the **United Irishmen** *(see p 29)*; John Moore, who was then appointed President of the Provisional Government of Connaught, is buried beside it. Great flax markets used to be held in the Town Hall.

EXCURSIONS

Windy Gap – *7mi/12km north of Castlebar by the minor road to Burren.* The steep and narrow road through the pass provides **views** of Castlebar and Lough Conn.

★**Errew Abbey** – *22mi/35km north of Castlebar by R 310 and R 315; turn right onto minor road. 20min there and back on foot across the fields.* The abbey ruins stand on a lonely and picturesque **site** on the very end of a spit of land extending into Lough Conn. Little remains of the abbey, which was founded in 1413 for the Augustinian canons; the 13C church with its piscina and trefoil windows pre-dates the cloister buildings.

Foxford Woollen Mills ⊙ – *15mi/24km northeast of Castlebar by N 5 and N 58.* The Woollen Mills were set up by Mother Arsenius, of the Irish Sisters of Charity, who came to Foxford (population 974) with a group of nuns in 1890 and, despite discouragement and adversity, including a fire in 1907, established the thriving mill which in 1987 became independent of the nuns.

The tour begins with an audio-visual presentation about the history of the mill and continues with a tour of the old machinery (1930s) which is now obsolete, and a view from the galleries of the various processes – carding, spinning, weaving, mending, washing and drying – involved in the production of the famous Foxford blankets, rugs and tweeds, which are on sale in the shop.

★**Pontoon Bridge View** – *10mi/16km northeast of Castlebar by R 310.* From the bridge there is an extensive **view**★ of Lough Cullin *(south)* and of Lough Conn *(north)*. Both lakes are known for angling (brown and white trout); Lough Cullin has safer sandy beaches for swimming.

Turlough Round Tower and Church – *5.5mi/8.8km east of Castlebar by N 5; at the crossroads turn left to Park.* Northeast of the village, above the wooded Castlebar River Valley stands a squat round tower, next to a ruined 18C church which incorporates a 16C window and a Crucifixion plaque (1625).

Strade – *12mi/19km east of Castlebar by N 5 and N 58.* An annexe to the modern church houses the **Michael Davitt Memorial Museum** ⊘ devoted to the life of Michael Davitt (1846–1906), the founder of the Land League, who was born in Strade and is buried in the churchyard: letters, photographs, Land League sash, books by and about Davitt.

The ruined **friary** was founded in the 13C for the Franciscans but transferred to the Dominicans in 1252. Although most of the building seems to be 15C, the chancel is 13C; there are several cross-slabs against the south wall and a beauti-fully-sculpted tomb in the north wall.

Michael Davitt (1846–1906)

Davitt was born in the middle of the Great Famine. When he was four years old his family was evicted for non-payment of rent and emigrated to Lancashire in England. At the age of nine he began work in a woollen mill but three years later his right arm had to be amputated as a result of an accident in the mill. The loss gave him time to attend a Wesleyan School and at 16, when he took up work in a printing business, he began to attend evening classes at the Mechanics' Institute and studied Irish history. He joined the Fenian movement and became organizing secretary in Northern England and Scotland but was arrested and imprisoned for seven years for smuggling arms. On his release in 1878 he returned to Co Mayo and helped to organize the tenants to wrest improvements from the landlords. Davitt persuaded Parnell to join the movement, and the Mayo Land League was formed in Daly's Hotel in Castlebar on 16 August 1879. The Irish National Land League was formed in October. During the ensuing Land War Davitt and others were arrested under the Coercion Act (1881). When the Land War ended in 1882 Davitt moved out of the limelight but continued to work as a reformer, teacher, writer and social thinker, with particular interest in the lot of the agricultural labourer and trade unionism; he was also involved in the formation of the GAA. He travelled widely and wrote several books – *Leaves from a Prison Diary* (1885), *The Fall of Feudalism in Ireland* (1904) and titles on working conditions in Australia and South Africa. He was elected to Parliament four times and used his position to advocate prison reform.

★★**Ballintubber Abbey** ⊘ – *8mi/13km south of Castlebar by N 84.* The abbey, which stands on the north shore of Lough Carra, is one of the few medieval churches where mass has been celebrated continually for over 750 years.
It was founded in 1216 by Cathal O'Conor, king of Connaught, as the Monastery of the Holy Trinity in the town of St Patrick's Well *(Baile Tobair Pádraig)* for a community of Augustinian canons; over the centuries it acquired extensive lands in Mayo. Although suppressed by Henry VIII in 1536, the abbey was reclaimed by the Augustinian friars in 1635. In 1653 the Cromwellians destroyed the conventual buildings and burned the timber roof of the church.
The nave of the **church** was rebuilt following a fire in 1265. The 13C west door and window, removed in the 19C, were restored by the Church of Ireland in 1964. The modern roof (1965) is a reproduction in Irish oak of a 15C Irish roof. The windows in the north transept depict St Patrick and St Bridget; there is a 13C piscina with a carved head in the Lady Chapel and two tomb slabs (15C and 16C) in the adjacent chapel. The modern altar bears a 17C figure of Christ. The de Burgo chapel (now the Sacristy) contains the tomb of Theobald Burke, Viscount Mayo *(see p 260)*, who was murdered in the locality in 1629. In the south transept the font, possibly a relic of the earlier church, dates from about 1200; high in the south wall is the doorway from which the night stair from the dormitory descended into the church; the west window depicts St Columba.
The **Cloisters** are in ruins. The ruined buildings in the east range, the Treasury and the Chapter House, date from the 13C. At the east end of the south range (early 15C) is the warming room with under-floor heating ducts and an external fire-place. A Celtic chapel and "Elizabeth's House", a small cottage-kitchen tucked under a wall, have been reconstructed in the abbey grounds.

For adjacent sights see ACHILL ISLAND, KILLALA, KNOCK, SLIGO, WESTPORT.

CAVAN

AN CABHÁN – Co Cavan – Population 3 509
Michelin Atlas p 97 and Map 923 – J 6

Cavan, the county town, lies in drumlin country – a tranquil, undulating, well-wooded landscape, scattered with countless small lakes which provide extensive coarse fishing and boating facilities. Nearby is Lough Oughter, the largest lake in Co Cavan, which is fed by the River Erne.

Literary Associations – Several famous penmen are connected with County Cavan. The playwright, **Richard Brinsley Sheridan**, was the grandson of Dr Thomas Sheridan, headmaster of Cavan Royal School and a good friend of Jonathan Swift, who often stayed at his home. An ancestor of **Edgar Allan Poe** (1809–49) emigrated to America from Killeshandra in the mid 18C. William James, a native of Baillieborough, who emigrated to America because he was a Presbyterian, was the grandfather of **Henry James** (1843–1916).

SIGHTS

Town Centre – At the north end of the town stands the Roman Catholic **cathedral** (1942), a composite of styles by Ralph Byrne, with sculptures by Albert Power. South stands the **Anglican Church**, an aisleless, galleried church with crenellations, a west tower and steeple, by John Bowden, who also designed the Classical **Courthouse** *(opposite)*. There is a Genealogical Centre at the Tourist Information Office.

Life Force Mill ⊘ – In the town centre on the River Cavan stands an old flour mill which ceased production in the early 1950s and has been restored to working order. A video *(25min)* presents the history of the mill and its restoration. The tour *(1hr)* starts with the participants mixing the dough for a loaf of soda bread, shows the milling machinery in operation and returns to the kitchen when the bread is cooked.

Cavan Crystal ⊘ – *On N 3 southeast of Cavan.* This, the second-oldest glass factory in Ireland, still produces its own lead-crystal glass. Visitors can watch the various processes – blowing, marking, hand-cutting, polishing – and buy the product in the shop.

EXCURSIONS

Ballyjamesduff – *10mi/16km south of Cavan by N 3, N 55 and a minor road via Cross Keys.* Population 53 000. The town is named after an English officer who was involved in the 1798 uprising. It clusters round the Market House (1813) at the junction of five broad streets; during the 18C, it was a lively place on the main coach road between Cavan and Kells with a weekly market, nine fairs a year and a reputation for selling black cattle.

Cavan County Museum ⊘ – The museum traces the history of County Cavan with archeological finds from the Stone Age to the Middle Ages (three-faced pre-Christian Corleck Head; 1 000-year-old dug-out boat), a display of 18C, 19C and 20C costume from the **Pighouse Collection**, a gallery on folk life, one on the Gaelic Athletic Association *(see p 37)* and another hung with banners and sashes belonging to various orders – Loyal Orange Lodge Royal Black Preceptory, the Apprentice Boys of Derry, the Ancient Order of Hibernians and the Irish National Foresters – showing religious scenes, King William III, Death of Schomberg, Mountjoy breaking the boom at the siege of Londonderry. The building is a converted 19C convent set in a typical conventual garden.

Carraig Craft Centre and Basketry Museum ⊘ – *Mount Nugent; 15mi/24km south of Cavan by N 3, N 55 and R 154.* This unusual little museum displays baskets of every sort – donkey creels (panniers), baskets for pigeons, eggs, turf, potatoes, fish, salmon and eel traps, egg laying, hens and ducks, bee skeps, flower baskets, potato sieves and serving dishes – made not only from willow but also from straw and reed which are less rigid and need a frame; the owner specializes in rush work using rush gathered each summer from Lough Sheelin. The tour begins with a short video on baskets and basket weaving.

Basketry

In past centuries in Ireland there was a willow tree – there are 260 sorts of willow – outside each house, mostly in Donegal, Mayo and Galway, to provide material for making baskets. The trees were coppiced to produce long straight shoots, known as withies. Natural withies are dark, stripped withies are white; boiled and stripped withies have a red tinge. Different patterns of weaving and design developed in different parts of the country.

Kilmore Cathedral ◷ –

2mi/3.2km west of Cavan by R 198. The Anglican cathedral, which stands isolated in rolling parkland, is dedicated to St Felim *(Fethlimidh)*, who brought Christianity to the region in the 6C; it is also known as the Bedell Memorial Church. It was completed in 1860 in the neo-Gothic style and incorporates *(north side)* a

William Bedell (1571–1642)

William Bedell was born in Sussex, studied at Cambridge and travelled widely in Europe, before being appointed Provost of Trinity College in Dublin in 1627. In 1629 he became Bishop of Kilmore and tried to introduce reforms. During the 1641 Rebellion he was imprisoned for two years by the Confederates in Clogh Oughter Castle.

12C Romanesque doorway which may have belonged to an earlier church or to the abbey on Trinity Island in Lough Oughter. On display in the chancel is a copy of the Old Testament (printed in 1685) translated into Irish by Bishop William Bedell (1571–1642), whose memorial is over the west door; he is buried in the neighbouring graveyard.

★ **Killykeen Forest Park** – *5mi/8km west of Cavan by R 198.* The Forest Park (600 acres/243ha), a patchwork of land and water, is in two sections linked by a footbridge. The woodland, which is mostly spruce grown for commercial exploitation, includes about 10% deciduous trees. There are three marked nature trails *(maximum 2mi/3.2km)* which follow the shore, identifying the trees and the habitats of birds and animals, and a wildfowl sanctuary in Sally Lake.

On Trinity Island at the southern end of Lough Oughter there is the ruin of a Premonstratensian Priory, established in 1250 by monks from Lough Key *(see p 89).* On an island in the northeast arm of the lake stands Clogh Oughter Castle, a 13C or 14C tower house.

For adjacent sights see CARRICK-ON-SHANNON, ENNISKILLEN, LONGFORD, MONAGHAN.

CLONMACNOISE ★★★

CLUAIN MHIC NÓIS – Co Offaly
Michelin Atlas p 90 and Map 923 – I 8
13mi/21km south of Athlone by N 6 and N 62

The monastery of Clonmacnoise, which was founded in 545 by St Kieran (Ciarán), was the burial place of the Kings of Connaught and Tara, and one of the most famous monastic sites in Ireland, second only to Armagh.

Its position beside the Shannon now seems remote and inaccessible but in earlier centuries transport was easier by water than over land. The old Pilgrims' Road approached from the north along the esker. On St Kieran's Day (9 September) people still make a pilgrimage to Clonmacnoise.

Monastic Settlement – As its reputation grew the settlement expanded from an original wooden oratory to a cluster of stone churches, numerous monks' dwellings and a round tower within an earth or stone enclosure. None of the surviving ruins is earlier than the 9C.

St Kieran

St Kieran, a native of Roscommon, went to train under St Finnian at Clonard in Co Meath and then to study under St Enda on Inishmore, one of the Aran Islands; there he had a vision of a great tree growing in the centre of Ireland which St Enda interpreted as a church founded by St Kieran on the banks of the Shannon. After spending some time on Hare Island in Lough Ree, St Kieran with seven companions settled at Clonmacnoise, the field of the sons of Nos, where he died only seven months later of the plague at the age of 33.

The monastery was plundered many times from the 9C onwards by the Irish, the Vikings and the Anglo-Normans, until it was finally reduced to ruin in 1552 by the English garrison from Athlone. A castle built by the Normans c 1212 on the river bank was slighted in the Cromwellian period.

TOUR *1hr*

Visitor Centre ◷ – The **Visitor Centre** displays the original **high crosses**, which have been replaced on site by replicas, and a collection of **grave slabs★** uncovered at Clonmacnoise which must have been an important stone-carving centre from the 8C to 12C.

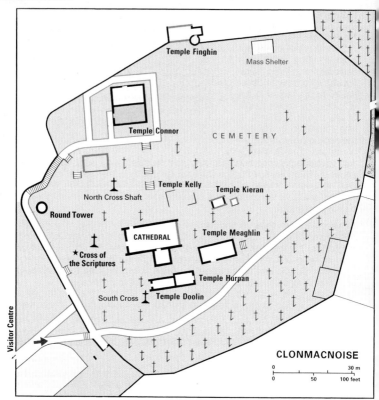

CLONMACNOISE

0 —————— 30 m
0 ————— 50 ————— 100 feet

South Cross – The cross (12ft/3.6m), which dates from the early 9C, bears a carving of the Crucifixion on its west face. The decorative spirals and interlacing are similar to those on the crosses at Kells *(see p 190)* and to those at Iona and Kildalton in Scotland.

Temple Doolin – The church, which is named after Edward Dowling, who restored it in 1689 to serve as a mausoleum, is probably pre-12C with antae and a round-headed east window. In the 17C Temple Hurpan was added to the east end.

Temple Meaghlin or Temple Rí – The east windows of this church, which dates from about 1200, are similar to those at Clonfert *(see p 235)* and O'Heyne's Church at Kilmacduagh *(see p 221)*; there was once a wooden gallery at the west end.

Temple Kieran – Parts of this tiny church, which is said to contain the grave of St Kieran, are pre-12C.
From the south side a stone path leads out of the enclosure to the Nun's Church *(see below)*. On the north side is the outline of **Temple Kelly** (12C).

North Cross Shaft – The shaft (c 800) is decorated with lions, biting their tails, and a cross-legged figure thought by some to be the Celtic god Cernunnos.

Cathedral – The simple rectangular building has been modified many times. The oldest parts probably date from the 10C when the original wooden church was replaced with a stone structure. The Romanesque west doorway dates from the 12C, the two-storey sacristy may be 13C; in the 15C the elaborate north doorway, surmounted by three plaques depicting St Dominic, St Patrick and St Francis, was constructed by Dean Odo and the chancel was divided into three vaulted chapels.

★**Cross of the Scriptures** – The cross, which is made of sandstone and is related to the crosses at Monasterboice *(see p 93)*, was erected in the 10C possibly by King Flann (d 916). The decoration includes the Last Judgement on the east face and the Crucifixion on the west; the lowest panel on the east face may represent St Kieran and King Diarmaid founding the first church, or Abbot Colman and King Flann setting up the cross or beginning the cathedral.

Round Tower – This is a good example of a round tower although it has lost its conical cap. It may have been built in the 10C by Fergal O'Rourke and been repaired in 1120 by Abbot O'Malone, but the arched doorway is most likely 12C.

Temple Connor ⊘ – The church may date from 1010 when it was endowed by Cathal O'Connor; the small window in the south wall is original. The building was restored in 1911 and is used by the Church of Ireland (Anglican) for services.

Temple Finghin – The 12C church consists of a nave and chancel. The Romanesque chancel arch was modified and strengthened in the 17C. It is unusual in having a south door and a mini round tower incorporated into the chancel.

From the centre of the enclosure follow the old path east across the extended graveyard and along the road; 10min there and back on foot.

Nun's Church – The ruined church consists of a nave and chancel and according to the Annals of the Four Masters *(see p 130)* it was completed in 1167 by Dervorgilla. The west doorway and the chancel arch are beautifully decorated in the Irish Romanesque style.

EXCURSION

Clonfinlough Stone – *2mi/3km east by the minor road and 0.5mi/0.8km south by the minor road; park by the church; 10min there and back on foot up the path and over the stile.* Near the edge of the field stands a large boulder which bears symbols similar to some Bronze Age rock art in Galicia in Spain. The natural indentations in the rock have been modified to suggest human figures.

To the south there is a **view** of the Brosna and Shannon river valleys where peat extraction is conducted on a large scale.

For adjacent sights see ATHLONE, BIRR, LOUGHREA, PORTUMNA, TULLAMORE.

Clonmacnoise

Slide File, Dublin

The length of time given in this guide
*   – for touring allows time to enjoy the views and the scenery;*
*   – for sightseeing is the average time required for a visit.*

CLONMEL ★

CLUAIN MEALA – Co Tipperary – Population 15 215
Michelin Atlas p 80 and Map 923 – I 10

Clonmel, the principal town of Co Tipperary, is set on the northern bank of the River Suir which at this point forms the boundary between Co Tipperary and Co Waterford. Directly to the south beyond the river rise the Comeragh Mountains, providing an impressive backdrop to the many historic buildings of the town.

HISTORICAL NOTES

The town is believed to pre-date the Vikings; its name comes from the Irish words for "a meadow of honey", an early Christian reference to the great fertility of the Suir valley. Viking longships sailed up the River Suir from Waterford in the early 10C and, according to tradition, a battle was fought at Clonmel in 916 or 917 between the local O'Neill clan and the Vikings. Edward I granted the town a charter and the walls were built in the early 14C. The town became an important stronghold of the Butler family, the Earls of Ormond *(see KILKENNY)*. The garrison at Clonmel put up more resistance to Cromwell in the mid 17C than any other Irish town.

Literary Associations – Four major figures in English literature had close associations with Clonmel. **Anthony Trollope** *(see p 102)* wrote his first two novels while living in the town from 1844 to 1848. **George Borrow**, who was at school in Clonmel, mentioned the town in two chapters of *Lavengro*. **Marguerite Power**, the Countess of Blessington, a noted early-19C literary figure, was born at Suir Island in 1789; she died in Paris in 1849. **Laurence Sterne** (1713-68), author of *Tristram Shandy*, was born in Mary Street; his family lived at Suir Island.

Bianconi Cars

Charles Bianconi (1786–1875), son of an Italian immigrant from Lombardy and twice Mayor of Clonmel, began a horse-drawn car service in 1815 linking Clonmel to Limerick and Thurles. Following the battle of Waterloo, horses were in plentiful supply at about £10 each; by 1844 he had over 100 in his stables. By 1851 his open long cars, known as Bians, operated in 22 counties with central depots in Clonmel, Galway and Sligo. At its peak the service employed 1 400 horses and 100 vehicles, painted crimson and yellow. It created a nation-wide revolution in the carrying of mail, freight and passengers, which was superseded only by the building of the railway network in the later 19C.

Bianconi retired in 1865 but one of the Bianconi horse-drawn mail cars was used between Clonmel and Dungarvan as late as the 1920s. A coach-horn from a Bianconi mail coach, together with the clock, now handless, by which the departures were timed, are displayed in the foyer of Hearn's Hotel (**A**).

SIGHTS

★**County Museum** ⊘ (**M¹**) – The display depicts the history of the South Riding of Co Tipperary from the Stone Age to the 20C – Roman coins found in Clonmel, the scrapbook associated with the Young Irelanders' trial held in Clonmel in 1848 and the uniform jacket of the Royal Irish Regiment, which had a depot in the town until it was disbanded in 1922 after the signing of the Anglo-Irish Treaty. There is also a small collection of paintings by Irish artists.

★**St Mary's Church** ⊘ – The present Anglican church, with its unusual octagonal tower, was built in the 19C, incorporating parts of earlier 14C buildings. Written references suggest the existence of a building as early as the 13C. In the grounds there are extensive sections of the town walls, mostly in good condition. The tower at the northwest corner of the churchyard was the last portion of the walls used defensively until 1805.

Riverside – The 17C *Old Bridge* (**18**) crosses the River Suir three times from Little Island and Suir Island *(downstream)* to Stretches Island *(upstream)*, derived from the name of 16C Italian immigrants called Stroccio.
The north bank from the Old Bridge to the 18C **Gashouse Bridge** (**12**) (so-called because of its proximity to the town's gas-works) forms the town **quay**, where ships used to unload their cargoes; it is marked by a memorial to the Manchester Martyrs *(see p 29)* of 1867 and is lined by terraces of **Georgian** houses and tall warehouses. On the south bank lies Denis Burke Park.

Main Guard – The three-storey, five-bay building is crowned by a cupola and bears the **Arms of Clonmel**. It was commissioned by the Duke of Ormond to replace the original 17C courthouse, which was destroyed during the Cromwellian siege in 1650.

CLONMEL

A Hearn's Hotel
M¹ County Museum
M² Museum of Transport

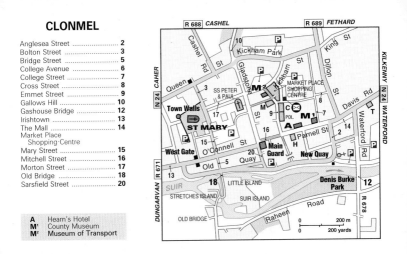

West Gate – The original 14C gate was rebuilt in 1831. The style is mock Tudor and the building has a castellated top.

Museum of Transport ⏱ (**M²**) – Two floors of a handsome six-storey mill building now house some two dozen vintage, veteran and classic cars as well as much motoring memorabilia.

EXCURSIONS

★★ **Nier Valley Scenic Route** – *Round tour of 40mi/64km. From Clonmel take R 678 south. After 5mi/8km turn right; after 4mi/6km make a detour left to a viewpoint. In Ballymacarbry turn right onto R 671 to return to Clonmel.*
The road climbs into the Comeragh Mountains – there are **views** of mountains and forests at most points on the route – before descending the Nier and Suir river valleys.

Carrick-on-Suir – Population 5 143. *13mi/21km east by N 24.* This bustling town has an enviable location on the tidal Suir between Slievenamon *(northwest)* and the Comeragh foothills *(south)*. Its 15C Old Bridge is evidence of its former importance as the lowest crossing point of the river before the estuary.
Carrick's great treasure is **Ormond Castle★** ⏱. The ruins of this 15C castle and adjoining Elizabethan mansion stand in a wooded park. The restored mansion, a very fine example of its type, was built about 1568 by the 10th Earl of Ormond, known as Black Tom, to receive his cousin, Queen Elizabeth, who never visited Ireland. The exterior has fine mullioned windows and gabled roofs; the interior is noted for its **ornamental plasterwork** and long gallery.

Ormond Castle, Carrick-on-Suir

Dúchas, Dublin

113

Kilkieran High Crosses – *17mi/27km east by N 24 and R 697*. The three crosses, which probably date from the 9C, mark the site of an early monastery. There are eight horsemen on the base of the **West Cross** which otherwise is decorated with interlacing and bosses. It bears an unusual cap, as does the East Cross which was probably not finished as it is undecorated.

★**Ahenny High Crosses** – *19mi/31km east by N 24 and R 697*. The two crosses, which bear unusual caps, may date from the 8C since the decorative interlacing and spirals are similar to those in the Book of Kells. The figures on the base represent seven clergy carrying croziers, led by a clerical cross-bearer.

Tipperary Crystal ⊘ – *10mi/16km east by N 24*. Visitors may watch the various stages in the process which produces hand-decorated crystal glassware.

★**Fethard** – *8mi/13km north by R 689*. Population 946. The small town retains several relics of the Anglo-Norman settlement and some sections of the late-14C town wall. **Fethard Castle** in the town centre is one of three keeps probably dating from the 15C. The **church**, which has a late-15C crenellated tower, includes earlier buildings much restored between 1400 and 1600. The huge roof-span of the nave is a notable architectural feature. There are many 16C and 17C tombs among the ruins of the 12C Augustinian priory.

The **museum** ⊘ in the old railway station has numerous items of rural and domestic life in Ireland in earlier centuries: farriery tools, an old jaunting car, Victorian perambulators, a thistle cutter, a beet gapper and a hay kicker for drying hay.

For adjacent sights see CAHER, CASHEL, DUNGARVAN, KILKENNY, YOUGHAL.

COBH ★

AN CÓBH – Co Cork – Population 6 468
Michelin Atlas p 78 and Map 923 – H 12

Cobh (pronounced Cove) began to expand during the late 18C, when Cork harbour became an assembly point for Royal Navy fleets engaged in the American War of Independence and later in the war against France. Its main architectural development, neo-Gothic villas and Italianate buildings, came in the early 19C when Cobh was a health resort. The elegant waterfront pavilion (1854) which used to be the home of the Royal Cork Yacht Club was designed by the architect Anthony Salvin; the RCYC, now based in Crosshaven *(see CORK)*, was the successor to the world's first yachting fraternity, the Water Club of 1720. In 1849 Cobh was renamed Queenstown in honour of Queen Victoria who visited the town in August of that year. Until the 1960s Cobh was a port of call for the *Queen Mary*, the *Queen Elizabeth* and other great ships from lines such as Hamburg Atlantic and North German Lloyd; photographs and paintings of that period hang in the bar of the Commodore Hotel. The traffic was not all tourist class; Cobh was also the port of departure for hundreds of thousands of Irish emigrants who sailed to North America in the late 19C and early 20C.

Cork Harbour ⊘ – There is a car ferry across the River Lee between Carrigaloe *(east bank)* and Glenbrook *(west bank)*. There are also cruises from Kennedy Pier via the harbour forts, Spike Island, the naval base and major harbour industries.

★**St Colman's Cathedral** ⊘ – The neo-Gothic Roman Catholic cathedral, which stands on the heights above the town, was designed by Pugin and Ashlin and built between 1868 and 1915. Its tall **spire**, which houses a carillon of 47 bells, is a landmark for miles. The interior is decorated with columns of polished marble, mosaic flooring and a detailed marble reredos.

★**Lusitania Memorial** – *Casement Square*. The 1 500 victims of the *Lusitania*, which was torpedoed in 1915 *(see KINSALE)*, are commemorated by an elaborate carving of an angel flanked by two sailors; it was designed by Jerome Connor (1876–1943), a Cork sculptor, and completed after his death by Seamus Murphy. In nearby Pierce Square a more modest memorial recalls the victims of the *Titanic*; the supposedly unsinkable liner made her last call at Cobh on 11 April 1912 before setting off on her fateful maiden voyage.

Cobh Heritage Centre: The Queenstown Story ⊘ – Part of Cobh railway station now houses an exhibition recalling the days when Cobh was a great port – evocation of shipboard life in the days of sail for emigrants and convicts; emigrant lodging houses in Cobh; audio-visual presentation on the development of Cork Harbour as a naval base; embarkation of troops for the Boer War and the First World War; introduction of steam ships in 1838 and the heyday of the great liners between the wars; the sinking of the *Titanic* and the *Lusitania*.

Cobh Museum ⊘ – A former Presbyterian Church houses a collection of local artefacts with a strongly maritime theme.

EXCURSION

★Fota Island – *4mi/6km north by R 624*. The island was the estate of the Smith-Barry family until 1975 when it was purchased by University College, Cork. The house, originally an 18C hunting lodge, was designed in the 1820s by Sir Richard Morrison and contains some of Ireland's finest Regency interiors.

The **Wildlife Park★** ⊘ (70 acres/28ha) was established by the Zoological Society of Ireland in 1983 with the main aim of conserving endangered species, like the cheetah which is one of its main attractions. Fota is one of the most popular establishments of its kind in Ireland, with a fine array of creatures, a few of which languish behind conventional bars. A grassy plateau in the centre of the island sufficiently resembles the savannah to provide a convincing habitat for giraffes, zebras and antelopes. Various species of monkey disport themselves on a series of islands on the lower part of the site, while flamingoes, pelicans, penguins and other waterfowl are accommodated on and around the surrounding pools. A "train" helps footsore visitors experience the whole of the extensive grounds and there is a playground with a zoo theme.

The **Arboretum** ⊘ is planted with many sub-tropical trees and shrubs which flourish in the mild climate; the collections have come from all over the world, including Australia, Chile, China, Japan and New Zealand. Unusual species of coniferous trees grow in the garden.

B Lynch /Bord Fáilte, Dublin

Fota Wildlife Park

For adjacent sights see CORK, KINSALE, MIDLETON, YOUGHAL.

CONG★

CONGA – Co Mayo – Population 197
Michelin Atlas p 89 and Map 923 – E 7

Cong, once the seat of the kings of Connaught, is an attractive village on the eastern fringe of the lakes and mountains of Connemara. It takes its name from its position on a narrow neck of land (*conga* in Irish) dividing Lough Mask from Lough Corrib. The lakes are linked by the River Cong which descends steeply (36ft/11m in 4mi/6.5km), mainly underground, creating caves in the porous limestone.

SIGHTS

Cong Abbey ⊘ – *Car park*. The Augustinian abbey, which stands beside the river on the south side of the village, was founded in the 12C, probably by Turlough O'Conor, King of Connaught and High King of Ireland, on the site of an earlier monastic foundation (6C or 7C). After the Dissolution of the Monasteries in 1542 the buildings fell into ruin. Little remains of the church except the chancel and a Romanesque doorway, erected in the north wall during restoration work carried out by Sir Benjamin Guinness in the 19C. Opposite is the sacristy with traces of the night stairs. Some of the capitals in the **cloisters**, which date from about 1200, were carved in the 19C. The **chapter house** in the eastern range below the dormitory contains some fine carved stonework. Beside the river stands the Guest Refectory with a twisted chimney stack. West of the abbey grounds on an island in the river is the **monks' fishing house** (12C); when a fish was caught in the net which was lowered through a hole in the floor, a bell rang in the kitchen.

> **The Quiet Man**
>
> *The Quiet Man* was written by Maurice Walsh (1879–1964), a native of Listowel who was employed in Customs and Excise. In 1952 his novel was made into a film, in which **John Wayne** played the part of Sean Thornton, an Irish prize fighter, who returns to his native Ireland after making his name in the USA. Many of Wayne's fans think it was his best role and in recent years they have made their way to Cong in such large numbers that there is now a *Quiet Man festival* held in June with a John Wayne lookalike contest and a costume ball.

Dry Canal

The dry channel which runs east of the town parallel with the river between Lough Mask and Lough Corrib has never carried a boat. A canal with three locks was proposed; for six years men doing relief work during the famine laboured on piece rates, some earning only 3p a day. In March 1854 work was suspended owing to rising costs, competition from the railways and the uncertainty of being able to seal the channel in the porous limestone rock.

The base of the cross erected in the 12C to mark the completion of the abbey now stands in the town centre. The cross it supports bears an inscription soliciting prayers for Niahol and Gillibard O'Duffy, Abbots of Cong in the 13C.

Ashford Castle ⊙ – *Pedestrian entrance south of the Abbey; vehicle entrance on R 346 east of Cong.* The superb **site** between the river and Lough Corrib is occupied by a castle, now a hotel, designed in the Victorian baronial style by James Franklin Fuller for Arthur Edward Guinness, Lord Ardilaun; it incorporates Ashford House, built in the style of a French château, and part of a 13C castle, built by the de Burgos *(see PORTUMNA)*. The grounds include a stone bridge leading to the castle, formal gardens with a terraced walk *(north)*, the Joyces Tower in a woodland setting *(east)* and a series of underground caves known as the Pigeon Hole *(northeast)*.

EXCURSIONS

★**Ross Abbey** – *9mi/14.5km south of Cong.* Although in ruins, Ross Abbey on the south bank of the Black River is one of the best-preserved Franciscan friaries in Ireland. It was probably founded in 1351, at the latest in 1469, and greatly enlarged and extended in 1496. The gatehouse and enclosure date from 1572. After the Reformation, except for a period during the Commonwealth from 1698 to 1715, the friars continued in residence until 1753 largely owing to the protection of the 2nd Earl of Clanrickard.

The **church** was decorated with frescoes on the walls and ceilings; the windows are 15C. The **water spout**, by the pillar supporting the transept arches, channelled rainwater from the roof to an underground cistern, later used as a tomb. In the Lady Chapel is a wall plaque (1646) bearing the arms of the O'Donnells who invited the Franciscans of Ross to found a friary in Donegal *(see DONEGAL)*. Above the chancel arch are two **corbel stones** on which lights burned continuously to illuminate the figures of the Crucifixion which stood in the rood loft above.

The buildings surrounding the **cloisters** *(entrance at the foot of the tower)* have survived in part to first-floor level. The west range contains the main entrance, flanked by the doorkeeper's room and the guests' dining room; above were the **library** and **scriptorium**, where manuscripts were copied and illustrated.

Beyond is a second courtyard with a postern gate for entry to the friary after dark. The **kitchen** contained a round **fish tank**, a great west door, now blocked, to the kitchen gardens and a north door opening into the mill; the huge fireplace backed onto a large circular oven in the adjoining **bakery**; above were a dormitory and the Chapter House.

The north range of the main cloister contained the east-facing **refectory** with a **wall lectern** and the **lavatorium**; above was a dormitory with a latrine at the north end over the mill stream. Along the east walk were the candle store, the Sacristan's laundry and the **sacristy** with the guesthouse or infirmary above; guests or invalids could see the high altar through a **hagioscope** on the landing.

The **central tower** (70ft/21.5m) was probably added in 1498; from the roof *(76 narrow wooden spiral steps)* there is a fine **view**★.

Annaghdown Church and Priory – *15mi/24km south of Cong by R 346, R 334 and N 84; 5.5mi/8.8km south of Headford turn right to Annaghdown.*
St Brendan of Clonfert *(see p 170)* founded a convent for his sister at Annaghdown. The 15C building at the southern end of the graveyard is the Cathedral incorporating earlier decorated stonework – a fine doorway and window (c 1200). The middle church is the oldest on the site (11C or 12C). The other ruined building was a parish church. The priory *(turn right into the lane beyond the graveyard)* is a good example of a fortified monastery (c 1195); there is some Romanesque carving in the church.

For adjacent sights see CONNEMARA, GALWAY, TUAM, WESTPORT.

New Michelin Green Guides:

Brussels, Chicago, Europe, Florida, Scandinavia Finland, Tuscany, Thailand, Venice and Wales

CONNEMARA ★★★
Co Galway
Michelin Atlas p 88 and Map 923 – C 7

Connemara is a wild and beautiful region of mountains, lakes, tumbling streams, undulating bog, sea-girt promontories, unspoilt beaches and panoramic views. It is a Gaelic-speaking region and has attracted many artisans, who can be visited at work in their studios – handweaving, knitting, screen printing, pottery, jewellery, marble inlay and carving.

The centre of Connemara is composed of mountain peaks, the **Twelve Bens** or **Pins**, which culminate in Benbaun (2 388ft/728m). The sharp grey peaks of quartzite rock, which is resistant to weathering, are too steep and hard to be clothed in blanket bog. The Bens are drained by mountain streams and ringed by a chain of lakes where trout are plentiful. The region is now largely uninhabited, although in the past the more fertile lowlands were cultivated and the uplands were used as pasture for cattle and sheep.

Between the foot of the Twelve Pins and the deeply indented southern coastline extends the level **Connemara Bog**, dotted with innumerable tiny lakes. On a bright day the stretches of water act like mirrors reflecting the sun; in the rain the whole environment seems to be made of water.

John D'Arcy (1785–1839)

In 1804 the D'Arcy estates in Connemara, then an inaccessible and sparsely populated region, were inherited by John D'Arcy, who had earlier converted to the established church to avoid exclusion as a Roman Catholic under the Penal laws. He was the seventh generation of a family of Anglo-Norman origin, which had settled in Galway in the reign of Elizabeth I. After the death of his first wife in 1815 he moved to Connemara and devoted the rest of his life to the development of a town, which he named Newtown Clifden. He importuned the authorities constantly for funds to build roads to link his new settlement to Galway and Westport.

CLIFDEN

Clifden (population 808) lies in a hollow at the head of Ardbear Harbour, a safe anchorage in a long sea-inlet on the west coast; the site was chosen deliberately as in the early 19C all heavy goods were carried by sea. The harbour **quay**, begun in 1822, was not completed until 1831 owing to lack of funds. The road to Galway, which runs east–west between the Twelve Bens and the Connemara bog, was built in the 1820s. As it passed through uninhabited country, tents and cooking utensils had to be supplied for the workmen. The railway from Galway, which was laid in 1895, closed in 1935.

NORTH CONNEMARA *Round tour of 60mi/96km – 1 day*
From Clifden take the cliff road west.

Clifden Bay – There is a long sandy beach on the north shore of Clifden Bay west of the harbour *(1.5mi/2.4km – car park)*.

★★**Sky Road** – A steep and narrow road climbs along the cliffs on the north side of Clifden Bay past the site of Clifden Castle, John D'Arcy's house. To the south across Clifden Bay rises the round hump of Errisbeg (987ft/300m).
As the road bears northwest over the ridge, a magnificent **view**★★ unfolds *(northwest)* of the indented coastline and the islands offshore *(viewing point car park)*. The road descends in a curve to the head of Kingstown Bay and then continues inland along the south shore of Streamstown Bay, a narrow inlet (4mi/6.4km long).

At the T-junction turn left onto N 59. Either make a detour (4mi/6.5km) west to Cleggan or continue north.

Inishbofin – Ferry ⊘ from Cleggan. The island of the White Cow, where St Colman of Lindisfarne founded a monastery in the 7C, is inhabited by farmers and fishermen. The fort was used by Grace O'Malley *(see p 260)*, whose ancestors seized the island from the O'Flahertys in the 14C.

★**Connemara National Park (Páirc Náisiúnta Chonamara)** ⊘ – *1.5mi/2.4km to car park*. The park (4 942 acres/2 000ha) covers part of the Twelve Bens range of mountains and consists of heath, blanket bog and grassland with some natural woodland of oak and birch. The flora ranges from Mediterranean species to alpine and arctic plants on the upper slopes. The **red deer**, once native to Connemara, and the **Connemara pony**, are being established in the park.

117

Out and about in Connemara

Visitors intending to walk in the hills should be properly equipped (map and compass, stout waterproof footwear, warm clothes and food) and should advise someone, preferably the National Park Visitor Centre, of their route and expected time of return; no one should walk alone.

There is a guided walk up to *(2hr)* and through *(2–4hr)* the **Pass of the Birds** (first Sunday in August) from Recess northeast up Owentooe River Valley, southeast of Maumeen Peak, through Pass of the Birds, past St Patrick's Bed and Holy Well, down into Failmore and Joyce River valleys.

The **Visitor Centre**, housed in old farm buildings, provides information on guided walks and nature trails, an audio-visual film and an interpretative exhibition about the Connemara landscape.

Rising behind the Visitor Centre is Diamond Hill (1 460ft/445m), the highest point, which provides a good view. At the foot of its east face the Polladirk River flows north from a large valley, Glanmore, and through a spectacular gorge.

Continue north on N 59. In Letterfrack make a detour left to Rinvyle.

Rinvyle Peninsula – At the end of the peninsula, which is dominated by Tully Mountain, stands **Rinvyle (Currath) Castle**, a ruined tower house, belonging to the O'Flaherty clan. The northeast corner has collapsed revealing a spiral stair, a vaulted third storey and a huge fireplace. There is a fine view of the Mweelrea Mountains *(northeast)* and of the islands offshore – Inishbofin *(west)*, Inishturk and Clare Island *(north)*. The Rinvyle House Hotel was once the home of the author, Oliver St John Gogarty.

Return to N 59 and continue east.

★**Kylemore Abbey** ⊘ – The name, *Coill Mhór* in Irish, which means the big wood, refers to the oak, birch, holly and conifers which grew on the north shore of Lough Pollacappul at the foot of Doughruagh Mountain. The turreted and crenellated neo-Gothic castle, built (1860–67) of Dalkey granite, now houses a community of Irish Benedictine nuns and a convent school. **Kylemore pottery** is made and decorated by hand in the Visitor Centre.

The lavish mansion was commissioned by Mitchell Henry (1826–1901) and his wife Margaret Vaughan of Co Down, who entertained on a grand scale until her death in 1874. The history of the castle and convent is traced in photographs and text and an audio-visual presentation in three rooms of the castle, including the entrance hall with its magnificent staircase and ceiling.

A walk *(10min there and back on foot)* along the wooded shore past rushing streams leads to the **Gothic church** (1868), a replica of Norwich Cathedral, which is used for ecumenical services and concerts.

Continue east on N 59.

Leenane – *Car park.* There is a fine view of **Killary Harbour** ★, a deep fjord which is the drowned estuary of the Erriff River. *(See also p 261).*

Leenane Sheep and Wool Museum ⊘ – The museum, which is housed in the Leenane Cultural Centre, demonstrates the processing of wool – from the fleece to the finished product – carding, spinning, dyeing with natural plant dyes and weaving. There is a selection of hand-made goods on sale in the shop. Outside, several different breeds of sheep, some very ancient, graze on the turf.

Take R 336 south; after 4.5mi/ 8km turn left onto a steep and narrow mountain road with occasional potholes.

Lough Inagh

★**Joyce Country** – This area takes its name from a Welsh family which settled in the mountains between Lough Mask and Lough Corrib after the Anglo-Norman invasion in the 12C. The route provides many beautiful perspectives of lake and mountain.

★**Lough Nafooey** – East of the watershed there is a superb **view** of Lough Nafooey at the foot of Maumtrasna (2207ft/671m). From the north shore there is a view of the waterfall at the west end of the lake.

Lough Mask – From the Ferry Bridge the full extent of Lough Mask is revealed stretching north at the foot of the Partry Mountains *(west)* towards the Plains of Mayo.

At the T-junction turn left. In Clonbur turn right onto R 345.

★★**Lough Corrib** – The wooded shore road provides a **view** of the lake and islands. In the northwest arm of Lough Corrib on an island stands the ruin of **Hen's Castle**, an O'Flaherty stronghold, which was twice defended by Grace O'Malley *(see p 260)*. In 1570 the Joyces, who had murdered her husband, Donal O'Flaherty, tried in vain to gain possession of the castle. Several years later, when it was besieged by English troops from Galway, Grace drove them back by pouring melted roof-lead on their heads and summoned help by sending a man through the underground passage, which linked the castle with the shore, to light a beacon on Doon Hill, a promontory on the north shore.

Alexander Nimmo (1783–1832)

Alexander Nimmo was a Scot who came to Ireland in 1809 to assist in bog surveys. In 1822 he was appointed engineer of the Western District and engineered the Galway to Clifden road; while work was in progress in the 1820s he lived at Corrib Lodge at Maam Cross. He also designed piers and harbours.

At the T-junction turn left onto R 336. In Maam Cross turn right onto N 59 to return to Clifden.

Maam Cross (An Teach Dóite) and **Recess (Sraith Salach)** – These are two popular angling villages on the Galway to Clifden road. Beyond Recess the many islands of **Derryclare Lough** come into view. North of this lake in the glaciated valley between the Maumturk Mountains *(east)* and two of the Twelve Pins, Bencorr and Derryclare *(west)*, lies **Lough Inagh** *(picnic places)*; the bog is dotted with turf stacks and sheep.

On the south shore of Ballynahinch Lake stands **Ballynahinch Castle** (now a hotel), formerly the property of the Martin family who acquired the estate from the O'Flaherty clan in the 16C; it was the home of Richard Martin, also known as "Humanity Dick", who founded the Society for the Prevention of Cruelty to Animals.

SOUTH CONNEMARA *Round tour of 75mi/121km – 1 day*
From Clifden take R 143 south.

Owenglin Cascade – On the southern edge of the town the Owenglin River plunges over a waterfall before entering Ardbear Harbour.
Continue south on R 341 for 2mi/3.2km.

Alcock and Brown Monument – The monument on the hill *(northwest)* commemorates the first non-stop transatlantic flight made in 1919 by Alcock and Brown who landed in Derryginlagh Bog *(south)*.
Continue south on R 341.

Ballyconneely (Baile Conaola) – The first transatlantic wireless telegraph station was established here by Marconi *(see p 303)*, whose mother came from Enniscorthy.
Continue on R 341.

Errisbeg – The outcrop of dense gabbro rock (987ft/300m) shelters two sandy coves.

★**Roundstone (Cloch na Rón)** – Population 281. The resort was laid out by Alexander Nimmo *(see above)*, a Scot, who invited fellow Scots to live there. On the south side of the town is a **craft village**, one of those established by the Industrial Development Authority. It is best known for the workshop of Malachy Kearns who makes the traditional goatskin drum (*bodhrán* pronounced "borawn") which accompanies folk music.
In Toombeola turn right onto R 342.

★**Cashel** – This attractive little resort, a good angling and shooting centre, nestles at the foot of a hill overlooking Bertraghboy Bay.
Turn right onto R 340.

Carna Peninsula – A string of villages punctuates the shoreline.
Offshore *(south)* lies **St MacDara's Island** ⊘ where the 6C saint founded a monastery; the church (restored), which was built of very large stones, has unusual antae meeting at the roof ridge; sailors used to dip their sails in veneration of St MacDara. It can be reached from **Carna**, a lobster fishing village. **Kilkieran** *(Cill Chiaráin)* on the east coast offers a fine view of the patchwork of islands and peninsulas which lie offshore.
7mi/11.3km north of Kilkieran, turn right (sign) to Patrick Pearse's Cottage.

Patrick Pearse's Cottage ⊘ – *Car park.* Nestling against a rocky outcrop on the west shore of Lough Aroolagh is the three-roomed thatched cottage built by Patrick Pearse *(see p 164)* where he spent his holidays and studied the Irish language.
Return to R 340; continue east. At the T-junction turn left onto R 386. In Maam Cross turn left onto N 59 to return to Clifden.
For a description of the road see NORTH CONNEMARA above.
For adjacent sights see ARAN ISLANDS, CONG, GALWAY, WESTPORT.

CORK ★★

CORCAIGH – Co Cork – Population 127 187
Michelin Atlas p 78 and Map 923 – G 12

Ireland's third-largest city, after Dublin and Belfast, Cork is a major commercial city, the administrative centre of Co Cork and a university town.
The city centre, built on reclaimed marshland, is flat but the northern suburbs, including **Montenotte**, Cork's most exclusive residential district, are set on the steep northern heights. The River Lee flows through the centre forming attractive channels on the western side; its estuary forms the largest natural harbour in Europe. Until the 19C many of the city streets were open waterways where ships moored; in 1780 Arthur Young compared Cork to Dutch towns.
The city has a strong historical and cultural identity. The people of Cork speak with a distinctive accent and relish two local specialities, black pudding *(drisheen)* and pig's trotters *(crúibíní – crubeens in English)*; both can be appreciated by a visit to the **English Market** where the stall holders have a lively line in Cork banter.

OUT AND ABOUT IN CORK

Tourist Information

Cork City Tourist Office, Áras Fáilte Tourist House, Grand Parade ☎ (00353) 021273251; Fax (00353) 021273504. Alternatively consult the website at www.iii.ie/iii

Public Transport

For **bus travel** contact the Bus Éireann Travel Centre, Parnell Place ☎ 021508188, or consult the website at www.infopoint.ie/buse/
For frequent use of the bus network, purchase a Bus Éireann Rambler ticket, available for 3–day, 8–day or 15–day periods.
For information on **rail travel** contact Iarnród Éireann, Travel Centre, 65 Patrick Street ☎ 021504888 or consult the website at www.club.ie/RailNet/

Cork Harbour

There is a **car ferry** ⊘ from Glenbrook (southeast of the city centre) to Carrigaloe near Cobh on Great Island. There are also **harbour cruises** ⊘ from Penrose Quay.

Shopping

Most of the well-known brands are to be found in **Patrick Street**, the main shopping street running through Cork City centre, and in **Merchants Quay Shopping Centre**, which is also in Patrick Street. **North Main Street** is one of the oldest shopping streets in Cork. For something a little different try the **Huguenot Quarter**, a bohemian district which houses a variety of cafés and boutiques, as well as several antique shops. The **English Market** *(just off Patrick Street)* offers market-lovers a wide range of fresh produce to choose from.

Festivals

Cork Guinness Jazz Festival is an annual jazz festival, established over 20 years ago, which takes place in the last week of October and attracts over 35000 visitors. For further details ☎ 021270463.

Murphys Cork Film Festival, which has been running for over 40 years, takes place in October and celebrates the best in world cinema. ☎ 021271711.

Entertainment

Everyman Palace Theatre, *MacCurtain Street* ☎ 021501673.

UCC Granary Theatre ☎ 021904275 – Range of amateur and professional productions.
The **Opera House**, *Emmet Place* ☎ 021270022 – Touring theatre companies and local productions.

Kino Cinema, *Washington Street* ☎ 021271571 – Wide selection of films.

The Half Moon Club, *just to the rear of the Opera House* ☎ 021 274308 – Variety of jazz, blues and rock music acts.

Triskel Arts Centre ⊘ (**Z F**), *Tobin Street* – Film shows, art exhibitions and other activities.

"A Marshy Place" – Cork derives its name from the Irish for a "marshy place", where St Finbar founded a church in 650 on the banks of the River Lee near the present site of University College. Its early development was disrupted in 860 by Viking raids, and in 1172 by the invasion of the Anglo-Normans who eventually broke the Danish hold on the city.

"Rebel Cork" – Owing to its commercial strength Cork early developed a political independence which has survived to the present day. In 1492 **Perkin Warbeck**, the pretender to the English throne, arrived in Cork; he won the support of the mayor and some leading citizens who accompanied him to England, where he proclaimed himself Richard IV, King of England and Lord of Ireland. Warbeck and his Cork supporters were hanged at Tyburn.
In the 1640s Cork supported the royal cause. Cromwell entered the city in 1649 causing much damage. Cork's humiliation was complete in 1690 when, after a five-day siege, the army of William III entered the city and the walls and other fortifications were destroyed.
In the early 18C Cork received many of the Huguenots who fled from religious persecution in France; their presence is recalled in the name of French Church Street.

CORK

In the 19C the city lived up to its reputation of rebelliousness by being a stronghold of Fenian agitation. The *Cork Examiner*, the city's daily newspaper, was founded in 1841.

The War of Independence and the subsequent Civil War were bitterly fought in and around Cork. In 1920 the Black and Tans set fire to a substantial portion of the city centre, which was later rebuilt in anonymous modern style. The political unrest was aggravated by the deaths of two Lord Mayors of Cork. Terence McSwiney died on hunger strike in Brixton Prison; Tomás McCurtain was shot in his bed by Crown Forces in the presence of his wife and children.

Commercial and Industrial Centre – Cork began its involvement in trade in the 12C exporting hides and cloth and importing wine from Bordeaux.

By the 18C the city had extended its commercial activities through the production and sale of butter to Great Britain, Europe and America. This lucrative export business ended only after the First World War. The **Butter Exchange** (1750), now the **Shandon Crafts Centre** (**Y A**), provided a centralized system for exports and in 1769 a Committee of Merchants was set up to control the trade; it established first three then six standards of quality and its influence prevailed until the late 19C.

In 1852 Cork staged Ireland's first national Industrial Exhibition, modelled on the Great Exhibition held in London the year before. In 1917 the Ford car company set up its first overseas factory at the Marina in Cork; **Henry Ford**, the founder of the American firm, was born at Ballinascarty, north of Clonakilty. The Ford factory closed down in 1980 at the same time as the Dunlop tyre plant, set up in the 1930s. Shipbuilding also came to an end in the 1980s. Commercial activity is now concentrated in computer manufacturing companies.

CITY CENTRE

★**Grand Parade** (**Z**) – The main business street of Cork contains some handsome late-18C bow-fronted buildings hung with grey slates. Until 1800 the street was an open channel of the River Lee lined by merchants' houses; the steps that led down to the boats can still be seen.

★**South Mall** (**Z**) – The Commercial Rooms, now incorporated in the Imperial Hotel at the eastern end of South Mall were built in 1813 for the merchants who ran the Butter Exchange; directly opposite, at the corner of Pembroke Street, is a doorway with the inscription *Cork Library* (**E**), the city's first major library, funded by private subscription.

Grand Parade, Cork City

Slide File, Dublin

122

★**St Patrick's Street** (Z) – Cork's main shopping thoroughfare offers a wide variety of departmental and speciality shops, supplemented by a large new shopping centre in Merchant's Quay.

★**Crawford Art Gallery** ⊘ (Y)– The gallery, which is named after its founding bene-factor, WH Crawford, presents a representative collection of 19C and 20C works by Irish artists such as William Conor, John Keating, Sir William Orpen and Seán O'Sullivan, together with works by John Hogan and Daniel Maclise, two noted 19C Cork artists, and works by modern Irish artists.

Other exhibits include late-19C Japanese Samurai armour and a collection of Classical casts from the Vatican. There are frequent touring exhibitions of contemporary Irish and European art.

The gallery building, erected in 1724 as the Custom House, was given in 1832 to the Royal Cork Institution, a scientific society, from which the gallery inherited its collection of casts.

Cork Archives Institute ⊘ (Z B) – *South Main Street.* The copious material held by the Institute consists chiefly of historical records relating to business, local government and trade union activities, as well as family and private papers, some of potential genealogical interest.

The archive is administered jointly by Cork Corporation, Cork County Council and University College, Cork.

It is housed in Christ Church, built in 1726 on the site of a medieval church destroyed in the 1690 siege; ancient gravestones survive in the old churchyard.

Cork Vision Centre ⊘ (Y) – This urban information centre, located in the deconsecrated 18C St Peter's Church, has displays on the past, present and future of Cork, arranged around a large model (1:500) of the city.

Beamish and Crawford Brewery (Z) – The attractive old-English half-timbered façade belongs to one of the two local breweries.

University College ⊘ (X) – University College Cork (UCC) was founded by charter in 1845, together with two other colleges in Galway and Belfast, and is now part of the National University. The original buildings were designed by Benjamin Woodward (1816–61). A walking tour starting from the main gates includes the Main Quadrangle building with its outstanding Stone Corridor, the Boole Library, the Honan Chapel which is noted for its **stained-glass windows★** by Harry Clarke, the Crawford Observatory, the Republican Grave Plot and Gaol.

Busker in Cork City

SOUTH CITY

★**Cork Public Museum** ⊘ (X M) – The exhibits, which are attractively presented in a house in Fitzgerald Park, trace life in the Cork area since prehistoric times. The entrance hall displays the City Coat of Arms, rescued from the old City Hall which was burned in a fire in 1920. The collection of maces and other Corporation regalia includes the 1500 **silver dart**, thrown into the sea by Lord Mayors to assert the limits of the city's jurisdiction. A model of the walled city shows the extent of Cork in 1185.

Prehistoric life is illustrated by a model of Iron Age metal-making methods. Local crafts include needlepoint lace made in Youghal and 18C Cork silver. The rare **Cork Republican Silver** dates from early 1922, when the fighting in the city made it impossible to send silver to Dublin to be assayed.

The adjoining park exhibits **sculptures** by five contemporary Irish sculptors.

St Fin Barre's Cathedral (Anglican) ⊘ (Z**) – Cork's most exuberant church build-ing (1865) was designed by William Burges in an early pointed French Gothic style and built in white limestone. It replaced an earlier church (1735) which was pre-ceded by a medieval structure. The church has three spires, the central one rising to 240ft/73m. The apse is lit by 18 windows of stained glass. A brass plate in the floor marks the burial place of Elizabeth Aldworth; she is said to have hidden in a clock-case during a Masonic lodge meeting in her husband's house in 1712 and was made a Mason to secure her silence.

The **cannonball** hanging south of the altar is said to have been fired at the tower of the previous church during the 1690 siege.

*Christ the King Church (**X D**) – *Turner's Cross*. This striking modern church was built in 1937 to a design by Barry Byrne, a Chicago-based Irish-American archi-tect, and his partner, JR Boyd Barrett. The interior is devoid of ornamentation but the façade has a Cubist-style sculpture of Christ by American artist John Storrs. From the front of the church there is a magnificent **panorama** of the city.

*Elizabethan Fort (**Z**) – Originally built in the 1590s for "overawing the citizens of Cork", the fort was rebuilt on its present lines in about 1624 and was converted to a prison in 1835. It was burned down in 1922 by the Anti-Treaty forces before they withdrew from the city. The extensive parapets provide one of the best vantage points in Cork.

Cork Lough (**X**) – Despite the proximity of the houses, the large grass-fringed lake is a thriving bird sanctuary inhabited by many species, including Mandarin duck, mallard, moorhen and a large population of swans.

Nano Nagle

This relative of Edmund Burke was born near Mallow but she spent her life in teach-ing and in feeding and clothing the poor children of Cork. She was an early educa-tional pioneer and in 1776 she founded South Presentation Convent, which contains her tomb and some of her perso-nal possessions.

South Chapel (**Z**) – The chapel (1766) contains a sculpture of the Dead Christ, beneath the high al-tar; it is the work of John Hogan (1800–58), who spent his boyhood in nearby Cove Street.

Red Abbey (**Z**) – The square tower is all that re-mains of Cork's oldest building, an Augustinian friary founded in 1300. Du-ring the siege of 1690, a cannon was mounted on top of the tower, then outside the city, to batter Cork's eastern walls.

Cork Heritage Park ⊘ (**X**) – *Blackrock; 2mi/3km east*. The centre is housed in the outbuildings of the Bessboro estate, the home of the Pikes, a local Quaker family.

The flora and fauna to be found on the estate and the adjacent Douglas estuary are presented in the Environmental Centre.

The Maritime Museum traces the history of the Pike family, who came from Newbury in Berkshire in England, their trading in wool, their shipbuilding yards and their charitable works during the Famine; it shows a scale model of Cork Harbour with its islands and tributaries, and accounts of shipwrecks.

Horse-drawn forms of transport are displayed in the stables.

The history of Cork City fire service is demonstrated with obsolete equipment.

NORTH CITY

Shandon Bells ⊘ (Y**) – *St Anne's Anglican Church*. Cork's most famous attrac-tion is the carillon of eight bells hung in 1752 in the church tower; among the tunes which visitors may play is Cork's own "anthem", *On the Banks of My Own Lovely Lee*.

The tower, which is faced in limestone on two sides and sandstone on the other two, is built of four blocks of diminishing size and has the largest clock faces in Cork. The church (1722), which has a wooden ceiling, replaces an earlier building destroyed in the 1690 siege; there has been a religious foundation on this site since 1100.

The interior houses a collection of 17C books – a 1648 medical textbook, the *Letters of John Donne* printed in 1651 and a Bible printed in Geneva in 1648 – which belonged to the Green Coat charity school built nearby in 1716.

Cork City Gaol ⊘ (**X G**) – *Convent Avenue*. The prison, designed by Sir Thomas Deane, opened in 1825 and closed in 1923. After 1878 it was used for women only, except during the period when Ireland gained its independence, when it housed men and women.

CORK

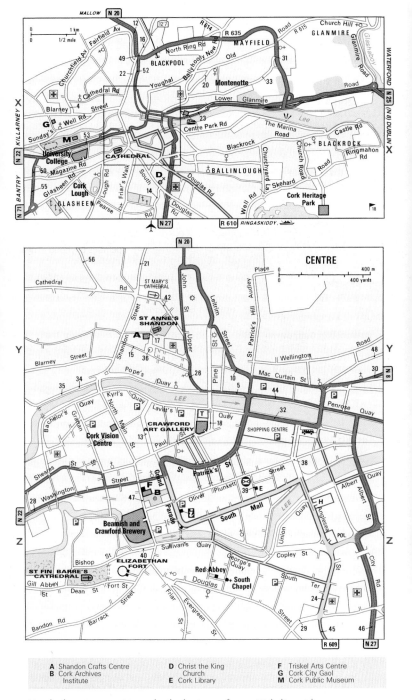

A Shandon Crafts Centre
B Cork Archives
   Institute

D Christ the King
   Church
E Cork Library

F Triskel Arts Centre
G Cork City Gaol
M Cork Public Museum

Use the key on page 4 to make the best use of your Michelin guide.

CORK

The display recalls the prison diet (porridge) and regime (oakum picking, tread-mill, solitary confinement), the sort of crimes the prisoners might have committed, the role of the school (1856–79) and the hospital, the graffiti left by 20C prisoners.

The audio-visual presentation, which takes place in the eastern rotunda, provides a dramatic insight into the social conditions of 19C Cork.

Railway Locomotive (**X**) – In the railway station entrance hall stands a steam **locomotive**, a 2-2-2 built in 1848; it was withdrawn in 1874 after 30 years of service.

Shandon Crafts Centre (**Y A**) – The old Cork Butter Market, the seat of the city's prosperity in the 19C, is now a crafts centre where visitors may watch such articles as crystal, jewellery and textiles being made.

EXCURSIONS

★**Dunkathel House** ⊘ – *3mi/5km east of Cork by N 8; after the Dunkettle/Glanmire roundabout turn left (sign)*. This Georgian house was built about 1790 and stands on rising ground with a superb prospect of the estuary of the River Lee. The lived-in interior is particularly appealing, with fascinating items of furniture including a rare barrel organ of 1880 which may be played. To the rear of the hall, where the ceiling and walls are hand-painted, is a bifurcating staircase with a cast of the *Three Graces* on the half-landing. An upper room is profusely hung with attractive water-colours by a daughter of the house, Beatrice Gubbins (1878–1944); some are of local inspiration; others were painted in the course of the travels which took her around the Mediterranean and to the West Indies.

Riverstown House ⊘ – *5mi/8km east of Cork by N 8; at the Dunkettle/Glanmire roundabout, turn left onto R 639 to Glanmire; at the crossroads in Riverstown turn right (sign)*.
In 1745 the original house (1602) was rebuilt with fine **plasterwork**★ by the Lafranchini brothers for Dr Jemmett Browne, Bishop of Cork.

Crosshaven – *15mi/24km southeast of Cork by N 28, R 611 and R 612*. This popular little resort, which is located at the point where the Owenabue River broadens to form a sheltered inlet of Cork Harbour, is a yachtsman's paradise and, since 1969, the home of the Royal Cork Yacht Club.
Boatbuilders thrive here; among their past achievements are the *Brendan (see p 170)* and the *Gypsy Moth* in which Sir Francis Chichester sailed round the world in 1971. **Fort Meagher**, a fine example of a coastal artillery fort, commands the approach from the sea while **Crosshaven House** (mid-18C) looks down on the activity of the waterfront.

Ballincollig Gunpowder Mills ⊘ – *Ballincollig; 4mi/6.4km west by N 22*. The display in the Visitor Centre and the audio-visual presentation describe the production of gunpowder, which was discovered by the Chinese, and illustrate the history of the gunpowder mills on the south bank of the Lee.
The guided tour includes a Change House, where the powder was stored temporarily, and one of the 24 mills, a wooden building, where the powder was incorporated by two vertical millstones turning in a circular trough; one waterwheel drove two mills and each pair of mills was isolated from the others by blast walls. Many of the original buildings still stand on the site and are being restored.

Lee Valley – *25mi/40km west of Cork by N 22. After 9mi/14.5km turn right (sign)*.

Farran Forest Park – The valley of the Lee upstream from Cork has been partly drowned to provide hydro-electric power but here in the forest park the surrounding landscape remains attractive.

Continue west by N 22; 1mi/1.5km before Macroom turn left onto R 584 towards Bantry; after 2mi/3km park in the lay-by (left). It is dangerous to venture off the causeway running from the lay-by without taking local advice; water-levels can change rapidly and many parts of the area are very swampy.

Gunpowder at Ballincollig

The mills were started in 1794 by Charles Henry Leslie, a Cork banker. In 1805, under the threat of invasion by Napoleon, the British Board of Ordnance bought the mills for £17 000, increased the production and capacity and dug a canal to provide water power and transport. On Napoleon's defeat in 1815 the demand for gunpowder decreased and the mills closed. In 1833 they re-opened and by the mid 1850s Ballincollig was one of the largest industrial establishments in the Cork area, employing about 500 men and boys with a wide range of skills – coopers, millwrights, carpenters – who lived in the workers' cottages nearby. The discovery of dynamite and nitroglycerine made gunpowder obsolete and in 1903 the mills closed.

The Gearagh – A great rarity, the post-glacial alluvial oak forest, known as the Gearagh, was also inundated but has recovered and is now protected as a National Nature Reserve. In the distant past, its many-branched stream, treacherous reed-beds, mud-banks and countless islands provided a refuge for fugutives from the law, notably distillers of illicit whiskey *(potheen)*. Today despite its forlorn appea-rance, with blackened tree-stumps protruding from the surface of the water, it is home to an extraordinary variety of flora and fauna, best visited from October onwards when vast numbers of migrant birds arrive, among them whooper swans and greylag geese, many species of duck, curlew, lapwing and golden plover.

For adjacent sights see COBH, KINSALE, MALLOW, MIDLETON, YOUGHAL.

DINGLE PENINSULA★★
Co Kerry
Michelin Atlas p 82 and Map 923 – AB 11

The Dingle Peninsula is a Gaelic-speaking area and contains a large number of ancient stone monuments, many from the early-Christian period. It is appreciated for its scenery and dramatic views. On the north coast rises Brandon Mountain (3 121ft/951m), the second-highest in Ireland; it is clothed in mountain blanket bog and takes its name from St Brendan of Clonfert *(see p 170)*, a 6C monk, who is reputed to have set out on a transatlantic voyage from the narrow sea-inlet at the west foot of the mountain.

HISTORICAL NOTES

From the 12C onwards Smerwick Bay and Ventry Bay were superseded by the great natural harbour of Dingle, which is almost totally enclosed. Its possibilities were quickly realized by the Anglo-Normans; in 1257 Henry III of England imposed customs duties on exports. The peak of its commercial importance was reached in the 16C when Dingle had particularly strong trading links with Spain; in 1583 the town received per-mission to build a wall of enclosure.

In the same year a long period of local rule by the house of Desmond came to an end when Gearóid, the rebel Earl, was killed. Three years earlier 600 Spanish and Italian troops sent to aid the Desmond Rebellion had been massacred by government forces at Dún an Óir on the west side of Smerwick Harbour. Following the rebellion of 1641 and the Cromwellian wars Dingle declined significantly as a port for nearly a century. During the late 18C the town had a substantial linen industry.

SIGHTS *In clockwise order from Dingle town*

★**Dingle (An Daingean)** – Population 1 272. Dingle, the principal centre of population, is an important commercial fishing port; when the catch is unloaded, the pier (0.25mi/0.4km long) is a scene of frantic activity; at other times it is ideal for a quiet stroll.

In recent years the town has developed as a tourist resort with numerous restau-rants and craft shops; there is also a **Craft Centre** ⊙ *(Ceardlann na Coille in Ventry Road)* with a cluster of workshops – jewellery, making of uilleann pipes and violins, knitting, feltwork, leatherwork, hand-weaving, upholstery, wood-turning and cabinet-making.

The fine collection of stained glass (1924) in **Presentation Convent Chapel★** ⊙ consists of 12 lights, featuring biblical scenes by Harry Clarke .

St Mary's Church★ dates from 1862 when the earlier church (1812) was replaced; the red sandstone was quarried near Minard Castle *(see below)* and substantial financial backing was provided by Clara Hussey, a prominent Dingle business-woman. Extensive renovation work was carried out between 1965 and the late 1970s.

In **Dingle Library** ⊙ *(next to St Mary's Church)* there is a large display of printed material relating to local history, as well as a permanent exhibition on Thomas Ashe (1885–1917), who took a leading role in the 1916 Easter Rising and was born at Lispole *(5mi/8km east)*.

The **Holy Stone** beside the pavement *(junction of Upper Main Street and Chapel Lane)* is a large stone (10ft/3m long) with several deep cup marks on it, which may have been cut in prehistoric times.

Slea Head (Ceann Sléibhe) – *10mi/16km west of Dingle by R 559 (sign: Ceann Sléibhe). The scenic route skirts the fine sandy beaches of Ventry Harbour.* On the south face of Mount Eagle (1 696ft/516m), both east and west of the ford at Glenfahan *(parking)*, there are many prehistoric remains – over 400 **beehive huts** ★ *(privately owned)* made with dry stone and mostly in perfect condition, nearly 20 souterrains and as many inscribed stones.

In good weather there is a fine **view** from Slea Head across the Blasket Sound to the Blasket Islands *(see below)*.

Blasket Islands Heritage Centre ○ – *10mi/16km west of Dingle by R 559 via Ventry and Dunquin or via Slea Head.* The stark modern building houses a display celebrating the fine Gaelic literary tradition of the Blasket Islands, based on local folktales, which attracted the interest of foreign scholars. The centre also illustrates the traditional way of life, based on farming, with spade cultivation and donkey transport, and on fishing in the island boats made of skin stretched over a timber frame. Some islanders emigrated to America; the last inhabitants moved to the mainland in 1953.

> **Blasket Island authors**
>
> Among the better-known works are *Twenty Years A-Growing* by Maurice O'Sullivan, *The Islandman* by Tomás Ó'Criomhthain, *Peig* by Peig Sayers (translated from Gaelic) and *Western Island* by Robin Flower.

Blasket Islands ○ – Accessible by boat from Dunquin. The group consists of four large and three smaller islands, as well as many rocks and reefs. The largest of the islands is the mountainous **Great Blasket** (4mi/6km x 0.75mi/ 1.2km), now a national historic park where some of the ruined buildings are being restored. Inishvickillane, which was owned by Charles Haughey from 1974 to 1997, has monastic ruins, a house and cottage and helicopter landing-pad but for most of the year is accessible only by air.

In 1586 two ships from the Spanish Armada – *San Juan* and *Santa Maria de la Rosa* – foundered near the Blaskets.

★**Corca Dhuibhne Regional Museum** ○ – *Ballyferriter; 8mi/13km west of Dingle by R 559.* The centre illustrates many details of life and history on the Dingle peninsula: ancient monuments, Blasket Island literature, 190 folk scenes.

★★**Gallarus Oratory** – *5mi/8km northwest of Dingle by R 559 (sign).* Built probably in the 9C in the shape of an inverted boat, using dry stone, this is a fine example of a corbel-built oratory in perfect condition. There are two openings, the west doorway and the east window; the doorway has a double lintel above which project two stones, each pierced with a round hole, indicating that the entrance may have been closed with a wooden door.

Gallarus Oratory

★**Kilmalkedar** – *5mi/8km west of Dingle by R 559 and minor road (right).* The ruined Romanesque church, probably built in the 12C, is part of a medieval religious complex and has an alphabet stone and an Ogam stone. Similar in style to Cormac's Chapel at Cashel, it has a tympanum on the east doorway and blind arcading in the nave, the walls of which survive to their full height.

The chancellor's house *(404yd/369m south)* was once occupied by the chancellor of the diocese of Ardfert *(see p 250)*. St Brendan's House, a two-storey ruin, may have been a priest's residence in medieval times.

From here an old track, the **Saint's Road** *(7mi/12km)*, runs up the southwest face of Brandon Mountain to the summit which is crowned by an oratory and shrine dedicated to St Brendan *(see p 170)*.

★★Connor Pass – *5mi/8km from Dingle by the minor road (sign) northeast.* From the highest mountain pass in Ireland open to vehicles (1 496ft/456m – *car park*) there are clear **views** *(south)* of Dingle Harbour and *(north)* of Brandon Mountain overlooking Brandon Bay and Tralee Bay separated by the Castlegregory Peninsula.

Brandon Bay – *North of Dingle via the Connor Pass.* The beautiful horseshoe bay is dominated *(east)* by Brandon Mountain and lined *(south and west)* by **Stradbally Strand ★★**, the longest sandy beach (12mi/19km) in Ireland; several trackways link the main road to the beach.

Offshore at the north end are the **Magharee Islands** ⊘, also known as The Seven Hogs. At low tide it is possible to walk from Illauntannig, the largest island, on which there is an early-Christian monastery, to Reennafardarrig Island.

Minard Castle – *9mi/14.5km east of Dingle by N 86; turn right onto a minor road (sign).* The ruin *(in a dangerous condition)* occupies an excellent vantage point overlooking Dingle Bay. The great square fortress was built by the Knight of Kerry in the 15C and largely destroyed by Cromwellian forces in the 17C.

For adjacent sights see IVERAGH PENINSULA, KILLARNEY, TRALEE.

DONEGAL

DÚN NA NGALL – Co Donegal – Population 2 296
Michelin Atlas p 100 and Map 923 – H 4

Donegal is an attractive small town at the mouth of the River Eske which rises in the Blue Stack Mountains. It is a good centre from which to explore northwards into the glens and mountains, westwards through dramatic coastal scenery or southwards to the seaside resorts on Donegal Bay.

The famous woollen Donegal tweed, which is made locally, is on sale in the shops; there are demonstrations of **hand-loom weaving** ⊘ in the summer season.

HISTORICAL NOTES

Donegal, the fort of the foreigners, was established by the Vikings. It then became the stronghold of the O'Donnell clan for 400 years until the flight of the Earl of Tyrconnell in 1607. In 1610 it was granted by the English crown to Sir Basil Brooke who laid out the town round the central triangular Diamond.

The Irish mounted an unsuccessful attack during the 1641 rebellion; during the Williamite war the town was burned by the Jacobite Duke of Berwick but the castle held out. In 1798 two French ships, carrying reinforcements for General Humbert's army *(see KILLALA)*, anchored in Donegal Bay but cut their cables on learning of his defeat. The anchor abandoned by the *Romaine* is now displayed on the quay.

SIGHTS

★Donegal Castle ⊘ – *The Diamond.* The castle stands on a bluff on the south bank of the River Eske. The O'Donnell stronghold consisted of a tower house which was largely destroyed by Hugh Roe O'Donnell to prevent it falling into the hands of the English. The remains were incorporated into the Jacobean mansion built in the courtyard by Sir Basil Brooke, who also built the gatehouse. The five-gable façade contained living accommodation on the first floor with the kitchens below. Above the original entrance to the O'Donnell tower a large mullioned bay

Donegal Castle

Slide File, Dublin

> **Four Masters**
>
> The four masters were Michael O'Cleary (b 1580), a Franciscan from Donegal Abbey, and three lay Gaelic scholars, who compiled the *Annals of the Kingdom of Ireland*, an account of Irish history known as the *Annals of the Four Masters*; the work was done in the 17C while the authors were in refuge at a Franciscan house by the River Drowes south of Bundoran *(see below)*. They are commemorated by the obelisk erected in 1967 in the Diamond in the town centre, and are also recalled in the dedication of the Roman Catholic church which was built in 1935 in local red granite in the Irish Romanesque style.

window was inserted to light the great hall on the first floor; its stone chimney-piece is carved with the Brooke family coat of arms. The tower has been re-roofed (1988–96), and the rooms are furnished in the style of the 1650s and present visual histories of the O'Donnell and Brooke families.

Donegal Railway Heritage Centre ⊘ – An exhibition in the old station house traces the history of the County Donegal Railway. From 1900 until its closure in 1959 its steam and later diesel trains took market produce, farmers, fishermen, shoppers and schoolchildren along the route from Derry and Strabane to the Atlantic Coast. Displays include photographs, contemporary film footage, timetables and a 1940s model of part of the railway. Carriages are being restored with a view to operating vintage train rides on a re-opened stretch of scenic line.

Donegal Friary (Abbey) – On the south bank of the estuary overlooking Donegal Bay are the ruins of a Franciscan house consisting of a church with cloisters and conventual buildings on the north side. The buildings were greatly damaged by an explosion in 1601 when the friary was occupied by the English and their ally, Niall Garbh. The friary church was used for Anglican worship until the present church in cut stone was built in 1828 beside the castle.

The friary, which was founded in 1474 by Red Hugh O'Donnell and his wife Nuala and richly endowed by the O'Donnell family, acquired a reputation as a centre of learning.

Drumcliffe Walk – From the river bridge there is a pleasant wooded walk downstream along the north bank of the River Eske overlooking the estuary.

EXCURSIONS

South of Donegal *Drive of 22mi/36km – half a day*

From Donegal take N 15 south. After 4mi/6.4km in Ballintra turn right onto R 231 to Rossnowlagh.

★★ Rossnowlagh Strand – A small village and a large hotel overlook the great sweep of sand (2.5mi/4km) which is excellent for bathing, surfing and horse riding; northwest across Donegal Bay rises Slieve League *(see p 131)*.

Continue south on R 231.

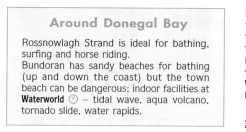

> **Around Donegal Bay**
>
> Rossnowlagh Strand is ideal for bathing, surfing and horse riding.
> Bundoran has sandy beaches for bathing (up and down the coast) but the town beach can be dangerous; indoor facilities at **Waterworld** ⊘ – tidal wave, aqua volcano, tornado slide, water rapids.

Abbey Assaroe – In the late 12C Cistercian monks from Boyle Abbey settled by the Erne estuary. The history of their monastery and mill is retold in an audiovisual presentation at **Water Wheels** ⊘ in the restored mill buildings.

Ballyshannon – Population 2 420. The town, which was created a Borough by Royal Charter in 1613, is set on a steep slope guarding an important crossing point on the River Erne. In 1597 the English under Sir Conyers Clifford *(see p 88)* were defeated here by Red Hugh O'Donnell.

William Allingham (1824–89), the poet, was born in the Mall and is buried in St Anne's churchyard at the top of the hill. Another famous native was "Speaker" Conolly *(see p 225)*, son of a local publican.

Upstream is **Assaroe Lake**, which has been formed by a dam to provide power for two generating stations.

From Ballyshannon take N 15 south.

Bundoran (Bun Dobhráin) – Population 1 463. Bundoran is one of Ireland's major seaside resorts with a fine view across Donegal Bay to Slieve League; to the south rises the distinctive square mass of Benbulben north of Sligo. The rocks at the north end of the resort have been fashioned into strange shapes by the waves. On the cliffs above there is a golf course where for many years Christy O'Connor was the professional.

For adjacent sights see DONEGAL COAST, DONEGAL GLENS, ENNISKILLEN, Lough ERNE, INISHOWEN PENINSULA.

DONEGAL COAST ★★
Co Donegal
Michelin Atlas p 100 and Map 923 – FGHI 2, 3

The coast of Donegal is a remote and sparsely inhabited region facing the full force of the Atlantic gales in winter. It has a rugged, broken coastline of deep sea-inlets and sandy beaches, backed by spectacular mountains and blanket bog. On the north coast the land is divided into fields by walls of huge round stones and dotted with tiny white houses, each with its own turf stack; the thatched roofs are roped down against the winter gales.

DONEGAL TO LETTERKENNY

Donegal to Naran *Drive of 70mi/113km – 1 day*

From Donegal take N 56 west. West of Dunkineely, after the turning to St John's Point, turn left; park beyond the old railway embankment.

Killaghtee Cross – A broad grass path leads from iron gates to the ivy-covered ruins of Killaghtee Church (12C); in the graveyard stands a 7C **cross-slab**.
Return to N 56 and continue west. After 3mi/4.8km turn left.

Killybegs – Population 1 522. The town, which is set on a steep hill, where the River Strager enters a deep sea-inlet, is a major port in the Irish fishing industry and very lively when the catches are landed. The town is also famous for the hand-tufted carpets which were first produced in the middle of the last century.
Within the gates of St Catherine's Church *(turn right uphill; car park)* which was designed by JB Papworth in about 1840, stands the **tomb slab** *(left)* of Niall Mor MacSweeney, showing several gallowglasses.
Continue west on R 263; after 3mi/4.8km turn left onto the Coast Road.

Kilcar (Cill Cárthaigh) – Population 1 307. Kilcar is a centre for Donegal tweed; visitors can watch the weaving and buy the cloth. It stands where two rivers meet in a narrow sea-inlet with several sandy beaches in the vicinity.
Continue west. In Carrick turn left to Teelin (Teileann); take the second right to Bunglass, a steep, narrow, gated road (passing places).

★★Cliffs of Bunglass – After climbing steeply (over 1 000ft/305m) and skirting Lough O'Mulligan the road reaches the cliff top *(car park)* facing one of the most spectacular views in Ireland: the south face of **Slieve League** (1 972ft/601m) dropping sheer into the sea. In winter the cliffs seem dark and menacing but on a fine day the sunlight picks out the different hues of the minerals in the rock face.
Return to Carrick and turn left onto R 263. After 2mi/3.2km bear left to Malin Beg (Málainn Bhig).

Glenmalin Court Cairn – *Park in the road; 5min return on foot over the stile and along the concrete path.* In marshy ground beside a small stream are the substantial remains of a court tomb, known locally as Cloghanmore meaning the Big Stone.
Continue to the crossroads; turn left along the coast.

★Trabane Strand – *Car park; steep steps.* The sheltered sandy bay faces south across Donegal Bay to Benbulben *(see SLIGO).*
Return to the crossroads and go straight ahead to Glencolumbkille.

★★Glencolmcille Folk Village ⊘ – The folk village was the idea of Father James McDyer (d 1987) who set up a cooperative to improve economic conditions in his poor and remote parish. Three cabins, each appropriate to a certain period – the 1720s, the 1820s and the 1920s – are furnished with items presented by the villagers reflecting the local way of life and the slow advance from rural poverty: household utensils, tools for spinning and weaving, items from the dairy, turf spades and fishing tackle. Local history can be traced in the School House. Local preserves and wines are on sale and available for tasting in the **Shebeen**.

The ordinary village of Glencolumbkille *(Gleann Cholm Cille)* (population 259) lies inland from its sandy beaches guarded by a Martello tower on Glen Head (745ft/227m). In this remote and rugged valley St Columba *(Colmcille* in Irish – *see p 136)* built himself a retreat house for quiet prayer. On his feast day (9 June) pilgrims make a penitential tour (3mi/5km) of the glen between midnight and three in the morning stopping at the Stations of the Cross, which are marked by cairns, boulders, pagan standing stones and early-Christian cross-slabs.

On the edge of the village stands the **Ulster Cultural Institute** *(Foras Cutúir Uladh)*, a centre for Gaelic studies and activities, with a display on local archeology, an archive of traditional music and a shop selling Gaelic books and tapes.

Take the road to Ardara. After 10mi/16km viewing point (left).

★★**Glengesh Pass** *– Car park at viewpoint.* From the head of the pass there is a fine view of the glaciated, green valley, enclosed between steep and rugged mountains. Hairpin bends carry the road down to join the river.

Glengesh

Ardara (Ard an Rátha) – Population 653. Ardara (pronounced with the accent on the last syllable) is an attractive market town on the Owentocker River at the head of a deep sea-inlet. It is an important centre for the production and sale of homespun Donegal tweed. The **Ardara Heritage Centre** ⊘ traces the history of the tweed industry, its devastation by government export restrictions in 1699 and its 19C revival, largely due to the efforts of philanthropists Ernest and Alice Hart. Weaving demonstrations are given and the products – rugs, jumpers etc – are on sale.

Take N 56 east.

Glenties (na Gleannta) – Population 802. Glenties is an angling centre at the confluence of the Owenea and Stracashel Rivers, and the home town of Patrick MacGill (1896–1937), known as the "Navvy Poet", who is honoured in a festival each August.

St Conall's Museum and Heritage Centre ⊘ is housed partly in purpose-built premises and partly in the adjoining Courthouse (1843) which contains the original court-room, still used once a month, and three basement cells. It traces the local history through slides, films and early photos, archeological artefacts, records of the Great Famine, relics of the Donegal Railway, 19C souvenirs of the relationship between landlord and tenants, obsolete implements and school equipment, and a display of local wildlife. St Conall, a cousin of St Columba, founded a monastery on Inishkeel *(see below)* where he died in 596.

Opposite the museum stands **St Conall's Church** (Roman Catholic) designed by Liam McCormack; beneath the steep pitched roof the windows descend to floor level revealing the surrounding water garden; the detached triangular shingled belfry echoes the sheltering conifers.

Take N 56 west. In Maas take R 261 west; after 3mi/5km turn right.

Naran and Portnoo – The twin resorts, which face Inishkeel in Gweebarra Bay, provide broad sandy beaches, cliff walks, surfing, sailing, fishing and golf.

Naran to Dunfanaghy *70mi/113km – 1 day*
East of Naran take R 261 east. In Maas take N 56 north.

★**Gweebarra Estuary** – A long bridge spans the beautiful estuary.
Continue north on N 56.

★**The Rosses** – Dunglow *(An Clochán Liath)* is an attractive small town (population 988), known as the capital of The Rosses, a bleak flat rocky Gaelic-speaking region (100sq mi/259km²) which is dotted with over 100 tiny lakes.
Take R 259 northwest.

Burtonport (Ailt an Chorráin) – Population 278. This remote and tiny harbour provides a regular ferry service *(2mi/3.2km)* to Arranmore Island.

Arranmore Island ⏱ – Population 1 000. The island has an annual festival in August. The scenic attractions are rugged cliffs on the northern and western shores, and several lakes. There are six pubs which hold regular traditional music sessions; local crafts – incuding Aran knitwear – are on sale.
Continue north on R 259. In Crolly turn left onto N 56. After 1mi/1.6km turn left onto R 258; turn left to Bunbeg.

Bunbeg (An Bun Beag) – Population 1 427. Beyond the signal tower on the narrow winding Clady estuary is the tiny harbour; old warehouses line the quay. Boats sail from here to Tory Island *(see below)*.
Take R 257 north.

Bloody Foreland Head – The headland owes its name to the reddish colour of the rocks, which is enhanced by the evening sun.
Beyond the headland is a wild and remote area with many abandoned houses. Offshore Inishbofin and its sister islands point north towards Tory Island.

Tory Island (Toraigh) ⏱ – *Access by boat from Meenlaragh (Magheroarty) and Gortahork; from Gortahork follow the signs (Bloody Foreshore) and turn right down a steep hill to the pier.* The island *(7mi/11km from the mainland)* is still inhabited by Gaelic-speaking fishermen. Little is left of the monastery founded in the 6C by St Columba (Colmcille): a round tower, a Tau cross and two ruined churches. At the Tory School of Primitive Art islanders produce striking paintings in a "folk" style, including depictions of ships at sea, in strong, simple shapes and colours. Examples can be seen at the Glebe House *(see DONEGAL GLENS)*.
Turn left onto N 56.

Ballyness Bay – This sheltered sea-inlet is overlooked by two Gaelic-speaking villages (population 951), **Gortahork** *(Gort an Choirce)* and **Falcarragh** *(An Fál Carrach)*.

Dunfanaghy – Population 280. The small town, sited on a flat isthmus in the shelter of Horn Head, was a busy fishing port until the harbour silted up; it is now a seaside resort, with extensive sandy beaches and facilities for sailing, surfing, water-skiing and fishing.

★**Horn Head Scenic Route** – *30min – viewpoint.* The headland, a breeding colony for a great variety of seabirds, rises to high cliffs (over 600ft/183m) on the north coast; there is a blow-hole known as McSwyne's Gun *(southwest)*.
The road circles the headland providing magnificent **views**: *(west)* Inishbofin, Inishdooey and Inishbeg, three islands, backed by Bloody Foreland Head; *(northwest)* Tory Island further offshore; *(east)* Sheep Haven Bay backed by the Rosguill Peninsula *(see below)*; *(northeast)* Melmore Head and Malin Head and on a clear day Scotland; *(inland)* Muckish Mountain and Errigal Mountain.

Dunfanaghy to Letterkenny *80mi/130km – 1 day*
From Dunfanaghy take N 56 east.

Portnablagh – From a scattered fishermen's hamlet Portnablagh began to develop into a seaside resort with the opening of the Portnablagh Hotel in 1923. The golf course is a links course designed in 1905 by Harry Vardon.

Ards Forest Park – The park (1 188 acres/481ha) extends along the north shore of the Ards Peninsula, rising to a headland, Binnagorm, overlooking Sheep Haven Bay *(bathing beaches)*. Several waymarked **walks** and **nature trails** (1.5mi to 8mi/2.5km to 13km) explore the many different features: mixed woodland, Lough Lilly where white and yellow water-lilies flower in August, the Derryart River, fenland, sand dunes, salt-marsh, red deer enclosure, dolmen, ringforts, viewpoints. The whole peninsula was once a huge estate (2 000 acres/4 942ha), bought in 1782 by Alexander Stewart, brother of the Marquis of Londonderry *(see p 330)*, from the eccentric William Wray who always made provision for 20 guests at dinner; in 1930 the southern part was bought by the Franciscans who replaced Ards House (c 1830) with the present Friary buildings (1966); the grounds are open to the public.
Continue south on N 56.

Creeslough – Population 299. The village sits in the shadow of Muckish Mountain (2 197ft/670m) which is reflected in the shape of **St Michael's Church** (Roman Catholic) designed in 1971 by Liam McCormack and Partners. Artists and writers such as William Butler Yeats, AE Russell, Percy French and GK Chesterton were frequent visitors.

In Creeslough turn left (east) onto a minor road.

★ **Doe Castle** ⊘ – The ruined castle stands in a strategic and beautiful position on a promontory in Sheep Haven Bay protected by the sea and a rock-cut moat which was spanned by a drawbridge. A bawn encloses a four-storey keep to which an L-shaped building, two round towers and a Great Hall were added later. It is difficult to date as it was frequently attacked, damaged and repaired until its military importance declined after the Battle of the Boyne (1690).

The initials over the east entrance belong to a relative of the Vaughans of Buncrana, General George Vaughan Harte, who had served with distinction in India. At the end of the 18C he made the castle habitable and mounted several cannon from the Siege of Serringapatam on the turrets and sea front.

The **tomb slab** standing against the tower near the entrance gate is carved with an elaborate cross; until 1968 it stood in the ruins of the neighbouring Franciscan monastery. It is thought to have belonged to one of the McSweeneys, medieval mercenaries from Scotland, who by 1544 held Doe Castle and allied themselves with the English or Irish in their family disputes for possession.

On leaving the castle turn left over a hump-backed bridge; turn left onto R 245.

Carrigart (Carraig Airt) – The village is a popular seaside resort on a deep inlet.

Take R 248 northwest.

★ **Rosguill Peninsula Atlantic Drive** – *9mi/14.5km.* The **Atlantic Drive** is a modern road which circles the Rosguill Peninsula. From the great curve of sand dunes flanked by the Rosapenna golf links, the road climbs to **Downies** *(Na Dúnaibh)*, a resort and centre for Donegal Tweed, and then skirts the high ground overlooking *(west)* the deep inlet of Sheep Haven Bay backed by Horn Head, *(northwest)* the sheltered beach of Tranarossan Bay, *(north)* the promontory extending to Melmore Head and *(east)* the sandy coves and islands in Mulroy Bay.

Hand-loom weaving, Co Donegal

Slide File, Dublin

In Carrigart take R 245 east.

The road follows the wooded west shore of Mulroy Bay to **Millford**, a good centre for fishing in Lough Fern and the Leannan River *(2mi/3.2km southwest).*

In Millford turn left onto R 246. 2mi/3.2km north of Carrowkeel fork left onto the coast road.

Fanad Peninsula – A string of hamlets lines the east shore of Mulroy Bay and Broad Water. North of Kindrum, grass-covered dunes, dotted with white cottages and small lakes, extend to the sandy shore. The lighthouse on Fanad Head *(no access)* marks the entrance to Lough Swilly. Dunaff Head, the Urris Hills and Dunree Head come into view on the opposite shore. **Portsalon** is a small resort at the north end of Warden Beach.

From Portsalon take R 246; after 1mi/1.6km turn left onto the coast road.

★ **Knockalla Viewpoint** – *Car park.* The north end of Knockalla Mountain (1 194ft/364m) provides a superb view: *(north)* Ballymastocker Bay and the Fanad Peninsula; *(northeast)* Lough Swilly and the Inishowen Peninsula.

At the junction bear left onto R 247.

Rathmullan (Ráth Maoláin) – Population 536. The **Flight of the Earls' Exhibition** , housed in the old Napoleonic battery beside the pier, recalls the incident in 1607 when Hugh O'Neill and Rory O'Donnell, the Earls of Tyrone and Tyrconnell took ship with their families in Rathmullan harbour, never to return to Ireland; they were bound for Spain but were forced by bad weather to land in France. In 1608 they arrived in Rome; they are buried before the high altar in the church of San Pietro in Montorio. Their confiscated estates were granted to new settlers from England and Scotland. The harbour was also the site of the kidnap of Red Hugh O'Donnell by Sir John Perrot in 1587.

By the shore stand the ruins of a Carmelite Priory, founded in the 15C by McSweeney, Lord of Fanad, who built the tower and chancel. In 1617 the Bishop of Raphoe *(see p 138)*, Knox, converted the nave and south transept into a residence, adding several windows, two corbelled corner turrets in the Scottish style and a new doorway bearing the date and his initials.

Continue southwest on R 247.

★**Rathmelton** (Ráth Mealtain) – Population 920. This very attractive town, on a salmon river flowing into Lough Swilly, was founded early in the 17C by William Stewart. The Mall, a tree-lined street, along the south bank of the river, opens into the Square; warehouses line the quay. The ruined 17C church at the top of the hill contains an interesting perpendicular east window and Romanesque carving from Aughnish Island further down the creek.

The **Mackemie Hall** *(Back Lane)*, which now houses the **Family History Research Centre** , was formerly a **meeting house** and is named in honour of the Revd Francis Mackemie, who was Rector in Rathmelton until he emigrated in 1683 to Virginia in America, where he founded the first Presbyterian church.

Take R 245 south to Letterkenny.

For adjacent sights see DONEGAL, DONEGAL GLENS, INISHOWEN PENINSULA, LONDONDERRY.

DONEGAL GLENS
Co Donegal
Michelin Atlas p 100 and Map 923 – I 3
Local map below

The centre of County Donegal is mountainous country traversed by long and sometimes serpentine glens: the Barnesmore Gap running south of the Blue Stack Mountains (2 205ft/672m) to Donegal, the Barnes Gap north of Kilmacrenan to the east of Muckish Mountain (2 197ft/670m), and Muckish Gap at the foot of the south face. The most spectacular of the high peaks is Errigal (2 466ft/752m), a cone of white quartzite, which towers over Dunlewy.

The county town is Lifford but **Letterkenny** is the largest town and, owing to its position, is a good centre from which to tour the county.

Newmills, Co Donegal

Dúchas, Dublin

135

SIGHTS *In rough clockwise order from Letterkenny*

Letterkenny – Population 7 166. The town on the River Swilly has the longest main street in Ireland and is the seat of the bishop of the Roman Catholic diocese of Raphoe. **St Eunan's Cathedral** was built from 1895 to 1900 in the neo-Gothic style; the interior is decorated with Celtic carving, and the ceilings in the choir and sanctuary chapels are the work of Amici, an Italian from Rome; the Four Masters *(see DONEGAL)* are among the figures on the pulpit, which is made of Carrara marble with Irish marble columns.

The **County Museum** ⊘ *(High Road)*, which is housed in the old 19C workhouse, traces the folk life and traditions of Donegal, its history, archeology and geology.

Newmills ⊘ – The corn mill and flax mill were operated by the water power of the River Swilly. The tour explains how the corn was dried and milled and how the flax was treated by retting, rolling, scutching and buffering to produce linen thread.

St Columba

St Columba (known in Irish as St Colmcille) (521–597), who was a native of Donegal, was active during the transition from pagan to Christian Ireland. He was born in Gartan of a noble family, the O'Neill, and in accordance with the custom of the times was fostered at Kilmacrenan as a boy. There are several sites in Donegal associated with his life. Over a period of 15 years he founded monasteries at Tory, Drumcliffe, Kilmore, Swords, Moon and Durrow (553). In c 560 he embraced the white martyrdom by giving up all he loved and left Ireland for Iona off the coast of Scotland, where he established a famous monastic community. He died in 597, the year in which Augustine landed in Kent.

Lake Finn – *19mi/31km west of Letterkenny by R 250 to Fintown.* From the roadside village, which faces the lovely Aghla Mountains across the lake, a track leads down to the pier where paddle boats are available for hire. The lakeside scenery can also be explored by taking a ride on the **Black Pig Train** ⊘ (An Mhuc Dhubh), which runs along a narrow-gauge track beside the lake *(30min there and back)*. The bumpy and noisy vintage snub-nosed carriages, which give the railway its name, are somewhat at odds with the serenity of their surroundings.

Colmcille Heritage Centre – *Church Hill; car park.* The modern building beside Gartan Lough presents a detailed exhibition on the life of St Columba (*Colmcille* in Irish). There is a detailed display on the preparation of materials required for producing illuminated manuscripts: parchment, ink, pigments.

★**Glebe House and Gallery** ⊘ – *Church Hill; car park.* The gallery stands in the attractive lakeside grounds of an old rectory (1828), which was bought by the artist, Derek Hill, in 1953; he was born in Southampton in 1916 and worked as a stage designer in Munich.

The **gallery** was built in 1982 to house the **Derek Hill Collection** of paintings by 20C artists, consisting of works by important Irish artists and inhabitants of Tory Island who paint in a primitive style producing striking "folk" works; textiles by William Morris and Middle Eastern ceramics.

The **house**, which is furnished with Japanese and Chinese prints from his travels, William Morris fabrics, William de Morgan tiles, a Tiffany lamp and Wemyss ware pottery, displays a bronze bust of Derek Hill by John Sherlock and works by Derek Hill, Victor Pasmore, Basil Blackshaw, Augustus John, Evie and Nathaniel Hone, Sir William Orpen, Oskar Kokoshka, Cecil Beaton and John Bratby.

St Colmcille's Oratory – On the hillside facing southeast over Lough Akibbon are the scanty remains of a monastery associated with St Colmcille: a holy well, two crosses and the ruins of a church in a graveyard.

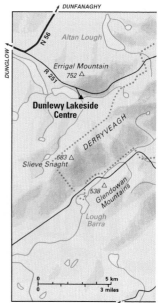

★★Glenveagh National Park 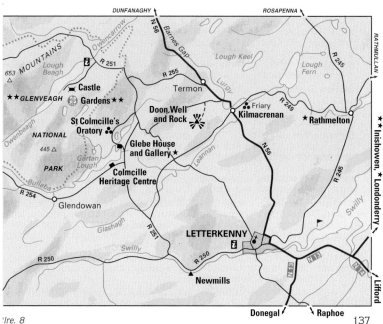 ⊘ – The park (23 887 acres/9 667ha) consists of Lough Beagh and the surrounding bog and open moorland and natural woodlands of oak and birch; in sharp contrast, on a promontory beside the lake are luxuriant gardens surrounding a romantic granite castle. The estate was created by John George Adair by the amalgamation of several smaller holdings from which he evicted all the tenants in 1861. In 1937 it was bought by Henry McIlhenny, of Philadelphia, USA, who sold the land to the Irish National Parks Service in 1975 and in 1983 donated the castle and gardens.

The **Visitor Centre**, a cluster of grass-topped pavilions, hidden in a depression, traces the history of the park and offers a short audio-visual show about the conservation of the flora and fauna, including the largest herd of red deer in Ireland contained by a fence (28mi/45km long).

The beautiful **gardens★★** were begun by Mrs Adair and cherished and extended over 40 years by Mr McIlhenny. The planting is designed to provide colour and interest at all seasons; the stone statues and ornaments add a formal note particularly on the **Terrace** (1966) and in the **Italian Garden** (1958). From the long lawn at the centre of the **Pleasure Grounds**, paths lead up to the **Belgian Walk** which was constructed during the First World War by convalescent Belgian soldiers staying in the house. The **walled garden** contains an Orangery (1958) designed by Philippe Jullian. From the south end of the gardens there is a long **view** up Lough Beagh to the head of the glen below the peak of Slieve Snaght (2 441ft/683m).

The castellated façade of the **castle** conceals a large Victorian house, designed in 1870 by John Adair's cousin, John Townsend Trench. It was lit by oil lamps until 1957 and heated by a boiler which was fed with turf every three days. The furnishings, left by the last American owners, include a carpet woven in Killybegs (see *DONEGAL COAST*) to match the **drawing room** furnishings; there are paintings by George Russell in the Library.

Dunlewy Lakeside Centre (Ionad Cois Locha) ⊘ – On the shore of the lake stands an old weaver's homestead, which offers weaving displays, a guided tour of the original weaver's cottage, pony treks and special activities such as story-telling boat trips. The restaurant has good views of Errigal Mountain.

The road from Dunlewy east to Letterkenny (R 251) offers wonderful **views** of the lake and its valley, known as the **Poisoned Glen**; a derelict white-stone church forms a striking landmark on the slopes.

Doon Well and Rock – *Car park.* The rags on the bush show that people still believe in the curative properties attributed to the well in the Penal Period. Until the 16C the **Doon Rock** was the place of inauguration of the O'Donnells, the chiefs of Tirconaill. Its flattened top *(5min there and back on foot)* provides a fine **view** of the surrounding country. It was near here that Sir Cahir O'Docherty *(see INISHOWEN PENINSULA)* was shot dead in 1608.

Errigal Mountain, Co Donegal

Kilmacrenan – Population 393. The **Lurgy Vale Thatched Cottage** ⊘ has been restored to its original state with an open hearth and flagged floor. Its **museum** displays obsolete domestic and farming implements. Musical evenings and demonstrations of traditional crafts are held in the barn. A nature **walk** explores the wooded banks of the Lurgy River.

St Columba built the first church here. The site, between the road to Millford and the Leannan River, is now marked by the ruins of a 17C church and traces of a friary, which was founded in 1537 by the local chieftain, Manus O'Donnell.

Raphoe – Population 1900. The village of Raphoe (pronounced with the stress on the last syllable) is grouped around an attractive triangular green. In the south corner stands **Raphoe Cathedral** ⊘, a Gothic church, with 18C tower and transepts, incorporating several carved fragments dating from the 10C to 17C. The see of Raphoe was established in the 12C at the monastery founded by St Adomnan (625–704), ninth Abbot of Iona, which lasted until 1835.

The gaunt ruin south of the church was the Bishop's Palace built in 1636 by Dr John Leslie with flanking towers similar to Kanturk and Rathfarnham; it was damaged during the 1641 Rebellion and the Williamite Wars but was repaired, only to be destroyed by fire in 1839.

Beltany Stone Circle – *Due south of Raphoe; west up a stone track (sign "Stone Circle"); park at the entrance to The Potato Centre; 10min there and back on foot.* The stone circle (150yd/137m circumference; about 4ft/1m high) dates from the Bronze Age; it consists of 64 stones although there were originally many more.

Lifford – Population 1359. The old **courthouse** *(Main Square)*, built in 1746, has been converted into the **Seat of Power Visitor Centre** ⊘, containing a genealogical centre and a display on local history and the evolution of the legal system from the period when the O'Donnell clan held sway, through the Plantation of Ulster to more recent centuries, using models, talking heads, artefacts, audio-visual reenactments of famous trials and a tour of the prison cells.

Cavanacor House ⊘ – *At Ballindrait, 2mi/3km west of Lifford by N 14; turn left at sign.* The house, the oldest in Donegal, was built c 1611 by Roger Tasker, whose younger daughter Magdalen was the great-great-great-grand-mother of James Knox Polk, 11th President of the USA. It was saved from destruction during the retreat of James II from the Siege of Derry in 1689 because he had earlier dined under a sycamore in the garden. The tour of the principal rooms shows a simple Plantation house; the outbuildings contain a museum about the history of the house and a display of hand-made pottery.

For adjacent sights see DONEGAL, DONEGAL COAST, INISHOWEN PENINSULA, LONDONDERRY.

DROGHEDA ★

DROICHEAD ÁTHA – Co Louth – Population 24 460
Michelin Atlas p 93 and Map 923 – M 6

Drogheda is a major port on the Boyne estuary; there are extensive beaches at Bettystown to the south and an attractive coastline to the north. Inland lies the **Boyne Valley**, rich in Irish history.

HISTORICAL NOTES

The town was founded in 911 by the Norsemen, under the Dane Thorgestr. In the late 12C Hugh de Lacy, Lord of Meath, developed it into an important Norman stronghold with two separate parishes, one in the diocese of Armagh and one in Meath. Little remains of the many monasteries which flourished in Drogheda in the Middle Ages; the roofless nave and crossing tower are the only relics of **St Mary's Abbey** (Y) which was founded in 452; the **Magdalene Tower** (14C) recalls the Dominican friary, founded in 1224, where in 1395 four Irish princes submitted to Richard II. Only the **Butter Gate** on Millmount and St Laurence Gate *(see below)* remain of the town walls which were begun in 1234.

Parliament often met in Drogheda and it was during one of these sittings that Poynings' Law was enacted in 1494.

Cromwell's Massacre – During the Confederate Rebellion Drogheda was twice besieged. In 1641 Sir Henry Tichborne and Lord Moore withstood the forces of Sir Phelim O'Neill until the Earl of Ormond brought relief. When the town was again besieged in 1649 by Cromwell it was stoutly defended by Sir Arthur Aston and 3 000 men. During the siege many people who had taken refuge in St Peter's Church were burned to death when the wooden steeple was set alight. Eventually the city wall was breached on the southeast side of Millmount near St Mary's Church and, according to Cromwell's own estimate, 2 000 died by the sword in the ensuing massacre. Most of the survivors were transported to Barbados.

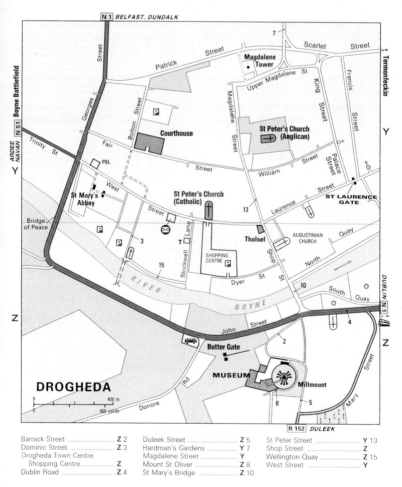

MILLMOUNT

The eminence on the south bank of the Boyne, possibly an ancient passage grave, was crowned by an Anglo-Norman motte and then by 18C fortifications. From the highest point there is a good **view** of the town centre on the north bank of the Boyne and of the **railway viaduct** which was built in 1855 across the Boyne estuary. Until then passengers travelling between Dublin and Belfast by rail had to leave the train on the south bank and take a coach over the river bridge to join another train on the north side.

The point where Cromwell breached the city walls is visible in the churchyard *(southeast)* of St Mary's Church (Anglican), which stands on the site of a Carmelite convent.

★**Drogheda Museum** ⊘ **(Z)** – The museum is housed in the old Officers' quarters (1820). The excellent display covers various aspects of local history: the medieval period; Drogheda's maritime activities; three **guild banners**; souvenirs of Friendly Societies and Temperance Groups; Victoriana; domestic utensils set out in a 19C kitchen; obsolete industrial equipment; local battles; geological collection.

TOWN CENTRE

The town centre is set on the steep north bank of the river; narrow lanes and flights of steps link the different levels.

★**St Laurence Gate (Y)** – Despite its name the structure is a barbican which protected the 13C gate; a section of the town wall still stands on the south side.

St Peter's Church ⊘ **(Y)** – The neo-Gothic building (1881) contains the shrine of Oliver Plunkett (1625–81), Roman Catholic Archbishop of Armagh, who was implicated in the Oates conspiracy, executed for high treason at Tyburn in 1681 and canonized in 1975: his head, his letters from Newgate gaol and his cell door.

St Peter's Church ⊘ **(Y)** – The Anglican church was built in 1753; the porch and spire were added by Francis Johnston in 1793. In the graveyard, beside the east gate, is a cadaver tombstone; beyond the gate are three rows of houses (c 1730) built for clergy widows.

Courthouse (Y) – The building with its distinctive weather vane was designed by Francis Johnston and completed in 1790.

Tholsel (Z) – The Tholsel stands at the crossroads in the town centre; a clock tower and a lantern surmount the limestone building (1770) where Corporation meetings and law courts were held until 1889.

Oliver Plunkett (1629–81)

Oliver Plunkett was a member of a notable Anglo-Irish family from Loughcrew in Co Meath. He was educated in Rome and trained by his kinsman Patrick who became Bishop of Meath. In 1670 he was appointed Archbishop of Armagh and Primate of Ireland. Using his family connections with the establishment, particularly Viceroy Berkeley, he began to impose his authority and reverse the effect of years of neglect following the Cromwellian era and the Penal Laws. He travelled extensively in the north of Ireland administering the Sacrament of confirmation; a school was set up for pupils of all ages, priests were ordained, bishops appointed.

In response to a new wave of repression, occasioned by the marriage of the Charles II's bother, James Duke of York, to Mary of Modena, a Roman Catholic, Plunkett chose to go into hiding. Anti-monarchists in London accused him of complicity in the 'Popish Plot' fabricated by Titus Oates; he was said to have organised an invasion of 40 000 men who would land in Carlingford. Plunkett was arrested in 1679 and brought to trial in Dundalk but no one would give evidence against him. He was later tried in London for treason and condemned to be hung, drawn and quartered at Tyburn. Through the intervention of his friends his body was preserved and eventually various relics were returned to Ireland.

EXCURSION

Whiteriver Mills  – *Dunleer; 9mi/14.5km north of Drogheda by N 1 and R 132.* On the southern edge of Dunleer stands a three-storey 18C mill, which has been lovingly restored to working order; all the processes involved in milling are expertly demonstrated.

For adjacent sights see BOYNE VALLEY, DUNDALK, FINGAL, KELLS, TARA, TRIM.

Cadaver tombstone, Drogheda

Slide File, Dublin

Michelin on the Net: www.michelin-travel.com.

Our route planning service covers all of Europe - twenty-one countries and one million kilometres of highways and byways – enabling you to plot many different itineraries from any starting point. The itinerary options allow you to choose a particular route – the quickest, the shortest or the one reocommended by Michelin.

The network is updated three times weekly, integrating ongoing road works, detours, new motorways, and snowbound mountain passes.

The description of the itinerary includes the distances and travelling times between towns, selected hotels and restaurants.

DUBLIN ★★★

BAILE ÁTHA CLIATH – Co Dublin – Population 470 838
Michelin Atlas p 93 and Map 923 – N 7, 8

The capital of Ireland is situated on the banks of the River Liffey; downstream the port of Dublin straddles the estuary on the shores of Dublin Bay. In the 18C Dublin enjoyed a period of prosperity from which it has preserved many of its neo-Classical buildings and elegant Georgian terraces. Several garden squares and the broad green acres of Phoenix Park, as well as the banks of the canals, provide oases of tranquillity. The residential suburbs extend north to the Ben of Howth and south to Dalkey Headland. For recreation Dubliners can retreat to the sandy beaches of the east coast, or inland to the rich farming country west and north, and the wooded heights of the Wicklow Mountains to the south.

OUT AND ABOUT IN DUBLIN

Tourist Information

The various tourist information centres provide information to people calling in person:

– **Dublin Tourism**, Suffolk Street;
– Irish Tourist Board (Bord Fáilte), Baggot Street Bridge;
– Dublin Airport, Arrivals Hall;
– Dún Laoghaire, New Ferry Terminal;
– Tallaght, The Square, Town Centre.

For information by phone:

– 1859 230 330 (Irish Tourist Board);
– 0171 493 3201 (Irish Tourist Board from London).

For information by fax:

– 066 979 2035.

For information by e-mail to: information@dublintourism.ie

For information via the internet consult the official Dublin website at www.visit.ie/dublin

For credit card accommodation reservations in Dublin:

– by e-mail to: reservations@dublintourism.ie

For credit card accommodation reservations International free phone:

– 00 800 668 668 66 (from Ireland,UK, France, Germany, Italy, Sweden and Norway);
– 011 800 668 668 66 (from the USA);
– 001 353 66 92082 (from other countries).

Public Transport

The **DART** (Dublin Area Rapid Transport) is a **rail service** along the coast from Howth in the north to Bray in the south. The service operates daily between 6am (9am Sunday) and 11.45pm with trains running every 5-10min during peak times and every 15min off-peak. All-day tickets available at any station – rail only up to £3.20 according to distance; rail and bus £4. Further details from 35 Lower Abbey Street; ☎ 01 836 6222.

Dublin Bus (CIE) operates the **bus network** which covers the whole city from the Central Bus Station (Busáras) in Store Street (behind the Custom House); any bus bearing the direction *An Lár* is going to the city centre. All-day tickets available either exclusively for bus travel or for bus and rail travel combined – bus only £2.80; all-day bus and rail £4. Further details from Dublin Bus, 59 Upper O'Connell Street; ☎ 01 873 4222.

Nitelink buses run from the City Centre to the suburbs, every Thursday, Friday and Saturday, at midnight, 1am, 2am and 3am.

Parking

In the city centre there are **paying car parks**, **parking meters**, **pay and display machines** and **disc parking areas**; an electronic panel, advertising parking spaces, is visible from the west side of St Stephen's Green.

There is **no parking** on **double yellow lines** at any time; no parking on **single yellow lines** during the hours indicated on the time plate; no parking in **clearways and bus lanes** during the hours indicated on the time plate.

Parking bays for the **disabled** may be used only if a disabled parking permit is displayed. Cars parked illegally may be **clamped**; declamping costs £65 payable by phone by credit card only or at the Parking shop (16 Bachelor's Walk, Dublin 1; ☎ 01 602 2500) by credit card, cash or cheque (with cheque card).

Sightseeing

A **Supersaver Card**, available from the Dublin Tourism Centre, provides entry to the following tourist attractions and saves up to 30% on admission prices: Dublin's Viking Adventure, Dublin Writers Museum, James Joyce Museum, Shaw Birthplace, Malahide Castle, Fry Model Railway and Newbridge House.

Three different **heritage trails**, walking tours with historical themes, are organized by Dublin Tourism; further details from the Dublin Tourism Centre or from the website *(see above)*.

A **historical walking tour** ⊘ of Dublin enables you to see all the famous Dublin landmarks while learning about key events in Irish history.

Several companies organize **circular bus tours** ⊘ of the city centre on an open-top bus; for a comprehensive tour (2hr 45min) including all the famous sights and a running commentary given by an approved guide, contact **Dublin Bus**; for **hop-on-hop-off bus tours** which give unlimited travel throughout the day, with the flexibility of stopping off and visiting various sights and then catching a later bus for no extra charge, contact **Dublin Bus**; **Gray Line Buses**; **Guide Friday**.

More active sightseers may consider a **bicycle tour** ⊘ (bicycles provided) of Dublin, accompanied by a guide, who will point out the cultural and historical sights and avoid the busier roads.

A ride in a **horse-drawn open carriage** ⊘ is a more romantic and leisurely way of seeing the city; departure point St Stephen's Green *(northeast corner)*.

For sightseers prepared to go further afield there are **steam train excursions** ⊘ starting from Dublin and travelling to various provincial towns and cities.

Shopping

The **central shopping** area extends from Grafton Street *(south bank)* to O'Connell Street *(north bank)*. Nassau Street *(parallel with the south side of Trinity College)* contains several good shops selling a range of **Irish goods** from high fashion to modest souvenirs – clothing, craftwork, pottery, Irish music and instruments, family crests.

North Earl Street, Dublin

Slide File, Dublin

The **Temple Bar** area offers an eclectic mix of individual little shops and outdoor stalls.

Market-lovers should try the **Moore Street market** or **Mother Redcaps Market**, the oldest market in Ireland, which offers a wide assortment of goods, including antiques, bric-a-brac, knitwear and crafts *(open Friday to Sunday, 10am to 5.30pm)*.

For **antiques** go to Francis Street.

Entertainment

The **National Concert Hall** *(Earlsfort Terrace)* has a regular programme of classical and modern orchestral music.

Smaller venues offering more specialized music, such as jazz, blues etc are to be found in Temple Bar; details from the Temple Bar Information Centre *(Eustace Street)*, ☎ 01 671 5717.

Theatre-lovers can enjoy performances at the historic **Abbey Theatre** or at the **Gate theatre**.

Cinema-goers will have plenty to choose from at several **cinemas**, including two art-house cinemas and a nine-screen complex in Parnell Street.

Sporting venues include **Croke Park**, the home of Gaelic games (football, hurling), and **Leopardstown** (south) and **Fairy House** (north) for horse racing.

The Real Irish Pub Crawl takes in both pubs and historic buildings; details from ☎ 01 493 2676 or 088 212 2020; or try the *Jameson Literary Pub Crawl* ☎ 01 670 5602.

Pubs and Restaurants

The greatest concentration of pubs is in Temple Bar. The following is a selection of pubs offering traditional Irish music:

North bank

Keatings Pub, *Jervis Street, Dublin 1* ☎ 01 873 1567 – Traditional music every Tuesday, Wednedsay, Thursday and Saturday night.

Clifton Court Hotel, *O'Connell Street Bridge, Dublin 1* ☎ 01 874 3535 – Traditional music every night.

South bank

Brazen Head Pub, *20 Lower Bridge Street, Dublin 8* ☎ 01 679 5186 – Traditional music every night in Ireland's oldest pub.

Castle Inn, *5-7 Lord Edward Street, Dublin 2* ☎ 01 475 1122 – Traditional music every Friday night.

Harcourt Hotel, *Harcourt Street, Dublin 2* ☎ 01 478 3677 – Traditional music every Monday, Tuesday and Wednesday.

The Norseman, *29 East Essex Street, Dublin 2* ☎ 01 679 8372 – Traditional music every night except Monday.

Oliver St John Gogarty, *Temple Bar, Dublin 2* ☎ 01 671 1822 – Traditional music every night (Saturday at 4.30pm; Sunday at noon).

O'Shea's Merchant Pub, *12 Lower Bridge Street, Dublin 1* ☎ 01 679 3797 – Traditional music every night.

Kitty O'Shea's, *23-25 Upper Canal Street, Dublin 4* ☎ 01 660 8050 – Traditional music every night except Thursday.

Northern Suburbs

Clontarf Castle Hotel, *Castle Avenue, Dublin 3* ☎ 01 833 2321 – Traditional music every Saturday night.

Abbey Tavern, *Howth, Dublin* ☎ 01 832 2006 – Traditional music every weekend, booking essential.

Southern Suburbs

Sean Doherty's, *Edmonstown Road, Rockbrook, Rathfarnham, Dublin* ☎ 01 493 1495 – Pub and restaurant *(20min south of the city centre)*.

Culturlann na hEireann, *Belgrave Square, Monkstown, Dublin* ☎ 01 280 0295 – Traditional music every Friday and Saturday night; *céili* every Friday night.

Johnny Fox's Pub, *Glencullen, Dublin* ☎ 01 295 5647 – Traditional music every night *(south by N 11 and R 116)*.

HISTORICAL NOTES

Viking Settlement – The name Dublin is derived from *Dubh Linn*, the Dark Pool at the confluence of the Poddle and the Liffey; the Irish name, *Baile Átha Cliath*, means the city by the hurdle ford. The first permanent settlement beside the Liffey was established by the Vikings in the 9C at Wood Quay; at the Battle of Clontarf on the north shore of Dublin Bay in 1014 their power was curbed by Brian Ború.

Anglo-Norman Stronghold – After the Anglo-Norman invasion late in the 12C Dublin was granted to the port of Bristol as a trading post by Henry II in 1172. Under constant harassment by the Irish tribes and an unsuccessful attack in 1316 by Edward Bruce of Scotland, the extent of the Anglo-Normans' influence waxed and waned but they never lost control of Dublin which gradually became the seat of Parliament and also the centre of government.

Georgian Dublin – In the relative peace of the 18C, restrictions eased and trade flourished. Buildings were constructed to house public bodies; elegant terraces of houses were erected first north and then south of the river; men of property, drawn to the capital on parliamentary and other business, commissioned fine mansions.
Under the activities of the Wide Streets Commissioners, established in 1758, Dublin developed into an elegant city, embraced by the Royal and Grand Canals and bisected by the Liffey, now embanked between quays and spanned by several bridges.

Capital of the Republic – With the Act of Union (1800) political affairs removed to London and, despite being known as the "second city of the Empire", Dublin stagnated. After the brief rage of the Civil War, the city restored the Four Courts, the GPO and the Custom House to something like their former glory. The refurbishment projects carried out in the last decades of the 20C mean that Dublin well deserved the title European City of Culture awarded in 1991 by the European Union. The major public buildings have been restored and are floodlit at night. Temple Bar was transformed from a dilapidated district into a network of pedestrian streets, vibrant with pubs, restaurants, hotels, craftshops and cafés. The district west of O'Connell Street is being regenerated under the Harp Project beginning in 1999.

Literary Dublin

Several Nobel Prize winners figure in the long roll of Dublin-born writers who have achieved international fame – Swift, Mangan, Wilde, Shaw, Yeats, Synge, O'Casey, Joyce, Behan, Beckett. Their places of residence are marked with plaques or converted into museums. The major figures are named together with their work in a literary parade in St Patrick's Park. The literary achievement, past and present, is analysed in the Dublin Writers Museum.

★★DUBLIN CASTLE ⊘ (HY) *South bank*

Symbol of British Rule – For 700 years until 1922 Dublin Castle represented British rule in Ireland. People under suspicion languished in its prisons; traitors' heads were exhibited on spikes over the gate. Early Lord Deputies **operated** from their own power bases in the Pale – Trim, Maynooth and Kilkenny – but in the 16C Sir Henry Sidney, who was four times Lord Deputy, took up residence in the castle and put it in good repair. Gradually the medieval fortress evolved into an administrative centre and vice-regal court. In the 19C the Lord Deputy usually resided in Vice-Regal Lodge in Phoenix Park *(see below)*, staying at the Castle only for the few winter weeks of the Castle Season which was a glittering round of levées, balls and receptions.

Construction – In 1204, 30 years after the Anglo-Norman landing in Ireland, King John ordered a castle to be built. The site chosen was high ground southeast of the existing town and protected to the south and east by the River Poddle. The original structure expanded into a rough quadrangle with a round tower at each corner on the site of the present Upper Yard. In 1684 much of the medieval castle was destroyed by fire. New apartments designed by Sir William Robinson were completed in 1688 but most of them were replaced in the middle of the 18C.

Under Attack – The most serious siege occurred in 1534 when Thomas Fitzgerald, known as "Silken Thomas" because of the silk embroidery on his men's apparel, was acting as Vice Deputy during his father's absence in London. On hearing a false report that his father had been beheaded, he relinquished the sword of state and threatened the citizens to allow him to lay siege to the castle in what was known as the Kildare or Geraldine Revolt. The citizens warned the Constable of the castle and supplied him with stores; when they heard that the king's men were coming they turned against Fitzgerald. The besieged proclaimed the arrival of the king's army and made a sortie; the besiegers took fright and scattered. Fitzgerald himself escaped but he was forced to surrender some months later and was executed in London together with his five uncles.
The last attack on the castle was during the Easter Rising in 1916 when the rebels commanded the approaches and main gate from the roof of the City Hall; after about three hours the regular soldiers regained command of the Upper Yard.

Drawing Room, Dublin Castle

Tour *1hr; entrance via Lower Yard*

State Apartments – *Upper Yard.* The upper floor on the south side of the Upper Yard was built between 1750 and 1780 and altered on several occasions. All the carpets were made in Killybegs *(see DONEGAL COAST).*

Beyond the hexagonal sentry boxes flanking the entrance the **Grand Staircase** ascends to the **Battleaxe Landing**, named after the weapons carried by the Viceroy's bodyguard.

A suite of rooms includes the one where James Connolly, one of the leaders of the Easter Rising, was held prisoner: Sheraton, Regency and Louis XV and XVI furniture and two fine Irish **plasterwork ceilings**, from Mespil House (demolished). The windows overlook Castle Green and Queen Victoria's Wall which was built to hide the stables. The **Apollo Room** is furnished with an original 18C mantelpiece and a ceiling (1746) depicting Apollo, the sun god and patron of the arts and music.

The modern colour scheme in the 18C **Drawing Room** is based on a late-Ming vase. The ovals and four roundels depicting Jupiter, Juno, Mars and Venus, which decorate the **Throne Room**, are attributed to Giambattista Bellucci, an early-18C Venetian. Portraits of the Viceroys and Venetian chandeliers hang in the **Picture Gallery**, originally the Dining Room.

Four black **Wedgwood plaques** ascribed to John Flaxman (1755–1826) adorn the Wedgwood Room; the three paintings are ascribed to Angelica Kauffmann (1741–1807).

The carpet in the **Bermingham Tower Room** echoes the rose, thistle and shamrock on the chandelier and ceiling (1777).

St Patrick's Hall was built after 1746 as a ballroom. Typical crests, helmets and banners hang above the stallplates recording the names of the members of the Order of the Knights of St Patrick. The ceiling, a symbolic representation of the relationship between Britain and Ireland, was painted by Vincenzo Valdré (1742–1814), an Italian who came to Ireland in 1774 with the Viceroy, the Marquess of Buckingham, for whom he had worked at Stowe.

Powder Tower Undercroft – *Lower Yard.* Excavations beneath the Powder Tower have revealed parts of the Viking and Norman defences – a 13C arch and relieving arch in the **Old City Wall** which enabled boatmen to enter the moat to deliver goods to the postern gate.

Church of the Most Holy Trinity – *Lower Yard*. The building, which stands on the site of an earlier and smaller Chapel Royal, was designed by Francis Johnston and consecrated in 1814. The exterior is decorated with over 100 heads carved in Tullamore limestone by Edward Smyth and his son John; the interior plaster-work is by George Stapleton and the woodwork by Richard Stewart. The scenes from the Passion of Christ in the east window are composed of old stained glass from the Continent. The arms of all the Viceroys from 1172 to 1922 are repre-sented in wood on the galleries and chancel walls and in stained glass in the gallery windows.

Castle Hall – *Upper Yard*. The attractive two-storey building *(not open)* on the north side of the upper yard was designed c 1750 by Thomas Ivory for the Master of Ceremonies. It incorporates the **Bedford Tower**, which was named after John Russell, Duke of Bedford and Lord Lieutenant, and built on the base of the west tower of the original castle gate. Four days before the state visit of Edward VII and Queen Alexandra in 1907 the Crown Jewels were stolen from the Office of Arms in the Bedford Tower; they have never been recovered.
Flanking Castle Hall are two gates surmounted by statues by Van Nost: *Fortitude* on the west gate and *Justice* on the east gate, which was the sole entrance until the west gate was opened in 1988 and a new bridge built; the fountain and pool recall the old moat. In wet weather the scales of Justice used to dip unevenly until holes were bored to drain the rainwater from the outer pan.

★★★**Chester Beatty Library** ⊘ – The collection of Islamic and Far Eastern Art, which is of international standing, was made by Sir Alfred Chester Beatty (1875–1968). The Library has a large and renowned collection of **Arabic, Persian and Turkish manus-cripts**. There are over 270 copies of the **Koran** among the Islamic manuscripts, including illuminations by some of the greatest master calligraphers.
Biblical material consists of Syriac, Armenian, Ethiopian and Coptic texts, also early Western Bibles and Books of Hours. Of international importance are the biblical papyri dating from the early 2C to 4C.
The **Japanese and Chinese collection** includes paintings and prints of the highest quality, including Japanese woodblock prints which influenced 19C European art, and a large collection of snuff bottles, *netsuke*, jade books and rhinoceros-horn cups.
The **Western European collection** contains many important printed books. The print collection includes works by Dürer, Holbein, Piranesi, Bartolozzi and many others.

OLD TOWN *South bank – 1 day*

The heart of old Dublin occupies the ridge between the Liffey and its southern tri-butary, the Poddle River, which now flows underground. The Vikings settled on the south bank of the Liffey at **Wood Quay** (**HY 196**) (4 acres/1.62ha), where the modern Civic Offices of Dublin Corporation now stand; excavations (1974–81) revealed the remains of 150 Viking buildings at 13 different levels (AD 920–1100). Dublin Castle was raised on the south side of the ridge overlooking the Poddle. The town expanded westwards along the **High Street** (**HY 78**) into the **Cornmarket** (**HY 49**), where vast quantities of grain were sold for export in the Middle Ages. Little remains of the old buildings in **Fishamble Street** (**HY 67**), where Molly Malone was born and Handel conducted the first performance of *Messiah* to raise funds for the Rotunda Hospital *(see below)*. The **Liberties** was the name given to the area further south and west, which lay outside the jurisdiction of the medieval city; here the buildings vary from 17C high-gable houses built by French Huguenot refugees to 19C mansion flats and 20C modern housing estates.

★★**Christ Church Cathedral** ⊘ (**HY**) – The cathedral, which is a combination of the Romanesque and Early English Gothic styles, is the seat of the Anglican Bishop of Dublin and Glendalough and the Metropolitan Cathedral of the Southern Province of the Church of Ireland, second only to Armagh. Until 1871 it was also the state church where the officers of the Crown were instituted. The foundation dates from 1038 when a wooden church was built by Dunan, the first Bishop of Dublin, on land provided by Sitric, the Viking King of Dublin. Soon after 1170 this building was replaced by a stone church built by the Anglo-Normans and served by a com-munity of Augustinian canons, who were replaced at the Dissolution (1541) by the Dean and Chapter.
In the 19C restoration, carried out under George Street, the Long Choir of John de St Paul (1358) was demolished. The floor is paved with encaustic tiles copied from the 13C originals in the Chapel of St Laud.
The elegant **Romanesque south door** overlooks the ruins of the Chapter House.
The **nave** was built early in the 13C in the Early English Gothic style; the north wall, supported by buttresses, is original but the south wall collapsed in 1562 and was rebuilt in the 19C. Some of the cathedral musicians are commemorated in the north-west corner. George Street converted the north porch into the **baptistery**; the **font** is composed of different-coloured Irish marble. The coat of arms in the north transept belongs to Sir Henry Sidney, Lord Deputy of Ireland under Elizabeth I.
The **brass eagle lectern** is medieval but the pulpit and the choir screen, which is sur-mounted by a replica of the Cross of Cong, date from 1872. The sanctuary contains the bishop's throne and the carved oak stalls for the canons. The ambulatory leads

to the Chapel of St Laud, which is paved with some of the original 13C tiles; hanging on the wall *(right)* is a casket containing the heart of St Laurence O'Toole, the second Archbishop of Dublin. The south transept shows the transition from Romanesque to Gothic.

The **"Strongbow" monument** in the south aisle commemorates Richard de Clare, Earl of Pembroke, known as "Strongbow", who initiated the building of the cathedral and died in 1176. The short stone figure is probably the original which was broken when the south nave wall collapsed; the full-length figure, which bears the arms of the FitzOsbert family from Drogheda, was supplied by Sir Henry Sidney; "Strongbow's" tomb" was frequently specified in legal contracts as the place of payment.

The 12C Norman **crypt** *(access in the south aisle)* was originally used for services, then let to shopkeepers and afterwards used for burials until the mid 19C; it now houses the **stocks** (1670) which formerly stood in the churchyard.

Dublinia ⊘ **(HY)** – The Synod Hall, which is linked to the cathedral by an arch, presents an informative review of the early years of local history (1170–1540) using artefacts on loan from the National Museum, a scale model of the city *(upstairs)* and reconstructions based on the dockside at Wood Quay and a medieval merchant's house.

From the top of St Michael's Tower *(96 steps)* there is a fine **view** of the city in all directions.

★★St Patrick's Cathedral ⊘ **(HZ)** – As John Comyn, who was appointed Archbishop of Dublin by Henry II in 1181, disliked living next to Christ Church *(see above)* under the jurisdiction of the City Provosts, he moved south to the site of a holy well where, according to tradition, converts were baptized by St Patrick in the 5C; the well was rediscovered in 1901 in St Patrick's Park. Comyn's immediate successor, Henry de Loundres, promoted the church to a cathedral and began a new building in the Early English style which was dedicated in 1254; the Lady Chapel was added c 1270. The present tower dates from 1370. Little of the original fabric remains owing to a fire in 1362 and extensive restoration work commissioned by the Guinness family in the 19C.

The tomb of **Jonathan Swift**, Dean of St Patrick's from 1713 to 1745, is marked by a bronze plaque in the floor near the main door beside that of his friend "Stella"; his epitaph which he himself wrote is inscribed over the door in the south wall next to his bust. In the north transept are displayed his death-mask, publications by and about him, his chair, altar-table and movable pulpit. He composed the inscription on the black marble tomb of the **Duke of Schomberg** *(see p 91) (north choir aisle)*, and put up a plaque *(south transept)* to his servant, Alexander McGee.

The vaulted **baptistery** in the southwest corner of the nave was probably the entrance to the church built by Comyn. The 13C floor tiles, transferred from the south transept in the 19C restoration, have been copied throughout the cathedral. At the west end of the nave stands the old door of the Chapter House; the hole was cut in 1492 so that the Earl of Kildare could "chance his arm" in a conciliatory gesture to Black James Ormond who had taken refuge in the Chapter House; they had

---

Jonathan Swift (1667–1745)

The famous Dean of St Patrick's Cathedral was born in Dublin in 1667 and educated at Kilkenny and Trinity College, Dublin. In 1689 he became Secretary to Sir William Temple of Moor Park in England but, impatient at failing to secure advancement, returned to Ireland, where he was ordained in 1694 and appointed as prebendary of Kilroot, near Carrickfergus; here he wrote his first book, *A Tale of a Tub*, a satire on "corruptions in religion and learning", published in 1704 together with *The Battle of the Books*. He tried a second time to advance his career in England but, on Temple's death in 1699, he again returned to Ireland; in 1701 he became Vicar of Laracor, south of Trim, and a prebendary of St Patrick's Cathedral; he was appointed Dean of St Patrick's in 1713.

Swift is still remembered as the author of *Gulliver's Travels* but he wrote many pamphlets on church matters, on politics and about Ireland, including the delightfully satirical *A Modest Proposal* (1729) for disposing of unwanted babies. His *Journal to Stella*, a collection of intimate letters, was addressed to Esther Johnson, whom he met in 1696 at Moor Park; she settled in Ireland with a companion Rebecca Dingley in 1700–1 but whether or not she and Swift married is uncertain.

Swift was also associated with Vanessa van Homrigh of Celbridge, whom he met in 1708; she died in 1723 apparently of a broken heart three years before Stella.

Swift spent one-third of his income on the poor and saved another third which he bequeathed for the founding of a hospital for the insane. At the end of his life he suffered from Ménière's disease and lost the use of many of his faculties.

quarrelled because Lord Ormond had been appointed Lord Deputy in place of Kildare who had failed to oppose Perkin Warbeck, a pretender to the English throne. The huge **Boyle Monument**, erected by the Great Earl of Cork in memory of his second wife Catherine, is the work of the sculptor, Edward Tingham. On the west wall are the arms of five of the Archbishops of Dublin between 1555 and 1678, painted in oil on wooden panels. One of the Celtic **cross-slabs** once marked the site of St Patrick's Well. An attractive sculpture commemorates **O'Carolan** *(see BOYLE)*, a friend of Swift.

In the north aisle stands a statue by Edward Smyth of the Marquess of Buckingham, Viceroy and first Grand Master of the **Order of St Patrick** instituted in 1783 by George III. Until 1871 the cathedral was the chapel of the Order; the knight's banners hang in the choir above the stalls which are labelled with their escutcheons. The arches along the east side of **St Patrick's Park** form a literary parade of Dublin-born writers, with their dates and major works; three won a Nobel Prize for Literature.

★★**Marsh's Library** ⊘ (**HZ**) – The building was designed in 1701 by Sir William Robinson to house the first public library in Ireland. A portrait of the founder, Archbishop Narcissus Marsh, hangs above the stairs. The dark oak bookcases, surmounted by a mitre, divide the long room into seven bays. Beyond the office are three "cages" where precious books can be consulted behind locked wire screens. The total of 25 000 books is composed of four individual collections: Marsh's own library including books on science, mathematics and music as well as texts in Hebrew, Arabic, Turkish and Russian; the library of Edward Stillingfleet (1635–99), Bishop of Worcester, which contains some of the earliest printed works; books on Protestant theology and controversy collected by the first Librarian, Dr Elias Bouhereau, a Huguenot who left France in 1685; the collection bequeathed by John Stearne (1660–1745), Bishop of Clogher, which contains Cicero's *Letters to his Friends*, a beautiful book, printed in Milan in 1472. The Library owns a copy of Clarendon's *History of the Rebellion* annotated by Swift and two volumes of the translation of the Old Testament into Irish by Bishop Bedell *(see CAVAN)* which Marsh helped to prepare for the printers.

★**Tailors' Hall** ⊘ (**HY**) – The Tailors' Hall, built between 1703 and 1707, is the only surviving guild-hall in Dublin; it is now the head office of *An Taisce*, an organisation devoted to the conservation of the Irish environment. The elaborate entrance gate, dated 1706, leads into a small garden containing plants imported or developed by Irishmen. The Great Hall has a stage and a handsome marble fireplace; an elegant pine staircase leads up to the minute gallery with a wrought-iron railing which overlooks the hall.

The Catholic Convention, convened here by the United Irishmen under the leadership of Theobald Wolfe Tone, came to be known as the Back Lane Parliament because of the name of the street.

★**City Hall** ⊘ (**HY**) – The City Hall (1769–79) was designed by Thomas Cooley as the Royal Exchange. It was bought by the City Corporation in 1852 when economic activity declined after the Act of Union (1800). The domed **rotunda** *(entrance hall)* is decorated with **frescoes** (1914–19) by James Ward, illustrating the city's history, and **a coffered ceiling** (18C) by Charles Thorp; Thorp also created the rich stuccowork above the doors and on the ceiling of the **east staircase**, which has an elegant wrought-iron balustrade and mahogany handrail. In 1916 the building was garrisoned by the insurgents *(explanatory panel on exterior west side)*.

St Audoen's Gate (**HY B**) – The river gate (1275) is one of the 32 gates which pierced the Norman city walls.

St Werburgh's Church ⊘ (**HY**) – The foundation dates from the 12C. The present building (1715) was remodelled in 1759; in 1810 the spire was dismantled as it overlooked the castle courtyard. Lord Edward Fitzgerald, who was mortally wounded while being arrested for his involvement in the 1798 rebellion, is buried in the vaults; his captor, Maj Henry Sirr, is buried in the graveyard. A plaque commemorates John Field (1782–1837), composer and creator of the Nocturne, who was born nearby in Golden Lane and baptized in St Werburgh's.

St Audoen's Church ⊘ (**HY A**) – The old church (Anglican) was founded by the Anglo-Normans and dedicated to St Audoen of Rouen in France. The west doorway dates from the 12C; the original 13C nave is lit by 15C windows.

Brazen Head (**HY S**) – The old public house, which dates from 1688, was the headquarters of the United Irishmen in the 18C.

TEMPLE BAR ⊘ (**HJY**) *South bank*

The area now known as Temple Bar (28 acres/11ha) takes its name from Sir William Temple, Provost of Trinity (1628–1699), who owned land which included a sand bar on the south bank of the river. A stroll through its medieval network of narrow streets and alleys and courts reveals a variety of old buildings – Georgian houses, warehouses and chapels – restored and converted to new uses, interspersed with new purpose-built property.

The area, a successful case of urban renewal, is being re-developed as a **cultural district** with theatres, cinemas, nightclubs and bars, seven centres – including Designyard, an applied arts centre, and the Irish Film Centre, a national centre for film in Ireland – galleries, "alternative" shops, ethnic restaurants, hotels and public and private residential accommodation. Open spaces have been created on derelict sites – Meeting House Square for open-air performances, Central Bank Plaza among the banks and insurance offices in Dame Street, and Temple Bar Square, a shopping centre.

The **Temple Bar Information Centre** *(18 Eustace Street)* ⊘ provides a list of interesting things to do and see. **Sunlight Chambers** *(corner of Essex Quay and Parliament Street)* was built as the headquarters of Lever Brothers with coloured terracotta friezes telling the story of soap. **Merchants' Hall** was designed by Frederick Darley for the Merchants' Guild, also known as the Fraternity of the Holy Trinity, the first of Dublin's 25 guilds; the arched passage through the building links Temple Bar with the river bank.

Viking Adventure ⊘ **(HY)** – The tour embarks on a simulated rough sea voyage which lands its passengers in Viking Dublin, where they are greeted by inhabitants who escort them on a guided tour explaining how at first they raided, then traded and then settled, building wooden houses, practising their crafts as jewellers, leatherworkers and cloth merchants, and building a church near a well as Christianity was introduced beside the old Norse religion.

A long ramp leads up round a model of an archeological dig to a model of a cross-section of a Viking ship and a film about the voyages made by the Vikings, who navigated by the sun and stars and travelled to Russia and Istanbul.

★**Liffey Bridge (JY)** – The delicate cast-iron footbridge linking the quays on the north and south bank was built in 1816 as the Wellington Bridge but its popular name, the **Ha'penny Bridge**, derives from the toll (a half penny) which was levied until 1919.

★★TRINITY COLLEGE ⊘ (JY) *South bank*
Entrances in Nassau Street and College Green

Trinity College, Dublin, sometimes known as TCD, was founded in 1592 by Elizabeth I on the site of All Hallows, an Augustinian monastery, suppressed at the Dissolution. It developed according to the tradition of the Oxford and Cambridge colleges and was an Anglican preserve until the late 18C. It stands in

Trinity College, Dublin

its own grounds, **College Park**, an open space devoted to sports – cricket, rugby, running and hurling – which has diminished as buildings to accommodate the science and medical faculties have been built at the east end.

★★★ **Old Library** ⓥ – The austere building (1712–32) was designed by Thomas Burgh, Chief Engineer and Surveyor-General of Her Majesty's Fortifications in Ireland, and paid for with a government grant of £5000. The library acquired its books by purchase or donation until 1801, when it became a copyright library. Since then the increased pace of acquisition has required new buildings: the Reading Room built in 1937 and the Berkeley Library designed by Paul Koralek in 1967. The ground floor, originally an open colonnade designed to protect the books from damp, was closed in to provide more book stacks in 1892; in 1992 part was converted to provide two galleries: The Colonnades for annual themed exhibitions, and the Treasury.

★★★ **Treasury** – This gallery displays the great treasures of Trinity College Library. The **Book of Kells**, the most famous of the library's treasures, is an illuminated manuscript of the four Gospels in Latin on vellum, produced c 800; although it was kept at Kells *(see p 190)* until the 17C, it is not known if it was produced in that monastery or elsewhere. The **Book of Durrow** (c 700) is another illustrated manuscript of the Gospels in a simpler style. The **Book of Armagh** (c 807) contains the complete text of the New Testament in Latin, as used by the Celtic Church, as well as the lives of St Patrick and St Martin and the Confession of St Patrick. The **Book of Dimma** contains both the Gospels and some liturgical text; its silver shrine dates from c 1150.

★★ **Long Room** – Above the entrance door at the top of the stairs are the **arms of Elizabeth I**, probably the only relic of the original college. The **Long Room** (209ft/64m x 40ft/12m) consists of 20 bays lined with bookcases surmounted by a gallery. The original flat ceiling was replaced in the mid 19C by the present higher wooden barrel vault to provide more shelving.
The **Irish harp** (restored), the oldest in Ireland, is at least 500 years old; it was found in Limerick in the 18C and is made of willow and has 29 strings.

Dublin Experience – Through photography, music and voices the audio-visual presentation *(40min)* gives an entertaining and informative account of a thousand years of Dublin history from the Viking settlement to the modern city.

Library Court – The **Campanile** (1853) was designed by Charles Lanyon. Among the trees in the centre is a sculpture by Henry Moore, *Reclining Connected Forms* (1969). The area behind the north range is called Botany Bay, after the Australian penal colony, possibly because of the students' unruly behaviour. The red-brick range on the east side, known as Rubrics, is the oldest building in the college. The south side is closed by the Library.

Front Court – Statues by Foley of Oliver Goldsmith and Edmund Burke flank the main gate. The gateway itself is paved with hexagonal wooden blocks.
The buildings date from the mid 18C; the wings terminate in the **Theatre** *(south)* and the **Chapel** *(north)*, both designed by Sir William Chambers with stuccowork by Michael Stapleton. The chapel is mainly lit by high semicircular windows; the organ case dates from the 18C. The theatre (1777-91) is used for degree ceremonies, Senate meetings and musical and theatrical performances; it is hung with portraits: Elizabeth I, Edmund Burke, George Berkeley, Jonathan Swift.

Provost's House – South of the entrance gates facing College Green stands an elegant Georgian house built for the Provost in 1758.

Museum – *South side of New Square.* The Museum (1850) was designed by Sir Thomas Deane and Benjamin Woodward in the Venetian style promoted by Ruskin; the delightful stone carving of flowers, leaves and animals is by the O'Shea brothers from Cork.

COLLEGE GREEN DISTRICT *South bank*

Until the Old Parliament was built in 1728 there was nothing east of the old town but the buildings of Trinity College facing College Green (**JY 45**), known as Hoggen Green, a triangular open space, formerly an old Viking burial ground *(haugen)* and meeting place *(thengmote)*.

College Green (**JY 45**) – At the centre stands a statue of **Henry Grattan** by John Foley (1879) and a modern iron sculpture designed by Edward Delaney in memory of **Thomas Davis** (1814–45), poet, leader of the Young Ireland movement and founder of *The Nation*.

★★ **Bank of Ireland** ⓥ (**JY**) – *Entrance in Foster Place.* Several architects contributed to this elegant building. The central block was designed by Pearce in 1728 to house the Irish Parliament; the south façade consists of an Ionic portico facing a square court which is flanked by two curved wings; above the pediment are replicas of three statues by Edward Smyth (1809) representing *Hibernia* between *Fidelity* and *Commerce*. James Gandon designed the east portico in 1785 and the west portico in 1797. In 1803 the building was converted by Francis Johnston for the use of the Bank of Ireland and in 1811 he designed the Armoury in Foster Place as a guardhouse for the bank.

In the **Story of Banking** an audio-visual presentation *(8min)* and exhibits of currency, bank notes and an old money cart form part of an excellent interpretation of the role of the Bank of Ireland in the commercial development of the country, since its establishment in 1783.

The old **House of Lords**, with its coffered ceiling, Irish glass chandelier (1788) and original oak mantelpiece to a design by Inigo Jones, is still intact; the tapestries (1733), woven by John Van Beaver and probably designed by Johann van der Hagen, depict William of Orange at the Battle of the Boyne and James II surveying the siege of Londonderry; the mace (1765) was retained by the last Speaker, sold by his descendants and bought from Christie's in 1937; a Bible (1772); coins, banknotes and scales for weighing sovereigns.

★**Grafton Street** (JYZ) – The most elegant shopping street in Dublin is now a pedestrian precinct; in the 19C it was paved with pine blocks to deaden the sound of carriage wheels. **Bewley's Oriental Café** ⊘ (**JY R**) with its distinctive mosaic façade and stained-glass windows by Harry Clarke was opened in 1927; the obsolete equipment in the **museum** *(top floor)* illustrates the evolution of the business which began c 1840. It stands on the site of Whytes School, which was attended by Robert Emmet, Thomas Moore, Richard Sheridan and the Duke of Wellington.

★**Powerscourt Centre** ⊘ (**JY**) – A most attractive modern shopping centre has been created in an 18C town house which contains some fine stucco ceilings. The house was designed in 1771 by Robert Mack for Viscount Powerscourt.

Civic Museum ⊘ (**JY M¹**) – The history of Dublin can be traced in the old City Assembly House. The Octagon Room displays maps, prints, postcards, photographs, relics of old buildings and a set of Malton's views of Dublin (1792–99). Early forms of transport are illustrated together with relics of earlier commercial practices.

St Ann's Church ⊘ (**JZ**) – The parish was founded in 1707 on a site provided by Sir Joshua Dawson. The building, one of the earliest Georgian churches in Dublin, was

DUBLIN
BUILT UP AREA

Adelaide Road	**BT** 3
Bath Avenue	**CT** 9
Benburb Street	**BS** 15
Berkeley Road	**BS** 16
Botanic Road	**BS** 19
Bow Street	**BS** 21
Canal Road	**BT** 30
Clanbrassil Street	**BT** 40
Conyngham Road	**AS** 48

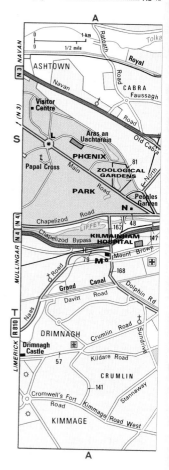

designed by Isaac Wills; the neo-Romanesque west front dates from 1868. The stained glass is Victorian; three windows in the south aisle are by Wilhelmina Geddes, a member of *An Tur Gloine (see p 55)*. The bread shelf in the chancel was established in 1723 by a charitable bequest to provide 120 loaves of bread each week for the poor.

Mansion House (JZ) – The house was built in 1705 by Joshua Dawson, a builder, and bought by the City of Dublin in 1715 as the residence of the Lord Mayor. The Round Room was added for the visit of George IV in 1821; it was here that the first Irish parliament met in 1919 to adopt the Declaration of Independence.

MUSEUM DISTRICT *South bank*

The district began to develop into a fashionable suburb in the 1750s when the Duke of Leinster built the first nobleman's house south of the river; his prediction that fashionable society would follow soon proved true.
In 1815 his mansion was bought by the Royal Dublin Society; the National Museum, the National Library and the National Gallery were built in the grounds. In the 20C the mansion was converted to house the new Republican parliament *(see below)* set up in 1922.

★★**National Museum** ⊘ (**KZ**) – *The collections of the National Museum are displayed here and at Collins Barracks (see p 160).* This museum, purpose-built in 1890 with a circular colonnaded portico, domed vestibule and elaborate decoration, concentrates on the display of the riches of the national archeological collections.

B	Shaw Birthplace
F	Bluecoat School
G	Waterways Visitor Centre
L	Phoenix Monument
M⁶	Kilmainham Gaol Museum
M⁷	Guinness Hopstore
N	Wellington Monument
Q	Portobello Hotel
V	Old Jameson Distillery
X	St Stephen's Church

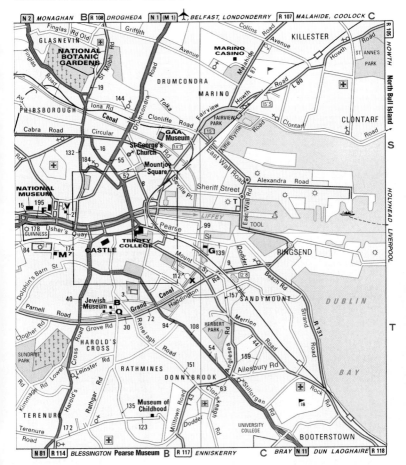

Ground floor – An audio-visual presentation *(15min)* helps put into context the masterpieces of Irish art brought together in **The Treasury★★**. Precious objects range in date from the Bronze Age to the 15C and include: a model boat in gold from the Broighter Hoard (1C); the Loughnashade Trumpet (1C BC) *(see p 285)*; the Ardagh Chalice (8C); the Tara Brooch (8C); the Shrine of St Patrick's Bell in bronze, gold and silver (c 1100); the "Cathach", a book shrine made to contain the Psalter of St Columba (Colmcille) (12C–15C); the Kavanagh Charter Horn of ivory and brass, the only surviving object associated with Irish kingship (12C–15C).

The section on Prehistoric Ireland has a reconstruction of a passage tomb as well as the huge Lurgan Longboat, hollowed from a tree-trunk around 2500 BC. **Ireland's Gold** displays a gleaming array of artefacts, some from hoards preserved for thousands of years in the Irish boglands.

The **Road to Independence** commemorates those involved in the Easter Rising in 1916 through photos, MSS, documents, uniforms and death-masks.

Upper floor – Among the objects shown in **Viking Ireland** are artefacts from the Viking settlement at Wood Quay in Old Dublin: iron, bone, wood utensils, clothing and ornaments. St Manchan's Shrine, a spectacular reliquary, is one of several ecclesiastical treasures on display in the section entitled **The Church**.

Small in number but superb in quality, the objects on show from **Ancient Egypt** benefit from their dramatically lit display. **Irish Glass** has fine examples of this craft in which the country has long excelled.

DUBLIN
CENTRE

A	St Audoen's Church
B	St Audoen's Gate
D	Number Twenty-Nine
E	St Michan's Church
G	Parliament
H	City Hall
M¹	Civic Museum
M²	Natural History Museum
M³	Heraldic Museum
M⁴	Hugh Lane Municipal Gallery of Modern Art
M⁵	National Wax Museum
M⁰	Dublin Writers' Museum
R	Bewley's Oriental Café
S	Brazen Head
T¹	Gate Theatre
T²	Abbey Theatre

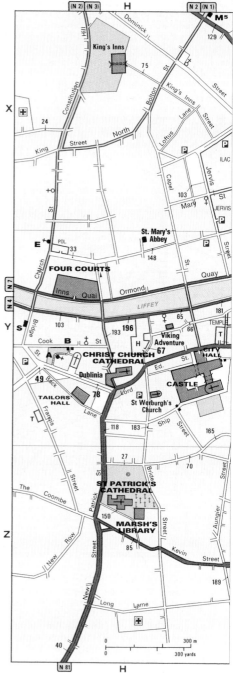

★★ **National Gallery** ⊘ (**KZ**) – *A list of the highlights of the collection is available at the entrance; multimedia service in Gallery 7.* The statue at the entrance is of William Dargan (1799–1867), the railway magnate who sponsored the Irish Industrial Exhibition (1853), which included a Fine Art Hall. The Gallery, which displays over 2 000 works, was refurbished and rehung in 1989. Although it contained no masterpieces when the Gallery opened in 1864 in the Dargan Wing designed by Francis Fowke, a representative collection of Dutch 17C masters was soon acquired. The Milltown Rooms were added to house the Milltown Collection *(see RUSSBOROUGH)* donated in 1897. Thirty-one Turner watercolours were presented in 1900 by Sir Henry Vaughan. Sir Hugh Lane enhanced the collection with gifts and bequests. George Bernard Shaw made a generous donation in his Will including royalties from *My Fair Lady*.

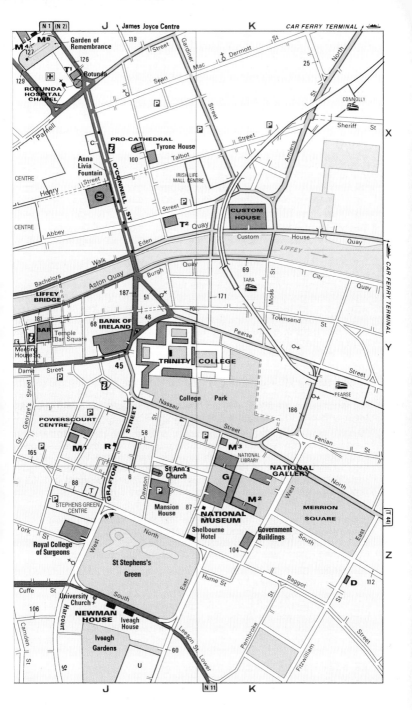

Ground Floor – The Shaw Room *(Room 1 a)* presents portraits and sculpture of Irishmen and women or by Irish artists – *a Statue of Shaw* by Paul Troubetzky (1866–1938), *Earl of Bellamont* by Joshua Reynolds (1723–92). The octagonal Milltown Rooms *(Rooms 2–8)* exhibit work including furniture by Irish artists – portraits and landscapes by Hugh Douglas Hamilton, Nathaniel Hone, Francis Darby, Jeremiah Mulcahy, Daniel Maclise, William Orpen (1878–1931), Jack B Yeats (1871–1957), Seán Keating (1889–1971), John Lavery (1856–1941), 20C painters and artists who worked in France. There is a fine collection of portraits *(Room 32)*. The rest of the **North Wing** *(Rooms 33–36)* are devoted to British Painting – Hogarth, Richard Wilson, Kneller, Angelica Kauffmann, Thomas Gainsborough, Joshua Reynolds, George Romney, Richard Bonington, John Crome.

First Floor – The Dargan Wing is devoted to Baroque painting *(Room 9)* and to **French painting** (17C–20C) *(Rooms 10–13 and 15–16)* which include works by Claude (1600–82), Chardin (1699–1779), Géricault (1791–1824) and Sisley (1839–99). The Italian collection *(Rooms 17–21)* includes works from the Early Renaissance to the 18C, as well as 16C Venetian paintings. The North Wing *(Rooms 23–31)* contains Greek and Russian icons, early Italian religious subjects and 17C Italian works, German and Early Netherlandish works, later Flemish, Dutch paintings – genre and marine, Rembrandt and his circle, Dutch landscapes – and 15C to 18C Spanish.

★**Merrion Square** (**KZ**) – *Floodlit at night.* The square was laid out in 1762 under the policy of the Wide Streets Commissioners. Delicate fanlights surmount the elegant doorways; commemorative plaques mark the homes of famous people. The mature gardens provide a welcome contrast to the busy streets.
The southeast vista is closed by **St Stephen's Church** ⊘ (**BT X**), designed in 1821 by John Bowden; above its Greek façade is a domed tower known as the "Pepper Canister".

★**Number Twenty-Nine** ⊘ (**KZ D**) – From 1794 to 1806 the 18C terrace house was occupied by a widow with three children, who bought it for £320 and sold it for £700.
Throughout, the house is furnished with original or reproduction wallpaper, carpets and curtains, and contemporary furniture and paintings.
Features of particular interest are a water filter, a sugar cone, a hastener (for accelerating the cooking of food) and wood, tin, pewter and Delftware vessels in the stone-floored kitchen; the typical cloak rail and massive door lock in the entrance hall; knife boxes, a wine cistern designed by Francis Johnston and a plate bucket in the dining room, where the early-19C table is laid for dessert; chandeliers and a spinet in the drawing rooms; a curved belly-warmer and hair and feather mattresses in the bedrooms; a stencilled floor in the governess' room; oilcloth and dolls' houses in the nursery.

Natural History Museum ⊘ (**KZ M²**) – On entering the pillared hall and galleries the visitor is confronted by three skeletons of the Great Irish Deer, now extinct. The specimens in the display cabinets cover the full range of mammals, birds, fish and insects ever to have lived in Ireland.

Heraldic Museum ⊘ (**KZ M³**) – The display presents: the banners of the recognized heads of Irish families; the arms of the provinces, counties, cities and towns; the colours of Irish Regiments which served in France in the 17C and 18C; the arms of the Presidents of Ireland; banknotes, coins, seals, livery buttons, glass, porcelain, silver and other heraldic artefacts. The building, designed in 1860 by Thomas Deane and Benjamin Woodward as the Kildare Street Club, bears unusual carvings by Charles W Harrison.

Parliament ⊘ (**KZ G**) – The two houses (**Dáil Éireann and Seanad Éireann**) meet in **Leinster House**, which was designed in 1745 by Richard Castle for the Duke of Leinster and converted to house the republican parliament in 1922. The public are admitted to the public gallery which overlooks the chamber of the lower house *(Dáil).*

Government Buildings ⊘ (**KZ**)– This imposing structure in Edwardian Baroque, opened in 1911 by George V, was the last major public building project carried out in Dublin under British rule. Until 1989 parts of the building were occupied by Trinity College. A major restoration programme, the provision of well-chosen modern furniture and the display of a fascinating range of contemporary art works make a fine setting for some of the business of government, carried out in committee and conference rooms and in the office of the Prime Minister *(Taoiseach).*

ST STEPHEN'S GREEN (JZ) *South bank*

Formerly common land first enclosed in 1663, the gardens (22 acres/9ha), a delightful combination of water, flower beds and lawns, were laid out in 1880 by Lord Ardilaun, whose statue stands on the west side. A bronze sculpture by Henry Moore was erected in memory of William Butler Yeats in 1967. The gateway in the northwest corner commemorates those who died in the Boer War.
The green is bordered by some buildings of note. The **Shelbourne Hotel** *(north side)* was built in 1867; exotic figures flank the elegant porch and entrance. The **Royal College of Surgeons** *(west side)*, designed by Edward Parke in 1806, was captured during the Easter Rising in 1916 by a party of insurgents led by Constance Markievicz *(see p 245)*. **Iveagh House** *(south side)*, designed by Richard Castle, is now the Department of Foreign Affairs.

Harcourt Street curving from the southwest corner is lined by elegant terraces of red-brick Georgian houses with handsome door frames and fanlights.
Much of the district south of St Stephen's Green is covered by elegant Georgian terraces.

★★ Newman House (JZ) ⊘ – The two 18C town houses are named after Cardinal Newman, the first Rector of University College, which started there in 1854. The smaller house was designed by Richard Castle in 1738 and was then flanked by gardens. It has regained its original 18C appearance: glazing bars designed by Castle, marble tiled floor, early Cuban mahogany staircase. The original colour scheme of the Apollo Room has been revealed through paint scrapes; the stucco figures of Apollo and the nine Muses are the work of the Lafranchini brothers. They also decorated the Saloon on the first floor; two of the nude figures were covered in 1883 when the room became a Jesuit chapel. The larger house, which dates from 1765, contains the Bishops' Room, which is furnished with a reproduction of the original wallpaper (c 1780), a portrait of Cardinal Newman and the chair given him as Rector of the University; the staircase is decorated with Rococo plasterwork – birds and musical instruments – by Robert West.

University Church ⊘ (JZ)– The church (1854) was designed at the behest of Cardinal Newman by John Pollen in the Byzantine and Italian early-Christian style advertised by John Ruskin.

Iveagh Gardens ⊘ (JZ) – *Access from Harcourt Street or Earlsfort Terrace*. The gardens form an unexpected haven of lawns and tree-lined walks, enhanced by statuesque fountains, a rosarium and a maze.

National Concert Hall (BT) – *Earlsfort Terrace*. The building, which was opened for its present purpose in 1981, was completed in 1865 as the Exhibition Palace to house the successful International Exhibition, which was opened by Queen Victoria. The Winter Gardens of glass and steel were later dismantled. The main auditorium (capacity 1 200) was inaugurated in 1865 with a concert of music by Handel, Mendelssohn and Haydn, followed four days later by a great ball. From 1908 to 1981 it was used mainly as an examination hall by University College (UCD). The new organ has four keyboards and a tracker action. The **John Field Room** (capacity 250), formerly the Sculpture Hall, is lit by a chandelier of 14 564 hand-cut pieces of Waterford crystal (20ft/6m high, 10ft/3m wide, 1 000lb in weight).

O'CONNELL STREET – PARNELL SQUARE (JKX) *North bank*

By the 18C this area had become the fashionable residential district of Dublin, centred on O'Connell Street, then known as Gardiner's Mall. The site of Parnell Square, formerly Rutland Square, was developed by Bartholomew Mosse to raise money for his maternity hospital, which occupied the south side. The houses on the other three sides were completed in the 1770s and inhabited by peers and bishops and members of Parliament. Public entertainments were held in the walled **pleasure gardens** extending behind the hospital; they were laid out with a wilderness, temples of refreshment and a terrace, called the Orchestra, where music was played. Funds were also raised from entertainments given in the **Rotunda**, designed in 1764 by John Ensor and now a cinema, and from functions held in the **Assembly Rooms**, designed by Richard Johnston in 1786 and now occupied by the **Gate Theatre** (JX T¹), founded in 1928 by Hilton Edwards and Micheál MacLiammóir.

Many of the once-elegant Georgian terraces in the neighbourhood, particularly **Mountjoy Square** (BS), have passed through neglect and decay to demolition or restoration. **St George's Church** (BS) where the Duke of Wellington married Kitty Pakenham in 1806 was designed by Francis Johnston in the Greek Ionic style (1802–14) with a marked similarity to St Martin's-in-the-Fields in London.

The tradition of **public entertainment**, begun in the 18C, continues in the cinemas and theatres.

★ O'Connell Street (JX) – The famous street, which is now lined with shops and cinemas, was laid out by Luke Gardiner in the 18C as a mall and then converted into a narrow residential square. Renamed Sackville Street, it developed into the most important street in 18C Dublin; later it was extended south to Carlisle Bridge (1794); the street and the present bridge (1880) were renamed after O'Connell in 1922.

Down the centre of the street stands a row of **monuments**: *(south to north)* statue by John Foley of Daniel O'Connell; William Smith O'Brien (1803–64), the leader of the Young Ireland Movement who was sentenced to death for treason in 1848; Sir John Gray, who organized Dublin's water supply; James Larkin (1876–1947), founder of the Irish Transport and General Workers' Union (1909); Father Theobald Mathew of the 19C temperance movement.

The **Anna Livia Fountain**, a female personification of the Liffey, soon nicknamed the Floozie in the Jacuzzi, was erected to commemorate Dublin's Millennium in 1988; it occupies the site of Nelson's Pillar (1808), which was damaged by a bomb in 1966 and demolished.

The **GPO building ★** with its Ionic portico was designed by Francis Johnston in 1814. It was the headquarters of the rebels in the Easter Rising in 1916 and still bears scars of the fighting.

The north end of the street is marked by a statue of Charles Stewart Parnell.

Parnell Square (JX) – The north end of has been converted into a **garden of remembrance** designed by Daithí P Hanly. Celtic motifs are incorporated into the design of the gates. The central sculpture by Oisín Kelly echoes Yeats' poem *Easter 1916* with the mythological theme of the transformation of the Children of Lir into swans *(see p 230)*. The broken spears in the mosaic reflect the Celtic custom of throwing weapons into water after a battle.

The site is significant; the plans for the 1916 uprising were made in a house *(plaque)* on the north side of the square and the rebels were held prisoner in the square overnight.

★**Hugh Lane Municipal Gallery of Modern Art** ⊘ (JX M⁴) – The gallery houses an extensive collection of late-19C and 20C works by Irish and Continental artists including the works collected by Sir Hugh Lane (1875–1915), who drowned on the *Lusitania*. The building, a three-storey mansion of Portland stone and granite, flanked by curved screen walls, was designed in 1762 by Sir William Chambers for an earlier connoisseur of art, James Caulfield, 1st Earl of Charlemont *(see p 312)*, who also built the Marino Casino *(see p 164)*.

The permanent collection includes many fine British and French paintings, among the latter several Impressionists as well as pictures by Corot and Courbet. Contemporary artworks include a characteristic project by Christo for swathing the pathways of St Stephen's Green but the most interesting rooms are perhaps those devoted to works by Irish artists. *Lakeside Cottage* (c 1929) is a typically atmospheric landscape by Paul Henry, while the dramatic canvas *The Rescue of the Prison Van at Manchester* by Maurice MacGonical reconstructs a famous Fenian attack in 1867 *(see p 29)*. A whole room is devoted to the paintings of Roderic O'Conor (1860–1940), a friend of Gauguin and an important link between artistic life in France and the British Isles; his pictures reflect the influence of his French colleagues, from Seurat to Van Gogh.

Dublin Writers' Museum ⊘ (JX M⁸) – The museum illustrates the personalities of those Irish writers who were associated with the city of Dublin. On display are personal items, photos, portraits, busts, manuscripts and copies of their major works. The museum also traces the written tradition in Ireland from the illuminated manuscripts of the Celtic Christian church such as the Book of Kells *(see Trinity College above)* to the present day through Jonathan Swift and his contemporaries, writers who made their names in England such as Oscar Wilde and Bernard Shaw, writers who lived abroad such as James Joyce and Samuel Beckett, the great names who promoted the 19C revival of interest in Irish folklore such as WB Yeats, Synge and O'Casey and those who lived and worked in Dublin such as Flann O'Brien, Brendan Behan and Patrick Kavanagh. Temporary exhibitions are held in the elegant reception rooms, readings and workshops in the children's section.

The museum occupies two Georgian terrace houses with **elegant stucco ceilings★**; the one in the library is by Michael Stapleton. Alterations made in 1891–95 by Alfred Darbyshire for George Jameson include stained-glass windows bearing the Jameson monogram, four female figures representing Music, Literature, Art and Science, and, in the first-floor saloon, a series of painted door panels by Gibson and an ornamental colonnade and gilded frieze.

★**Rotunda Hospital Chapel** ⊘ (JX) – The exuberant Rococo chapel is decorated with superb stuccowork by Bartholomew Cramillion and carved mahogany woodwork by John Kelly. It is lit by an 18C lantern and a Venetian window which is filled with modern stained glass and surmounted by the Lamb of God on a book with seven seals and the figure of Charity with three children. The chapel is part of the lying-in hospital designed by Richard Castle in 1752 for Dr Bartholomew Mosse (1712–59).

James Joyce Centre ⊘ (JX) – *35 North Great George's Street.* The centre, which aims to promote an interest in the life and work of James Joyce, offers talks, conducted tours of the house and walks through the north inner city. As a boy Joyce lived nearby in Fitzgibbon Street and attended Belvedere College *(Denmark Street)*. The centre is housed in a restored terrace house, which was built in 1784 by Francis Ryan as the town house of Valentine Brown, Earl of Kenmare; the very fine plasterwork is mostly by Michael Stapleton. Portraits of members of the Joyce family line the staircase; there are family photographs in the exhibition room.

National Wax Museum ⊘ (HX M⁵) – The display of waxwork figures combines fantasy and reality. The tableaux on the upper floor illustrate traditional fairy tales. Those on the ground floor are peopled by national figures such as O'Connell, the heroes of the Easter Rising, the Presidents of Ireland, theatrical stars, church leaders, poets and writers, politicians, sportsmen and pop stars.

★**Pro-Cathedral** ⊘ (JX) – The Church of the Conception of the Virgin Mary, which is in the style of a Greek temple with a Doric portico and a dome, was completed in 1821. The design has been attributed to John Sweetman, who went into exile after the 1798 rebellion, but the architect may be Louis Hippolyte le Bas, who worked for Napoleon. St Mary's has been known as the Pro-Cathedral since the 1880s, as the title of cathedral was granted by the Pope to Christ Church in the 12C.

In 1851 John Newman made his profession of faith to Cardinal Cullen in this church. The Palestrina Choir was endowed in 1902 by Edward Martyn *(see LOUGHREA)*; one of its early members was John McCormack *(see ATHLONE)*.

Tyrone House (**JX**) – The elegant mansion, now occupied by the Department of Education, was designed by Richard Castle in 1741.

Abbey Theatre (**JX T²**) – The foyer is hung with portraits of the actors and writers who have contributed to the Irish Theatre. The Abbey, which first opened in 1904 under the direction of William Butler Yeats and Lady Gregory, now occupies a modern building (1950s), which includes the smaller Peacock Playhouse (157 seats).

★★**Custom House** ⊘ (**KX**) – *Entrance in south front; floodlit at night.* The Custom House, with its long façade and central dome, is one of the most impressive pieces of architecture in Dublin. It was designed by James Gandon and completed in 1791. The building has been extensively restored, after being seriously damaged by fire in 1921, and houses government offices. The **Visitor Centre** occupies the ceremonial vestibules behind the south portico, little altered since Gandon's day. The detailed and fascinating display examines the construction of the building, the fire and restoration, Gandon's career and the work of the government offices which were housed there – excisemen, roads, canals and railways.

Famine Memorial – Six bronze figures by Rowan Gillespie, standing on the quay beside the River Liffey, recall the mixed emotions – ranging from despair through suffering to hope – of the many victims of the Great Famine *(see p 29)*.

FOUR COURTS DISTRICT *North bank*

This part of the north bank of the Liffey, which was known as Oxmantown, had been settled by Norsemen. In the Middle Ages it was dominated by St Mary's Abbey. In the 17C it was built up on a grid plan around Oxmantown Green, now Smithfield, and provision was made for a hospital and free school, now the Bluecoat School.

Four Courts

Four Courts (HY) – The building (1785), which housed five courts – Chancery, King's Bench, Judicature, Exchequer and Common Pleas – was designed by Thomas Cooley and James Gandon. In 1922 during the first hostilities of the Civil War, exploding mines and ammunition gutted the building and destroyed the Public Records Office which contained national archives dating from 1174.

St Michan's Church ⓒ (HY E) – The first church on the site was probably built by the Danes as St Michanl1418 is thought to be a Danish saint. The present church dates from 1095 but its present appearance from 1686.

The **vaults** beneath the church contain some **mummified corpses** which have been preserved for over 300 years by the very dry air and the constant temperature. The **interior** displays several features of interest: the **organ** (1724), which was played by Handel; a wooden panel carved with **musical instruments** on the organ loft; the 18C **font** where Edmund Burke was baptized; the 18C **pulpit** with its curving stair; the **Penitents' Pew** where malefactors knelt to make public acknowledgement of their guilt; the **Ten Commandments** flanking the Venetian east window; the stone effigy of a **12C bishop** *(south chancel wall)* which may mark the tomb of Samuel O'Haingli (d 1121), appointed Bishop of Dublin in 1095.

Old Jameson Distillery ⓒ (BS V) – Part of the old distillery, last used as such in 1971, has been converted to show current and earlier methods of production of whiskey. A video *(8min)* is followed by a tour *(20min)* which passes from the centre of a kiln, through the yard where the barley was delivered from the farms to the grain store; the mystery of worts and wash-backs in the process of making and maturing whiskey is explained. The tour ends in the bar where visitors are invited to take part in a whiskey tasting.

St Mary's Abbey ⓒ (HY) – All that remains of the abbey are the **Slype** and the rib-vaulted Chapter House, which now contains a reconstruction of the 15C cloister arcade (the pieces were recovered in 1975 from a 17C building in Cork Street) and information about the foundation, architecture and history of the abbey and the Cistercian way of life.

St Mary's was founded in 1139 by Benedictines from Savigny but in 1147 the community adopted the Cistercian Rule and eventually came under the control of Buildwas Abbey in Shropshire, England.

It became the richest monastery in the Pale, with extensive estates both north and south of Dublin, and was closely associated with the city, acting as a repository, treasury and meeting place for the Council of Ireland. It was here that Silken Thomas renounced his allegiance to Henry VIII in 1534 and precipitated the Kildare Revolt, also known as the Geraldine Revolt.

★ **Bluecoat School** (BS F) – The building, which is now owned by the Incorporated Law Society, was designed by Thomas Ivory in 1773; his tall central tower was replaced by the squat dome for reasons of economy. Until 1970 the building housed the Hospital and Free School of King Charles II, which was founded in 1670 for the education of poor boys; it was usually known as the Bluecoat School because the pupils wore a military-style blue uniform.

King's Inns (HX) – The building where barristers used to live as well as study was begun in 1795 and completed in 1827. It is the last great public building designed by James Gandon and the dining room is the only Gandon interior to survive. The west front overlooks an extensive park.

Dublin Waterways

The urban landscape of Dublin is greatly enhanced by the five waterways which traverse the city – **River Liffey**, personified as Anna Livia Pluribella, which bisects the centre as it flows out to sea in Dublin Bay; two tributaries, the **River Dodder** on the south bank and the **River Tolka** on the north bank; and two canals, the **Grand Canal** (1757–1803) which passes through the southern suburbs to join the Shannon at Shannon Harbour, north of Birr, and the **Royal Canal** (1790–1817) which passes through the Northside to join the Shannon west of Longford.

WESTERN SUBURBS *North to south*

★★ **National Museum** ⓒ (BS) – *The collections of the National Museum are displayed here and at Kildare Street (see p 152).* This great complex, which once housed 3 000 men and 1 000 horses, was built in 1700 on the orders of King William III and designed by Thomas Burgh. It was intended to be "plain and useful, without any unnecessary ornament" and in its day was the largest institution of its kind in the British Isles, a progressive alternative to the contentious practice of billeting soldiers on the population. It has been converted to provide accommodation for several sections of the National Museum including the decorative arts, folklife, history and geology.

As well as space for temporary exhibitions, the **West Block** has galleries devoted to the work of the museum, and an enthralling array of special treasures – 25 highly varied pieces grouped together under the heading of **Curators' Choice**; they include a rare astrolabe from Prague, an elongated late-13C or early-14C wood statue of St Molaise *(see p 246)* and Bow figurines made by Thomas Frye, some of them modelled on his fellow London Irishmen.

The **South Block** has three floors of galleries: *(third floor)* Irish country furniture and woodcraft, with period furniture showing the development of furniture from Baroque to Modern, including the fascinating late-19C style unique to Ireland, Neo-Celtic, inspired by objects like the Tara Brooch discovered in 1850; *(second floor)* scientific instruments; *(first floor)* Irish silver from the early 17C to the striking work of modern silversmiths.

★★**Phoenix Park** (**AS**) – *Restricted access by car*. The park (1 752 acres/709ha), the largest enclosed urban park in Europe, derives its name from the Gaelic for clear water *(Fionn Uisce)*. The land, confiscated from Kilmainham Priory *(see below)* in 1543 by the Crown, was enclosed in 1662 by the Duke of Ormond who introduced a herd of fallow deer which still roam the Fifteen Acres (actually approximately 300 acres/121ha).

The history of the park is presented in the **Phoenix Park Visitor Centre** ⊙, housed in an old stable block, beside a 17C tower house which was for many years the residence of the park keeper before being incorporated into a private house (now demolished). The southeast gate is flanked by the **Wellington Monument** (**N**) designed by Sir William Smirke in 1817 and the **Peoples' Garden** *(right)*, a flower garden sloping to a small lake. Opposite are the **Zoological Gardens** *(see below)* designed initially by Decimus Burton. The main road, lit by gas lamps, leads to the **Phoenix Monument** (**L**) which was erected by Lord Chesterfield in 1745. To the south stands the residence of the Ambassador of the USA and the **Papal Cross** erected to mark the visit of Pope John Paul II in 1979. To the north stands the **official residence** ⊙ of the President of Ireland (**Aras an Uachtaráin**), formerly Vice-Regal Lodge, which was built (1751–54) as a private house by Nathaniel Clements and in 1815 acquired its Ionic portico by Francis Johnston. It was near here in 1882 at the height of agitation over the Land Act that the newly-appointed Chief Secretary, Lord Frederick Cavendish, and the Under-Secretary, Thomas H Burke, the intended victim, were stabbed to death by the "Invincibles", members of a secret society.

★**Zoological Gardens** ⊙ (**AS**) – *Phoenix Park*. The Zoo, which was founded in 1830, is set in attractive parkland (30 acres/12ha). As well as keeping animals of many types from all parts of the world, it is involved in breeding programmes with other zoos and is under constant development. The **World of Cats** presents snow leopards as well as lions and other felines, while the **World of Primates** with its vivacious monkeys and sad-faced orang-utans exercises a constant appeal. Arctic foxes and snowy owls inhabit **Fringes of the Arctic**, while the lakes and their banks provides a habitat for water fowl, flamingoes, penguins and sea-lions. **City Farm** and **Pets Corner** are especially popular with children.

★**Guinness Hopstore** ⊙ (**BT M⁷**) – *Crane Street*. A free glass of the famous dark stout with the creamy head is served in the visitors' bar in the **old hop store**, at the end of a fascinating survey of the Guinness production process. The history of the Guinness family firm is traced through 140 years by means of a film *(20min)* supplemented by text, pictures, obsolete machinery and equipment.

Further west in Thomas Street is the house built by Arthur Guinness in the 18C next to the main gate of the brewery where the new date is painted up every year. St James' Gate, which pierced the old city wall, has given its name to the brewery which straddles the road. The old windmill is known as St Patrick's Tower.

Irish Museum of Modern Art ⊙ (**AT**) – *Military Road. Car park*. The role of the museum (opened in 1991) is to present 20C Irish and international art and allied theatrical and musical performances, and to establish a permanent collection through purchases and commissions. The inaugural exhibition included works by Braque, Delaunay, Miró, Mondrian and Picasso; by Ellsworth Kelly, Richard Serra and Sol LeWitt; by Evie Hone, Jack B Yeats and Louis Le Brocquy. The range of buildings facing the south front of the museum has been converted into artists' studios.

The museum is housed in **Kilmainham Hospital** ★★, the earliest-surviving Classical building in Ireland. It was commissioned by the Duke of Ormond, James Butler of Kilkenny, who was appointed Viceroy in 1669 after living in exile in France, and inspired by Les Invalides in Paris. The architect was William Robinson, Surveyor-General since 1670, who designed (1680–84) four ranges of buildings round a courtyard providing accommodation for 300 old soldiers, the last of whom left in 1929.

The **North Range** is occupied by the Master's Quarters, Great Hall, now used for concerts and government receptions, and Chapel.

The **Great Hall**, the soldiers' dining and recreation room, is hung with portraits specially commissioned between 1690 and 1734. The stained glass (1908) is the work of AE Child. Over the door is an oak carving (1683) by Jacques Tabary. The **chapel**

Dúchas, Dublin

Kilmainham Gaol, Dublin

ceiling is a papier mâché replica, made in 1903, of the unique Baroque stucco ceiling created in 1687 by English plasterers; after three centuries some of the fruit and vegetable motifs (max 12in/30cm long) had begun to break off. The altar, reredos and rails (1686) were carved by Tabary in Irish oak. The north front overlooks the formal gardens, designed (1710–20) by Edward Pearce to represent the crosses of St George and St Andrew.

The site, once part of Phoenix Park, was previously occupied by a monastery, founded in the 7C by Irish monks, which in 1100 passed to the Knights of St John and was later used as the Vice-Regal Lodge until demolished in 1670.

★★Kilmainham Gaol Museum ⊘ (**AT M⁶**) – *Inchicore Road*. An excellent display documenting the Irish struggle for political independence is housed in the prison where so many Irishmen were incarcerated for offences against the Crown.

A modern hall, occupying the Governor's garden, presents an exhibition of souvenirs, photographs, letters and press cuttings, which explains and illustrates the many incidents and rebellions which took place between 1796 and 1924 and their social and political context.

The **tour** includes the Central Hall (1862) which contains 100 cells and replaced the original East Wing, the chapel with an audio-visual presentation on the history of the prison, individual cells in the 1798 corridor, and the yards where the prisoners were confined and executions were carried out.

Grand Canal, Dublin

The New Gaol, as it was known for many years, was built in 1792 and consisted of a central range flanked by an east and a west courtyard divided into exercise yards; one contains the *Asgard (see p 173)*. In 1862, when the east wing was rebuilt, a high outer wall was constructed.

Drimnagh Castle (**AT**) – *Long Mile Road*. Drimnagh is a 13C moated castle consisting of a medieval Great Hall over a vaulted undercroft, flanked by a battlemented tower. It has been restored to its medieval appearance with a formal 17C garden – box hedges, lavender bushes and herbs – at the rear.

SOUTHERN SUBURBS *East to west*

Waterways Visitor Centre ⊘ (**CT G**) – The modern building, which stands on an island in the Grand Canal basin, houses a display which explains canal engineering and the history of the countrywide network of canals which was established in the 18C. The flat roof provides a view of the warehouses lining the canal basin.

Museum of Childhood ⊘ (**BT**) – *Palmerston Park*. The museum, which is housed in a special building at the end of a suburban garden, has grown from a small-scale hobby to a comprehensive private collection of nursery toys: teddy bears, farm animals, soldiers, Dinky toy vehicles, Hornby trains, dolls' houses and dolls galore. There are many dolls' houses, originally an adult enthusiasm, which became popular for children after 1856 when Charles Dickens introduced the idea to Queen Victoria. Some of the miniature furniture was made by Duncan Phyffe, the best-known late-19C exponent of the craft.

Shaw Birthplace ⊘ (**BT B**) – *33 Synge Street*. The modest house, where George Bernard Shaw (1854–1949) was born and spent his early years, is furnished in the style of the mid 19C.

Jewish Museum ⊘ (**BT**) – *Walworth Road*. The museum was opened in 1985 by Chaim Herzog, President of Israel and son of the first Chief Rabbi of Ireland, in the old Walworth Road Synagogue (1917–c 75). The showcases on the ground floor display material on the history of the Jews in Ireland from the 11C to the 20C. In the kitchen, which is fitted with separate sinks for meat and milk, the table is laid for the Sabbath evening service.

The **synagogue** upstairs retains all its ritual fittings. The women's gallery has been converted to display religious artefacts: Torah Scrolls with their handles and covers, an Ark Cover (c 1750), the wedding canopy, skullcaps and prayer shawls, circumcision instruments, candlesticks, ram's horns, tabernacles and a Hebrew clock.

★**Rathfarnham Castle** ⊘ – *3mi/5km south of Dublin by N 81 and R 115*. The magnificent but forbidding exterior gives no hint of the elegant 18C interior designed by Sir William Chambers and James "Athenian" Stuart. The rectangular central keep with four flanker towers was built c 1593 by Adam Loftus, a Yorkshireman who became Dean of St Patrick's Cathedral, Archbishop of Armagh and then of Dublin (then a more important see than Armagh). The remodelling of

the interior in the 1770s was commissioned by Henry Loftus. After being abandoned in the early 20C and then occupied by a Jesuit seminary, the castle was in need of restoration. The tour enables visitors to see this painstaking work in progress, to admire the 18C plaques in the Front Hall, the grand dimensions, original fireplaces and curved doors of the Drawing Room, the bow window in the Dining Room where the work of Chambers and Stuart seems to overlap, the elaborate Stuart ceilings in the Boudoir and in the Gilt Room.

Pearse Museum ⊙ – *4.5mi/7.2km south of Dublin by N 81. In Terenure fork left. In Rathfarnham bear left (direction: Bray); turn first right onto Grange Road; after 0.5 mile/0.8km turn right onto Sarah Curran Avenue. 10min there and back on foot from the car park by the footpath parallel with the road.*

Through pictures and manuscripts the museum traces the life of Patrick and William Pearse, founder members of the Irish Volunteers (1913), who were executed in 1916 for their leading role in the Easter Rising.

The house (1797) was acquired by the Pearse brothers in 1910 for their boys' school, named after St Enda of Aran *(see p 76)*. Their desire to encourage Irish culture and to allow children to develop their talents free from the pressure of exams was reflected in the curriculum, which included Gaelic language, literature and history, theatrical performances, nature study and games.

The **grounds** contain an avenue of trees, called Emmet's Walk in memory of Robert Emmet who courted Sarah Curran in the grounds, a walled garden, where the pupils grew vegetables, and a nature walk, called *The Wayfarer*, which follows the river from the lake where the pupils used to swim, to the car park.

Patrick Pearse (1879–1914)

He was the second of four children born to Margaret Brady, whose family had moved to Dublin from County Meath during the Great Famine, and James Pearse, a stone carver from England, who came to Ireland in the 1850s, during a boom in church building. From his father's library he acquired a love of English literature and from his maternal great-aunt, Margaret, a love of the Irish language. In 1895, aged sixteen, he joined the **Gaelic League** and in 1903 became editor of the League's newspaper. Two years later he went to Belgium to study bilingualism in the schools. He wrote many articles proposing the same policy for Ireland and set up his own school for boys. Great names – William Butler Yeats, Patrick MacDonagh and Padraic Colum – took an interest in the pupils' theatrical productions. Pearse spent his holidays in Rosmuc *(see p 120)* in order to study Gaelic. Over the years his original intention simply to promote a pride in things Irish evolved into more active political engagement. In November 1913 he joined the Irish Volunteers to campaign for Home Rule and in February 1914 he joined the IRB. He took a prominent part in the Easter Rising and was executed at Kilmainham Gaol on 2nd May 1914, not knowing that his brother was to be executed the following day.

NORTHERN SUBURBS *West to east*

★★**National Botanic Gardens** ⊙ (**BS**) – The gardens were established in 1795 on an attractive site beside the Tolka River. The glasshouses include the **Curvilinear Range** (1843–69), designed by Richard Turner, and the **Great Palm House** (1884). There is a delightful **walk** along the river bank from the **rose garden**, past the mill race, through the **peat garden** (walled) and the **bog garden** beside the ornamental pond to the **arboretum**. The specimens in the rock garden, cactus house and fern house are among the 20 000 species grown here.

GAA Museum ⊙ (**BS**) – *Clonliffe Road*. **Croke Park** is the home of the national games of Ireland – hurling and Irish football. The museum traces the development of the **Gaelic Athletic Association** *(see p 37)* and its influence on the sporting, cultural and social traditions of Ireland. Touch-screen technology provides a view of the highlights of past games, the great men in action and the information stored in databanks.

★★**Marino Casino** ⊙ (**CS**) – The charming Palladian casino, designed by Sir William Chambers in 1765, was built in the grounds of Marino House (demolished 1921), the country seat of James Caulfield, Earl of Charlemont *(see pp 158 and 312)*, who had met Chambers while making the Grand Tour (1746–54). The casino is built of Portland stone in the French neo-Classical style in the shape of a Greek cross on a rusticated basement; 12 Doric columns support a frieze and cornice topped by pediments, statues and urn-shaped chimneys. The sculpture is by Simon Vierpyl and Joseph Wilton.

The interior contains four state rooms, decorated with elaborate plaster ceilings and inlaid floors using eight different kinds of wood, and four small bedrooms on the upper floor; plans of the building are displayed in the basement service rooms.

North Bull Island ⊘ – *North of Dublin by the coast road to Howth.* The island, which accommodates two golf links and attracts many summer visitors to its sandy beaches, consists of sand dunes, salt-marshes and mud-flats. It is an important **nature reserve** where many wildfowl and wading birds spend the winter; at high tide the 30 000 shore birds which feed in Dublin Bay all roost on North Bull Island. An exhibition on the wildlife and natural habitats of the island is housed in the **Interpretive Centre** *(at the end of the central causeway).* For many years the only link with the mainland was a plank bridge to the southern end of the island. Since the Bull Wall was built in the late 18C to protect Dublin harbour from silting up, the island, which at first was only a sandbank covered at high tide, has grown to its present size (3mi/4.5km long) and continues to increase in width seawards.

For adjacent sights see DÚN LAOGHAIRE, FINGAL, KILDARE, MAYNOOTH, POWERSCOURT, RUSSBOROUGH, TARA, TRIM, WICKLOW MOUNTAINS.

DUNDALK

DÚN DEALGAN – Co Louth – Population 25 843
Michelin Atlas p 98 and Map 923 – M 5, 6

Dundalk, the county town of Louth, is also a port on the south bank of the Kilcurry estuary. The salt-marshes and mud-flats *(east)* are a vast bird sanctuary; further south is Blackrock, a seaside resort flanked by sandy beaches.
The Normans seem to have settled at Dún Dealgan *(1mi/1.5km west of Dundalk by N 53)* where their motte is now covered in trees. Dundalk is a medieval town which was granted a charter in 1189 and flourished until destroyed by the forces of Sir Henry Tichbourne in 1642. Charles II granted all the corporation property to Viscount Dungannon, who was succeeded as landlord by the Hamiltons, Earls of Clanbrassil, and the Jocelyns, Earls of Roden.

Town Centre – Dundalk was laid out c 1740 by James, 1st Earl of Clanbrassil. South of the river bridge *(Church Street)* stands **St Nicholas' Church** (Anglican); the tower is 14C but the body of the church was rebuilt in 1707 and the transepts were added in the 19C; the spire is by Francis Johnston. In the graveyard is the tomb of Agnes Burns, near to a pillar erected in memory of her brother Robert Burns (1759–96), the celebrated poet who wrote in the Scots dialect.
The **Courthouse** *(south)* was designed in the Doric style (1813–18) by Park and Bowden. An elaborate porch-screen *(Roden Place – east)* leads to **St Patrick's Church** (Roman Catholic) which is modelled on King's College Chapel in Cambridge; mosaics decorate the sanctuary and the side chapels.
The **Louth County Museum** ⊘ *(Jocelyn Street)* in an 18C warehouse (restored) traces local history (farming, industry, the port and railway) through audio-visual presentations, touch-screens, films and graphics.
Northeast *(Castle Road)* stands the **bell-tower** (known locally as the Castle) of a Franciscan Friary, which was founded c 1240, burned by the soldiers of Bruce in 1315 and razed to the ground in 1539. Further east is the seven-storey conical stump of a **windmill** *(inaccessible)* devoid of its sails.

EXCURSIONS
Cooley Peninsula

The Cooley Peninsula is a mountainous granite promontory, which provides magnificent land- and seascapes – *(south)* over Dundalk Bay and – *(north)* over Carlingford Lough which forms the boundary between the Republic of Ireland and Northern Ireland.
From 1873 to 1926 Greenore, at the entrance to Carlingford Lough, was the terminal of a ferry service to Holyhead; since 1960 the port has handled freight. There is a safe south-facing beach at Giles Quay.

★**Proleek Dolmen** – *5mi/8km north of Dundalk by N 1 and east by R 173. Park in the grounds of the Ballymascanlon Hotel; 20min there and back on foot through the yard and along the tarmac path between the fields.* The massive capstone (40 tons/47 tonnes) on its two supports dates from 3000 BC; according to legend the wish will be granted of anyone who can make three pebbles land on the top. Nearby is a wedge-shaped gallery grave.
Continue east and turn left into the mountain road north to Omeath.

★**Windy Gap** – The road climbs towards Carlingford Mountain (1 932ft/587m). Beyond the site of the Long Woman's Grave *(plaque)* the road enters the aptly-named **Windy Gap**, a narrow pass between rocky crags; fine view south over Dundalk Bay. Further north there is a **viewpoint** *(car park)* overlooking the mouth of Newry River at Warrenpoint and the Mourne Mountains rising from the eastern shore of Carlingford Lough.

Omeath – Population 315. Once a Gaelic-speaking fishing village, Omeath is now a little resort with a rocky shoreline, where one can savour freshly-caught seafood. In summer jaunting cars carry fares to the outdoor Stations of the Cross at the monastery of the Rosminian Fathers, and the Carlingford Lough Ferry plies across the border to Warrenpoint.

Traditional cottage, Carlingford

From Omeath take the coast road south.

Carlingford – Population 650. This attractive resort was founded by the Vikings and settled by the Normans. The old road winds through the village, whereas the newer coast road runs through a disued railway cuttting underneath the castle entrance. Local history from the Vikings to the present day is traced in the **Carlingford Heritage Centre** ⊘, housed in the deconsecrated Anglican church, which is the starting point for a guided tour of the town centre. There is a marina and there are boat trips on Carlingford Lough.

The ruins of **King John's Castle** stand on a bluff on the north side of the harbour commanding the entrance to Carlingford Lough; the western bailey was probably built by Hugh de Lacy, before King John's visit in 1210, while the eastern apartments were added in 1261.

Overlooking the harbour is **Taaffe's Castle**, a late-15C square tower fortified with machicolations, crenellations, arrow slits and murder holes; the vaulted basement may have been a boat-house since the tide used to reach the foundations. It was built by the Taaffe family, created Earls of Carlingford in 1661.

South of the town square stands the **Mint**, a 15C fortified house *(right)* with Celtic-style designs on the door and window mouldings; although it is known as the Mint, there is no proof that the local mint, founded in 1467, ever operated there.

Spanning the street is a gateway, once three storeys high, known as the **Tholsel**, where Parliament is said to have promulgated laws for the Pale *(see TRIM)*.

South and West of Dundalk

★**St Mochta's House** – *9.5mi/15km southwest of Dundalk by N 52; bear right onto R 171 to Louth.* In a field behind the ruins of a Franciscan friary (14C–15C) stands a stone oratory with a **corbelled** roof. Between the steep roof and the vaulted ceiling is a tiny chamber reached by a steep stone stair. The oratory, which has been much restored, probably dates from the second half of the 12C; it is said to have been built in a night as a resting place for St Mochta who died in 534. The little village, which has given its name to the county, was the centre of the kingdom of Oriel in the 11C and 12C.

★**Dún A' Rí Forest Park** – *21mi/34km west of Dundalk by R 178 and R 179.* The forest park, until 1959 part of the Cabra estate, is set in a valley beside the Cabra River. A **nature trail** and four sign-posted **walks** reveal its secluded features: red deer enclosure; a waterfall downstream from Cromwell's Bridge; a wishing well; Cabra Cottage, the Pratt family mansion until Cabra Castle *(east)* was built in 1814; a ruined flax mill; an ice house; the ruins of Fleming's Castle (1607), named after an Anglo-Norman family who lost their land for supporting James II *(see p 93)*.

Carrickmacross – *14mi/22km west of Dundalk by R 178.* Population 1 678. The town grew up round a castle built by the Earl of Essex to whom the land was granted by Elizabeth I. It has a reputation for angling and hand-made lace.

Carrickmacross Lace Gallery ⊘ *(Market Square at the north end of the main street)* displays examples of the local work which is a "mixed lace", composed of cambric patterns applied to machine net and embellished with point stitches and loops; both traditional and modern designs are executed. The Roman Catholic church (1866) was designed by JJ McCarthy, with stained glass (1925) by Harry Clarke.

Inniskeen – *10mi/16km west of Dundalk by R 178 turning north in Chanonrock.* The village on the Fane River is the birthplace of Patrick Kavanagh (1904–67), poet, author and journalist, who is buried in the churchyard; his death mask is displayed in the local **folk museum** ⊘. The remains of a round tower mark the site of a 6C monastery founded by St Daig.

Ardee **(Baile Átha Fhirdhia)** – *13mi/21km south of Dundalk by N 52.* Population 3 269. The name means the Ford of Ferdia *(see p 34)*. On the east side of the main street stand two fortified buildings: **Hatch's Castle**, a late-medieval fortified house; and **Ardee Castle**, built in 1207 by Roger de Peppard, although much of the present building dates from the 15C. In the 17C the castle was granted to Theobald Taaffe, Earl of Carlingford.

Roodstown Castle – *13mi/21km south of Dundalk by N 52; before reaching Ardee turn left.* Beside the road stands a 15C **tower house** with well-preserved carved window surrounds. The corner tower beside the entrance contains a spiral stair and the other a latrine chute.

For adjacent sights see BOYNE VALLEY, DROGHEDA, KELLS, MOURNE MOUNTAINS, NEWRY.

DUNGARVAN

DÚN GARBHÁN – Co Waterford – Population 7 175
Michelin Atlas p 79 and Map 923 – J 11

The thriving town occupies an attractive **site** astride the Colligan estuary overlooking Dungarvan Harbour flanked by the Drum Hills *(south)* and the Monavullagh and Comeragh Mountains *(north)*.

West Bank – **King John's Castle**, built by the king in 1185 not long after the Anglo-Norman invasion, consists of a large circular **keep** surrounded by fortified walls, much modified in subsequent centuries.
There is a fine view from here and from the broad promenade over the Harbour to Cunnigar Point.
The **Dungarvan Museum** ⊘ housed in the Municipal Library has a nautical theme; local shipwrecks are well documented, especially the *Moresby* which went down in Dungarvan Bay on 24 December 1895 with the loss of 20 lives.

East Bank (Abbeyside) – The **shell house** and its garden are decorated with ornaments made from sea shells.
The holy water font outside St Augustine's Roman Catholic Church dates from 1865. On the seaward side of the church stands the now-ruined 13C **Augustinian priory** which was founded by the McGraths, who also built the 12C or 13C **castle**, of which only the west wall still stands. The walk on the seaward side of the graveyard provides fine **views**★ across Dungarvan Harbour south to Helvick Head.

EXCURSIONS

Cunnigar Peninsula – *5mi/8km south of Dungarvan by N 25 and R 674.* The sandy spit of land extending into Dungarvan harbour may be walked from end to end *(1.5mi/3km)*.

Ringville (An Rinn) – *8mi/13km south of Dungarvan by N 25 and R 674.* Population 265. This small village is the centre of an Irish-speaking area, the **West Waterford Gaeltacht**. From the road there are excellent **views**★ across Dungarvan harbour to the Monavullagh Mountains to the north.

★**Helvick Head** – *8mi/13km southeast of Dungarvan by N 25 and R 674.* Helvick Harbour, a small but busy port backed by a row of fishermen's cottages, shelters below the headland which, despite its modest height (230ft/82m), provides outstanding **views**★ of the coastline from Mine Head *(south)* to Brownstown Head *(northeast)*.

Mine Head – *10mi/15km south by N 24 and R 674; in Ringville turn right; in Loskeran turn left.* Mine Head provides impressive **views** of the cliffs and *(southwest)* across Ardmore Bay to Ram Head.

Master McGrath Monument – *2mi/3.2km northwest of Dungarvan by R 672.* The only monument in Ireland to a dog commemorates a locally-bred greyhound which won the Waterloo Cup in England three times between 1868 and 1871. In a career of 37 races, the dog was beaten only once.

For adjacent sights see ARDMORE, CLONMEL, LISMORE, WATERFORD, YOUGHAL.

DÚN LAOGHAIRE

Co Dún Laoghaire-Rathdown – Population 55 540
Michelin Atlas pp 87 and 139 and Map 923 – N 8

The town, which is the main port of entry to Ireland from Britain, is named after Laoghaire (pronounced Leary), the High King of Ireland in the 5C, who built a fort here. The growth of trade with Britain in the 18C turned the small fishing village into a busy port.

The **harbour** (251 acres/101ha) was designed by John Rennie and begun in 1817; the main work, built of Dalkey stone, was complete by 1842.

For 100 years the port was known as **Kingstown** in honour of **George IV** who landed here in September 1821; an **Obelisk**, erected in memory of the king's visit to Ireland, stands on the waterfront south of the harbour.

SIGHTS

National Maritime Museum of Ireland ⊘ – *Haigh Terrace*. The museum is housed in the Mariners' Church (1835–60) on the south side of Moran Park. The exhibits include a cannon from the Spanish Armada; a French longboat, painted red, white and blue, captured during an attempted landing in Bantry Bay in 1796; the lamp from the Baily lighthouse *(see p 173)* in working order; the chart used by the Commander of the German U-boat which landed Roger Casement on Banna Strand; models of a Guinness barge, Irish coastal curraghs, a Rosslare cot (a sea-going flat-bottomed boat), Galway and Donegal hookers (sailing ships – *see p 178*), an Arklow schooner, racing skiffs, ferries, cargo ships, the first transatlantic steam ship *Sirius* (1838); the Halpin Collection, including a model of the *Great Eastern*, and the Cornelissen Collection of model ships showing the evolution from a Greek trireme to the fighting ships of the Second World War.

James Joyce Museum ⊘ – *0.5mi/0.8km east of Dún Laoghaire by the coast road to Sandycove*. The Martello Tower (1804) on the point at Sandycove now houses a **Joyce Museum**: first editions, letters, photos, his death-mask, piano, guitar, cabin trunk, walking stick, wallet and cigar case. Joyce stayed there for six days in 1904 as the guest of the poet Oliver Gogarty who had rented the tower from the government. The upper room which was the location of the breakfast scene in Ulysses is furnished appropriately, while the **view** from the roof embraces Dún Laoghaire Harbour *(north-west)*, the coast to Dalkey Island *(southeast)* and the Wicklow Mountains *(southwest)*.

Dalkey Village – *1mi/1.6km south of Dún Laoghaire by the coast road*. Dalkey (pronounced Dawkey), now incorporated in Dún Laoghaire, was once a walled town with seven fortified buildings. **Bulloch Castle** by the shore was built in the 12C by the monks of St Mary's Abbey in Dublin to protect the harbour. Two late-medieval tower houses survive in the heart of the village. **Archbold's Castle** stands opposite the **Goat Castle** which now houses the **Dalkey Heritage Centre** ⊘ with excellent displays on local history and a splendid all-round view from the battlements. A modern extension has been sensitively integrated with the adjoining graveyard of the ruined **St Genet's Church**, which may date from the 8C. Many writers, among them LAG Strong, Lennox Robinson, James Joyce and Hugh Leonard, have associations with Dalkey; as a child (1866–74) George Bernard Shaw (1856–1950) lived in Torca Cottage on Dalkey Hill and learnt to swim at Killiney beach. Offshore lies **Dalkey Island**, which is now a bird sanctuary.

From the coast road south of Sorrento Point there is a magnificent **view**★★ of Killiney Bay extending south to Bray Head.

Killiney Hill Park – *Entrance and car park on the northwest side of Dalkey Hill. The park, which covers the south end of Dalkey Hill*, was once the property of Col

John Mapas who lived in Killiney Castle, now a hotel; it was opened to the public in 1887 to celebrate Queen Victoria's Jubilee. A **nature trail** winds through the trees and over the heath to the **obelisk**, which was built by John Mapas in 1742 to provide work for his tenants: fine **view** *(south)* to Bray Head and the Little and Great Sugar Loaf Mountains, *(east)* to Dalkey Island, and *(north)* to Dún Laoghaire and Dublin Bay backed by Howth Head.

For adjacent sights see DUBLIN, MAYNOOTH, POWERSCOURT, RUSS-BOROUGH, WICKLOW MOUNTAINS.

Dalkey Island and Vico Road

B. Lynch /BORD FÁILTE, Dublin

ENNIS

INIS – Co Clare – Population 15333
Michelin Atlas p 83 and Map 923 – F 9

Ennis, the county town and administrative centre of Co Clare, has much of historic interest in its narrow winding streets.

Harriet Smithson, the wife of Hector Berlioz, was born in Ennis; her father was the manager of the first theatre built in the town in the late 18C.

Traditional folk dancing and music are demonstrated in **Cois na h'Abhna**, a modern circular building on the Galway road *(N 18)*.

Royal Origins – The town traces its origins back to the 13C when the kings of Thomond built their royal residence nearby and one of the O'Brien royal family founded the Franciscan friary. Because of its central position Ennis became the county town of Clare during the shiring of Ireland in the reign of Elizabeth I. In 1610 the town was granted permission to hold fairs and markets; two years later it received a corporation charter from James I.

Famous Statesmen – Two famous Irishmen are commemorated in the town. A great Doric column was erected in 1867 in O'Connell Square where **Daniel O'Connell** was declared MP for Clare in 1828.

A modern statue of **Eamon de Valera**, who was first elected to Parliament as MP for Ennis in 1917, stands in front of the old Courthouse (1850), a neo-Classical building with a pedimented Ionic portico *(Galway Road N 18)*.

SIGHTS

★Ennis Friary ⊘ – This 13C church originally consisted of a nave and chancel, to which a south transept and central tower were added in the 15C. The east window consists of five lancets. An **Ecce Homo** *(junction of the nave wall and the east wall of the south transept)* shows Christ with the Instruments of the Passion. A carving of St Francis *(northeast corner of the nave)* shows him with a cross-staff in his left hand and the stigmata on his right hand, side and feet. The most notable feature is the Creagh tomb (1843) in the chancel; it consists of five carved panels showing the Passion, taken from the MacMahon tomb (1475), and figures of Christ and the Apostles from another tomb. In the 14C the Franciscan friary was occupied by 350 friars and its school had over 600 students. It was finally suppressed in 1692. Until 1871 the church was used by the Anglican Church but was returned to the Franciscans in 1969.

De Valera Museum and Library ⊘ – The Presbyterian church (1853) has been converted into the Ennis town museum which contains 18C and 19C paintings of local interest, a cabin door from a Spanish Armada ship sunk off the Clare coast in 1588, the decorated barrow and inscribed spade with which Charles Stewart Parnell turned the first sod for the construction of the West Clare railway, and the pen used by de Valera and Chamberlain to sign the Anglo-Irish financial agreement of 1938.

Cathedral – The Roman Catholic Cathedral, dedicated to St Peter and St Paul, was built between 1831 and 1843 in Tau-cross shape; the tower with its spire was added between 1871 and 1874. Rows of pointed arches divide the nave and aisles and support the decorated panelled ceiling.

Railway Locomotive – *Railway Station.* On a plinth stands one of the steam engines from the West Clare railway, immortalized by Percy French's song *Are You Right There, Michael, Are You Right?* The railway, which ran to Kilkee *(see KILRUSH)* closed down in 1961 and the station is now used only for freight and buses.

EXCURSIONS

Dromore Wood National Nature Reserve ⊘ – *Barefield; 8mi/13km north by N 18 (signed).* This nature reserve (1 000 acres/400ha) encompasses a variety of habitats, including lakes, limestone pavement and turloughs, river, fen and semi-natural woodland, together with several examples of human habitation, notably the ruins of the 17C O'Brien castle. A guidebook available from the visitor centre describes species such as the grey heron, badger and pine marten living near to the two self-guided trails.

★Dysert O'Dea – *6mi/10km north by N 85, R 476; after 4mi/6.4km turn left (sign); after 1mi/1.6km turn right.*
The **Archeology Centre** ⊘ and a small **museum** devoted to the prehistoric and later culture of the neighbourhood *(audio-visual film (20min); leaflet of walks)* are housed in a 15C tower house, which has a murder hole above the entrance. From the roof there is a fine **view** of the surrounding country and nearby ruins.

The Brendan Voyage

St Brendan of Clonfert , also known as Brendan the Navigator, was a seafaring monk, who in the 6C set sail from Brandon Creek, the narrow sea-inlet at the west foot of Brandon Mountain *(see p 127)* on the Dingle Peninsula. His account of the voyage, *Navigatio*, written in medieval Latin, was usually thought to be fanciful until Tim Severin built the *Brendan* and set sail with a small crew, to prove that the earlier voyagers could have reached America several hundred years before Christopher Columbus. The exploits of the 20C adventure, which in many respects substantiate the 6C narrative, are recorded in *The Brendan Voyage*.

In a neighbouring field *(access on foot or by car)* stand the late-12C **White Cross of Tola** showing the Crucifixion and a bishop on its east face, the stump of an 11C **round tower** and much of the chancel arch and outer walls of an 11C **church**; the Romanesque doorway is a reconstruction of the original. They were built on the site of a monastery founded by St Tola in the 8C.

★**Clare Heritage Centre** ⊙ – *Corrofin; 8.5mi/14km north by N 85 and R 476.* The centre, housed in the former Anglican church, illustrates life and work in Co Clare in the 19C through text and exhibits – a flax teaser, a butter spade, a melodeon and the workhouse keys. A section of oak trunk is marked with the dates of historic events which took place during the growth of the tree.

Extensive genealogical records make it possible to trace people who emigrated from Clare in the last century; in the aftermath of the Great Famine between 1851 and 1871 at least 100 000 people left the region.

Clare Abbey – *1mi/1.6km southeast by R 469; turn right before the railway station, then left; park at the corner; 0.5mi/0.8km on foot over the level crossing and right.* On the west bank of the River Fergus stand the substantial ruins of an Augustinian friary founded in 1189 by Dónall Mór O'Brien, last king of Munster; they include the central tower, much of the nave and a tall chimney stack, part of the domestic buildings, leaning at a steep angle.

★**Quin Franciscan Friary** ⊙ – *6.5mi/10.5km southeast by R 469; in Quin turn left.* The extensive ruins of the friary, built about 1430 by Sioda McNamara, include the **cloisters**, the tower and the south transept. The friary was built on top of a ruined Norman castle (1280–86) which had three round towers and was built on the site of an earlier monastery.

★**Knappogue Castle** ⊙ – *8mi/13km southeast by R 469.* The castle (restored), which from 1467 to 1815 was the seat of the McNamara family, is now used for medieval banquets. The gardens and orchards have been replanted.

★**Craggaunowen Centre** ⊙ – *11mi/18km southeast by R 469 (sign).* Various prehistoric Irish constructions have been re-created in a lakeside setting: a Crannóg, a wooden marsh track *(togher)*, a ringfort, a cooking site. The project was started

Brendan

by John Hunt, a medievalist, some of whose Collection is housed in the **tower house** ; most of it is on display in the Hunt Museum in Limerick *(see p 215)*.

The last exhibit is the *Brendan*, an ocean-going curragh built of wood and leather, in which Tim Severin and his crew sailed the Atlantic in 1976–77; the patch where the leather hull was holed by an ice floe is clearly visible.

An enclosure in the woodlands nearby is home to a group of Wild Boar *(Porcus sylveticus)*; other early breeds, such as the goat-like Soay sheep, can be seen grazing in fields near the entrance to *Craggaunowen – the Living Past*.

For adjacent sights see ADARE, The BURREN, KILLALOE, KILRUSH, LIMERICK, TRALEE.

ENNISCORTHY

INIS CÓRTHAIDH – Co Wexford – Population 3788
Michelin Atlas p 81 and Map 923 – M 10

Enniscorthy, which is built on the steep slopes of the River Slaney, has a special place in the history of Ireland, because of its involvement in the 1798 rebellion.

It has two public buildings of exceptional interest in its castle and cathedral; its many 19C architectural characteristics have been little changed in the intervening years.

The surrounding country is well suited to the growing of soft fruits, and the Strawberry Fair in early July attracts people from miles around.

Monastic Foundation – In the 6C St Senan arrived from Scattery Island *(see KILRUSH)* in Co Clare to found a monastic settlement at Templeshannon. In 795 the Vikings pillaged the monastery. From the 12C its fortunes were controlled by the Normans, who ruled from their castle in Enniscorthy until some time in the 15C when a local clan, the MacMurrough Kavanaghs, gained control. In the latter part of the 16C Queen Elizabeth I appointed two of her own men to put an end to local rule.

Commercial Development – Commercial exploitation was started in the 16C by Queen Elizabeth's men. Sir Henry Wallop felled timber in the rich woodlands and exported it to France and Spain through the port of Wexford; Philip Stamp set up an ironworks, which survived until the 1940s, and brought many English families to settle in Enniscorthy, which expanded across the River Slaney. Towards the end of the 18C distilleries and breweries were set up; by 1796 Enniscorthy had 23 malthouses. Today Enniscorthy is noted for its bacon curing, fruit growing, cutlery and potteries.

> ### Vinegar Hill
>
> 21 June 1798 is the most well-known date in the history of Enniscorthy. Following the rebellion that year, centred mostly in Co Wexford and Co Wicklow, the insurgents, known as the pikemen after their weapons, took their last stand on Vinegar Hill, which they held for nearly a month.
>
> The 20000 insurgents, accompanied by many women and children, were faced by an equivalent number of English troops led by General Lake; the armed men killed in the battle on 21 June were far outnumbered by the defenceless people killed by the English army. The defeat at Vinegar Hill marked the end of the 1798 rebellion.

SIGHTS

★**Enniscorthy Castle** – The present building, which dates from 1586, houses the **County Museum★** ⊘. The local history section includes the **1798 room**, containing a collection of pikes, and the **1916 room**, displaying many photographs and other material illustrating Enniscorthy's active participation in the Easter Rising. Among the model ships is one of a 19C emigrant ship wrecked on the Blackwater sandbar near Youghal. The old-style kitchen and dairy are equipped with old artefacts such as butter churns. The original castle was built either by Raymond le Gros, who led the first Anglo-Norman soldiers into the town in 1169, or by the Prendergasts early in the 13C. It was held by the Prendergast family until the mid 15C when it was won in battle by the MacMurroughs. In 1581 the castle reverted to the crown and was leased to Edmund Spenser, the poet, for three days. Early this century the present castle was restored as a residence by the Roches, a local family of maltsters.

St Aidan's Cathedral – The Gothic-style building, which stands on the site of the former parish church, was designed by Pugin. The foundation stone was laid in 1843 and the building was roofed in 1846. Many of the stones used in its construction came from the ruined Franciscan friary in Abbey Square, dissolved in 1544.

Memorials – The 1798 memorial *(Market Square)*, designed by Oliver Sheppard, shows Fr Murphy, a leader of the uprising, and a pikeman. The 1916 Easter Rising memorial *(Abbey Square)* portrays Seamus Rafter, a local commander.

Enniscorthy

EXCURSIONS

Carley's Bridge Potteries ⊘ – *1mi/1.5km west of Enniscorthy past the grey-hound track.* Carley's Bridge Potteries, the oldest in Ireland, were founded in 1659 by two brothers from Cornwall. The local clay is used to make a variety of earthenware pots. It takes three months to make enough pots to fill the kiln and four days for them to be fired and cooled.

Also at Carley's Bridge are the Hillview Potteries.

★**Ferns** – *8mi/13km northeast of Enniscorthy by N 11.* The small village of Ferns (population 859), once the capital of the province of Leinster, is renowned for its **ruins.** The tower, square at the bottom and round at the top, and part of the north wall of the church are all that remain of an abbey founded in the 12C by the King of Leinster, Dermot MacMurrough Kavanagh, which was burned down in 1154; he rebuilt it in 1160 and gave it to the Augustinians. Little remains of the cathedral where MacMurrough is said to be buried in the graveyard.

The 13C **castle**, one of the best of its kind in Ireland, has a rectangular keep and circular towers; the first-floor **chapel** has a fine vaulted ceiling.

Bunclody – *12mi/19km north of Enniscorthy by N 11 and N 80.* Population 1 316. The town is attractively sited on the River Clody, a tributary of the Slaney, at the north end of the Blackstairs Mountains. The broad central mall is bisected by a stream that falls in steps. The Church of the Most Holy Trinity, consecrated in 1970, is an interesting modern design by EN Smith.

Bunclody was the last bastion in Co Wexford of the Irish language, which was in widespread use in the town until a century ago; even today Gaelic is quite often used in shops, notices and signs.

★**Mount Leinster** – *17mi/28km north of Enniscorthy by N 11 and N 80. In Bunclody take the minor road west; after 4mi/6.4km turn left onto the summit road which ends 0.25 mile/0.4km from the peak.*
From the summit (2 602ft/793m) on a clear day there are the best views in southeast Ireland: much of Wexford and Wicklow and even the mountains of central Wales across the sea.

For adjacent sights see NEW ROSS, WEXFORD, WICKLOW MOUNTAINS.

The star ratings are allocated for various categories:
– regions of scenic beauty with dramatic natural features
– cities with a cultural heritage
– elegant resorts and charming villages
– ancient monuments and fine architecture, museums and picture galleries.

The area north of Dublin, which re-adopted the ancient name of Fingal in 1994, consists of rich farmland fringed by a long coastline. The seaside resort of **Skerries** (population 7 339) has a colony of grey seals and a fishing harbour where famous Dublin Bay prawns are landed. **Portmarnock** (population 9 175) is another popular resort; to the south extends a long sandy spit, consisting of a beach known as the **Velvet Strand** and a championship golf course. In the Middle Ages Fingal formed part of **The Pale** *(see TRIM)* and contains several historic sites, elegant parks surrounding old stately homes and the charming town of Malahide.

SIGHTS

★**The Ben of Howth** – The Ben of Howth is a steep rounded peninsula of rock rising from the sea on the north side of Dublin Bay.
From the high point on the west side of the headland *(car park)* there are two **cliff walks**: south past the Baily Lighthouse on the point and along the cliffs for a fine **view★** over Dublin Bay; or north past the Nose of Howth and Balscadden Bay to the picturesque village of **Howth**, which clings to the steep north face of the headland. At its heart are the ruins of **St Mary's Abbey** ⊘; in the chancel is the splendid tomb of a late-15C knight and his lady. Below is the harbour (1807–09), which now shelters sailing craft and fishing boats; for 20 years from 1813 it was the packet boat station until Dún Laoghaire (then Kingstown) took over in 1833. Offshore lies **Ireland's Eye** ⊘, now a bird sanctuary, where the early Christians built a church (in ruins) in the 6C.

West of the village is Howth Castle Demesne. In the grounds is the **National Transport Museum** ⊘, a varied and comprehensively-labelled collection of commercial and military vehicles, horse-drawn or motorized, neatly parked in a large shed.

Struggle for Independence

In July 1914, 900 rifles and 25 000 rounds of ammunition for the Irish Volunteers were landed at Howth from the *Asgard* which belonged to Robert Erskine Childers, a Republican politician, who was arrested by the Provisional Government in 1922 and condemned to death and executed by a firing squad for possessing a revolver; his novel *The Riddle of the Sands* has been made into a film.

The castle *(private)*, a medieval keep with a 15C gatehouse, contains work by Morrison and Lutyens. Legend has it that when Grace O'Malley *(see p 260)* was refused hospitality on her return journey from London, she abducted the Earl of Howth's son and returned him only when the Earl promised always to keep his door open to her family at mealtimes.
South of the Castle and the golf clubhouse are the **Howth Castle Gardens** ⊘, a wall of seasonal colour created by about 2 000 different varieties of **rhododendrons** growing on a steep cliff face. The soil required for the first plantings in 1850 was imported in sacks by the garden staff of Howth Castle. The cliff top commands a fine view of the coast.

★★**Malahide Castle** ⊘ – The castle was the home of the Talbot family for 791 years, except for seven years (1653–60) under Cromwell; in 1177 the land at Malahide was granted to Richard Talbot who came to Ireland with Henry II; in 1976 the house and grounds (268 acres/108ha) were bought by Dublin County Council. The house, which consists of the original 14C tower, the 15C Great Hall and 18C reception rooms, still contains some of the original furniture and is hung with portraits from the National Portrait Collection.
The dark-panelled **Oak Room** includes a 16C Flemish carving of the *Coronation of the Virgin* and early-17C Dutch or Flemish carvings of *Adam and Eve*.
The Small and Large Drawing Rooms were created between 1765 and 1782; the **Rococo plasterwork** is probably by Robert West of Dublin. The larger room displays a Chinese carpet, two gilt settees (1770) in the French style, and a pair of carved and gilt Irish side-tables with lacquer tops (1740) which belonged to the Talbots. Among the paintings are a *Self-Portrait* by Nathaniel Hone, who lived at St Doolagh's Park *(2mi/3.2km south)*, and a portrait of Edmund Burke by Sir Joshua Reynolds.
The turret room is decorated with six pastels and 12 oils by Hugh Douglas Hamilton, an Irish artist; the frames were probably designed by Frederick Trench who commissioned these oval portraits of his family.
Hanging in the Staircase Hall are a portrait of *James Gandon*, the architect, and *The Battle of Ballynahinch* by Thomas Robinson which was painted in 1798, the year of the battle.

The 15C **Great Hall** is dominated by the *Battle of the Boyne* by Jan Wyck; it is said that 14 of the Talbot cousins, all Jacobites, who breakfasted at Malahide on the morning of the battle, were killed in the fighting. Facing the minstrels' gallery is a collection of family portraits.

Fry Model Railway Museum ⊘ – *Malahide Castle Yard*. The model engines and rolling stock made by Cyril Fry of Dublin are displayed in the first room together with information on the development of railways in Ireland.

The second room contains a working-gauge model railway incorporating replicas of Belfast Central Station, Cork Station, Heuston and Conolly Street Stations in Dublin, the DART, Dublin and Howth trams, the car ferry terminal, the Liffey and the Guinness dock.

★Newbridge House ⊘ – This early-18C Georgian house, designed by George Semple, stands on the western edge of Donabate in extensive grounds, one of the finest remaining examples in Ireland of a landscape park.

It has been the home of the Cobbe family since it was built *c*1740 for Charles Cobbe (1686–1765), who came to Ireland in 1717 as Chaplain to the Lord Lieutenant, his cousin the Duke of Bolton, and became Archbishop of Dublin in 1746.

Many members of the family travelled abroad, including Frances Power Cobbe (d 1909) who toured in Egypt and Greece and earned her living as a journalist.

The **guided tour** passes through the inner hall, which is hung with family portraits, and the study to the austere entrance hall where the Cobbe coat of arms appears over the fireplace; a portrait of Archbishop Cobbe hangs above an 18C Irish hand-carved mahogany table with an Italian marble top.

The dining room was redecorated soon after 1765 with a **Rococo ceiling**; the Greek key pattern on the two Chinese Chippendale side-tables is reflected on the walls. The chairs bear the Cobbe family crest. The black Kilkenny marble mantelpiece displays 17C and 19C China blue porcelain; the silverware and items from a 200-piece Mason ironstone dinner service belonged to the family. The late-18C plate-warmer was heated with charcoal or methylated spirits.

The Library has a Baroque ceiling depicting the Four Seasons in the four corners. The family **museum**, begun in 1790, displays souvenirs and trophies from foreign parts. The Chinese decor (restored) and the cabinets are original.

The **Red Drawing Room**, a fine example of a Georgian interior, has hardly changed since the wallpaper, curtains and carpet were installed in 1820. The Rococo plasterwork is attributed to Richard Williams, a pupil of Robert West. Much of the furniture was supplied by Dublin craft firms. The room was added to the house in about 1760 by the Archbishop's son, Thomas, and his wife, who entertained on a large scale and needed a gallery for their **art collection**.

The basement **laundry** displays the equipment used in the washing, ironing and mending of the household clothes; the magnificent 18C **kitchen** is fitted with its original screen wall, dresser, table and open hearth, a mid-19C iron range and many implements: wooden dough trough, water filter, whiskey still, duck press, copper pans, mouse- and rat-traps.

Traditional Farm – The courtyard and adjoining buildings have been restored and are now a museum of traditional rural life. Round the large cobbled **courtyard** (1790) are the dairy (19C), an estate worker's dwelling, the carpenter's shop, the forge, the stables and coach house containing a park drag, which could carry 13 passengers, and the Lord Chancellor's State Coach (1790).

Beyond the courtyard, the haggard and the farmyard have displays of farm implements and machinery, and pigs and domestic fowl can be seen. A string of paddocks in the parkland is inhabited by a Connemara pony, donkeys, sheep and cattle, and draught horses. The large walled garden, which once provided the demesne with all its vegetables and fruit, was converted to an orchard during the emergency of 1939–45.

Ardgillan Castle ⊘ – *Parking at the entrance to the park and beside the house*. On the coast north of Skerries lies the demesne (198 acres/80ha) of a country house, acquired in 1737 by the Revd Robert Taylor, Dean of Clonfert; it remained the home of the Taylor (also Taylour) family until 1962. His ancestor Thomas Taylor, a professional surveyor, had come to Ireland from Sussex in 1650 to work on the Down Survey.

The original Georgian house, the basement of which extends under the south lawns, was enlarged in the late 18C. The tour of the ground floor includes the billiard room, drawing room, dining room, morning room and library, which contain some mementoes and furniture of the Taylor family. Kitchens, larder and scullery occupy the extensive basement.

There is an exhibition on the **Down Survey** on the upper floor.

Down Survey

The survey, which took 13 months (1655–6) and was conducted by Sir William Petty *(see pp 27 and 190)*, was known as the Down Survey because it noted down on paper an account of ownership of the Baronies and Parishes of Ireland at the time of the redistribution of land following the Cromwellian Settlement. The maps were individually drawn and coloured and several sets were made. While at sea between Dublin and London in 1707 the Petty set was captured by the French. The barony maps were presented to the French King's library and are now in the French National Library; the rest were sold.

North of the house are the rose gardens containing standards and climbing varieties and the walled gardens which are laid out with lawns and flowers and vegetables in geometric plots. The west front is screened by a row of 21 Irish yew trees, one of which is gold. The great sweep of the grass and woodland down to the shore is a sanctuary for many species of birds and mammals.

Swords (Sord) – Population 22 314. The bustling county town of Fingal has a history going back to the 6C when St Columba founded a monastery on a low hilltop just to the west of the modern town centre. Its site is marked by the Anglican church, a 9C **round tower** and a 12C **Norman tower**. At the northern end of the town stands **Swords Castle** ⏱, the summer palace of the Archbishops of Dublin; there are substantial remains of the curtain wall, gatehouse, apartments, banqueting hall and chapel; the craggy twin-towered Constable's Tower has been fully restored.

Lusk Heritage Centre ⏱ – *Lusk*. The centre is housed in the tower of Lusk Church, which incorporates an earlier round tower; it presents the history of Lusk monastery and the medieval churches of the area, and the magnificent 16C effigy tomb of Sir Christopher Barnewall and his wife Marion Sharl.

For adjacent sights see BOYNE VALLEY, DROGHEDA, DUBLIN, KELLS, TARA, TRIM.

GALWAY ★★

GAILLIMH – Co Galway – Population 57 241
Michelin Atlas p 89 and Map 923 – E 8

Galway is not only a county town but also the largest conurbation in the west of Ireland. Its position at the mouth of the Corrib River in the northeast corner of Galway Bay makes it an excellent port; from the original quays on the east bank of the river the docks have extended southeast into Lough Atalia where they are still expanding. Galway has grown from a medieval core of narrow streets into a lively cathedral and university city with many modern industries. The **Galway Arts Festival** held annually in July (10 days) now commands more interest than the traditional **Oyster Festival** in late September. Galway is well placed as a centre for excursions in all directions.

City of the Tribes – The city was founded on the east bank of the river late in the 12C by the Anglo-Norman family de Burgo (later Burke) *(see p 235)*; it attracted many Welsh and Norman merchants who enclosed the city within a defensive wall. Under the control of the 14 leading families, known as the "tribes", an extensive trade developed not only with the Continent, importing French and Spanish wine, but also with the West Indies. This prosperity however did not survive the religious disputes of the Reformation and their political consequences. After two lengthy sieges – by the Cromwellians in 1652 and by William of Orange's forces in 1691 – Galway went into decline.

The Claddagh – Long before the arrival of the Normans there was a fishing village on the west bank of the Corrib River, an Irish-speaking community which preserved its own traditions and elected its own leader, known as the King. The name derives from the Gaelic word *cladach* meaning a rocky or pebbly shore. The men fished by night while by day the women sold the catch on the Spanish Parade. The picturesque whitewashed thatched cottages sited at random were replaced in the 1930s by a modern uniform housing scheme. The Claddagh finger ring, which bears the device of a heart enclosing two clasped hands, is popular throughout Ireland.

Gaelic Galway – The city adjoins the most extensive Gaelic-speaking region in Ireland: the Aran Islands, Connemara and the Joyce Country. The 19C revival of interest in the language brought many visitors to the region; two of the oldest summer schools were founded at the turn of the century at Spiddal *(west)* and Tormakeady on the west shore of Lough Mask.

Out and about in Galway

Galway is known for good theatre, including the **Druid Theatre** ⊘ (**BZ K**), *Courthouse Lane*, which specializes in experimental/ avant-garde works, and the **Irish Theatre** (An Taibhdhearc na Gaillimhe) ⊘ (**BY F**), *Middle Street*, which stages Irish productions – music, singing, dancing and folk drama. There are **boat trips** from Wood Quay to Lough Corrib *(see below)*.

Access to the Aran Islands – There is an air service from the airfield at Inverán *(20mi/32km west of Galway by R 336)* and a ferry service from Wood Quay.

Since the founding of the Republic, the Gaelic character of the region has been reinforced: University College, Galway, founded in 1849 as Queen's College, was created a bilingual institution in 1929 and is an important centre for the study of Gaelic language and literature; a state-sponsored Irish Theatre *(Taibhdhearc na Gaillimhe)* was launched by Micheál Mac Liammóir and Hilton Edwards; the offices of the Gaelic Development Authority were moved to Na Forbacha in 1969 and Gaelic Radio has been operating from Casla since 1972.

Literary Galway – Galway city and its environs have produced or fostered several literary personalities. Patrick O'Connor (1882–1928), who wrote short stories in Gaelic, Nora Barnacle (1884–1951), who lived in Bowling Green and married James Joyce, and Frank Harris (1856–1931) are natives of the city. Violet Martin, the second half of the Somerville and Ross partnership, lived at Ross House on the west shore of Lough Corrib. In 1896 Edward Martyn who lived at Tullira Castle in south Galway introduced William Butler Yeats to Lady Gregory; together they co-founded the Irish Literary Theatre, which became the Abbey Theatre in Dublin.

SIGHTS

★**St Nicholas' Church** ⊘ (**BY**) – The medieval church, which was dedicated to St Nicholas of Myra, the patron saint of sailors, was begun c 1320 and frequently enlarged, especially in the 15C and 16C. According to tradition Christopher Columbus once worshipped in the Lady Chapel. The **exterior** is decorated with gargoyles and carved mouldings over the doors and windows. The **interior** includes a medieval water stoup, a font and numerous tombstones, some with vocationed marks. The south transept was extended to include the Lynch tomb which bears the family crest. The **Lynch Memorial** (**A**) recalls the legend that in the 15C Judge James Lynch condemned his son Walter to death for murder and acted as hangman since no one else would carry out the sentence.

★**Lynch's Castle** (**BY**) – The 16C building belonged to the most powerful of the 14 tribes. The grey stone façade bears some fine carving: gargoyles, hood mouldings over the windows, medallions bearing the lynx, the family crest and a roundel bearing the arms of Henry VII.

★**Roman Catholic Cathedral** (**AY**) – The cathedral, which is dedicated to Our Lady Assumed into Heaven and St Nicholas, was designed by John J Robinson in 1957 and built of black Galway "marble", the local limestone which takes a good polish. A copper dome surmounts the crossing. Above the altar in St Nicholas' Chapel in the east transept are the early-17C carved stone plaques, depicting the three persons of the Trinity surrounding the Virgin, which were rescued during the Cromwellian period from St Nicholas' Church.

Spanish Arch (**BZ**) – The name is a reminder of the city's trading links with Spain. The arch itself seems to have been part of a bastion, incorporating four blind arches, one of which was opened in the 18C to give access to a new dock beside Eyre's Long Walk. Part of the medieval **town wall** (20yd/20m long) is visible on the south side of the arch, together with the tidal quays dating from 1270.
The adjoining buildings house the **Galway City Museum** ⊘, a miscellany of articles illustrating daily life in the area in past centuries. A spiral staircase leads to the rooftop terrace *(open in fine weather only)* which provides a fine view of the River Corrib as it enters inner Galway Bay.

Nora Barnacle's House ⊘ (**BY**) – Nora Barnacle, the wife of James Joyce, lived in this two-up-two-down cottage until she left Galway to work in Dublin, where she met Joyce – souvenirs, photos and letters.

Salmon Weir Bridge (**AY**) – The bridge was built in 1818 to link the old prison (1802–1939), which stood on the cathedral site, with the **County Courthouse** (**B**), built (1812–15) on the site of the Franciscan Abbey. Upstream is the **salmon weir**; beyond are the pontoons of the Galway-to-Clifden railway viaduct (1890–1935).

Eyre Square (**BY**) – The focal point of the modern city between the old town and the docks centres on a small park, named after John F Kennedy, President of the USA, who visited Galway in 1963 *(plaque)*. There are several monuments: the

GALWAY

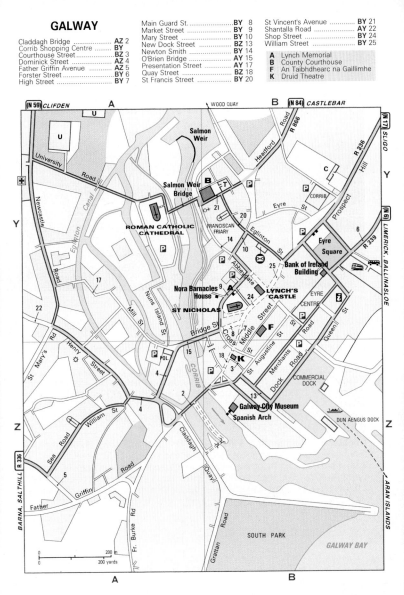

Browne doorway removed from their house in 1906; cannons from the Crimean War presented to the Connaught Rangers; a statue by Albert Power RHA of **Patrick O'Connor** (1882–1928); a statue of **Liam Mellows** who took part in the 1916 Easter Rising and was executed by the Free State army during the Civil War.

The **sword and mace★** of the city corporation, which was instituted by Richard III in 1484 and abolished in 1841, are displayed in the **Bank of Ireland Building** ⊙; the sword (1610) bears two Galway silversmiths' marks; the mace, a massive highly-decorated piece made in Dublin (1710), was presented by Edward Eyre in 1712.

EXCURSION

★★Lough Corrib

By road 17mi/27.5km northwest of Galway by N 59; by boat ⊙ from Wood Quay in Galway.

Lough Corrib, the second-largest lake in Ireland (36mi/58km long), is dotted with numerous islands, known as **drumlins**, varying in size from a tuft of grass to Inchagoill which was once the site of a monastery. To the west extends the wild mountainous country of Connemara; east and south lies the fertile Galway plain.

★Aughnanure Castle ⊙ – *16mi/26km northwest of Galway by N 59; turn right (sign). Car park; 5min there and back on foot.* The ruins of Aughnanure, an Irish tower house and bawn, stand on an outcrop of rock, partially defended but also

Galway Hooker

undermined by the Drimneen River. It was probably built by Walter de Burgo. The inner ward, of which only the circular **watch tower** remains, was later enclosed by the larger outer ward. Most of the **Banqueting Hall** collapsed into the river when the rock caved in but the east wall with its decorated windows remains. The **keep** rises through six storeys from a battered base to Irish-style crenellations with a machicolation on each side. A gun loop and murder hole defend the entrance. From the ground-floor guard-room and store room a spiral stair *(73 steps)* climbs past the sleeping accommodation to the top-floor living room with its fireplace. The garderobe on this floor leads into the space above the third-floor vault. From the roof there is a fine view of Lough Corrib.

★**Oughterard** *(Uachtar Ard)* – Population 711. The small town on the lake shore is a famous angling resort and an attractive and popular tourist centre.
The shore road north of the village, which ends near the head of the lake at Curraun *(8mi/13km there and back)*, provides an ever more spectacular **view**★★ of the lake and its many islands backed by the mountains of the Joyce Country.

For adjacent sights see ARAN ISLANDS, The BURREN, CONG, CONNEMARA, LOUGHREA, TUAM.

GLENDALOUGH ★★★
GLEANN DÁ LOCHA – Co Wicklow
Michelin Atlas p 87 and Map 923 – M 8

This once-remote valley among the Wicklow Mountains where St Kevin sought solitude and later founded a great monastery has long been a place of pilgrimage and
continues to attract innumerable visitors. The "Glen of the Two Lakes" is one of the
most evocative of all Irish monastic sites, both for the beauty of its setting and for
the array of buildings, intact or in ruin, which conjure up a vivid picture of the early
days of Christianity in Ireland.

Glendalough

The monastery founded by St Kevin flourished for many years after his death around
617, drawing pilgrims who were deterred from making the journey to Rome by the
unstable conditions of the time. Seven pilgrimages to Glendalough were said to be the
equivalent of one to far-off Rome. Despite repeated raids and destruction by both
Vikings and Irish the monastery enjoyed a golden age in the 10C and 11C, a period
of Celtic revival. Glendalough also prospered under the reforming leadership of
St Laurence O'Toole (1128–80), who became abbot at the age of 25 and was made
Archbishop of Dublin in 1163. Decline began in the 13C and an English attack in 1398
caused much destruction. Dissolution followed during the reign of Henry VIII but the
pilgrimages continued until the disorderly behaviour of many participants caused their
suppression in the 1860s.

The two lakes at Glendalough were once one. They are set in a valley whose dramatic
contours were shaped by an Ice Age glacier descending from the Wicklow Mountains.
The splendidly-wooded southern shore of the Upper Lake, the site of several features
associated with St Kevin, is particularly striking, with cliffs (100ft/30m) dropping precipitously into the dark waters of the lake. For many years the area was the scene of
mining activity, with the woods being cut to smelt lead, zinc, iron, copper and silver
ores. The Miners' Road, which runs along the northern shore of the lake to a deserted
mining village at the top of the valley, provides the best view of St Kevin's Bed and
the ruins of Temple-na-Skellig.

TOUR *2–5hr*

Visitor Centre ⊘ – This spacious modern building has a number of displays including a fine model, based on Glendalough, of a typical monastery complex as it would
have appeared in medieval times. Old photographs show the site as it was before
restoration and reconstruction took place in the late 19C; an audio-visual show
traces the monastic history of Ireland.

★★★ **Monastic Site** – The ruins of the later monastic settlement, east of the Lower
Lake, form the most important part of the Glendalough site. It is approached
through the gateway, the only surviving example in Ireland of such an entrance to
a monastic enclosure. Set in the wall just beyond the first of two arches is a great
slab of mica schist with an incised cross, probably marking the point at which sanctuary would be granted to those seeking it.

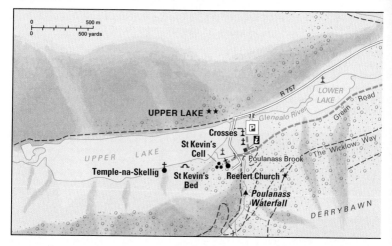

★★ Round Tower – This fine example of a round tower (100ft/30m high) is the dominant feature of the site. Probably constructed in the early 10C, it would have served as landmark, storehouse, bell-tower, look-out and refuge; its entrance is some way above the ground (12ft/4m). The thick walls (3ft/1m at the base) taper slightly towards the tip. Internally the tower was divided into six storeys, connected by ladders.

★★ Cathedral – This roofless structure, once the focal point of the communal life of the monastery, is still a substantial presence on the site, its nave one of the widest of early Irish churches. Built in stages, perhaps from the late 10C onwards, it consists of a nave and chancel with a small sacristy attached to the latter on the south side. The principal features of the nave are the corner pilasters, the west doorway and the south windows. A gravestone set against the north wall of the chancel bears carved crosses and inscriptions in Irish; an adjacent slab has outstanding scroll designs.

St Kevin's Cross – This early, undecorated Celtic high cross (12ft/3.5m high) is the best preserved of the many crosses on the site.

★★ St Kevin's Church – This early Irish oratory with its high-pitched roof of overlapping stones dates from the 11C. Its alternative popular name – St Kevin's Kitchen – is because of its unusual circular tower resembling a chimney or perhaps because of the scullery-like sacristy at its eastern end. The sacristy was once entered from a chancel, now demolished, whose outline can be traced in what remains of its foundations and in the line where its roof met the wall of the nave. Inside there is a sturdy barrel vault with a croft between it and the roof.

St Kieran's Church – The remains of a very small nave and chancel were discovered in 1875 close to St Kevin's Church but outside the stone wall surrounding the monastic enclosure.

★ St Saviour's Priory – *East of the Lower Lake by the Green Road*. The Priory may have been founded by St Laurence O'Toole, Abbot of Glendalough, but is probably earlier in origin. The buildings (reconstructed in 1875), now enclosed within a

St Kevin

Probably born around the middle of the 6C, the young Kevin soon attracted attention for his miracle-working abilities. He was put into the care of three clerics but he escaped his tutors into the bosom of Nature, supposedly dwelling in the hollow of a tree above the Upper Lake at Glendalough. Though persuaded to take up his studies again, Kevin had fallen under the spell of Glendalough, and it was to the lower part of the valley that he returned with a group of monks to found a monastery. The foundation flourished under the leadership of Kevin as abbot but, tiring of his fame, he once more retired to the wilderness, living in complete solitude "in a narrow place between the mountain and the lake", probably the area above the Upper Lake now known as Temple-na-Skellig. The story is told of the blackbird who lays her egg in the saint's hand as he stands in ascetic contemplation, his arms outstretched in the shape of the Cross, a posture he holds

" in the sun and rain for weeks
   until the young are hatched and fledged and flown" (Seamus Heaney).

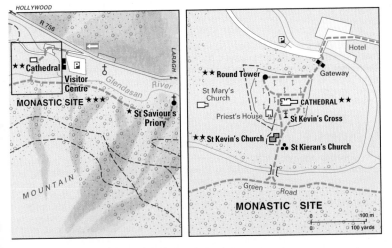

forestry area, include a nave and chancel with a small group of domestic buildings on the north side. The chancel arch and the east window are impressive features in the Irish Romanesque style with much fine carving.

★★Upper Lake – *1.5mi/2.5km on foot west of the Visitor Centre by the Green Road – or 0.5mi/0.8km on foot from the Upper Lake car park. The approach to St Kevin's Cell is by a pathway which is steep and even muddy in places. There is no access to St Kevin's Bed or Temple-na-Skellig, which are best viewed from the far side of the lake.*

Crosses – *East shore of Upper Lake.* The crosses, which originally marked the boundary of the monastic site, were later used as Stations of the Cross when Glendalough became an important pilgrimage centre.

★Reefert Church – Traditionally the burial place of kings, and even perhaps of St Kevin himself, this roofless church is set among the oak and hazel woodland of the lower slopes above the lake. With a plain but beautiful chancel arch, round-headed windows in the south wall of the nave and an imposing granite doorway with sloping jambs, the building may date from the late 10C. In the graveyard are grave slabs and two crosses, one with fine interlaced carving.

St Kevin's Cell – Nothing remains of the cell where St Kevin dwelt alone save for a ring of foundation stones, colonized by three oak trees. His lonely abode was probably built with corbelled stones *(see p 52)* on the pattern of the beehive dwellings on Skellig Michael. The doorway faced eastward down the valley and there may have been a window overlooking the lake.

St Kevin's Bed – This tiny cave in the rockface (30ft/9m above the lake) was probably a Bronze Age tomb. Believed to be the place where St Kevin would go to pray and fast, it used to be the focal point of a pilgrimage to Glendalough; having arrived at Temple-na-Skellig by boat, the pilgrims would make their way along the lake shore, climb steps hewn in the cliff and then be helped, one by one, into the "bone-rock bed of the austere saint" (Richard Hills).

Temple-na-Skellig – The first church on this site (about 20ft/6m above the lake) may date from the time of St Kevin himself, though the present ruined structure was probably a 12C rebuilding and was restored in the 1870s. It has an east window with narrow round-headed twin lights and a huge granite lintel above the incomplete west doorway. The huts of the earliest monastic community were probably built in the raised enclosure to the west of the church.

Poulanass Waterfall – From close to the cottage housing the National Park Information Centre, a path follows the miniature chasm of the Lugduff Brook steeply upstream to a lovely waterfall set among the oaks and holly trees of the surrounding forest.

For adjacent sights see ATHY, KILDARE, POWERSCOURT, RUSSBOROUGH, WICKLOW, WICKLOW MOUNTAINS.

HOOK HEAD PENINSULA

Co Wexford

Michelin Atlas p 80 and Map 923 – L 11

A remote location, quiet beaches and distinctive landscapes have long drawn holiday-makers to the Hook Head Peninsula, bounded to the west by Waterford Harbour and to the east by Bannow Bay. There is angling, scuba-diving; in spring and autumn when more than 200 species have been recorded the peninsula is an important bird-watching location.

The first Anglo-Norman expedition to Ireland landed in 1169 at Bannow Island and the peninsula contains many reminders of medieval demesnes, both lay and ecclesiastical.

SIGHTS

★**Dunbrody Abbey** ⊘ – *5mi/8km north of Duncannon. Key at Furlong's cottage by the main road entrance.* Close to the village of Clonmines, a deserted medieval borough with remains of tower houses, fortified church and Augustinian priory, are the handsome ruins of the abbey founded in 1170 by Hervey de Montmorency, the uncle of famous Strongbow. The roofless but well-preserved cruciform abbey church, pleasantly set above an inlet of the river Barrow, has a low turreted tower and six transept chapels with slender single-light windows. Slight traces exist of some of the outlying buildings.

The abbey was built in 1182 by Cistercian monks from St Mary's Abbey in Dublin. It had the right of sanctuary and the abbot sat in the House of Lords. The last abbot was Alexander Devereux, elevated to the bishopric of Ferns in 1537.

After the Dissolution, the abbey passed into the hands of the Etchingham family; there are substantial remains of the fortified dwelling they erected around the Norman keep built to defend the abbey. In its grounds is a new-grown maze of yew.

★**Tintern Abbey** – *5mi/8km east of Duncannon by R 737, R 733 and R 374 to Saltmills. Restoration in progress.* The ruined Cistercian abbey, a daughter house of Tintern Abbey in Monmouthshire, whence its name, was founded in 1200 by William the Earl Marshal in thanksgiving for his safe crossing from England in a violent storm. At the Dissolution of the Monasteries in the 16C the abbey was granted to the Colclough family who took up residence in the nave and tower.

Ballyhack Castle ⊘ – Overlooking the ferry crossing from Passage East on the west bank of Waterford Harbour is an imposing tower house (15C or 16C); steep stairs in the thickness of the wall link the five floors, of which the ground and first floor are vaulted and the others open to the sky. The site originally belonged to the Knights Templar from whom it passed to the Knights Hospitaller and then came into the possession of the Earl of Donegall.

Kilmokea Gardens ⊘ – Hervey de Montmorency established himself on Great Island, linked to the mainland since land reclamation took place in the 19C. A rect-angular earthwork on the island probably represents the outline of his stronghold. Another enclosure within earthen ramparts (20 acres/8ha) was the site of an Early Christian monastic foundation. Within it stands a handsome Georgian glebe house; its gardens, developed over half a century, offer a delightful contrast between formal areas close to the house and a luxuriant, carefully created and maintained jungle extending along the narrow valley of a tiny stream.

★**Duncannon** – This small seaside village (population 339), partly built on a penin-sula, has an attractive sandy beach. **Duncannon Fort** ⊘ (3 acres/1.2ha) was first selected for defensive purposes by the Anglo-Normans in the 12C. In 1588 the fortress was strengthened as part of the precautions against the Spanish Armada. In 1690 both James II and William III took ship from Duncannon following the Battle of the Boyne.

Slade – The minute fishing village has a small double harbour and is a popular scuba-diving centre. On the pier are the remains of 18C salthouses where sea water was evaporated to make salt. Beside them stand the ruins of **Slade Castle**, consisting of a tower house (15C–16C) and a house (16C–17C), built by the Laffan family.

Hook Head Lighthouse – At the seaward end of the narrow limestone promon-tory terminating in Hook Head stands an extraordinary structure, one of the oldest lighthouses in Europe, where a light was maintained almost continuously for 1 500 years. The cylindrical keep (82ft/25m) was built by the Normans in the early 13C to aid navigation up Waterford Harbour to their port at New Ross. It is topped by a more conventional structure erected early in the 19C.

Fethard – This little place (population 267), the largest town on the peninsula, was founded by the Anglo-Normans. The entire façade of Jimmy O'Leary's garage is decorated with shells; in the forecourt is the anchor from the *Tempo*, an Italian ship wrecked in 1880.

For adjacent sights see CLONMEL, ENNISCORTHY, KILKENNY, WATERFORD, WEXFORD.

INISHOWEN PENINSULA ★★

INIS EOGHAIN – Co Donegal
Michelin Atlas p 101 and Map 923 – J, K 2

The Inishowen Peninsula is triangular in shape, flanked on the east by Lough Foyle and on the west by Lough Swilly; projecting from the north coast into the Atlantic Ocean is Malin Head, the most northerly point in Ireland. The landscape is composed of rugged mountains covered in blanket bog, terminating along the coast in steep cliffs or broad sweeps of sand. Flocks of sheep graze the stony ground. In the fishing villages the traditional cabins are roofed with thatch, tied down with ropes against the wind.

The peninsula is named after a son of Niall of the nine hostages, Eoghain, who was a contemporary of St Patrick in the 5C. The Vikings made several raids but were expelled. By the 15C the O'Dochertys held sway but when Sir Cahir O'Docherty, the young clan chief, was killed at Kilmacrenan *(see p 138)* in 1608, a year after the *Flight of the Earls (see p 135)*, the way was open to Sir Arthur Chichester, who took possession of the whole peninsula.

INIS EOGHAIN SCENIC DRIVE

100mi/160km – from Moville to Letterkenny – 1 day

Moville (Bun an Phobail) – Population 1 392. Moville (pronounced with the accent on the second syllable), once a bustling port where emigrant ships set sail for the United States, is now a seaside resort. **St Pius' Roman Catholic Church** (1953) is an impressive granite building with a handsome mahogany interior. The cliffs and beaches overlooking Lough Foyle have been incorporated into a landscaped coastal walk, **Moville Green**, interspersed with lawns and shrubberies and sporting facilities. At **Cooley** *(2mi/3.2km southwest)* at the graveyard gate stands a **high cross** (10ft/3m) with a hole in its head through which people clasped hands to seal an undertaking. The graveyard contains a **mortuary house**, a tomb shrine known as the Skull House and thought to be associated with St Finian, the abbot of the monastery, which was founded by St Patrick and survived until the 12C.

From Moville take R 241 north.

Greencastle – Population 588. A fine beach makes this a pleasant and popular resort. North of the town on the cliffs opposite Magilligan Point commanding the narrow entrance to Lough Foyle stand the overgrown ruins of a castle built in 1305 by Richard de Burgo, the Red Earl of Ulster, so-called because of his florid complexion. It was captured by Edward Bruce in 1316, fell into the possession of the O'Donnells in the 14C and was granted to Sir Arthur Chichester in 1608; the adjoining fort (1812) was used in the defence of Lough Foyle until the end of the 19C.

Continue north past the golf course; bear left uphill.

★**Inishowen Head** – The headland (295ft/90m) above the tiny harbour next to the lighthouse on Dunagree Point commands a fine view east along the Antrim coast as far as the Giant's Causeway. *Clifftop footpath to Kinnagoe Bay.*

Return south by the upper inland road; on the edge of Greencastle turn right to Kinnagoe Bay.

Viewpoint – *Car park.* The view embraces open moorland used for turf cutting and sheep pasture extending east to Lough Foyle.

Kinnagoe Bay – The sandy beach is sheltered by steep headlands. A map *(at the road junction)* plots the sites of the many ships of the Spanish Armada which were wrecked on the Irish coast; many interesting military relics were found in *La Duquesa St Anna* and *La Trinidad Valencia*, which were wrecked in the bay.

Follow the road inland; at the junction turn right to Tremone Bay (sign); west of Tremone Bay at the T-junction turn right to Culdaff; immediately turn left; after 3.5mi/5.5km turn right at the T-junction and then left.

Carrowmore High Crosses – The site of a monastery founded by Chionais, St Patrick's brother-in-law, is now marked by two **high crosses**, a decorated slab and a boulder inscribed with a cross.

Return to the junction, turn left and then right.

Clonca Church and Cross – *Path across a field.* In the 6C St Buodán founded a monastery at Clonca. The ruined church dates from the 17C or 18C but the carved lintel is earlier. Inside is a 16C tombstone showing a sword and a hurley stick and bearing a rare Irish inscription. In the field opposite the church door is **St Buodán's high cross** depicting the miracle of the loaves and fishes *(east face)*.

At the end of the road turn right onto R 238 and then left.

Bocan Stone Circle – In a field *(left)* are the remains of a stone circle which originally may have consisted of 30 standing stones.

Return to the junction; turn right onto R 238; take the second right and second left.

Dunmore Head – The headland overlooks the sandy beaches of Culdaff Bay.

Culdaff – The houses cluster round the village green.

In Culdaff turn right to Glengad along the coast road; at Glengad Head follow the road inland; turn right to Malin Head.

★★ Malin Head – The tiny fishing village shelters from the prevailing wind in the lee of the great headland, the most northerly point in Ireland, which figures in the shipping forecasts. On the cliffs stands a tower, originally built in 1805 by the British Admiralty to monitor shipping and later used as a signal tower by Lloyds.

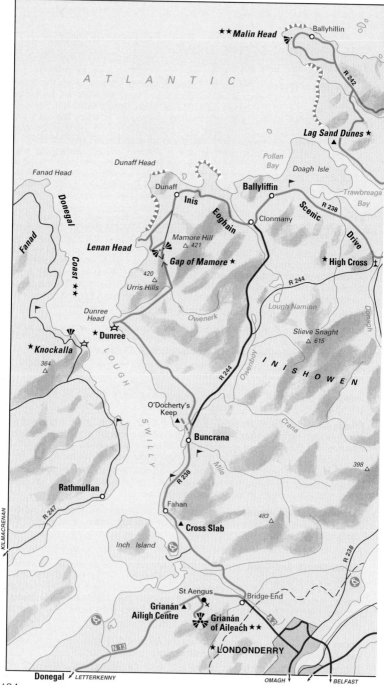

North across the sound *(1.5mi/2.4km)* lies Inishtrahull Island, once the site of a hermitage but now deserted. The road circles the headland providing dramatic **views**★★ *(southwest)* across the water to Pollan Strand and Dunaff Head.

Take R 242 to Malin.

★**Lag Sand Dunes** – Massive sand dunes rise up on the north shore of Trawbreaga Bay, the estuary of the Donagh River.

Malin – The 17C Plantation village is centred on a triangular green.

South of Malin bear right onto R 238. In Carndonagh turn right over the river.

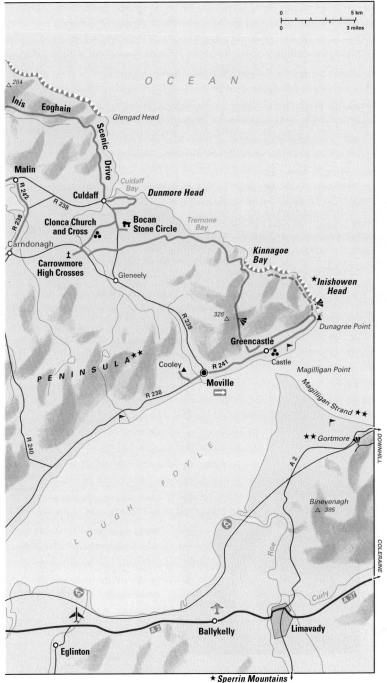

★Carndonagh High Cross – At the top of the hill next to the Anglican church *(left)* stands an 8C **high cross**, decorated with an interlaced cross and a Crucifixion and flanked by two **pillars**, one of which shows David with his harp. In the graveyard stands a **cross pillar**, known as the Marigold Stone, which is decorated with a seven-pointed star, resembling a marigold, on one side and a Crucifixion on the other.

Continue northwest on R 238.

Ballyliffin (Baile Lifín) – Population 334. This attractive resort is set slightly inland from Pollan Bay and Pollan Strand, a long sandy beach backed by a golf course on Doagh Isle, a flat sandy peninsula.

In Clonmany turn right to Dunaff. Bear right to Lenan Head.

Lenan Head – The headland, where a gun battery (1895) used to command the entrance to Lough Swilly, is disfigured by a ruined army camp.

Take the road past Lenan Strand; turn right to the Gap of Mamore.

★Gap of Mamore – From the **viewpoint** *(car park – left)* there is an extensive view north to Dunaff Head. From the saddle between Mamore Hill *(left)* and the Urris Hills *(right)* the road descends past rocky outcrops and grazing sheep into the valley and follows the Owenerk River downstream *(right)*.

Turn right to Dunree Head.

★Dunree Fort ⊘ – *Car park within the military compound.* A drawbridge spans the narrow defile which separates the fort from Dunree Head. The fort itself has been converted into a **military museum** containing the original guns; a film explains their role in a coastal defence battery; 180 years of records illustrate the evolution of the fort from a fortified earthen embankment, built in 1798 under the threat of French invasion, to an important element in a chain of forts on the shores of Lough Swilly defending a British Naval Base at Buncrana. In 1914 the entire British Grand Fleet sheltered behind a boom in the Lough. Knockalla Fort is visible across the narrow channel on the opposite shore.

Take the coast road south to Buncrana.

Buncrana (Bun Cranncha) – Population 3118. This seaside resort has a long sandy beach facing west across Lough Swilly to the mountains of Donegal.
At the north end of the seafront an old six-arched bridge spanning the Crana River leads to **O'Docherty's Keep**, a Norman tower which was repaired in 1602 by Hugh Boy O'Docherty in anticipation of a Spanish invasion. It was burned in the English counter-attack but granted by Chichester to the Vaughans who restored it as their family residence. The nearby mansion of seven bays and two wings, which stands at the top of the rise overlooking the sea, was built by Sir John Vaughan in 1718. The **Vintage Car Museum** ⊘ contains a small but varied collection of vehicles: 1929 Rolls-Royce landaulette, 1915 Model T Ford, 1957 Chevy Sports coupé, 1951 Alvis DHC, bone-shaker bicycle (1875), Irish jaunting car (1920), Morris doctor's coupé (1933), Hillman Minx Convertible (1953), Mustang (1966), model car collection and several other cars and carriages.

Take R 238 south to Fahan.

Fahan Cross-Slab – On the south side of the village (population 309) in the old graveyard beside the Anglican church stands a 7C **cross-slab**, which is decorated on each face with a cross formed of interlaced bands; one of them is flanked by two figures. It marks the site of a monastery which was founded by St Mura in the 7C and survived until at least 1098.

Continue south on R 238; in Bridge End turn right onto N 13. After 2mi/3.2km turn left; after 0.5mi/0.8km turn right; after 1.5mi/2.4km turn left.

B Lynch /Bord Fáilte, Dublin

Grianán Aileach

★★Grianán of Aileach – *Car park.* The circular stone fort, which crowns the exposed hilltop and provides an excellent protection against the wind, is a reconstruction dating from 1870. A tunnel pierces the stone wall (13ft/4m thick) which contains small chambers and steps to the ramparts and encloses a circle (77ft/23m in diameter). It is not known to what extent this structure resembles the original stone fort, which was built early in the Christian era and served as the royal seat of the O'Neill clan from about the 5C to 12C. It was destroyed in 1101 by the King of Munster, Murtogh O'Brien, in retaliation for the destruction of his own royal seat at Kincora near Killaloe. From the ramparts there is an extensive **view★★** *(east)* of Londonderry and the Sperrin Mountains, *(northeast)* of Lough Foyle, *(north)* of the Inishowen Peninsula, and *(west)* of Inch Island, Lough Swilly and Knockalla Mountain.

The circular shape of the stone fort is echoed at the foot of the hill in **St Aengus Church**, which was designed by Liam McCormack.

Return to N 13; turn left towards Letterkenny.

Grianàn Ailigh Centre ⊘ – *Burt; beside N 13.* An exhibition of storyboards and models relating the legends associated with the site is housed on the upper floor of a redundant Anglican church, which has been converted into a restaurant. Other displays describe similar Irish stone forts and the restoration of the church.

Coirrgend, the warrior

His punishment for murdering the king's son was to carry the body and a burial stone to Grianán Mountain. The burden killed him and he died crying "Á, leac!" ("Alas, stone!") – the origin of the name of the site.

Continue southwest by N 13 to return to Letterkenny.

For adjacent sights see DONEGAL, DONEGAL COAST, DONEGAL GLENS, LONDONDERRY, SPERRIN MOUNTAINS.

IVERAGH PENINSULA ★★

Co Kerry
Michelin Atlas p 76 and Map 923 – ABC 11, 12

The Iveragh peninsula in southwest Kerry, also known as the Waterville promontory, rises to some of the highest peaks in Ireland. "The Ring of Kerry", the road (N 70) which skirts the entire coastline between Killorglin in the north and Kenmare in the south, presents a succession of picturesque land- and seascapes.

★★RING OF KERRY
126mi/203km – 1 day

Most coach tours on this route travel from north to south but passing is difficult as the road is narrow.

Take N 70 west to Killorglin.

Killorglin (Cill Orglan) – Population 1 229. The town is best known for the **Puck Fair**, which takes place every August; it is one of the three great fairs of Ireland (the other two are Ballycastle and Ballinasloe – *see p 372*). A large billy-goat from the locality is enthroned on a chair in the town square during three days and nights of revelry. The **Puck Fair Exhibition** ⊘, displayed in the basement room of a private house *(turn left before crossing the bridge at the foot of the hill)*, consists of souvenirs, photos, press cuttings etc.

St James's Church (Roman Catholic), built in 1837 with a thatched roof, was rebuilt in 1887 in the Gothic style with a slate roof.

Continue west on N 70; turn left to Caragh Lake, then right and left to Lickeen.

★Lough Caragh – The road along the west shore affords attractive views of the lake, which provides good salmon and trout fishing; southeast rise the Macgillycuddy's Reeks (3 414ft/1 038m).

Return to N 70 and continue west; in Caragh Bridge turn right.

Cromane Strand – The long spit of sand provides a good view of Castlemaine Harbour.

Continue west on N 70; on the far side of Glenbeigh take the minor road west across the bridge to Rossbeigh Strand.

Rossbeigh Strand – The long strand (3mi/5km) faces west over Dingle Bay. In the small hamlet at the landward end there is a pub and a shop; there are extended walks in Rossbeigh Woods.

Continue west on N 70; in Kells turn right onto the minor road to Kells Bay (1mi/1.6km).

Kells Bay – This small secluded beach is a popular bathing place with excellent views across Dingle Bay to the Dingle Peninsula.

Continue west on N 70.

The gaunt ruins of **Daniel O'Connell's Birthplace**, Carhan House (right), are in a very dilapidated condition.

Cahersiveen (Cathair Saidhbhín) – Population 1 213. The native town of Daniel O'Connell is a relatively new development in Irish terms since it dates from the early 19C. The **O'Connell Memorial Church** was built in 1888 of Newry granite with dressings of local black limestone; the tower was never completed. Although rejected at first by the church authorities as too elaborate, the plans were approved by Pope Leo XIII.

The old police barracks by the bridge, burnt out in 1922, have been restored to house the Tourist Information Centre.

Take the minor road north towards Cooncrome harbour; after crossing the river turn left (2mi/3.2km).

Cahergall Fort – The walls of this large stone fort are stepped on the inside as at Staigue *(see below)*. They enclose two drystone buildings, a beehive hut and a rectangular house.

On foot continue west; turn right into a private road.

Leacanabuaile Fort – This partly-reconstructed prehistoric drystone fort was inhabited during the Bronze and Iron Ages; from the top of the ramparts there are excellent **views**★★ of the coast.

Return to Cahersiveen and continue west on N 70.

To visit Valencia Island EITHER turn right to Renard Point and take the ferry to Knight's Town OR continue on N 70, turn right onto R 657 to Portmagee and cross the bridge over the Portmagee Channel.

Valencia Island ⊘ – Although the island is small (7mi/11.3km x 2mi/3.2km), its name is well known to all who listen to the shipping forecasts relayed by the British Broadcasting Corporation.

Knight's Town (population 204), the main village, named after the Knight of Kerry, a former landowner, consists of a single street ending at the weather-boarded clock tower by the harbour; the **anchor** on view was retrieved in 1971 from the wreck of the four-masted barque, the *Crompton*, which went down off the island in 1910. A steep narrow road north of the church leads *(2.5mi/4km)* to a grotto created in the inverted V-shaped mouth of a disused slate quarry; from the headland there is a view of Beginish Island in Doulus Bay backed by Doulus Head.

Skellig Experience ⊘ brings to life the history of the Skellig Islands through an exhibition and an audio-visual presentation *(16min)*. In the 7C St Finian founded a monastery which survived for 500–600 years on Skellig Michael; the ruins – the church, two oratories and six beehive cells – are perched on a narrow natural platform at the top of a flight of several hundred steps. In 1996 Skellig Michael was designated a World Heritage Site. From 1820 to 1987, when the lights were automated, the lighthouses were attended by keepers who lived for long periods on the islands. The natural history sections describe the sea bird colonies and the underwater life of the Skellig Islands.

B Lynch /Bord Fáilte, Dublin

Beehive Huts on Skellig Michael

The western extremity of Valencia Island, Bray Head, is marked by Bray Tower *(30min on foot up a track from the end of the road)*, a 16C stone watchtower, which gives views *(south)* to the Skellig Islands and *(north)* to the Dingle Peninsula.

Take the bridge over the Portmagee Channel to Portmagee (An Caladh); turn right to take the coast road south.

The road climbs behind Glaneragh (1 044ft/318m) and then plunges in steep narrow zigzags down to St Finan's Bay; in fine weather there is a view of the **Skellig Islands ★★** – **Great Skellig**, also known as **Skellig Michael**, and **Little Skellig**, its smaller neighbour – two steep barren islands, outcrops of rock rising sheer from the sea west of Bolus Head.

Continue south on R 567.

Ballinskelligs (Baile an Sceilg) – This very small Irish-speaking village is noted for its minute harbour and long golden strand (4mi/6km).

Continue east on R 567; at the junction turn right onto N 70.

Waterville (An Coireán) – Population 475. The little resort is built on an isthmus between **Lough Currane** and the sea; it boasts a long promenade (0.5mi/0.8km). Many photographs of Charlie Chaplin's frequent visits are to be found in the foyer of the Butler Arms Hotel, redolent of the 1950s in its decor.

Coomakesta Pass – The winding pass (700ft/213m) offers striking views of the coast.

★★**Derrynane National Historic Park** ⊘ – The house and surrounding parkland formerly belonged to Daniel O'Connell (1775–1847), the Great Liberator.
The **park** (298 acres/121ha) which borders Derrynane Bay includes a bathing beach, a bird sanctuary and Abbey Island which is accessible at low tide. Near the house there are walks through flower gardens and woodlands.
The south and east wings of the slate-fronted **house** are presented as they were when built by O'Connell in 1825. The dining room *(ground floor)* is furnished with its original long table, chairs and sideboards, and hung with family portraits. A nearby small room contains many mementoes of O'Connell, such as his quill pen and correspondence relating to the return to Ireland of his body after his death in Genoa in Italy. The centrepiece of the drawing room *(first floor)* is the elaborate **table** presented to O'Connell when he was an alderman of Dublin Corporation. The top is made of walnut and the base, made from Irish oak, features Irish wolfhounds and a harp; the carving took four years to complete. The elaborate leather-covered chair was often used by O'Connell. The chapel adjoining the house was built by O'Connell in 1844 in thanksgiving for his release from prison, and the huge triumphal chariot, in which O'Connell was paraded through Dublin, has been restored to its full gilded magnificence.

From Derrynane take N 70 east, in Castlecove turn left at the Staigue Fort House hotel.

★**Staigue Fort** – *Narrow approach road; 20p donation "for trespass".* This 2 000-year-old drystone fort (restored) is one of the finest in Ireland. It was built as a centre of communal refuge probably before the 5C. The walls (18ft/5m high and up to 13ft/4m thick) are stepped on their interior face to provide access to the parapets. The entire fort is surrounded by a bank and ditch.
Northwest rises Tooreenyduneen mountain (1 436ft/431m high).

Continue east on N 70.

★**Sneem (An Snaidhm)** – Population 292. This attractive village is set at the head of the Sneem Estuary. Monuments to Cearbhall O'Dálaigh (1899–1976), former President of Ireland, who lived in Sneem, have been erected in the two large grass-covered squares which are linked by a narrow bridge.
The **Anglican Church** ⊘ is a charming small building dating from 1810 with a tower and a small spire supporting a salmon-shaped weathervane. Among the few ornaments in the white-painted interior are a number of brass pew plates, bearing the names of former parishioners.

Continue east on N 70.

Kenmare Lace

Kenmare lace is needlepoint lace, a technique introduced from Italy in the 17C. It is the most difficult kind as it is worked in needle and thread without any supporting fabric. The design is drawn on parchment or glazed calico and outlined with skeleton threads which are later removed together with the backing. Its distinctive characteristics are braided outlines and the use of linen rather than cotton thread. Raised point is created by using buttonhole stitches over cords or horsehair.

Kenmare (Neidín) – Population 1 366. The small market town is set in a horseshoe of mountains where the Roughty River widens into the Kenmare River. The attractive site was chosen by Sir William Petty (1623–87), a man of many talents, who arrived in Ireland as physician-general in Cromwell's Army and organized the Down Survey *(see p 175)*. In 1775 the first Marquess of Lansdowne laid out the two principal streets, which intersect one another to form an X-shape, with space for a market at the point of intersection. Kenmare is a popular tourist centre, with elegant shops (jewellery, linen, delicatessen, books and foreign newspapers).

The **Kenmare Heritage Centre** ⊘ *(Main Street)* traces the history of Kenmare, originally called Nedeen, and its buildings, its sufferings during the Famine and the story of the Nun of Kenmare. There is a display of antique Kenmare lace. The **Lace and Design Centre** gives demonstrations of lace-making and sells lace made by a local cooperative working from the designs created by the nuns.

On the edge of the town *(Market Street)* there is a prehistoric **stone circle** consisting of one central stone surrounded by 15 upright stones.

South of the town *(cross the Kenmare River and turn left – sign)* are the **Sheen Falls** where the Sheen River swirls and tumbles over rocks and boulders before joining the Kenmare River.

Take N 71 north to return to Killarney.

For adjacent sights see BEARA PENINSULA, KILLARNEY, TRALEE.

KELLS ★

CEANANNAS MÓR – Co Meath – Population 2 183
Michelin Atlas p 92 and Map 923 – L 6

Kells is an attractive market town in the valley of the River Blackwater, which owes its fame to its monastic past. The Courthouse and the Roman Catholic Church were designed by Francis Johnston.

The Book of Kells – The famous illuminated manuscript of the Gospels, now in Trinity College library *(see DUBLIN)*, was produced in the local monastery in the 8C; it was stolen from the sacristy in 1007 but found two months later minus its gold ornament. The monastery was founded by St Columba *(see DONEGAL GLENS)* in the 6C; in 807 monks from Iona sought refuge at Kells from the Vikings and in 877 St Columba's relics were moved to Kells. In the 10C, however, Kells itself was raided by the Vikings. Further raids, by the Irish, occurred in the 11C and the monastery was burned in 1111 and 1156. The Synod of Kells in 1152 raised the monastery to the status of a diocese but it was later reduced to a parish.

SIGHTS

★★**Round Tower and High Crosses** – *Market Street*. In the churchyard of **St Columba's Anglican Church** ⊘ stand various relics of the early monastery.

The **round tower**, built before 1076, has lost its conical cap, and the heads carved on the doorway are severely weathered.

Next to it stands the **South Cross**, probably 9C, which depicts Daniel in the Lions' Den, the Three Children in the Fiery Furnace, Cain and Abel and Adam and Eve *(south face)*, the Sacrifice of Isaac *(left arm)*, St Paul and St Antony in the desert *(right arm)*, David with his harp and the miracle of the loaves and fishes *(top)*, the Crucifixion and Christ in Judgement *(west side)*; interlacing, foliage and birds and animals fill the interstices. Nearby stands the stump of a cross showing various biblical scenes and geometric decoration. South of the church stands an unfinished cross with raised panels ready to be carved and the Crucifixion on one face. North of the church is a medieval church tower with grave slabs inserted at the base. Detailed information about the monastery, the crosses, the Kells crozier *(in the British Museum)* and the Book of Kells is displayed in the gallery of the church.

★**St Columba's House** – *Keys available at the house with the vehicle entrance in the lane beside the east churchyard gate.* Higher up the lane stands an ancient stone oratory with a corbelled stone roof which probably dates from the 11C or 12C. The original entrance is visible in the west wall; the intervening floor is missing. Between the ceiling vault and the steep roof there is a tiny chamber *(access by ladder)*.

EXCURSIONS

St Kilian's Heritage Centre ⊘ – *8mi/13km north of Kells by R 164*. The centre celebrates the life of St Kilian (640–689), the "Apostle of the Franks" who became the patron saint of Würzburg and died a martyr's death. North of Mullagh stands a ruined church known as Kilian's church *(Teampall Ceallaigh)*. People still pray at his holy well, although formal observances ended early in the 19C.

Castlekeeran High Crosses – *5mi/8km west of Kells by R 163; after 3mi/5km turn right at the crossroads. Park beside the road. Through the farmyard and across the field and stile.* Round the edges of the graveyard are three undecorated early crosses which pre-date the scriptural crosses at Kells. Beside the yew tree stands an Ogam Stone. They mark the site of an early monastery which grew up round the hermitage of Kieran, a monk from Kells.

St Kilian

Kilian was born in the 7C in Mullagh in Co Cavan and was educated at the monastic school in Rosscarbery *(see p 210)* in Co Cork. As a pilgrim for Christ, he went to Würzburg in Franconia to convert the people to Christianity. According to tradition he disapproved when the local ruler, Gozbert, whom he had converted, married his brother's wife and so she had St Kilian beheaded. In 782 his remains were moved to a round church on the Marienberg but in 1991 they were returned to Mullagh.

★**Loughcrew Passage Graves** ⊘ – *15mi/24km west of Kells by R 163. Beyond Ballinlough bear right onto R 154; after 3mi/5km turn left onto L 3. After 3mi/4.6km turn left; after 0.5mi/0.8km turn left again onto narrow rough road. Car park.* The cemetery covers two adjoining peaks, Cairnbane East and Cairnbane West, on either side of the road, on Slieve na Calliagh (908ft/277m). It consists of at least 30 graves, some of which have been excavated. Most of them date from between 2500 and 2000 BC, although excavations in 1943 in Cairn H on Cairnbane West uncovered objects bearing Iron Age La Tène style decoration. **Cairn T** (120ft/37m in diameter), the largest grave on Cairnbane East, is decorated with concentric circles, zigzag lines and flower motifs.

For adjacent sights see BOYNE VALLEY, CAVAN, DROGHEDA, DUNDALK, MULLINGAR, TARA, TRIM.

KILDARE ★

CILL DARA – Co Kildare – Population 4 278
Michelin Atlas p 86 and Map 923 – L 8

The small cathedral town, which has the same name as the county, developed from a 5C religious community, founded by St Brigid and St Conleth; it was one of the few convents for women in the Celtic period.

★★**Cathedral** – The present cathedral building is a late-19C reconstruction, incorporating portions of a 13C structure. The plain unplastered interior is relieved by ancient tombs with effigies, a medieval stone font and stained-glass windows.
The **round tower** (108ft/30m high) has been substantially restored in recent years; from the top there are **views** over the Curragh and the surrounding Midland counties.
A minor road opposite the cathedral leads to **St Brigid's shrine** and **well**.

EXCURSIONS

★★**Irish National Stud** ⊘ – *1mi/1.5km southeast of Kildare (sign).* Lord Wavertree, a wealthy Scotsman from a brewing family, began breeding horses at Tully in 1900; in 1915 he gave his stud to the British Crown and it continued as the British National Stud until it was handed over to the Irish Government in 1943. The stal-

---

The Curragh

The Curragh, an extensive plain of short springy turf dotted with clumps of yellow gorse, is the headquarters of Irish racing. Its name is derived from the old Irish word *(cuirrech)* meaning racecourse and the area has been associated with horse racing since the pre-Christian era. The first recorded prize is the Plate donated in 1640 by the Trustees of the Duke of Leinster. By the mid 19C there were some 25 courses at the Curragh ranging from a short course (2 furlongs/440yd/402m) for yearlings to "Over the Course" (4mi/6km).
The area was also used for military manoeuvres. The barracks at the Curragh Camp, built in 1855 to train soldiers for the Crimean War, are now used by the Irish army.

lion boxes, with their lantern roofs, were built in the 1960s. In the Sun Chariot yard, finished in 1975, pregnant mares are stabled during the stud season and yearlings are housed from July to October. Mares and foals can be seen in the paddocks from the Tully Walk *(2mi/3km long)*.

The most outstanding exhibit in the **Irish Horse Museum** is the skeleton of Arkle, the Irish racehorse with an outstanding record of wins whose career ended in a fall at Kempton Park in England on 27 December 1966. The other exhibits, which include a 13C horse skull found at Christchurch Place in Dublin and harness made in Dublin between the 13C and 15C, trace the history of the horse, horse racing and steeple-chasing *(see p 24)*.

The grounds of the stud contain an extensive lake, created by Eida *(see below)*, and the ruins of the **Black Abbey**, founded as a preceptory of the Knights Hospitaller of St John after the Anglo-Norman invasion of Ireland in 1169. According to tradition it is connected by a tunnel (1mi/1.5km) to Kildare Cathedral. When the abbey was suppressed in the mid 16C, it passed into the possession of the Sarsfield family and it was here c 1650 that Patrick Sarsfield *(see p 213)*, leader of the Irish at the Siege of Limerick, was born.

Slide File, Dublin

Flat Racing at the Curragh (1987)

★★Japanese Gardens ⊘ – *In the grounds of the National Stud (see above).* The gardens were created for Lord Wavertree between 1906 and 1910 by the Japanese gardener Eida and his son Minoru. The main garden depicts the story of the life of man, beginning with the **Gate of Oblivion** and the **Cave of Birth**, continuing across the bridges of engagement and marriage to the **Hill of Ambition** and the **Well of Wisdom**. The garden used to conclude with the **Gateway to Eternity**. The **Garden of Eternity** (1974) depicts the conflict of human nature. The **Zen meditation garden** (1976) is not designed to suggest any particular thought; visitors are encouraged to generate their own concepts.

Peatland World ⊘ – *Lullymore; 12mi/19km north by R 401 and R 414.* The Centre, housed in the stables of an old estate, presents the history of the estate and of the Midland bogs. The display explains peat cutting by hand for the home, and by machine to fuel the peat-powered electricity generating stations. Among the exhibits are bog wood and bog butter and a pre-Christian bog-oak canoe, turf cutting spades, cloth made from peat fibres, products derived from peat such as oil, wax, candles, toilet articles such as shampoo, toothpaste and soap from Germany. Upstairs the display illustrates the flora and fauna of the peat bogs and their conservation.

Hill of Allen – *6mi/10km north by R 415.* The summit of the 19C tower (676ft/206m) provides **views** of the Bog of Allen *(northwest)*.

Robertstown ⊘ (Inis Robertaig) – *10mi/16km north by R 415. Barge trips from Old Canal Hotel; cruisers for hire from Lowtown Marina.* Population 235. The village consists of the waterfront buildings facing the canal, which reached Robertstown in 1785. Near Binns Bridge stands the Old Canal Hotel, built in 1803 to serve the passengers on the flyboats *(see p 25)*; it now houses an exhibition.

Grand Canal, Robertstown

Punchestown Standing Stone – *15mi/24km east by N 7 to Naas and R 411.* North of the racecourse *(Woolpack Road)* stands a granite long stone (20ft/6m high) which is thought to date from the early Bronze Age.

Kilcullen – *7mi/11km west by R 413.* Population 1 664. The **Hide Out Bar**, designed in the style of a jungle hut, preserves the black and withered right arm of prize-fighter Dan Donnelly (1786–1820), who won a spectacular bout on The Curragh on 13 December 1815. The pub also displays a collection of old maps, deer heads, hunting guns and knives.

For adjacent sights see ATHLONE, ATHY, BIRR, CARLOW, CLONMACNOISE, MULLINGAR, RUSSBOROUGH, TULLAMORE, WICKLOW MOUNTAINS.

To plan a special itinerary:
– consult the Map of Touring Programmes which indicates the recommended routes, the tourist regions, the principal towns and main sights;
– read the descriptions in the Sights section which include Excursions from the main tourist centres.
Michelin Map no 923 shows scenic routes, interesting sights, viewpoints, rivers, forests...

KILKENNY ★★

CILL CHAINNIGH – Co Kilkenny – Population 8 507
Michelin Atlas p 80 and Map 923 – K 10

Kilkenny, the county town, is Ireland's most outstanding medieval city, set on the banks of the River Nore and dominated by its castle and its cathedral, which face each other across the city centre. Narrow alleys, know locally as slips, recall the medieval street pattern.

The city's historical legacy, which is keenly preserved in several ancient buildings, all admirably restored, is matched by a strong artistic tradition, expressed in modern themes in the Kilkenny Design Centre. The Kilkenny Arts Festival, held annually in August, is now one of the most important arts events in Ireland.

The most famous pupil of Kilkenny College, a boarding school founded in 1666 by the first Duke of Ormond, was Dean Swift.

Capital of the Kingdom of Ossory – The city is named after St Canice, who founded a church here in the 6C. From the 2C to the 12C Kilkenny was the capital of the Gaelic Kingdom of Ossory; the ruling MacGiolla Phadruig family was engaged in a constant struggle for the kingship of Leinster.

Statutes of Kilkenny – Following the Anglo-Norman invasion in the 12C Kilkenny quickly became strategically and politically important; it was a major venue for Anglo-Irish parliaments. Under Anglo-Norman rule the native clans and the invaders lived side-by-side in reasonable co-existence despite frequent incomprehension. Over the centuries many of the Anglo-Norman families, led by the dominant Butler family, tended to become absorbed into the native Gaelic culture. In 1366 a parliament in Kilkenny passed the **Statutes of Kilkenny** to prohibit the Anglo-Normans from intermingling with the Irish but the process was so far advanced that observance of the new laws was most impractical.

Confederation of Kilkenny – Kilkenny's most outstanding period was from 1642 to 1648, when the Confederation of Kilkenny functioned as an independent Irish parliament, representing both the old Irish and the Anglo-Irish Roman Catholics. Later the Confederation split and the Anglo-Irish side supported the English Viceroy, while the Old Irish relied on the military support of Pope Innocent X. The Old Irish, led by Owen Roe O'Neill, were eventually defeated; following Cromwell's siege of Kilkenny in 1650 the Irish army was permitted to march out of the city.

Nationalist Tradition – Kilkenny has always had a strongly nationalistic tradition and played a key role in the movement for independence earlier in the 20C. **William T Cosgrave**, first president of the Executive Council of the Irish Free State, was Sinn Féin member for Kilkenny, first at Westminster and then in the Irish Parliament (Dáil).

★★KILKENNY CASTLE AND GROUNDS ⊙ (Z)

The castle was built by William the Earl Marshal between 1192 and 1207 on a most imposing site overlooking the River Nore. Uniquely among Irish castles, it was a nobleman's residence, the main seat of the Butler family, Earls and Dukes of Ormond, for over five centuries from the 14C until 1935. In the 19C it was extensively modernized but in 1967, when it was handed over by the 6th Marquess of Ormond to the people of Kilkenny, it was in a derelict state.

Interior – The hall, paved with Kilkenny marble and hung with portraits, leads to the mahogany stairs installed in 1838. The Library and Drawing Room have been restored to their Victorian appearance with some of the original furniture and some reproduction pieces. The Dining Room is furnished in the style of the 18C.

The Long Gallery was designed in the 19C by John Pollen with a double fireplace in Carrara marble; the hammerbeam roof of Norwegian timber is decorated in the pre-Raphaelite style with neo-Celtic motifs. It is hung with 17C-to-19C portraits (on loan) and four Gobelin tapestries (1660) designed by Rubens. The bedrooms display hand-painted Chinese silk wallpaper and a mahogany bed with a horsehair mattress. In the 19C the castle was staffed by 93 servants who came and went through a tunnel under the road to the stables.

Butler Gallery ⊙ – *Basement*. These rooms house a collection of 19C and 20C Irish art and visiting exhibitions of contemporary art.

Park ⊙ – The extensive park (50 acres/20ha) provides many beautiful walks.

Kilkenny Design Centre ⊙ – *Castle Stables*. The Design Centre, which is housed in the monumental 18C stable buildings of the Castle, functioned for a quarter of a century as a focal point for improvement in the design of ceramics, textiles, furniture and jewellery. With its objectives largely achieved, it is now a major retail outlet for high-quality souvenirs and continues to provide accommodation for a variety of craftspeople. It has a shop in Dublin in Nassau Street.

Dúchas, Dublin

Kilkenny Castle

★★ST CANICE'S CATHEDRAL ⊘ (Y)

The cathedral stands upon a small hill, which may be the site of St Canice's 6C church, and is best approached by St Canice's Steps *(southeast)* which date from the early 17C.

It was built in the 13C in the early English Gothic style and has been periodically restored, first after 1650 when Cromwell damaged the monuments, destroyed the roof and stabled horses in the nave, second in the mid 18C and 19C, and again from 1959 to 1961 when the roof and organ were renovated.

Interior – The many architectural features of the cathedral, the second-longest in Ireland, are best appreciated from the west end of the nave. Among the many fine tombs the best-known *(south transept)* is that of Piers Butler, Earl of Ormond and Ossory, who owned the town and died in 1539, and his wife Margaret Fitzgerald: her effigy has a finely jewelled and embroidered girdle.

The oldest tomb (13C) *(north transept)* has no inscription but still bears part of the original dog-tooth ornament. The oldest slab, found under the High Street in 1894, is the **Kyteler slab** *(north aisle)*, inscribed in Norman French in memory of Jose Kyteler, probably the father of Dame Alice Kyteler, who was tried for witchcraft in 1323.

Round Tower – The **round tower**, built between 700 and 1000, has wooden stairs leading to the top (100ft/30m high) which gives an overall view of Kilkenny and its surrounding countryside.

St Canice's Library – The library *(northwest)* contains some 3 000 books dating from the 16C and 17C.

TOWN CENTRE

Shee Alms House (Z) – The 16C building makes a fascinating home for the tourist information office.

★**Black Abbey** ⊘ (Y) – The church, one of the few **medieval churches** in Ireland still in use, was founded soon after 1226 for the Dominicans. The interior is decorated with fine early-14C window tracery in the south transept, particularly the five-light Rosary window. Although inscribed 1264, the alabaster carving of the Most Holy Trinity beside the altar is thought to date from c 1400. In the graveyard are 10 stone coffins dating from the 13C and 14C.

Near the abbey is the **Black Freren Gate**, Kilkenny's only remaining medieval gate.

★**Rothe House** ⊘ (Y) – The house was built in 1594 by a local merchant, John Rothe. In the 17C it was used as a meeting place by religious and political leaders during the Kilkenny Confederation. It now houses the local museum which presents

Brewing in Kilkenny

As early as the 14C a light ale was being brewed by the monks of St Francis Abbey, a Franciscan foundation (1234), which was destroyed by Cromwell in 1650; only the ruined tower and chancel survive in the grounds of the **St Francis Abbey Brewery**, which was founded in 1710 by John Smithwick and is now owned by Guinness.

many historical curiosities, including letters written by Daniel O'Connell when he was MP for Kilkenny City in 1836–37, an 18C penal cross and the Carlingford Screw, all that remains of the first Irish aeronautical patent, taken out in 1856 by Viscount Carlingford, a local landowner. There is a small costume collection on the top floor.

Tholsel ⊘ (**Y**) – The Tholsel *(see p 56)*, built in 1761 (restored), contains examples of mayoral regalia dating back two centuries. The first tholsel was constructed around 1400, when the city walls were built.

Courthouse (**Y**) – The courthouse was built above Grace's Castle (1210) which was converted into a prison in 1568.

St Mary's Cathedral (**Y**) – The Roman Catholic cathedral was built in the 19C of limestone with a high tower (200ft/61m).

Kyteler's Inn (**Y**) – Dame Alice Kyteler *(see above)* is said to have been born here in 1280. In 1324 the half-timbered building became an inn.

Tynan's Bridge House Bar (**Y**) – The pub has a distinctive Victorian exterior and has retained its marble counter and low wooden ceiling painted red.

KILKENNY

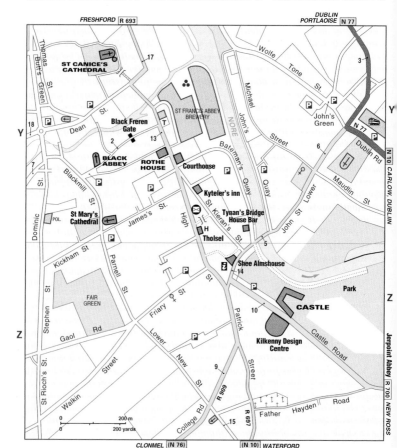

EXCURSIONS

Thomastown – *11mi/18km south of Kilkenny by R 700.* Little twisting streets focus on the market-like main street close to the old bridge over the Nore, half-obliterated by its modern concrete deck. There are remains of the medieval town walls and castle.

Behind a modest frontage on a side street is the surprise of **Ladywell Water Garden** , an intricate mixture of trees, shrubs and aquatic plants.

The magnificent estate of **Mount Juliet** ⊘ (1 400 acres/567ha) offers a variety of sporting facilities including a golf course designed by Jack Nicklaus; the house (c 1780) is a hotel, open only to residents.

★**Kilfane Glen and Waterfall** ⊘ – *14mi/23km south of Kilkenny by R 700 and N 9 north from Thomastown.* This is an unusual and fascinating garden, a romantic creation from the late 18C. Lost in its wooded ravine, it seems to have fallen into decay quite early in the 19C but has been restored and linked in poetic counterpoint to more formal contemporary gardens and modern sculpture placed in the woodland. A barn-like structure among outbuildings, the work of the American artist, James Turrell *(see p 241)*, invites visitors to look anew at the heavens; modern sensibility is left far behind among the rock outcrops, deep shade and rushing stream of the ravine. Precipitous walks, steps and bridges, a winding stairway, a waterfall and, above all, a delightful thatched cottage orné, set in a grassy glen, all testify to the advanced taste of the Power family, in touch in this seemingly remote place with the latest trends in landscaping of the 1790s.

The ruined church in the village contains a famous effigy, the **Cantwell Knight** ★, a fine carving of a Norman nobleman, placed upright in the roofless nave; his head turned, his tall form (8ft/2.44m) clad in mail, his long shield bearing his coat of arms, he makes an awesome presence in this lonely spot.

★★**Jerpoint Abbey** ⊘ – *12mi/19km south of Kilkenny by R 700 and N 9 south from Thomastown.* The ruins on the banks of the Little Arrigle River, near its confluence with the Nore, are probably the most interesting and least ruined Cistercian remains in Ireland. Jerpoint was founded, probably as a Benedictine house, between 1160 and 1170 by one of the Kings of Ossory. In 1180 it became a daughter house of the Cistercian monastery at Baltinglass *(see ATHY)*.

In 1228 the community numbered 36 monks and 50 lay-brothers. After the Dissolution in 1540 the abbey was leased to the Earl of Ormond until the mid 17C.

The **Visitor Centre** presents an explanatory model of the abbey buildings.

The cruciform **church** has an aisled nave supported on stout Romanesque pillars; the transepts, which belong to the original late-12C construction, each have two chapels. In the **chancel** are the effigies of two bishops, one believed to be Felix O'Dulany, first abbot of Jerpoint and bishop of Ossory (1178–1202). On the north wall are remains of a 15C–16C wall painting showing the heraldic shields of some of Jerpoint's main benefactors. From the south transept a flight of wooden steps, on the site of the

B Lynch /Bord Fáilte, Dublin

Jerpoint Abbey Cloisters

night stairs, leads to the roof of the east range of the monastic buildings. The tower with its stepped Irish battlements dates from the 15C.

The columns of the 14C or 15C **cloisters** (restored) bear remarkable carvings of animals, saints and secular figures showing the clothing and armour worn in Ireland at that period.

★**Kells Priory** – *8mi/13km south of Kilkenny by R 697.* Beside the Kings River are the extensive ruins (5 acres/2ha) of a 14C–15C priory with a fortified enclosure. Little remains of the original monastery founded in 1193 by Geoffrey de Marisco with four Augustinian canons from Bodmin in Cornwall.

Edmund Rice Centre ⊘ – *Callan; 10mi/16km southwest of Kilkenny by N 76*. A museum is now housed in the cottage **birthplace** of Edmund Ignatius Rice (1762–1844), founder of the Christian Brothers, a teaching order which has played an important role in Irish education. The kitchen has a stone-flagged floor, open hearth and spinning wheel, as in Rice's day: the other rooms are similarly preserved with furniture of the period.

In the town of Callan (population 1 246) there are substantial remains of a 15C Augustinian priory.

Bród Tullaroan ⊘ – *10mi/16km west of Kilkenny by a minor road*. This heritage centre, the "Pride of Tullaroan", set in deep countryside, is devoted to the memory of **Lory Meagher**, the "prince of hurlers" who dominated the sport in Co Kilkenny in the 1920s and 1930s. The thatched farmhouse where he was born and lived has been restored and furnished to evoke the period around 1884, the year in which the Gaelic Athletic Association *(see p 37)* was founded, by Lory's father among others. The adjoining **Museum of Hurling** presents the regional history of the sport in fascinating detail.

Kilcooly Abbey – *21mi/32km northwest of Kilkenny by R 693; from Urlingford take R 689 south for 3.5mi/5.5km; 500yd/0.5km on foot from parish church car park*. The substantial ruins of this Cistercian abbey, which was founded around 1200, include a massive tower over the crossing and a cloister. Among a number of fine monuments is the carved effigy of a knight. The abbey is protected by a ha-ha and formidably buttressed. In the field stands a large dovecot.

★ Dunmore Cave ⊘ – *7mi/11km north of Kilkenny by N 77 and N 78*. One of the few large caves in Ireland, it has fascinating formations, including stalagmites and stalactites. The visitor centre explains its geology and history. In 928 the Vikings massacred 1 000 people in the cave, which is known in legend as one of the three darkest places in Ireland.

Castlecomer – *11.5mi/19km north of Kilkenny by N 77 and N 78*. Population 1 396. The village was laid out in the Italian-village style in 1635 by Sir Christopher Wandesforde, whose family mined the coal in this region for three centuries. The coalmining industry is now defunct but in Reddy's Coalmine Lounge, where the main bar is decorated like a mine, lumps of Castlecomer coal are on show, together with items of mining equipment such as lamps, picks and shovels.

For adjacent sights see CAHER, CARLOW, CASHEL, CLONMEL, NEW ROSS.

KILLALA ★

CILL ALA – Co Mayo – Population 713
Michelin Atlas pp 94–95 and Map 923 – E 5

Killala is a quiet seaside resort overlooking Killala Bay at the mouth of the River Moy, which is partially blocked by Bartragh Island, a narrow sandbank. It has a sandy beach, and land and water sports facilities; the harbour **warehouses** show that it was once a busy port. The remote little town enjoys a place of disproportionate importance in the history of Ireland, as it was here that the French first halted when they invaded in 1798.

The Year of the French

In August 1798 a force of 1 067 French revolutionaries under General Humbert landed at Kilcummin, a hamlet on the west shore of Killala Bay. In Killala John Moore was appointed President of the Provisional Government of Connaught by General Humbert. As the French advanced inland they were joined by a growing number of enthusiastic but ill-equipped Irishmen.

The first place of importance to fall to them was Ballina where their capture of the town is commemorated by the Humbert Monument.

Then came their first encounter with General Lake, who was in command of a vastly superior force of militia and yeomanry. Despite being outnumbered General Humbert routed his opponent and the retreat of General Lake's cavalry became known as the **Races of Castlebar**.

Another monument at Carrignagat *(south of Sligo on the N 4 before Collooney, east side)* marks the site of their third victory over the English. Humbert then moved southeast in the hope of avoiding the English army and of joining up with the United Irishmen but the latter had already been defeated and he himself was overcome at Ballinamuck, near Longford. The French were taken prisoner; the Irish were hanged as traitors.

The events of the 1798 Rebellion were re-enacted in Killala in 1981 during the filming of Thomas Flanagan's historical novel, *The Year of the French*.

To the west lies North Mayo, one of the most remote and least inhabited regions of Ireland. The north coast confronts the Atlantic with a line of dramatic sea cliffs broken only by **Broad Haven**, a broad bay of sandy coves, narrow sea-inlets and tiny habitations, flanked by **Benwee Head** (829ft/253m – *east*) and **Erris Head** (285ft/87m – *west on the Belmullet Peninsula*). Inland the country is largely covered in Atlantic blanket bog (400sq mi/1 036km²), which is extensively exploited to gene-rate electricity; the turf is harvested by machine to fuel the power station at Bellacorick which is supplemented by wind turbines. In fine weather the bog gleams gold in the sun but when the sky is overcast the prospect is bleak like the entrance to the under-world.

Killala Cathedral – The present Anglican **cathedral** *(floodlit at night)* was erected in 1670 by Thomas Ottway, Bishop of Killala, using rubble and stones from the ruined medieval cathedral – south doorway and Gothic east window – and is fur-nished with box pews. In the graveyard stands a 12C **round tower**, which is built of limestone (84ft/25m high); the cap is a 19C reconstruction; it is all that remains of the monastery founded by Muiredach, the first bishop of Killala, who was appointed by St Patrick in the 5C. There is also a 9C **souterrain** with many cham-bers *(unfenced)*.

Killala Harbour

Slide File, Dublin

EXCURSIONS

North Mayo Coast

Rathfran Abbey – *3mi/4.8km north of Killala by R 314; after crossing the river turn right; at the crossroads turn right.* The ruins of a Dominican friary, which was founded in 1274, lie close to the shore. The long rectangular church, which has a panel depicting the Crucifixion over the west door, was lit by lancet windows. In the 15C some of the south windows were built up, an aisle was added and part of the nave was rebuilt. Little remains of the two cloisters and the 16C conven-tual buildings. Although the friary was suppressed and the buildings burned by Sir Richard Bingham, the English Governor of Connaught in 1590, the friars remained in the neighbourhood until the 18C.

Breastagh Ogam Stone – *5mi/8km north of Killala by R 314. After crossing the river turn right. Climb the stile into the field (left).* The stone (8ft/2.5m high), pro-bably a Bronze Age standing stone, is marked with the linear Ogam script but the inscription is only partially legible.

★**Downpatrick Head** – *25mi/40km north of Killala by R 314; after crossing the river turn right; continue via Carrowmore, Killogeary and Rathlackan.* North of Killogeary the road follows the coast providing a fine view of the broad sands of Lackan Bay and then of Downpatrick Head projecting flat-topped and blunt into the sea against the backdrop of Benwee Head.

Turn right to Downpatrick Head; 20min there and back on foot from car park to cliff.

The projecting headland is undermined by the sea which appears at the bottom of a **blow hole** *(fenced off)*. Just offshore stands Dunbriste, a rock stack surmounted by a prehistoric earthwork, which was probably detached from the mainland in 1393. The view includes *(east)* Benbulben and the Dartry Mountains north of Sligo, *(southeast)* the Ox Mountains (Slieve Gamph), *(southwest)* the Nephin Beg Mountains, *(west)* the cliffs to Benwee Head and the Stags of Broadhaven offshore.

Céide Fields ⊙ – *22mi/36km north of Ballina by R 314 via Ballycastle.* Under the blanket bog, which covers most of North Mayo, lies an extensive Stone Age monument – the stones of the houses and the walls which divided the gardens and fields of people who lived near the Céide Cliffs over 50 centuries ago and were contemporaries of the people who built the tombs in the Boyne Valley *(see BOYNE VALLEY)*. Using iron probes and bamboo markers the fields have been mapped over a wide area (4sq mi/10km²) although they extend even further.

The **Visitor Centre** explains the geological structure of the terrain, the development of the bog which now covers the site to a depth of 13ft/4m and the archeological interpretation of the site. From the evidence found on the site – a primitive type of plough, postholes – deductions can be made about the lifestyle of the Stone Age farmers, who cleared the land of primeval forest and piled up the stones to create enclosed fields and houses. From the roof gallery there is a good view of the site.

Belderrig Prehistoric Farm ⊙ – *West of Belderrig by the coast road (sign).* The centrepiece of the **visitor centre** is a large and twisted Scots pine 4 400 years old, which was found in the vicinity. In the prehistoric era this site was a farming estate; it is now reduced to a circle of earth marked with post-stones and hearth-stones.

Moy Estuary

★**Moyne Abbey** – *1mi/1.6km southeast of Killala by the coast road; 10min there and back on foot across the fields.* The ruins, which stand near the water, are those of a Franciscan friary, founded in the mid 15C. Although part of the original plan, the six-storey tower was added later. The church has been considerably enlarged on the south side. The cloisters date from the end of the 15C; the east range consists of the sacristy and the chapter-house; the kitchen and refectory on the north side are built over a stream. Although the buildings were burned by Sir Richard Bingham, the English Governor of Connaught in 1590, some friars continued in residence until the 17C; the last one died in about 1800.

★**Rosserk Abbey** – *4mi/6.4km south of Killala by R 314; after 1.5mi/2.4km bear left.* The well-preserved ruins on the Rosserk River, a tributary of the Moy, belong to the first Franciscan house (mid-15C) to be built in Ireland. The decorative features of the church include the carved west door, the east window, the south transept window and the carved piscina in the chancel which shows a round tower, angels and the instruments of the Passion. From the cloisters, stairs lead up to the dormitories and refectory above the vaulted rooms on the ground floor. In the 16C the friary was burned by Sir Richard Bingham, the English Governor of Connaught.

Ballina – *7.5mi/13km south of Killala by R 314.* Population 6 563. Ballina, the largest town in North Mayo and the seat of the bishop of the Roman Catholic diocese of Killala, straddles the River Moy. The **cathedral** of St Muiredach on the east bank between the bridges was built in the 19C next to the ruins of a late-14C Augustinian **friary** founded by the O'Dowd family; the decorated west door and window of the friary church date from the 15C.

For adjacent sights see ACHILL ISLAND, CASTLEBAR, KNOCK, SLIGO, WESTPORT.

The length of time given in this guide
– for touring allows time to enjoy the views and the scenery;
– for sightseeing is the average time required for a visit.

KILLALOE★

CILL DALUA – Co Clare – Population 972
Michelin Atlas p 84 and Map 923 – G 9

The village, a popular fishing centre, at the end of Lough Derg, is the southern limit for cruising and yachting on the Shannon.

★**St Flannan's Cathedral** ⊙ – The **cathedral**, which stands on the site of a monastery founded in the 6C by St Molua and dedicated to his successor, was begun by Dónall Mór O'Brien in 1185. By 1225 it had been rebuilt in the present mixture of Romanesque and Gothic. It contains a 12C **Romanesque doorway**, a 12C High Cross from Kilfenora *(see The BURREN)*, a cross shaft carved c 1000 bearing a dual inscription in both **Ogam** and **Viking Runic script** asking for a prayer for Thorgrim, and an oak screen erected in 1885.

St Flannan's Oratory – Beside the cathedral stands the vaulted nave of a 12C Romanesque church incorporating a loft beneath the stone roof.

St Molua's Oratory – The oratory, which stands beside the Roman Catholic church at the top of the hill, was built c 1000 on Friar's Island in the Shannon; it was transferred stone by stone when its original location was submerged by the hydro-electric scheme in the 1920s.

Heritage Centre ⊙ – The display traces in pictures and text the history of Killaloe from the birth of Brian Ború, through many years of fishing and cruising to the Civil War and the building of the Ardnacrushna dam to provide electricity.

EXCURSIONS

Graves of the Leinstermen – *4mi/6.4km northeast of Ballina by R 494 and a minor road (sign); car park*. The group of prehistoric stones on the west face of Tountinna (1 512ft/461m) is probably one of the first inhabited places in Ireland. There are commanding **views**★ over much of Lough Derg to Slieve Bernagh.

Béal Ború Earthwork – *1mi/1.6km north by R 463; turn right (sign) into a track (0.5mi/0.8km); cross the fields*. This large circular earthwork surrounded by a deep ditch and a grove of beech and pine trees is set immediately above the Lough Derg shoreline. From its name, which means "Pass of the Tributes", Brian Ború took his title.

Tuamgraney – *10mi/16km north by R 463*. The village is known as the birthplace of the novelist, Edna O'Brien *(see p 62)*. The **East Clare Heritage Centre** ⊙, which documents the local history, is housed in St Cronan's Church (Anglican), which is believed to be the oldest church in continuous use in Ireland or Great Britain. The west portion with its lintelled doorway dates from c 969; the east end of the building is 12C; note the Romanesque windows. Beside it stands a 15C tower house *(restoration in progress)*. The **Memorial Park** *(300m west of the village)*, is planted with the indigenous trees and shrubs of Co Clare in commemoration of the famine victims of the Great Hunger of 1845–52.

★**Holy Island** ⊙ – *16mi/26km north by R 463. Accessible by boat from Mount-shannon*. The **round tower** (80ft/24m high) and the extensive remains of six churches mark the site of a monastic settlement founded by St Caimin in the 7C. The **bargaining stone** has a hollow channel through which monks would apparently shake hands to seal an agreement.

For adjacent sights see BIRR, ENNIS, LIMERICK, NENAGH.

KILLARNEY★★

CILL AIRNE – Co Kerry – Population 8 809
Michelin Atlas p 77 and Map 923 – D 11

Killarney is set on the east shore of Lough Leane in Killarney National Park. The site is dominated by the Macgillycuddy's Reeks which include the **Gap of Dunloe** and culminate in the highest peak in Ireland, Carrauntoohill (3 414ft/1 041m). The town is an ideal touring centre not far from Farranfore airport *(north)*.

Founding of Killarney – Early in the 17C Sir Valentine Browne (1591–1633) moved from Molahiffe *(north)*, acquired in 1584 by his English grandfather, to Ross Castle and began to develop a village round Killarney church. By the 1620s the village was described as having 40 "good English houses"; 20 years later the Cromwellian wars brought destruction. Thomas Browne (1726–95), the 4th Viscount Kenmare, laid out the present street plan and created a neat town of slated houses and shops. He also introduced linen and woollen manufacturing. Tourism began in the 19C.

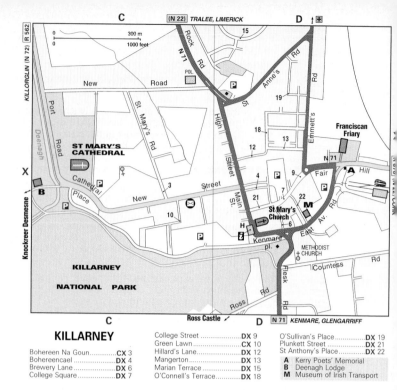

KILLARNEY

SIGHTS

★**St Mary's Cathedral** (**CX**) ⊙ – The Roman Catholic cathedral spire (285ft/87m high) is a prominent local landmark. The church was designed by Augustus Pugin; the austere unplastered interior reveals the various hues of the limestone. Although the foundation stone was laid in 1842, work was discontinued between 1848 and 1853 and the building was used as a shelter for famine victims. The cathedral was consecrated in 1855 and adapted for the new liturgy in 1972–73.

Museum of Irish Transport ⊙ (**DX M**) – The many veteran and vintage cars, posters and magazines on display make this museum a Mecca for motor enthusiasts. The Silver Stream, designed in 1907–09, is the only car of its type ever built; the 1910 Wolseley which belonged to Sir Jocelyn Gore Booth *(see p 245)* was driven by Countess Markievicz and William Butler Yeats. Mercedes produced the 540K (1955) and the 300SL (1938) gullwing models.

> ### Cinematic History
>
> *The Dawn*, a famous Irish film set in the War of Independence, was shot in Killarney between 1933 and 1934, with a cast of 250, mainly local amateurs; its initiator was Tom Cooper, a local cinema owner. Shooting usually took place on Thursdays, early closing day. Photographs of this production, of *The Quiet Man*, filmed in 1952 at Cong, and of *Ryan's Daughter*, shot at Banna Strand in 1968, can be seen in the bar of the Three Lakes Hotel.

St Mary's Church (**DX**) ⊙ – The Anglican church was built in 1870 in the Early-English style on the site of an earlier 17C church. One of the stained-glass windows is a reproduction of Holman Hunt's *Light of the World*. Among the several interesting memorials is one *(north side of the nave)* to the Revd Arthur Hyde, great-grandfather of Douglas Hyde *(see BOYLE)*, first president of Ireland.

Franciscan Friary (**DX**) – The friary, built in 1860 in a style similar to Muckross Friary *(see below)*, contains a stained-glass window *(entrance hall)* by Harry Clarke.

Kerry Poets' Memorial (**DX A**) – The memorial was created in 1940 by Seamus Murphy to commemorate Co Kerry's four best-known Gaelic poets.

EXCURSIONS

★★★❶ **Killarney national park** ⊙

Round tour of 30mi/48km. South of Killarney by N 71. Information Centre at Knockreer House and Muckross House and also Torc Waterfall (July to September only).

The park (39sq mi/101km²) embraces the three lakes – Lower (Lough Leane), Middle (Muckross Lake) and Upper which are linked by the Long Range River – the foreshore and the mountain slopes south and west. The varied landscape of gardens and woodland, lakes and mountains, peat bogs and heathland provides many miles of beautiful **walks** to suit all tastes. The nucleus of the National Park was the Muckross Estate, presented to the Irish State in 1932 as the Bourn Vincent Memorial Park (9 984 acres/4 000ha), to which have been added Knockreer, Ross Island and Innisfallen, formerly part of the Kenmare Estate. In 1981 the park was designated a Biosphere Reserve by UNESCO.

> ## Out and about around Killarney
>
> The **National Park** may be explored on land or by water. There are many miles of **walks** to suit all tastes at Ross Castle, Muckross House and through the Gap of Dunloe. Trips in a **jaunting car** are available at Muckross House and through Gap of Dunloe, which may also be explored on foot or astride a **pony**. There are **boat trips** on Lough Leane from Ross Castle or as part of the trip through the Gap of Dunloe. There are **information centres** at Muckross House and at Torc Waterfall *(summer only)*.

Knockreer Demesne ⊙ – *Footpath to Ross Castle (see below)*. The grounds of Knockreer House extend westwards from Killarney to the shore of Lough Leane; the entrance from the town is marked by a thatched cottage, **Deenagh Lodge** (**CX B**).

★**Ross Castle** ⊙ – *1mi/1.6km south by N 71 and a minor road west (sign). Boat trips to Innisfallen Island. Footpath to Knockreer Demesne (see above)*. The castle, the last castle in Munster to hold out against Cromwellian forces (1652), who cap-

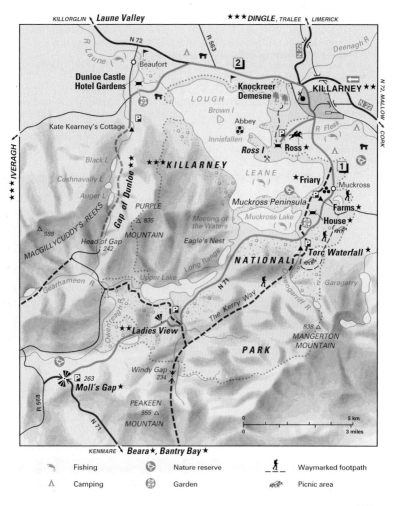

⤸	Fishing	⊛	Nature reserve	🚶	Waymarked footpath
Λ	Camping	⊛	Garden		Picnic area

tured it only by attacking it from armed boats, was built on the shore of Lough Leane in the 15C by one of the O'Donoghue Ross chieftains. A fortified bawn reinforced by circular flanking towers surrounded the rectangular keep. The four floors, containing the parlour, the bedchamber and the Great Hall, have been restored using medieval building techniques and furnished in the style appropriate to the early-15C to late-16C period.

Ross Island – The promontory, where there were active copper mines in the early 19C, extends into Lough Leane and is traversed by a profusion of tree- and flower-lined alleys. Shelley was particularly impressed by the arbutus (strawberry tree) during his visit in 1813. There are fine views of Lough Leane in its mountain setting and of the islands.

On **Innisfallen** *(access by boat from Ross Castle)* are the ruins of an abbey on the site of a 7C monastery.

★**Muckross Friary** ◷ – *Car park; footpath to Muckross House.* The friary, also called Muckross Abbey, was founded for the Franciscans in 1448 and constructed over a period of 59 years; it features a mid-15C nave and choir – the latter lit by a widely splayed window of four lights crowned by intersecting bar tracery – a broad central tower and a south transept built about 1500. The 22-arch cloisters north of the church were built in four different phases; the domestic buildings include the dormitory, refectory and kitchen. The three-storey building north of the choir probably contained the Sacristy and the Sacristan's lodging.

★**Muckross House and Farms** ◷ – *Car park; footpath to Muckross Friary.* Many of the rooms in the Elizabethan-style mansion (1840–43) are furnished in the style of the early 20C: the **drawing room**, **library** and **dining room**, with their lavish decorations; the nursery containing dolls made c 1870, an old-fashioned bathroom and a bedroom with a four-poster bed.

In the **basement** the old wine cellar is filled with ancient bottles; butter churns are preserved in the dairy. Regional crafts are recalled in **working displays**: cobbling, bookbinding, woodcarving and weaving *(cloth on sale in the craft shop)*. The printing room displays wooden and metal type and hand-operated presses.

The beautiful **gardens** extend down to the lakeside.

The **Muckross Peninsula**, which divides Lough Leane from Muckross (Middle) Lake, contains one of the finest yew woods in Europe *(nature trails)*.

The **traditional farms** *(1hr on foot)* are worked in the manner which prevailed in Ireland in the early 20C. There are several buildings, from the large farm to the labourer's cottage, all furnished in the appropriate manner with dressers, presses, settle-beds, domestic utensils and farming equipment. Live animals inhabit the yards and fields. Indoors turf fires burn in the hearths and the staff, in period costume, describe how it used to be and demonstrate bread-making, washing clothes by hand etc.

Muckross Gardens

SLIDE FILE

Torc Waterfall

Slide File, Dublin

★**Torc Waterfall** – *Car park.* The **cascade** (60ft/18m) is one of the highest in Ireland. The adjacent viewpoint *(173 steps)* provides a fine view of the lakes.

★★**Ladies View** – *Car park.* The panoramic views of Macgillycuddy's Reeks and of the Upper Lake dotted with islands appealed greatly to Queen Victoria and her entourage when they visited Killarney in 1861.

★**Moll's Gap** – *Car park.* The pass (863ft/263m) provides *(north)* a striking view of the Gap of Dunloe in Macgillycuddy's Reeks and *(south)* a glimpse of the Kenmare River.

★★② Gap of Dunloe

Round tour of 24mi/38km. From Killarney take N 72 west; after 4mi/6km turn left. As the narrow unsurfaced road through the gorge is unsuitable for vehicular traffic, park at the north end of the gorge at Kate Kearney's Cottage and proceed on foot or hire a **pony** *or* **pony and trap***.*

There are also **organized round trips** ⊘ *(6–7hr) from Killarney by bus to Kate Kearney's Cottage, by pony or pony and trap through the Gap to Lord Brandon's Cottage, by boat across the three lakes and by bus back to Killarney.*

The jarvies and their carriages plying for hire throng the roadsides and the forecourt of **Kate Kearney's Cottage** ⊘, originally an old coaching inn kept by the beautiful Kate, who served illicit whiskey *(potheen)* to 19C tourists.

The road through the narrow rock-strewn gorge, a U-shaped glacial breach (1500ft/457m deep), leads up past Black Lake, Cushnavally Lake and Auger Lake to the Head of the Gap (794ft/242m).

As the track descends into the Gearhameen Valley, where red deer graze, there is a fine view of the Upper Lake, bordered by native oakwoods and backed by Mangerton Mountain (2756ft/838m).

Laune Valley

Dunloe Castle Hotel Gardens ⊘ – *5mi/8km west of Killarney by N 72; after 4mi/6km turn left.* From the modern hotel the luxuriant gardens, partly enclosed by grey stone walls, extend to the 13C tower house overlooking the River Laune and the River Loe with a clear view of the Dunloe Gap.

The botanic collection consists of exotic specimens from all parts of the world – the Killarney Strawberry tree, South African lilies, Australian gums, New Zealand cabbage trees and cherries, Japanese maples, North American dogwood, Chilean fir trees, South American fuchsias.

There are also rare specimens such as the Chinese swamp cypress and the "Headache" tree with its aromatic leaves.

Kerry Woollen Mills ⓥ – *9mi/14km west of Killarney by N 72; after 8mi/13km turn right at sign; after 1mi/1.6km turn left and then right.* Woollen goods have been produced here for over 200 years. The original mill buildings contain the showroom and retail shop. Visitors may tour the modern mill and watch the spinning, dyeing and weaving which results in rugs and blankets for people and horses, tweeds for clothes and furnishings, scarves and shawls, knitwear and knitting yarn.

For adjacent sights see BANTRY BAY, BEARA PENINSULA, DINGLE PENINSULA, IVERAGH PENINSULA.

KILMALLOCK ★

CILL MOCHEALLÓG – Co Limerick – Population 1 311
Michelin Atlas p 84 and Map 923 – G 10

This small town on the River Loobagh in the Golden Vale, which grew up round an abbey founded by St Mocheallog in the 7C, has preserved many of its historic buildings; from the 14C to the 17C it was the seat of the FitzGeralds, Earls of Desmond, and one of the most important towns in the province of Munster. In 1568 James Fitzmaurice set fire to Kilmallock to prevent it from being taken by the English. During the Cromwellian wars in the 1640s it surrendered to Cromwell's forces; the extensive walls were later restored but large sections were finally destroyed in the 1690 Williamite wars.

SIGHTS

★**Kilmallock Abbey** – The 13C Dominican foundation was lavishly endowed and was given to the Corporation of Kilmallock by Queen Elizabeth I following the Dissolution of the Monasteries (1540). A fine transept window survives; the tower (90ft/27m high) is gracefully supported by narrow arches but a substantial part of one corner has collapsed. At the entrance to the abbey is a small town **museum**.

★**Collegiate Church** (Roman Catholic) – In the 13C church, dedicated to St Peter and St Paul, the walls and arches of the nave and south transept are largely intact; the tower is part of an ancient round tower.

Blossom's Gate – The sole survivor of the five gates, which pierced the walls of the medieval town, spans the entrance to the town from the west.

Town Walls – A substantial portion of wall survives intact between Blossom's Gate and the vicinity of the Collegiate Church.

King's Castle – The 15C tower house occupies the site of an earlier fortress built to guard the Loobagh valley. During the Parliamentary Wars (1645–51) it was used as an arsenal by the Irish and later as a hospital by the Cromwellians.

15C House – *Wolfe Tone Street.* In this building next to the river bridge in 1795 there died a Gaelic poet of great renown, Aindrias Mac Craith, who composed *An Mangaire Súgach*; he was buried in the graveyard of the Collegiate Church *(see above)*.

EXCURSIONS

★**Monasteranenagh Abbey** – *14mi/22.5km north of Kilmallock by R 512; in Holycross turn left.* The impressive ruins, parts of which survive to roof level, lie beside the River Camoge. The Cistercian monastery, colonized by monks from Mellifont, was founded in the 12C by Turlough O'Brien, King of Thomond, as a mark of thanksgiving for defeating the Danes in the Battle of Rathmore in 1148.

★**Lough Gur Interpretive Centre** ⓥ – *10mi/16km north of Kilmallock by R 512; in Holycross turn right.* The area around the lake is one of the longest-inhabited districts in Ireland; excavations have contributed information about life in the Stone Age. Many Stone and Bronze Age relics, as well as models of stone circles and burial chambers, are on display in the **visitor centre**, which also provides an audio-visual film illustrating the life of Neolithic man in this region.

Irish Dresden ⓥ – *15mi/24km west of Kilmallock by R 515.* The delicate and elaborate porcelain figures represent musicians and dancers, ladies in flounced skirts made of layers of simulated net, angels and figures for the Christmas crib, and birds and animals. The inspiration for such delicate craftsmanship originated in Vollestedt in Germany. After the Second World War, the business struggled on until 1960, when Johanna, great-niece of the founder, and her husband, Oscar Saar, moved to Dromcolliher, where they trained a new workforce who use the old German master moulds and have also created new ones reflecting the factory's new surroundings.

De Valera Museum ⊘ – *Bruree ; 6.5mi/10km north-west of Kilmallock by R 518.* The museum and heritage centre, which celebrates Eamon de Valera, former President of the Republic, is housed in the old national school in **Bruree** (population 265) between the ancient six-arch bridge over the River Maigue and the old mill with its perfectly-preserved mill wheel. On display are de Valera's school copy-books and his desk with his initials carved

---

Eamon de Valera (1882–1975)

As a young boy Eamon de Valera (1882–1975) lived with his uncle near Bruree where he attended the village school, which has been converted into a museum in his memory. He played a leading part in the Easter Rising in 1916 for which he was condemned to death but was saved from execution by his American birth. He was first elected to Parliament for Ennis in 1917. Later he became Prime Minister *(Taoiseach)* and then President of the Republic.

---

into the top. Among the other relics are many 19C artefacts and tools, such as a thatcher's comb and querns for grinding corn.

De Valera walked to school from the **cottage** where he lived with his uncle *(1.5mi/2.4km north on the road to Athlacca).*

For adjacent sights see ADARE, LIMERICK, MALLOW, TIPPERARY.

KILRUSH ★

CILL ROIS – Co Clare – Population 2 740
Michelin Atlas p 83 and Map 923 – D 10

Kilrush, the second-largest town in the county and the trading centre of southwest Clare, is situated on the north bank of the Shannon Estuary and linked to the south bank by the Shannon Car Ferry. Lively horse fairs are often held in the main square. In the 19C the area became popular with the people of Limerick as a holiday resort. There are good beaches at Cappa and Brew's Bridge and a marina at Merchant's Quay. In summer families of bottle-nosed dolphins can be seen sporting in the Shannon Estuary.

Kilrush Heritage Centre ⊘ – *Main Square.* The Market House (1808) now presents a display explaining the role of the local landlord, the Vandeleur family, from the building of Kilrush in the 18C, through the Napoleonic Wars and the Great Famine, to the evictions of 1888.

Kilrush Forest Park ⊘ – *Ferry Road.* The magnificent woodlands (420 acres/

In and around Kilrush

The marina at Merchant's Quay provides 120 berths, a boatyard and yacht hire; there are **boat trips** to Scattery Island as well as cruises and deep-sea fishing expeditions; **Dolphin watch trips** ⊘ depart from Kilrush Marina and from Carrigaholt.

The **Shannon car ferry** ⊘ *(from Killimer 5.5mi/8.8km east of Kilrush) carries vehicles and passengers to the south shore of the Shannon Estuary.*

168ha) of the Vandeleur demesne remain but the family mansion (1803) was destroyed by fire in 1897. The stables and old walled garden are being restored.

Scattery Island Visitor Centre ⊘ – *West of Merchant's Quay.* The centre provides information about the history and wildlife of Scattery Island *(see below).*

EXCURSIONS

★**Scattery Island** ⊘ – *Accessible by boat from Kilrush.* Its 6C monastery, founded by St Senan, whose most famous pupil was St Ciaran of Clonmacnoise, and the remains of five medieval churches are dominated by the **round tower** (115ft/33m high), which has its doorway at ground level.

West Clare Railway ⊘ – *Moyasta: 4mi/6.4km northwest of Kilrush by N 67 opposite Clancy's pub.* Visitors may take a short ride on a restored section of the West Clare Railway, which originally ran between Ennis *(see ENNIS)* and Kilkee. There are plans to restore more of the line.

Kilkee *(Cill Chaoi) – Population 1 315. 8.5mi/13.5km northwest of Kilrush by N 67.* This seaside resort is set deep in Moore Bay with a long promenade embracing a wide horseshoe-shaped sandy beach with a gentle slope. The Duggerna rocks at the entrance to the bay are accessible at low tide.

Slide File, Dublin

Kilkee Beach

Loop Head Peninsula – *Poor road surface in places*. West of Kilrush and Kilkee the land forms a peninsula, terminating in Loop Head. The treeless landscape is divided into fields by earthbanks rather than the hedges or flagstones found further inland.

On the south coast **Carrigaholt Tower House** stands beside the pier. It was built in the 16C by the McMahon family, who once controlled the peninsula, and was last besieged in 1649. From the top of the tower there are fine **views** south to the north Kerry coast *(3mi/5km)*.

Off the north coast near Moneen a huge natural arch, the **Bridge of Ross ★** *(sign)*, formed by the action of the sea, is visible from the edge of the cliffs.

Loop Head is surmounted by the lighthouse (277ft/84m above sea-level) which was built on the headland in 1854; in 1869 the light was changed from fixed to intermittent. It is the third light on the site; the first, built in about 1670, was one of four stone-vaulted cottage lights which had a coal-burning brazier on a platform on the roof.

For adjacent sights see ADARE, ENNIS, LIMERICK, TRALEE.

KINSALE ★★
CIONN TSÁILE – Co Cork – Population 2 007
Michelin Atlas p 78 and Map 923 – G 12

Kinsale is a most attractive town with narrow lanes and slate-hung houses overlooking the broad estuary of the River Bandon. It is also the gourmet capital of Ireland with many excellent restaurants; a **gourmet festival** is held in October.
There are attractive views of the town from the tree-lined walk up to the **Carmelite Church**.

HISTORICAL NOTES

In 1223, soon after the Anglo-Norman invasion of Ireland, Kinsale passed by marriage to the de Courcy family. In 1333 the town received its first charter from Edward III. The most outstanding event in the town's history was the **Siege of Kinsale** in 1601–02, when a Spanish force occupied Kinsale and was besieged by English armies; an Irish attempt to raise the siege was defeated. The defeat at Kinsale meant the beginning of the end of the old Gaelic order and clan system. In 1641 the town declared for Cromwell and so was spared much damage. Until the end of the 18C no native Irish were to settle within its walls.

Similar lack of success attended James II who landed at Kinsale in March 1689 in an attempt to regain his kingdom; after the Battle of the Boyne *(see p 91)* he returned to exile in France from Duncannon in Waterford Harbour.

During the 17C Kinsale flourished as a shipbuilding port for the Royal Navy, which constructed *HMS Kinsale* here in 1700. The 18C trend towards larger ships rendered the docks obsolete. The closure of the railway line from Cork in 1931 also caused a decline in the economy, but since the 1960s Kinsale has enjoyed a considerable revival as a centre for tourism, yachting and deep-sea fishing.

SIGHTS

★**St Multose Church** (Anglican) ⊘ – The original church was built about 1190 and dedicated to St Multose or Eltin, the patron saint of Kinsale, who lived in the 6C. The tower doorway is 12C Irish Romanesque; the west doorway was built at a slightly later date. A statue of St Multose stands in a niche over the west door. The interior contains some interesting 16C gravestones.

★**Kinsale Regional Museum** ⊘ – Housed in the late-17C town hall, which is surmounted by distinctive Dutch gables, the museum has many relics of old Kinsale, including several royal charters. In the loggia is the Toll Board listing charges on goods coming to market, and a gun from *HMS St Albans*, which foundered in Kinsale harbour on 8 December 1693. The great hall is associated with the famous inquest on the victims of the *Lusitania (see below)*. The exhibition room displays a variety of items: Kinsale-made lace which, like the Kinsale cloak, was popular for over a century; footwear and cutlery belonging to the Kinsale giant, **Patrick Cotter O'Brien** (1706–1806), who made a lucrative career on the English stage. There are additional displays at Desmond Castle and at Charles Fort *(see below)*.

Desmond Castle ⊘ – The three-storey tower house was built in the late 15C or early 16C by the Earls of Desmond as a custom-house, as the site was then close to the harbour. During the siege of Kinsale it was used as a magazine and then reverted to being a custom-house until 1641. Subsequently it was used as a gaol for French and other foreign prisoners, hence its other name the "French Prison". It now houses a **Museum of Wine** reflecting the days when Kinsale was a port, bringing in wine from the continent of Europe.

EXCURSIONS

★**Kinsale Harbour**

There is a pleasant walk *(1.5mi/2.4km)* along the east bank of the Bandon estuary to **Summercove**; the single village street dips down to a minute harbour where English ships landed guns and supplies for their army during the siege of Kinsale (1601–02). From the graveyard of St Catherine's Anglican Church there are extensive **views**★ across to the west side of the harbour.

The star-shaped fortress, **Charles Fort**★ ⊘ *(up the hill)*, was begun about 1670 and in use until 1922. Many of the buildings now surrounding the quadrangle of greensward are derelict but the old ordnance-store houses an exhibition, and a 19C fire engine occupies the Fire Engine House (restored). From the fort there are extensive **views** of Kinsale harbour.

The harbour was guarded on the west side by **James Fort** *(cross the bridge over the Bandon River and turn left; after 0.5mi/0.8km park; 0.5mi/0.8km on foot)* which was built in 1604 but is less well preserved than Charles Fort; only the central tower, blockhouse and portions of the defensive walls are still partially intact.

Slide File, Dublin

Kinsale

> **Lusitania ★**
>
> On the seabed (12mi/19km south) lies the wreck of the *Lusitania*, torpedoed on 7 May 1915; its sinking precipitated the entry of the United States into the First World War. Among the 1 500 who lost their lives was Sir Hugh Lane, who established the Municipal Gallery of Modern Art in Dublin.

The harbour entrance is protected by the **Old Head of Kinsale** *(from the river bridge take R 600 west and R 604 south)*. On the top of the headland stand the ruins of a 15C de Courcy fort. The road stops just short of the modern lighthouse, which replaced one built in 1683.

★Carbery Coast *38mi/61km west of Kinsale by R 600*

The south coast of Co Cork is penetrated by a number of sea-inlets, some framed by woodland, and offers many attractive views of land and sea.

★**Timoleague** – Population 304. The village on the Argideen estuary is dominated by a ruined **Franciscan friary ★**, founded in 1320 and plundered by Oliver Cromwell in 1642. The extensive ruins include the cloisters and the outer yard, and *(0.5mi/0.8km south)* the ruins of a 12C leper hospital.
The ruins of **Barrymore Castle** (13C) are now surrounded by **gardens★** ⊘, maintained by the Travers family for the past 170 years, in which palm trees and mild-weather shrubs thrive.

★**Courtmacsherry** – *3mi/5km detour east by R 601*. Population 204. There is only one street, overlooking the estuary. The railway station closed in 1961. There are walks in the woods leading to Wood Point, and a pebble beach at Broadstrand Bay.

From Timoleague take R 600 west. Before the junction with the main road (N 71) turn left (sign).

Lios na gCon ⊘ – The 10C ringfort has been restored according to the evidence uncovered by a team of archeologists who conducted an excavation in 1987–88. The souterrain is still intact and the enclosing ditch and bank are well preserved and give a wide **view** of the surrounding country.

Clonakilty (**Cloich na Coillte**) – Population 2 576. The market town, founded in 1598, is renowned for its **black puddings**, which were first produced in the 1880s by Philip Harrington at 16 Sovereign Street (now Pearse Street). The celebrated water pump, known as the Wheel of Fortune *(at the junction of Connolly Street and Lamb Street Lower)*, was provided by the Earl of Shannon in 1890.
The town centre is distinguished by **Emmet Square**, an 18C Georgian square with a central garden, and by the use of Gaelic on many of the renovated shopfronts.
The **West Cork Heritage Centre★** ⊘, in the converted schoolhouse, traces the local history – minute-books of Clonakilty Corporation dating from 1675, photographs of *St Maloga*, the extraordinary steam engine that once worked the railway line to Courtmacsherry, extensive material on the War of Independence and on Michael Collins who was born at Sam's Cross *(3mi/5km west)*.
The **West Cork Model Railway Village** ⊘, which is set in the 1940s, is a delight for young children, who should enjoy following the trains round the track and reading the historical and environmental captions at each station and halt.
The peninsula, Inchydoney Island *(3mi/5km south by the causeway road)*, is renowned for its sandy beaches; the large grass-covered spit of land jutting south into the sea is known as the "Virgin's Bank".

From Clonakilty take N 71 west.

Rosscarbery – Population 455. This small village is built round an enormous quadrangular square. **St Fachtna's Cathedral** ⊘ (Anglican) is a 12C Romanesque building, restored in 1612, with an elaborately-carved west doorway. In AD 590 St Fachtna, bishop and abbot, founded a monastic school at Rosscarbery. It was here that St Kilian *(see p 191)* was educated before setting out as a missionary to Würzburg in Germany. Two centuries later, in the 8C, St James, a monk from Würzburg, established a Benedictine community in Rosscarbery.

From Rosscarbery take R 597 west towards Glandore; after 4mi/6.4km turn left to the Drombeg Circle (sign).

★**Drombeg Stone Circle** – This is probably the most impressive of the 60 stone circles built in prehistoric times in west Cork. It has 14 evenly-spaced stones which form an enclosed circle (30ft/9m in diameter); usually the number of stones was uneven.
Of similar antiquity is the nearby cooking pit *(fulacht fiadh)*; hot stones can bring the water in the basin to boiling-point within 15 minutes.
Continue west on R 597 to Glandore.

★**Glandore** – The original Irish name for this small village, Cuan Dor meaning the "harbour of the oaks", recalls the extensive woods that covered much of west Cork 300 years ago.

The semicircular harbour faces two minute islands in the estuary called Adam and Eve; old sailing directions told sailors to "avoid Adam and hug Eve". A walk up the hill *(300yd/274m)* leads to Glandore's upper level.

For adjacent sights see COBH, CORK, SKIBBEREEN.

KNOCK

AN CNOC – Co Mayo – Population 2 575
Michelin Atlas p 95 and Map 923 – F 6

Until the end of the last century Knock was a quiet little village set on a wind-swept ridge in the middle of a blanket bog. Now it is always thronged with pilgrims visiting the Shrine and the Basilica and the souvenir shops.

Apparition at Knock

On a wet August evening in 1879 two of the village women reported seeing three figures – Mary, Joseph and St John – bathed in light against the south gable of the church. They called others to share the vision. A church commission examined the witnesses and accepted their account. Pilgrimages began the following year and many miraculous cures were reported. A second commission in 1936 confirmed the earlier finding. In 1957 the church was affiliated to the Basilica of St Mary Major in Rome and special indulgences are granted to pilgrims. In 1979, on the centenary of the apparition, Pope John Paul II visited Knock.

SIGHTS

Apparition Church – The south gable of the church where the apparition was seen has been glassed in to provide protection against the weather. Early pilgrims used to take away pieces of the wall plaster, believing it to have miraculous powers.

★**Basilica of Our Lady, Queen of Ireland** – The huge hexagonal church (48 687sq ft/4 524m²), which can hold 12 000 people, was consecrated in 1976 and designed by Dáithí P Hanly. A slender spire surmounts the tower which contains the Blessed Sacrament Chapel.

Inside above the chapel entrance hangs a large tapestry depicting the apparition, designed by Ray Carroll in the form of a hand-woven Donegal carpet. The centre of the church is occupied by the high altar.

The rest is divided into five chapels dedicated to the Sacred Heart, St John the Evangelist, Our Lady of Knock, St Joseph and St Columba, each represented by a statue. Each partition wall contains a replica of a church window from one of the four provinces of Ireland.

A covered ambulatory surrounding the church is supported on 12 pillars of red Mayo granite, and 32 pillars of stone from each of the 32 counties of Ireland.

Folk Museum ⊘ – A modern building, bearing the shields of the four provinces of Ireland – Ulster, Connaught, Leinster, Munster – houses a well-presented display illustrating life in the west of Ireland at the time of the Apparition; the exhibits are grouped under various themes: fishing; farming; craft tools; examples of Irish lace and Aran knitting; Irish glass and fine bone china; a cottage interior; transport; schoolroom; the development of Knock shrine and the life and times of Mgr James Horan, parish priest (1963–87). A life-size beehive cell, made by sculptress Imogen Stuart in Western Red cedarwood, recalls the dark domed dwellings used by the monks in the Celtic era.

EXCURSION

Connaught Airport – *9mi/14.5km north by N 17.* The first scheme (1950s) for an airport at Knock proposed a grass airstrip for domestic flights. Convinced that the Pope's visit to Knock in 1979 would attract even greater numbers of pilgrims, the parish priest, Mgr James Horan, launched a more ambitious project. Despite great public scepticism and government refusal to provide financial assistance, the airport opened in 1985. Since then it has been in constant use not only by pilgrims to Knock but by tourists to the west of Ireland. As the runway (8 000ft/2 438m) is long enough to accommodate jumbo jets, the airport is used for pilot training.

For adjacent sights see BOYLE, CASTLEBAR, CONG, ROSCOMMON, SLIGO, TUAM, WESTPORT.

LIMERICK ★★

LUIMNEACH – Co Limerick – Population 27 098
Michelin Atlas p 84 and Map 923 – G 9, 10

Set astride the River Shannon, Limerick, the main administrative and commercial centre of the mid-west region, is the fourth largest city in Ireland. The historic centre, known as English Town or King's Island, which contains many examples of medieval architecture, is set on the north bank of the Abbey River, an eastern tributary of the Shannon; Irish Town developed on the south bank; in the 18C the city extended further south with the construction of Newtown Pery (1769). In 1848 the city was linked to Dublin by rail. Many of Limerick's characteristic industries, such as bacon curing and grain milling, were developed during the last four decades of the 19C. After the foundation of the Irish Free State in 1922 the city suffered economic decline and heavy emigration, which have since been reversed owing to the construction of the hydro-electric scheme on the Shannon at Ardnacrushna *(east)*, which was completed in the 1920s, the opening of Shannon Airport in 1945, and the arrival since the 1960s of many new industries, notably computer manufacture and electronic engineering.

OUT AND ABOUT IN LIMERICK

Tourist Information Centre

Tourist Information Centre, Arthur's Quay ☎ 061 317 522; Fax 061 317 939.

Public Transport

For bus travel contact **Bus Eireann** ☎ 061 313 333; e-mail buse@cie.iol.ie or consult the website at www.infopoint.ie/buse

Sightseeing

Guided **walking tours** ⏱ of Limerick depart from St Mary's Action Centre, 44 Nicholas Street.

Shopping

The main shopping areas are **O'Connell Street** and **William Street**. The **Arthur's Quay Centre** is a shopping complex, housing more than 30 stores. Market-lovers should visit the **Milk Market**, Limerick's market quarter; the Saturday morning market offers a range of fresh produce, and every Friday there is an Arts and Crafts Market.

Entertainment

The **Belltable Arts Centre** is host to various theatre productions; for details of events ☎ 061 319 866. The **Theatre Royal** in Upper Cecil Street is popular for music and other forms of entertainment; for full listings ☎ 061 414 224. The **Savoy Cinema**, Bedford Row, boasts five screens – ☎ 061 311 900. The **Irish Chamber Orchestra** is now based in Limerick, although it does also tour; for a full programme ☎ 061 202 620. The University Concert Hall has a regular and varied programme of music; for bookings ☎ 061 331 549. There are several art galleries which mount temporary exhibitions – **Belltable Arts Centre** *(see above)*; The **Dolmen Gallery**, Honan's Quay, ☎ 061 417 929; The **Bourne Vincent Gallery**, Foundation Building, University of Limerick ☎ 061 202 700; **Angela Woulfe Gallery**, 16 Pery Square ☎ 061 310 164.

HISTORICAL NOTES

City of Sieges – Limerick takes its name from the Norse word *Laemrich* meaning "rich land". In 922 the Danish Vikings established a settlement from which they plundered the rich agricultural hinterland. For over a century the town was repeatedly attacked by Irish forces until Brian Ború, High King of Ireland, sacked it and banished the settlers. The Normans, who captured Limerick in 1194 following the death of Dónall Mór O'Brien, King of Munster, built 400 castles in the city and in the countryside and raised extensive city walls, some of which survive (**YZ**). During the relative calm of Norman rule Limerick gave strong allegiance to the English throne. Under King Henry II the kingdom of Thomond (North Munster) was split between the Normans, who were allocated the land south of the River Shannon in Co Limerick, and the O'Briens who had the land to the north in Co Clare.

In Tudor times the city had rich trading links with France and Spain but in 1571 James Fitzmaurice Fitzgerald led the Geraldine revolt against English rule.

In 1642 confederate forces occupied the city; in 1651 Ireton, a Cromwellian commander, laid siege to Limerick for six months until it was betrayed by some of its garrison officers. After the Battle of the Boyne in 1690 the defeated Irish forces retreated to Limerick pursued by William of Orange who laid siege to Irish Town, but he was unsuccessful in his several attempts to capture the city.

Sarsfield's Ride

During the Siege of Limerick by William of Orange in 1691, Patrick Sarsfield, the Irish leader, acting on information from a deserter, slipped out of the city with 600 cavalry. They headed north and then east; they forded the Shannon upstream of Killaloe Bridge, which was held by the Williamites, and travelled south through the Silvermine Mountains to Glencar where they camped while scouts went out on reconnaissance. At midnight Sarsfield's troop set out via Cullen to Ballyneety *(18mi/30km south of Limerick)* where they intercepted the Williamite siege train – eight heavy cannon, five mortars and 200 wagons of ammunition and supplies. The noise of its destruction was heard in the city.

Treaty of Limerick – In 1691 after a two-month bombardment from the north and south by another Williamite army led by General Ginkel while an English fleet blockaded the river, Sarsfield sued for peace and signed the Treaty of Limerick. He then became a soldier in the French army and was killed in battle at the age of 43.

18C to 20C – Despite considerable agrarian revolt in the region in the 18C, the City Corporation decided that Limerick no longer needed to be fortified and in 1760 most of the city walls were demolished.

The 18C was also marked by the last flowering of the old Irish culture; after the severe 19C famine and subsequent emigration Gaelic ceased to be the vernacular language of Limerick. Gerald Griffin (1803–40), who was born in Limerick *(plaque in St Augustine's Place)*, made his name as a novelist and poet in English.

During the struggle for independence, Limerick and its county provided three leaders for the 1916 Easter Rising. The most famous was **Eamon de Valera** (1882–1975), later Prime Minister *(Taoiseach)* and then President of the Republic.

In 1919 at the start of the three-year War of Independence a general strike took place in Limerick in protest against British military rule in Ireland. In the same year a soviet was set up in the city.

KING'S ISLAND

★★**St Mary's Cathedral** ⊘ **(Y)** – Limerick's oldest-surviving building, the Anglican cathedral, was founded on King's Island in the River Shannon in 1168 by Dónall Mór O'Brien, King of Munster.

Parts of the king's palace were incorporated in the original cruciform church which was built in the transitional Romanesque style; the Romanesque west doorway may have been the palace entrance.

Interior – The black oak choir stalls and their misericords in the Jebb Chapel, both dating from the 15C, are the only surviving examples of their kind in Ireland. The reredos of the high altar was carved by the father of Patrick Pearse. The north transept contains fine 15C carvings on the **Arthur Memorial** *(below the window)*, which commemorates Geoffrey Arthur (d 1519), the cathedral Treasurer, and a small rectangular lepers' squint *(right)*. In the south transept is the 15C Galway-Bultingfort tomb. The pillar near the south door bears a memorial to Dan Hayes, 18C Limerick gentleman of means, who is described as "an honest man and a lover of his Country". The earliest of the peal of eight bells was cast in 1673; the bell-tower is structurally unsafe.

★**Limerick Museum** ⊘ **(Z M²)** – The museum, which occupies the ground floor and basement of two restored 18C houses, depicts the history of the city, particularly during the later 19C and early 20C.

Many photographs record life in Limerick between 1870 and 1910; others were taken during the turbulent War of Independence (1919–21). Old guild and trade union memorabilia and regalia are preserved.

The **Nail** from the Old Exchange *(see below)*, on which commercial transactions were settled, is made of limestone with a brass top; "paying on the Nail" was a common feature of English trading centres. An extensive collection of 18C silverware recalls a now-defunct Limerick craft. The examples of Limerick **lace** include tambour, needlepoint and tape lace.

★**King John's Castle** ⊘ **(Y)** – The castle, a fine example of fortified Norman architecture, stands on the east bank of the River Shannon guarding Thomond Bridge. It was built between 1200 and 1216 without a keep; massive round towers

King John's Castle, Limerick

reinforce the gateway and the curtain walls, which were higher in those days to withstand the contemporary siege machines. After 1216, when it was extensively repaired after siege damage, the castle featured frequently in Irish annals and English State papers as an important stronghold.

In the 17C a diamond-shaped gun bastion (1611) was built by Josias Bodley at the southeast corner, and the other towers and the wall-walks were lowered to accommodate cannon. The repairs carried out after the structure was bombarded by General Ginkel in 1691 can still be seen from Thomond Bridge. In the mid 18C barracks (demolished) were built within the castle walls and c 1793 the east wall and part of the southeast bastion were dismantled to enlarge the parade ground. The history of the castle and the city is traced through multi-media displays, including an audio-visual presentation, in the modern **Visitor Centre**, which is supported on piles to reveal the archeological excavations below – pre-Norman fortifications and three houses.

In the courtyard are reproductions of war engines – mangonel, trebuchet and battering-ram. The sentry walk on the battlements between the Gate Tower and the Northwest Tower provides good views of the Shannon, the city and its surroundings.

Old Bishop's Palace ⊘ **(Y)** – The house, the oldest-surviving dwelling in Limerick, was designed in the Palladian style by Francis Bindon (c 1690–1765), who was a native of Limerick. It now houses the Limerick Civil Trust.

Almshouses (Y) – Limerick is unusual among Irish towns in possessing two sets of almshouses north and south of the castle. The **Villiers Almshouses** *(north)*, founded in 1826 for 12 poor Protestant widows, each to receive £24 per annum, were designed by James Pain to form three sides of a courtyard built in the Bishop's garden. The **Corporation Almshouses (A)**, also known as the 40-shilling (£2) Almshouses or the Widows' Almshouses, were built for the use of 20 widows by Limerick Corporation in 1691.

Old Exchange (Y B) – All that remains of the Limerick Exchange *(see above)*, built in 1673, is seven Tuscan columns, bricked up to form a wall.

Toll House (Y) – The Gothic-style building with castellated parapets by the eastern bridgefoot was built in 1839 at the same time as the Thomond Bridge, which is by James Pain.

Treaty Stone (Y) – *By the Thomond Bridge on the west bank of the river.* The 1691 Treaty of Limerick *(see above)* was said to have been signed on this block of limestone, which used to stand on the opposite side of the road, in front of the Black Bull public house, where it was used as a mounting-block and despoiled by souvenir hunters. In 1865 it was mounted on a pedestal and moved to the riverside.

CITY CENTRE

The old Irish town which grew up on the south bank of Abbey River, outside the walls of the English town, now forms the centre of modern Limerick.

The district south of Irish town is a fine example of 18C town planning – broad parallel streets lined with **red-brick terraces** – and named **Newtown Pery** after Edmond Sexton Pery (1719–1806), Speaker of the Irish House of Commons from 1771 to 1785.

LIMERICK

A   Corporation Almshouses
B   Old Exchange
D   St Saviour's Dominican
    Church
M¹ Limerick City Gallery of Art
M² Limerick Museum

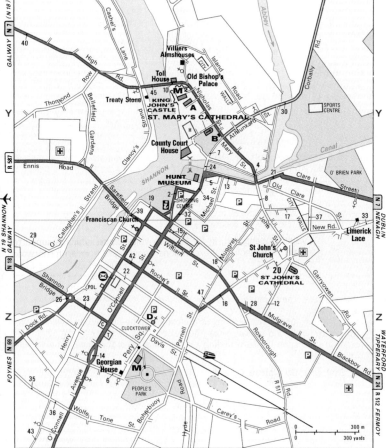

★★ **Hunt Museum** ⊘ (Y) – The restoration of the 18C Custom House designed by Italian architect Davis Duchart has provided a fitting home for this outstanding collection of art and antiquities, the life's work of John and Gertrude Hunt, which they donated to the people of Ireland. The award-winning assemblage is now sensitively displayed with expert Docents (guides) in attendance so that visitors may explore the collection and the lives of the collectors. The exhibits span every age and include works from the immense to the miniature but in particular they reflect the Hunts' personal love of Medieval and Religious Art, fields in which they were acknowledged experts. Highlights on the **First Floor** include the wooden carved *Apollo – Genius of the Arts*, a small bronze *Horse*, attributed to Leonardo da Vinci, and a startling self-portrait by Robert Fagan (c 1745–1816), a painter of the English school and dealer in antiquities in Rome. The **Second Floor** is dedicated to the archeological collection, embracing the ancient civilizations of Egypt, Greece and Rome, together with Irish treasures such as the Cashel Bell *(see CASHEL)* and Antrim Cross and a Jewellery Gallery where the Mary Queen of Scots Cross is exhibited. Religious Art on the **Ground Floor** is dramatically displayed in the Treasury; here among the gleam of silver and precious stones is a Greek coin, traditionally thought to be one of the "Thirty Pieces of Silver".

★**Georgian House** ⊘ (**Z**) – *2 Pery Square*. Built by the Pery Tontine Company in the late 1830s, the terrace of six Georgian town houses facing People's Park is the epitome of Limerick's Newtown Pery district. One of the houses has been restored as a splendid example of Georgian architecture and decor and now contains a museum of Georgian life in the city.

★**John Square** (**Z 20**) – Started in 1751, the square is bordered on three sides by terraces of three-storey houses. The plain limestone buildings have shouldered architraves above the main doorways and plain architraves surrounding the red-brick niches.

Originally the houses were occupied by the wealthy citizens of Limerick, who spent the summer in Kilkee *(see KILRUSH)*. The terraces (restored) are now mainly used by the city's legal and medical professions.

The fourth side of the square is closed by **St John's Church** (deconsecrated), built of limestone in 1843.

★**St John's Cathedral** ⊘ (**Z**) – The Roman Catholic cathedral on the southern fringe of what was the old Irish town was built in the neo-Gothic style in 1861. The spire (280ft/85m high) was completed in 1883 and is the tallest in Ireland. The earliest reference to a church on this site was in 1205 when the Cathedral Chapter of the Diocese of Limerick was founded by Bishop Donatus O'Brien.

Limerick City Gallery of Art ⊘ (**Z M¹**) – This two-storey building, once the Carnegie Library, set in a corner of the People's Park now houses a permanent collection of leading Irish artists, such as Sean Keating, Jack B Yeats and Evie Hone. There are frequent visiting exhibitions.

> **Limerick Lace** ⊘
>
> The traditional craft of lacemaking was introduced to Limerick in the 1820s by English lacemakers. At its 19C peak the local lace factory employed 900 girls. The elaborate Celtic patterns were outlined on machine-made cotton net in thin or thick thread and filled in with decorative stitches. The craft is still practised at the Convent of the Good Shepherd *(for visiting apply to the TIC)*.

Franciscan Church ⊘ (**Z**) – It is difficult to obtain a full perspective of the impressive Corinthian portico owing to the narrowness of Henry Street. The foundation stone was laid in 1876 but work was not completed until 1934.

The apse, one of the last sections of the church to be finished, is lined with multi-coloured marble and mosaic work. Representations of many of the saints of the order are placed in the surrounding niches; the **shrine of St Anthony** is a miniature of the chancel.

St Saviour's Dominican Church ⊘ (**Z D**) – Built in the Romantic Gothic style in 1816, the church holds a 17C statue of Our Lady of Limerick brought from Flanders in 1640 and presented to the Dominicans in the city as a mark of atonement by a Limerick merchant, whose uncle had sentenced Sir John Burke to death for allowing a priest to say Mass in his house during a time of severe religious persecution. Also preserved in the church is the 1649 Kilmallock chalice.

The Stations of the Cross and the fresco over the chancel arch were painted by Fr Aengus Buckley, a local priest in the Dominican order.

EXCURSIONS

Cratloe Woods House ⊘ – *5mi/8km west by N 18*. A red gate-lodge marks the entrance to the estate, which provided the oak timber for the roof of Westminster Hall in London.

The house (1600) is a rare example of the Irish long house *(see p 57)*. In the early 1700s, in order to provide more privacy, a passage was added on the north side, together with a new staircase fashioned by a ship's carpenter; in 1884 the rear entrance was enclosed in a porch and became the front door. The interior displays furniture and souvenirs of the owners, direct descendants of Brian Ború and the O'Briens, the leading family of the region – portraits, local landscapes by Mulcahy, painted maps of the estate, pieces of Limerick lace and Clare embroidery. On the north side of the road covering the lower slopes of Woodcock Hill is **Cratloe Wood**; as well as the lake and forest walks there is a fine **view★** *(0.75mi/1.2km to car park)* of the Shannon Estuary.

★**Castleconnell** – *7mi/11km east by N 7; bear left (sign) to Castleconnell*. Population 1 391.

The well-kept small village by the Shannon offers excellent salmon fishing and riverside walks under the trees.

★**Clare Glens** — *13mi/21km east by N 7 and R 503; east of Newport turn right (sign). Car parks both sides of the river.*
The Clare River descends from the Slievefelim Mountains in a series of **waterfalls** cascading through wooded glens.

Glenstal Abbey — *12mi/19km east by N 7 and R 506; on the north side of Murroe turn right through the park gates.*
Impressive grounds and lakes surround the castle which is now a Benedictine monastery and school *(private)*.
The modern **church** ⊘ is known for its surrealistic decor and for the Ikon Chapel in the crypt.

For adjacent sights see ADARE, ENNIS, KILLALOE, KILMALLOCK, KILRUSH, TIPPERARY.

LISMORE ★

LIOS MÓR – Co Waterford – Population 715
Michelin Atlas p 79 and Map 923 – I 11

Lismore is set on the south bank of the River Blackwater at its confluence with its tributary, the Owennashad. The small but attractive town in the shadow of Lismore Castle has one of Ireland's oldest cathedrals and some interesting domestic architecture, created during the 19C in an old-English Tudor style. The River Blackwater offers salmon, sea and brown trout fishing in idyllic rural surroundings; there is a picturesque walk along its south bank east of the bridge, which was designed in 1775 by Thomas Ivory (c 1720–86) of Cork.

HISTORICAL NOTES

The monastery founded by St Carthach in the 7C became one of Europe's most distinguished universities. In the 8C Lismore reached its academic peak, when it had 20 seats of religion or learning within its walls. In 978 the Danish Vikings raided the town and burned the monasteries.
In 1171 Henry II of England came to Lismore to receive the submission of many chiefs from Munster and Leinster, as well as those of the bishops and abbots of Ireland. Two years later Raymond le Gros completed the destruction of the monastic city. King John built a castle at Lismore in 1185 and a prosperous town grew up around its walls. In 1589 the castle passed into the hands of Sir Walter Raleigh, who sold it to Richard Boyle, the "Great" Earl of Cork. Like most of the town, it was destroyed by Cromwellian forces.
It was eventually rebuilt in the mid 19C in spectacular style by Sir Joseph Paxton, who had designed the Crystal Palace in London and was also the gardener of the Duke of Devonshire, the new owner of the castle. It rises dramatically, a magnificent neo-Tudor fantasy, over the park-like valley of the River Blackwater with its elegant bridge by the Dublin architect Thomas Ivory.

SIGHTS

★**Lismore Castle Gardens** ⊘ – The gardens, where Spenser is said to have composed part of *The Faerie Queene*, straddle the Riding Gate entrance to the castle. The lower garden, known as the Pleasure Grounds, dates from c 1850 although the Yew Walk is much earlier; it is at its best in spring – camellias, rhododendrons and magnolias. The terraced upper garden was laid out in the 17C. The central grass walk is aligned on the spire of the cathedral, and flowers and vegetables grow in the plots screened by yew, beech and box hedges. Against the north wall are greenhouses (1858) designed by Sir Joseph Paxton. The Broghill Tower *(southwest corner)* provides a fine view.

★**St Carthage's Cathedral** (Anglican) ⊘ – Much of the present structure dates from the early 17C although three other religious edifices previously occupied the site. Stone fragments at the front of the west wall are all that remains of the Great Church of Lismore, mentioned in 1173. A new cathedral built in 1207 was razed during the Desmond rebellion in 1579. In 1633 Sir Richard Boyle decided to have the ruined church repaired. In 1679 Sir William Robinson was called in to complete the rebuilding. Two of the south transept windows date from this period, while the **ribbed ceilings** were built by Sir Richard Morrison about 1820 and the fine **tower** and **ribbed spire** were added in 1826 by the Payne brothers, architects in Cork. At the west end of the church there are fragments of 9C tombstones; the enormous Macgrath family **table-tomb** dates from 1548. Beside the 19C Gothic monument in the south transept is a **stained-glass window** by the pre-Raphaelite artist Sir Edward Burne-Jones. Pebbles from the Isle of Iona in Scotland are set into the floor of St Columba's Chapel.

St Carthach's Church (Roman Catholic) ⊘ – Designed by WG Doolin in 1881, it is one of the most outstanding Lombardo-Romanesque churches in Ireland, richly detailed and built of red sandstone with white limestone dressings. The square tower, adjacent to the main buildings, is in a campanile style. Over the main west door is a mosaic of Christ. The **interior** of the church features a wooden beam ceiling and a spacious gallery.

Facing the west entrance to the church is a fine row of 19C artisans' cottages.

Lismore Heritage Centre ⊘ – The Old Courthouse provides an introduction to the history of Lismore through models and an audio-visual presentation.

EXCURSIONS

★**The Gap** – *10mi/16km north by R 688.* The road through the V Gap in the Knockmealdown mountains offers fine **views★**. On the north slopes of Sugar Loaf mountain (2 144ft/653m) stands **Grubb's Grave**, the burial cairn of Samuel Grubb, a local Quaker who died in the 1920s. The sugar-loaf construction enabled him to be buried upright overlooking his estates.

★**Mount Melleray Abbey** ⊘ – *8mi/13km northeast by N 72, R 669 and a minor road right.* As this abbey is a Cistercian monastery only the public church and part of the Community **church** are open to the public.

The monastery was founded in 1832 and derived its original monks from Melleray in France, where the community was threatened with suppression unless the foreign monks, who were mostly Irish, left. The monks are devoted to prayer but they also pursue a number of crafts, such as baking their own bread.

There are impressive views south from the slopes of the Knockmealdown Mountains across the Blackwater Valley.

In 1980 an extensive grotto was built in a quarry south of the monastery by the bridge. From the bridge there is an attractive walk beside the Glenshelane River.

For adjacent sights see CAHER, CLONMEL, COBH, CORK, DUNGARVAN, MALLOW, MIDLETON, YOUGHAL.

LONGFORD

AN LONGFORT – Co Longford – Population 6 393
Michelin Atlas p 91 and Map 923 – I 6

The county town of Longford lies on the Camlin River a few miles east of its confluence with the Shannon. Longford derived its name and its existence from a fortress *(long-phort)*, built by the O'Farrells, but neither it nor the priory, which they founded in 1400, has survived.

The last engagement of the 1798 rebellion *(see p 29)* was fought at Ballinamuck *(10mi/16km north)*, where General Humbert's French and Irish volunteers were defeated by the English forces under General Lake.

SIGHTS

St Mel's Cathedral ⊘ – *Dublin Street.* The cathedral, designed by Joseph Keane in 1840 in the Italian Renaissance style, resembles a Greek temple surmounted by a tall domed belfry. The interior is supported on a double row of Ionic columns. The **Diocesan Museum** ⊘ *(right transept)* houses **St Mel's Crozier** (10C), a stick of yew encased in bronze, inset with studs and decorated with animal motifs, foliage and interlacing; it was found at old St Mel's Church in Ardagh *(see below)* in 1860 and may originally have consisted of four sections. Among the other exhibits of local provenance are a number of Penal Crosses and the Ballinderry gaming board with 49 peg holes in seven rows of seven.

Maria Edgeworth (1767–1849)

She is best known for her novels on Irish life – *Castle Rackrent* (1800), *The Absentee* (1812) and *Ormond* (1817) – in which she developed the regional and historical novel; she also wrote English novels and stories for children. In her day her influence was acknowledged by Jane Austen, Macaulay, Ruskin, Thackeray, Turgenev and Sir Walter Scott, who described her as "the great Maria" and visited her in 1825. Apart from some time in England at school, she lived all her life (1767–1849) at the family home in Mostrim, also known as Edgeworthstown (8.5mi/14km east), where her circle included the Pakenhams of Tullynally and the Lefroys of Carrigglas. She was the eldest daughter of Richard Lovell Edgeworth, a wealthy landlord, who had four wives and 22 children. He was an eccentric man with an interest in science, who installed a central heating system at Tullynally Castle.

Town Centre – From the **Courthouse**, designed in 1791 in the Renaissance style with a pedimented central door surmounted by a Venetian window, the main street descends to the river and then climbs the north bank past the barracks adjoining the present castle (1627) and the 18C Anglican **Church of St John** ⊘ *(right)*.

EXCURSIONS

Carrigglas Manor ⊘ – *3mi/5km east of Longford by R 194.* The castellated mansion is the home of the Lefroys, a family of Huguenot descent. It was designed in 1837 by Daniel Robertson of Kilkenny in the neo-Gothic style for Thomas Lefroy, Lord Chief Justice of Ireland and youthful inamorato of Jane Austen.

The outstanding feature of the interior (restored) is the **corniced and moulded ceilings** in the reception rooms. The house contains some fine early Dutch furniture, artefacts and pictures including many family portraits.

The **Costume Museum** *(stable buildings)* displays costumes worn by past generations of Lefroys and a collection of **lace**, some made by the ladies of Carrigglas.

The magnificent **double stable and farm yard** *(restoration in progress)* was designed by James Gandon in 1790; the stable yard is enclosed by four ranges of two storeys, with pedimented and rusticated arches, adjoining the farm yard where the lower storey is gradually absorbed into the rising ground.

The woodland garden, which contains an interesting collection of plants, was inspired by the great Victorian designer, William Robinson.

Ardagh – *20mi/32km southeast of Longford by N 4 and R 393.* The charming little estate village was largely rebuilt in the 1860s by Lady Fetherstone, who lived at Ardagh House.

The ruins of a simple stone church, St Mel's Cathedral, are said to stand on the site where the saint was buried. He was appointed bishop by St Patrick, his uncle, who founded a church in Ardagh in the 5C.

Ardagh Heritage Centre ⊘ in the old schoolhouse traces the history of Ardagh from the pre-Christian era of folk tales, through the arrival of Christianity, the internal rivalries of the local O'Farrell tribe and the 1619 Plantation.

Corlea Trackway ⊘ – *10mi/16km south of Longford by N 63 and R 397; in Keen turn right (sign).* The ancient trackway *(togher)* was discovered in the 1980s. It consisted of oak planks secured by pegs and was wide enough to carry wheeled vehicles for the transport of animals and personal effects across the bog. It dates from 147-8 BC and lasted for only about 10 years as it was too heavy to remain on the surface of the bog. A section of it has been preserved and relaid under cover on its original site. Its excavation by an international team of archeologists and its preservation are described in an audio-visual film; it is set in its Iron-Age context by the accompanying exhibition.

For adjacent sights see ATHLONE, CARRICK-ON-SHANNON, MULLINGAR, ROSCOMMON, STROKESTOWN.

Corlea Trackway

Dúchas, Dublin

Goldsmith Country

The country around Lough Ree is where Oliver Goldsmith (c 1731–74), poet, playwright, historian and naturalist, spent the first 20 or so years of his life, visiting relatives and going to school in Elphin, Mostrim, Athlone and Lissoy.

The road from Ardagh to Athlone (N 55) links a number of sites connected with his life and work.

In **Ardagh** he himself experienced the plot of his play *She Stoops to Conquer*, by mistaking the big house for the village inn.

The site of his first boyhood home at **Pallas** is marked by a statue by Foley.

Until 1731 Goldsmith's father was Rector of **Forgney** church, which contains a stained-glass window depicting "sweet Auburn".

After her husband's death in 1747, Goldsmith's mother lived in **Ballymahon** on the Inny River.

It was in **Tang** that Goldsmith first went to school near the mill.

The pub, known as **The Three Jolly Pigeons**, preserves the name of the inn in Goldsmith's play *She Stoops to Conquer*.

Lissoy Parsonage, now in ruins, was the house where the Goldsmith family lived from 1731 to 1747; **Lissoy** village is recalled as "sweet Auburn" in his poem *The Deserted Village*.

LOUGHREA

BAILE LOCHA RIACH – Co Galway – Population 3 360
Michelin Atlas p 89 and Map 923 – G 8

The town lines the north shore of Lough Rea facing the Slieve Aughty Mountains. Its origins lie in a Norman stronghold built in about 1300 by Richard de Burgo, who also founded the **Carmelite Priory**, now in ruins, where General St Ruth, who died at the Battle of Aughrim, is said to be buried under the tower. Part of one of the medieval **town gates** stands on the edge of the cathedral precinct.

★**St Brendan's Cathedral** ⊙ – The cathedral of the Roman Catholic diocese of Clonfert *(see p 235)* was designed by William Byrne in the neo-Gothic style in 1897. The interior is richly decorated in the spirit of the Celtic Revival. The work was commissioned by Edward Martyn *(see p 55)* and his relatives, the Smyth family of Masonbrook.

The stained glass is by Sarah Purser, Hubert McGoldrick and Evie Hone working

for **An Túr Gloine** *(see p 55)*, and by Patrick Pye and Michael Healy.

The textiles were designed and woven by the Dun Emer Guild, which was founded by Evelyn Gleeson. The sculpture is from the hands of John Hughes and Michael Shorthall. The furnishings, metalwork and wood-carving are the work of William Scott.

The diocesan **museum** displays a collection of vestments (15C–20C), chalices (16C–19C), statues, penal crosses, rosaries, crucifixes and missals.

EXCURSIONS

Kiltartan Country *South of Loughrea*

★**Thoor Ballylee** ⊙ – *12mi/19km southwest of Loughrea by N 66 (sign)*. The 16C tower house, which was William Butler Yeats' summer house for 11 years, became a powerful symbol in his poetic work, as the inscription on the wall facing the road records. In 1917, the year of his marriage to Georgie Hyde-Lees, he was looking for a property near to Lady Gregory's house at Coole Park, where he was a frequent visitor. He spent most of that summer converting the tower; on the ground floor, facing the stream, was a small dining room; winding stairs led up to the living room *(first floor)* and bedroom *(second floor)*; the third floor was occupied by the strangers' room, known as the secret room. In 1928 increasing ill health and other interests forced Yeats to abandon the tower. In 1961 the local Kiltartan Society began its restoration and it was opened by the poet Pádraic Colum on 20 June 1965. The adjoining miller's cottage and millwheel have also been restored.

St Joseph by Michael Healy in Loughrea Cathedral

B Lynch /Bord Fáilte, Dublin

Coole Park ○ – *16mi/25km southwest of Loughrea by N 66 and north by N 18.* Coole is a national park with a deer enclosure, a nature trail and a forest walk *(0.5mi/0.8km)* to the lake, where petrified trees protrude from the water.

In the walled garden stands a great copper beech, the **autograph tree★**, on which many of the significant figures in the Irish Literary Renaissance – William Butler Yeats, George Bernard Shaw, G Russell (AE), John Millington Synge and Sean O'Casey – cut their initials while guests of the former owner Augusta, Lady Gregory (1852–1932); the house has been demolished.

★**Kilmacduagh Churches and Round Tower** – *19mi/30km southwest of Loughrea by N 66 to Gort and R 460; car park.* The ruins of the monastery, which was founded in the 7C by St Colman, son of Duagh, straddle the road. The monastery suffered from many Viking attacks in the 9C–10C; after the Reformation it became the property of Richard, 2nd Earl of Clanrickard.

The **Glebe House**, a two-storey 13C building, was probably the Abbot's lodging. South of it stands the **Church of St John the Baptist**, a small 12C building with rounded and pointed windows and a later chancel.

Beside the well-preserved inclined **round tower** stands the **cathedral**; its west gable dates from the 11C–12C, the nave from 1200; the south doorway with a bishop's head above it, the two transepts, the west window and the chancel probably date from the 15C; the folk art Crucifixions were moved from the south to the north transept after 1765. **St Mary's Church**, across the road, was built c 1200.

O'Heyne's Church *(northwest)* contains early-13C carving on the chancel arch and east windows.

★**Dunguaire Castle** ○ – *20mi/32km west of Loughrea by N 6 to Craughwell and southwest by R 347 to Kinvarra; car park.* The four-storey tower house with adjoining bawn, which stands by the shore at the head of Kinvarra Bay, was built in 1520 by the descendants of Guaire, King of Connaught in the 7C. The Martyns of Galway owned it from the 17C to 20C, when it was restored by Oliver St John Gogarty (1924) and by Christobel Lady Ampthill (1954). Traces of the wickerwork support used in its construction are visible on the ground-floor vault. The first and second floors are furnished for medieval banquets, the top floor *(76 steps)* as a 20C sitting room. The castle faces **Kinvarra** (population 425), a charming little port at the head of the bay.

North and east of Loughrea

★**Athenry** (Baile Átha an Rí) – *11mi/18km northwest of Loughrea by R 349 and R 348.* Population 1 612. Now a quiet agricultural town on the Clarinbridge River, Athenry, meaning the King's Ford, was an important Norman stronghold. In the town centre stands a 15C market cross depicting the Crucifixion.

The **North Gate** is the best preserved section of the town walls (1211).

The **castle** ○ built by Meiler de Bermingham c 1239 consists of a stout wall rein-forced by two towers enclosing a central keep which has a vaulted undercroft supported on pillars and a main entrance at first-floor level.

Beside the river on the east side of the town are the ruins of a **Dominican friary** ○ founded in 1241 by Meiler de Bermingham. The choir of the church, which was dedicated to St Peter and St Paul, is 13C with lancet windows, but the pillars and aisle arches date from a 14C rebuilding in which the chancel was extended and a new east window was inserted. The tomb niches date from the 13C to the 15C. The north transept was probably added during repairs after a fire in 1423. In 1574 the friary was confiscated and burned by the Burkes. In 1627 it was returned to the friars, who restored the buildings, and in 1644 it became a university. Eight years later, however, the friars were expelled by the Cromwellians.

★**Turoe Stone** – *4mi/6.4km north of Loughrea by R 350; in Bullaun turn left to Kiltullagh; after 0.25mi/0.4km turn right; park in gateway.* In the middle of a field *(right)* stands a granite boulder (3ft/1m high). Its domed cap is carved in relief with curvilinear La Tène motifs and a "step" pattern arranged in four panels. Motifs include a stylized bird's head and the **triskele**, a three-pointed symbol of fertility connected with Brigid, the Irish goddess of fertility, which has been converted into the four-pointed symbol known as St Brigid's cross. It is presumed to be a Celtic ritual stone and was found in a nearby hillfort, known as the Rath of Fearmore (Rath of the Big Man), which dates from the last pre-Christian centuries.

Kilconnell Franciscan Friary – *13mi/21km northeast of Loughrea by R 350 and R 348. Plan of layout in the nave.* The ruins are the remains of a monastery founded in 1353 for the Franciscans by William O'Kelly on the site of an earlier monastery in the 6C by St Conall. The west doorway and the windows date from the 15C. There are two fine tomb niches: one bears the figures of six saints, named in a manner which suggests a French influence; the other in the choir belongs to the O'Daly family. The tower was added later, possibly by the founder's daughter who is also said to have built the main part of the church. The remains of the cloister include the refectory in the northwest corner. Although the friary was dis-solved in 1541, there were still friars in residence shortly before the Battle of Aughrim in 1691.

Battle of Aughrim

Aughrim was the last great battle in the War of the Two Kings *(Cogadh an Dá Rí)* between King James II of England, supported by Louis XIV of France, and King William III of England and his allies. After retreating west following the Battle of Athlone, the Jacobite forces, under the French general St Ruth, took up a defensive position at Aughrim against the army of William III of England, under the Dutchman General Ginkel. On 12 July 1691 45 000 men (20 000 Jacobites composed of Irish, French, Germans and Walloons and 25 000 Williamites composed of Irish, English, Dutch, German and Danish) met and fought; 9 000 died. The death of St Ruth at the height of the battle caused disarray among the Jacobites and gave victory to the Williamites. According to legend, the Williamite dead were buried at Clontuskert Priory while the Jacobite dead were stripped and left to rot and their bones were smashed on the walls of Kilconnell Friary.

Battle of Aughrim Centre ⊙ – *Aughrim; 14mi/23km east of Loughrea by N 6.* The Interpretative Centre uses audio-visual, three-dimensional displays and many relics to recreate the bloody battle of Aughrim, based on the account of Captain Walter Dalton, one of the combatants.

Clontuskert Augustinian Priory – *22mi/35km northeast of Loughrea by N 6 and south by R 355. 5min on foot from roadside car park (left).*
The first monastery on the site was founded by St Baedán (dc809). The Augustinians, who arrived in the 12C, had by the end of the 13C established one of the richest monasteries in the diocese. Later they grew corrupt and the building was burned.
Most of the present ruined building dates from the 15C – east window, roodscreen, west door which bears carvings of St Michael, St John, St Katherine and an abbot or bishop. Although the building passed to the de Burghs at the 16C Dissolution, the monks returned in 1637 and made repairs to the fabric.

For adjacent sights see BIRR, CLONMACNOISE, GALWAY, PORTUMNA, ROSCOMMON, TUAM.

MALLOW ★

MALA – Co Cork – Population 6 434
Michelin Atlas p 78 and Map 923 – G 11

Mallow is attractively sited above the River Blackwater, sometimes described as the "Irish Rhine". It is a busy market town, noted for agricultural processing. Rathduff *(10mi/16km south)* is known for its cheese. The Duhallow Hunt was founded in Mallow in 1745.

HISTORICAL NOTES

The castle, built in the late 12C, had by the 16C become the seat of Sir John Norreys, Lord President of Munster. The town, which dates from 1298, was granted a charter in 1688 by King James II.

As the spa declined the town became a centre of considerable nationalistic political activity, helped by the fact that **Thomas Davis**, the mid-century political writer, was born *(no 73 Main Street)* and brought up in Mallow; so too was **William O'Brien** (1852–1928), a noted nationalist MP, who was born in what is now known as William O'Brien's House.

Mallow has literary connections with **Anthony Trollope**, who was a resident for some years; with **Canon Sheehan**, one of Ireland's most prolific and popular authors in the late 19C and early 20C, who was born in 1852 in Mallow *(no 29 O'Brien Street)* and went to school in the town; and with Elizabeth Bowen.

Mallow Spa

From 1730 to 1810 Mallow was a popular spa with a fast reputation; its male patrons were known as the **Rakes of Mallow**. During the season, which lasted from April to October, visitors would take the waters before breakfast and during the afternoon; the evenings were spent in dancing and playing cards. Balls, music meetings and other diversions were held in the Long Room in emulation of the entertainment available in Bath, Tunbridge and Scarborough in England. By 1828 when the Spa House was built in the Tudor style with a pump-room, a reading room and baths, the popularity of Mallow was in decline.
The curative properties of the local water – it was reputed to be efficacious in purifying the blood – were discovered in 1724; the temperature varies from 66°F to 72°F according to the season.

Elizabeth Bowen (1899–1973)

For the first seven years of her life, Elizabeth Bowen used to spend the winter in Dublin, where she was born, and the summer at Bowen's Court (demolished), the family seat, built by Henry Bowen c 1775 near Kildorrery *(northeast of Mallow)*. Although she spent her later childhood and married life in England, she entertained many guests at Bowen's Court during the summer months until 1959 when the difficulty of maintaining such a large house obliged her to sell.

She wrote of her early childhood days in *Seven Winters* (1942) and told her family history in *Bowen's Court* (1942). In *The Last September* (1929) she drew on her experience of country house life in Ireland. Her most widely-read and best known works are *The Death of the Heart* (1947) and *The Heat of the Day* (1949).

SIGHTS

★**St James' Church** ⊙ – The modern Anglican church dates from 1824 but in its grounds are the substantial ruins of a much older building, St Anne's, for which the foundations were laid in 1291. In this older church Thomas Davis, the Protestant patriot, was baptized in 1814.

Fitzgerald Statue – JJ Fitzgerald (1872–1906) was described as a scholar, patriot and champion of all oppressed. The quotation on the statue – "Ireland has not in our time lost a more able or unselfish young patriot" – is by William O'Brien.

Clock House – *Main Street*. The curiously out-of-place half-timbered Tudor-style building (1855) consists of four storeys with an adjacent clock tower.

Mallow Castle Grounds – The castle *(private)* stands in **extensive** grounds, including a deer park, which extend to the River Blackwater with its impressive weir. At the entrance to the demesne stands the ruin of a 17C four-storey castle.

EXCURSIONS

★**Buttevant Friary** – *7mi/11km north of Mallow by N 20*. The ruins of a Franciscan friary, built in 1251, stand beside the River Awbeg next to St Mary's Roman Catholic Church. The building, which was used until recently as a place of burial, has two crypts, one above the other; the chancel walls are still largely intact.

★**Doneraile Wildlife Park** ⊙ – *6mi/10km northeast of Mallow by N 20 and R 581.* The walled demesne (395 acres/160ha) is noted for its herds of red, fallow and sika deer. Clumps of trees in this rolling parkland are broken by ornamental lakes. Doneraile Court was built c 1700 and remodel-

Steeplechasing

The first recorded **steeplechase** took place from Buttevant in 1752, using the steeple of the Anglican Church as the starting point of a race to St Leger Church near Doneraile (4.5mi/7km).

led in its present form in the early 19C; its lawn is complemented by fine old larch trees.

A stone arched vault and spiral staircase are all that remains of **Kilcolman Castle**, once the residence of Edmund Spenser.

Outside the Roman Catholic church in Doneraile (population 815) stands a **statue** to Canon Sheehan, author of *My New Curate*, who was the parish priest from 1895 to 1913.

★**Annes Grove Gardens** ⊙ – *11mi/18km east of Mallow by N 72; in Castletownroche turn left onto the minor road*. The woodland gardens surrounding an 18C house and lawns overlooking the River Awbeg include a fine collection of rhododendrons and magnolias, as well as many rare trees and shrubs. Winding paths lead to the cliff garden overlooking the lily pond and the extensive river garden; in the walled garden with its 19C hedges there are herbaceous borders and water gardens.

Longueville House – *3mi/5km west of Mallow by N 72; turn right at sign*. This magnificent house (1720), now a hotel open to non-residents, features a dual staircase. The interior is hung with 18C and 19C political portraits: **Henry Grattan** and **Daniel O'Connell** in the anteroom; the presidents of Ireland, Douglas Hyde, Sean T O'Kelly, Eamon de Valera, Erskine Childers, Cearbhall ó Dálaigh and Patrick Hillery in the **Presidents' Room** restaurant.

Kilcolman Castle

The four-storey tower house near Doneraile was probably built by the 6th Earl of Desmond when he received the property from an uncle in 1418; the ruins show signs of some later additions. In 1586 a perpetual lease of the lands (3 028 acres) and castle of Kilcolman was granted to Edmund Spenser, under the scheme for the plantation of the confiscated Desmond lands in Munster with English Protestants loyal to the Crown. Spenser was a Londoner, a graduate of Cambridge and a rabid anti-papist; as secretary to the Lord Deputy, Spenser had participated in the masssacre of the expeditionary force of 600 Spaniards and Italians who had surrendered unconditionally at Smerwick in 1580. He held a post in the Dublin Court of Chancery which he resigned in 1588. It was at that time that he probably took up residence at Kilcolman Castle, where he lived, apart from visits to England, until 1598. In the summer of 1589 Spenser was visited by Sir Walter Raleigh. During his years at Kilcolman Spenser wrote poetry – the fourth, fifth and sixth books of The Faerie Queen, the Amoretti (love sonnets of his courtship of his second wife Elizabeth Boyle) and the Epithalamion, commemorating their marriage on Midsummer's Day in 1594, as well as his Veue of the State of Ireland (1596) and memoranda on the Irish situation. Although he had little sympathy for the Irish, Spenser's work reflects his sensitivity to the beauty of the landscape. A defensible building with scant comfort, such as Kilcolman Castle, was the usual abode of a settler in the 16C, who was in constant danger of attack. During the Rising in 1598 Kilcolman Castle was attacked and burned by insurgents; some of Spenser's MSS may have perished, including a seventh book of The Faerie Queen of which only fragments are known; the poet and his family fled to Cork and thence to England. It is doubtful whether the castle was inhabited after the fire of 1598, and in 1630 Kilcolman was sold by Spenser's son to Sir William St Leger.

In the courtyard at the back of the house there is a 150-year-old **maze**; the estate (500 acres/202ha) includes a **vineyard** (3 acres/1.2ha), the only one in Ireland; in a good year its grapes produce a Riesling-type wine.

★ **Kanturk (Ceann Toirc)** – *13mi/21km west of Mallow by N 72 and R 576.* Population 1 870. This small market town has three interesting **bridges:** the six-arch humpback structure (1760) spanning the River Dalua; the nearby six-arch Greenane bridge (1745) over the River Allua; the four-arch Metal Bridge built in 1848 by Sir Edward Tierney over the River Dalua, at the western end of the town, near the Church of the Immaculate Conception built in the French Gothic style.

The **castle ★** ruin *(south by R 579)* is still substantial. According to legend, in about 1609 the local chieftain, MacDonagh MacCarthy, built the biggest mansion to belong to an Irish chief; the English Privy Council ordered the work to stop on the grounds that "it was much too large for a subject"; when MacCarthy heard the news, he was so enraged that he threw away the blue glass tiles destined for the roof.

For adjacent sights see COBH, CORK, KILMALLOCK, LISMORE, MIDLETON.

MAYNOOTH
MAIGH NUAD – Co Kildare – Population 6 027
Michelin Atlas p 93 and Map 923 – M 7

Maynooth is a small town on the Royal Canal, which for centuries was the seat of the Fitzgeralds, who were made Earls of Kildare in 1316 and Dukes of Leinster in 1766; they were descendants of a Norman-Welsh adventurer who arrived in Ireland in 1169; they became one of the most powerful families in Ireland, holding the position of Lord Deputy from 1471 to 1534; the most famous was Garret Mór, the Great Earl of Kildare (d 1513). Maynooth is also famous as the site of the best-known seminary in Ireland.

SIGHTS

Maynooth Castle – At the west end of the main street stand the ruins of a castle, consisting of a massive keep surrounded by fragments of towers, walls and the entrance gate. It was built at the end of the 12C by the Fitzgeralds who occupied it, except for 17 years following the rebellion of Silken Thomas in 1535, until 1656, when it was abandoned in favour of a new house at the east end of the main street. This house, known as Carton *(private)*, was rebuilt c 1739 by Richard Castle and remodelled c 1815 by Sir Richard Morrison.

Maynooth College ⊘ – The college, now part of the National University, was founded in 1795 as St Patrick's College, a seminary for the Irish priesthood on property offered on advantageous terms by the Duke of Leinster; an earlier college, founded by the Fitzgeralds in Maynooth in 1521, was suppressed in 1538.

A second court, added in 1845, was designed in the neo-Gothic style by Pugin. It contains the chapel which was designed in 1875 by Pugin's pupil, JJ McCarthy. The history of the college is presented in the **Visitor Centre**, which organizes guided tours of the Chapel, Stoyte House, the Pugin building and the gardens.

EXCURSION

★★Castletown House

Celbridge; 4mi/6.4km southeast of Maynooth by a minor road.

Beside the road *(left)* stands the **Castletown Obelisk**, also known as the **Conolly Folly**, an obelisk mounted on two tiers of arches, which commands a view to the south of the roof of Castletown House. It was built to designs by Richard Castle and erected in memory of Speaker Conolly. Its construction was paid for by his wife, Katherine Conolly, to create employment during the severe winter of 1739.

> ### "Speaker" Conolly
> William Conolly (1662–1729) was a lawyer from Ballyshannon *(see p 130)*, who made a fortune dealing in forfeited estates after the Battle of the Boyne. He became Member of Parliament for Donegal in 1692, Commissioner of the Revenue in 1709, and in 1715 was elected Speaker of the Irish House of Commons.

Castletown House ⊘ – The first great Palladian mansion to be built (1722) in Ireland faces south over the Liffey Valley to the Wicklow Mountains. As the drive approaches at right angles to the main axis, the façade, a 13-bay central block linked by curved colonnades to two pavilions, is revealed obliquely. The central block was designed by Alessandro Galilei (1691–1737) of Florence, and the wings and colonnades by Sir Edward Lovett Pearce who supervised the construction work. The house was commissioned by William Conolly, who became Speaker of the Irish House of Commons. As he and his wife Katherine were childless, the property was inherited by his great-nephew, Tom Conolly, who in 1758 married Lady Louisa Lennox (15 years old); she completed the interior decoration and replaced the formal gardens with serpentine walks and garden buildings. The house remained in the Conolly family until 1965; in 1967 it was bought and partially restored by the Hon Desmond Guinness and is now owned by the Irish state and managed by Dúchas, the Heritage service.

Interior – A portrait of Galilei, the architect, hangs in the **hall**, which has not been altered since first designed by Pearce. The stairwell was empty until the cantilevered staircase of Portland stone was installed in 1760; its brass banisters were a novelty which started a fashion. The Baroque plasterwork (1759) is by the Lafranchini brothers.

The original 18C scheme of interior decoration, which used only local wood and stone, is preserved in the **Brown Study** – coved ceiling, tall narrow oak doors and pine panelling stained to resemble oak.

During the 1760s the ground-floor reception rooms were remodelled to the designs of Sir William Chambers to create the **dining room**, which is decorated in the neo-Classical style, and the **drawing rooms**. Flanking the central door in the green **drawing room** are portraits of William Conolly and of his wife, Katherine, with her niece, by Jervas. The japanned lacquer cabinet (1740) with painted Italianate panels belonged to Katherine Conolly.

The **print room** was decorated by Lady Louisa who began collecting the prints of old masters' work in 1762; she began in 1768 and the work was completed in the 1770s.

The most impressive room is the **Long Gallery**. The Pompeian decor dates from the mid 1770s and was carried out by two English artists, Charles Reuben Riley and Thomas Ryder, who used vivid blue, red and green in the scheme.

The chandeliers are of hand-blown glass from Murano near Venice. The portrait of Tom Conolly is a copy of the one painted in Rome in 1758 by Mengs. In Louisa's day the room was furnished with books, musical instruments and a billiard table, and was used by the family in winter as an all-purpose living room where they also took their meals. From the windows the obelisk *(see above)* is visible completing the vista to the north.

Long Gallery, Castletown House

Wonderful Barn – The barn *(private)* which closes the northeast vista *(3mi/5km east by R 403 and R 404)* was built for Mrs Conolly in 1743 by John Glinn. It is a conical structure, consisting of four diminishing brick domes with an external spiral staircase; it was used for drying and storing grain.

Steam Museum ⊘ *5mi/8km south of Maynooth by R 406*

The museum is housed in the old railway engineers' Gothic church, transferred from its original site in Inchicore. The Model Hall contains the Richard Guinness Collection of over 20 prototype locomotive models, dating from the late 18C. The hall is hung with the portraits of inventors and famous engineers. The Power Hall contains four live steam stationary engines and one marine engine – a six-pillar independent type beam engine from the Midleton Distillery, an architectural single-column beam engine purchased at the Manchester Exhibition in 1847 for Smithwick's Brewery in Kilkenny, a duplex steam pump from the Jameson Brewery in Dublin, a Victor Coates Mill engine used in the Frazer & Haughton bleaching and dyeing factory in Northern Ireland, and a triple-expansion marine engine from SS Divis of Belfast made by Workman Clark in 1920. Children usually enjoy working the hand pump in the courtyard.

Coolcarrigan Gardens ⊘
10mi/16km southwest of Maynooth by R 408 via Donadea to Timahoe; 1mi/1.6km south of Timahoe turn right (sign)

The parkland laid out in the 19C has been much embellished by extensive planting of **shrubs** and **trees**, all clearly labelled: pine trees, clipped Irish yews, a tulip tree, acers, elaeagnus, *cedrus Atlantica, pinus silvestris*, buddleia, philadelphus, camellia, syringa, fuchsia, daphne and box. Roses and herbaceous borders are arranged in the formal gardens near the house. The **glasshouse** contains a vine, a passion flower, peaches and nectarines. At the end of the **woodland walk** *(30min)* through the forest there is a fine view across the Bog of Allen. The **church** (1881), which is surrounded by a moat and approached through a lych gate, is in the Hiberno-Romanesque revival style and decorated with stained glass.

For adjacent sights see DUBLIN, DÚN LAOGHAIRE, FINGAL, KILDARE, MULLINGAR, POWERSCOURT, RUSSBOROUGH, TARA, TRIM.

The length of time given in this guide
 – for touring allows time to enjoy the views and the scenery;
 – for sightseeing is the average time required for a visit.

MIDLETON

Midleton is a pleasant market town, dating from 1180, set in the rich fertile plain of East Cork on the main road from Youghal west to Cork city. It is now the centre of Irish whiskey production, where all the famous brands – except Bushmills *(see p 305)* – are distilled.

Old Midleton Distillery ⊘ – The home of Jameson Irish Whiskey is a modern distillery, built by Irish Distillers in 1975, beside the 19C buildings, which were used as a woollen mill and barracks before becoming a distillery in 1825. The tour begins with an audio-visual presentation on the history of the distillery and ends with a whiskey tasting; Irish whiskey, which is distilled three times, is smooth to the palate without the distinctive smokey flavour of Scotch. In between there is a guided tour of the old buildings and equipment – kiln where the malted barley is dried, five-storey storehouse where the grain is stored and turned, the water-wheel (1852) which operated five pairs of millstones, the **largest copper pot still** (1825) in the world (capacity 33 000 gallons/1485hl), oak casks in which the spirit is matured to add tannin and vanillin for colour and taste, office where records were kept and payments made through a small window.

EXCURSIONS

★**Cloyne Cathedral** ⊘ – *5mi/8km south by R 630 and R 629*. The first church at Cloyne (population 731) was founded by St Colman (522–604). The **round tower** (100ft/30m high) dates from the 10C and may be climbed by visitors. The 14C cathedral (restored) contains a memorial in the north transept to its most famous bishop, **George Berkeley** (1684–1753), the distinguished philosopher, who was born at Thomastown *(see p 197)* and was bishop of Cloyne for 19 years from 1734; his line "Westward the course of empire takes its way" inspired the naming of Berkeley in California. Several interesting late-medieval tombs adorn the austere nave. A notice records that the cathedral's Coat of Arms was erected in 1722 and that the carver, Mr Maguire, was asked to complete the job for not more than £10. A small building near the cathedral is believed to be a reconstruction of St Colman's oratory.

Stephen Pearce Pottery ⊘ – *9mi/14.5km southeast by R 630 and R 629*. The village of Shanagarry is the home of the famous Stephen Pearce pottery where visitors may watch the production process; the finished articles are on sale in the shop.

Midleton Distillery

227

Out and about in East Cork

There are beaches and coves for bathing from Roche's Point eastwards to Knockadoon Head. Trabolgan recreation complex *(at Roche's Point)* offers an indoor swimming pool, plunge pool, sauna, solarium, fitness centre, tennis, 10-pin bowling and an indoor sports hall.

Sailing enthusiasts will find plenty of activity in Ballycotton Bay, at Roche's Point and in Cork Harbour. Anglers may choose between shore and lake fishing.

For those who prefer dry land there are many golf courses and pleasant walks, particularly along the cliffs from Roche's Point to Ballycotton.

Ballycotton – *11mi/18km southeast by R 630 and R 629.* Population 444. The fishing village with its small harbour offers cliff walks overlooking Ballycotton Bay and the lighthouse on Ballycotton Island.

Rostellan Wood – *6mi/9.7km southeast by R 630.* There are pleasant forest walks on the shore of Cork Harbour in what was once the demesne of Rostellan House (demolished).

Barryscourt Castle ⊘ – *4mi/6.4km west by N 25 and R 624. Restoration in progress.* The ruined castle occupies a strategic site on the main route from Cork to Waterford. The keep, which dates from 1420, is surrounded by a bawn, which incorporates the ruined wall of a 13C great hall. After an attack on the castle in 1580 by Sir Walter Raleigh *(see YOUGHAL)*, the keep was reinforced by the addition of the southwest and northeast towers. The castle takes its name from Philip de Barri of Manorbier in Wales, to whom the land was granted c 1180 by his uncle, Robert Fitzstephen, one of the first Norman adventurers in Ireland. Another member of the de Barri family was **Gerald of Wales** (c 1146–1233), also known as Giraldus Cambrensis or de Barri, an important Welsh cleric and a member of the Fitzgerald (Geraldine) family; he travelled in Ireland with Prince (later King) John and published two works – *Topographia Hibernica*, a description of the country and its people, and *Expugnatio Hibernica* (1188), an account of Henry II's conquest of Ireland.

For adjacent sights see COBH, CORK, KINSALE, YOUGHAL.

MONAGHAN
MUINEACHÁN – Co Monaghan – Population 5 628
Michelin Atlas p 98 and Map 923 – L5

Monaghan is the commercial centre and the county town of Co Monaghan, which was part of the original province of Ulster and projects deep into Northern Ireland as far as the Blackwater River. The town is a popular angling centre. In the 14C the McMahons established their headquarters on an artificial island (crannóg) in the lake and they dominated the area until the arrival of British settlers in the 17C.

Monaghan was granted a charter in 1613. Most of the grey limestone buildings lining the narrow streets date from the 18C when the town became an important centre for the linen industry; in the 19C the Ulster Canal and the Ulster Railway brought further prosperity.

SIGHTS

St Macartan's Cathedral ⊘ – *Dublin Road.* On a hill southeast of the town stands the Roman Catholic cathedral (1859–92) of the diocese of Clogher. It was designed by JJ McCarthy in the decorated French Gothic style and is built of local grey limestone. The exterior is dominated by the soaring spire (250ft/76m) and decorated with statues of saints and bishops. Beneath the splendid **hammerbeam roof** the interior has been refurbished following Vatican II with three **tapestries** on the east wall, illustrating the Christian life and the life of St Macartan, and with a massive altar in the shape of a Tau cross, a lectern and an ambo in South Dublin granite.

Charles Gavan Duffy (1816–1903)

Duffy, who was born in Monaghan *(no 10 Dublin Street)*, became a journalist and co-founded *The Nation*. He worked through the Young Ireland movement to repeal the Act of Union, formed the Tenant Right League and was elected as MP for New Ross. Disillusioned by the lack of response from Westminster, he emigrated to Australia where he became Prime Minister of the State of Victoria (1871) and worked for federation of the states.

County Museum ⊘ – *Hill Street near the Tourist Office.* The modern museum displays the **Cross of Clogher** (14C) together with local crafts (lace) and historic and prehistoric items; art gallery.

Town Centre – The elegant **Market House** (1792), designed by Samuel Hayes, an amateur architect, in the local grey limestone with round-headed arches and decorative carved panels, now houses the Tourist Office.

Church Square *(east)* is marked by the **Courthouse** (1830) by Joseph Welland, a handsome Classical building of stone quarried in the north of the county, which bears the scars of the Civil War, and by **St Patrick's Anglican Church** (1831), designed by William Farrell in the Regency Gothic style; the east window (1862) is the work of Fred Settle Barff of Dublin.

East of Church Square is the **Diamond**, the original market place against the north wall of the 17C castle (demolished); the **Rossmore Memorial**, an elaborate neo-Gothic drinking fountain (1875) was erected to the 4th Baron Rossmore *(see below)*.

At the south end of Dublin Street stands the 17C **Market Cross** in the form of a sundial; the head is upside down and the indicators are missing.

St Louis Convent – The history of the religious community from its foundation in France in 1842 is told in the **St Louis Heritage Centre** ⊘. There is a **crannóg** in Spark's Lake in the convent grounds.

EXCURSIONS

Rossmore Forest Park ⊘ – *2mi/3.5km south of Monaghan by N 54 and R 189.* The Forest Park, a delightful landscape of woods and water with rhododendron walks, was originally the demesne of the Earls of Rossmore.

Clones – *12mi/19km southwest of Monaghan by N 54.* Population 2094. Clones (pronounced as two syllables) is a pleasant market town and angling centre on the slope of a hill. In the central Diamond, below the Anglican church (1822), stands a **high cross** (c 10C) depicting *(west face)* Daniel in the Lions' Den, Cain and Abel and Adam and Eve, and *(east face)* the Crucifixion, the Last Supper and the Adoration of the Magi. It probably belonged to the monastery founded by St Tighernach in the 6C; the ruins *(bisected by Abbey Street)* include a **round tower**, a **monolithic shrine** and a 12C **church**.

The **Ulster Canal Stores** ⊘ building has been converted to house a display of **Clones lace**, a crochet lace, in which individual motifs are connected by areas of Clones knot.

Lough Muckno Leisure Park – *15mi/24km southeast of Monaghan by N 2 to Castleblaney.* The island-studded waters of Muckno Lake are surrounded by a wooded park (91 acres/37ha) laid out with **nature trails**. It was formerly the grounds of Blaney Castle, also known as Hope Castle, as it was bought in the late 19C by Thomas Hope, a London banker; in 1830 he purchased a

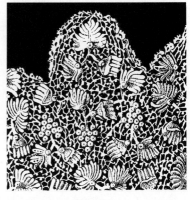

Clones Lace

B Lynch /Bord Fáilte, Dublin

45.5 carat diamond which was subsequently known as the Hope Diamond and is now in the Smithsonian Institution in the USA; it was apparently formed from the French Blue, which disappeared when the French crown jewels were stolen in 1792. The first castle, round which Castleblaney (population 2029) developed, was built on the orders of James I by Sir Edward Blaney, Governor of Monaghan. The 11th Lord Blaney (1784–1834) built the Georgian **Courthouse** and the Anglican church (1808).

Castle Leslie ⊘ – *Glaslough; 6.5mi/10km northeast of Monaghan by N 12 and R 185.* The house, a modest mansion for those days with about 70 rooms, was designed by WH Lynn in 1870 overlooking the lake and surrounding woodland. The historical tour of the reception rooms and bedrooms, including the haunted room, explains the history and connections of the Leslie family – the family Bible of Bishop John Leslie who settled at Glaslough (population 305) in the 17C, jewellery inherited from Mrs FitzHerbert, the morganatic wife of George IV, a baby dress worn by Sir Winston Churchill, a kilt in the Leslie tartan, a fireplace by Francesco della Robbia and a chest and fireplace from Perugia, acquired during a three-year stay in Florence.

For adjacent sights see CASTLE COOLE, CAVAN, ENNISKILLEN, Lough ERNE, NEWRY.

MULLINGAR

AN MUILEANN GCEARR – Co Westmeath – Population 8 040
Michelin Atlas p 91 and Map 923 – J, K7

The county town of Westmeath is an important agricultural market in the middle of prime cattle country. It is a good centre for anglers as it lies in a loop of the Royal Canal on the west bank of the River Brosna between Lough Owel and Lough Ennell. During his student days **James Joyce** spent some time in Mullingar where his father was reorganizing the electoral rolls; he had already begun to write and the town provided him with settings for scenes in *Ulysses* and *Stephen Hero*.

HISTORICAL NOTES

In the 2C AD there was a royal residence on **Uisneach Hill** *(6mi/9.6km west by R 390*, an ancient druidic sanctuary, where the Celts held ritual assemblies, particularly the Maytime festival. The **Catstone** marks the meeting point of the five provinces of ancient Ireland. When the Normans arrived in the 12C, they constructed several mottes and baileys in the region as well as stone castles; a Corporation was established in Mullingar with a seal, discovered in 1880. In the 16C under Henry VIII Meath was divided in two and Mullingar became the county town of Westmeath.

SIGHTS

Cathedral of Christ the King ⊙ – *Mary Street*. At the end of the street, in parkland extending to the Royal Canal, rise the twin towers (140ft/43m), surmounted by crosses, of the Roman Catholic cathedral, which was dedicated in 1939 and thoroughly restored from 1993 to 1997. It was designed by Ralph Byrne with a Classical portico above the main door; the tympanum contains a **sculpture** in Portland stone by Albert Power of the Virgin Mary handing a model of the previous cathedral, dedicated to St Mary, to Christ who is flanked by St Peter, St Patrick and Pope Pius XI. The **mosaics** in St Anne's and St Patrick's Chapels are by Boris Anrep, a Russian.
The **cathedral museum** *(upstairs – ask the Verger)* displays a letter written by Oliver Plunkett *(see p 140)*, his vestments; catechisms in Irish; a model of the earlier cathedral (1834–1936); penal crosses; chalices and monstrances.

Town Centre – In the market square stands the attractive 18C **market house**, which now houses the local Tourist Information Office.
The handsome **Courthouse** *(Mount Street)* dates from 1825. The prison was erected opposite at the same time but demolished at the end of the century and replaced by the County Buildings (1920). Public hangings took place in the intervening space. All Saints' Church (Anglican) *(Church Avenue or Church Lane)* was built on the site of the Augustinian Priory founded in 1227 by Ralph le Petit, Bishop of Meath. The church, which incorporates some of the priory stonework, was reconstructed late in the 17C and again in 1814 when the transepts and spire were added and the rectory was built.

EXCURSIONS

★**Multyfarnham Franciscan Friary** – *8mi/13km north of Mullingar by N 4; in Ballynafid turn right.* The outdoor Stations of the Cross are composed of life-size figures set in a grove of evergreens beside a swiftly flowing stream.

Taghmon Church – *7mi/11.5km north of Mullingar by N 4 and R 394; in Crookedwood turn right.* Between the stream and the foot of the slope on the site of a monastery founded by St Fintan Munna stands a fortified church, which probably dates from the 15C; the four-storey tower contains living accommodation and has two sculpted heads incorporated in the north and west walls.

★**Tullynally** ⊙ – *15mi/24km north of Mullingar by R 394 to Castlepollard and R 395 west; ramped drive (0.75mi/1.2km) from gateway to house.* Tullynally has been the seat of the Pakenham family since 1655. The drive winds through the park to a great grey pile of turrets and crenellations, formerly known as Pakenham Hall. The original fortress with its masonry walls (10ft/3m thick) was converted early in the 18C into a country house. In the 19C Francis Johnston added a Gothic façade (1801–05); the central tower and the two wings (1840) – for the Dowager Countess and the servants – linking the house to the stable block were designed by Sir Richard Morrison.

> ### The Children of Lir
> Tullynally is the old Irish place name, which means the Hill of Swans, and Tullynally Castle is set on high ground sloping south to Lough Darravaragh, where, according to Irish legend, the Children of Lir spent 300 years after they were changed into swans by their jealous stepmother.

The tour of the castle includes the **drawing room**, designed by Francis Johnston in 1806, which displays a Chinese cabinet, hand-painted by an Irishwoman in Cork, and a dinner service donated to Admiral Sir Thomas Pakenham by grateful German merchants for relief from pirates; the **Great Hall**, designed in 1820 by James Shiel, which rises through two storeys to a vaulted ceiling and originally had red and blue painted woodwork; the octagonal **dining room**, with wallpaper designed by Pugin for the House of Lords and country-style Chippendale furniture; the extensive **library**.

The Victorian service wings display the various equipment required to run a large country house – butler's room; **kitchen** splendidly equipped with ovens, copper pans, a great pestle and mortar and an ice chest; **laundry** fitted with lead-lined sinks, wash-ing boards and a huge box mangle; **ironing room; drying room** with vertical racks; **boiler room**. The family coach (restored) is on display in the courtyard.

By 1760 the early-18C formal layout with canals and cascades had been replaced by **gardens** designed in a more natural landscape style; the terraces were

created in the Victorian era for tennis and croquet. The **woodland garden** contains a beech tree, that produces both cut-leaved and normal foliage, and a grotto made of local limestone; from the seat there is a distant **view** of Knockeyon hill at the southern end of Lough Derravaragh.

The **flower garden** dates from 1740; a "weeping pillar" embellishes the lily pond. Two sphinxes (1780) made of Coade stone flank the gate into the huge walled **kitchen garden**; its former glory is still appreciable in the fruit trees trained against the walls, in the Regency glasshouses, where grapes and peaches were grown, and in the avenue of Irish yews linked by a variegated hedge of box, yew and holly, so dense that moss can grow on its surface.

From the stretch of ornamental water a **forest walk** leads past a waterfall to the lower lake (herons, swans and wild duck) and a **view** of the castle.

★**Fore Abbey** – *15mi/24km north of Mullingar by R 394 to Castlepollard and R 195 east; turn right to Fore*. The ancient monastic site of Fore was inhabited from the 7C to the 16C. It was enclosed within a wall, under a charter of murage (1436), to protect it from attack by the Irish. The ruins of the south and west gates are visible beside the road. Various features have traditionally been known as the **"Seven Wonders of Fore"** and described in miraculous terms.

The chief wonder, the "monastery in a bog", is the **abbey** founded in 1200 by the de Lacys for a community of Benedictine monks from Normandy, which stands on an island of firm ground surrounded by a marsh. The 15C cloister arcade, part of which was re-erected in 1922, is bordered by the ruins of the 13C church, sacristy and chapter-house, and the 15C refectory and kitchen. Two towers containing living accommodation were added when the abbey was fortified in the 15C. From the top of the west tower *(75 steps)* there is a good **view**; east stand the remains of a **columbarium** and of the **watergate**.

The "water that will not boil" refers to water from **St Fechin's Well** in the shade of a "tree that will not burn" with "no more or less than three branches", representing the Trinity; only one branch survives.

The "stream that flows uphill" appeared when St Fechin beat the ground with his crozier beside Lough Lene on the south side of the hill, to supply water power to the "mill without a race", which had been built at his command on dry ground; the mill ruins stand near the road beside a stream that flows from an underground source.

The "hermit in the stone" was Patrick Beglen, the last anchorite in Ireland, who lived in the 17C in an old medieval watchtower, which was incorporated in 1680 into a **chapel mausoleum** for the Nugent family.

The "stone raised by St Fechin's prayers" is the huge lintel marked with a Greek cross over the west doorway of **St Fechin's Church** *(south)*, an 11C or 12C building named after the founder who died in 665. The figure of a seated monk is carved in the moulding *(north side)* of the chancel arch (1200 – re-erected in 1934).

Mullingar Bronze and Pewter ⊘ – *5mi/8km east of Mullingar by N 4; after 4mi/6km bear left towards Killucan to The Downs*. Visitors may watch the craftsmen at work, moulding, soldering, turning, polishing and blackening, and admire and purchase the finished articles in the showroom.

★**Belvedere House and Gardens** ⊘ – *3.5mi/5.6km south of Mullingar by N 52 – half a day*. The beautiful site on the steep east bank of Lough Ennell is graced by an elegant villa (1740) which was probably designed by Richard Castle as a fishing lodge for Robert Rochfort, known locally as the Wicked Earl. From 1912 to 1960 the house became the property of Col Charles Howard-Bury.

Everest Expedition

In 1921 Col Charles Howard-Bury led an expedition to Everest. Dressed in Donegal tweed his party came within 2 000ft/609m of the summit, took the first photos of the mountain and brought back stories told by the local porters of "abominable snowmen" clad in their own hair.

The elegant **interior** (unfurnished) is embellished with finely-carved wooden chimney-pieces and window frames and a curving staircase balustrade. The ceilings in the hall and reception rooms are fine examples of Rococo plasterwork.

The **gardens** include three terraces overlooking the lake, added by Charles Brinsley Marly, Robert's great-great-grandson. The **walled garden** was started by Marly and developed by Col Bury, who also introduced peacocks. The **woodland walk** *(2mi/3km)* on the north side of the house includes an **octagonal gazebo**, a **Gothic arch**, an **ice house** and two **stone bridges** over the stream. The 18C plantations of beech have been supplemented by exotic conifers and other rare and ornamental trees introduced by Col Bury. The **jealous wall** (148ft/45m high), designed as a mock-Gothic ruin, was built in about 1760 by Robert to blot out the view of Tudenham House (now in ruins), the residence of his brother George. Behind it are the stables, converted into craft studios and a teashop.

The Wicked Earl

Robert Rochfort (1708–79), created 1st Earl of Belvedere in 1757, was a quarrelsome man. In 1836, following the death of his first wife, he married Mary Molesworth, aged 16; she was reluctant but her father was keen on the title and Robert's position at court; four children were born. As Robert spent more and more time at court, Mary turned in her need for company to her brother-in-law Arthur and his wife. Rumours of an affair between Mary and Arthur reached Robert. He brought an action against his brother for £20 000 damages; as Arthur was unable to pay, he went abroad for a number of years but on his return he was arrested and spent the rest of his life in prison. Mary was confined at Gaulstown, seeing no one but the servants. Once she escaped but her parents in Dublin sent her back to Gaulstown, where she stayed until Robert's death in 1774 when she was released by her son. Robert's rare visits to Gaulstown ceased completely once he had built another house, Belvedere on Lough Ennell. While living there he quarrelled with his other brother George and built the jealous wall to hide his brother's house from view.

For adjacent sights see ATHLONE, BIRR, KELLS, KILDARE, LONGFORD, TARA, TRIM, TULLAMORE.

NENAGH ★

AN TAONACH – Co Tipperary – Population 5 645
Michelin Atlas p 84 and Map 923 – H 9

Nenagh, the administrative centre of Tipperary North Riding, is located a few miles southeast of Lough Derg and bounded to the west and south by the Silvermine and Arra Mountains.

The town was first settled by the Anglo-Normans in the 12C; in the 19C it became a substantial garrison town. The 13C Franciscan friary, one of the most important in Ireland, was dissolved during the reign of Queen Elizabeth I and subsequently fell into ruin leaving only the walls of the church standing.

★**Nenagh District Heritage Centre** ⊘ – The Centre, which also operates the Tipperary North Genealogical Service, is housed in the old prison which was built in 1842. The **Gatehouse** contains the condemned cells and the execution room, which displays tableaux and biographical notes of the 17 men executed between 1842 and 1858.

The octagonal **Governor's House** has been converted into a local museum: *(basement)* relics of the traditional dairy industry; *(middle floor)* schoolroom with wooden desks, inkwells, blackboard and a tape recording of a class reciting sums; display on Lough Derg; scale model of the prison complex in the former chapel; *(top floor)* museum of rural life – craftsmen's tools, agricultural implements, laundry and kitchen utensils, tradesmen's tools.

★**Castle** – Opposite the Heritage Centre stand the ruins of Nenagh Castle, a fine Anglo-Norman structure built about 1200. Little remains but the circular keep (100ft/30m high), which was once part of the curtain walls.

EXCURSION

Newtown Water Mill – *4mi/6.4km west of Nenagh by R 494; turn left.* The mill, which is driven by a back-shot wheel, only recently ceased to grind corn and saw timber.

For adjacent sights see BIRR, CASHEL, KILLALOE, LIMERICK, ROSCREA, TIPPERARY.

NEW ROSS

ROS MHIC TREOIN – Co Wexford – Population 5012
Michelin Atlas p 80 and Map 923 – L 10

Despite its late-19C appearance New Ross is one of the oldest settlements in Co Wexford and dates from the late 6C. Its narrow streets, many linked by footpaths incorporating flights of steps, rise steeply from the quays on the east bank of the wide River Barrow to Irishtown, an earlier monastic settlement, on the heights above. Rosbercon is a small suburb on the west bank of the river. New Ross is still an important inland port; its industries include the manufacture of fertilizer which began in the 1950s.

HISTORICAL NOTES

In the late 6C or early 7C St Abban founded a monastery on the heights near Irishtown. New Ross itself was founded in about 1200 by William le Marshall, Earl Marshal of Ireland, and his wife, Countess Isabelle de Clare, daughter of Strongbow. The first bridge across the River Barrow was built in 1211 and in 1265 the first town walls were constructed. By the 14C New Ross had become the principal port of Ireland but was overtaken in importance by Waterford by the end of the 17C. In 1649 the town was captured and devastated by Cromwell but in the 1798 rebellion it was successfully defended against the insurgents. During the mid 19C New Ross had a substantial maritime trade, its ships going as far afield as Newfoundland and the Baltic ports.

SIGHTS

★**St Mary's Church** ○ – The early-19C Anglican church was built on the site of the nave and crossing of what was probably the largest parish church in medieval Ireland, and belonged to an abbey founded by William le Marshall and his wife Isabelle between 1207 and 1220. The extensive abbey ruins are surrounded by a large unkempt graveyard. The south transept was restored in the 15C but the tower collapsed in 1763. The ruined chancel contains some striking late-13C and early-14C effigies.

Roman Catholic Parish Church – The design of the church with its high ceiling and Corinthian columns was inspired by that of St Mary's Church *(adjacent)*; the frieze and cornice above the altar were made by craftsmen from Bannow. Construction began in 1832 but was interrupted by the cholera epidemic in that year which killed 3000 people in New Ross. The first building on the site was an Augustinian residence (1725); a chapel was erected in 1728. From the front of the church there are views over the town and river.

Medieval Gates – At Fair Green there are substantial remains of the 15C Maiden Gate; the Mural Tower and the Three Bullet Gate nearby date from the 14C. Cromwell entered the town in 1649 through the latter gate.

Tholsel ○ – This building, surmounted by a tower and a weather-vane, was built in 1749 and rebuilt in 1806, when the ground subsided. It houses the local council, which holds many volumes of corporation minutes dating from the 17C, as well as the mace of Charles II (1699) and the charter of James II (1688). Opposite the building is a statue of a **croppy boy**, a local term for the insurgents in the 1798 rebellion, owing to their short hair; it commemorates the uprising and the subsequent battle of New Ross.

Old Town Walks – There are two steep but rewarding climbs into the heart of the old town: flights of steps lead up from the Hotel New Ross towards the parish church, which may also be approached by a steeply-climbing footpath from Mary Street.

EXCURSIONS

★**Graiguenamanagh** – *11mi/18km north of New Ross by N 30, R 700 and R 705.* Population 1 395. The riverside quays, once the site of much commercial activity, provide good walks beside the Barrow, a fine fishing river. The Duiske Inn (prounced Dooishka), near the bridge, displays many old photographs showing aspects of life in Graiguenamanagh in the earlier decades of this century.

★★**Duiske Abbey** ⊘ – The most outstanding feature of the restoration is the high-pitched church roof, constructed from unseasoned timbers of oak and elm with wooden pegs to secure the joints. The effigy of the Knight of Duiske, cross-legged, sword-seizing, dates from about 1300 and is one of the most impressive anywhere in Ireland; the knight's identity remains a mystery.

The Abbey Centre houses a museum, which displays some of the Abbey plate and other items relating to the abbey, and a gallery exhibiting the work of contemporary artists on Christian themes using a variety of media.

The abbey, which once covered most of the present town, was established early in the 13C by William le Marshall, Earl of Pembroke. Although it was suppressed in 1536, monks continued to occupy it for many years afterwards; the tower collapsed in 1774.

★**Inistioge** – *10mi/16km north of New Ross by N 30 and R 700.* Population 261. Inistioge (pronounced Inisteeg), one of the most attractive villages in the locality, is set on the west bank of the Nore which is spanned by a 10-arch bridge; there are riverside walks *(picnic areas)*.

The ruins of a 1220 **castle** once the borough courthouse, stand between the river and the **square** which contains the remains of a cross erected in 1621 and damaged in 1798; on the west side next to the ruined Tholsel is the **Armillary Sphere**, a device said to have been invented by Eratosthenes in 250 BC to demonstrate the movements of the earth and moon. The 19C almshouse was built by Lady Louisa Tighe. The Roman Catholic church contains stone carvings *(near the entrance)* of uncertain date, said to illustrate the legend of the mermaid being taken from the River Nore in the village in 1118; up the lane is **St Colmcille's Well**.

Adjoining the Anglican Church are the tower, nave and Lady Chapel of an **Augustinian priory**, founded in 1210 and dedicated to St Mary and St Columba *(Colmcille)*. In the graveyard is the elaborate tomb erected in memory of Mrs Mary Tighe, a locally famous poet, who died in 1810.

Woodstock Forest Park *(1mi/1.6km southwest of Inistioge)* is the former Tighe family demesne offering forest walks, an old tiled Japanese garden and a conical dovecote; the house is largely ruined.

★**Kennedy Arboretum** ⊘ – *7.5mi/12km south of New Ross by R 733 and R 734; turn right (sign).* The arboretum (667 acres/252ha), opened in 1968 in memory of John F Kennedy, President of the USA, is divided into the plant collection, forest plots and mountain heathland. The many varieties of shrubs and trees are arranged in two circuits, one mainly conifers, the other broadleaf. When complete the collection should total 6 000 species. There are extensive walks through the arboretum, and a scenic road winds to the summit of Slieve Coillte. The views are superb, taking in the rich pattern of enclosed farmland, the Hook Peninsula and mountain ranges. Footpaths radiate from the car park, one of them leading to the **Mountain Viewpoint**, where a memorial stone commemorates the 1798 rebels who camped here.

Kennedy Homestead ⊘ – *Dunganstown; 4mi/6.4km south of New Ross by R 733 and the minor road west.* The whitewashed cottage *(privately owned)* was the birthplace in 1820 of the great-grandfather of John F Kennedy, President of the USA (1961–63). One room of the original four or five displays photographs and mementoes of the President's visit to Co Wexford in the summer of 1963, including the wreath he laid on the graves of the leaders of the 1916 Easter Rising at Arbour Hill in Dublin.

For adjacent sights see CLONMEL, ENNISCORTHY, KILKENNY, WATERFORD, WEXFORD.

PORTUMNA ★

PORT OMNA – Co Galway – Population 984
Michelin Atlas p 90 and Map 923 – H 8

Portumna, meaning the port of the oak, is a major crossing point on the River Shannon where it enters Lough Derg, the lowest and most attractive of the Shannon lakes, which is a wildlife sanctuary. There are facilities for coarse angling and game fishing and for boating on the lake.

★**Portumna Castle** ⊘ – The castle, which stands in the northeast corner of the park, was the seat of the Burke family. The approach passes through a series of formal gardens divided by an Adam Gate (partially ruined), a Gothic Gate and a Tuscan Gate *(nearest the house)*; the beds are planted with rose trees. The handsome fortified house (restored) dates from 1518 and was accidentally destroyed

Portumna Castle

by fire in 1826. The exhibition traces the history of the family, the house and its restoration. The castle caught fire in 1826 and was abandoned; a new house, designed by Sir Thomas Deane, was built but has left no trace.

The gate lodge *(opposite Reception)* displays a cannon, left by Patrick Sarsfield after the Battle of Aughrim *(see p 222)*.

De Burgo – de Burgh – Burke

The illustrious name of Burke derives from de Burgo, of Norman origin. In 1193 William de Burgo, who came to Ireland with Prince John in 1185, married the daughter of Donal Mor O'Brien, king of Thomond; his son was made Lord of Connaught; in 1265 Walter de Burgo was created Earl of Ulster. In the 14C the property passed to a descendant of Richard, Lord of Connaught, who adopted the name de Burgh by royal licence and was made Earl of Clanrickard in 1543. John, the 9th Earl, abandoned the family tradition of loyalty to the crown and fought with the Jacobites; he was taken prisoner at Aughrim (1691) and his lands confiscated but they were redeemed 12 years later for £25000. On the death of Hubert de Burgh Canning (1832–1916), who was a bachelor recluse, the title passed to the Marquess of Sligo and the land to Henry Lascelles, 6th Lord Harewood who married the Princess Royal, daughter of George V and Queen Mary.

Portumna Priory – South of the castle stand the ruins of a priory, originally a Cistercian chapel, which was granted to the Dominicans by O'Madden, the local chieftain. The north and south windows at the eastern end of the church, probably part of the Cistercian building, date from the 13C. The rest of the priory is 15C and contains some fine windows. The north transept seems to have been used as living accommodation. Parts of the cloisters were re-erected this century.

Portumna Forest Park – The park (1 400 acres/566ha), which extends west along the north shore of Lough Derg, combines a deer park with forest walks, nature trails, an observation tower, a marina and yacht club.

EXCURSIONS

★**Clonfert Cathedral** ⊘ – *17mi/27km northeast of Portumna by N 65, R 355, R 356 via Eyrecourt and a minor road east; key available at the lodge.* The church was built in the 12C, probably for Conor O'Kelly, on the site of a monastery founded in 563 by St Brendan the Navigator *(see p 170)*. The **west doorway**★★ is a masterpiece of Hiberno-Romanesque decoration in red sandstone. It is surmounted by a triangular hood, containing alternating human heads and triangles above a row of arches, and is framed by six recessed orders decorated with a variety of motifs and animal heads. The sixth order was added in the 15C, at the same time as the tower, south transept and sacristy. The chancel arch, also 15C, is carved with angels, a rosette and a mermaid; the beautiful east windows are Romanesque. The Romanesque south transept is in ruins; the Gothic north transept has been demolished.

The grounds *(through the rear churchyard gate; turn left)* contain an ancient **yew walk**, now suffering from storm damage and exposure; it was probably planted by the monks in the shape of a cross over 400 years ago. The ruined Bishop's Palace belonged to Sir Oswald Mosley from 1951 to 1954 when it was destroyed by fire. The charming circular oratory serves the Emmanuel Retreat House.

Meelick Franciscan Friary – *7mi/11km northeast of Portumna by N 65, R 355 and a minor road east.* The friary was built in the 15C on a slight rise overlooking the Shannon. In 1986 the ruins were restored and the church roofed and equipped for worship. Most of the walls, the west door and two arches in the south wall are original; between the arches is a small figure of St Francis which was added later. The west window and sacristy door were inserted in the 17C, the date of several wall tablets in memory of local families. During the restoration four quills were found in a chimney in the dwelling house which dates from 1732.

A short walk *(0.5mi/1km east)* leads to Meelick Weir and Victoria Lock, the largest lock on the Shannon.

Lorrha – *6mi/10km east of Portumna over the Shannon Bridge ⊙ by R 489 and a minor road south.* The tiny village contains three ruined churches. On the east side stands an ancient church, part of which is used for Anglican worship. On the west front there are antae and a 13C doorway framing a 15C doorway carved with a pelican vulning (pecking at her breast). It stands on the site of a monastery founded by St Ruadhán (d 845), a disciple of St Finian of Clonard. **St Ruadhan's Church** is a 15C building with an ornate west doorway, handsome east and west windows and a vaulted sacristy. On the south side of the village, next to the Roman Catholic church, are the remains of a church belonging to a Dominican priory founded by Walter de Burgo c 1269. The chancel was lit by a five-light east window and several lancets in the south wall.

For adjacent sights see BIRR, CLONMACNOISE, LOUGHREA.

POWERSCOURT ★★

Co Wicklow

Michelin Atlas p 87 and Map 923 – N 8 – Local map p 159

The estate takes its name from Eustace le Poer, a Norman knight. In 1609 the land was granted to Sir Richard Wingfield by James I who made him Viscount Powerscourt. In 1961 the estate was sold to Mr and Mrs RCG Slazenger.

Gardens ⊙ – The gardens were created on a steep south slope facing the Sugar Loaf Mountain (1 654ft/503m); they are well known for roses and flowering shrubs, an extensive range of conifers, a stand of Eucalyptus trees planted in 1897 and an avenue of beech trees which leads up to the front of the house.

Powerscourt Estate

Powerscourt Gardens

The house, designed by Richard Castle in 1730 to incorporate an earlier castle, was accidentally burned out in 1974. The ground floor has been restored and now houses a terrace café overlooking the gardens and an **exhibition** with video on the history of the estate and its owners.

Turn right along the terrace.

At the west end of the terrace is the entrance to the memorial garden, created in 1931 in memory of Julia, widow of the 7th Viscount, by her son; the four busts of Michelangelo, Cellini, da Vinci and Raphael are copies of the Vatican originals. The Bamberg Gate is a fine example of Viennese ironwork (1770). Several walled gardens descend the hillside to the pets' corner and the rhododendron grove.

The **terraces** were begun in 1843 by the 7th Viscount and designed by Daniel Robertson, a gouty eccentric, who directed the work from a wheelbarrow. The beach at Bray provided the black and white stones for the mosaic. Many of the statues were collected by the 6th Viscount (1815–44) who travelled extensively in Europe. Children take great delight in rolling down the steep grass banks, which descend to a lake where a Triton spews a jet of water (100ft/30m high) into the air; in summer the water lilies are in flower.

From the east bank the paths plunge into the jungle-like profusion of the **Japanese Garden** which was created in 1908 on reclaimed bogland. The stone **tower** *(54 steps)* provides an interesting view of the house and terrace and of the surrounding treetops.

Take R 760 south; after 2mi/3.2km turn right (sign); at the crossroads drive straight on for 2mi/3.2km to Valclusa.

★★**Waterfall** ⊘ – *5min on foot from car park to foot of waterfall; climbing the rock face is dangerous.* The waterfall is formed by the Dargle River which plunges (400ft/122m) in a spray of thick white spume down a jagged grey rock face in a horseshoe of hills. There are pleasant walks and nature trails by the river, and swings and slides for children at the visitor centre.

For adjacent sights see DUBLIN, DÚN LAOGHAIRE, MAYNOOTH, RUSSBOROUGH, WICKLOW MOUNTAINS.

ROSCOMMON

ROS COMÁN – Co Roscommon – Population 1 432
Michelin Atlas p 90 and Map 923 – H 7

Roscommon, the county town, is an important market in the middle of rich cattle and sheep country. Its name, which means Comán's wood, refers to St Comán, who was the first Bishop of Roscommon and abbot of Clonmacnoise. He founded a monastery of Augustinian canons in Roscommon; traces of it may have been incorporated into the Anglican church.

SIGHTS

Town Centre – In the fork at the top of the main street stands the **old courthouse** (1736), now the Bank of Ireland, which was used as the Roman Catholic church from 1833 to 1903.

On the north side of the square stands the **old county gaol**, erected in the 18C, where executions were carried out by "Lady Betty", the last hangwoman in Ireland, who used to draw her clients in charcoal on the prison walls before they died. She had murdered her lodger for his money, as she was starving, and given herself up when she realized that the dead man was her adopted son. She was condemned to death. When the hangman failed to arrive, she offered to hang the other convicts in exchange for her life and continued as hangwoman until the 19C.

★**Roscommon Castle** – *North of the town on N 61. From the car park 2min on foot over a stile and across a field.* On rising ground stands the impressive ruin of a Norman castle, originally protected by a lake or swamp which has since been drained. Its massive walls, which are defended by round bastions at each corner, enclose a large rectangular area. The entrance gate is in the west wall. The mullion windows were inserted in the 16C by Sir Nicholas Malby who made other alterations.

The castle was built in 1269 by Robert de Ufford. During the next three centuries it passed through many hands, English and Irish, until it was occupied, probably in 1578, by Sir Nicholas Malby, Governor of Connaught. In 1645 it was captured by the Confederates under Preston but he surrendered in 1652 to the troops of Cromwell who ordered its destruction.

Dominican Friary – *South of the town off N 63.* The ruined friary was founded in 1253 by Felim O'Conor. The traceried windows were inserted in the 15C when the north transept was added.

In a recess in the north wall of the chancel is a late-13C carved effigy of Felim, his feet resting on a dog; below is a panel, probably 15C, which depicts eight soldiers, possibly gallowglasses, armed with swords although one carries a battle-axe; above them in the spandrels are angels.

EXCURSIONS

Ballintober Castle – *14mi/22.5km northwest of Roscommon by N 60 and R 367*. The village (population 857) is dominated by the ruins of a castle built by the O'Connors about 1300. Two projecting turrets guard the entrance gate on the east side. The high walls, fortified by a polygonal tower at each corner and originally surrounded by a moat, enclose a large rectangular courtyard. The northwest tower, in which there is an inscribed fireplace, was partially rebuilt in 1627. In 1652 the castle was captured by the Cromwellians but returned to the O'Connor Don *(see below)* in 1677 and inhabited until the 19C.

Clonalis House ⊘ – *20mi/32km northwest of Roscommon by N 60 via Castlerea*. Clonalis is a Clan House, the ancestral seat of the O'Connor Don (Don means king or leader), descendant of the High Kings of Ireland and head of the O'Connor of Connaught, whose possession of the land goes back over 1500 years. The present house, which stands on rising ground beside the River Suck, was designed in 1878 by Pepys Cockerell in a Victorian Italianate style.

Beside the front door *(left)* stands the inauguration stone of the O'Connor clan which was formerly at **Rathcroghan** *(see below)*.

The **tour** *(1hr)* of the house presents several souvenirs of the O'Connors. Over the stairs hangs the Standard of St Patrick which was carried by the O'Connor Don at the coronation of George V. Among the portraits are Hugh O'Connor, who founded Tucson in Arizona, and Maj Maurice of Ballintober *(see above)* whose lands were confiscated under Cromwell, returned by Charles II and mortgaged to raise troops for James II.

Percy French (1854–1920)

The famous songwriter and gifted painter was born at Cloonyquin *(11mi/18km north of Roscommon by N 61)*. It was while studying engineering at Trinity College in Dublin that he began to write the songs which capture the humour and spirit of his native land. For seven years he was inspector of loans to tenants in Cavan and worked elsewhere in Ireland before moving to England in 1908; he died in Formby in Lancashire.

The **drawing room** displays a handsome collection of Meissen, Limoges and Minton porcelain figures. The **library** shelves hold some 5000 books: 18C diaries of Charles O'Connor (1710–90), written in Irish; facsimile of the *Book of Armagh*, the *Book of the Dun Cow*, the *Book of Fenagh* and the *Book of Hours of Anne de Bretagne*; O'Connor archives consisting of some 100000 letters and documents. The **dining room** furniture is Irish Sheraton except for the sideboards; the dinner service is Mason ironstone; the recesses beside the fireplace held logs.

Slide File, Dublin

Castlestrange Stone

The **bedrooms** display four-poster and tester beds, tapestries, 18C bonnets, 19C children's dresses and lace from Mount Mellick, Limerick, Brussels and Malta.

Two relics from the Penal Period are displayed in the **chapel**: the altar which comes from an earlier chapel built among the outbuildings of the previous house; the chalice which unscrews into two separate pieces for easy concealment and was used by Bishop O'Rourke who travelled as a farm labourer under the name of Fitzgerald.

The **billiard room** now displays some of the O'Connor archives: facsimile of the death warrant of Charles I; a grant of O'Connor lands under James II; letters from Louis XIV about an officer's commission; famine documents; letters from Douglas Hyde, Daniel O'Connell, Samuel Johnson, William Gladstone, Charles Parnell, Laurence Sterne, Anthony Trollope, Napper Tandy; O'Carolan's **harp**, his concerto and his portrait.

Rathcroghan – *15mi/24km north by N 61 and N 5.* The hill, on which there are several earthworks, is claimed to be the inauguration place of the Kings of Connaught and the prehistoric capital of Ireland.

★**Castlestrange Stone** – *7mi/11km south of Roscommon by N 63 and R 362 north. Turn right and left onto a private drive.* In a field *(right)* is a rounded granite boulder decorated with curvilinear designs in the Celtic style of ornament known as La Tène which dates from 250 BC.

For adjacent sights see ATHLONE, BOYLE, KNOCK, LONGFORD, STROKESTOWN, TUAM.

ROSCREA ★

ROS CRÉ – Co Tipperary – Population 4 170
Michelin Atlas p 85 and Map 923 – I 9

Roscrea is a prosperous agricultural town on the steep banks of the Bunnow River. It was founded in the 7C by St Cronan and developed into a medieval borough. The principal medieval relics are the castle and monastery.

SIGHTS

Roscrea Castle ⊘ – The 13C **castle** is an irregular polygonal enclosure surrounded by curtain walls and two D-shaped towers. It was originally entered through a gate-tower (c 1280), topped by 17C gables and chimneys; the portcullis winding gear is visible in the Great Hall. The gatetower now houses the **Roscrea Heritage Centre**, which presents an exhibition on the history of Norman castles in Ireland, including Roscrea.

★**Damer House** – Standing within the castle walls is an elegant 18C three-storeyed house containing a handsome pine staircase. It was started in 1715 by Joseph Damer, the richest man in the country when he died in 1720 and a member of a Plantation family which came to Ireland in 1661. The house was completed in the 1720s and became the residence of the Anglican Bishop of Killaloe. In 1798 it was used as a military barrack. After remaining vacant for many years this century, it was saved from demolition to make way for a council car park. The rooms house exhibitions of local historical interest and a computerized genealogical service.

St Cronan's Church and Round Tower – *Church Street.* The site of a monastery, founded by St Cronan during the early 7C and destroyed four times during the 12C, is marked by the west façade of a 12C church; the carved figure above the doorway is probably St Cronan. North of the ruins stands a 12C **high cross** bearing two carved figures at the foot of the north and south faces of the shaft. The 8C **round tower** (60ft/18m high) lost its conical cap in 1135; another piece (20ft/6m) was destroyed in the fighting in 1798.

Franciscan Friary – The present Roman Catholic church of St Cronan, set on a slight incline, is approached through the bell-tower of the original 15C friary. The east and north walls of the earlier chancel and part of the nave arcade have been incorporated into the modern church.

EXCURSION

Monaincha Abbey – *1mi/1.6km west by N 7 and minor road from the roundabout.* The ruined abbey church stands on a raised site, once an island in a bog; it has a finely carved 12C west doorway and chancel arch, of sandstone. The sacristy dates from the 15C or 16C. The monastery was probably founded in the 6C by St Cainnech of Aghaboe in Co Laois but was also associated with St Cronán of Roscrea.

Devil's Bit Mountain – *15mi/24km south of Roscrea by N 62.* Legend has it that the gap at Devil's Bit Mountain was scooped out by the devil to form the Rock of Cashel. Reality is more prosaic; the hollow was created by glacial action. There is an easy climb to the summit of the mountain (1 577ft/479m), rewarding for the extensive views of the Golden Vale to the south and east.

For adjacent sights see ATHY, BIRR, KILKENNY, NENAGH.

RUSSBOROUGH ★★★
Co Wicklow
Michelin Atlas p 87 and Map 923 – M 8

The magnificent Palladian mansion stands on slightly rising ground facing a stretch of water backed by the Wicklow Mountains. The grass terraces to the rear are part of the original landscaping. The short drive passes the old riding school before the full façade, consisting of a central block built of Wicklow granite, linked to two pavilions by curved colonnades, is revealed to view.

The house (1741–51) was designed by Richard Castle; following his death in 1757, the work was completed by Francis Bindon. It was commissioned by Joseph Leeson, made Earl of Milltown in 1763, who in 1740 had inherited a fortune from his father, a wealthy Dublin brewer. His caricature in stucco appears above the door from the staircase hall to the entrance hall.

Beit Art Collection

The paintings, which are displayed in the main rooms, were collected in the late 19C by Alfred Beit (1853–1906). In 1875 he went to South Africa where he became a friend of Cecil Rhodes; together they founded the De Beers Diamond Mining Company. On his death he left his collection to his younger brother, whose son, Sir Alfred Beit, bought Russborough as a home for the collection in 1952. The collection has a strong emphasis on works from the Dutch, Flemish and Spanish schools but also contains Italian, French and English paintings, Italian bronzes, European porcelain, furniture, tapestries and carpets.

TOUR ⊙ *1hr*

The ground floor is richly decorated with stucco ceilings, probably by the Lafranchini brothers, in the saloon, library and music room. The Dining Room and the barrel vault in the Tapestry Room are probably the work of pupils. An unknown and less accomplished hand created the very thick and ornate stucco on the staircase, depicting a hunting scene. The drawing room is probably the work of Francis Bindon; the decorative stucco panels on the walls were designed for the four Vernet seascapes now back in their original places after being sold in 1926. Such richness is complemented by ornate mantelpieces and extensive use of carved mahogany for the doors, dados, staircase and saloon floor, which is inlaid with satinwood.

The bedrooms on the upper floor contain maple and bamboo furniture and displays of porcelain and silver.

For adjacent sights see ATHY, DUBLIN, DÚN LAOGHAIRE, GLENDALOUGH, KILDARE, MAYNOOTH, POWERSCOURT, WICKLOW MOUNTAINS.

Salon, Russborough

Bord Fáilte, Dublin

SKIBBEREEN
SCIOBAIRÍN – Co Cork – Population 1 926
Michelin Atlas p 77 and Map 923 – E13

This busy market town owes its existence to Algerian pirates, who raided the neighbouring settlement of Baltimore in 1631. Some of the English settlers were captured but the remainder fled inland and set up two settlements, known as Bridgetown and Stapleton, which grew into Skibbereen.

The town suffered severely during the 19C famine but has regained a certain economic vitality in the last 20 years.

Regular arts events are held at the **West Cork Arts Centre** ⊙ in North Street.

EXCURSIONS

★**Creagh Gardens** ⊙ – *3.5mi/5km west of Skibbereen by R 595*. The gardens (30 acres/12ha) were created in 1945 on gently sloping ground leading down to a sea-estuary. They are designed for the Romantic in the Robinsonian style with woodland glades. There are many rare and tender plants, traditional walled kitchen gardens and exotic farmyard fowl.

"Keeping an eye on the Czar of Russia"

In the 1890s a leader in the *Skibbereen Eagle* remarked that the paper was "keeping an eye on the Czar of Russia". The comment, outrageously bombastic for a small provincial newspaper, was picked up by the international wire services and went around the world. Still quoted today, it turned out to be the most famous line ever written in an Irish newspaper. The files of the old *Eagle* may be inspected by appointment at the offices of the *Southern Star* newspaper in Ilen Street.

Liss Ard Experience ⊘ – *2mi/3km south of Skibbereen by R 596*. The estate is tended so as to enhance the natural flora and fauna. Each element is isolated from the rest to create a series of open-air "rooms" where visitors are invited to linger long in contemplation of the colours, shapes and sounds – the subtle colours in the wild flower meadow, the rustle of leaves in the woodland walk, the ripples on the surface of the lake, the chuckling of the waterfalls or the silence of the grass arena and oval of sky in the Crater, created by James Turrell *(see p 197)*.

Somerville and Ross

The village of Castletownshend was once a stronghold of the Protestant Ascendancy, whose way of life in west Cork was comically portrayed by Edith Somerville and Violet Martin, second cousins, who wrote in partnership as **Somerville and Ross.** They are buried in the graveyard of St Barrahane's Church. Their most successful work, *Some Experiences of an Irish RM* (1899), led to *Further Experiences of an Irish RM* (1908) and *In Mr Knox's Country* (1915). Their novel *The Real Charlotte* (1894) is in a much less light-hearted vein. *The Big House at Inver* (1925) is the best of the novels written by Edith Somerville after Violet Martin's death.

★**Castletownshend** – *5.5mi/8km southeast of Skibbereen by R 596*. Population 147. The steep Main Street of this tiny village descends to the water's edge where a small pier offers views across the Castle Haven estuary.

St Barrahane's Church (Anglican) ⊘ is attractively set at the top of four flights of steps *(50)* at the foot of the Main Street; the Nativity Window was designed by Harry Clarke

Lough Hyne Nature Reserve – *6mi/10km southwest of Skibbereen by R 595 and a minor road south. Extensive observation facilities in preparation. The presence of sea urchins makes barefoot paddling dangerous.* Set among low hills this marine

Baltimore

nature reserve containing unpolluted salt water provides a unique ecosystem; over 60 species have been recorded, including the redmouth goby otherwise found in Portugal. From the north side of the lough a track leads to a prominent viewpoint in the forest providing extensive panoramas of the area.

Baltimore – *8mi/13km southwest of Skibbereen by R 595. Ferries to Skull and Sherkin and Cape Clear Islands.* Population 217. The fishing village offers some of the safest anchorages on the southwest coast. Overlooking the two piers – one old, one new – are the ruins of the early-17C fortified house built by Sir Fineen O'Driscoll. On the headland *(1mi/1.6km south)* stands **Lot's wife**, a medieval beacon, shaped like a rocket and painted white; from its immediate vicinity there are panoramic **views** of Sherkin Island.

*★***Sherkin Island** Ⓥ – *Access by ferry from Baltimore or Skull (see below). A full day is needed to explore the island; if the weather turns stormy visitors may be marooned for a night or more.* Population 70. The **marine research station**, a privately-owned undertaking, monitors the marine environment and organizes courses on pollution.

Sherkin has three pubs, a number of guesthouses and four roads leading north and west from the harbour. The extensive ruins of a Franciscan **friary** near the harbour date from 1460.

Cape Clear Island Ⓥ – *Access by mailboat from Baltimore harbour. At least two days, more in bad weather, are needed to visit the island. Basic accommodation for visitors is provided by the bird observatory.* Population 150. The vast seabird colonies attract many ornithologists to Cape Clear Island. The north and south harbours are divided by an isthmus; the one tiny village is called **Cummer**. The island is one of the last bastions of the Irish language in west Cork. Many of the people living here are called O'Driscoll or Cadogan, which presents problems for the postman.

Mizen Peninsula

Tour of 35mi/56km west of Skibbereen – 1 day

From Skibbereen take N 71 west. After 10mi/16km turn left.

Ballydehob – Population 260. The steeply-sloping Main Street is lined with many brightly-painted houses. The 12-arch railway bridge, part of the Skull and Skibbereen light railway which closed in 1947, has been converted into a **walkway**.

Take the minor road north uphill bearing west and south to Mount Gabriel and Skull.

Road Bowls

The ancient Irish sport of road bowling is still played on Sundays in Co Cork and Co Armagh. A heavy iron ball (28oz/794g; 7in/18cm) is hurled along a stretch of quiet winding country road in as few throws as possible; the ball may hurtle through the air at shoulder height. Betting is heavy.

Mount Gabriel – This mountain (1 339ft/408m) offers a challenging climb. The traces of Bronze Age copper mining on the slopes contrast with the modern technology of the two globes near its summit which are aircraft tracking stations.

Take the road south to Skull.

*★★***View** – Beyond the pass there is a fine view of Skull and Roaringwater Bay.

*★***Skull (Schull)** – *Ferries to Baltimore and Cape Clear Island (see above).* Population 579. This small market town and commercial fishing centre is popular with yachtsmen. Skull can also claim two bookshops. The **planetarium** Ⓥ presents an exhibition, regular astronomy shows *(60 seats)* and holds telescope viewing nights.

Continue west; in Toormore turn left into R 591 to Goleen and Crookhaven. Turn right (sign) at the entrance to the village of Goleen.

The Ewe Ⓥ – This residential art centre welcomes visitors to its gallery and delightful sculpture garden overlooking the sea.

Crookhaven – This small hamlet set by the water's edge on the way to Streek Head can claim little more than two pubs, a few houses and the ruins of a 17C pilchard palace used for storing fish. From the harbour the extensive ruins of the late-19C copper mines are clearly visible on the north side of the inlet.

Take the minor road along the east side of Barley Cove.

Barley Cove – The deep inlet with its **sandy beach** between the cliffs makes a splendid holiday resort; the many chalets do not detract from the overall view.

After crossing the causeway at the head of Barley Cove turn left to Mizen Head.

Mizen Vision ⊘ – *10min steep descent on foot from car park.* A suspension bridge (150ft/46m above sea-level) spans the chasm between the mainland and Cloghane Island where a Fog Signal Station was built in 1910. It presents the work of the station and of lighthouse keepers, local marine life – dolphins, seals, basking sharks and whales and seabirds – and wrecks, the Fastnet Race and the building of the Fastnet Rock Lighthouse *(southeast – 9mi/14km).*

For adjacent sights see BANTRY BAY, CORK, KINSALE.

SLIGO ★★

SLIGEACH – Co Sligo – Population 17786
Michelin Atlas p 96 and Map 923 – G5

Sligo is a large and busy market town on the short River Garavogue which drains Lough Gill into the sea. It is surrounded by beautiful and varied scenery – green and wooded valleys, lofty mountains, sandy seashores. **Strandhill** (population 654) is good for wind-surfing but bathing can be dangerous. **Rosses Point** *(An Ros)* (population 707), a sandy peninsula projecting into Drumcliff Bay, provides a championship golf course and two beautiful sandy beaches for bathing and wind-surfing.

A Turbulent History – In 807 Sligo was plundered by the Vikings; following the Norman invasion in the 13C it was granted to Maurice Fitzgerald who built a castle and the abbey; for 200 years its possession by the O'Conors was disputed by the O'Donnells; a fort was built by the Cromwellians; Patrick Sarsfield reinforced the defences so that Sligo was one of the last places to capitulate after the Battle of the Boyne (1690); the Battle of Carrignagat (1798) was fought south of the town.

> ### Out and about in Sligo
>
> There are **waterbus trips** ⊘ on **Lough Gill**, particularly to the Isle of **Innisfree**, from Doorly Park and Parke's Castle. There are also boat trips offshore to **Inishmurray** from Rosses Point and from Mullaghmore *(north of Sligo).*

A Prosperous Port – In the 18C and 19C Sligo developed into a busy trading port which saw many emigrants set out for the New World. Several buildings date from that period: warehouses by the docks; the Courthouse (**B**), built in 1878; the City Hall (**AB H**), built in 1865 in the Italian Renaissance style. The stone building (**A**) with a rooftop look-out turret, now known as **Yeats Watch Tower**, once belonged to the Pollexfen family.

SIGHTS

★**Sligo Abbey** ⊘ (**B**)– *Key available at 6 Charlotte Street.* The original Dominican friary, founded by Maurice Fitzgerald in 1252 or 53, was accidentally destroyed by fire in 1414; the present buildings (1416),

> ### Yeats' Country
>
> The beauty of the landscape is reflected in the poetry of William Butler Yeats and in the paintings of his brother, Jack B Yeats. They often spent the summer holidays with their Pollexfen cousins at Elsinore Lodge on Rosses Point, and would spend time watching their grandfather's ships in the bay from the top of his warehouse, now called the Yeats Watch Tower *(private property).* William B Yeats, who is buried at Drumcliff *(see below),* recorded in verse his visits to Lissadell House *(see below)* on Drumcliff Bay.

which were spared by Queen Elizabeth on condition that the friars became secular clergy, were deliberately set on fire in 1641 by Sir Frederick Hamilton. The nave, which contains an elaborate altar tomb *(north wall)* belonging to the O'Creans (1506), is separated by a 15C rood screen (partially restored) from the 13C chancel, which has eight original lancet windows, a 15C east window and altar and the 17C O'Conor monument. The tower was added in the 15C and the transept in the 16C. North of the church are the 13C sacristy and chapter-house and part of the carved 15C **cloisters.**

County Museum and the Niland Gallery ⊘ (**B**) – The old manse (1851) houses the **Yeats Memorial Collection** containing manuscripts, photographs and letters.
The **collection of modern Irish art** includes work by George Russell, Maurice McGonigal, Norah McGuiness, Estella Solomons, Paul Henry and Augustus John; the small gallery *(upstairs in the adjacent library)* is mainly devoted to the paintings of Jack B Yeats and Seán Keating.

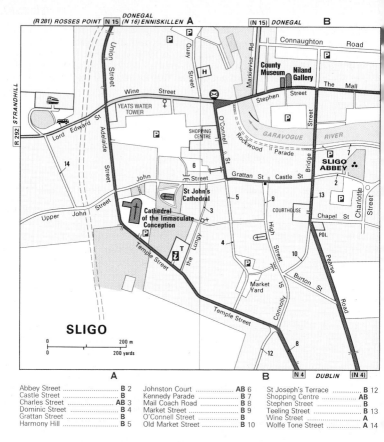

DONEGAL
(R 281) ROSSES POINT [N 15] (N 16) ENNISKILLEN **A** [N 15] DONEGAL **B**

SLIGO

0   200 m
0   200 yards

A   **B** [N 4] *DUBLIN* [N 4]

St John's Cathedral ⊘ (**A**) – This unusual structure was designed in 1730 by Richard Cassels; the tower is unaltered but the apse and the windows in the church were replaced during remodelling in the Gothic style in 1812. A brass tablet *(north transept)* commemorates WB Yeats' mother, Susan, who was married in the church; the tomb of her father, William Pollexfen, is near the main gates.

Cathedral of the Immaculate Conception ⊘ (**A**) – The Renaissance Romanesque building (1874) was designed by George Goldie. The lighting effect of the 69 stained-glass windows, made by Loblin of Tours in France, is best seen in the evening or early morning. By the main door is a small wooden statue of St Asicus.

EXCURSIONS

Sligo Peninsula

★**Carrowmore Megalithic Cemetery** ⊘ – *3mi/5km southwest of Sligo by a minor road.* Carrowmore is the largest Stone Age cemetery in Ireland; it consists of over 60 passage graves – dolmens and stone circles and one cairn, which is the largest grave; the oldest dates from 3200 BC, 700 years earlier than Newgrange *(see BOYNE VALLEY)*. The Visitor Centre contains an exhibition about Stone Age man and the excavations.

★**Knocknarea** – *7mi/11km west of Sligo by R 292. After 6mi/10km bear left; after 1mi/1.6km park at the side of the road; 1hr 30min there and back on foot to the summit.*
The approach road climbs up "The Glen", a natural fault in the limestone creating a special habitat in which rare plants thrive. On the summit of **Knocknarea** (1 076ft/328m) is a massive **cairn** (197yd/180m round), visible for miles, which probably contains a passage grave. Tradition says it is the burial place of Maeve, Queen of Connaught in 1C AD (also known as Queen Mab) but it is more likely that she was buried at **Rathcroghan** *(see p 239)*. On a fine day the **view**★★ from the top of the cairn is panoramic: in the foreground *(north)* Benbulben, *(east)* Sligo and Lough Gill, *(southwest)* the Ox Mountains; on the horizon *(north)* Slieve League, *(southeast)* the Curlew Mountains and *(southwest)* Croagh Patrick.

★★Lough Gill

Round tour of 30mi/48km east of Sligo – half a day

From Sligo take N 4 south; after 0.25mi/0.4km bear left (sign) to Lough Gill.

Tobernalt – *Car park (right) at the road junction.* The holy well shaded by trees marks an old Celtic assembly site where a festival was held in August (Lughnasa). *Continue on the shore road; at the T-junction turn left onto R 287.*

Dooney Rock Forest – *Car park.* The top of Dooney Rock provides a view of the islands in Lough Gill and of Benbulben *(north).*

At the crossroads turn left; after 2mi/3.2km turn left; 2mi/3km to car park.

Innisfree ⊙ – The tiny lake isle of Innisfree, immortalized by Yeats' poem, lies a few yards from the jetty; view of Lough Gill and Parke's Castle *(see below).*

Return to R 287 and continue east.

Dromahair – *Population 329.* This attractive riverside village lies between the shell of Villiers Castle (17C) and a ruined abbey.

Creevelea Abbey – *Park behind the Abbey Hotel (left); 6min there and back on foot across the bridge.* An avenue of evergreens beside the Bonet River leads to the ruins of a Franciscan friary which was founded by Owen O'Rourke in 1508. The church presents well-preserved east and west windows and west door. Carved pillars in the cloisters on the north side show St Francis with the stigmata and with birds perched on a tree. In the 17C the tower was turned into living quarters.

Continue on R 287 (car park and viewpoint).

★**Parke's Castle** ⊙ – The castle was built in 1609 by Capt Robert Parke, who became an MP in 1661; it was captured in 1647, surrendered to Coote in 1652 and soon abandoned. Extensive work has restored the stone slate roof, the mortice-and-tenon woodwork, the wainscoting and the window glazing. The bawn wall enclosing the yard supported the less substantial thatched outbuildings. There was a postern gate and a water gate to the lake; the water-level was higher (10ft/3m) in the 17C. The yard contains traces of an earlier tower house which probably belonged to the O'Rourkes. A limestone beehive **sweat house** stands by the shore.

Continue west on R 286 (car park and viewpoint); after 7mi/11.3km turn left.

Hazelwood – A nature trail explores the wooded peninsula which provides attractive views of the lake; the Palladian house *(private)* was designed by Richard Castle in 1731.

Continue west on R 286 to return to Sligo.

Benbulben

Round tour of 44mi/71km north of Sligo – 1 day

From Sligo take N 15 north.

★**Drumcliff** – *Car park.* In the churchyard at Drumcliff, where his great-grandfather had been rector, is **William Butler Yeats' grave** *(left).* Although he died in Roquebrune in the south of France in 1939, his body was interred here in 1948, as he had wished, and he himself composed the epitaph inscribed on his tombstone.

The site under the square escarpment of Benbulben (1 730ft/526m) by the Drumcliff River was also chosen by St Columba for the foundation of a monastery in about 575; the **round tower** was damaged by lightning in 1396; the **high cross**, which was probably erected c 1000, shows Adam and Eve, Cain killing Abel, Daniel in the Lions' Den and Christ in Glory on the east face, and the Presentation in the Temple and the Crucifixion on the west.

Make a detour left via Carney.

Lissadell House ⊙ – The austere neo-Classical house, designed in 1830 by Francis Goodwin, stands on the north shore of Sligo Bay surrounded by woods. It is still the home of the Gore-Booth family, which settled in the district in the reign of Elizabeth I.

The oval gallery, which is hung with paintings collected on the Grand Tour,

Countess Markievicz

The most remarkable member of the Gore-Booth family was Constance (1868–1927), who was an artist like her Polish husband, Count Markievicz; Constance was condemned to death in 1916 for her involvement in the Easter Rising but reprieved two years later; she was the first woman elected to the House of Commons in Westminster but never took her seat.

Benbulben

was designed as a music room and visitors may be invited to test the excellent acoustics at the grand piano. More paintings, by and of the family, hang in the rooms overlooking the garden. The influence of the Egyptian Revival is evident in the great marble chimney-pieces. The quaint mural portraits in the dining room were executed by Count Markievicz. Souvenirs of the family are displayed in the billiard room.

Leave the grounds by the north gate; turn left; after 1mi/1.6km turn left to Raghly (sign – 3mi).

Ardtermon Castle – Standing within its bawn wall is an early-17C house (restored) built by Sir Nathaniel Gore. The entrance is flanked by two round towers; the stair-case is contained in a semicircular projection at the rear facing the road.

Return to N 15 and continue north.

The road passes **Streedagh Point**, a sand bar (3mi/5km) lying parallel with the shore, where three ships from the Spanish Armada – *Juliana*, *La Levia* and *La Santa Maria de Vision* – were wrecked; over 1 300 men are thought to have died.

In Cliffony turn left to Mullaghmore.

Mullaghmore – Population 124. Sandy beaches flank the approach to the rocky headland pointing north into Donegal Bay. The village on the sheltered east side is grouped round the stone-walled harbour, built in 1842 by Lord Palmerston, who also built **Classiebawn Castle** (1856) which rises on the exposed west shore. Several members of the Mountbatten family were murdered here in 1979 by the IRA.

Inishmurray ⊘ – *11mi/18km offshore; access by boat from Mullaghmore pier and from Rosses Point near Sligo (see above).* St Molaise founded a settlement here in the 6C; remains of his monastery, which are surprisingly intact, include the Women's Church *(Teampall na mBan)*; rectangular and "beehive"-style dwellings; the main or Men's Church; underground passages and stone altars. Elsewhere on the island are pillar stones which may be pre-Christian, 57 inscribed stone slabs and 16 Stations of the Cross, spaced around the rocky perimeter. The island has a long history of human habitation – a decorated container found here dates back to 2000 BC – and not until 1948 did the last people leave, defeated by wartime fuel restrictions, which ended the regular supply-boat trips from Killybegs *(see p 131).*

From Mullaghmore return inland bearing left at the first fork and right at the second. At the crossroads turn left onto N 15; car park opposite.

★**Creevykeel Court Cairn** – *Car park.* The well-preserved court tomb, which dates from the Late Stone Age (c 2500 BC), consists of an open court leading into a double burial chamber surrounded by a wedge-shaped mound of stones. Two other chambers, entered from the side, were probably made later.

At the crossroads turn left inland.

Gleniff Horseshoe Scenic Drive – The road makes a loop *(6mi/10km)* into the Dartry Mountains along the west face of **Truskmore** (2 120ft/644m), over the streams at the head of the valley behind **Benbulben** (1 730ft/526m).

Turn left onto the minor road. After 6mi/9.5km turn left onto N 15; before reaching Drumcliff turn left onto a minor road.

★**Glencar Waterfall** *– Car park left; access path right; 5min there and back on foot.* The waterfall, which is more impressive after rain, tumbles over layers of rock to a sheer drop (50ft/15m) into a round pool.

Continue east. At the junction turn right into N 16 to return to Sligo.

For adjacent sights see BOYLE, CASTLEBAR, DONEGAL, ENNISKILLEN, Lough ERNE, FLORENCE COURT, KILLALA, KNOCK.

STROKESTOWN ★

BÉAL NA MBUILLÍ – Co Roscommon – Population 568
Michelin Atlas p 90 and Map 923 – H 6

Strokestown is a fine example of an estate village. The broad main street, supposedly modelled on the Ringstrasse in Vienna, was laid out at the beginning of the 19C to complement the new Georgian Gothic entrance to Strokestown Park House; the site of the earlier village is marked by a ruined church (1236) in the park east of Strokestown Park House.

In 1635 the land at Strokestown was confiscated from the Gaelic O'Connor Roe, part of whose bawn survives in the building which now houses the restaurant. In 1659 approx 6 000 acres was granted to Capt Nicholas Mahon (d 1680) for his services as one of Cromwell's 49 militia officers; the estate was extended after the Restoration in 1660 by Charles II to guarantee Mahon's support.

Mahon Family

Nicholas Mahon's grandson, Thomas Mahon MP, incorporated parts of an earlier dwelling in a magnificent new mansion, which was enlarged by Thomas' son, Maurice. Unlike his father who had opposed the Act of Union, Maurice accepted a Union peerage in 1800, becoming Baron Hartland of Strokestown. In 1845 the property passed to Major Denis Mahon, who was shot dead in 1847 by some of his tenants, possibly in mistake for his over-zealous agent or for organizing the assisted emigration to America of two-thirds of his destitute tenants during the Great Famine *(see below)*. The last member of the family to live at Strokestown was Mrs Olive Hayes Pakenham Mahon, who left in 1979.

★**Famine Museum** ⊙ – The museum, which is housed in the stable yard, presents a comprehensive and detailed display, based on State archives and the Strokestown estate records for the famine years, which were used by Cecil Woodham-Smith in compiling her book *The Great Hunger*.

The detailed and balanced exhibition traces the history of the family and the estate, and explains the political, economic and natural events in the mid 19C which produced the Great Famine and Emigration, comparing conditions in 19C Ireland with those in the Third World in the 20C.

★**Strokestown Park House** ⊙ – The house, a fine Palladian mansion designed by Richard Castle in the 1730s, consists of a central three-storey block with a pillared portico, linked by curving corridors to the service wings, and incorporates parts of an earlier house.

Most of the furniture was bought in 1779 after the house had been extended.

The tour includes the **hall and staircase** with their cornice and expensive white panelling by **Castle** and a coffin table; the **drawing room**, which is hung with a portrait of Thomas Mahon and his wife and a portrait of the Duke of Wellington bearing the Duke's seal and signature; the **library**, a well-proportioned room with a coved ceiling and its original brown and gold Paris wallpaper, added early in the 19C as a ballroom with a bowed wall to accommodate the musicians; the **dining room**, furnished with the original red damask wallpaper, a sideboard from Dublin, late-18C chairs, plate buckets, a wine warmer and a wine cooler.

On the first floor are the **mistress's bedroom** and the **master's bedroom;** a **schoolroom**, a child's bedroom and a **display of toys**, although children's rooms were usually on the top floor. The great **kitchen** *(north wing)* is fitted with a dresser displaying Belleek pottery *(see p 317)* and with spits and ovens for baking, roasting and smoking; it is overlooked by a **gallery**, which led to the housekeeper's room from a stair in the service corridor.

The splendid **vaulted stables** *(south wing)* were linked in the 19C by an underground passage to the yard on the north side of the house.

County Roscommon Heritage Centre ⊙ – At the north end of the village stands St John's Church (Anglican – deconsecrated), an octagonal structure designed in 1820 to resemble a medieval chapter-house; it now houses a genealogical research service and presents a historical interpretation of Strokestown.

For adjacent sights see BOYLE, CARRICK-ON-SHANNON, LONGFORD, ROS-COMMON.

TARA ★

Co Meath
Michelin Atlas p 93 and Map 923 – M 7
24mi/38km north of Dublin by N 3

The name of Tara conjures up the spirit of Irish Celtic greatness; the Hill of Tara, also known as Tara of the Kings, played a significant part in Irish legends. Its origin as a religious site is lost in prehistory; it achieved its greatest prestige under the pagan High Kings of Ireland, and even after the introduction of Christianity it retained its significance as the nominal seat of the High King until it was abandoned in 1022.

During the 1798 rebellion a skirmish took place on the hill. In the 19C O'Connell chose it as the site of one of his monster meetings in the cause of Roman Catholic emancipation; 250 000 people came to hear him speak.

The **bare hill** ⊙ pockmarked with earthworks does not readily suggest a royal palace. An effort of the imagination is required to envisage the many small buildings, of wood or wattle and daub, where the king held his court.

TOUR ⊙ *30min*

The history of Tara is recounted in an audio-visual presentation in the early-19C **St Patrick's Church,** which incorporates a medieval window.

In the churchyard stands a red sandstone pillar stone, known as **St Adamnán's Cross,** which bears a carved figure which may be the ancient Celtic god Cernunnos.

West of the graveyard is the **Rath of the Synods**, a ringfort with three banks. Further south is an Iron-Age ringfort, enclosed by a bank and a ditch, known as the **Royal Enclosure**. Within it is the **Mound of the Hostages**, a small passage grave which dates from about 1800 BC. In the centre of the enclosure are two ringforts, known as the **Royal Seat and Cormac's House**; at the centre of the latter, beside a statue of St Patrick, is a standing stone known as the **Lia Fáil**, which was moved from its original position near the Mound of the Hostages to be a memorial to those who died in 1798.

South of the Royal Enclosure is part of another earthwork known as **King Laoghaire's Rath.** To the north of the churchyard is a hollow flanked by two long parallel banks, which may have been the grand entrance but which is known as the Banqueting Hall. On the west side are three circular earthworks; the first is known as Gráinne's Fort, the other two as the Sloping Trenches.

South of the hill *(0.5mi/0.8km – visible from the road)* is part of another ringfort, known as **Rath Maeve**, surrounded by a bank and ditch.

For adjacent sights see BOYNE VALLEY, DROGHEDA, FINGAL, KELLS, MAYNOOTH, TRIM.

TIPPERARY

TIOBRAID ARANN – Co Tipperary – Population 4772
Michelin Atlas p 84 and Map 923 – H 0

Tipperary is a pleasant country town on the River Ara in the Golden Vale, prime dairy farming country. The Normans built a motte and bailey, still visible northwest of the town. Its excellent modern sporting facilities contrast with its status as a heritage town and the conservation of its traditional 19C shop fronts. Tradition is also maintained by the **Genealogical Service**, housed in the old prison, and the clans office in James Street.

Old IRA Exhibition ⊙ – *Canon Hayes Sports Complex.* The display commemorates the exploits of the 3rd Tipperary brigade of the old IRA which fought many battles during the War of Independence.

EXCURSION

★**Glen of Aherlow** – *6mi/10km south of Tipperary by R 664.* The road climbs through thick woodland over the Slievenamuck Ridge; gradually, as it descends the south face, the magnificent prospect is revealed. From the **viewpoint** *(parking)* one can see the beautiful glen (11mi/18km long), which follows the course of the River

Aherlow as it flows east to join the River Suir. To the south rise the Galty Mountains, which provide delightful woodland trails in the forests on the lower slopes, and good climbing and hill walking among the corrie lakes and peaks of the upper slopes.

New Tipperary

In the late 19C the town was a centre of Land League agitation. When the rents were raised in 1889 by Hugh Smith Barry, the local landlord, some tenants rebelled. West of the town centre, on land belonging to another landlord, they built a new town, assisted by tenants from all over Ireland who voluntarily gave a week's labour. The shopping arcade has been demolished but some of the properties still stand in Emmet Street and Dillon Street. In the former the buildings were designed so that, at a later date, the shop could be demolished leaving an ordinary house; Daltons (no 9) has been restored to its original state.

For adjacent sights see CAHER, CASHEL, KILMALLOCK, LIMERICK, NENAGH.

TRALEE

TRÁ LÍ – Co Kerry – Population 19 056
Michelin Atlas p 83 and Map 923 – C 11

Tralee, the county town of Kerry, is situated at the head of Tralee Bay on the northern approach to the Dingle peninsula. As the town was largely destroyed during the 17C wars, its architecture dates from the 18C. During the last three decades it has developed as the main commercial centre of north Kerry. Barnacle geese graze on the springy turf of Tralee Bay. The Vale of Tralee *(northeast)*, which was thickly wooded in Tudor times, now provides rich pasture for the black Kerry cattle.

Desmond Stronghold and Denny Fief – Tralee grew up around the castle built by the Anglo-Norman, John Fitzgerald, in 1243; it became the principal seat of his descendants who in 1355 received the title Earl of Desmond. Following the Desmond rebellion the town and neighbouring land (6 000 acres/2 428ha) were confiscated and granted to Sir

Out and about in Tralee

The performances of the **National Folk Theatre of Ireland** ⊘ (Siamsa Tíre), founded in 1974, draw on the rich local Gaelic tradition to evoke in music, song, dance and mime the seasonal festivals and rural way of life in past centuries. The past is also reflected in the ultra-modern theatre building which is shaped like a ringfort; a round tower gives access to the upper catwalks.
There are indoor water facilities at the **Aqua Dome** ⊘ and beaches west and north in Tralee Bay.

Henry Denny, in recompense for his services to the English Crown at the massacre of Dun an Oir on Smerwick Bay in 1580 when the 15th Earl of Desmond was killed. For the next 300 years Tralee was controlled by the Dennys; the town became strongly nationalistic in outlook.

SIGHTS

Kerry – The Kingdom ⊘ – *Ashe Memorial Hall.* In **Geraldine Tralee** *(downstairs)* the sights, sounds and smells of the medieval town, the seat of power of the Anglo-Norman Fitzgeralds (1300–1500), are recreated for visitors who are carried through a partial reconstruction of Tralee in time cars equipped with multi-lingual commentary.
In the **Kerry County Museum** *(upstairs)* the countryside north of Tralee and its history are illustrated by local artefacts and an audio-visual presentation – *Kerry in Colour.* The surrounding **town park** contains the ruins of the **Geraldine castle** and a statue of William Mulchinock (1820–64) *(see below).*

Tralee-Blennerville Light Railway ⊘ – The Centenary Year of the old Tralee–Dingle Light Railway (1891–1953) was marked by the re-opening to passenger traffic of the first stretch *(1.5mi/2.4km)* of the narrow-gauge (3ft/1m) line between Tralee and Blennerville *(see below).* The train is composed of three original carriages drawn by one of the original steam locomotives, no 5, a 2-6-2 built by Hunslett of Leeds.

Rose of Tralee

Every August the town is host to the International Rose of Tralee Festival which attracts visitors, particularly emigrants, from many parts of the world; all girls of Irish descent are eligible for the title. A statue of William Mulchinock (1820–64), who wrote the song *The Rose of Tralee*, stands in the Town Park.

"She was lovely and fair
as the rose of the summer
Yet t'was not her beauty alone that won me
Oh no t'was the truth in her eye ever dawning
That made me love Mary, the Rose
of Tralee."

Dominican Memorial – *Dominic Street*. The commemorative figure of a Dominican, by local sculptor Noel Fitzgibbon, is backed by an arcade, carved by local apprentices in 1987–88 in the style of the original abbey, which was founded by John Fitzgerald in 1243 and destroyed by Cromwellian forces in 1652. The present Dominican Church *(Rock Street)* dates from 1861 when the Dominican order returned to Tralee.

Courthouse – This building (restored) was designed in the mid 19C by Sir Richard Morrison in the Greek Revival style. The two lions gracing the entrance steps are dedicated to Irish soldiers who died in India and the Crimea.

EXCURSIONS

★**Blennerville Windmill** ⊙ – *2mi/3.2km south of Tralee by R 559*. The five-storey windmill (60ft/18m high), built by the local landlord, Sir Rowland Blennerhassett, c 1800 and derelict by 1880, is again in working order with a new cap and sails and two sets of grinding stones; an electric engine takes over when the wind fails. Information on windmills and milling is displayed on the ground floor.

The **Emigration Exhibition** in the adjoining building illustrates the experience of the many thousands who left Ireland for America in the 19C – embarkation, the sea voyage, food, medical matters, quarantine on arrival.

In the **craft workshops** visitors can see artists at work and buy the finished product – pottery, enamels etc.

★**Crag Cave** ⊙ – *11mi/18km east of Tralee by N 21 to Castleisland (Oileán Ciarraí); take the minor road north for 1mi/1.6km (sign)*. The complex of limestone caves (4170yd/3813m), discovered in 1983, is thought to be over a million years old. A short descent *(62 steps)* leads to the tunnels and chambers of the show cave (383yd/350m); lighting enhances the natural beauty of the many calcite formations – stalactites, stalagmites, columns, curtains, drip stones and flow stones. The myriad shimmering white straw stalactites in the **Crystal Gallery** provide a magical climax.

★**Ardfert** – *5.5mi/9km north of Tralee by R 551*. Population 677. Ardfert was established as a missionary base as early as the 5C. The stone church, founded in the 6C by St Brendan the Navigator *(see p 170)* as part of a monastery, was damaged by lightning in 1046 and destroyed by fire in 1089. Under the Normans Ardfert became an important borough; two major ecclesiastical ruins have survived from this period. The **cathedral** ⊙ was built c 1150, extended in the 15C, 16C and 17C and destroyed by fire in 1641 during the Cromwellian wars. The south transept (15C), which was used as a parish church from 1671 to the mid 19C, contains an exhibition on the history of the site. In the chancel there are graduated lancet windows in the east wall and a row of nine lancets in the south wall. The nave walls contain effigies of two 13C bishops by the main east window. The doorway and decorated arch in the west gable, a remnant of an earlier church, are in the Irish-Romanesque style.

Temple na Hoe, the Church of the Virgin, is a Romanesque church, without its chancel; the window in the south wall preserves some patterns of petalled flowers, geometrical designs and small decorative bosses.

In Temple na Griffin (15C) the jamb of the window at the east end of the north wall is decorated with carved griffins.

The round tower (119ft/36.5m high) collapsed in 1771.

Ardfert Friary, a Franciscan house, was founded in 1253 and substantially rebuilt in 1453; much of the tower and of the chancel with its nine lancets in the south wall and five-light lancet in the east wall are still intact.

Opposite **St Brendan's Church** (Roman Catholic), built in 1855, stands a memorial to the victims of Black and Tan atrocities committed in the district during the War of Independence (1919–21).

Fenit Sea World ⊙ – *8mi/13km north of Tralee by R 551 and R 558*. At the bend of the L-shaped pier *(0.5mi/0.8km; parking)*, where fish and oil products are landed, stands the aquarium. Every few minutes a wave of water crashes in above the entrance door to keep the water moving in the tanks. All the myriad species of fish displayed are named and identified. The touch-tank presents cockles, mussels, urchins, crabs, limpets and starfish.

★**Banna Strand** – *7.5mi/13km northwest of Tralee by R 551.* The vast stretch of sandy beach (5mi/8km) was used for the filming of *Ryan's Daughter* in 1968. A memorial at the entrance commemorates Sir Roger Casement (1864–1916), who landed on the beach on 21 April 1916 from a German submarine with a consignment of arms for the Easter Rising.

★**Rattoo Round Tower** – *13mi/21km north of Tralee by R 556.* The round tower, which is very well preserved, and the ruined 15C church mark the site of an abbey founded in 1200 for the Knights Hospitaller of St John the Baptist. In 1202 it became an Augustinian house, which was burned in 1600.

The **Rattoo-North Kerry Museum** ⊘ at Ballyduff *(2mi/4km north)* displays relics illustrating the history of the locality from the Mesolithic Age to the 1950s – Bronze Age (2000 BC) ferry boat carved from a split oak trunk; medieval shoe, wooden cream-cooling pan, thatching needle and comb.

Listowel (Lios Tuathail) – *17mi/27km north of Tralee by N 69.* Population 3347. The exceptional literary reputation of the market town of Listowel and of North Kerry is celebrated in **Writers' Week**, which is held annually in May and attracts worldwide participation. In the huge central square stands **St John's Art and Heritage Centre** ⊘, formerly the Anglican parish church, which offers live performances of music and theatre, film shows and various exhibitions about art, literature, history; the permanent display, consisting of collected texts, archive recordings and audiovisual presentations, covers the work of John B Keane, Brian McMahon, Brendan Kennelly and other local writers.

In the northeast corner of the square is the striking **plasterwork façade** of the Central Hotel.

Ballybunnion – *20mi/32km north of Tralee by R 556 and R 551.* Population 1346. This seaside resort has many amusement arcades and several beaches; it is also noted for its outdoor baths, where seaweed is used for therapeutic purposes. From the ruins of **Ballybunnion Castle**, built in 1583, there are extensive **views** *(north)* to Loop Head and *(south)* to the Dingle peninsula.

★**Carrigafoyle Castle** – *27mi/43km north of Tralee by N 69 to Listowel, R 552 to Ballylongford and a minor road north.* Once the principal seat of the O'Connor clan, who ruled most of north Kerry, the castle stands beside a sea-inlet on what was once an island; it was finally destroyed by Cromwellian forces in 1649. One of the flanker towers is fitted out as a dovecot. A spiral staircase leads to the top of the tower (80ft/29m high) for extensive **views** of the Shannon estuary.

Lislaughtin Abbey – *26mi/42km north of Tralee by N 69 to Listowel and R 552 via Ballylongford.* This Franciscan foundation dates from the 15C; the church has an attractive west window and three well-preserved sedilia; traces of the refectory and dormitory remain on the east side of the cloisters; the lavatories were housed in the tower at the north end.

Tarbert – *28mi/45km north of Tralee by N 56 via Listowel.* Population 679. **Tarbert Bridewell** ⊘, built 1828–31, has been converted into a museum describing through wax tableaux in the courtroom and cells the legal and penal systems in force in Ireland at that time.

The **woodland walk** *(starting from the car park)* leads through the grounds of **Tarbert House** ⊘ (17C), which has seen such notable guests as Benjamin Franklin, Charlotte Brontë and Daniel O'Connell, and continues along the wooded shore to Tarbert Old Pier. The new pier is the departure point for the **Shannon car ferry** ⊘ which crosses to Killimer near Kilrush.

For adjacent sights see ADARE, DINGLE PENINSULA, IVERAGH PENINSULA, KILLARNEY.

On the cover of Michelin Green Guides,
the coloured band on top indicates the language:
    pink for English
    blue for French
    yellow for German
    orange for Spanish
    green for Italian etc.

TRIM ★

BAILE ÁTHA TROIM – Co Meath – Population 1740
Michelin Atlas p 92 and Map 923 – L 7

Trim straddles the River Boyne by an ancient ford. In the 12C Hugh de Lacy, appointed Lord of Meath by Henry II in 1172, chose the town as his headquarters, where Parliament sometimes met. He controlled his territory, which stretched from the Irish Sea to the Shannon, by dividing it into baronies which he granted to his knights.

SIGHTS

★★**Trim Castle** ⊘ – *South bank; access through the Town Gate or along the river bank from the bridge*. The magnificent ruins of this medieval castle stand on the south bank of the River Boyne. The central **keep**, which was built between 1220 and 1225, consists of two great halls with sleeping accommodation above; the entrance is in the east tower facing the Dublin Gate. The castle walls date from c 1250; the holes for the beams which supported a wooden sentry walk are best seen in the east section near the river.

> ### The Pale
> In the Middle Ages the Irish who lived outside the Anglo-Norman jurisdiction were said to be beyond the Pale. The term derives from the Latin word *palus* for a stake. Its use to describe the part of Ireland under effective English rule dates from 1446. The settlement made under Henry II (1154–89) comprised Louth, Meath, Trim, Dublin, Kilkenny, Tipperary, Waterford and Wexford, but by the late 15C the Pale had shrunk to only four counties, Louth, Meath, Dublin and Kildare.

The **Dublin Gate** was protected by two drawbridges and a barbican; the upper floors served as a prison where Henry IV was held by Richard II until he escaped and captured the English throne. Westwards along the wall are a 17C limekiln, two sally ports and a small square building where cannon balls were made in the Cromwellian period to be fired from a cannon mounted on the in-filled tower.

The west-facing **Town Gate** has a medieval flagstone floor, a portcullis groove and barrel-vaulted arches. The smaller breach in the river wall was caused by Cromwell's troops and the larger stretch collapsed in the Big Wind in 1839; in between is an underground chamber.

Across the river stands a stone arch, the medieval **Sheep Gate** where tolls were levied on flocks bought and sold at the great sheep fairs.

Yellow Steeple – *North bank; access from the High Street*. The ruined late-14C tower, which gleams in the sun, marks the site of **St Mary's Abbey**, an Augustinian community, founded by St Malachy of Armagh in the 12C near the point where St Patrick landed in the 5C and converted Foitchern, the son of the local chieftain and later first Bishop of Trim. Many pilgrims were attracted to the abbey by Our Lady of Trim, a wooden statue with a reputation for effecting miracles, which disappeared in the Cromwellian period.

In 1425 the west cloisters of the abbey were converted by Lord Lieutenant Talbot into a fortified house, **Talbot's Castle**, which bears the Talbot coat of arms on the north wall. After the Reformation the house became a Latin School, later attended by Sir Rowan Hamilton, the mathematician who discovered quaternions, and the Duke of Wellington, later MP for Trim, whose family home was at Dangan *(southeast)*.

Cathedral – *North bank; 1mi/1.6km east at Newtown Trim*. Among the graves of New-

Trim Castle

town Cemetery is a **tomb** bearing the recumbent figures of Sir Luke Dillon, in his Renaissance armour, and his wife, Lady Jane Bathe, in an Elizabethan gown; people leave pins on the tomb in the belief that their warts will disappear.

Further west are the ruins of a **cathedral**, dedicated to St Peter and St Paul; it was built early in the 13C to replace the church at Clonard *(southwest)*, which was burned by the Irish at the end of the 12C. The founder, Simon de Rochfort, the first Anglo-Norman Bishop of Meath, was buried under the high altar. The foundations show that the original cathedral was very large with a long nave, aisles and transepts. The south wall collapsed in the Big Wind in 1839.

Southwest of the cathedral are the remains of a **priory**, also founded by Simon de Rochfort, for a community of Canons Regular of St Victor, who originated in Paris. The south and west walls of the refectory still stand, next to the 14C kitchen; the foundations of the chapter-house doorway are also visible.

Crutched Friary – *South bank; 1mi/1.6km east at Newtown Trim.* On the south bank of the Boyne are the ruins of a 13C hospital built by the Crutched Friars, an order of mendicant friars who wore a cross on their habits. The buildings consist of a keep with several fireplaces, a ruined chapel with a triple-light window and the hospital and stores beside the river.

EXCURSION

★**Bective Abbey** – *5mi/8km northeast by R161 (T26); after 4mi/6.4km turn right. Park beyond the abbey near the bridge.* The impressive and extensive ruins stand in a field on the west bank of the Knightsbrook River. The abbey, one of the earliest Cistercian houses in Ireland, was founded in 1150 by the King of Meath, Murcha Ó Maolsheachlainn, and dedicated to the Blessed Virgin; its abbot was a member of the Parliament of the Pale and Hugh de Lacy was buried here in 1195. Little remains of the 12C buildings. The **cloisters**, the tower and the great hall in the south wing date from the 15C when the buildings were altered and fortified. The film *Braveheart*, about Robert Bruce, was shot among these ruins and also at nearby Dunsoghly Castle.

For adjacent sights see BOYNE VALLEY, FINGAL, KELLS, MAYNOOTH, MULLINGAR, TARA.

The length of time given in this guide
– for touring allows time to enjoy the views and the scenery;
– for sightseeing is the average time required for a visit.

Dúchas

TUAM

TUAIM – Co Galway – Population 3 446
Michelin Atlas p 89 and Map 923 – F 7

The small city of Tuam, with its two cathedrals, is the ecclesiastical capital of Connaught. In 1049 the O'Connor kings of Connaught made it their headquarters and in the 12C, when Turlough and Rory O'Connor were High Kings of Ireland, it was virtually the capital of the whole country.

In 1252 the right to hold markets was granted to the Archbishop by Henry III; in 1613 James I granted a charter and the city was laid out to its present plan, with all the streets converging on the central diamond.

SIGHTS

★**St Mary's Cathedral** ⊘ – *West of the town centre*. The site, which is enclosed by a high wall, is that of a monastery founded late in the 5C by Jarlath, a follower of Benen of Kilbennan *(north)*. The original cathedral was founded in 1130 but most of the present Anglican church was designed by Sir Thomas Deane in 1860 in the neo-Gothic style, with a tower and a hexagonal spire (200ft/61m). In the north aisle by the west door stands the shaft of a 12C **high cross**; the inscription asks for prayers for the king, Turlough O'Connor, for the craftsman and for Jarlath's successor, Aodh Ó'hOisín, for whom the cross was made. The complete 12C cross, which formerly stood in the town square, is only partly composed of original pieces; one face depicts the Crucifixion and the other an abbot or bishop. All that remains of the original church is the red sandstone **chancel**; the two windows and the chancel arch with its five rows of moulding are fine examples of 12C Irish-Romanesque architecture. East of the cathedral is a 14C building, which was badly damaged by the Cromwellians and has been restored in its original castellated style to serve as a Synod Hall.

Cathedral of the Assumption ⊘ – *East of the town centre*. The foundation stone of the Roman Catholic cathedral was laid in 1827, a year before the Emancipation Act. Funds were subscribed by the local inhabitants regardless of denomination. The cruciform neo-Gothic structure was designed by Dominic Madden. The Stations of the Cross, thought to be by Eustache Le Sueur, a 17C portrait painter, were bought by Archbishop John McHale (1791–1881), an eminent Gaelic-speaking churchman, whose statue stands outside the entrance *(north)*. The east window (1832) by Michael O'Connor of Dublin depicts St Mary and the Evangelists; the fourth window in the north aisle (1961) shows Jarlath who was advised by St Brendan of Clonfert to build where the wheel of his chariot broke. The four windows, depicting the Ascension, the Crucifixion, the Assumption and the Apparition at Lourdes, are from the Harry Clarke Studios.

Mill Museum ⊘ – *West of North Bridge*. The 17C corn mill on a tributary of the Clare River has been converted into a milling museum; three sets of mill-wheels are driven by an undershot spur wheel. There is an audio-visual presentation on the history of Tuam and its locality.

St Jarlath's Churchyard – *West of town centre*. Irish yews grow among the graves surrounding the ruins of the 13C parish church, which was dedicated to the patron saint of Tuam; the west tower contained a lodging for the priest, and after the Reformation Roman Catholic clergy were buried in a side chapel. Some of the tombstones are inscribed with symbols showing the occupation of the deceased.

EXCURSION

★**Knockmoy Abbey** – *12mi/19km southeast of Tuam by R 332; after 9mi/14.5km turn right at the crossroads onto N 63. In Knockmoy village turn right. After crossing the river turn right and park by the cemetery. 15min there and back on foot by a path and four stiles.*

In the fields on the north bank of the River Abbert are the substantial ruins of an abbey which was founded in 1189 for the Cistercians of Boyle by Cathal O'Connor, king of Connaught, and dedicated to the Blessed Virgin Mary.

The church consists of the nave, a transept with two chapels and the **chancel** which is decorated with some fine stone carving and a 13C tomb niche. Behind a protective grill is a rare **fresco** (1400) of the medieval legend of the Three Live Kings, who are dressed for hawking, and the Three Dead Kings, who bear the inscription "We have been as you are, you shall be as we are". Two partition walls, inserted in the 14C or 15C, have spoiled the east window of the chapter-house in the east wing of the conventual buildings; little remains of the refectory in the south wing and even less of the cloisters.

For adjacent sights see CONG, GALWAY, LOUGHREA, ROSCOMMON.

TULLAMORE

TULACH MHÓR – Co Offaly – Population 8 622
Michelin Atlas p 91 and Map 923 – J 8

The town of Tullamore has been the county town of Co Offaly since 1833. It is bisected by the Tullamore River and in 1798 was linked by the Grand Canal to Dublin and the River Shannon. To the south rise the Slieve Bloom Mountains.

Tullamore Dew

The distillery, which was founded in 1829 by Michael Molloy, has produced two enduring spirits. In 1887 Daniel E Williams, who had been steeped in whiskey production since joining the staff at the age of 15, became general manager and gradually acquired overall control of the business. He used his own initials to provide a brand name – *Tullamore Dew* – for the distillery's pot still whiskey and from that flowed the advertising slogan – *Give every man his Dew*. In the 1950s, when sales were low, the distillery began to produce *Irish Mist*, a whiskey-based liqueur, inspired by a traditional Irish recipe for heather wine made with pot still whiskey, herbs and heather honey.

SIGHTS

Town Centre – The entrance to the **canal harbour** is spanned by Bury (Whitehall) Bridge, the last of the canal bridges to survive unaltered. The old warehouses have been demolished but the harbour-master's house still stands on the corner of St Brigid's Place. The **Roman Catholic church** (1985) is roofed with great lengths of timber and contains some stained glass by Harry Clarke. **St Catherine's Church** was designed by Francis Johnston and contains a memorial (1767) to the first Earl of Charleville by John van Nost.

Charleville Forest Castle ⊘ – *On N 52 going south; restoration in progress*. The house was designed by Francis Johnston in 1798 and is a fine example of the neo-Gothic style in grey limestone. The central stairs rise straight up in a broad high hall to the reception rooms. The most impressive is the **gallery**, which extends the full width of the garden front and is decorated with fine plasterwork and the original fireplaces. The dining room, decorated in William Morris style, the morning room and music room are also of imposing dimensions. The library, which is housed in a turret, forms an ante-room to the chapel.
Radiating from the house are five avenues of Irish yew trees terminating in a bank and ha-ha; there are some fine trees including an oak tree said to be 700 years old.

EXCURSIONS

Durrow High Cross – *4mi/7km north of Tullamore by N 52; 10min there and back on foot along the drive*. A causeway passes over the swampy ground through a tunnel of trees to a graveyard.
The 10C **high cross** depicts the Sacrifice of Isaac on the east face together with Christ in Glory flanked by David with his harp *(left)* and David killing the Lion *(right)*; the west face shows the Crucifixion and associated events.
There are fragments of two other crosses, 9C to 11C grave slabs, and the ruins of a small 18C church which may contain parts of earlier churches belonging to the monastery founded in 556 by St Columba.
The *Book of Durrow*, an illuminated manuscript, which is now in Trinity College Library in Dublin, was produced at Durrow c 650; it was rescued from a farmer who used to dip it in water and then touch his sick cattle with it.

Locke's Distillery ⊘ – *Kilbeggan; 7.5mi/12km north of Tullamore by N 52*. On the west bank of the River Brosna, which is fed by springs in Lough Ennell, stand the extensive buildings of the distillery (1757–1953) established by John Locke, possibly the oldest licensed distillery. In the **cooperage** craftsmen make the oak casks in which whiskey, produced at Cooley, is matured. The process of distilling whiskey is explained and much of the original equipment is still in place: three sets of mill-stones for grinding barley; the mash tuns (known as kieves) for making wort; the huge wooden vats (washbacks) for fermentation; the hogsheads for maturing the whiskey; coopers' tools; the under-shot water-wheel, and the steam engine which replaced it when the water-level was too high or too low.

Clara Bog – *7mi/10km northwest of Tullamore by N 80; in Clara take a minor road south; car park at the end of a short causeway; visitors should not stray from this causeway unless accompanied by a knowledgeable guide*. This raised bog (1 640 acres/665ha; 23ft/7km maximum depth) is one of the finest and largest raised bogs remaining in Ireland and is of international interest. In 1987 it was designated a National Nature Reserve and preserved from exploitation by Bord na Mona for peat production. It has a diverse flora, including at least 10 different bog mosses; in wet areas carnivorous plants, like sundews and bladderworts, entrap unwary insects.

For adjacent sights see ATHLONE, ATHY, BIRR, KILDARE, TRIM.

WATERFORD★

PORT LÁIRGE – Co Waterford – Population 42 540
Michelin Atlas p 80 and Map 923 – K 11

Waterford is a large seaport, with a strong industrial tradition, situated on the south bank of the River Suir, upstream of its confluence with the River Barrow in Waterford Harbour. The city is best known for its glassware, **Waterford Crystal**, which has been the main contributor to the economic prosperity of Waterford since the 1950s when the industry was revived.

> ## Out and about in Waterford
>
> The **Waterford Light Opera Festival** is held annually in September in the Theatre Royal. Throughout the year regular art exhibitions, recitals and theatrical productions are staged in the **Garter Lane Arts Centre** ⊘ (**Y E**). **Walking Tours** ⊘ of the city are organized by the Tourist Board. There is a **car ferry** ⊘ across Waterford Harbour from Passage East *(southeast of Waterford by R 683)* to Ballyhack.

Viking Settlement – The Danish Vikings established a settlement in 853 called *Vadrefjord*, which means weather haven. Despite constant warfare with the local Irish, the Danes retained control of their settlement until 1169 when the Anglo-Normans arrived. Under their rule Waterford became the second most important Anglo-Norman town in Ireland after Dublin. In 1649 Waterford was unsuccessfully besieged by Cromwell but it fell to his general, Ireton, the following year.

SIGHTS

★**Waterford Crystal** ⊘ – *1.5mi/2.5km south by N 25.* Waterford Glass in the original style was first produced in 1783; the factory is now the largest glassworks in the world.
The factory tours take in all aspects of production, starting with the moulding of the molten glass and concluding with the delicate polishing. A collection of crystal is on display; there are videos of the production process for sale.

★**City Walls** (**YZ**) – The watchtower (35ft/10m high) surveys a well-preserved section of the very extensive city walls. As well as the Norman extensions, which are mostly 13C, there are traces of the 9C and 10C Danish walls, including the sallyports in Reginald's Bar near Reginald's Tower.

City Hall (**Z H**) **and Theatre Royal** ⊘ (**Z T**)– The **City Hall**, originally the city exchange, was designed by John Roberts in 1788. The first-floor council chamber displays a complete dinner service of 18C Waterford crystal, a cut-glass chandelier of similar vintage and a painting of Waterford city in 1736 by a Flemish artist, William van der Hagen.

The building incorporates the **Theatre Royal** (1876); its Victorian decor is rare in Ireland. The three-tier horse-shoe design (seating capacity 650) rises to an impressive dome; the specially-designed Waterford Crystal chandelier was presented by Waterford Crystal in 1958.

Reginald's Tower Museum ⊘ (**Z**)– This stone fortress, in a commanding location overlooking the River Suir, was built by the Vikings in 1013 as part of the town's defences. Its three floors, linked by a stair built within the thickness of the walls, contain displays on towers and fortifications.

Waterford Crystal

Terry Murphy Photography

Waterford Treasures ⊘
(Y F) – *The Granary.* The building houses a display of Viking and medieval finds from local excavations – coins, leather-work, jewellery, woven cloth, pottery, bone needles, wooden bowls and spoons and a plan of a Viking house. Also on display are the city charters and regalia.

French Church ⊘ **(Z B)** – The tower and chancel walls belonged to a Francis-

Famous Sons

Thomas Francis Meagher (1822–67) was a wealthy lawyer, who joined the Young Ireland Uprising. He received a death sentence for his part in the rising at Ballingarry in Co Tipperary, which was commuted to transportation to Tasmania. He escaped to the USA where he founded the Irish Brigade and fought in the American Civil War.
William Hobson (1783–1842), who was born in Lombard Street near The Mall, became the first Governor of New Zealand.

can foundation, built in 1240, which remained in the friars' possession until 1539. The Holy Ghost hospital occupied part of the building from 1545 to 1882 when it moved to the outskirts of the city. With the arrival of French Huguenot refugees in Waterford in the late 17C a Huguenot chapel was in use between 1693 and 1815. Many of Waterford's most distinguished families are buried within the precincts.

WATERFORD

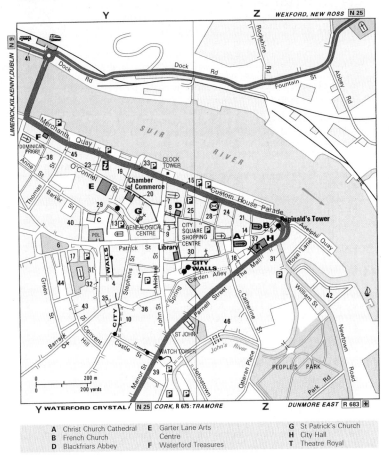

A	Christ Church Cathedral	**E**	Garter Lane Arts	**G**	St Patrick's Church
B	French Church		Centre	**H**	City Hall
D	Blackfriars Abbey	**F**	Waterford Treasures	**T**	Theatre Royal

Waterford Christ Church Cathedral ⊘ (**Z A**) – The present building was designed by John Roberts (1714–96) in the 18C English Classical style; it was completed in 1779. In 1891 the galleries and square pews were removed and more light was introduced. Within is a model of the original Viking church, which stood on the site from 1050 to 1773, and also several monuments from the medieval church – the tomb of James Rice showing his body a year after his death with signs of decay and vermin; two monuments by John van Nost to the Fitzgeralds and to Susanna Mason.

Medieval Waterford – *First level below the City Square Shopping Centre.* During construction of the modern shopping centre 12 layers of housing were found resting on Viking foundations. Stones mark the site of St Peter's church (12C), the earliest example of an apsed church in Ireland. The mural depicts the area in c 1100.

Municipal Library ⊘ (**Y**) – The Waterford Room provides an extensive selection of information in print and on microfilm about historic and modern Waterford.

Blackfriars Abbey (**Y D**) – Only the square tower survives of the Dominican abbey, which was founded in 1226 and later used as a courthouse until the late 18C.

St Patrick's Church (**Y G**) – The church, which dates from the Penal Period, was deliberately constructed to resemble a house from the outside.
The **Genealogy Office** is housed in the section facing Jenkin's Lane.

Chamber of Commerce ⊘ (**Y**)– The fine Georgian building was designed by John Roberts, a noted 18C Waterford architect, and built in 1795; over the door are the words Waterford Harbour Commissioners; the interior contains a well-preserved dome, staircase and carvings.

EXCURSIONS

Passage East – *8mi/13km east of Waterford by R 683 and L 157. Car ferry to Ballyhack.* Population 542. Formerly a fort, the fishing village is built beneath a high escarpment with small squares and streets; there are no fewer than three quays: Boathouse Quay, Hackett's Quay and Middle Quay.

Geneva Barracks – *8mi/13km southeast of Waterford by R 683 and R 685.* On the west shore of Waterford Harbour stands an impressive 18C ruin; its four walls (each 0.25mi/0.4km long) are still remarkably intact. It was part of a new town built in 1793 by the Government for Swiss metalworkers, who left soon after the project was completed. During the 1798 rebellion the buildings were infamous for the atrocities committed against the rebels held within.

★**Dunmore East** – *12mi/19km southeast of Waterford by R 683 and R 684.* Population 1 038. The fishing village, built in the Breton style, has several thatched cottages and a number of coves, including Badger's Cove and Ladies' Cove. At the entrance to the large fishing and yachting harbour is an anchor recovered from Waterford Harbour and believed to have come from an 18C merchantman. There are forest walks beside the Ballymacaw Road (0.25mi/0.4km west).

Tramore (Trá Mhór) – *9mi/14.5km south of Waterford by R 675.* Population 6 069. Tramore is one of Ireland's main holiday resorts with a large amusement park (50 acres/20ha) and a long sandy beach (3mi/5km) overlooking Tramore Bay. The town is built on steep hills rising from the beach.
There are fine walks, with extensive sea views, along the Doneraile cliffs *(south).* Great Newtown Head *(west)* across the bay is crowned by three early-19C navigational pillars, one of which is surmounted by the **Tramore Metal Man**, a cast-iron figure (14ft/4m high), with pale blue jacket and white trousers, erected in 1823 as a warning to shipping.

For adjacent sights see CLONMEL, DUNGARVAN, HOOK HEAD PENINSULA, NEW ROSS, WEXFORD.

WESTPORT★★

CATHAIR NA MART – Co Mayo – Population 4 253
Michelin Atlas p 94 and Map 923 – D 6

Westport occupies an attractive site on the meandering Carrowbeg River and is an excellent centre for touring the west coast of Mayo; there are facilities for sailing, fishing, walking and horse-riding, and sandy beaches to the southwest.
Charming and elegant, it was planned and built c 1780 for the local landlord, John Denis Browne, of Westport House. Until the arrival of the railway in the 19C, Westport Quay on the estuary was a busy port lined with imposing 18C warehouses.

★★WESTPORT HOUSE ⊘ *1hr 30min*

The house is the work of several architects: Richard Castle, who designed the east front in 1730, Thomas Ivory who was responsible for the south elevation (1778), and James Wyatt who added the west front c 1780; the Greek columns on the south front are replicas *(see below)* erected in 1943. It replaces an earlier house built in 1650 on the site of an O'Malley castle. Originally the sea came right up to the house; the lake was created in the 18C by damming the Carrowbeg River. The garden terraces were built in the early 1900s.

Interior – The hall with its barrel ceiling is by Castle although the original black fireplace was replaced this century. The Pompeian frieze and cloud-painted ceiling in the drawing room *(restaurant)* were commissioned by the 2nd Marquess in about 1825.

A collection of **family portraits** hangs in the Long Gallery. The large dining room is the work of James Wyatt; the mahogany for the doors came from the

After photo A. F. Kersting

Westport House

family estates in Jamaica; the sideboards and wine coolers were made for the 2nd Marquess; Col John Browne's silver dinner service is displayed together with Georgian goblets, Waterford glass finger bowls, Worcester china, 18C silver dish rings and a unique **centrepiece** of bog oak and beaten silver. As well as a collection of engravings depicting Sir Anthony Browne copied from the murals at Cowdray Castle, the small dining room contains the **Mayo Legion Flag** which was brought to Mayo in 1798 by General Humbert *(see p 198)*. The **oak staircase** and its ceiling are by James Wyatt, as is the mantelpiece in the morning room. The **marble staircase** was installed for the 3rd Marquess by Italian workmen; on the walls are two paintings of Westport House by George Moore (1761) and several local landscapes by James O'Connor, part of a collection commissioned in 1818 by the 2nd Marquess. Two chalk drawings of the children of the 2nd Marquess by F Wilkin and *The Holy Family* by Rubens are on the landing. The wallpaper in the **Chinese Room** is 200 years old. The **basement** includes the dungeons of the O'Malley castle, now furnished with attractions for children.

Grounds – The old walled garden, containing a mulberry tree planted in 1690, now houses a small zoo. A **craft shop** is located in the Farmyard Buildings Holiday Centre and there are fishing and rowing boats on the lake.

The Brownes of Westport

Twelve generations of Brownes have lived at Westport and their activities are recorded in the family archives which cover 400 years. The family is descended from Sir Anthony Browne of Cowdray Castle in Sussex, whose younger son John came to Mayo in the reign of Elizabeth I. The first house was built by his great-grandson, Col John Browne (1638–1711), a Jacobite, who was made bankrupt by the Williamite victory; his wife was the great-great-granddaughter of Grace O'Malley *(see below)*. His grandson, John Browne (1709–76), was brought up as a Protestant to avoid the sanctions of the Penal Laws and ennobled as Earl of Altamont. Two generations later, John Denis (1756–1809) was made Marquess of Sligo at the time of the Act of Union in 1800. The 2nd Marquess, Howe Peter (1788–1845), a friend of Lord Byron, returned from a tour of Greece in 1812 with the two columns from the doorway of the Treasury of Atreus in Mycenae; in 1906 they were discovered in the basement, identified and presented to the British Museum.

WESTPORT TOWN

★**Town Centre** – From the **Octagon**, where the weekly market is held round a Doric pillar once crowned by a statue of George Glendinning, a local banker and benefactor, the main street descends to the **Mall**, a tree-lined stretch of the Carrowbeg River spanned by a narrow hump-backed bridge.

Holy Trinity Church ⊘ – The church, consecrated in 1872 on a site donated in 1868 by the 3rd Marquess, is in the neo-Gothic style with a pencil spire over the east door. Under the hammer roof the interior is richly decorated with murals in marble mosaic by Italian craftsmen depicting scenes from the Gospels: a copy of da Vinci's *The Last Supper* above the west door. The chancel is decorated with Carrara marble; the pulpit is carved in alabaster washed up by the sea in Westport Bay. From 1892 to 1913 the rector was Canon James Owen Hannay, whose pen-name was George A Bermingham.

Clew Bay Heritage Centre ⊘ – *Westport Quay*. The small museum gives an insight into the history of the area – the capture of the town in 1798 and pilgrimages to the top of Croagh Patrick – and of some local figures – Grace O'Malley *(see below)*;

John MacBride (1868–1916), born in Westport, who was executed in Kilmainham Gaol for his part in the Easter Rising; William Joyce, who lived near Ballinrobe (1909–21) and broadcast from Germany as Lord Haw-Haw during the Second World War; the grandfather of Grace Kelly, wife of Prince Rainier of Monaco, who emigrated to America from a homestead near the road to Castlebar.

EXCURSIONS

★★Murrisk Peninsula *Drive of 51mi/82km south of Westport – 1 day*
From Westport take R 335 west.

The road descends the hill to Westport Quay and skirts the wooded shore, crossing the Owenee River at Belclare where the O'Malley chiefs *(see below)* had their seat; there is a good view of the drumlins in Westport Bay.
After 5.5mi/9km turn right.

Murrisk Abbey – By the shore are the ruins of an Augustinian Friary founded by the O'Malleys in 1457 and suppressed in 1574, although a chalice was made for the monastery by Grace O'Malley's son Theobald in 1635. The crenellated church, which has a beautiful east window and a 17C west door, is flanked by a domestic wing.
Return to R 335.

★Croagh Patrick – *Car park; 2hr on foot to the summit.* The conical peak of Croagh Patrick (2503ft/763m) dominates the south shore of Clew Bay. According to legend all the snakes in Ireland plunged to their death when St Patrick rang his bell above the south precipice. A procession of pilgrims, some barefoot, climbs the stony slopes to the church on the summit on the last Sunday in July (Garland Sunday); they used to climb by torchlight, possibly an echo of the old Celtic festival of Lughnasa. On a fine day the **view** from the top embraces *(north)* Clew Bay with its many islands, *(west)* Clare Island, and *(south)* the Sheeffry Hills flanked by the Mweelrea Mountains *(west)* and the Partry Mountains *(east)* and backed by the Twelve Pins of Connemara.
Continue west on R 335.

Louisburgh – Population 177. The central octagon of this charming little 18C town on the Bunowen River was laid out by the 1st Marquess of Sligo, whose uncle Henry had fought against the French at the Battle of Louisburgh in Canada.
Turn right at the central crossroads.

Folk and Heritage Centre ⊘ – *Louisburgh.* The centre traces the family tree of the O'Malleys, the history of the clan and their territory, and the life of Grace (1530–1603), the most famous member of the family.
Take the road south to Killadoon; make a detour west to Roonagh Quay for the ferry to Clare Island.

Clare Island ⊘ – *Ferry service from Roonagh Quay; bicycles for hire at the islanad harbour; accommodation* ⊘ *available.* The hilly bulk of Clare Island commands the entrance to Clew Bay. Grace O'Malley spent her childhood in the castle by the quay; she may be buried in the Carmelite friary which was founded on the island by the O'Malleys in 1224, although the ruins are of later date. The sandy beach near the harbour is safe for bathing and waters sports. Traditional Irish music is played in the island pubs.

Granuaile

Granuaile is the Irish name of **Grace O'Malley** (1530–1603), who for many years resisted English domination while elsewhere in Ireland the Gaelic system succumbed to English rule. From her strongholds in Clew Bay, where the many islands made pursuit difficult, she commanded a fleet of privateers which preyed upon the shipping in Galway Bay, imposing pilot charges or confiscating cargoes. She was imprisoned by the English from 1577 to 1578. She had two sons and a daughter from her first marriage (c 1546–c 1564) to Donal O'Flaherty, who owned castles at Ballynahinch and Bunowen in Connemara; in 1566 she married Iron Richard Burke and, although she divorced him the following year, she retained possession of Carrigahowley Castle *(see below)*, where she spent the majority of her time and brought up her youngest son, Theobald Burke. She repulsed an English expedition from Galway which in 1574 attempted to besiege the castle. In the autumn of 1593 she sailed to Greenwich to present a successful petition to Elizabeth I for the release of her brother and her son Theobald Burke, who was made Viscount Mayo *(see p 107)* by Charles I in 1627.

SLIDE FILE

Bunlahinch Clapper Bridge

Return to the road to Killadoon and continue south.

Killeen – A cross-inscribed stone stands in the northwest corner of the graveyard.
Turn right at the crossroads; after 0.5mi/0.8km turn right and park.

★**Bunlahinch Clapper Bridge** – Beside a ford stands an ancient stone footbridge
of 37 arches constructed by laying flat slabs on stone piles.
*Return to the crossroads. EITHER go straight across OR turn right to make a
detour (10mi/16km there and back) to Silver Strand.*
Beside the road *(left)* stands a **cross-inscribed stone.**

Silver Strand – The vast sandy beach (2mi/3.2km) is sheltered by dunes.
Return to the crossroads and turn right.

Altore Megalithic Tomb – Beside the road *(left)* overlooking Lough Nahaltora are
the remains of a wedge-shaped gallery grave.
At the T-junction turn right onto R 335.

★**Doo Lough Pass** – The road, which was constructed in 1896 by the Congested
Districts Board, descends from the pass to Doo Lough (2mi/3.2km long) which is
enclosed by the Mweelrea Mountains (2 668ft/817m) *(west)* and the Sheeffry Hills
(2 504ft/761m) *(east)*; at the southern end of the lake rises Ben Gorm
(2 302ft/700m).

Delphi – The 2nd Marquess of Sligo renamed his fisheries on the Bundorragha
River near Fin Lough after visiting Delphi in Greece.

★**Aasleagh Falls** – *Car park left and right.* At the narrow head of the fjord the Erriff
River gushes over a broad sill of rock. The fight in *The Field* was filmed at Aasleagh.
Turn right onto N 59.

★**Killary Harbour** – The harbour is a magnificent fjord, a narrow arm of the sea
(13 fathoms deep) extending inland (8mi/13km) between high rock faces; it broadens out opposite Leenane on the south shore. *(See also p 118).*

Clew Bay *Drive of 25mi/40km – half a day*
From Westport take N 59 north.

Newport – Population 521. This charming little angling resort is dominated by the
disused railway viaduct (1892), which has been converted into an unusual walk
spanning the Newport River. The broad main street climbs the north bank of the
river to St Patrick's Church, built in the Irish-Romanesque style in pink granite
(1914) and containing a fine **stained-glass window** by Harry Clarke.
Continue north on N 59; after 1mi/2.4km turn left.

★**Burrishoole Abbey** – By a narrow inlet where the waters of Lough Furnace drain into the sea lie the ruins of a Dominican Friary, founded in 1486. A squat tower rises above the church, which consists of a nave, chancel and south transept. The east wall is all that remains of the cloisters. In 1580 the friary was fortified and garrisoned by the English under Sir Nicholas Malby.

Burrishoole was an important port even before the arrival of the Normans but was abandoned as Westport harbour was developed.

Continue north on N 59; after 2.5mi/4km turn left.

Carrigahowley (Rockfleet) Castle – The 15C or 16C four-storey tower house is built on a most attractive **site** on flat rocks beside a sea-inlet commanding Clew Bay. The living room was on the fourth floor separated from the lower storeys by a stone vault. In 1566 the owner, Richard Burke, became the second husband of Grace O'Malley *(see above)*.

Take N 59 east; after 1mi/1.6km turn left.

★**Furnace Lough** – A narrow switchback road loops north between Lough Furnace and Lough Feeagh. At the salmon leap where the waters of Lough Feeagh tumble, golden and foaming, over the rocks into Furnace Lough, census work on the numbers of fish moving up- and down-stream is conducted by the Salmon Research Trust of Ireland. From the narrow spit of land dividing the two lakes there is a splendid **view** north to Nephin Beg (2065ft/628m).

For adjacent sights see ACHILL ISLAND, CASTLEBAR, CONNEMARA, KNOCK.

WEXFORD ★

LOCH GARMAN – Co Wexford – Population 9533

Michelin Atlas p 81 and Map 923 – M 10

Wexford is the county town and the commercial centre of the southeast region. It is a town of great antiquity – it was first granted a charter in 1317 – with narrow streets and alleyways, set on the south bank of the River Slaney where it enters Wexford Harbour. The town has a strong cultural tradition and is known internationally for its annual **opera festival**.

Wexford Festival Opera

The **Opera Festival** is an annual event, lasting 18 days in late October; during this time it puts on three productions and over 50 events. It has gained an international reputation for the quality of its performances and for its policy of specializing in rare or unjustly neglected operas. The company of artists and the audiences are truly international, being drawn from all over the world. The productions are staged in the **Theatre Royal** ⊙ (**Z T**).

Concerts, plays and art exhibitions are held in the **Wexford Arts Centre** ⊙ (**Y**) throughout the year.

Organized walking **tours** ⊙ of Wexford depart from Crescent Quay.

HISTORICAL NOTES

In his 2C AD map of Ireland Ptolemy named the site of Wexford Menapia after a Belgic tribe which settled in the region in prehistoric times.

The name Wexford is derived from *Waesfjord* (the harbour of the mud-flats), the name the Vikings gave to the settlement which they established in 950.

When the Anglo-Normans invaded in 1169 Wexford was captured and the first Anglo-Irish treaty was signed at Selskar Abbey. In the 13C the earthen ramparts of the Norse town were replaced by a stone wall.

In 1649 Cromwell entered Wexford; Selskar Abbey was destroyed and 200 citizens were massacred in the market place by Cromwell's forces.

During the rebellion of the United Irishmen in 1798 Wexford was a stronghold of the insurgents, who held it for a month until it was recaptured with much bloodshed by the Crown forces.

In the 19C, led by local shipping companies, Wexford built up a strong maritime trade but it went into decline early in the 20C.

A native of Ballysampson in Co Wexford, **John Barry**, who became senior commodore of the US navy (1794–1803), is commemorated by a statue (**Z**) presented to the town by the American government in 1956.

SIGHTS

★**Main Street (YZ)** – The commercial centre of Wexford is a narrow street, mainly pedestrianized, so narrow that the shops and houses on each side, fronted in the grey slate characteristic of the area, almost seem to touch. Many of the small shops retain the traditional 19C design and style of country town establishments; the once-proud boast of O'Connor's bakery (**Y A**) – "Bread is still the Staff of Life" – appears above the premises. Kelly's bakery (**Z B**) features window displays of traditional Irish loaves, such as wheatsheaves and ducks. The **Bull Ring (Y)** was originally used for bull baiting, a popular sport among the Norman nobles of 12C and 13C Wexford. The 1798 **memorial** shows the bronze figure of a pikeman, created by Oliver Sheppard.

★**Franciscan Friary** ⊘ **(Z)** – The church founded by the Franciscans in 1230 was confiscated in 1540 at the Dissolution of the Monasteries but returned in 1622. The present church (restored) contains an attractive stucco ceiling and works by contemporary Irish artists, including a striking modern sculpture – **The Burning Bush Tabernacle** – created by Brother Benedict Tutty of Glenstal Abbey *(see p 217)*. The adjacent convent claims to hold the remains of St Adjutor, a boy martyr of ancient Rome, together with a phial of his blood.

★**St Iberius' Church** ⊘ **(Y D)** – The Anglican church stands on an ancient Christian site dating back 1 500 years, at that time at the water's edge. The present church was built in 1760 in the Georgian style, with an Ionic reredos and two Corinthian columns screening the sanctuary. The Venetian-style façade was added in the mid 19C.

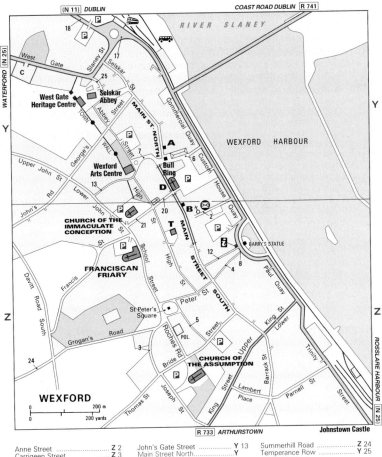

Selskar Abbey (Y) – The abbey, which was founded c 1190 by Sir Alexander de la Roche on his return from the Crusades, was dissolved in 1538. The outer walls and the square tower are well preserved. During Lent in 1172 Henry II, king of England, did penance at Selskar for the murder of Thomas à Becket.

West Gate Heritage Centre ⊘ **(Y)** – The West Gate is the only one of the five original fortified gates still standing; it was built by Sir Stephen Devereux c 1200 and closed to traffic in the late 16C. The Norman rooms in the tower give access to a battlement walk to Selskar Abbey; the cosmopolitan history of Wexford is traced in an audio-visual presentation.

★**Twin Churches (Z)** – The foundation stones of the **Church of the Assumption** in Bride Street and the **Church of the Immaculate Conception** in Rowe Street were laid on the same day in 1851. Both churches were designed by Augustus Pugin in an almost identical Gothic style and their towers are the same height (230ft/70m).

EXCURSIONS

Wexford Wildfowl Reserve ⊘ – *3mi/4.8km north of Wexford by R 741; turn right along the coast.* For eight months of the year most of the world's population of Greenland White-fronted Geese winters on the north shore of Wexford Harbour.

★**Curracloe** – *6mi/9km north of Wexford by R 741 and R 742.* Thatched cottages, sand dunes and sandy beaches (7mi/12km) overlook Wexford Bay.

Rosslare (Ros Láir) – *10mi/16km south of Wexford by N 25 and R 740.* Population 847. The pleasant and popular seaside resort of Rosslare boasts a most attractive long beach (6mi/9.5km) and various sporting facilities.
The **ferry terminal** at Rosslare Harbour *(5mi/8km southeast)* provides passenger services from Ireland to South Wales and the ports of northern France.

Lady's Island – *11mi/18km south of Wexford by N 25 and minor road from Killinick.* A place of pilgrimage, the island has the ruins of an Augustinian friary and a Norman castle; the tower of the latter leans at a greater angle than that at Pisa.

Tacumshane Windmill ⊘ – *11mi/18km south of Wexford by N 25 and minor road from Killinick.* The windmill, which was built in 1846, was restored complete with sails in the 1950s.

★★**Irish Agricultural Museum, Johnstown Castle** ⊘ – *5mi/8km southwest of Wexford by N 25; after 4mi/6.4km turn right (sign).* The Johnstown estate was donated to the Irish State in 1945. **Johnstown Castle** *(not open)*, designed by Daniel Robertson, now houses an agricultural research centre.
The park (50 acres/20ha) contains **ornamental grounds** with over 200 species of trees and shrubs, three ornamental lakes, walled gardens, hothouses and a picnic area. The old farmyard buildings now house a well-presented museum displaying many examples of obsolete agricultural machinery. The transport section includes tub traps, widely used in rural Ireland until the arrival of the motor car in the 1920s, a jaunting car made in Gorey, Co Wexford, about 1880, carts, traps and harness; corn winnowing machines and old tractors, which heralded the revolution in farming. There are sections on dairying, haymaking and poultry keeping; reconstructions of a cooperage, a harness-maker's workshop, a blacksmith's forge and a carpenter's shop; a re-creation of 19C Irish rural living and a display of fine Irish country furniture.
The **Famine Exhibition** is a thorough science-based interpretation of the causes, effects and aftermath of the Great Famine (1845–49), with re-creations of a rural home and the lazy-beds in which potatoes were grown, as well as explanations of how life could be surprisingly well sustained on a monotonous diet of potatoes and dairy products and how the disaster affected different regions of the country. A reconstruction of a soup kitchen evokes relief work, and a reconstruction of a field laboratory demonstrates how the fight against disease was conducted.

★**Kilmore Quay** – *15mi/24km southwest of Wexford by N 25 and R 739; boat trips* ⊘. Population 424. This fishing village retains much of its 19C atmosphere, as about 15 houses still have thatched roofs. The *Wooden House* pub has an extensive collection of historic photographs.
The **maritime museum** ⊘ in the former *Guillemot* lightship, moored in the harbour, contains many relics of the Wexford seafaring tradition, including old maps and a 200-year-old compass and binnacle, a whale's backbone and a large-scale model of *HMS Africa*, sister ship to Nelson's *Victory*.

★**Saltee Islands** ⊘ – *Boat trips from Kilmore Quay; 3mi/4.8km offshore.* The Great and Little Saltee Islands (each about 0.5mi/0.8km long), normally uninhabited, form Ireland's largest bird sanctuary, home for many thousands of gannets, guillemots and puffins (200 000 birds) as well as seals and dolphins.

★**Irish National Heritage Park** ⊘ – *Ferrycarrig; 2.5mi/4km northwest of Wexford by N 11 going north across the River Slaney.* Nine thousand years of Irish history are brought to life by 16 separate sites, mostly reconstructed, linked by a visitors' trail and a nature trail. The **Stone Age**, 7000-2000 BC, is represented by a Mesolithic camp site, an early Irish farmstead and a portal dolmen. The **Bronze Age** is illustrated by a cist burial chamber and a stone circle. The Celtic and early-Christian ages, the most extensively reconstructed, are represented by an early-Christian monastery, an **Ogam stone** showing the earliest form of writing in Ireland, and a **crannóg**, an artificial island protected by a palisade. The horizontal watermill is a reconstruction of one dating from 833 in Co Cork. The round tower is a replica, built in 1857 to commemorate Wexford men killed in the Crimean War (1854–56).

The only real historic relic is the Norman earthworks and fortifications, built by Robert FitzStephen in 1169.

For adjacent sights see ENNISCORTHY, HOOK HEAD PENINSULA, NEW ROSS, WATERFORD, WICKLOW MOUNTAINS.

WICKLOW
CILL MHANTÁIN – Co Wicklow – Population 6416
Michelin Atlas p 87 and Map 923 – N 9

Wicklow is the county town and the main commercial centre for the northern part of Co Wicklow. It is also an attractive seaside town set at the eastern foot of the Wicklow Mountains *(see below)*. Leading off the narrow main street, which in the centre of the town divides into two levels, are numerous side streets descending to the riverside quay on the Vartry estuary, the large harbour and beach.

HISTORICAL NOTES

The Irish name of the town recalls St Mantan, a missionary who established a church in the 5C. In the 9C the Danish Vikings set up a port, which developed into an important trading centre. The English name of the town is derived from the Danish words for Viking meadow (Wyking-alo).

After the 12C Anglo-Norman invasion, the area of the town was granted to Maurice Fitzgerald, and for the next five centuries the two Irish clans living in the district, the O'Byrnes and the O'Tooles, fought repeated battles with the English for possession. Although the local people played a minor part in the Nationalist rebellion of 1798, many of the participants were tried in the Wicklow courthouse; such uprisings (1798, 1803, 1848, 1867) are commemorated by the statue of a pikeman in the Market Square.

SIGHTS

Harbour – From the attractive tree-lined mall beside the Vartry, streets of 19C fishermen's dwellings *(Bath Street, Bond Street)*, lead to the harbour with its breakwater and rocky beach.

Black Castle – The castle, which stands on a rocky promontory immediately south of the harbour, was built by Maurice Fitzgerald in 1176 and was the subject of frequent attacks by local clansmen until the 16C. The ruins form a fine vantage point for **views** over the town and the coast of north Co Wicklow.

Anglican Church ⊙ – The 18C building has an onion-shaped copper cupola, donated in 1777, and incorporates a 12C Irish-Romanesque doorway. The interior contains a fine king-post roof, a 12C font, an organ, transferred in the late 18C from the Anglican cathedral in Cashel, and a memorial tablet to Captain Halpin *(see below)*. The title "the Church of the Vineyard" recalls the vines planted by the Normans on the "Vineyard Banks" which descend to the River Vartry.

Franciscan Friary – The extensive ruin of this friary, founded by the Fitzgerald family in the 13C, stands in the grounds of the parish priest's house. After the 16C Dissolution of the Monasteries, the building became a courthouse. In 1812 the buildings were given to the local parish priest, as a reward for his services in the Battle of Salamanca in Spain.

Halpin Memorial – The obelisk of polished granite commemorates Captain Robert C Halpin (1836–94), a native of the town, who commanded the *Great Eastern*, the ship built by Brunel that laid the first transatlantic telegraph cable. Mementoes of Halpin are displayed at his residence, Tinakilly House, now a hotel *(2mi/3km northwest by N 11).*

Wicklow Historic Gaol ⊙ – The formidable stone-built prison dates from 1702, the time of the Penal Laws and was used as a prison until 1924. It now houses elaborate exhibits which bring to life some of the more dramatic aspects of Ireland's history. A warder inducts visitors into the ghastly conditions suffered by prisoners in the 18C; British soldiers ponder how to crush the 1798 Rebellion; local gentleman-rebel Billy Byrne awaits his execution; the life of convicts in the 19C, both here and in Australia, is evoked; stern Captain Betts shows how to deal with recalcitrant prisoners on board the transportation vessel *Hercules*.

The Murrough – *0.5mi/0.8km north on the east bank of the estuary.*
A long shingle beach (3mi/5km) backed by a broad grass bank is flanked by the sea and the **Broad Lough**, a lagoon noted for its wildfowl and golden plover.

For adjacent sights see GLENDALOUGH, WICKLOW MOUNTAINS.

The Wicklow Mountains south of Dublin provide high peaks and spectacular views, lakes, reservoirs and waterfalls, open moorland and verdant valleys, some landscaped into elegant gardens. The rolling heights are covered in peat bog where the rivers form broad shallow treeless corridors; on the harder schist they create deep and narrow wooded gorges, like Dargle Glen, Glen of the Downs and Devil's Glen.

There are electricity generating stations in the Wicklow Gap (Turlough Hill) and on the Poulaphouca Reservoir; ⏱ the Vartry Reservoir supplies water to Dublin.

Along the coast, which is formed by a shingle ridge covered by sand dunes liable to severe erosion, are a string of seaside resorts and strands: Bray, Greystones, Wicklow *(see above)* and Arklow.

INLAND *North to south*

★**Killruddery** ⏱ – The **formal gardens** at Killruddery were designed by a Frenchman in 1682. The central feature is a pair of parallel canals (550ft/168m long), the **Long Ponds**; their axis is prolonged by the **Lime Avenue** which leads uphill to the 18C park. The ponds are flanked to the east by the **Angles**, a number of intersecting walks lined with high hedges, and to the west by a wilderness of trees bisected by broad walks. Nearer the house are a **sylvan theatre**, enclosed by a bay hedge, and the **beech hedge pond**, two concentric circular beech hedges, surrounding a round pond (60ft/18m in diameter) and a fountain; the four 19C statues represent the four seasons. West of the house lie two 19C ornamental gardens bordered by box hedges. The octagonal ornamental building was originally a dairy. East of the house a natural outcrop of rock is planted with shrubs. The **house**, which dates from the 1650s, was considerably remodelled in the 1820s by Richard and William Morrison and the statue gallery was added in 1852. Above the stableyard entrance is a clock and striking mechanism, both operated by water power and built by members of the family in 1906–09.

The estate was granted in 1618 to Sir William Brabazon, created Earl of Meath in 1627, whose ancestors arrived in England with William the Conqueror and whose descendants still live at Killruddery.

Out and about in the Wicklow Mountains

There is an **Information Point** ⏱ for the Wicklow Mountains at the Upper Lake in Glendalough. Boat trips and other water sports are available at the Blessington Lakes Leisure Centre on the **Poulaphouca Reservoir** ⏱. The **Tiglin Adventure Centre** in the Devil's Glen offers courses in caving, canoeing, hang gliding, hiking, mountaineering, orienteering, rock climbing, snorkelling and surfing. The **Clara Lara Fun Park** ⏱ in the Vale of Clara offers a variety of activities for children – assault course, adventure playgrounds, radio-controlled boats, bathing, boating and fishing, picnic meadows. The **Wicklow Way** is a long-distance footpath which runs from north to south of the mountain chain.

Kilmacanogue – Population 763. The shop and factory of **Avoca Weavers** ⏱ stand on the site of a house, Glencormac, built in 1864 by James Jameson of the famous whiskey family. The grounds, which he laid out with the assistance of a landscape gardener called Sheppard, contain many rare species – a weeping cypress, Blue Atlantic cedars, 13 yew trees which are said to be 700 to 800 years old and originally formed part of an avenue leading to Holybrook Abbey, several Wellingtonias and various types of eucalyptus and pine.

★★**Sally Gap** – The crossroads on the Military Road gives splendid views of the surrounding blanket bog on the Wicklow Mountains.

★**Loughs Tay and Dan** – The two lakes are linked by the Cloghoge River.

Roundwood – Population 437. The village (780ft-/238m above sea-level) consists of little more than a broad main street with several pubs and craft shops; a pub and a café both claim the honour of being the highest in Ireland.

Military Road

After the 1798 Rebellion the British Government built a military road running south from Dublin through some of the most rugged and isolated parts of the Wicklow Mountains. The original barracks in Glencree now house **St Kevin's**, an organization which seeks to promote reconciliation between people of different religious traditions on both sides of the border.

Glenmacnass Waterfall

Annamoe – There are pleasant walks beside the Annamoe River. It was here at the age of seven that Laurence Sterne *(see CLONMEL)* fell into the mill race and emerged unscathed.

Charles Stewart Parnell (1846–91)

After an unpromising school career Parnell entered Parliament in 1875 and soon attracted the attention of the Nationalists. He became Vice-President of the Home Rule Confederation of Great Britain. As President of the Land League he campaigned for the tenants to keep a firm grip on their home-steads and went on a fund-raising trip to America and Canada; he was so well received that he was dubbed the "uncrowned king of Ireland". In September 1880 he proposed the policy of "moral Coventry" which advo-cated what came to be known as boycotting, after Capt Boycott who was the first to feel its effect. Parnell used his own newspaper *United Ireland* to attack government policy. In 1882 he founded the National League to cam-paign for Home Rule. In 1886 he took up residence with Mrs Kitty O'Shea, whom he had met in 1880, and in 1889 Captain O'Shea won an uncon-tested case for divorce, citing Parnell as co-respondent. Parnell was called upon to resign but he refused and his party split. He died in October 1891 four months after marrying Kitty O'Shea.

★**Glenmacnass Waterfall**– *Car park*. The mountain river streams down an inclined rock face.

★★**Wicklow Gap** – The road west from Glendalough to Hollywood follows the course of the medieval pilgrims' path, **St Kevin's Road**, through the Vale of Glendasan. Where the modern road loops northeast, hikers may follow the old direct route *(2mi/3km)* closer to Lough Nahanagan. The motor road rejoins the old route to pass through the Wicklow Gap between Tonelagee (2 686ft/816m *north*) and Table Mountain (2 302ft/700m *west*).

★**Devil's Glen** – The Vartry River makes a spectacular **waterfall** (100ft/30m) by cascading into the Devil's Punchbowl, a deep basin in the rock. There are **walks** in the immediate vicinity and good views of the coastline.

Samuel Hayes

Avondale was inherited by the Parnell family from Samuel Hayes, a plantsman, whose Chippendale bureau is on display in the house. In 1788 Hayes presented a bill to Parliament "for encouraging the cultivation of trees" and in 1904 Avondale became the national forestry training centre.

★Mount Usher Gardens ⊙ – Set on the outskirts of Ashford village (population 878), the natural-style gardens (20 acres/8ha), which are planted with over 5 000 species, many sub-tropical, are renowned for the collections of eucryphia and eucalyptus. They were laid out in 1868 by Edward Walpole, a member of a Dublin linen-manufacturing family, and totally restored following severe flood damage in 1986.

Two suspension bridges lead to the woodland walks on the east bank of the River Vartry, which has been attractively developed with the addition of weirs.

Vale of Clara – The road, which follows the course of the Avonmore River, a trout stream, links Laragh (population 249), a meeting point of many roads and glens, to the attractive village of Rathdrum (population 1 175).

★Glenmalur – The road beside the upper reaches of the Avonbeg River ends in a remote and desolate spot at the northeast foot of Lugnaquilla, Ireland's second-highest mountain (3 039ft/926m high).

★ Avondale ⊙ – The Avondale estate was the birthplace and family home of **Charles Stewart Parnell**, the 19C Nationalist leader (1846–91). The two-storey neo-Classical **house** has been restored to its appearance during Parnell's lifetime when it was much used for social occasions. It was designed in 1759 by Samuel Hayes, with a large two-storey hall, served by twin stairways, one for the family and one for the servants, and Coade stone ornamentation by the **Lafranchini brothers** in the dining room. The life of Charles Parnell, the history of his family in Ireland, his role in 19C Irish politics, particularly his direction of the Land League and his promotion of Home Rule, are traced by a video in the morning room. Among the furniture and memorabilia are Parnell's chair (he was 6ft 3in/1.90m tall), his stick, the Parnell family tree, photos of Parnell and Kitty O'Shea, her wedding ring of Avonmore gold mined by Parnell, a set of folding library steps made of Irish bog oak.

The **forest park** (512 acres/207ha) covers a steep slope facing east across the Avondale River. The oldest surviving trees – two gigantic silver firs by the river as well as oaks, beeches and larches – were planted by Samuel Hayes in the 18C. The stump of a beech tree, planted nearly 250 years ago, has its rings delineated in relation to subsequent historical events. There are several trails and woodland walks ranging from the **Pine Trail** (0.5mi/0.8km), which is suitable for disabled people, to the **River Walk** (4mi/6.4km), which passes through the massed conifers on the banks of the Avonmore River and along the Great Ride.

★Meeting of the Waters – The confluence of the rivers Avonbeg and Avonmore is set amid the forests of south Co Wicklow; nearby stands the tree beneath which the poet Thomas Moore (1779–1852) is said to have composed *The Meeting of the Waters* in 1807.

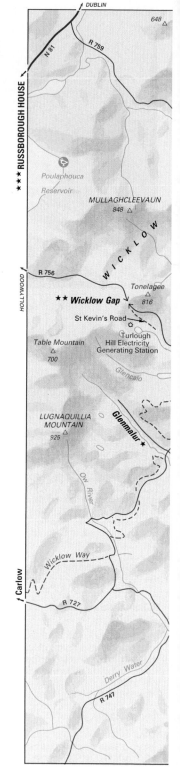

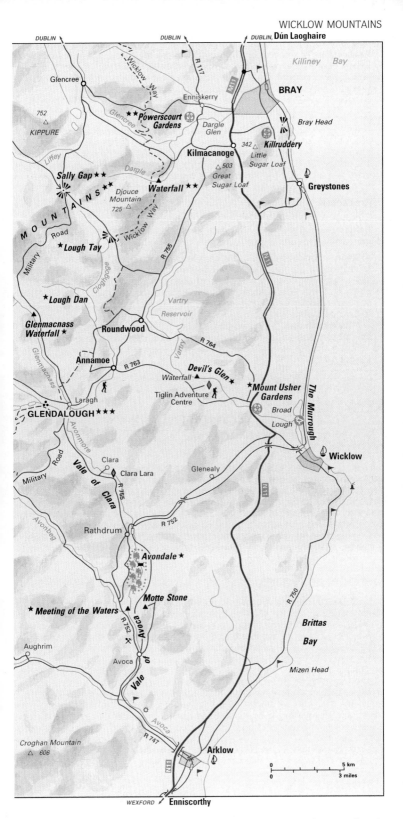

Motte Stone – The name of the large glacial boulder is derived from the French for half (moitié), as it used to mark the half-way point on the Dublin-Wexford road before the advent of mileposts.

Vale of Avoca – There are forest walks in the wooded river valley. At the **Avoca Weavers Mill** ⊘, founded in 1723 and therefore the oldest surviving business in Ireland, visitors may watch the production of textiles by traditional methods.
The village of Avoca has attracted visitors in great numbers, after it was chosen as the setting for the hugely popular television series, *Ballykissangel*.

ON THE COAST *North to south*

Bray – Population 25 096. Bray is an old-established resort with a sand and shingle beach at the south end of Killiney Bay; in recent years it has become a dormitory town for Dublin. The public park on Bray Head provides a fine **view** of the coastline. The **Heritage Centre** ⊘ in the Town Hall traces the local history through photographs, maps and artefacts. The **National Sea-Life Centre** ⊘, on the sea-front, presents more than 30 displays populated by an array of marine and freshwater creatures.

Greystones – Population 9 649. The resort has developed from a fishing village with a harbour flanked by shingle beaches.

Brittas Bay – The long sandy beach (3mi/5km), backed by dunes, is one of the most popular resorts on the east coast.

Arklow – Population 7 987. The seaside resort, founded by the Vikings on the south bank of the Avoca estuary, is also an important east-coast fishing harbour and a base for Ireland's main fleet of coastal trading ships. The most famous product of the local boatyards is **Gypsy Moth III**, the yacht in which Sir Francis Chichester sailed around the world in 1967. There are attractive walks by the harbour and along the south bank of the river.
The **Maritime Museum** ⊘ displays about 200 exhibits connected with Ireland's maritime history and traces the development of local commercial shipping since the 1850s; a video *Eyes to the Sea* tells the maritime history of Arklow.

Arklow Rock *(2mi/3.2km south)* provides a fine **view** of the coastline.

For adjacent sights see CARLOW, DÚN LAOGHAIRE, ENNISCORTHY, GLENDALOUGH, KILDARE, POWERSCOURT, RUSSBOROUGH, WICKLOW.

YOUGHAL ★
EOCHAILL – Co Cork – Population 5 630
Michelin Atlas p 79 and Map 923 – I 12

Youghal (pronounced yawl) occupies an attractive **site** on the west bank of the Blackwater estuary. It derives its name from the Irish for yew wood, a reference to the great forests that surrounded the town in medieval times.
Strategically placed for the landing of forces from England and always vulnerable to the threat of invasion from France and Spain, Youghal became one of England's most strongly-defended Irish seaports, enclosed by impressive town walls.
Several buildings of historical interest have survived, although the **North Abbey**, a Dominican establishment dating from 1268, is reduced to the west chancel wall standing in the main town graveyard.

HISTORICAL NOTES

First occupied by the Danish Vikings in the 9C, Youghal was later settled by the Anglo-Normans at the end of the 12C. The town supplied King John with three fighting ships and received its first charter in return. In the 13C it was completely enclosed on three sides by elaborate walls, the fourth side being protected by the River Blackwater.
In the late 16C, while mayor of Youghal, **Sir Walter Raleigh** introduced the tobacco and potato plants into Ireland. Following the Cromwellian invasion of 1649 Youghal passed through a particularly difficult period. In the 18C the closed borough was totally dominated by members of the Protestant minorities; Roman Catholics were utterly deprived of religious, political and civil rights, the cause of successive rebellions.
During the 19C Youghal developed a commercial tradition – in brick-making, now extinct, and lace-making, a nearly vanished craft. In the latter part of the 19C some 150 sail-powered schooners traded from the port; sailors from Youghal could recognize one another throughout the ports of the world by their distinctive whistle. This once-strong tradition began to decline early in the 20C with the silting-up of the estuary and the building of steam-powered freight ships.

SIGHTS

★★**St Mary's Collegiate Church** ⊘ – It is probable that the first church on the site, a wooden building, was erected by followers of St Declan of Ardmore in c 400. The present early-13C edifice was pronounced "one of Ireland's most impressive churches" by the late Claud Cockburn, writer and long-time Youghal resident; it replaced an 11C Danish-built church destroyed in a great storm soon after its

YOUGHAL

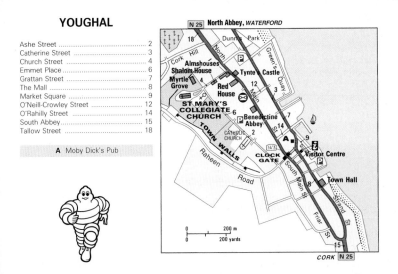

A Moby Dick's Pub

construction. During the late-15C wars, the forces of the Earl of Desmond occupied the building and removed the roof of the chancel. Large-scale restoration, including the re-modelling of the chancel, took place between 1851 and 1858.
The east window dates from 1498; the font in the nave is also from this period. The church contains a large collection of **grave slabs** and **effigies**, including some from the 13C and 14C with Norman-French inscriptions.
In the south transept stands a vast **monument** to the first Earl of Cork, his three wives and 16 children. He arrived in Ireland nearly penniless towards the end of the reign of Elizabeth I and became so rich that he is often described as one of Europe's first capitalists.

★**Town Walls** – Youghal has the best-preserved town walls in Ireland, more extensive even than the city walls of Londonderry. They were built in the 13C and extended in the 17C; large sections are still in excellent condition, although only three of the 13 medieval towers remain. The portion restored in the 19C with a turret and a cannon is accessible from the churchyard; the sentry walk provides a fine **view** of the town and the harbour. The full length of the walls is best seen from the road at the rear *(Raheen Road)*.

★**Clock Gate** – The unusual four-storey building straddling the Main Street was constructed by the corporation in 1777 to replace the Iron Gate, also known as Trinity Castle, part of the walls. The new tower was used as the town gaol until 1837; such was the state of insurrection in the late 18C that it soon became overcrowded; rebels were hanged from the windows as an example to the rest of the populace.

The Red House – This fine example of early-18C Dutch domestic architecture creates a marked contrast with its neighbours. The red brick façade with white stone quoins is surmounted by a triangular gable and a steep mansard roof. It was designed in 1710 for the Uniacke family by a Dutch architect-builder Claud Leuvethen.

Youghal Heritage Centre ⊘ – The old Market House now houses the Tourist Information Office and an exhibition on the history of the walled port of Youghal. In the Market Square stands a memorial commemorating the *Nellie Fleming*, the last of the old Youghal sailing vessels.
In the pub on the corner, **Moby Dick's (A)**, are many photographs taken during the filming of *Moby Dick* on location in Youghal during the summer of 1954.

Benedictine Abbey – All that remains of the abbey is the east gable wall pierced by a moulded Gothic doorway with ornamental spandrels; in the passageway are the arched piscina and square aumbry from the original church. The abbey was founded in 1350 and used by Cromwell as his winter headquarters in 1649–50.

Almshouses – The Elizabethan almshouses were erected in 1610 by the Earl of Cork who provided "five pounds apiece for each of ye six old decayed soldiers or Alms Men for ever". They are still used for residential purposes, as is the neighbouring former Protestant **asylum**, dated 1838 and now called Shalom House.

Tynte's Castle – This 15C battlemented building has a device over the front door for pouring boiling oil on rebels and other unwelcome visitors. Once on the waterfront, it is now some distance (200yd/182m) from the river.

For adjacent sights see ARDMORE, COBH, CORK, DUNGARVAN, LISMORE, MIDLETON.

271

Giant's Causeway

S Chirol

Northern Ireland

ANTRIM

Antrim, a linen-spinning centre, was once the county town of the administrative area which bears its name. It lies on the Six Mile Water, a good trout stream, beside Lough Neagh. On the lake shore there is a championship golf course and a marina which provides cruises on Lough Neagh *(see p 336)*. The town was burned by General Monro in 1649 and attacked during the 1798 Rebellion by a force of 3500 United Irishmen under Henry Joy McCracken, a Belfast cotton manufacturer, who was defeated.

SIGHTS

★ Round Tower – *Steeple Park.* Among the trees stands a well-preserved round tower (90ft/27m); the conical cap has been restored. It was probably built c 900 and is all that remains of an important 6C monastery, abandoned in 1147.

Pogue's Entry ⊘ – *East end of the main street.* In a narrow alley stands the simple cabin where Alexander Irvine (1863–1941) spent his childhood. The front room served as kitchen, living room and workshop where his father made and repaired shoes; there was a bedroom at the back and the children slept in the loft. Irvine became a missionary in the Bowery in New York; his book, *My Lady of the Chimney Corner*, is about his mother's struggle against poverty.

Antrim Castle Gardens ⊘ – *West end of the main street.* Beyond the Market Place and the Court House (1726) stands a magnificent Tudor gate, the entrance to the former seat of the Clotworthy family, ennobled in the 17C as Lords Massereene. Memorials to members of the family and to their dogs and horses stand in the grounds, which were laid out late in the 17C in a formal arrangement with long ornamental stretches of water, screened by high pleached hedges. Between the Norman motte and the stone bridge over the river are the remains of the castle, accidentally burnt down in 1922.

Shane's Castle Grounds ⊘ – *0.25mi/0.4km west by A 6.* On the shore of Lough Neagh stand the ruins of **Shane's Castle**, the seat of the O'Neill family since 1607 when James I settled the estate on Shane McBrian O'Neill. A burial vault, built in 1722, is linked by a tunnel to the ruins of the castle which burned down in 1816. A superb collection of camellias over 100 years old is housed in the surviving conservatory, which has an arcade of round-headed windows beneath a castellated parapet terminating in square towers; it was designed by John Nash and is an exact copy of the one he built at his property in East Cowes on the Isle of Wight. He also designed the **terrace**, which is furnished with cannons from a British man o'war which sank in Lough Foyle, and provides a good view of Lough Neagh. In the **Nature Reserve** (80 acres/32ha) are rare breeds of cattle – Irish moiled (hornless), Highland and Belted Galloway, and a herd of feral fallow deer *(viewing area)*; a nature trail skirts the lake shore.

EXCURSIONS

Patterson's Spade Mill ⊘ – *5mi/8km southeast by A 6 via Templepatrick.* The only surviving water-powered spade mill in Ireland was founded in 1919; five generations of Pattersons worked at the mill until 1990. The tour includes all the stages involved in producing spades in the traditional way – the forge for heating the metal billet, the huge tilt hammer for shaping the blade which is then sharpened and tempered, the riveting of the blade to the shaft, and the painting – all done by two men. Beside the mill are the ruins of associated industrial buildings.

Ballance House ⊘ – *11mi/17km south by B 101, A 26 and A 30 via Glenavy.* The house was the birthplace of John Ballance (1839–93), who emigrated to Birmingham and thence to New Zealand, where he became a journalist and then entered politics, becoming the first Liberal Prime Minister. The parlour is furnished in the style of 1850 as it was during John Ballance's childhood. The upper floor is devoted to the Ulster–New Zealand connection, particularly the continuing link between the Royal School in Dungannon and Dilworth School in New Zealand, and to Maori culture.

Templetown Mausoleum ⊘ – *Templepatrick; 5mi/8km east of Antrim by A 6. Park at the end of the drive.* A short avenue of evergreens leads to a walled graveyard enclosing a mausoleum, which was designed by Robert Adam in the Palladian style c 1770 for Sarah Upton in memory of her husband Arthur. It contains tablets to later generations of Uptons who received the title Viscount Templetown.

Finishing Shop, Patterson's Spade Mill

Immediately before the entrance is the grave of Sir John Campbell who wrote the history of Castle Upton while renting the property, which he wanted to buy. South of the mausoleum lies the grave of Josias Walsh (1598–1634), Minister of Templepatrick c 1622–34 and grandson of John Knox.

The name Templepatrick derives from an earlier church dedicated to St Patrick who is supposed to have baptized converts at a nearby Holy Well in about 450.

Slemish – *16mi/26km northeast by A 26 to Ballymena, A 42 east and B 94; after 1mi/1.6km turn left; after 3mi/4.8km turn right (Carnstroan Road); after 0.25mi/0.4km turn right. From the car park 1hr there and back on foot.* The distinctive bare silhouette of Slemish (1 437ft/438m), an extinct volcano, rises abruptly from the flat landscape. On St Patrick's Day (17 March) it is a place of pilgrimage since tradition has it that **St Patrick** spent six years here in captivity herding swine for the local chieftain Miluic. From the top there is a fine **view** including the ruins of Skerry Church *(northwest)*, the burial place of the O'Neills, supposed to have been founded by St Patrick himself.

Arthur Cottage ◷ – *17mi/27km northwest by A 26 to Ballymena and B 62 to Cullybackey. Cross the river and turn sharp right onto a narrow lane.* At the end of the lane stands an isolated one-storey cottage with the traditional split door. The floor is of clay and the roof of flax-straw thatch. From here the father of Chester Alan Arthur, 21st President of the USA, emigrated in 1816 to Vermont where he became a Baptist clergyman. The furniture is in period; in summer there are demonstrations of traditional domestic crafts. The large outbuilding contains collections of local agricultural and domestic implements from the past, and a display on Chester Alan Arthur's family and 19C emigration from Ireland.

Gracehill – *11mi/18km northwest by A 26 to Ballymena and A 42.* Population 449. The Georgian architecture and attractive layout of this village are the work of the Moravians, who came via London from Bohemia where their church was persecuted. Their settlement, started in 1759 and grouped round a central square, included a church, the minister's house and communal houses for single men and women. The boarding schools for girls and boys acquired an enviable reputation far outside their locality. Men and women sat on separate sides in church and were buried in separate sections of the graveyard.

Randalstown Presbyterian Church – *5mi/8km west by A 6.* The charming oval church was built of dark stone with pointed windows in 1790. The porch, containing curved flights of steps to the internal gallery, was added in 1829 and the row of oval oculi was inserted in 1929 when the height of the walls was raised.

For adjacent sights see ANTRIM GLENS, BELFAST, CARRICKFERGUS, LOUGH NEAGH.

Co Antrim

Michelin Atlas p 103 and Map 923 – N, O 2, 3

A drive up the **Antrim Coast** offers a great variety of scenery and a sense of expectancy at each approaching headland. Seaward are attractive villages, long flat strands, steep basalt or limestone cliffs, and a distant prospect of the Mull of Kintyre in Scotland. Inland are the glens created by the tumbling mountain streams which descend from the uplands of heath and bog, now punctuated by forestry plantations. In the glens, where the underlying sedimentary rocks are exposed, the farms are arranged like ladders climbing the valley sides so that each has a share of the good land near the river and of the poorer upland pasture.

For many years this was the most isolated and least anglicized part of the country owing to the difficult terrain. There had always been a track along the coast, which still makes a good walk, but the first coast road, passable to coaches in all weathers, dates from 1832 when the Grand Military Road from Carrickfergus to Portrush was built under the supervision of William Bald.

Two narrow-gauge railway lines (3ft/1m) were laid down in the 19C to carry the increasing output of the Glenariff mines, which opened in the late 1860s. One, the railway built by the Glenariff Iron Ore & Holding Co, ran from Inverglen down Glenariff to the southeast end of Red Bay, where the bed of the track is still visible; when mining declined it closed. The other ran from Ballymena up the Clogh Valley to Retreat (1876) but was never extended further, owing to the steep gradient down Glenballyemon to the coast; it turned to carrying passengers and opened up the glens to the tourist trade before ceasing operations in 1930.

Larne to Ballycastle *70mi/113km – 1 or 2 days.*

Larne – *Larne Lough Ferry* ○ *to Island Magee (see p 300).* Population 17 575. The town, the southern gateway to the Glens of Antrim, is a busy port with a regular ferry service to Stranraer and Cairnryan in Scotland. In the 9C and 10C, landings were made by the Vikings, who called the lough Wulfrichford.

South of the harbour on the spit of land called Curran Point stand the ruins of a square, four-storey 16C tower house, now called **Olderfleet Castle** (derived from Wulfrichford) although its original name was Coraine; it was one of three castles which protected the entrance to the lough in the early 17C.

The **Chaine Memorial Tower**, a modern replica of the traditional Irish round tower, erected in honour of James Chaine, a local MP and benefactor, stands on the shore at the northern entrance to the harbour.

From Larne take A 2 north.

Carnfunnock Country Park ○ – The Park (473 acres/190ha) was once a private demesne north of Drains Bay village. Set among the flowers and shrubs in the walled garden are 12 sundials showing GMT, Summer Time or local time. A viewing platform overlooks the interior of the **maze**, which echoes the shape of Northern Ireland. The **limekiln walk** *(1hr)* includes the old ice house and the Look Out; there is also a walk through the forest. Opposite the park entrance on the shore are a marine promenade and boat slip.

Continue north on A 2.

Ballygally Castle – The Ballygally hotel was originally a planter's castle, built in 1625 by James Shaw; the twin bartizans are original but the sash windows were introduced later. Inland rises a natural amphitheatre, Sallagh Braes; the fine walk above the Braes along the plateau edge *(access via Carncastle and Ballycoose Road)* forms part of the Ulster Way.

Continue north on A 2.

Glenarm Village – Population 650. This attractive village, which wears a light coating of white dust from the local limestone quarries, is the oldest village in the Glens. The main street runs inland past the 19C barbican gateway of **Glenarm Castle** *(private)*, the seat of the Earl of Antrim, which was begun in 1606 and re-modelled in the Elizabethan style by William Vitruvius Morrison early in the 19C.

The **Forest Park** at the top of the street *(car park)* provides a view of the castle, and pleasant walks by the stream in the upper woodlands beyond the belt of conifers.

Return to A 2; turn left onto B 97.

Glenarm – The road passes through open farmland on the west slope facing Glenarm Forest across the glen. At the top, Slemish *(see p 275)* is visible to the south.

At the T-junction turn right onto A 42.

Glencloy – The road descends through gently sloping pastures to the coast.

Turn left into A 2.

MA Boet /Jacana

Seal

Carnlough – Population 1 493. The large sandy bay makes this an attractive resort. Until the 1960s, limestone from the quarries above the town was transported by rail to the tiny harbour which is now full of pleasure-boats. The line was carried across the main road by a low bridge *(plaque)* which, together with the adjoining clock tower and former courthouse, was built by the Marquess of Londonderry *(see p 330)* in 1854.

Red Bay – Beyond Garron Point, the beautiful expanse of Red Bay comes into view, backed by the distinctive steep-sided, flat-topped silhouette of Lurigethan (1 154ft/352m). The bay is called red because of the colour of the sandstone in the neighbouring hills, which is washed down into the sea by the mountain streams.

Glenariff (also **Waterfoot**) – Population 300. The village, which lies at the mouth of the Glenariff River, is the site of the Glens of Antrim Feis, an annual festival of Gaelic sport and culture. Just north of the village, on the headland, stand the ruins of Red Bay Castle, built by the Norman Bisset family, above the Red Arch road tunnel.

From Glenariff take A 43 inland.

★ **Glenariff** – From the broad patchwork of fields at its foot to the narrow gorge at its head, the "**Queen of the Glens**" is enclosed between steep hanging crags.

★★ **Glenariff Forest Park** ⊘ – The forest (2 298 acres/930ha) consists of woodland, land reserved for future planting or too poor to grow trees, turbary areas and several small lakes and rivers. The visitor centre beside the garden and aviary has an excellent display on forestry, local wildlife, the 19C iron ore and bauxite mines and their railways.

The **waterfall**★★ known as Ess na Larach *(1hr there and back on foot from the north side of the car park)* tumbles through a wooded gorge created by the Glenariff River; from the Fog House the waterfall can be viewed through panels of tinted glass which impart a sunlit glow, a moonlit chill or a green, luminous light. Below the fall the Glenariff is joined by the River Inver; the path up Inverglen returns through the garden and aviary to the car park.

Continue southwest on A 43; at the junction turn right onto B 14.

Glenballyemon – After emerging from an evergreen forest into open moorland the road passes through Retreat on the north slopes of Lurigethan.

Cushendall – Population 1 285. At the crossroads in the centre of this charming village stands a red sandstone tower, known locally as the Curfew Tower, which was built as a watchhouse in 1809 by Francis Turnly of the East India Company.

Take Layde Road, the steep coast road going north to Cushendun.

Layd Old Church – The ruins of the church stand in a graveyard beside a swiftly flowing stream which plunges directly into the sea. The church is thought to have been founded by the Franciscans but from 1306 to 1790 it was a parish church. There are MacDonnell memorials in the graveyard.

As the coast road continues uphill there is a fine view south across Red Bay to Lurigethan and Garron Point, west into Glencorp and northeast to Scotland.

At the T-junction in Knocknacarry turn left onto B92 and left again onto A 2.

Glencorp – The name of this short glen, aligned north–south, translates as the glen of slaughter.

After 1.5mi/2.4km turn right onto Glenaan Road. Turn left onto a lane (sign "Ossian's Grave"); car park beyond the farmhouse; 20min return on foot.

Ossian's Grave – The stones in the field *(right)* are the remains of a Neolithic court tomb, consisting of a semicircular forecourt opening into a bi-cameral burial gallery, originally enclosed in an oval cairn. Ossian was an early Christian warrior-bard, the son of Finn McCool, whose legendary feats are recounted in the Ossianic Cycle.

Continue west up the glen.

Glenaan – The Glenaan River flows down from the slopes of Tievebulliagh *(south)* where Neolithic men made axe heads from the hard porcellanite rock.

At the crossroads turn right onto Glendun Road to Cushendun.

★**Glendun** – The Brown Glen is the wildest of the nine glens; its river, which is noted for sea trout and salmon fishing, flows parallel with the road under the viaduct designed by Charles Lanyon in 1839 to carry the main coast road.

Cushendun – Population 50. The houses of this picturesque village, which is now preserved by the National Trust, cluster at the southern end of a sandy beach flanked by tall cliffs. The most distinctive architecture is the work of Sir Clough Williams-Ellis (1883–1977), who designed Portmeirion in North Wales and was employed here by Ronald McNeill, Lord Cushendun. Glenmona Lodge (1923), which stands in a pine grove on the north side of the village facing the sea, is in the neo-Georgian style with an arcade supported on Tuscan columns. The three terraces of small, white houses facing onto a square date from 1912; the row of slate-hung cottages was erected in 1925 in memory of Lord Cushendun's Cornish wife, Maud.

From Cushendun take the coast road, a winding, steep and narrow road north. After 5mi/8km fork right onto Torr Road.

Torr Head – *Car park.* The low promontory is crowned by a look-out post, which is the nearest point to the Scottish coast (12mi/19km).

Continue northwest along the coast road; after 2.5mi/4km turn right.

★★★**Murlough Bay** – *1mi/1.6km to the upper car park; smaller car park lower down the cliff face.* This is the most beautiful bay on the Antrim coast, set in the lee of **Fair Head** (Benmore) at the foot of steep and towering cliffs. From the shore, grassy

Murlough Boy and Fair Head

slopes dotted with birch and rowan trees climb steeply to the escarpment. The stone cross is a memorial to Sir Roger Casement. From the lower car park there are two paths *(waymarked)*: one leads north to some long-abandoned coal mines before returning along the shore past the remains of the miners' cottages and the ruins of Drumnakill Church; the other leads south past an old lime kiln, bears inland through the wood to avoid Murlough Cottage *(private)* and ends at Benvan farmhouse.

From the upper car park there is a path *(waymarked)* along the clifftop to **Fair Head** (Benmore) which provides a wide **view★★★** of Rathlin Island *(north)* and the Mull of Kintyre *(northeast)*; to return to the car park the path swings inland across the rough and often wet ground of the plateau, past a **crannóg** in Lough na Cranagh *(right)*, the farm buildings *(car park)* at Coolanlough and Lough Fadden *(left)*.

Return to the coast road; turn right to Ballycastle.

Bonamargy Friary – Well-sited beside a stream stand the ruins of a Franciscan friary (c 1500), now surrounded by Ballycastle golf course. The first of the roofless buildings is the **gatehouse**, which has an upper room with a fireplace and window and was set in a boundary bank. The **church** was lit by an impressive east window, grooved to receive glazing; the round-headed cross in the nave is thought to mark the grave of Julia McQuillan, a 17C recluse known as "the black nun". The **MacDonnell vault** was added south of the altar in 1621 but probably modified at a later date. Nothing remains of the **cloisters**, which were probably built of wood, except the corbels and the roof line. The **east range** consists of two storeys linked by a flight of steps built in the thickness of the wall; the small barrel-vaulted chamber probably served as the sacristy; the larger vaulted chamber was the refectory and day room; the vaults are now exposed in the dormitory on the upper floor.

On the edge of Ballycastle turn left onto B 15; after 0.25mi/0.4km bear right uphill onto Dunamallaght Road.

Glenshesk – The road overlooks the Glenshesk River and skirts the southern edge of Ballycastle Forest. From Breen Bridge, at the foot of the south face of Knocklayd Mountain, a waymarked footpath, the **Moyle Way**, a spur of the Ulster Way, leads north over the summit of Knocklayd (1 695ft/514m) to Ballycastle *(4mi/6.4km)*.

From Breen Bridge take B 15 west.

Armoy Round Tower – In the graveyard of St Patrick's Church stands the base of a round tower (30ft/9m), which dates from 460 and was part of a monastery founded by Olcan, a disciple of St Patrick.

From the crossroads take the minor road north to Ballycastle.

Glentaisie – The glen skirts the west face of Knocklayd.

Turn right onto A 44 to Ballycastle.

For adjacent sights see CARRICKFERGUS, CAUSEWAY COAST, GIANT'S CAUSEWAY.

ARMAGH ★★

ARD MACHA – Co Armagh – Population 14 265
Michelin Atlas p 98 and Map 923 – L, M⁴

Armagh lies in a fertile district of fruit orchards planted by 17C settlers from the Vale of Evesham in England. It has many fine Georgian buildings and two cathedrals, each set on a hill, the seats of the Anglican and Roman Catholic archbishops of Ireland. In July 1994 this county town was raised to city status by royal command.

Royal and Religious Centre – Armagh, derived from Ard Macha meaning Macha's Height, is named after a legendary pagan queen who built a fortress on the central hill of Armagh. Although the major pre-Christian power centre of Ulster was nearby Navan Fort *(see below)*, the settlement of Armagh grew in prominence after Navan's destruction in AD 332.

In his mission to convert Ireland to Christianity, c 445, St Patrick arrived in Armagh and chose it as the centre of the new religion; he declared that it should take precedence over all other churches in Ireland and from that time it has been the ecclesiastical capital of the whole country.

In the following centuries Armagh developed into an important centre of religion and learning under teachers such as St Malachy, St Celsus and St Concord; its reputation was such that in 1162 an ecclesiastical Synod decreed that only those who had studied at Armagh could teach theology elsewhere in Ireland. The school was suppressed at the Reformation under the Dissolution of the Monasteries but the scholastic tradition was revived in 1608, when James I founded the Royal School, which moved in 1773 from Abbey Street to new buildings designed by Thomas Cooley on College Hill.

Architectural Elegance – In the peaceful conditions of the 18C and early 19C, farming and commerce flourished; Armagh acquired some of its finest architecture under the benevolent patronage of two Anglican Primates: Richard Robinson, later Lord Rokeby, who became Archbishop in 1765 and attempted to establish a university in Armagh; and Lord John George Beresford, who was appointed Archbishop in 1822.

SIGHTS

★**St Patrick's Cathedral** (Anglican) ⊘ (**Z**) – The present building, which incorporates some medieval elements, was restored by Archbishop Robinson in 1765, and again by Archbishop Beresford between 1834 and 1837, when it was faced with a cladding of sandstone and the steeple demolished. It is now a plain building in the Perpendicular Gothic style with a squat crenellated central tower.

The **exterior** is decorated with a series of grotesque medieval stone heads and a sundial which dates from 1706. When King Brian Ború and his son, Murchard, were killed at the Battle of Clontarf (1014), on the north side of Dublin Bay, they were buried according to the king's wishes at Armagh *(plaque on west wall of north transept)*.

The **interior** contains a collection of 18C monuments by Roubiliac, Rysbrack, Nollekens and Chantrey, and pieces of an 11C market cross.

★**St Patrick's Cathedral** (Roman Catholic) ⊘ (**Z**) – The twin-spired cathedral stands on a hill approached by a long flight of steps *(44 steps)*, flanked at the top by statues of Archbishop Crolly and Archbishop McGettigan, under whom it was built. Construction began in 1840 in the Perpendicular Gothic style of Thomas J Duff but the Great Famine brought work to a halt until 1854; the cathedral was completed in 1873 in the Decorated Gothic of JJ McCarthy. The statues in the niches on the west front represent the Apostles.

The **interior** is lavishly decorated with a painted vaulted roof, stained-glass windows and mosaics on the walls; the spandrels frame the heads of Irish saints. The sanctuary was renovated in 1981–82 under the architect, Liam McCormick.

Slide File, Dublin

Cricket in the Mall, Armagh

★**The Mall** (**YZ**) – The Mall is a most attractive urban feature, a long stretch of grass with a pavilion and cricket pitch bordered by elegant terraces. In the 8C it was common grazing land, as its former name, The Commons, implies, and it was used for horse racing, bull-baiting and cock-fighting until these gambling activities were stopped by Archbishop Robinson in 1773 and the land converted to public walks. The Classical-style **Courthouse** was designed in 1809 by Francis Johnston.

The remaining stone was used to build the Sovereign's House (**M²**) which now contains a military museum *(see below)*; the office of Sovereign was equivalent to that of Mayor but the title ceased to be used in 1850.

Beresford Row was designed by John Quinn between 1810 and 1827 and named after Lord John Beresford; the houses have elegant iron balconies.

Charlemont Place, one of the finest Georgian terraces, was designed by Francis Johnston in 1827.
The Ionic portico, set back from the street behind a lawn, was designed by Francis Johnston in 1833 as the entrance to a school which now houses the County Museum *(see below)*.
A long tree-lined drive leads up to **St Mark's Church**, also designed by Francis Johnston in 1811.
His nephew, William Murray, designed the small **Savings Bank** building with an un-pedimented portico in 1838. The old **Gaol** was erected in 1780 on the site of the barracks.

★**Armagh County Museum** ⓥ (**Y M¹**) – The political and social history of the area is illustrated by a series of displays: prehistoric weapons and implements; early-Christian relics including illustrations of the three Tynan crosses *(see below)*; local buildings, both extant and demolished; 18C and 19C costumes and military uniforms; jewellery, clocks and watches; local crafts – lacemaking, embroidery and crochet, linen making and corn weaving; woodcraft – bowls, cups, four-handled vessels (methers) for drinking, spades; the railway; local geology, flora and fauna; paintings and portraits of local interest.

★**Museum of the Royal Irish Fusiliers** ⓥ (**Y M²**) – The history of five regiments, which were raised in 1793 to fight the French and merged into one regiment with five battalions in 1881, is illustrated by an excellent presentation of flags and standards, uniforms, medals, weapons, silver, portraits and paintings.

Palace Demesne (**Z**) – From the 17C to the 20C the estate was the residence of the Anglican Archbishop of Armagh.
The buildings surrounding the stable yard now house the **Palace Stables Heritage Centre** ⓥ. A 19C town coach stands at the entrance. The display presents a typical day in the life of the stables and the palace, in fact 23 July 1776 when Arthur Young, the famous agricultural improver, and other guests were entertained by Archbishop Richard Robinson.
The **Primate's Chapel**, a superb example of Georgian neo-Classical architecture, was commissioned by Richard Robinson, begun in 1770 by Thomas Cooley but, owing to his death, completed in 1786 by Francis Johnston. It is built of local limestone with an Ionic portico and contains some very fine carved oak panelling, a fireplace of Armagh marble and an ornamental plaster ceiling of rosettes surrounded by a frieze. The gallery for choir and musicians is at the east end and the chapel, which is deconsecrated, is used for concerts.
Nearby are the conservatory, an ice house and a tunnel providing access to the house for the servants. There is an eco-trail through the park.
The house, which is now the offices of Armagh District Council, was also begun by Cooley and completed in 1786 by Johnston, who later added a third storey for Lord John George Beresford.
Near the demesne entrance are the ruins of **Armagh Friary**. In accordance with Franciscan practice it was extremely long and narrow, the longest-known in Ireland (180ft/50m x 21ft/7.6m); a tower was added later at the junction of the nave and chancel.
There are two tomb recesses in the north wall at the east end. The Franciscans were established in Armagh in 1263 or 1264. After the Dissolution the buildings fell into ruins; in 1618 the site became part of the archbishop's demesne.

St Patrick's Trian ⓥ (**Y**) – The Trian (pronounced Tree-an) was one of the administrative divisions of the city. The display traces the history of Armagh in association with the theme of religious belief through tableaux and an audio-visual presentation. The *Land of Lilliput* is an interpretation of *Gulliver's Travels*, whose author Jonathan Swift often visited the area.
The Trian also contains a Geneaological Research Centre, art exhibitions and the Tourist Information Centre.

Armagh Planetarium ⓥ (**Y**) – The planetarium is housed under a dome (50ft/15m in diameter) which serves as a hemispherical screen for the projection of films of the sky at night. The Hall of Astronomy contains 12 computer stations presenting information on planets, constellations and space flight. The Planetarium was set up in 1968 by Dr Lindsay, Director of the Observatory (1937–74), who invited Patrick Moore to be its first director.
In the grounds stands the **Observatory**, founded and endowed in 1789 by Archbishop Robinson; it is one of the oldest meteorological stations in the British Isles.

Armagh (Robinson) Public Library ⓥ (**Y A**) – The library, which was founded by Archbishop Robinson in 1771, is housed in a building designed by Thomas Cooley; the Greek inscription on the façade means "the healing of the mind". The library contains a copy of *Gulliver's Travels* annotated by Swift and many other

ARMAGH

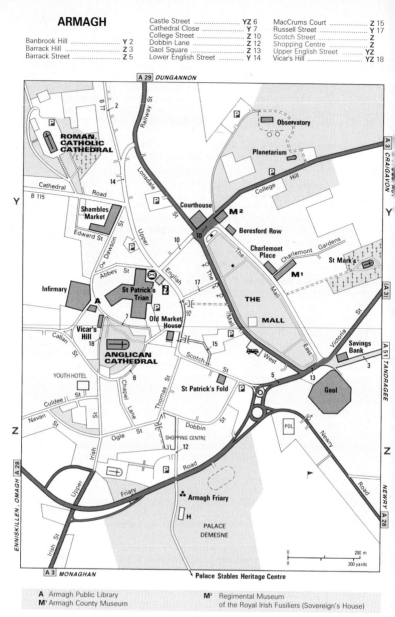

A Armagh Public Library
M¹ Armagh County Museum
M² Regimental Museum
of the Royal Irish Fusiliers (Sovereign's House)

In Northern Ireland parking in the town centre may be restricted to attended vehicles only.

ancient books and manuscripts; it also contains the Rokeby Collection of 18C engravings as well as maps of historical interest, including a complete set of the 1838 edition Ordnance Survey Maps of the 32 counties of Ireland.

Infirmary (Y) – The infirmary, another of Archbishop Robinson's foundations, was designed by George Ensor *(see below)* and completed in 1774; it is still in use.

Vicar's Row (YZ) – The terrace of small houses on the west side of the cathedral close was begun in about 1720 as accommodation for female clergy dependants.

Old Market House (Z) – A technical school now occupies the Market House, which was commissioned in 1815 by Archbishop Stuart from Francis Johnston, and originally consisted of only two storeys.

St Patrick's Fold (Z) – The house, which is thought to stand on the site of St Patrick's first church in Armagh, was designed in 1812 for Leonard Dobbin, MP for Armagh from 1833 to 1838, by Francis Johnston to whom the houses (1811) in nearby Dobbin Street are also attributed.

Shambles (Y) – As is written over the entrance, the building was erected in 1827 by Archbishop Beresford; it was designed by Francis Johnston and is still used as a meat market.

Staircase Hall, The Argory, Co Armagh

A von Einsiedel /National Trust Photographic Library

EXCURSIONS

★**The Argory** ⊘ – *10mi/16km northeast of Armagh by A 29 and a minor road right.* The Argory house on the Derrycaw estate beside the River Blackwater was built in about 1824 by Walter McGeough, who took his paternal grandmother's name of Bond. It passed to his second son, Ralph Shelton McGeough Bond, known after 1873 as Captain Shelton.

The house contains a number of family portraits. The cast-iron stove in the entrance hall has a descending flue which passes under the floor to the drawing-room chimney. The **drawing room** is elegantly furnished with a rosewood grand piano by Steinway. The two *pietra dura* round tables, one showing the Bond coat of arms and the other a series of rare butterflies, are part of Lady Bond's collection of Continental inlaid furniture. Her portrait as a young girl by JJ Shannon hangs above the late-17C Spanish chest in the corner; most of the watercolours are by her mother, Mary Nichols.

Each generation has contributed to the comfortable informality of the **study**: 18C bookcase, William IV chairs. The dado in the **billiard** room is painted to resemble panelling and the shutters grained to imitate walnut veneer. The table, cue stand, rests and scoreboard are early 19C. The **dining room** is furnished with two round-topped tables in mahogany adjusted by a system of internal pulleys, two side tables, beneath which stand two plate buckets and a tea caddy; there is a warming cupboard beside the fireplace *(left)*.

The cabinet **barrel organ** *(upstairs)* is by James Bishop and was commissioned in 1824. The original six barrels, of which three survive, are typical of the period; Samuel Wesley was consulted over their selection.

The distinctive **light fittings** on the dressing tables in the bedrooms date from 1906 when an acetylene gas plant was installed to provide artificial light.

The **Gardens**, which extend to the Blackwater River, comprise old roses set in box-lined beds surrounding a sundial dated 1820, and yew tree arbours, a cedar of Lebanon and a tulip tree growing in the Pleasure Grounds which are flanked by a Garden House and a Pump House. A lime tree walk describes a long curve from the bottom of the lawn to the main drive.

The **Stable Block** (1820), the most elegant of the many outbuildings, is surmounted by a cupola housing an eight-day striking turret clock and capped by a weather-vane.

Ardress House ⊘ – *7mi/11km northeast of Armagh by B 77.* Ardress, which was inherited by the architect, George Ensor, on his marriage in 1760, is a simple 17C manor house, consisting of five bays, enlarged and embellished in the 18C with the addition of two wings, elliptical urns on the parapet and the pedimented and pillared porch.

The house displays glass from Dublin, Cork and Belfast, and some fine furniture, including Irish Chippendale chairs. The front door has retained its original brass furnishings.

Ardress House Yard, Co Armagh

The symmetry and proportions of the elegant **drawing room** are enhanced by the delightful stuccowork by Michael Stapleton on the walls and ceiling. The symmetrical design in the Adam style surrounds Aurora in her Chariot. The frieze moulding and the wall plaques seem to be stock Stapleton patterns representing the Seasons and Classical figures. The present colour scheme is based on the original drawings (in the National Museum in Dublin).

The cobbled **farmyard** with its central pump is alive with chickens, ducks and peacocks, a pig in the sty and some goats. The surrounding farm buildings include a milking shed, a dairy with pottery and wooden skimming dishes, churns and measures, a forge, a threshing barn and a display of old farm implements including baskets and bee skeps.

Orange Order Museum ⊙ – *6mi/10km northeast of Armagh by A 29 and B 77 to Loughgall; half way up the west side of the main street; caretaker's house on the right of the museum.* The museum is housed in a single narrow room overflowing with mementoes of the Orange Order: sashes, caps, waistcoats, banners, the table on which the first warrants were signed, guns and pikes used in 1795 at the Battle of the Diamond *(3mi/5km northeast)*. The room, formerly Jim Sloane's pub, was converted into a museum in 1961.

Tayto Potato Crisp Factory ⊙ – *11mi/18km east of Armagh by A 51; factory entrance next to the police station on entering Tandragee.* The factory is housed in Tandragee Castle, which dominates the town (population 2 871); it was built in 1837 by the 6th Duke of Manchester.

The tour *(1hr)* starts in the warehouse in which great cliffs of potatoes are stored; it then passes the washing, peeling and slicing machines to where the raw white wafers enter a tunnel of hot sunflower oil and emerge as wavy golden crisps. At the next stage the crisps acquire a flavour and are packed by ingenious machines, one of which swathes stacks of cardboard boxes in polythene film like mummies.

★**Gosford Forest Park** ⊙ – *7mi/11km southeast of Armagh by A 28 to Markethill; two car parks: one near the entrance and the other between the Castle and the Walled Garden.* The Forest Park was formerly the demesne of the Earl of Gosford whose family name was Acheson. Contemporary with the building of the present castle, a huge pseudo-Norman pile designed by Thomas Hopper in 1819, are the **arboretum**, which contains many magnificent mature trees from all over the world, and the **walled gardens**, which are beautifully laid out with flowers and shrubs, and contain a brick **bee house** with niches to protect the straw skeps from the damp. A **nature trail** round the park includes various forestry plantations, two raths *(see p 55)* and a stretch of the Drumlack River with a waterfall at **Swift's Well**.

An interesting feature of the original gardens is the **Dean's Chair**, an artificial sun trap created by making a semicircular hollow protected by a yew hedge in a south-facing bank; it is named after Jonathan Swift who spent over a year at Gosford between 1728 and 1730 as a guest of Sir Arthur Acheson.

Little remains of the old Manor House which burnt down early in the 19C, except the water wheel in the car park, an old stone building known locally as the laundry house, the mill ponds, now inhabited by a great variety of water fowl, and the gate lodge consisting of two apartments, one on either side of the entrance arch.

Navan Fort Excavations

Excavations carried out between 1961 and 1971 showed traces of human activity as early as 2000 BC; in c 400 BC a round wooden house and yard was built, which was replaced many times during the next 300 years. In c 100 BC a huge wooden structure (125ft/40m in diameter) was erected consisting of an outer timber wall and five concentric inner rings of large posts; the remains of a very large central post made it possible to date the structure, which was probably roofed. Soon after it was built it was filled with limestone boulders and set on fire and the remains covered with earth to form a mound, probably as part of a religious ritual. Navan Fort seems to have been part of a religious complex. The four Iron Age bronze trumpets (one is now in the National Museum in Dublin), which were found in the 18C in the water at the edge of Lough na Shade *(northwest of the Fort beyond the quarries)*, may have been deposited in the lake as an offering to the gods. Excavations carried out in 1975 show that the King's Stables *(northwest of the Fort)* was an artificial pool used for ritual deposits in the Late Bronze Age.

The **Gosford Heritage Poultry Collection** aims to conserve in their natural surroundings the native poultry breeds that would have been found in the 18C poultry yard of a large estate.

★**Navan Fort** ⊙ – *2mi/3.2km west of Armagh by A 28*. The fort is an impressive earthwork, surrounded by sacred places and settlement sites, which in the late Bronze Age was the most important place in Ulster. Navan is thought to be synonymous with Emain Macha, the capital of legendary Ulster, mentioned in the *Ulster Cycle (see p 34)*.

The exhibition in the **Visitor Centre** traces the archeological study of the fort and its associated sites and shows how they were used by their Neolothic builders. Two films provide further information – *The Dawning* evokes the pre-Christian and early-Christian era in Ireland with its tradition of storytelling; the second film recounts and illustrates the myths and legends associated with Navan.

The fort itself *(5min on foot from the Visitor Centre or by road; car park)* consists of a massive bank and inner ditch enclosing a circular area. Within is a high mound on the highest point of the hill, flanked by a low circular mound surrounded by an infilled ditch.

Tynan High Cross – *7mi/11km west of Armagh by A 28 and B 210; turn left uphill into the village and then right*. The cross stands southwest of the church outside the churchyard wall. It dates from about 700–900 and was probably a boundary stone belonging to Tynan Abbey; the lower front section depicts Adam and Eve. Photographs of three similar local crosses *(private property)* are displayed in Armagh County Museum.

Road Bowls

The ancient Irish sport of road bowling is still played on Sundays in Co Cork and Co Armagh. A heavy iron ball (28oz/794g; 7in/18cm) is hurled along a stretch of quiet winding country road in as few throws as possible; the ball may hurtle through the air at shoulder height. Betting is heavy.

For adjacent sights see DUNGANNON, MONAGHAN, Lough NEAGH, NEWRY, SPERRIN MOUNTAINS.

BANGOR

BEANNCHAR – Co Down – Population 52 437
Michelin Atlas p 99 and Map 923 – O P 4 – Local map Strangford Lough

Bangor lies on the south shore of Belfast Lough at the north end of the Ards Peninsula. Now partially a dormitory town for Belfast, Bangor developed from an early-17C Scottish Plantation into a 19C seaside resort with safe sandy beaches, a sea-water swimming pool, several yacht clubs and a golf course.

HISTORICAL NOTES

Bangor Abbey – The abbey founded at Bangor by St Comgall in 558 became one of the most famous abbeys in western Christendom. Its monks founded other monasteries in Ireland and abroad. One of them, St Columbanus, founded monasteries in Luxeuil, Annegray and Fontaines in France before falling into disfavour; after spending some time at St Gall in Switzerland he moved to Bobbio in Italy where he founded another monastery; here he died in 613.

In the 9C Comgall's tomb was desecrated in Viking raids; Malachy, appointed abbot in 1124, built a stone church and introduced the Augustinian Order. The 14C tower, the only structure to survive Dissolution in 1542, is now part of **Bangor Abbey Church** ⊘.

Scottish Settlement – On the accession of James I, Bangor was granted to Sir James Hamilton, later Viscount Clandeboye, who founded a town with settlers from his native Ayrshire. In 1710 his estates passed by marriage to the Ward family of Castle Ward on the south shore of Strangford Lough. Two generations later Col Robert Ward improved the harbour, promoted the textile industry and founded a boys' school. When the railway arrived in 1865 Bangor developed into a seaside resort with a pier (demolished 1981).

SIGHTS

★**North Down Heritage Centre** ⊘ – The Centre is housed in the service wing of Bangor Castle. The ground-floor galleries trace the history of Bangor Abbey (9C Irish bronze hand bell), the Scottish settlement, the local landed families and Bangor's heyday as a seaside resort. The first floor illustrates the Prehistoric Period, the Bronze Age and the Viking invasions with local archeological exhibits. Almost all the items in the **Jordan Collection** of Far Eastern objets d'art are 19C and 20C Chinese.

Bangor Castle, now the Town Hall, was built by Robert Edward Ward (1818–1904); 1852, the date of completion, is inscribed above the door. The Elizabethan–Jacobean revival style – mullioned windows, oriels crested with strapwork, steep gables with finials and a battlemented tower with a pyramidal clock turret – suggest that the architect may be William Burn; the stables may be the work of Anthony Salvin.

Old Custom House and Tower – In 1620 Sir James Hamilton was granted a warrant to establish a maritime port in Bangor including the nearby creeks. By 1637 with financial assistance from the Crown he was building a Custom House (now the Tourist Centre) in the Scottish Baronial style with flanking watchtowers, a crow-stepped gable and a quarter-round corbelled turret.

EXCURSIONS

Crawfordsburn Country Park ⊘ – *7mi/11km west of Bangor by B 20*. The country park, like the picturesque village, takes its name from the Crawford family from Scotland who were tenants of Sir James Hamilton in the early 17C. In 1674 they bought the estate, which they landscaped and planted with rare species.

The history and flora and fauna are illustrated in the **Park Centre**, which also has a 3-D show on bees and wasps, a colony of leaf-cutter ants, and an array of brightly-coloured interactive exhibits.

The **glen walk** *(30min there and back on foot)* starts in a mature beechwood underplanted with laurel. From the old salmon pool it passes under the viaduct, designed by Sir Charles Lanyon in 1865, which carries the railway across the glen on five arches (80ft/24m). Upstream is the waterfall, a rushing torrent after heavy rain, which formerly drove corn, flax and saw mills and in 1850 generated electricity to light the glen.

Grey Point Fort – *Accessible by footpath (1hr there and back) within the Country Park or by residential roads (Coastguard Avenue)*. The fort, which was built in 1907 and taken out of service in 1963, commands the sea approaches to Belfast and was manned during both World Wars by the Royal Artillery. Panels outline its history and a solitary six-inch gun, a gift from the Government of the Republic of Ireland, is mounted in one of the massive reinforced concrete gun emplacements.

★★**Ulster Folk and Transport Museum** ⊘ – *8mi/13km west of Bangor by A 2*. The grounds of Cultra Manor have been converted into an extensive museum bisected by the coast road *(A 2)*; the folk section is on the south side inland, and the buildings housing the transport section are on the north side extending to the seashore.

Folk Museum – Since 1958 various buildings mostly from the Ulster countryside have been re-erected to form a vast open-air museum. **Demonstrations** of cooking, weaving, spinning and agricultural work are given in season.

The dwellings, which are furnished as they would have been at the turn of the century, range from a one-room farmhouse, shared by the family with the cows, to a substantial 17C farmhouse with panelled walls. The working premises include a forge, a flax-scutching mill and a spade mill, a weaver's house and a bleach green watchman's hut to shelter the person protecting the webs of linen, spread out on the green to bleach, from theft or damage by animals. A village is being assembled round a school, a market-cum-courthouse, a church and a rectory, together with two terraces of urban cottages including a shoemaker's workshop and a bicycle repair shop.

Rectory and Church, Ulster Folk Museum

NITB, Belfast

In the **Gallery** *(three floors)* the traditional Ulster way of life is illustrated with original domestic, industrial and agricultural implements.

Transport Museum – The **Irish Railway Collection**, the most comprehensive of its kind in the whole of Ireland, is housed in a vast hangar with a first-floor viewing gallery. Visitors may walk at track or platform level and enter some of the exhibits – *Maeve (Maebh)* (1939), a 4-6-0 800 Class; *Dunluce Castle*, a 4-4-0 Class U2. Printed wall panels provide information on the history of Irish Railways.

The exhibits of the **Road Transport Galleries** occupy two further hangars, richly furnished with all types of transport memorabilia – two-wheelers of all kinds, from the draisiennes and velocipedes of early days to the stylish scooters of the 1960s or the massive mounts of tattooed ton-up bikers. Buses include a 1973 Daimler Fleetline, burnt out but lovingly restored, while the most extraordinary vehicle is perhaps No 2 of the Bessbrook and Newry Tramway Co, built in 1885 and still carrying passengers in the 1940s.

The final gallery is devoted to *The Car in Society* – from the 1898 Benz Velo Confortable, the oldest petrol vehicle in Ireland, to one of the glamorous cars produced in 1981 by the short-lived De Lorean company, with the emphasis as much on car culture as on the vehicles themselves; many tentative answers are provided as to why a nominally functional object should play such a dominant part in people's lives.

The **Dalchoolin Transport Galleries** present a miscellany of exhibits. **Gallery 1** – Shoulder creels and wooden sledges, carts and jaunting cars. **Gallery 2** – Horse-drawn vehicles from a dogcart to a dress chariot. **Gallery 3** – A selection of cars and motorcycles spanning the century; description of the internal combustion engine. **Gallery 4** – The ingenious machines designed by Rex McCandless which challenged conventional motorcycle design; ships and aircraft, including the Short SC1, a pioneering VTOL (Vertical Take-off and Landing). The **Titanic Gallery** describes how the great liner, built at Belfast's famous Harland and Wolff shipyard, sank on her maiden voyage after being holed by an iceberg, and shows pictures of the wreck obtained by divers in 1985.

Somme Heritage Centre ⊘ – *3mi/5km south of Bangor by A 21.* The time tunnel carries the visitor back to the outbreak of the First World War in 1914 and to one of the bloodiest battles, the Somme offensive (1916), where nine Irish regiments drawn from all over the country fought side by side in a common cause.

The display recaptures through photos and exhibits the volunteers being issued with uniforms, kit and weapons and embarking for France; reconstruction of the trenches and the sights and sounds of war over noman's land.

Groomsport – *1.5mi/2.5km east by coast road.* Population 900. Groomsport is an attractive little seaside resort, flanked by sandy beaches and modern bungalows and caravan parks. In the harbour, yachts ride the water beside the fishing boats.

Fishing is still an important activity but only two fishermen's cottages, one thatched, still stand beside the harbour; they now house an **art gallery**. In the 17C there was enough traffic in the port to justify a customs officer and a Watch House to guard against smuggling.

In 1689 the Duke of Schomberg landed at Groomsport; his army of 10 000 men probably came ashore at Ballyholme or Bangor where he spent the first night as a guest of Sir James Hamilton *(see above)*, before proceeding south to the Battle of the Boyne, where he was killed.

Donaghadee – *7mi/11km east of Bangor by B 21.* Population 4455. The picturesque, winding streets lead to the **parish church** which dates from 1641. The huge harbour, now full of pleasure boats, was built in 1820 to accommodate the mail ships, which were transferred to Larne in 1849. From the 16C to 19C Donaghadee-to-Portpatrick was the most popular route between Ireland and Scotland as it is the shortest crossing (21mi/34km). The Norman **motte** near the shore was probably raised by William Copeland, a retainer of John de Courcy; it is crowned by a stone building (1818) used as a gunpowder store during the building of the harbour. From the top there is a fine **view** of Donaghadee, the Copeland Islands offshore and the coast of Galloway across the North Channel.

Copeland Islands ⊘ – *Accessible by boat from Groomsport or Donaghadee.* The nearest and largest island was inhabited until the 1940s, when the last inhabitants moved to the mainland and the island was left to the sheep and weekend cottages. Lighthouse Island is now a bird sanctuary in the care of the National Trust; a modern lighthouse was built on Mew Island in 1884.

★**Ballycopeland Windmill** ⊘ – *10mi/16km southeast of Bangor by B 21 and A 2; in Millisle turn right. Car park. The mill is not open to the public when the machinery is working owing to the risk of accident.* In the late 18C, when grain was

grown extensively in the Ards Peninsula, the landscape was thickly dotted with windmills but few have survived. The one at Ballycopeland was probably built in 1780 or 1790 and worked until 1915. It is again in working order; the neighbouring miller's house provides an explanatory display. Beside the mill is a dust-house and the kiln where the grain was dried before being milled.

Ards Peninsula – The peninsula is a long narrow tongue of land *(23mi/37km x 3-5mi/5-8km)* extending west and south of Bangor to Ballyquintin Point which marks the southern tip.

Owing to its soil and climate the low-lying land is one of the best grain-producing regions of Ireland, divided into larger-than-usual farms. By contrast the southern end of the peninsula presents an austere landscape of marsh and heath.

The east coast is swept by bracing sea breezes; the **coast road**, which follows the bare shoreline, skirting frequent sandy beaches and occasional rocky outcrops, is almost constantly in sight and sound of the sea. **Portavogie** is the home base for one of Northern Ireland's three fishing fleets, where fish is sold on the quayside when the fleet is in port.

For adjacent sights see BELFAST, MOUNT STEWART, STRANGFORD LOUGH.

Ballycopeland Windmill

Syndication International

BELFAST ★

BÉAL FEIRSTE – Co Antrim – Population 379 237
Michelin Atlas p 99 and Map 923 – O 4

Belfast, since 1920 the capital of Northern Ireland, is an industrial and predominantly Victorian city which owes its rapid expansion during the 18C and 19C to the textile, engineering and shipbuilding industries.

It is also a large port on an ideal site where the River Lagan flows into Belfast Lough, a long arm *(12mi/19km)* of the North Sea, sheltered on both sides by hills.

Modern Belfast is a good shopping centre for linen and woollen goods, glassware and pottery and other crafts.

Belfast has a lively cultural life; the annual Belfast Arts Festival is held in November at Queen's University. There are four theatres. Regular performances are given at the **Grand Opera House**, designed by Frank Matcham in 1894 with a gilt-and-red plush interior (restored in the 1980s); it is also the venue for the Northern Ireland Opera spring and autumn seasons. The Ulster Orchestra gives concerts at the **Ulster Hall**, designed in 1860 by WJ Barre, which has a good organ.

OUT AND ABOUT IN BELFAST

Tourist Information Centre

For advance information: Tourism Development Office, Belfast City Council, The Cecil Ward Building, 4-10 Linenhall Street, Belfast BT2 8BP ☎ 0123 2 320 202 ext 3585/3583.

For immediate information:
– Belfast City Airport ☎ 01232 457 745
– Belfast International Airport ☎ 01849 422 888
– Northern Ireland Tourist Board, *St Anne's Court, 59 North Street, BT1 1NB* ☎ 0123 2 246 609.
– Alternatively consult the website at www.belfastcit.gov.uk

Public Transport

For travel within the city of Belfast apply to **Citybus** ☎ 0123 2 246 485 (24hr information) or call at the Citybus kiosk, *Donegall Square West.*
For travel outside Belfast apply to **Ulsterbus** ☎ 0123 2 333 000.

Sightseeing

Various **Citybus tours** ⊘ are organized between June and September from Castle Place.

There are various themed walking tours of the city, including:

Belfast – The Old Town of 1660–1685 – Easter to October, Saturday, 2pm from the Tourist Information Centre, NITB, *59 North Street* ☎ 0123 2 246 609.

Bailey's Historical Pub Tour of Belfast – Saturday, 4pm and Tuesday, 7pm from Flannigan's (upstairs in the Crown Bar), *Great Victoria Street* ☎ 01846 683 665 (Judy Crawford) or ☎ 01247 882 596.

Belfast Town and Gown Tour – June to September, Saturday, 10.30am from the Wellington Park Hotel ☎ 01232 491 469 (Kathleen Chandler) for group bookings.

Belfast City Centre and Laganside Walk – June to September, Friday, 2pm from the front gates of City Hall ☎ 01232 491 469 (Kathleen Chandler) for group bookings.

Laganside Walk – From the **Lagan Lookout** there is a tow-path walk beside the river extending upstream to Lisburn *(7mi/12km).*

Shopping

Shops are generally open from 9am to 5.30pm, Monday to Saturday, with late-night shopping until 9pm on Thursday. Shops in the city centre are also open from 1pm to 6pm on Sunday.

The main shopping area is around **Donegall Place**, with many High Street stores and a selection of local shops. Through Queen's Arcade to the left of Donegall Place you will find the **Fountain Area**, a number of streets with a diverse range of shops and produce. The **Castlecourt Centre** in Royal Avenue boasts over 70 shops, including many High Street brands, all under one roof, as well as several food shops.

Lovers of markets and antiques should head for the **Donegall Pass**, located off Shaftesbury Square, home to several antique shops and a weekly bric-a-brac market. Other markets worth visiting include **St George's Market** (Friday mornings), for fresh produce, and the **Variety Market** next door, where you can find just about anything you are looking for.

Entertainment

Cinema-goers can choose from several cinemas including:

Queen's Film Theatre, *University Square Mews* ☎ 01232 244 857 – A 2-screen arthouse cinema.

Virgin Cinema, *Dublin Road* ☎ 0541 555 176 – A 10-screen complex.

The Movie House, *Yorkgate, York Street* ☎ 0123 2755 000.

The Curzon Cinema, *Ormeau Road* ☎ 01232 641 373.

The Strand Cinema, *Holywood Road* ☎ 01232 673 500.

Lovers of the arts can choose from several venues and art forms including:

Belfast Waterfront Hall ☎ 01232 334455 (Box Office); ☎ 01232 334 400 (Information and reservations) – A wide and varied programme of entertainment, offering something for lovers of contemporary and classical music alike.

The Grand Opera House, *Great Victoria Street* ☎ 0123 2249 129 (24hr information).

The Lyric Theatre, *Ridgeway Street* ☎ 01232 381 081.

Belfast Civic Arts Theatre, *Botanic Avenue* ☎ 01232 316 900 – Musicals, contemporary drama and concerts.

Old Museum Arts Centre, *College Square North* ☎ 01232 233 332 (Ticket Line) – Drama, poetry, dance and workshops.

The Crescent Arts Centre, *University Road* ☎ 01232 242 338 – Various workshops in what was originally a Victorian school.

Cultúrlann Macadam Ó Fiaich, *Falls Road* ☎ 01232 239 303 – Irish Language arts centre featuring concerts and exhibitions.

Ulster Hall, *Bedford Street* ☎ 01232 323 900 – Pop concerts, sporting events and a regular venue for the Ulster Orchestra.

King's Hall, *Balmoral* ☎ 01232 665 225 – A major venue which can accommodate up to 7 000 people.

Pubs

Pubs in Belfast are generally open from 11.30am to 11pm, Monday to Saturday, and noon to 10pm on Sunday. A selection of pubs worth a visit includes:

Robinson's Bar, *Great Victoria Street*.

The Duke of York, *Commercial Court*.

The Empire, *Botanic Avenue* – Different types of music plus a comedy club.

Kitchen Bar, *Victoria Square, Belfast 1* – Opened in 1859 and renowned for its music – traditional live music Friday and Saturday nights.

Maddens, *Berry Street* – Musical instruments adorning the walls give some idea of the role that music plays in this pub, where there is traditional live music Wednesday and Sunday nights.

The Liverpool – Traditional live music Wednesday and Sunday nights.

The Blackthorn, *Skipper Street* – Traditional live music Thursday nights.

Katy Daly's, *Ormeau Avenue* – All types of live music.

Pat's Bar, *Princes Dock Street* – Traditional live music.

Bittles Bar, *Victoria Square* – A whimsical triangular building dating from 1861 (formerly *The Shakespeare*).

The Garrick, *Chichester Street* – Portraits of golfing heroes now adorn the walls of this recently restored pub which lies in the heart of Belfast's commercial area.

Kelly's Cellars, *Bank Street* – Established in 1720 and recognizable by its attractive red-and-cream exterior.

HISTORICAL NOTES

Belfast takes its name from the ford by the sandbank (*bealfeirste* in Irish), where John de Courcy built a castle when he invaded Ulster in 1177. The castle was destroyed by Edward Bruce in 1315 and the town was held by the O'Neill clan until their possessions were forfeited following the Flight of the Earls in 1603. Belfast then passed to Sir Arthur Chichester and remained in the family until his descendant, the Marquess of Donegall, went bankrupt in the late 1840s.

Port of Belfast – The development of the port began with the construction of a quay under a royal charter (1613) and was promoted by the purchase from Carrickfergus in the 1630s of the monopoly of imported goods in the northeast of Ireland. A corporation for improving the port was established in 1784 and the Victoria Channel from the port to Belfast Lough was dredged in 1849. Shipbuilding, a significant element of the local economy, began in 1791. The Harland and Wolff shipyard, the largest shipbuilding and repair yard in the UK, bears the names of Edward James Harland, an engineer from Yorkshire, who came to Belfast in 1850, and Gustav Wilhelm Wolff, a marine draughtsman from Hamburg.

Short Brothers, the second-largest employer, produced the Sunderland flying boat and the first VTOL jet; their airstrip in the docks now doubles as Belfast City Airport.

Industrial Development – The local linen industry benefited greatly from the new methods, introduced by French Huguenot refugees in the 17C, and grew steadily in importance. Cotton spinning, introduced in 1777, also prospered, particularly during the American Civil War. The success of the textile and allied engineering industries promoted a revival in shipbuilding in 1833.

Religious and Political Dissent – Owing to the predominance of the Presbyterian Church, its cultural links with Scotland and its commercial wealth, Belfast early became a centre for intellectual activity and sometimes dissent. Belfast had the first printing press in Ireland (c 1690) and published the first Irish newspaper, the *Belfast News Letter*, in 1737; it is the oldest morning paper in the British Isles.

It was in Belfast in 1791 that Wolfe Tone helped to found the Society of United Irishmen; in 1792 they published the Northern Star, a newspaper which expressed radical opinion and first promoted the idea of the Irish nation.

UNIVERSITY DISTRICT

★★Ulster Museum ⊙ (AZ M¹) – The national museum and art gallery of Northern Ireland is housed in a modern building (1972), added to the previous premises built in 1929 in the Botanic Gardens. The nucleus of the present collections was first put on display in 1831 by the Belfast Natural History Society in a museum building in College Square North.

Visitors are advised to take the lift to the fourth floor and descend through the galleries which are linked by ramps.

Art Galleries – Two views of the Giant's Causeway by Susanna Drury (c 1740), the first artistic representation of the site, which brought it to the attention of the public, hang in the small collection of British and Continental painting before 1900, which includes works by JMW Turner (1775–1851) and portraits of local gentry by Sir Joshua Reynolds (1723–92), George Stubbs (1724–1806) and Pompeo Batoni (1708–87). Portraits and landscapes by Irish artists or on Irish subjects are periodically presented together with Irish furniture in the **Irish Gallery**: among the artists represented are Hugh Douglas Hamilton (1740–1808), Joseph Peacock (c 1783–1837), Sir John Lavery (1856–1941), Roderic O'Conor (1860–1940), Sir William Orpen (1878–1931). The collection of **prints, drawings and watercolours** contains works by the Irish artists Andrew Nicholl and Richard Dunscombe Parker and a set of 10 compositions by John Henry Fuseli (1741–1825), many with his wife as his model.

Craft Galleries – The collections cover glass including pieces commemorating personalities and incidents in Irish history, ceramics including the products of Belleek *(see p 317)*, silver pieces of Irish manufacture from the 17C to 19C, jewellery ranging from the 16C to 20C with an extensive collection of 19C Irish jewellery, and a costume and textile collection covering fashionable costume from the 18C to the present as well as lace, embroidery and household linen.

Geology of Ireland – A skeleton of the extinct Giant Irish Deer dominates this excellent gallery, which with the sections on Irish Flora and Fauna and the Living Sea gives a comprehensive view of the landscape of Ireland.

Antiquities – Human activity from the Prehistoric Era to the Middle Ages is traced through artefacts excavated from archeological sites, notably the River Blackwater: the **Shrine of St Patrick's Hand★**, a 14C or 15C silver-gilt hand studded with glass and rock crystal and stamped with animal figures; Neolithic axe heads; late Stone Age pottery; a Bronze Age cauldron and a pair of horns which still produce a musical note; early Iron Age sword scabbards decorated in the "Celtic" style; an early Christian brooch.

BELFAST

A Union Theological College
M' Ulster Museum
U Queen's University

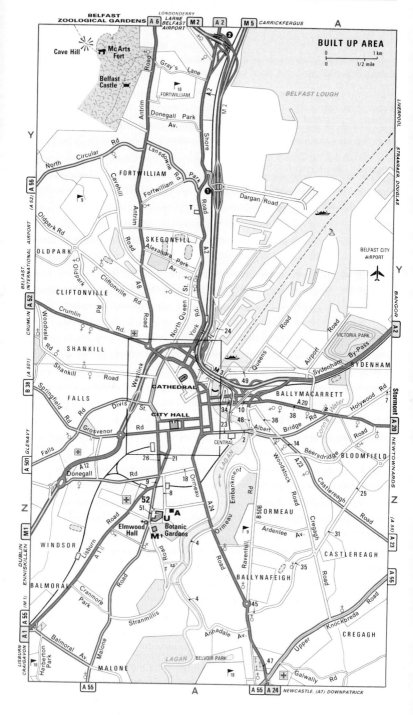

Pride of place goes to the **Spanish Armada treasure★★**, excavated from shipwrecks on the Irish coast: cannon and shot, a gold salamander set with rubies, gold chains, rings and crosses and coins.

BELFAST

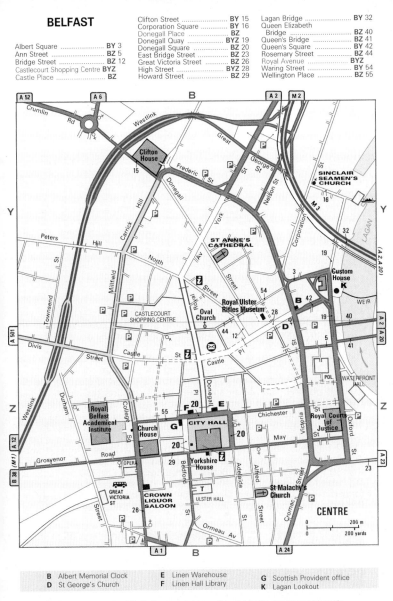

B Albert Memorial Clock	**E** Linen Warehouse
D St George's Church	**F** Linen Hall Library

G Scottish Provident office
K Lagan Lookout

In Northern Ireland parking in the town centre may be restricted to attended vehicles only.

Local History – The major part of this gallery traces the history of Ulster from c 600 to the present day. There is also a section on coins minted in Ireland up to 1690 and another on the Post Office displaying the portable desk used by **Anthony Trollope** (*see p 102*) to write his novels. The "Made in Belfast" gallery is devoted to the history of industry in the city and the northeast of Ireland.

Textile Gallery – Here the process of turning flax into linen is explained by means of texts and diagrams and 11 of the original machines.

Botanic Gardens ⊘ (**AZ**) – At the entrance to the Botanic Gardens stands a statue of Lord Kelvin (1824–1907), a native of Belfast, who invented the absolute scale of thermodynamics, the Kelvin Scale.

The gardens (28 acres/11ha), consisting of a bowling green, sweeping lawns, shrubberies, flower beds and a rose garden with pergola, slope gently to the River Lagan. Although the gardens were originally laid out for the study of plants by the Botanic and Horticultural Society, founded in 1827, many other activities and entertainments were organized to meet the constant need for funds. In 1895 the Gardens became a public park.

★ **Palm House** – This beautiful cast-iron and curvilinear glass structure, one of the earliest of its type, was designed by Charles Lanyon and completed in 1840. It was constructed by Richard Turner, who later collaborated with Decimus Burton on the construction of the Great Palm House at Kew. The dome was added in 1852. From the outset the east wing was a stove house while the west wing was a cooler greenhouse.

Tropical Ravine House – The present house is an extension of the older Fernery established in 1887 by the curator, Charles McKimm. In 1900 a stove section was added; two years later the lily pond was created over the boiler house. An internal gallery enables the plants to be viewed from both above and below.

Queen's University (**AZ U**) – Queen's College, Belfast, was incorporated in 1845 and established as a university in 1908. The red-brick Tudor-style building by Charles Lanyon is reminiscent of Magdalen College in Oxford.

Opposite stands **Elmwood Hall**, now an examination hall, an Italianate building with an arcaded façade in polychromatic freestone which was designed in 1862 by John Corry as a Presbyterian Church. The tower (1870) rises in three multi-columned stages to a needle spire.

University Square (**52**) is an attractive mid-Victorian terrace, now occupied by the Faculty of Arts, with fanlights over the front doors and magnolia trees in the gardens. Charles Lanyon also designed the **Union Theological College** (**A**) of the Presbyterian Church in Ireland (1852–55), where the first parliament of Northern Ireland sat in 1923. It is an unusual Italianate building of Scrabo stone *(see p 352)*, with a taller central portico, supported by four massive engaged Tuscan columns.

CITY CENTRE

★**City Hall** ⊘ (**BZ**) – The City Hall was begun in 1898 and completed in 1906 to celebrate Belfast's new city status, which was granted by Queen Victoria in 1888. The Portland stone building, which stands on the site of the old White Linen Hall (1784), was designed by Sir Brumwell Thomas in the Classical Renaissance style round a courtyard. The great copper-covered dome, capped by a stone lantern (173ft/53m) dominates not only the building but the whole square.

The guided tour of the **interior** starts at the foot of the grand staircase; the decor, which is enriched with Italian and Greek marble, depicts the history of Belfast Corporation and its coat of arms in the stained-glass windows, and the founding of the city and its principal industries in a mural painted by John Luke, a Belfast artist, to celebrate the Festival of Britain in 1951. Patrick MacDowell (1790–1870), a native of Belfast, sculpted one of the two memorials of the Marquess of Donegall (1827–53), who devoted the proceeds of his music and poetry to good works.

The Council Chamber is panelled in hand-carved Austrian oak; the Reception Hall displays the original Charter of Belfast granted by James I on 27 April 1613; above the carved oak panelling in the Banqueting Hall are stained-glass portraits of former mayors; the stained glass in the Great Hall shows the shields of the Provinces of Ireland and portraits of sovereigns who have visited Belfast.

Belfast City

W Webster /National Trust Photographic Library

Crown Liquor Saloon

★**Donegall Square** (**BZ 20**) – The hub of Belfast is Donegall Square, a vast rectangle of grass and flower beds formally laid out round the City Hall; here all the buses converge on the edge of the pedestrian shopping precinct.

The gardens at the centre of the square contain several statues: Queen Victoria stands on a pedestal flanked by two bronze figures representing shipbuilding and spinning; a group commemorates the *Titanic*, which was built in Belfast by Harland and Wolff and sank on her maiden voyage in 1912 after colliding with an iceberg; in front stands Sir Edward Harland.

Bordering the square are *(north side)* the **Linen Hall Library** ⓥ (**F**), which was founded in 1788 as the Belfast Library and Society for Promoting Knowledge and has retained its old-fashioned interior; an old linen warehouse (**E**) (1869) built of pink stone in the Venetian style; *(south side)* **Yorkshire House** which is decorated with roundels containing low-relief heads of famous men and gods and goddesses; *(west side)* the Scottish Provident office block (**G**) (1899–1902), designed by the Belfast architects, Young and Mackenzie.

★**St Anne's Cathedral** ⓥ (**BY**) – Belfast's Anglican Cathedral is built of white stone on the basilical plan in an adapted Romanesque style designed by Sir Thomas Drew and followed by Sir Charles Nicholson. Although begun in 1899 it was not completed until 1981.

Exterior – The West Front is pierced by three doors surmounted by carving: Christ in Glory *(centre)*, the Crucifixion *(north)* and the Resurrection *(south)*. The north transept incorporates a huge Celtic cross, the key to reconciliation.

Interior – A mosaic showing five angelic musicians adorns the tympanum above the west door. The Baptistery *(north aisle)* was the first part of the cathedral to be completed; the windows illustrate the Sacrament of Baptism, and the mosaic vault the Creation. The Chapel of the Holy Spirit *(south aisle)* commemorates St Patrick's mission to Ireland, shown in the mosaic above the entrance; the altar of inlaid wood is a replica of an early-Christian style. The capitals of the columns supporting the nave depict different aspects of Belfast life.

The **north transept chapel** is dedicated to the Royal Irish Rangers, the stained-glass window being a memorial to those who died in war.

The **East Window**, depicting the story of the Good Samaritan, comes from the earlier church, which was finally demolished in 1903.

★**Crown Liquor Saloon** ⓥ (**BZ**) – The Victorian interior is richly decorated with coloured glass and brightly coloured and moulded tiles, reflected in the arcaded mirrors behind the long curved marble bar. Carved animals top the doorposts of the panelled snugs. The ornate ceiling is supported on hexagonal wooden columns with feathered ornament. Inspired by his travels in Spain and Italy, Patrick Flanagan built the public house as a railway hotel in 1885; it is now owned by the National Trust.

★**Sinclair Seamen's Church** ⊘ (**BY**) – The church's service to the maritime community is reflected in its position near Belfast docks and its interior decoration. The present church, which opened in 1857, was designed by Sir Charles Lanyon; it consists of a nave and north transept, with the pulpit across the corner facing both arms of the L-shaped church. The tower containing the stairs to the gallery is linked to the church by a half-bridge resembling the Bridge of Sighs in Venice. The ship's bell from *HMS Hood* is rung at the beginning of the evening service; the collection is taken up in model life-boats instead of the pole boxes which now hang on the walls; a ship's wheel and a capstan stand in front of the pews; a ship's binnacle once served as a font; the reading desk is shaped like the prow of a ship; the pulpit and organ are adorned with port and starboard lights, a mast-head light, a ship's clock and a barometer.

★**St Malachy's Church** ⊘ (**BZ**) – The red-brick crenellated Roman Catholic church was built in 1844. Its austere fortified exterior gives no hint of the ornate interior, which is dominated by a white stucco Rococo ceiling of roundels and pendants.

Oval Church ⊘ (**BZ**) – The First Presbyterian Church, the oldest church in Belfast, opened in 1783 on the site of two previous Meeting Houses. Its elliptical plan was designed by Roger Mulholland; the entrance porch was enlarged in the 1830s. The line of the box pews echoes the curve of the galleries, which are supported on columns with Corinthian capitals. The Lewis organ (1907) retains its tubular pneumatic action and is of special interest to visiting musicians.

ADDITIONAL SIGHTS

Lagan Look-out ⊘ (**BY K**) – The display in the glass look-out describes the history of the River Lagan, its history as a major shipbuilding centre, its flora and fauna, the modern weir which controls the tides and creates a lagoon in the heart of the city.

Church House (**BZ**) – The headquarters of the Presbyterian Church in Ireland was designed by Young and Mackenzie (1905), Belfast architects, in the 15C Gothic style. The massive corner tower, which derives from St Giles' Cathedral in Edinburgh, contains a peal of bells. The semicircular Assembly Hall with its two galleries (refurbished in 1991) can seat about 1500 people.
The **Presbyterian Historical Society museum** contains old communion plate, pitch pipes and communion tokens, originally lead, now card. The Society keeps records and information about the Presbyterian Church in Northern Ireland but has little information from the 17C and 18C.

Royal Ulster Rifles Museum ⊘ (**BY**) – The small museum celebrates the military exploits of the regiment through weapons, sporting and shooting trophies, medals, 19C uniforms and a collection of drums including the Lambeg *(see p 325)*.

Royal Belfast Academical Institute (**BZ**) – The inter-denominational boys' school, commonly known as "Inst", is set back from the street behind pleasant gardens. The main block presents a long three-storey brick façade relieved by four pairs of plain pilasters and a recessed doorcase at the back of a Doric porch. It was probably designed by Sir John Soane and completed in 1814.

Clifton House (**BY**) – The wrought-iron entrance gate opens into a pleasant garden in front of a red-brick building with stone dressings set on a half-basement. It was designed by Robert Joy and opened as the Belfast Poorhouse in 1774, the date on the weather-vane which tops the octagonal stone spire.

Custom House (**BY**) – The building was designed by Charles Lanyon and erected in 1857 on the west bank of the River Lagan overlooking the docks; the two wings and central porch make an E-shape facing the city.

Royal Courts of Justice (**BZ**) – The massive building of Portland stone was designed by JG West and built between 1929 and 1933.

Albert Memorial Clock (**BY B**) – Owing to subsidence the tower has inclined slightly from the vertical since it was built in 1865 by WJ Barre; a statue of the Prince Consort stands in a niche in the west side facing up the High Street.

St George's Church (**BYZ D**) – The church was designed by John Bowden in 1816; the Classical portico comes from the palace which the Earl Bishop started to build at Ballyscullion after 1787.

EXCURSIONS

★★**Belfast Zoological Gardens** ⊘ – *5mi/8km north of Belfast by A 6. Car park; footpath to McArts Fort (see below).* The Zoo, which opened in 1934, lives up to its full name since the animal enclosures are set in the former Hazlewood Gardens, surrounded, where possible, by dry ditches or water-filled moats. There are spacious green areas for the big cats, the various types of deer and kangaroos; an aquatic complex is subdivided to house penguins, sea-lions and polar bears; water fowl and flamingoes congregate round the large lake. A large walk-through aviary enables visitors to see free-flying birds at close quarters. The zoo is in a state of continuous development; recent additions include an otter park and buildings housing groups of chimpanzees and gorillas.

Belfast Castle ⊘ **(AY)** – *4mi/6.4km north of Belfast by A 6. Turn left into Innisfayle Park to Belfast Castle.* In a superb location on the lower slopes of Cave Hill, this great mansion in Scottish Baronial style was built for the Donegall family in 1867–70 by WH Lynn; the external Baroque staircase was added to the east front in 1894. The interior now houses a restaurant and reception rooms, as well as a **Heritage Centre** on the top floor, with displays on the history of the castle and its surroundings. The commanding views over the city in its setting can be enjoyed by use of a remote camera with a powerful zoom lens. The castle has formal gardens and is one of a number of starting points for the waymarked trails through **Cave Hill Country Park**.

Cave Hill (AY) – *4mi/6.4km north of Belfast by A 6. Accessible on foot from several car parks, including those at Belfast Castle and at the Zoological Gardens; various waymarked paths lead to the summit.*
North of Belfast rears the black basalt cliff, known as Cave Hill (1 182ft/360m), which marks the southern end of the Antrim plateau and is said to resemble the profile of Napoleon. The headland, which is separated by a deep ditch from the rest of Cave Hill, is marked by an ancient earthwork, known as **McArts Fort**, after a local 16C-to-17C chieftain who was probably killed by the Elizabethans; it has served as a watchtower and place of refuge for the native Irish against Vikings and Anglo-Normans. In 1795 Wolfe Tone and his fellow United Irishmen spent two days and nights in the fort planning the independence of Ireland. Fine view of Belfast city and Belfast Lough and, on a clear day, of County Down and Strangford Lough *(southeast)*, Lough Neagh and the Sperrin Mountains *(west)*, and Scotland *(northeast)*.

Stormont ⊘ – *4mi/6.4km east of Belfast by A 20.* The Northern Ireland Parliament, a plain white Classical building with a central portico, which was de-signed by A Thornley, stands prominently on a hill approached by a broad avenue (1mi/1.6km long) through rolling parkland. A statue of Sir Edward Carson (1854–1935) stands at the centre of the roundabout. Parliament met regularly from 1932, when the building was opened, until 1972 when direct rule from Westminster was imposed. Stormont Castle, in the Scottish baronial style *(right)*, houses other government offices.

Glencairn People's Museum ⊘ – *Fernhill House; 4mi/6.4km west of city centre by Shankhill Road, Woodvale Road, Ballygomartin Road, Forthriver Road and Glencairn Road to Glencairn Park.* Set in a mid-Victorian butter-merchant's mansion, with wide views across Glencairn Park to the city centre, this museum includes an exhibition on the social history of the Shankhill area, with fascina-ting photographs of residents and their houses, and *(upstairs)* a history of Unionism.

For adjacent sights see ANTRIM, BANGOR, CARRICKFERGUS, LISBURN.

CARRICKFERGUS

CARRAIG FHEARGHAIS – Co Antrim – Population 22 786
Michelin Atlas p 103 and Map 923 – O 3

The largest and best-preserved Norman castle in Ireland dominates this pleasant seaside town on the north shore of Belfast Lough. A broad promenade runs along the front, between the bathing beach and the Marine Gardens; and a marina packed with yachts and fishing boats and rowing boats for hire now occupies the harbour where, until the development of Belfast, there was a thriving port. Medieval banquets and the annual Lughnasa Fair are held in the castle.
The district has nurtured three literary figures: Jonathan Swift wrote his first book at Kilroot; William Congreve and Louis MacNeice lived in Carrickfergus as children.

HISTORICAL NOTES

The name Carrickfergus, meaning the Rock of Fergus, recalls the ruler of the ancient kingdom of Dalriada, Fergus Mór, who was drowned in a shipwreck off the coast c 531.
The town grew up in the shadow of the castle and shared its history. The castle was built late in the 12C by the Anglo-Norman, John de Courcy, and completed by Hugh de Lacy c 1240. In 1315 it was captured after a year-long siege by Lord Edward Bruce from Scotland. The English recaptured it and held it for the next 300 years, withstanding many attacks by the local Irish and by invading Scots troops.

CARRICKFERGUS

In 1688 the castle and the town were held for James II by Lord Iveagh but were captured in 1689 by Schomberg. On 14 June the following year William of Orange landed in Carrickfergus harbour *(plaque)* on his way to the Battle of the Boyne *(see p 91)*. A bronze statue of William III was unveiled in 1990 to commemorate the tercentenary of his landing.

In February 1760 the town was held briefly by a French squadron under Thurot. In 1778 the American privateer John Paul Jones in his vessel *Ranger* attacked *HMS Drake* in an offshore engagement.

★★CASTLE ⊘

The castle stands on a basalt promontory, originally protected by the sea on all but the landward side. Its position commands the entrance to Belfast Lough. It was begun soon after the Anglo-Norman invasion in 1177 and twice extended to secure the whole promontory by the middle of the 13C.

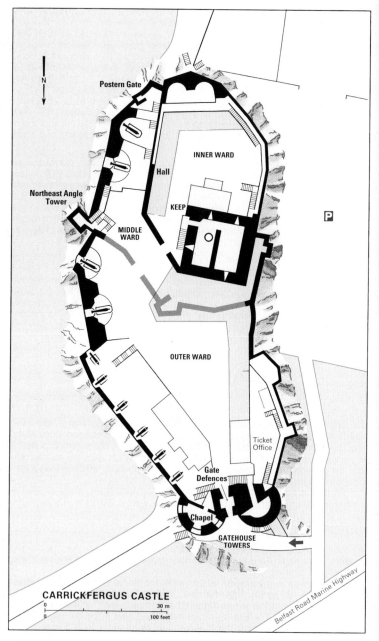

CARRICKFERGUS CASTLE

Carrickfergus Castle

Life-size figures of the castle's inhabitants and garrison illustrate its 800 years of active use.

The oldest part of the castle, built by John de Courcy between 1180 and 1200, is the **inner ward** which is enclosed by a high curtain wall; there was a hall against the east wall. The brick-built gunports were introduced in the 16C; the 19C gun platforms at the southern end provide a view of the castle and its surroundings: up the coast to Whitehead *(east)*, to Cave Hill and Belfast *(southwest)*, across Belfast Lough to Bangor *(southeast)*.

The **keep** provided living accommodation for the lord of the castle. The life led here is evoked in a variety of ways; there is a large model of the castle at the time of Schomberg's siege in 1689; an audio-visual show *Feasts and Fasts* in the Banqueting Hall, and, on the banner-hung top floor, the opportunity to dress up in period costume.

The wall enclosing the **middle ward,** now partly reduced to its foundations, was built to improve the castle's defences soon after it had been successfully besieged by King John in 1210. The northeast angle tower is a fine example of 13C defensive work with an impressive array of arrow slits. There is a postern gate in the southeast corner. The **outer ward** was probably built by Hugh de Lacy, between 1228 and 1242, to enclose the whole promontory and make the castle less vulnerable to attack from the land. Originally it probably contained living quarters but these were replaced in the 19C by ordnance stores supporting gun platforms.

The **gatehouse towers,** which were completely circular when they were built at the same time as the Outer Ward, were cut back some time after the Elizabethan period. The room over the entrance passage contains the portcullis winding-gear and a "murder hole". The Chapel on the first floor of the east tower is so called because of its elaborate east window.

TOWN CENTRE

★**St Nicholas' Church** ⊘ – The late-12C pillars in the nave are part of the original structure which was built by John de Courcy. After several centuries of turbulence the church was heavily restored in 1614. The west tower, the bell-tower, which was begun in 1778, was completed in 1962 as a memorial to both World Wars. In the north transept is a marble and alabaster monument to Sir Arthur Chichester (1563–1625), Governor of Carrickfergus, and his wife and son. The stained glass in the south side and west end of the nave is 16C from Co Meath.

North Gate and Town Walls – Carrickfergus was enclosed with defensive walls and ditches between 1607 and 1610 by Lord Deputy Arthur Chichester. The big arch of the North Gate is still largely 17C work but the structure has been repaired and altered many times; the pedestrian arch and crenellations are a 19C addition. A good stretch of wall survives to the east in Shaftesbury Park.

Knight Ride ⊙ – Visitors are carried in knights' helms on a monorail above the shopping precinct and into the dark ride, where the history of Carrickfergus is recalled in a strong local accent, from the legendary shipwreck of Fergus, through the invasions of Vikings, Normans and Williamites, to the present day. The static exhibition includes a scale-model of the town.

EXCURSIONS

Andrew Jackson Centre ⊙ – *2mi/3.2km north of Carrickfergus by A 2; turn right onto Donaldsons Avenue.* Between the road and the sea stands a 17C single-storey cottage near the site of the Jackson family's homestead *(plaque in southwest corner of the car park)*. The property has been restored to its original condition: earthen floor, wattle-and-daub canopy over the open hearth, hanging crane; the furniture dates from the 1850s.

The gallery traces the Ulster-American connection, in particular the life of Andrew Jackson, whose parents emigrated in 1765 to South Carolina, where Andrew was born in 1767. In 1829 he was elected 7th President of the USA and served two terms of office.

The adjoining exhibition centre presents the story of the **US Rangers** who were formed in Northern Ireland in 1942, with the task of acting as a Spearhead force for the invasions of the Second World War.

Dalway's Bawn – *6mi/10km north of Carrickfergus by A 2, B 149 and B 90.* South of Ballycarry beside the road *(left)* stand the remains of a bawn, with three flanker towers built by John Dalway c 1609 and now part of a farm.

Whitehead – *5.5mi/9km northeast of Carrickfergus by A 2.* Population 3 761. This seaside resort is sheltered between the cliffs of White Head and Black Head. It has a pebble beach backed by a promenade and two golf courses.

The town is also one of the bases of the **Railway Preservation Society of Ireland** ⊙ which owns a unique collection of steam locomotives and coaches, and operates steam rail tours to all parts of Ireland during the summer season.

Island Magee – *6mi/10km north of Carrickfergus by A 2. Ferry from Larne* ⊙ *(see p 411).* Although not an island, the peninsula (7mi/11km long), which separates Larne Lough from the North Channel, feels quite detached. The road *(B 90)* along the west side of the peninsula provides a good view across Larne Lough. At its north end in the front garden of a private house *(right)* stands the **Ballylumford Dolmen★**, a Neolithic burial monument, consisting of four stones supporting a capstone. The north end of the peninsula is marked by **Brown's Bay**, a sandy beach sheltered between low headlands, with a view of the shipping entering and leaving the port of Larne, and on a clear day the coast of Scotland *(north)*. On the east coast lies **Portmuck**, a small bay and harbour beside a farm on the headland reached by a narrow winding road. Further south are **The Gobbins**, two miles of cliffs which plunge precipitously into the sea; in 1641 the local inhabitants were flung over the edge by the soldiers from the garrison in Carrickfergus.

Glenoe Waterfall – *12mi/20km north of Carrickfergus by B 58 and B 99; car park (right) in Waterfall Road half way down the hill.* The gorge is so deep and so well screened by trees that the waterfall is audible before it is visible. The river falls in a double cascade into a deep pool before flowing on through the village under an old stone bridge. A path and steps lead up beside the fall, and a wooden bridge carries the footpath over the river into the village, which is now preserved by the National Trust.

For adjacent sights see ANTRIM, ANTRIM GLENS, BELFAST.

Help us in our constant task of keeping up-to-date.
Send your comments and suggestions to

Michelin Tyre PLC
Tourism Department
38 Clarendon Road
WATFORD, Herts
WD1 1SX
Tel: 01923 415000
Fax: 01923 415250
Web site: www.michelin-travel.com

CASTLE COOLE ★★★

Co Fermanagh
Michelin Atlas p 97 and Map 923 – J 4
1.5mi/2.4km southeast of Enniskillen by A 4

Probably the finest neo-Classical house in Ireland, Castle Coole was designed by James Wyatt and completed in 1798. The house, which is set on a rise sloping to the lake, consists of a central block containing the formal rooms, flanked by two single-storey wings containing the family rooms.

In the 1980s it was restored to something like its early-19C appearance by the recladding of the exterior, using the original or new Portland stone, and by the redecoration of the interior, in accordance with the original intentions of Wyatt or of Preston, one of the leading Dublin upholsterers of the period, who refurbished the interior between 1807 and 1825.

The stable yards (restored), built out of sight below the level of the house and linked to it by a tunnel, were designed in 1817 by Richard Morrison. On display is Lord Belmore's coach, built in 1863 and still used in the 1940s to fetch guests from the station.

The Corrys of Coole

John Corry, a Belfast merchant, originally from Dumfriesshire, purchased the manor of Coole in 1656 and in 1709 built a new house near the lake incorporating parts of an early-17C castle. In 1741 the estate passed to Armar Lowry-Corry, created 1st Earl of Belmore in 1797, who commissioned Wyatt to design the present house; his son, the 2nd Earl of Belmore, was responsible for the interior decoration and the Regency furnishings.

TOUR *1hr*

The spaciousness and sense of proportion experienced in the **entrance hall** are repeated throughout the house. Family portraits are hung in some of the main rooms; the Breakfast Room contains many important pictures.

James Wyatt's scheme of decoration and furnishings is best seen in the **library**, where the writing desk, the drum pier-tables and the bookcases are original, and in the **dining room**, where the decoration and the furniture have altered little since Wyatt's day: restrained ceiling, frieze and dado; sideboard bearing a silver salver and a pair of covered cups; urns on pedestals painted by Biagio Rebecca; oval wine cooler, known in the 18C as a sarcophagus owing to its size. The **oval Saloon**, the most important room in the house, is decorated with elaborate plasterwork; the curved doors, which are made of mahogany veneered with satinwood, are hung on pivots. Wyatt specified the ceramic stoves which have the same decorative motif as the friezes.

Preston's more flamboyant style is evident in the porphyry colour used in the hall, on the staircase and in the lobby on the first-floor landing. He provided the hangings and furniture in the drawing room and the saloon, and substituted a larger table in the dining room.

Christopher Hill / National Trust Photographic Library

State Bedroom, Castle Coole

The **Bow Room** on the first floor, also known as the Work Room, was used by the ladies of the house for sewing, talking, reading or playing the piano. The door lintel matches the chimney-piece. The wallpaper and the curtains, which are hung in the original manner with the pattern running vertically in the centre, are reproductions of the originals specified by Preston, who also supplied a set of 12 satinwood armchairs, a pair of glass-fronted cabinets and a pair of convex mirrors. The bamboo settee and chairs also date from this period.

The decoration and furnishing of the **State Bedroom** by Preston were in anticipation of George IV's visit to Ireland in 1821. Four massive lions' paws support the bed, which is made in Grecian form of Spanish mahogany. The gold fringes and borders are original although the scarlet silk hangings and the bed canopy have had to be restored.

For adjacent sights see ENNISKILLEN, Lough ERNE, FLORENCE COURT, SPERRIN MOUNTAINS.

CASTLE WARD ★★
Co Down
Michelin Atlas p 99 and Map 923 – P4

The house at Castle Ward is unique, an architectural compromise combining the conventional Classical idiom with the first example of Georgian Gothic in Ireland. It reflects the conflicting tastes of Bernard Ward and his wife, who married in 1747 but later separated. The three-storey rectangular block with a semi-octagonal bay at each end is built of Bath stone and was designed by an unknown architect in the early 1760s. From the Gothic front there is a fine **view** of Strangford Lough.

Ward Family

Late in the 16C Bernard Ward from Capesthorne in Cheshire bought the Castle Ward estate from the Earls of Kildare. In 1610 Nicholas Ward built a tower house, Old Castle Ward, on the shore of Strangford Lough. No trace remains of the 18C house built in the sixth generation by Michael Ward, who promoted the linen trade, developed the lead mines on his estate and became a Justice of the Court of the King's Bench in Ireland. In 1812 the property passed to Robert Ward, who abandoned Castle Ward in favour of his other house, Bangor Castle. In 1827 the 3rd Viscount Bangor (the title was bestowed in 1781) began to restore the house and estate. On the death of the 6th Viscount Bangor in 1950 the house was received by the state in lieu of death duties and presented to the National Trust.

TOUR *2hr*

The car park near the house is linked by a drive to another by the lake shore (Old Castle Ward).

House – The original entrance in the southwest Classical front opens into the **hall** which is highly decorated with stuccowork – partly the work of Dublin plasterers and partly in a more robust style by local workmen – and now in what is thought to be the original colour scheme.

The rooms on the northeast side of the house are decorated in the Gothic style favoured by Lady Bangor. The **fan vaulting** in the boudoir is based on that in Henry VII's Chapel in Westminster Abbey. The glass window panels in the **saloon** are thought to be 17C Flemish. The Gothic **morning room** contains a landscape of Castle Ward in 1785 by William Ashford and two drawings of the present house by its architect. The **dining room** is on the Classical side of the house. In 1827 the 18C panelling was painted, grained and parcel-gilt. The dining chairs (c 1760) are in the Chippendale style.

A tunnel leads from the basement to the **stable yard** where the ground level was lowered to hide the buildings from the house. The **laundry** is an 18C building with 19C equipment: wash tubs, a copper boiler, a stone mangle.

Grounds – In 1902 the **Sunken Garden** near the stable yard consisted of 61 flat beds producing flowers, several beds of roses on the terrace and a collection of begonias. Beyond were the Yew Terraces, planted in 1720 with Florence Court yews, and a Pinetum.

When the new house was built in the 1760s, an informal landscape with broad sweeps of grass and clumps of trees and a deer park was substituted for the earlier formal landscape, of which the chief feature, the **Temple Water**, remains; it was

Gothick Boudoir, Castle Ward

A von Einsiedel /National Trust Photographic Library

created in 1724 and aligned on the tower of Audley's Castle *(see p 349)*. The Queen Anne house had stood on the east side of the Water near the **ice house**. Opposite on a hill stands the **Temple**, a Classical summer house with a Doric portico (1750), next to the Walled Garden, which originally produced flowers, fruit and vegetables for the house and now contains pens for the **Wildfowl Collection**, reflecting the wildfowl to be found on Strangford Lough.

The 17C **tower house**, known as Old Castle Ward, was the first dwelling built on the estate by a Ward. It is now surrounded by the farmyard buildings, most of which were built in a matching castellated style in the mid 19C: cattle byre, turnip house, grain and coal store, drying kiln, sawmill and **grain mill** ⊘. The original 18C mill, which was a tidal mill, was later driven by water from the Temple Water. Another building houses the **Strangford Lough Wildlife Centre** ⊘.

For adjacent sights see DOWNPATRICK, STRANGFORD LOUGH.

CAUSEWAY COAST ★★

Co Antrim

Michelin Atlas p 102–103 and Map 923 – L M N 2

The north coast from Ballycastle westwards begins as dramatic cliffs and ends in a long sand dune extending into Lough Foyle; in between are the volcanic rock formations of the Giant's Causeway, superb views, major and minor resorts and many sandy beaches (at Portballintrae, Portstewart and Castlerock).

The geological importance of the Causeway Coast is recognized by its designation as a National Nature Reserve; it was at Portrush that the evidence was found which settled the long-standing controversy about the origin of such features as the Giant's Causeway.

BALLYCASTLE TO MAGILLIGAN STRAND *40mi/64km – 1 day*

Ballycastle – Population 4005. The attractive resort is situated at the foot of Knocklayd Mountain with a view over Ballycastle Bay to Rathlin Island. It has a long sandy beach, salt- and fresh-water angling, golf links and other sports facilities.

An Irish Music and Dance Festival is held here in June; the Ould Lammas Fair in August combines livestock sales with street stalls selling two traditional sweet confections – **Yellowman**, a sort of toffee, and **Dulse**, a dried edible seaweed. In 1898 Marconi *(see p 120)* and his assistant George Kemp set up a wireless link between Ballycastle and Rathlin Island; a stone memorial, symbolizing aerials and radio waves, stands at the west end of the harbour.

The town centre is graced by **Holy Trinity Church** ⊘, an elegant 18C building with a balustraded tower and steeple built in 1756 by Col Hugh Boyd and maintained by his family for many years.

On the cliffs east of the town is the **Corrymeela Centre**, which works for reconciliation between the two cultural traditions in Northern Ireland; it contains a semi-underground heart-shaped oratory.

Rathlin Island ⊙ – *Access by boat from Ballycastle.* Population 100. The island lies north of Ballycastle across Rathlin Sound (5mi/8km), a rough and dangerous crossing except on a calm day. An additional hazard is the whirlpool off Rue Point which nearly claimed the life of St Columba (Colmcille) in the 6C. The traditional occupations are fishing and agriculture, supplemented in the past by smuggling and now by tourism. In the 17C the island passed from the MacDonnells to the Gages, whose memorials adorn St Thomas' Church.

The sheltered harbour, where seals sometimes bask on the rocks, is set in the angle facing south across Church Bay and backed by the village. Three roads radiate to the outlying homesteads and the lighthouses.

The L-shaped fillet of land is treeless, pitted with shallow lakes and almost entirely surrounded by high white cliffs, where in early summer the sea-birds congregate in their thousands; the fields are divided by dry white stone walls. Tradition has it that here in 1306 Robert the Bruce received his famous lesson in perseverance from a spider while taking refuge in one of the many caves *(accessible only by boat)*.

From Ballycastle take B 15 west. After 5mi/8km turn right to Larry Bane Bay and Carrick-a-rede Rope Bridge.

Carrick-a-rede Rope Bridge ⊙ – *From the car park 30min there and back on foot. People cross the rope bridge at their own risk; dangerous in a high wind; remember the return journey.* During the walk along the Larry Bane Cliffs sea birds wheel and scream over the waves below and Rathlin Island is in full view. The rope bridge (66ft/20m long) bounces and sways as one ventures gingerly along the planks above the rock-strewn water (80ft/25m below). In the past there was only one handrail but accidents seem to have been few during the bridge's 200 years of existence.

Carrick-a-rede Rope Bridge

Christophe Boisvieux

The rope bridge is put up every spring for the fishermen who operate the island salmon fishery between April and September. As the migrating salmon swim west along the shore seeking their freshwater spawning grounds in the River Bush or River Bann, they are deflected north by the island (*Carrick-a-rede* means Rock-in-the-Road) straight into the nets which are always set in the same place.

The rocks were formed by a volcanic explosion at about the same time as that which created the Giant's Causeway. From the island there is a good **view** *(east)* of Fair Head, *(northeast)* of Rathlin Island, and *(west)* of Sheep Island and Ballintoy church and harbour, backed by Benbane Head.

Continue west on B 15; beyond Ballintoy turn right.

Ballintoy Harbour – The small white church with its unusual pinnacled tower overlooks a small harbour; the rocks have the same volcanic formation as the Giant's Causeway.

Return to B 15 and continue west; 1mi/1.6km after rejoining A 2 turn right to car park.

White Park Bay – Although the current makes the inviting stretch of sand unsafe for bathing, there is interest for the geologist in the fossil ammonites found on the beach, for the archeologist in the burial mounds and flint implements found on the collapsed chalk terrace, and for the biologist in the plant and animal life.

Continue west by A 2; after 0.25mi/0.4km turn right to Portbradden.

Portbradden – St Gobhan's *(private)* is the smallest church in Ireland.

Return to A 2; continue west; after 0.5mi/0.8km turn right onto B 146; after 1mi/1.6km park in the lay-by (right) by the cottages.

Dunseverick Castle – *From the castle there is a narrow cliff path (about 5mi/8km) west to the Giant's Causeway; as it is difficult in bad weather, stout shoes are required and children should be attended by an adult.*

The importance accorded to this castle in the written records is supported less by the scanty ruins than by the impressive site, a promontory separated from the mainland by two defiles. Dunseverick, which means the royal fort of Sobhairce, was visited by St Patrick in the 5C and was linked to Tara in Co Meath by the road through the Moyry Gap *(see p 339).*

Continue westwards on B 146.

A magnificent **view**★★ is gradually revealed of the coastline extending west beyond Portrush and Portstewart to Magilligan Strand and the mountains of Donegal.

★★★**Giant's Causeway** – *See p 321.*

Continue southwest by B 146 and A 2 to Bushmills.

Bushmills Distillery ⊘ – *Car park.* The prominent feature of Bushmills (population 1 348) is the distinctive caps of the kilns in the **distillery** on the eastern edge of the town. The original licence to distil was granted to Sir Thomas Phillips in 1608, although the earliest mention of distilling on the site goes back to 1276. Using its own supply of water from St Columb's Rill, a tributary of the River Bush which rises in peaty ground, the distillery produces two blended whiskeys and one malt. The tour includes the main stages in the production of whiskey: mashing, fermentation, distillation, maturing in oak casks, blending and bottling. Tasting takes place in the Potstill Bar where a small museum has been created in the old malt kilns.

From Bushmills take A 2 west.

★★**Dunluce Castle** ⊘ – *Car park.* The jagged silhouette of the ruins of Dunluce Castle rises from the cliff edge above the sea (100ft/30m). The site, an isolated rock stack separated from the mainland by a wide deep defile (20ft/7m), makes a perfect natural fortress. The castle was captured from the MacQuillans in the 16C by the MacDonnells from Scotland. In 1584 it was badly damaged by the English Lord Deputy but Sorley Boy MacDonnell restored the family position and he and his son James repaired and strengthened the castle to withstand artillery fire. The **pound**, the grassy area below the drawbridge, leads into a cave beneath the castle rock communicating with the sea; it was used as a retreat in the Early-Christian period.

The mainland courtyard was built in the 17C to provide accommodation for store rooms, a forge and stabling. Contemporary structures in traditional style house ticket office and an audio-visual theatre. The converging walls create a funnel from which a drawbridge spanning the defile gave access to the late-16C **gatehouse**, built in the Scottish style with corbelled corner turrets. A stone in the wall *(left)* at the inner end of the gatehouse bears an etching of a **masted galley**. Vestiges of a late-16C **loggia** survive *(right)*. The oldest parts of the castle, the two east towers and the south wall, date from the 14C. The **great hall**, which now almost fills the upper yard, was added in the 17C by the Earls of Antrim; it is built in a grand style with bay windows on the west front and two fireplaces. Northeast of the hall is the **kitchen** which has a vast fireplace, stone-built ovens, cupboard recesses and stone drainage. The cobbled **lower yard** is surrounded by service buildings including the bakery. In 1639 part of the castle, either here or near the kitchen, collapsed into the sea causing several deaths; this led to the castle being abandoned for a less perilous site near the car park. From the lower yard there is a superb **view** *(east)* of the Causeway coast, and *(west)* of The Skerries out to sea.

Continue west on A 2.

Portrush – Population 5598. The town is a popular seaside resort set on a peninsula, which is flanked by several sandy beaches and ends in Ramore Head, a haunt of bird watchers. There are various forms of indoor and evening entertainment, many sports facilities on land and on the water, and excursions by boat to visit the caves in the limestone cliffs at **White Rock** *(east)*, and to **The Skerries**, a chain of offshore islands densely populated by sea birds.

The **Dunluce Centre** ⊘, in the same prominent pavilion as the Tourist Information Centre, contains such lavish revisions of traditional end-of-the-pier entertainments as Turbotours and Earthquest.

The **Countryside Centre** ⊘, located in an old Victorian bath-house, introduces the ecology and marine life of the locality; visitors can observe the denizens of the seabed from within the "wreck" of the Nautilus.

Portstewart – Population 6459. Although quieter than its neighbour, Portstewart with its picturesque harbour was a fashionable watering-place in the 19C, dominated by O'Hara's Castle, a Gothic-style mansion (1834), which is now a Dominican college. From the promenade, paths lead west along the cliffs to Portstewart Strand *(2mi/3.2km)*. Regular exhibitions are held at the Flowerfield Arts Centre.

From Portstewart take A 2 inland to Coleraine.

Coleraine – Population 20721. Coleraine, a university town since 1968, is an excellent shopping centre and market town at the head of the Bann estuary, with a bird sanctuary and a marina on the river, which is a good place from which to watch the local regattas. The town first became prosperous in 1613 when the land was granted by James I to the City of London Companies *(see p 341)*.

A pedestrian precinct in the town centre contains **St Patrick's Church**, which has a high porch and pinnacled tower. The original church was founded in the 5C but burnt down in 1177; parts of the present building date from 1613.

Further west stands the Town Hall (1857–59), a robust building in ochre sandstone with Baroque window surrounds and chimney decorations, and a slender tower reminiscent of St Mary-le-Strand in London; it was designed by Thomas Turner, brother of Richard Turner who built the Palm House in Belfast.

From Coleraine take B 67 east via Ballybogy for 5.5mi/9km.

★**Benvarden** ⊘ – Benvarden House, home of the Montgomery family since 1798, opens its garden and grounds to the public every summer. A walled garden (2 acres/0.8ha), parts of which may date back to the original fortified enclosure, features rose beds, a formal hedged garden, a vinery and a pergola walk. Beyond are the kitchen gardens, with Victorian hothouses and the old gardener's bothy. A wild garden and azalea walk form part of the grounds, which lead down to the River Bush; this is spanned by a Victorian stone and cast-iron bridge, rare of its type in Ireland.

Return to Ballybogy. Turn left onto B 62 towards Ballymoney (sign at by-pass roundabout).

Leslie Hill Open Farm ⊘ – This mixed-farming estate has been in the ownership of the same family since the mid 18C. The agricultural writer Arthur Young stayed at Leslie Hill in 1776 and devoted no fewer than 18 pages of his *Tour in Ireland* to a description of the progressive farming practised here. The array of buildings and implements dating from most periods of the farm's existence give a vivid picture of its evolution. The cathedral-like Bell Barn contrasts with the modest two-room cabin lived in by the coachman's family. A little museum contains a fascinating collection of farm and family memorabilia. A track, hidden from view from the imposing Georgian house by a ha-ha, leads to the walled garden with its pit-house, hot wall, and the remains of the heating arrangements for growing peaches.

From Coleraine take A 2 west; 1mi/1.6km beyond Articlave at the Liffock crossroads turn left into the car park.

Hezlett House ⊘ – *Castlerock, on the northwest corner of the crossroads.* Hezlett House, which was built in 1691 probably as a clergyman's residence, is a long, single-storey thatched cottage with battered, rough-cast walls, an attic and cruck truss roof. It was taken over by the Hezlett family in 1761 and aquired by the National Trust in 1976.

Visitors are led through the tiny kitchen, pantry, dining room, bed-sized bedrooms and parlour and up into the attic, where the servants slept. Furnishings date from the 19th century and include balloon chairs (with holes for women's bustles) and prayer chairs, allowing women to kneel in hoop skirts while retaining their dignity. The walls and roof have been stripped back in places to show the timbers, peat infill and plastering techniques. A small museum in the outbuildings shows Victorian farming implements.

Continue west on A 2.

★**Downhill** – The buildings on the cliff top at Downhill were erected by the Earl Bishop. A charming glen planted with flowers and shrubs, many presented by visitors, leads up to the cliff top.

By the **Bishop's Gate** stood a mausoleum *(left)*, by Michael Shanahan, supporting a statue by Van Nost of the 3rd Earl of Bristol, which was blown from its pedestal in a high wind.

The **Mussenden Temple**★ ⊘, an elegant Classical rotunda, based on the Temple of Vesta at Tivoli, built of local basalt faced with sandstone from Ballycastle, perches precariously on the very edge of the high cliffs. It was erected in 1785 as a memorial to Mrs Mussenden, the Bishop's cousin; he used it as his library and allowed the local Roman Catholic priest to say Mass in the basement.

From here there is a splendid **view** *(east)* of the Bann estuary and the sands at Portstewart, *(below)* of the railway entering a tunnel, and *(west)* of Magilligan Strand and the mountains of Donegal.

The great house was destroyed in a fire in 1851, after which it was rebuilt, but since 1951 it has been a roofless shell.

Continue west on A 2.

Earl Bishop

The Earl Bishop was the eccentric Bishop of Derry, Frederick Hervey, who on the death of his elder brother became the 4th Earl of Bristol. He travelled extensively on the Continent and many a Hotel Bristol is named after him.

He commissioned the house at Downhill, known as **Downhill Castle**, in 1772 from Michael Shanahan, his favourite architect, to house the large collection of sculpture and paintings which he collected during his Continental journeys; most of it was destroyed in a fire in 1851.

He began a second large house in Ireland after 1787 at Ballyscullion on the west shore of Lough Beg; the portico now stands at the entrance to St George's Church in Belfast. The Earl Bishop also created an eccentric house on the family estate in England, Ickworth Place in Suffolk, which was started in 1795.

Beyond the Lion Gate there is a fine view of the sea and the strand where the Bishop held horse races and the present generation indulges in surfing.

Bear left into the Bishop's Road.

★★**Gortmore Viewpoint** – *Car park.* The road climbs steeply up the northeast slope of Binevenagh Mountain. There is a superb **view** of Magilligan Strand extending across the mouth of Lough Foyle towards the Inishowen Peninsula; in the last century it was used as the base line for the Ordnance Survey of Ireland.

Return downhill; turn left onto A 2.

★★**Magilligan Strand** – The long stretch of golden sand dunes (6mi/10km) is equipped with sports facilities at Benone. Much of the land is reserved for military purposes. The Point, where a Martello Tower (1812) was built during the Napoleonic Wars, is now a Nature Reserve.

For adjacent sights see ANTRIM GLENS, GIANT'S CAUSEWAY, SPERRIN MOUNTAINS.

Use the key on page 4 to make the best use of your Michelin guide.

DOWNPATRICK

DÚN PÁDRAIG – Co Down – Population 10 113
Michelin Atlas p 99 and Map 923 – O 45 – Local map Strangford Lough

The name Downpatrick recalls an early pre-Christian fort (*dún* in Irish) and St Patrick, the patron saint of Ireland. The fort developed into an ecclesiastical city with many religious foundations clustered round the cathedral which still dominates the region.

St Patrick

When St Patrick returned to Ireland in 432 to convert the population to Christianity, his ship was carried by the wind and tide into Strangford Lough and he landed near Saul after sailing up the River Slaney, now a mere stream. He converted the local chief, Dichu, who gave him a barn (*sabhal* in Irish, pronounced Saul) to use as a church. St Patrick was very attached to Saul and returned there to die in 461. Some records state that he was also buried in Saul, rather than in Downpatrick.

Downpatrick is an important historical town, which until recently was almost entirely surrounded by water; its narrow medieval streets – English, Irish and Scotch Street – converged on the town centre where the market house once stood. Despite losing its status as a county town in 1973, Downpatrick is still a busy market town serving the surrounding agricultural area, which to the south is known as the Lecale Peninsula.

SIGHTS

★Down Cathedral ⊘ – There is no trace of the monastery which grew up over the centuries since the time of St Patrick, although a round tower survived until 1780. In the 12C John de Courcy replaced the incumbent Augustinians with a community of Benedictine monks from Chester, rebuilt the abbey church, changed the dedication to St Patrick, to please the native Irish, and renamed the town Downpatrick. He claimed he had found the bodies of Patrick, Colmcille and Brigid and reburied them in his new church. This building was destroyed in 1316 by Edward Bruce and in 1538 its successor was set on fire by the English Lord Deputy Lord Grey.

In 1790 the building was restored and the west tower was built using the stones of the round tower. The cathedral now consists of the chancel of the abbey church. The original dedication to the Holy and Undivided Trinity was restored by James I in 1609.

Exterior – At the east end stands a granite High Cross, dating from the 10C or 11C, which until 1897 stood in the town centre. It is badly worn but the top panel represents the Crucifixion.

The three niches above the east window probably once contained statues of the three most famous Irish saints – Patrick, Brigid and Columba (Colmcille) – who, according to tradition, were buried in the same grave in Downpatrick.

A stone bearing their three names stood in the graveyard south of the cathedral until early this century, when it was replaced by the present slab of granite marking the traditional site of **St Patrick's Grave.**

St Patrick's Gravestone

In the 18C John Wesley preached to large crowds on the hillside south of the graveyard, in the Grove which was planted by Edward Southwell.

Interior – The granite font in the narthex was previously used as a watering trough and originally was probably the base of a cross.

Beside the Chapter Room door are two figures in ecclesiastical robes, which date from 1150 and are unique in Ireland.

The **organ**, which is mounted on the choir screen in a unique Georgian Gothic case, was built in the late 18C by Samuel Green for George III who presented it to the Cathedral in 1802. Despite several rebuildings it has not been substantially altered. The **choir screen** over the eight canons' **stalls** is the only one of its kind remaining in Ireland.

Opposite the **bishop's throne** stands the Judge's Stall, a reminder of the importance of Downpatrick as an assize town; it may have been used by the judge when courts of law were held in churches.

The **coats of arms** of the Diocese of Down and of the County families adorn the walls.

★ **Down County Museum** ⊘ – *The Mall.* The museum is housed in the old Down County prison, which was built between 1789 and 1796; Thomas Russell, the United Irishman, was hanged in the gateway in 1803. When a new prison was built in the 1830s the old buildings were occupied by the South Down Militia and then by the army until the mid 20C. Surviving **cells** form part of the museum display.

The **gatehouse** contains the **St Patrick Heritage Centre** which tells the saint's history in words and pictures, and illustrates *(video)* the many local sites connected with St Patrick.

The display in the former **Governor's House** in the centre of the courtyard traces the history of Co Down from 7000 BC and describes the local wildlife.

The Mall – To avoid the deep dip between the Cathedral and English Street the road was raised (15ft/5m) in 1790.

Well below the level of the road stands the **Southwell Charity**, which was founded in 1733 as a school and almshouses by Edward Southwell, the Secretary of State for Ireland, who by his marriage in 1703 became Lord of the Manor of Down. The buildings are of brick with sandstone quoins and plinth; the main block consists of a coach arch, surmounted by a cupola, flanked by the almshouses and terminating at each end in a schoolroom, one for boys and one for girls. The two teachers' houses are set well forward and linked to the main block by low quadrant walls. Opposite are the **Judges' Lodgings** *(nos 25 and 27)*, two late Regency-style houses built soon after 1835.

English Street – East of the Museum stands the Courthouse (1834), a large two-storey stuccoed block approached by a wide flight of granite steps and flanked by a gateway arch *(west)*, the sole relic of a new prison constructed behind the courthouse in 1835. East of the courthouse is a low two-storey building, originally designed with vaulted cells on the ground floor to hold prisoners but converted in 1798 into the **Downe Hunt Rooms**; the Hunt has unbroken records dating from 1757. The Clergy Widows' Houses *(nos 34–40)* date from 1730 and 1750 although their appearance was altered early in the 19C. The **Customs House** *(no 26)* was built in 1745 by Edward Southwell. Closing the lower end of the street are the red-brick Assembly Rooms designed in the Venetian Gothic style in 1882 by William Batt of Belfast.

Mound of Down – A second great Iron Age earthwork rises from the marshy levels around the town. The tree-covered mound sheltered an urban settlement destroyed by the Norman knight de Courcy in 1177.

EXCURSIONS

Saul – *2mi/3.2km east of Downpatrick.* The hilltop site, where St Patrick is said to have made his first Irish convert, is now crowned by **St Patrick's Memorial Church** ⊘, which was built in 1932 to commemorate the 1500th anniversary of St Patrick's landing near Saul in 432. It was designed by Henry Seaver of Belfast and is built of Mourne granite, with a characteristic Irish round tower incorporated as the vestry. Opposite the west door are the remains of a gable wall, probably part of the medieval abbey, occupied by Augustinian canons from the 12C until the Dissolution in 1540.

In the graveyard there are two cross-carved stones and two small mortuary houses.

Slieve Patrick – *3mi/4.8km east of Downpatrick. Car park. 15min there and back on foot to the top of the hill.* A statue of St Patrick was erected on the top of the hill in 1932 to commemorate the 1500th anniversary of St Patrick's landing near Saul in 432. The path up to an open-air altar is marked by the Stations of the Cross. From the top there is a fine **view** of Strangford Lough and the Ards Peninsula *(north)*, across the Lecale Peninsula to the Irish Sea *(east and south)*, and to the Mourne Mountains *(southwest)*.

St Tassach's (Raholp) Church – *4mi/6.4km east of Downpatrick.* In a field are the ruins of St Tassach's Church, also known as Templemoyle. It dates from the 10C or 11C and was in ruins by 1622; some restoration took place in 1915. The east window lintel is inscribed with crosses and the altar is flanked by recesses. It is here that Bishop Tassach is said to have administered the last sacrament to St Patrick.

★**Struell Wells** – *2mi/3.2km southeast of Downpatrick.* The site, in a secluded rocky hollow by a fast-flowing stream, comprises five buildings: an unfinished 18C church; a circular Drinking Well with a domed roof built on a wicker supporting arch; a rectangular Eye Well with a pyramidal corbelled roof; a Men's Bath-house, with a stone roof and a dressing room with seats next to the bath; and a Women's Bath-house without a roof – its dressing room is in the men's bath-house.

Although the oldest of these buildings dates only from c 1600, there is written reference to a chapel on the site in 1306. A strong tradition associates the site with St Patrick. Since streams and springs were important in Celtic pagan religion Struell has probably attracted pilgrims since the pre-Christian period but it was most popular from the 16C to 19C.

Ardglass Harbour

Christopher Hill, Belfast

★**Ardglass** – *7mi/11km south of Downpatrick by B 1.* Population 1 651. Ardglass stands on the south side of a natural harbour and has an active fishing fleet. In the 15C it was the busiest harbour in Ulster. Its importance as a fishing and commercial port in the medieval period is evident from the number of fortified buildings that were erected to protect this Anglo-Norman enclave from the native Irish.

Jordan's Castle ⊘, an early-15C tower house in the middle of the town overlooking the harbour, houses a collection of antiquities made by FJ Bigger, a solicitor and antiquarian from Belfast, who restored the building in 1911. The entrance is protected by two machicolations between the projections. In the Elizabethan period it withstood a three-year siege under its owner, Simon Jordan, until relieved by Mountjoy *(see p 27 and 330)* in June 1601.

Two other castles, King's Castle and Isabella's Tower, are mainly 19C structures. A row of fortified warehouses on the south side of the harbour has been converted into the clubhouse of the local golf course.

Killough – *7mi/11km south of Downpatrick by B 176.* Population 500. A broad central avenue runs through this quiet but attractive village on the south side of a deep se-inlet. In the 17C it was known as Port St Anne after Anne Hamilton, whose husband, Michael Ward of Castle Ward, developed the port to facilitate the export of lead and agricultural products from his estates.

St John's Point – *10mi/16km south of Downpatrick by B 176, A 2 and a minor road.* Near the point are the ruins of a 10C or 11C church built on the site of an early monastery. It is a pre-Romanesque building; the west door has sloping jambs and a lintel; the high gable carried a roof supported on antae. The lighthouse stands on the southernmost point of the Lecale Peninsula; there is a fine **view** across Dundrum Bay *(west)* to Newcastle at the foot of the Mourne Mountains.

Ballynoe Stone Circle – *3mi/5km south of Downpatrick. Park opposite the old railway station (east); 6min there and back on foot by the track (west) between the fields.*
The large circle is composed of low close-set stones round an oval mound which contained a stone cist at either end in which cremated bones were found during excavations in 1937–38. Nothing certain is known about its date but it was probably built by the late-Neolithic Beaker people c 2000 BC.

For adjacent sights see CASTLE WARD, HILLSBOROUGH, MOUNT STEWART, MOURNE MOUNTAINS, NEWCASTLE, STRANGFORD LOUGH.

DUNGANNON

DÚN GEANAINN – Co Tyrone – Population 9 190
Michelin Atlas p 98 and Map 923 – L 4

Dungannon, which is the administrative centre of the district, is set on a hill surrounded by rich farmland. The chief industry is agriculture: dairy farming and fruit growing with their attendant processing and packing activities and a weekly livestock market. There are many manufacturing industries; one of the oldest, textiles, has brought international fame to the name of Moygashel (founded in 1875).

Plantation Town – Under the O'Neill clan Dungannon was little more than a collection of huts grouped round Castle Hill but early in the 17C the English and Scottish settlers began to build a modern town. A charter was granted in 1612; in 1614 the Royal School was founded. When the native Irish rebelled in 1641 they were at first successful; the settlers' buildings were burned and their farms and orchards destroyed; the population dropped to 130. A new plantation followed the re-

> ### Victorious O'Neill
>
> Two important military engagements took place south of Dungannon. At the **Battle of the Yellow Ford** on the River Callan in 1598 Hugh O'Neill defeated the English forces under Sir Henry Bagnall; only about 1 500 Englishmen out of over 4 000 survived. In 1646 at the **Battle of Benburb**, fought at Derrycreevy west of Benburb on the north bank of the River Blackwater, the Scottish army of General Monroe was outmanoeuvred by Owen Roe O'Neill and 3 000 Scots were killed.

storation of peace in 1653. After the Battle of the Boyne (1690) Dungannon expanded rapidly; in 1692 the town was purchased by Thomas Knox, whose expansionary regime coincided with the development of the coalfields at Drumglass and the digging of the local canal.

SIGHTS

Tyrone Crystal ⊘ – *Northeast in Killybrackey Road (A 45).* Tyrone Crystal opened in 1971, exactly 200 years after an earlier glasshouse had started production at Drumreagh, Newmills *(north)*, under Benjamin Edwards. The nascent enterprise faced closure in the late 1970s' recession but local financial support was found and the factory moved into its present premises in 1990.
The **tour** covers the various stages in the process of producing hand-blown glass: preparing the molten glass, shaping the pieces by blowing, cooling, inspection for faults, bevelling, marking, cutting and polishing.

Heritage World ⊘ – *Main Street.* The stone building at the head of the sloping main street houses a genealogical research centre, with extensive computerized archives enabling people to "discover the path to their Irish roots".

EXCURSIONS

Cornmill Heritage Centre ⊘ – *Coalisland; 4mi/7km northeast of Dungannon by A 45.* The landscape around Coalisland is still marked by the extractive and other industries which once flourished here. Coal was being dug from bellpits as early as the 17C but severe faulting problems led to the closure of the last mine in 1970. Other industries included weaving, milling and a fireclay works; the Coalisland Canal had the first inclined plane to be built in the British Isles. The big brick cornmill, which dominates the centre of the town, was built in 1907 and has been extensively refurbished to serve as a community and heritage centre. The "Coalisland Experience" brings to life the past of this industrial area, unique in Ireland.

Donaghmore – *Donaghamore; 5mi/8km north of Dungannon by B 43*. In the centre of this quiet village stands an ancient sandstone cross (AD c 700-1000), associated with a former abbey; it is composed of the base and shaft of one cross and the shaft and head of another, which is decorated with motifs and biblical scenes: New Testament on the east face and Old Testament on the west. Originally it belonged to a nearby monastery said to have been founded by St Patrick. Its history is traced with cuttings and pictures in the nearby **Donaghmore Heritage Centre** ⓥ, housed in the former primary school.

Donaghmore clergy

The Revd **George Walker**, Rector of Donaghmore in 1674, was governor of Derry during the siege and died at the Battle of the Boyne.
Charles Wolfe *(blue plaque)* was curate of Donaghmore when he wrote his poem about the Burial of Sir John Moore at Corunna, which appeared in the *Newry Telegraph* in 1817.

Castlecaulfield – *5mi/8km northwest of Dungannon by A 4 and a minor road north*. Population 350. On the southeast edge of the village stand the stark ruins of a Jacobean **mansion** built (1611–19) by an ancestor of the Earls of Charlemont, Sir Toby Caulfield, who commanded Charlemont Fort *(see below)* and whose arms appear over the gatehouse, an earlier structure defended with murder holes above the main door. The house was burned by the O'Donnells in 1641 but occupied for another 20 years by the Caulfields.

Moy – *5.5mi/9km south of Dungannon by A 29*. Population 850. "The Moy" is an attractive Plantation town which was laid out in the 1760s by James Caulfield, Earl of Charlemont *(see p 158)*, on the model of Marengo in Lombardy, which he had seen while making the Grand Tour.
Horse chestnut trees line the main road where it passes through the broad central green, once the site of the great monthly horse fairs which lasted a whole week. The road slopes down to the Blackwater River past the screen and entrance gates to Roxborough Castle (destroyed by fire in 1921), the 19C seat of the Earl of Charlemont. On rising ground on the south bank stand the ruins of Charlemont Fort which was built in 1602 by Lord Mountjoy. Most of the fort was burned down in 1922; the gatehouse still stands at the end of a short avenue of trees; star-shaped ramparts are visible near the river.

Benburb – *7mi/11km south of Dungannon by A 29 to Moy and west by B 106*. The ruins of **Benburb Castle** (access on foot from priory grounds or just inside priory entrance) occupy a dramatic site, a rocky ledge above the River Blackwater, which tumbles through the tree-lined gorge (120ft/37m below). The castle, which was built by Sir Richard Wingfield in 1611, replaces an earlier O'Neill stronghold. The entrance is flanked by two rectangular towers containing rooms with fireplaces; the walls, which are pierced by musket-loops, enclose an irregular rectangular bawn containing a 19C house *(private)*; the round tower overlooking the river contains a stair leading to a postern gate.

★**Parkanaur Forest Park** ⓥ – *7mi/11km west of Dungannon by A 4. Car park*. The herd of **white fallow deer** at Parkanaur are direct descendants of a white hart and doe given by Elizabeth I in 1595 to her goddaughter, Elizabeth Norreys, who married Sir John Jephson of Mallow Castle *(see p 223)*. In 1978 five white fallow

Fallow deer

deer – a mature buck, a pricket and three does – were purchased from Mallow and established at Parkanaur. Fallow deer vary greatly in colour, from almost black through dark chestnut to light fawn with prominent white spots, and even pure white; the winter coat is usually much darker than the summer.

Formerly the property of the Burgess family, Parkanaur is an old estate with several unusual specimen trees; two parasol beeches with branches like corkscrews grow beside the front drive. The woodland is being developed as an oak forest. The walks and nature trail include the formal Victorian Garden, the stone archway, the wishing well and the stone bridge and weir on the Torrent River. The farm buildings (1843, later restored) contain a display of forestry machinery.

Simpson-Grant Homestead ⊙ – *11mi/18km west of Dungannon by A 4; just before Ballygawley turn left to Dergenagh. Car park.* On the west side of the road stands the 17C homestead of the ancestors of Ulysses S Grant, President of the USA (1869–77). The **Visitor Centre** tells the story of the Ulster-Scots Plantation, the Simpson family and the Ulster-American connection through an audio-visual film.

The house, restored in 1978 to its mid-19C state, has an ashpit for cooking potatoes before the hearth. The shed contains the appropriate farm implements; hens range in the yard and ducks dabble in the pond.

Across the road are the eight fields of the smallholding (10 acres/4ha): three for grazing a horse, a goat and two "mountainy" cattle; one for root crops (potatoes, turnips); one for a grain crop with the straw for bedding and thatching; three for a cash crop such as flax for the linen industry; there was also a flax hole or dam for "retting" the flax.

Errigal Keerogue Cross – *16mi/25km west of Dungannon by A 4; 1mi/1.6km west of the Ballygawley roundabout turn right to Errigal Keerogue (sign); at the crossroads in Ballynasaggart continue west; after 2mi/3.2km turn right.* In the graveyard stands the **high cross**; the carving is unfinished, probably owing to a fault in the stone. Two yew trees grow in the ruins of the medieval church, thought to be a Franciscan foundation (1489) which replaced an earlier monastery associated with St Kieran.

Augher – *18mi/29km west of Dungannon by A 4.* Population 400. The village is set on one of the most beautiful stretches of the Blackwater River which provides good fishing. On the north side of the lake stands Spur Royal, now a hotel; it began as a bawn on the site of an earlier stronghold in 1615, was restored after a fire in 1689 and enlarged in 1832 by William Warren, an architect from Sligo.

★**Clogher Cathedral** ⊙ – *20mi/32km west of Dungannon by A 4.* The cathedral, which dominates the village (population 550) from its hilltop site, was built from 1740 to 1745, in the austere Classical style with a squat tower topped by a balustrade and four pinnacles. Two **stone crosses** dating from the 9C and 10C stand in the graveyard outside the west door. A 7C **stone cross** *(outer porch)*, which is also thought to be a sundial for timing the services of the Celtic church, has a fish, an early Christian symbol, carved on the base. The **Golden Stone** *(inner porch)*, which was a famous oracle in pagan times, is known in Irish as **Clogh-Oir**, which may be the origin of the name Clogher. Clogher claims to be the oldest bishopric in Ireland, founded in the 5C. According to legend, its first bishop, to whom the cathedral is dedicated, was St Macartan or Macartin, a disciple of St Patrick.

Southwest of the cathedral stands Park House (1819), formerly the Bishop's Palace.

★**Knockmany Passage Grave** – *21mi/34km west of Dungannon by A 4 and north by B 83; 1.5mi/2.4km north of the crossroads turn right onto a track. Car park; 20min there and back on foot.* The hilltop site commands a superb view south over Knockmany Forest into the Clogher Valley. In 1959 a concrete bunker and skylight were built to protect the cairn from the weather but the stones of the burial chamber are visible through the grill: the decoration of circles, spirals and zigzags is typical of passage grave art.

For adjacent sights see ARMAGH, Lough NEAGH, SPERRIN MOUNTAINS.

ENNISKILLEN

INIS CEITHLEANN – Co Fermanagh – Population 11 436
Michelin Atlas p 97 and Map 923 – J 4

Enniskillen is a lively commercial town, which occupies an attractive island site between Lower and Upper Lough Erne. It makes an ideal base for exploring Lough Erne, for embarking on the Shannon–Erne Waterway *(see p 89)*, for fishing the Fermanagh lakes or for touring the Sperrin Mountains.

SIGHTS

Town Centre – In 1688 the **East Bridge**, which has almost disappeared under later alterations, replaced the drawbridge built by the planters on the site of an old ford in 1614. From the bridge the street passes the **Courthouse** *(left)*, radically remodelled in 1821–22 by William Farrell of Dublin; a squat Doric portico shelters the entrance to the five-bayed façade.

At the top of the hill in The Diamond stands the **Town Hall** *(right)*, designed by William Scott in 1898; a dragoon and fusilier stand in the two niches of the six-storey tower which dominates the surrounding streets.

The **Buttermarket**, which is further along in Down Street *(turn right at the junction of High Street and Church Street)*, has been converted into a craft and design centre. The main street *(Church Street)* continues to **St Macartin's Anglican Cathedral** standing in its graveyard *(right)*; it was completed in 1842 although the tower was part of the earlier 17C church. Opposite is **St Michael's Roman Catholic Church**, completed in 1875; the façade of this French Gothic Revival building by John O'Neill lacks the spire which was intended to crown the tower; more impressive is the external view of the apse rising above the sub-structure, supported by flying buttresses (1921). The street descends towards the **West Bridge** (completed in 1892); to the left is the **Castle** *(see above)* and to the right the Old Militia Barracks (1790), now occupied by the Royal Ulster Constabulary.

Enniskillen Castle ⊘ – Until the 18C the castle stood on its own island protected by a deep ditch spanned by a drawbridge. The central **keep** incorporates part of the first castle, built in the 15C by Hugh Maguire. In 1607 Captain William Cole rebuilt the castle, which had been damaged in war, and c 1615 he erected on the outer walls a turreted building, known today as the **Watergate**, which is best seen from the lake. There is no sign of its ever having contained an entrance but it may have been built near an earlier gate giving access to the lake. In the 18C the Cole family moved from Enniskillen Castle to their property at Portora *(northwest of the town centre where the river enters the lough)* and thence to Florence Court. Under the threat of French invasions new buildings were erected against the curtain wall west of the Watergate (1796) and along the north moat (c 1825). Exhibitions in the Watergate show the ancient monuments and castles of Fermanagh, and the pilgrim's trail to Devenish Island *(see p 315)*.

In the courtyard stands a German 21cm mortar captured in 1914.

Christophe Boisvieux

Watergate, Enniskillen Castle

The **Heritage Centre** illustrates the history of Fermanagh and its rural landscapes and wildlife using audio-visual presentations and local artefacts – yew horn (8C-10C) with bronze mounts.

The **keep** houses *(ground floor)* an exhibition on the history of the castle and a video on the Maguire family. A 3-D representation of Enniskillen, based on an OS map of 1833, takes up the whole of one wall. Downstairs, the storage vaults, sole survivors of the earliest (15C) castle, house life-size figures in vignettes showing the cramped conditions of castle life in the 15C and 17C.

The **Regimental Museum of the Royal Inniskilling Fusiliers** ⊘ *(ground and first floors)* traces the history of this famous regiment, which was formed in the late 17C together with the Inniskilling Dragoons – uniforms; weapons (swords, bayonets and rifles); badges and medals, including VCs; colours; musical instruments (drums, pipes and bugles); ceremonial silver and porcelain.

Forthill Park – *Southeast of the town centre.* This conical-shaped hill, known formerly as Camomile Hill or Commons Hill or Cow Green, received its present name from a star-shaped fort with four bastions and cannon built in 1689 during the Williamite Wars. In 1836 the hill was enclosed and planted with trees. The delightful Victorian **bandstand** is an oriental-looking cast-iron structure with an octagonal canopy, supported on eight slender columns and surmounted by a clock. The centre of the fort is now occupied by **Cole's Monument** ⊘, erected between 1845 and 1857, in memory of General the Hon Sir Galbraith Lowry Cole (1772–1842), brother of the 2nd Earl of Enniskillen of Florence Court; he was a close friend of the Duke of Wellington and fought in the Peninsular Wars. Within the fluted Doric column a spiral stair *(108 steps)* climbs to a platform: extensive **view** of Enniskillen and the surrounding countryside.

> **Portora Royal School**
>
> The school was founded in 1608 by James I at Lisnakea *(south)*. In 1643 it moved to Enniskillen and in 1777 to a site near **Portora Castle** (17C), which was partially destroyed by an explosion caused by schoolboys in 1859. Among its pupils were Oscar Wilde and Samuel Beckett.

For adjacent sights see CASTLE COOLE, CAVAN, Lough ERNE, FLORENCE COURT, SLIGO.

LOUGH ERNE★★
Co Fermanagh
Michelin Atlas p 97 and Map 923 – I 4

Lough Erne is the largest stretch of water (50mi/80km long) in the Fermanagh Lakeland. It is fed by the River Erne, which rises at Lough Gowna south of the border and flows northwest until it reaches the sea at Ballyshannon, also in the Republic. Relics of ancient monasteries survive on some of the 154 islands; fortified houses and stately mansions were erected on the shore.

Owing to its extent and configuration Upper Lough Erne rarely feels crowded. Boats are available for hire and there are many jetties and quays along the shore. Fishing is popular and the lake is used for water sports of various kinds. The recreational attractiveness of the Lough as a cruising centre was greatly enhanced in 1994 by the re-opening of the **Shannon-Erne Waterway** *(see p 89)*.

Out and about on Lough Erne

The best source of information about activities on or around the lake is the **Lakeland Visitor Centre** *(Shore Road on the west side of the town centre)*.
Lough Erne Waterbus Cruises ⏰ depart from the **Round 'O' Jetty** in Brook Park on the west bank of the River Erne *(northwest of the town centre)*.
Upper Lough Erne Cruises ⏰ *(1hr 30min)* in replicas of a Viking longship depart from the Share Centre in Lisnakea *(east shore of Upper Lough Erne)*.
There is a **Lakeland Canoe Centre** on Castle Island, Enniskillen.
The principal marinas are on Lower Lough Erne at **Kesh** *(east shore)* and on Upper Lough Erne at **Bellanaleck** *(west shore)* and **Carrybridge** *(east shore)*.
Day boats ⏰ for **fishing** are available in Enniskillen, Killadeas, Kesh, Belleek, Garrison, Bellanaleck, Teemore and Newtownbutler.
The **Lakeland Forum** offers facilities for swimming, squash, volley-ball, basket-ball, badminton, table tennis, bowls, archery, soccer, judo and keep-fit.
The **Lady of the Lake** festival takes place in Irvinestown in July.

LOWER LOUGH ERNE *Round tour of 66mi/106km – 1 day*
From Enniskillen take A 32 north; after 3mi/5km turn left to Trory Point.

★**Devenish Island** ⏰ – *10min there and back by ferry.* The island monastery, one of the most important, was founded in the 6C by St Molaise. It suffered from Viking raids and local feuds and in the 12C was occupied by a community of secular canons. In the 16C they and the neighbouring priory of Augustinian canons Regular were suppressed. The **museum** displays some of the loose stones from the site and traces the history of the monastery, with miniature models illustrating the seasonal activities of the monks.

The **round tower** dates from the 12C (81ft/25m high). The cut stones of the doorway have a flat moulding and there is a cornice below the cap with a carved face above each of the four windows. The view from the top floor *(key from the Caretaker)* is limited by the narrowness of the windows.

The **Lower Church** (Teampull Mór), nearest to the jetty, began as a short building c 1225 but was later extended. A dwelling for the canons was added to the north side and a mortuary chapel to the south for the Maguires of Tempo, whose arms are visible near the entrance and on the east wall. The oldest gravestone is a long flat slab with a two-armed cross in the southeast corner.

The smallest and oldest building, **St Molaise's House**, dates from the 12C although it is based on an earlier wooden church.

St Mary's Priory dates from the 15C although the tower is later. The two doorways at first-floor level gave access to a rood screen dividing the monks' chancel from the laymen's nave; bell ropes passed through the holes in the vault. There are traces of the cloisters on the north side of the church. A most unusual 15C **high cross** stands in the graveyard.

Devenish Island, Lough Erne

Continue north by B 82 along the east shore of the lake.

Killadeas – Ancient crosses stand in the churchyard.

★**Castle Archdale Country Park** ⊘ – The park on the lake shore includes extensive woodlands including over 20 kinds of trees and shrubs, which provide a habitat for fallow deer, red squirrels, badgers, otters, game birds and wildfowl. There are several relics of the Archdale family from East Anglia who were granted the land in 1612: an arboretum incorporating some fine specimens over 200 years old; a walled garden for flowers and fruit; the 19C pleasure grounds with a rockery and Irish yews; a cold plunge bath and sweathouse; the former outbuildings, now housing a Visitor Centre and a display of agricultural implements, adjacent to the site of the house (1773). Modern additions include a butterfly garden, a Japanese garden, a marina, and a camping and caravan site converted from a Second World War base for Sunderland and Catalina flying boats which patrolled the North Atlantic sea lanes. The ruins of the original

Christophe Boisvieux

Festival of the Lady of the Lake

dwelling, **Old Castle Archdale**, damaged in 1641 and abandoned in 1689, stand near the northeast entrance to the park *(car access from the road)*. The **bawn** still has its original gateway, a rare survival.

★**White Island** ⊘ – Offshore lies White Island which was an early ecclesiastical site. Within a large pre-Norman monastic enclosure stand the remains of a 12C church with a handsome Romanesque doorway. The eight **stone figures** set up against the north wall are definitely Christian but otherwise the subject of speculation; they probably date from the 9C or 10C and, as they have sockets in the heads and stumps on the feet, they may have been supportive members of a pulpit or shrine in an earlier church. In the 12C church they were used as building blocks.

After photo Ch. Boisvieux

Janus Figure, Boa Island

Continue north by the scenic route; north of Kesh bear left onto A 47. Near the western end of Boa Island park beside the road and follow sign to cemetery (about 550yd/500m there and back on foot).

★**Janus Figure** – The squat and ancient stone figure with two faces probably dates from the Iron Age.

Continue west on A 47.

Castle Caldwell Forest Park ⊘ – The forest covers two long fingers of land at the western end of Lough Erne and is managed with a threefold purpose: timber production, nature reserve and appropriate recreational activities such as shooting. The area is the main breeding ground of the Common Scoter duck and the islands are recognized bird sanctuaries. At the entrance stands the **Fiddler's Stone**, a memorial to a drunken fiddler who fell off a Caldwell boat in 1770 and was drowned. Beside the Visitor Centre is a **Fermanagh cot**, a flat-bottomed boat used until 1970 to transport cattle and sheep to and from the islands on the lake; the name originally applied to a boat made by hollowing out a large oak log. The castle, now in ruins, was built by Sir Edward Blennerhassett in 1612. The property was sold in 1662 to the Caldwell family who spent large sums on extensions and improvements. Owing to a decline in their affairs, the contents of the castle were auctioned in 1876.

Continue west on A 47.

Belleek – The village stands at the point where the waters of the Erne flow swiftly westward in a narrow channel towards the nearby border to enter the sea in Donegal Bay.

Belleek Pottery ⊘ – The pottery, which has an international reputation for its distinctive highly-decorated Parian ware, takes its name from the small border village of Belleek (population 369).

The **tour** begins where the slip, a mixture of feldspar, china clay, frit (glass) and water, is moulded and trimmed. Gum arabic is added to produce the extruded raw material used to make the ornaments and the basketware which is woven by hand. By individual choice this is men's work; the women prefer to do the hand painting. All serve a five-year apprenticeship. The results of their craftsmanship are on show and for sale in the Visitor Centre.

> ### Belleek Parian Ware
>
> The pottery in its handsome building was founded in 1857 by John Caldwell Bloomfield, who had just inherited Castle Caldwell and needed to increase his income. He was a keen amateur mineralogist and realized that the estate contained the necessary ingredients to make pottery – feldspar, kaolin, flint, clay, shale, peat and water power. At first only earthenware was produced; the first Parian ware was the result of 10 years of experiment. Belleek won its first Gold Medal in Dublin in 1865.

ExplorErne ⊘ – The exhibition, which is housed in the purpose-built Tourist Information Centre, introduces visitors to the history, landscapes and ecology of the Lough, from legendary beginnings to the harnessing of its waters to generate hydroelectric power and control the capricious changes in level, which once meant that "in the summer Lough Erne is in Fermanagh, and in the winter Fermanagh is in Lough Erne".

Leave Belleek by A 46 going east.

The road skirts the southern shore of Lough Erne beneath the high Cliffs of Magho.

After 10mi/16km turn left to Tully Castle.

★Tully Castle ⊘ – The castle, a good example of a fortified planter's house, was built in 1613 by Sir John Hume from Berwickshire but captured and abandoned in 1641.

The partially-paved bawn is protected by walls and corner towers with musket loops; each corner tower was also a house. A 17C-style garden has been made inside the bawn. The three-storey house has a vaulted room on the ground floor containing the kitchen fireplace, an unusually large staircase leading to a reception room on the first floor and a turret stair to the floor above. The projecting turrets are best seen by walking round the outside.

Return to A 46 and immediately turn right onto B 81 and then second right to the Lough Navar Scenic Drive. After 3mi/5km turn right opposite Correl Glen.

★★★Cliffs of Magho Viewpoint – The Scenic Drive *(7mi/11km – one way)* through **Lough Navar Forest** ⊘ leads to a viewpoint *(car park)* on the top of the Cliffs of Magho. The view embraces the north end of Lower Lough Erne with the Blue Stack Mountains in Donegal visible on the horizon *(north)*.

Return to A 46 and continue south.

Ely Lodge Forest – There are trails along the shore through the mixed woodland.

Continue south on A 46; turn right to Monea Castle.

Monea Castle – *Proceed up the drive; after 0.25mi/0.3km turn right at the gates of the house.* The ruined castle, one of the largest and best-preserved of the 17C tower houses, was built on a rocky bluff in 1618 by Malcolm Hamilton. The bawn wall, added in 1622, has two flanker towers; the one in the northwest corner beside the entrance gate has internal compartments which suggest it served as a dovecote. The entrance to the three-storey castle is protected by two circular towers. The crow-stepped gables and the corbelling on the towers and turrets are characteristic of the late-medieval Scottish style. Inside are vaulted kitchens on the ground floor and five chambers on the upper two floors.

On leaving turn left; in Monea turn left onto B 81 to return to Enniskillen.

UPPER LOUGH ERNE

Crom Estate ⊘ – *21mi/34km south of Enniskillen by A 4 and A 34; in Newtownbutler turn right onto a minor road.* The estate, which is a National Nature Reserve, lies on the east shore of Lough Erne. It offers parkland, oak woodland (1 800 acres/728ha) and wetland and lake shore (12mi/19km), unimproved fen meadows with reed beds, and a large heronry.

Crom boat-house

The **Visitor Centre** presents an exhibition about the history of the estate, its owners, the Creighton family from Scotland, later ennobled as Earls of Erne, the 17C planter's castle and the present 19C castle *(private)* designed by Edward Blore in 1838, the yachting parties held in the 19C.

The **Culliaghs Trail** passes through the oak woodland which contains a hide for mammal- and bird-watching. The longer trail *(1hr)* follows the lake shore to the remains of Crom Old Castle (17C) and two ancient yew trees once part of a formal garden, to the Boat House, across the White Bridge to the old Garden Orchard and Walled Garden on Inisherk, back to the mainland to the Old Boat House, the summer house, the Turf House, the Riding School and Stable Yard, before crossing the main drive and skirting the deer park.

For adjacent sights see CASTLE COOLE, CAVAN, DONEGAL, ENNISKILLEN, FLORENCE COURT, SLIGO, SPERRIN MOUNTAINS.

FLORENCE COURT ★★
Co Fermanagh
Michelin Atlas p 97 and Map 923 – I 5
58mi/13km southwest of Enniskillen by A 4 and A 32

This charming Palladian mansion stands in its own extensive parkland at the foot of Cuilcagh Mountain.

The original three-storey house, designed by an unknown architect at an unknown date, probably in the 1740s, is vigorously accented with stone quoins and elaborate window surrounds. The projecting central section contains the door surmounted by a triangular pediment and flanked by two narrow windows; above is a Venetian window between two niches. The wings are composed of seven-arched colonnades and canted pavilions, which were probably designed in the 1770s by Davis Ducart, a Sardinian, who spent most of his working life in Ireland. The property was transferred, largely unaltered, to the National Trust in 1955.

The Cole Family

The Coles came to Ireland from Devonshire, in the reign of Elizabeth I. They lived first at Enniskillen Castle and then at Portora Castle *(see p 315)*. It was Sir John Cole (1680–1726) who settled at Florence Court, named after his wife, Florence Wrey, a wealthy heiress from Cornwall. Their son, also John Cole (1709–67), made Lord Mount Florence in 1760, built the present central block; the wings were added by his son, William Willoughby Cole (1736–1803), later Viscount and then Earl of Enniskillen, who made the Grand Tour in 1756–57.

TOUR ⏱ 1hr 30min

House – The glory of the house is the exuberant **Rococo plasterwork**, in the style of Robert West. Some of it, including the nursery ceiling which was adorned with drums and rocking horses and other toys, was destroyed by fire in 1956. The entrance door with its original brass fittings opens into a spacious stone-flagged **hall.** The stone chimney-piece echoes the triangular pediment over the door and the frieze of triglyphs on the walls; the doors are surmounted by panels containing swags of drapery. A broad and richly decorated arch leads to the staircase and the rear rooms. The hall and most of the rooms are decorated with portraits, photographs, drawings and other memorabilia, returned from the family home in Scotland in 1997, after 25 years' absence.

The **Library** is lined with 18C pinewood bookshelves which complement the original plasterwork of the cornice, ceiling and door panel.

The **Drawing Room** cornice of bucolic motifs is original but the centrepiece was destroyed in the fire. The neo-Classical chimney-piece was introduced in 1946.

The **Dining Room** ceiling was saved from collapse during the fire by the drilling of small holes through which the water could drain. A surround of trailing foliage encloses the central panel where the four winds, represented by puffing cherubs, encircle an eagle. The cornice is similar to the one in the drawing room.

The decorative plasterwork is at its most exuberant on the **staircase:** wall panels overflowing with scrolls of foliage between a horizontal band of scrolls and a cornice formed of pendants. The handrail of the stairs is of yew and the fluted balusters, three to a tread, of pear-wood. Recesses on the landing are hung with a colourful collection of Japanese woodblock prints, and there are more family portraits in the room lit by a Venetian window, where decorative themes used elsewhere in the house are repeated in the cornice and ceiling.

Grounds – The Pleasure Grounds south of the house were mostly planted by the 3rd Earl early in the 19C. North of the house beside the drive is a walled garden; the original ornamental section has been retained whereas the vegetable plot has been laid out as lawn with shrubs and ponds. An 18C summerhouse has been meticulously rebuilt and there is a fascinating brick-lined ovoid ice house as well as a working sawmill (restored).

Forest Park ⊙ – Since 1975 the estate grounds have been developed as a forest park. In the woodlands southeast of the house stands the famous **Florence Court Yew**, also known as the Irish Yew, a columnar-shaped freak, which can be reproduced only by cuttings as seedlings revert to the common type. There are several trails of different lengths signposted with coloured indicators; the longest extends to the moorland to the southwest and gives access *(9hr there and back on foot)* to the top of Cuilcagh Mountain (2 198ft/670m).

EXCURSION

★★ Marble Arch Caves and Forest Nature Reserve ⊙ – *3mi/4.8km west of Florence Court.*
The cave system was formed in a bed of Dartry limestone by three streams on the northern slopes of Cuilcagh Mountain; they converge underground to form the Cladagh River which emerges at the Marble Arch and flows into Lough Macnean Lower.

The **reception centre** presents an exhibition on caving and a video *(20min)*, which covers the same ground as the tour and is a good substitute for those who cannot manage the many steep slopes and steps involved in the tour itself.

The **cave tour** includes a short boat trip on an underground lake which opens the way into a fantastic subterranean decor of stalactites, stalagmites, columns, flow stones, cascades, draperies and curtains, with picturesque names such as the Porridge Pot, Streaky Bacon, Cauliflowers, Tusks and Organ Pipes. The skilful illumination of these superb geological features is sometimes enhanced by reflection in pools of water. The longest stalactite (7ft/2m) is named after Edouard Martel, a famous French cave scientist who explored the caves in 1895.

The **nature reserve** *(car park at the cave entrance and on the Blacklion–Florence Court road)* consists of the wooded Cladagh gorge created by the collapse of caves eroded by the river. A path *(1hr there and back on foot)* along the east bank links the **Marble Arch**, a natural limestone arch, where the turbulent brown stream emerges from the ground, and the **Cascades**, where more water gushes forth. The forest is composed of ash, oak and beech and some conifers; in the spring the floor is a sea of bluebells.

For adjacent sights see CASTLE COOLE, CAVAN, ENNISKILLEN, Lough ERNE, SLIGO.

GIANT'S CAUSEWAY ★★★

Co Antrim
Michelin Atlas p 102 and Map 923 – M 2

The Giant's Causeway is the most famous tourist attraction in Northern Ireland. It was, however, little known until about 1740 when a local artist, Susanna Drury, painted two views of the Causeway, from the east and the west, which are now in the Ulster Museum in Belfast. Engravings of her work aroused great speculation among British and French geologists about the origins of the Causeway.

The Causeway itself is the most spectacular of a series of similar geological features to be found all along the North Antrim Coast. These were caused by a volcanic eruption which took place some 60 million years ago and affected not only northeast Ireland but also western Scotland, the Faroes, Iceland and Greenland. Several flows of lava exuded from fissures in the chalk and solidified into layers of hard basalt which cracked as they contracted, forming masses of adjoining columns; the majority are hexagonal in shape although some have four, five, seven, eight and even nine sides.

Early Tourism

In the early days visitors to the Causeway travelled by boat or on horseback. Numbers greatly increased with the advent of the railway line from Belfast to Portrush. In 1883 a hydroelectric narrow-gauge tramway, powered by the River Bushmills, was built from Portrush to Bushmills and extended to the Causeway in 1887; it closed in 1949 unable to compete with road transport. Some people came on day trips from Belfast; others stayed in one of the two hotels or the nearby boarding-houses.

The Causeway swarmed with souvenir sellers and unofficial guides who repeated fantastic legends about the formation of the Causeway and invented fanciful names for the different features.

Visitor Centre ⊘ **1** – This attractive modern building, which echoes the roofline of the Bushmills Distillery *(see p 305)*, contains a restaurant and a shop and an excellent video and exhibition about the Causeway Coast: geological formation, flora and fauna, mining and kelping, and various other local activities such as the Ballycastle Lammas Fair.

★★★**Giant's Causeway** – *20min there and back on foot; bus-shuttle service* ⊘ *in season*. The Causeway proper extends from the foot of the cliffs into the sea like a sloping pavement. According to legend it was built by the giant Finn McCool so that the Scottish giant could accept his invitation to Ireland for a trial of strength. When the latter had returned home defeated, the causeway sank beneath the sea. Similar rock formations are to be found in Fingal's Cave on Staffa in Scotland. The Causeway consists of about 40000 hexagonal columns, resembling stacks of old threepenny bits, and has been divided by the action of the waves into three sections: the Little Causeway, the Middle Causeway and the Grand Causeway. The columns themselves are split horizontally, forming concave and convex surfaces. The individual features are not easily recognizable by their local names: the **Wishing Well (1)** was a natural freshwater spring in the Little Causeway; the **Wishing Chair (2)** on the Middle Causeway is formed by a single column, the seat, backed by a semicircle of taller columns; the **Giant's Gate** is the natural gap carrying the coastal path through the **Tilted Columns (3)**.

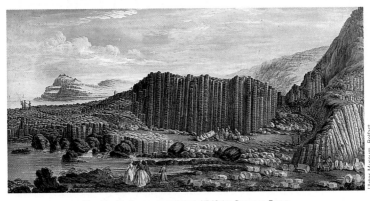

The Giant's Causeway painted 1740 by Susanna Drury

Ulster Museum, Belfast

East across Port Noffer the columns (40ft/12m) of the **Organ** (**4**) are visible in the cliff face; the **Chimney Tops** (**6**) are silhouetted against the skyline.

The Giant's Causeway painted c 1740 by Susanna Drury

For a bird's-eye view of the Causeway continue into the middle of Port Noffer and take the Shepherd's Path (steps) up to the clifftop; return to the Visitor Centre.

The headland, Aird Snout, gives an excellent view of the Causeway from above. From the next headland, Weir's Snout, there is a view across Port Ganny *(east)* to the Causeway and down into Portnaboe *(west)* where a volcanic dyke, known as the Camel's Back, is visible in the sea beyond the slipway where early visitors to the Causeway used to land.

Benbane Head **2** *– Round tour – 5mi/8km – 2hr there and back on foot. The path*

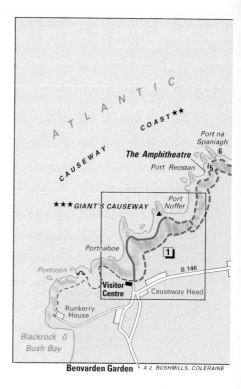

is liable to erosion and the steps at Benbane Head are steep. Stout shoes are required and children should be accompanied by an adult. The first part of the walk as far as the Shepherd's Path turning is described above.

This walk includes many of the associated volcanic formations along the Causeway Coast.

From Port Noffer the path continues into the next bay, Port Reostan, where the curved columns of the **Harp** (**5**), a product of the first lava flow, are set in a natural **amphitheatre**. The next headland is distinguished by the **Chimney Tops** (**6**), three rock

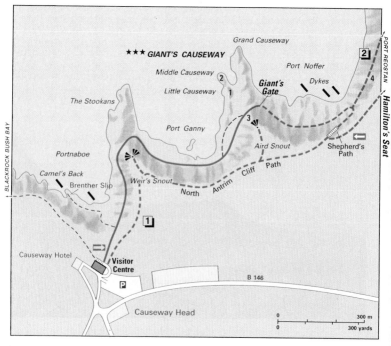

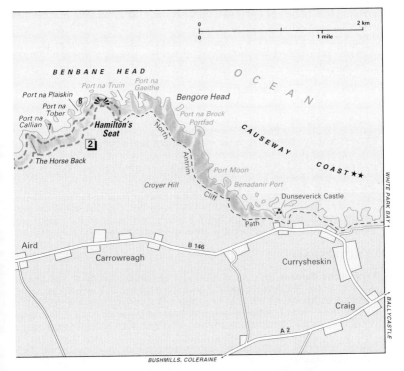

stacks formed by the second lava flow. Through a passage in the rocks the path enters Port Na Spaniagh where the *Gerona*, a galleass of the Spanish Armada, was wrecked in 1588 with no survivors; the treasures recovered by diving on the wreck in 1968 are now in the Ulster Museum in Belfast. Beyond the next headland, the Horse Back, lies Port na Callian; the further promontory consists of the **King and his Nobles (7)**, a file of figures apparently riding in from the sea. After skirting the next two bays the path climbs up past the **Horseshoe (8)** in the rocks *(left)* to **Hamilton's Seat** on Benbane Head. It is named after Dr William Hamilton who published his *Letters concerning the Northern Coast of Antrim* in 1786, and is a perfect place from which to survey the geological formations and admire the **view★★**, which on a clear day reaches to the mountains of Donegal *(west)*, and Rathlin Island and in Scotland the Mull of Kintyre *(east)*.

From here there is a path east along the cliffs (2hr) which rejoins the road (B 146) at Dunseverick Castle (see p 305).

The clifftop path back to the Causeway Centre provides a bird's-eye view of the volcanic formations.

For adjacent sights see CAUSEWAY COAST.

HILLSBOROUGH ★

CROMGHLINN – Co Down – Population 2 407
Michelin Atlas p 99 and Map 923 – N 4

This charming town, set on a hill round a central square, acquired its Georgian aspect under Wills Hill (1718–92), created Marquess of Downshire in 1789. Sir Hamilton Harty (1879–1941), the conductor, whose father was church organist, is buried in the churchyard.

★ Hillsborough Fort ⊙ – The gates on the east side of the square open into a drive leading to the fort, which was begun c 1630 to command the chief roads in Co Down, and was completed in 1650 by Col Arthur Hill who was appointed hereditary constable with 20 warders in 1650 by Charles II who declared it a royal fort. It is laid out as a square (270ft/82m x 270ft/82m) with a spear-shaped bastion at each corner to provide flanking fire from heavy cannon.

In 1770 Wills Hill created another entrance in the northeast rampart, surmounted by a gazebo with tracery windows, and converted the gatehouse in the northwest rampart into a little fort in the Gothic style with pointed doors and windows and hood-mouldings supported on grotesquely-sculptured heads; large-scale entertainments were held on the first floor of the gatehouse or in the open enclosure.

The central ditch is part of a circular trench revealed by excavations (1966–69) which suggest that the site had been occupied since c 500–1000.

Hillsborough Castle – The house, which was begun in 1760 by Wills Hill, later became the residence of the Governor of Northern Ireland and is now used for state functions. It stands on the west side of the square behind an elegant wrought-iron screen with gates, erected in 1936 but originally designed in 1745 for Richill Castle in Co Armagh, probably by the Thornberry brothers.

Court House ⓥ – In the centre of the square stands a two-storey block pierced by an archway which was built as a market house in 1760; two wings were added in about 1810 to contain the courthouse and a larger market hall.

The informative **exhibition on justice and law** begins with a summary of Brehon law tracing parallels with modern penal policy, reviews the origins of Common Law via written panels and an audio-visual presentation *(10min)*, and describes the traditions of legal dress with life-size mannequins.

St Malachy's Church – The Anglican church, built in 1662 on the site of its predecessor (1636–41), was enlarged (1760–73) by Wills Hill, who added the main tower and spire and the two subsidiary towers, and furnished the interior with Irish oak Gothic woodwork and box pews which are raised in the transepts.

EXCURSION

★**Rowallane Gardens** ⓥ – *10mi/16km east of Hillsborough by B 178 towards Carryduff, B 6 to Saintfield and A 7 south.* The gardens (52 acres/21ha), which are famous for massed plantings of azaleas and rhododendrons, are the work of a plantsman, Hugh Armitage Moore, who inherited the estate in 1903. During the next half-century he turned the drumlins with their light acid soil into a natural garden: a rock garden on a natural outcrop of stone; patches of wild flowers to attract butterflies; a spring ground and a stream ground; walled garden with fuchsias and shrub roses. In the old wood the stone walls between the original fields are still standing. The pleasure grounds behind the house (National Trust headquarters) extend in a great grass sweep to a small pond.

For adjacent sights see DOWNPATRICK, LISBURN, STRANGFORD LOUGH.

Walled garden, Rowallane

The town is situated in the middle of the linen-producing district in Ulster, and throughout the 19C it produced half of the linen woven in Ulster. Louis Crommelin made it his headquarters when he was appointed Linen Overseer of Ireland by William III.

In 1707 most of the town was destroyed by fire, except for the Assembly Rooms at the top of the market square.

> ### Sir Richard Wallace
> From 1873 to 1885 the MP for Lisburn was Sir Richard Wallace, owner of the Wallace Collection in London, whose mansion, built in imitation of Hertford House in London, stands opposite the entrance to the Castle Park.

SIGHTS

★**Irish Linen Centre and Lisburn Museum** ⊘ – Lisburn's Assembly Rooms have been adapted and extended to house the town's museum as well as extensive and attractive displays, which tell the story of the area's linen industry from its origins in the 17C to the present. The emphasis is not only on technique, but on the beauty and adaptability of the product and on the lives of the people involved in its manufacture. There are reminders of the role of linen in the ancient world in the form of material from Tutankhamun's tomb. In the Middle Ages Irish flax was exported to England to be woven into cloth. Then in the 17C English and Scottish weavers helped establish the weaving industry, eventually under the direction of Crommelin, whose portrait hangs in the main hall of the Assembly Rooms. There are live demonstrations of spinning and weaving, a re-creation of a family at work in a late-18C-early-19C spinner's cottage, and a vivid reconstruction of the weavers' toil in "Webster's", a hypothetical 19C mill, where conditions, however harsh, were nevertheless preferable to life on the farm –

> *"I'll ne'er despise the weaving trade,*
> *The shuttle's lighter than the spade".*
> John Dicky (1818).

Exquisite traditional items in diaper and damask are contrasted with their contemporary equivalents, where the creative potential of the computer has been harnessed to produce designs of great appeal and originality.

Temporary exhibitions draw on the extensive local history and other collections from the town museum.

Christchurch Cathedral ⊘ – The town is dominated by the cathedral, a good example of Planters' Gothic (1623, reconstructed in 1708); in the graveyard *(south side)* is the Crommelin tomb.

Lisburn Castle Park – North of the cathedral is the site of the **castle**, now a small public park enclosed within the surviving walls; from the parapet there is a good view of the Lagan winding past below.

EXCURSION

Lagan Valley *9mi/14.5km – half a day*

The valley of the River Lagan, which flows north through Belfast and enters the sea in Belfast Lough, is one of the most fertile areas in Northern Ireland. It now forms a Regional Park, traversed by the **Lagan Canal** *(towpath walk 9mi/14.5km from Lisburn to Belfast)* which was built to bring coal from Coalisland via Lough Neagh to Belfast; ironically it was mostly used to carry coal imported through Belfast. Under the Lagan Navigation Company, founded in 1843, it became Ulster's most successful waterway but its use declined in the 1930s; it was closed in 1958 and its course west from Lisburn to Moira turned into a motorway.

From Lisburn take A 1 north; in Hilden turn right (sign).

Hilden Brewery Visitor Centre ⊘ – The brewery occupies a Georgian house, once visited by William Wordsworth, adjoining a pleasant courtyard. An exhibition in the restaurant covers the history of beer-drinking and brewing, Hilden Village and the brewery building. The guided tours of the brewery take place before and after lunch.

Continue north on A 1 and turn right under the railway bridge onto B 103 to Lambeg.

Lambeg – This attractive village has given its name to the huge drums (over 30lb/14kg) with painted decoration which are played in the Orange Day parades; they were introduced to Ireland from the Netherlands by William III's army.

Continue on B 103 to Drumbeg. Car park (left) opposite the church.

Drumbeg Church ⊘ – From the magnificent Lych Gate (1878) the footpath passes through arches of yew up to the church which stands on a knoll. The lower courses of the tower date from 1798. The upper part was built in 1833 to replace an earlier wooden spire which blew down in a gale in 1831. The present church (1870) is cruciform with a shallow apsidal chancel and an interesting wooden

Lambeg Drums

roof. The entrance porch contains a stone, marked "A Free Howse 1675", to which is attached a touching love story retold alongside. The earliest record of a church here dates from 1306 but the dedication to St Patrick and its position by a ford suggest that a church was in existence much earlier.

Continue north on B 103.

Drumbridge Lock-Keeper's House – Beside the Ballyskeagh High Bridge which spans the Lagan River and Canal stands *(left)* the Lock-Keeper's House (1757), a two-storey cottage with sandstone dressings and brick-arched round-headed recesses extending into the upper storey and framing the windows; it was designed by Thomas Omer, the Lagan Canal engineer.

Dixon Park – *Car park.* The park is famous for the rose trial grounds (11 acres/4ha) which contain about 30 000 roses. The final judging of the trial roses takes place during **Belfast Rose Week** (mid July) which attracts breeders from many parts of the world. Originally the grounds of a private house on the River Lagan, the park was presented to Belfast Corporation by Lady Edith Stewart Dixon in 1959 so that its mature trees, woodland, copses and rhododendrons could be enjoyed by all.

Continue north on B 103. At the roundabout turn right onto the dual carriageway and right again.

Malone House ⊘ – *Car park.* In 1603 James I granted the Barnett demesne to the Chichester family, later to become Earls of Donegall. Since then three houses have occupied the hilltop overlooking the Lagan crossing. The present house, which was severely damaged by terrorist bombs in November 1976, was built in the late 1920s and probably also designed by William Wallace Legge, who later bought the lease of the whole demesne. Owing to the existence of accurate records it was possible to rebuild the house to its original design.

The plain and unpretentious exterior, relieved only by the entrance portico and a shallow central bay on the garden front, belies the elegant and spacious interior. The broad T-shaped hall leads to a stone staircase with crinoline-bowed iron balusters set in an apsidal stairwell, with sculpture niches flanking the tall arched window. The doorways are framed by Classical surrounds with decorative reliefs and console brackets supporting triangular pediments.

From the upper windows there is a magnificent view over the garden to the wooded grounds, which slope south down to the modern road bridge spanning the Lagan, beside the five stone arches of **Shaw's Bridge** (1711), which replaced an oak bridge built by Captain Shaw in 1655 so that Cromwell's cannon could cross the river.

On leaving the park turn right; after crossing the bridge turn right; take the road along the south bank to Edenderry (sign).

Edenderry – The road ends beside the river among five terraces of red-brick cottages and a chapel; the weaving mill which they served no longer exists.

Return to the last T-junction; turn right onto Ballynahatty Road; after 1mi/1.6km turn right (sign "Giant's Ring").

Giant's Ring – *Car park.* The Ring is a huge bank of gravel and boulders enclosing a circle (600ft/183m in diameter) with a megalithic chambered grave in the middle. Its purpose is unknown but it may have been a place of assembly or worship and its construction would have required large resources.

For adjacent sights see ANTRIM, BELFAST, HILLSBOROUGH, NEWRY.

LONDONDERRY ★

DOIRE – Co Londonderry – Population 72 334
Michelin Atlas p 101 and Map 923 – K 3

Londonderry is often known by its original name, Derry, meaning an oak grove; the prefix "London" was added in the 17C when large areas in the north of Ireland were granted to the London livery companies for development.
The old city, which stands on a hill on the west bank of the River Foyle, is still surrounded by its 17C walls.
Southeast rise the smooth rounded Sperrin Mountains; west and north lies the wild grandeur of the mountains of Donegal.

Monastic Foundation – According to tradition, the monastery of Derry was founded in 546 by St Columba (*Colmcille* in Irish). Derry was occupied by the English in 1565 and 1600. During the four-month rebellion of Sir Cahir O'Doherty in 1608, his forces attacked and captured Derry but could not sustain their momentum after his death at Kilmacrenan in Donegal.

The Irish Society – Under the scheme for the colonization of Ulster *(see p 27)* with settlers from Britain, The Honourable The Irish Society was constituted by Royal Charter in 1613 to plant the County of Coleraine, which was renamed County Londonderry. Most of the land was parcelled out to the 12 main livery companies of London but the towns of Derry and Coleraine were retained by the Society, which still uses its income from fisheries and property to support projects of general benefit to the community.

Siege of Londonderry

In the uncertainty created by James II's flight to France and William of Orange's landing in Devon, 13 Derry apprentices locked the city gates against a Jacobite regiment under the Earl of Antrim sent to garrison the town in December 1688. The citizens declared for William and received an influx of supporters although food supplies were low. In March James II landed in Ireland with an army of 20 000 and in April besieged the city, erecting a boom across the river which held the relief ships at bay for seven weeks.
After the departure of Lundy, who had proposed surrender, Major Henry Baker and the Revd George Walker took command. On 10 July a shell bearing terms for surrender was fired into the town by the besiegers; the defenders raised a crimson flag on the Royal Bastion to signify "No surrender".
The siege lasted 15 weeks during which thousands of the 30 000 within the walls died of starvation. On 28 July 1689 the boom was broken and the relief ships sailed through to the quay. Three days later the Jacobite army retreated.

THE WALLED CITY

★★**City Walls and Gates** ⊙ – The walls (1mi/1.6km long) enclosing the Plantation town were built from 1613 to 1618 by The Irish Society and originally pierced by four gates. **Ferryquay Gate** was closed by the 13 Apprentice Boys at the beginning of the siege in 1688; **Shipquay Gate** is surmounted by five of the cannon which defended the city during the Great Siege; southwest of **Butcher's Gate** stands the **Royal Bastion** on which Col Michelburn hoisted the crimson flag to signify "No surrender"; **Bishop's Gate** was rebuilt in 1789 as a triumphal arch to commemorate William of Orange. The other three openings were created later.

★**St Columb's Cathedral** ⊙ (**Z**) – The decision to build was taken by The Irish Society in 1613 but the cathedral was not begun until 1628; it was consecrated in 1634, the first cathedral to be built in the British Isles since the Reformation. The original plans made provision for a chancel but it was not added until 1887. The cathedral is in the late-Perpendicular style with a fully embattled exterior. The tower houses a peal of 13 bells and is surmounted by an early-19C spire (191ft/58m).
The **mortar shell** containing terms for surrender which was fired into the city during the siege in 1689 is preserved in the porch.
The Baptistery *(left)* commemorates Mrs CF Alexander (1818–95), wife of the Bishop of Derry; she wrote several well-known hymns which are illustrated in one of the windows in the north wall.
The window in the Choir Vestry *(right)*, presented in 1913 by the descendants of the defenders of the city, depicts the Closing of the Gates in 1688 *(left)*, the Relief of the city in 1689 *(centre)*, and the Centenary celebrations in 1789 *(right)*. The superb open-timbered **nave roof** is supported on stone corbels carved to represent the Bishops of Derry from 1634 to 1867 and the Revd George Walker. The mahogany organ case dates from 1747. In the north aisle are several interesting wall tablets; the fourth one incorporates the mortuary symbols of the period.

LONDONDERRY

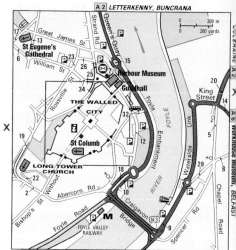

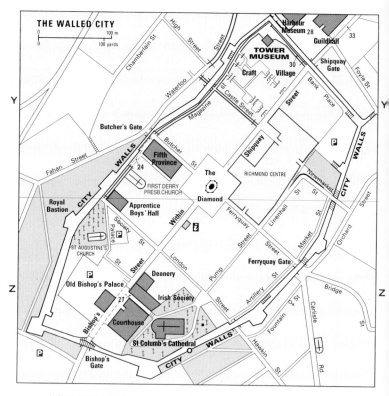

In Northern Ireland parking in the town centre may be restricted to attended vehicles only.

The **bishop's throne**, unusually placed in the nave in 1861, is a splendid mahogany chair of Chinese Chippendale (18C), probably given by the Earl Bishop *(see p 307)*. On the chancel arch above the pulpit is a **Cross of Nails**, a gift from Coventry Cathedral, signifying peace and reconciliation. Below the east window of the Ascension is a reredos of Caen stone; the mosaics in the wings represent the four Evangelists and St Patrick and *(second from right)* St Columba. The coats of arms in the hand-made carpet are those of The Irish Society, the See of Derry and Raphoe, and the See of Derry. The two flags were captured from the French during the Siege in 1689; only the wire work and the poles are original.

The **chapter house** *(for access ask the Verger)* was built in 1910 and contains several items of interest: padlocks and keys of the original city gates; cannon balls; Governor Walker's sword; fragments of the crimson flag of Col Michelburn; silver

328

plate, some of which dates from 1613; a pair of pistols and a kidney-shaped desk, thought to belong to the Earl Bishop; portraits of Mrs Alexander and her husband; a copy of her book *Hymns for Little Children*.

★**Tower Museum** ⊘ **(Y)** – The medieval-style modern building houses a comprehensive display about the history of the city of Derry using historical artefacts, wall panels and audio-visual and theatrical devices.
A brick-built tunnel, typical of the 17C houses, leads to the monastic origins of Derry in an oak grove, the 17C Plantation, the Siege of Derry and its aftermath, 19C emigration, the Partition of Ireland, the Second World War and the present troubles.

Fifth Province ⊘ **(Y)** – *Butcher Street*. Embedded in the modern Calgach conference and office centre is this ambitious and imaginative evocation of the history and culture of the Celts. A wide variety of contemporary techniques, including exciting voyages by module and space shuttle, give magical life to the past and demonstrate its relevance to present-day people of Irish descent.

Craft Village (Y) – Neglected back yards have been artfully transformed into a web of picturesque alleyways, centred on a little square and lined with a variety of traditionally styled buildings housing cafés and specialist shops.

City Centre – *Shipquay Street* **(Y)**, one of the steepest commercial streets in the British Isles, contains several imposing buildings and basement bars.
The **Diamond (Y)**, where the Town Hall used to stand, is marked by a war memorial. The four main streets lead to the four main gates.
The **Apprentice Boys' Hall (YZ)** stands on the site of the original Shambles.

Bishop's Street Within (Z) contains several fine buildings. The offices of **The Irish Society** are housed in a dignified Georgian building (1764). Next door is **The Deanery**, an elegant Georgian house with a splendid doorway. The **courthouse** is a white sandstone building in the Greek revival style with an Ionic portico. Opposite stands the former **bishop's palace** (now the Freemasons' Hall), built of red brick by the Earl Bishop; it stands on the site of the house occupied by Col Henry Baker who was in command of the defences of the city during the siege.

ADDITIONAL SIGHTS

★**Long Tower Church** ⊘ **(X)** – This is the oldest Roman Catholic church in Derry (1784–86). The present building has an interesting Rococo interior with extensive steeply-sloping galleries. It stands on the site of Templemore, a great medieval church built in 1164, and its name recalls the Long Tower (10C), all that remained when the medieval church was destroyed by an explosion in 1567. From the churchyard there is a fine view of the Royal Bastion.

★**Guildhall** ⊘ **(Y)** – The Guildhall, which has twice been severely damaged – in 1908 by fire and in 1972 by bombs, was erected in 1890 in the late-Gothic style with a loan from the Irish Society. The river façade is richly ornamented; the corner tower contains a large four-faced clock. A reproduction of Follingby's painting of the Relief of Derry decorates the marble-faced vestibule. The stained-glass windows are the work of Ulster craftsmen: London scenes on the stairs, early views of Derry in the Great Hall, which is panelled in oak and has a richly decorated ceiling.

Harbour Museum ⊘ **(Y)** – The grandiose 19C building, which once housed the meetings of the Londonderry Port and Harbour Commissioners, is now a museum with paintings, models and all kinds of maritime memorabilia. The dominant exhibit is the largest curragh ever built, constructed in 1963 to recreate the legendary voyage of St Columba to Iona.

St Eugene's Cathedral ⊘ **(X)** – Northwest of the city centre, between a district of elegant Georgian terraces and the green peace of Brooke Park, stands the Roman Catholic Cathedral which was dedicated to St Eugene in 1873 by Bishop Keely, to whom the great east window is a memorial. The building was designed in the Gothic revival style by JJ McCarthy in 1853 and finally completed with a cross on the top of the spire in 1903.

Foyle Valley Railway Centre ⊘ **(X M)** – Londonderry was once the focal point of no fewer than four railway companies, including the Londonderry and Enniskillen, "possibly the least efficient if not the most dangerous railway ever to operate in Ireland". Here too was the terminus of the County Donegal Railway, which was the most extensive of all the Irish narrow-gauge systems (125mi/200km). The Centre has steam engines, coaches, an old goods wagon, signals, signs and luggage. Excursion trains drawn by diesel car (1934) operate on a stretch of narrow-gauge line (2mi/3.2km) beside the Foyle. It is proposed to extend the line upstream to St Johnston (9mi/14.5km).

★**Workhouse Museum** ⊙ – *23 Glendermott Road, Waterside.* The city workhouse, designed by George Wilkinson and opened in 1840 with 800 inmates, now houses a library on the ground floor and a museum on the two floors above. The first stage has excellent displays and film footage about the role played by the city in the Second World War, and particularly in the Battle of the Atlantic. On the upper floor, the grim 19C workhouse conditions have been recreated; an original display compares the 1845–49 Irish famine with the modern famines of the Horn of Africa and especially Somalia.

For adjacent sights see CAUSEWAY COAST, DONEGAL GLENS, INISHOWEN PENIN-SULA, SPERRIN MOUNTAINS.

MOUNT STEWART★★★

Co Down

Michelin Atlas p 99 and Map 923 – P 4

A belt of trees on the east shore of Strangford Lough shelters the famous Mount Stewart **gardens** which complement the house, designed by George Dance and William Vitruvius Morrison. The banqueting house, an imitation of the Tower of the Winds in Athens, was designed by James "Athenian" Stuart.

Soldiers and Statesmen

The Mount Stewart estate was bought in 1774 by Alexander Stewart, whose Scottish forebears were granted land near Moville on the Inishowen Peninsula in the 17C. He built a house called Mount Pleasant, which was enlarged by his son Robert, made Marquess of Londonderry in 1816. The best-known member of the family is his elder son, Lord Castlereagh, who entered politics in 1790, aged 21, and rose to be Foreign Secretary and leader of the House of Commons at Westminster. His half-brother, the third Marquess, fought in the Peninsular Wars and became ambassador in Vienna. Later generations have followed in their footsteps as soldiers and as politicians at Westminster or Stormont.

TOUR ⊙

Gardens – The gardens were created by Edith, Lady Londonderry, in the 1920s to enhance the immediate surroundings of the house and to absorb some of the surplus labour after the First World War. The plants are drawn from all over the world; the more formal arrangements are closer to the house.
An arched wistaria walk leads to the Tasmanian Blue Gum trees of the **Fountain Walk.** The huge Irish Yews near the house look down on the **Italian Garden** which contains mainly herbaceous plants since roses proved unsuccessful; it is enclosed at the east end by the **Dodo Terrace,** which is decorated with stone animals, recalling the nicknames, not always complimentary, given by Lady Londonderry to some of her friends who were members of the Ark Club, which she founded in London during the First World War. To the south is the **Spanish Garden** designed after a ceiling pattern in the Temple of the Winds *(see below).* The **Peace Garden** *(west),* a graveyard for the family pets, leads to the **Lily Wood.** Steps and a gate, based on an illustration in a book by Kate Greenaway, lead to the **Sunk Garden** overlooked by the west front of the house; it is based on a design by Gertrude Jekyll and surrounded on three sides by a stone pergola. The theme of the **Shamrock Garden,** named for its shape, is Ireland: a topiary harp and a bed in the shape and colour of the Red Hand of Ulster.
The hill which overlooks the **lake,** created in 1846–48, provides a superb **view** over Strangford Lough. The **Jubilee Walk,** east of the lake, is planted in red, white and blue to commemorate the Silver Jubilee in 1936; a genuine Japanese pagoda stands beside the **Ladies' Walk,** an old path to the dairy and kitchen gardens.

House – The west wing was built in 1804-05 by George Dance. The major part of the house (1825–35) is the work of William Vitruvius Morrison, who produced a symmetrical design in the same dark stone with lighter dressings and added a balustrade at roof level to create a sense of unity. A giant Ionic portico wide enough to take a carriage screens the entrance.
The interior is richly decorated with portraits of the family and their racehorses, Irish and English furniture, collections of porcelain and Classical sculpture.
The portraits in the **Dining Room** include Lord Mountjoy (in armour; *see p 27*), William of Orange and Schomberg. Lining the wall are the 22 Empire chairs used by the delegates at the Congress of Vienna in 1815; they are embroidered with the arms of those present and of the nations they represented.

J Cornish /National Trust Photographic Library

Italian Garden, Mount Stewart

The next room displays **souvenirs of Lord Castlereagh** who as Foreign Secretary attended the Congress of Vienna in 1814 and the Peace of Paris in 1815: his portrait after Lawrence over the fireplace, engravings of his contemporaries in the Irish House of Commons and of his associates while Foreign Secretary, nine miniatures in one frame of the chief delegates to the Congress of Vienna, seven statuettes and busts of contemporary political figures by Jean-Pierre Danton (1833), a bust of Napoleon. The five 18C angle chairs made of padouk wood are Goanese.

Much of the **woodwork** in the west wing is by John Ferguson: in the Castlereagh Room – the shutters, six Regency mahogany bookcases, dado rail and double doors; in the Music Room reflecting the curved plaster ceiling – the inlaid wooden floor in oak, mahogany and bog-fir; in Lady Londonderry's Sitting Room – the wooden shutters, delicately decorated with rosettes set in circles, ovals and ellipses, and the floor which is inlaid with oak, bog-fir, yew, holly and other woods; on the staircase – the mahogany handrail inlaid with ebony and ending in satinwood rosettes. Dance's delicate touch is evident in the cast-iron balustrade and in the broad shallow arches supporting the first-floor gallery and the skylight dome.

The **Rome Bedroom** reflects the 1920s taste for strong colours and rich materials. The spacious **Drawing Room**, created by Morrison out of three smaller rooms, contains portraits of Viscount and Viscountess Castlereagh. The room is furnished with three Aubusson carpets, two 18C Italian pier-glasses at the ends, a large Austrian inlaid walnut writing-desk, a Boulle bracket clock in red tortoiseshell and brass. The lamps include several translucent alabaster and Carrara marble urns and vases, and a pair of tripod candlesticks carved with winged lions, all fitted with electricity. The room displays many objects of virtu.

Temple of the Winds – *30min there and back on foot from the house or 200yd/183m southeast by road to the car park and 4min there and back on foot.* The temple stands on a mound with a clear view across Strangford Lough to Scrabo Hill where the stone for it was quarried. It was designed as a banqueting house for the 1st Marquess of Londonderry by James "Athenian" Stuart in 1783 and is an accurate copy of the Temple of the Winds in Athens except for the balconies.

A cantilevered spiral stair rises under an elegant coffered ceiling in the rear turret. The inlaid wooden floor of the first-floor room matches the coffers, scallops and scrolls of the plasterwork ceiling. The domestic offices where the meals were assembled are concealed underground and linked to the vaulted basement by a passage.

For adjacent sights see BANGOR, CASTLE WARD, DOWNPATRICK, STRANGFORD LOUGH.

331

Co Down

Michelin Atlas p 99 and Map 923 – N O 5 – Local map below

The Mourne Mountains, which reach their highest point in Slieve Donard (2 796ft/852m), dominating Dundrum Bay, extend westwards to Carlingford Lough and north into rolling foothills. The **Kingdom of Mourne** was the name given to the strip of land between the mountains and the sea, a region of small fields divided by dry-stone walls where for centuries a life of farming and fishing continued largely undisturbed by external events. The Anglo-Normans built castles at Newcastle and Greencastle but only the latter, once the capital of the kingdom, has survived.

Exploring the Mourne Mountains

The beautiful scenery can be appreciated by walking the moors or by touring the coast and mountain roads by car.

Information on the area is available from the **Mourne Countryside Centre** ⊘, *91 Central Promenade* in Newcastle, which also organizes a programmme of hill walks in the summer months.

In summer there is a bus tour by the **Mourne Rambler** ⊘ to the Silent Valley Reservoir from Newcastle bus station.

There are bathing beaches at Newcastle and Cranfield.

The **Boley Fair**, a traditional sheep fair, takes place in Hiltown *(Tuesday after 12 July)*.

The **Maiden of Mourne Festival** takes place in Warrenpoint with fireworks in the evening *(several days in early August)*.

INLAND

★**Tollymore Forest Park** ⊘ – Tollymore (1 235 acres/500ha) straddles the Shimna, an excellent salmon river which rises in the foothills of the Mourne Mountains.

There are many walks exploring the azalea walk, arboretum, wildfowl enclosure on the lake, cascade (30ft/9m), salmon leap, mill ponds and a weir on the river, Old Bridge (1726), Hermitage, Clanbrassil barn (c 1757) resembling a church, Gothic Gate (1786) and Barbican Gate (1780) approached by an avenue of Himalayan cedars. The commercial forest area provides a habitat for foxes, otters, badgers, red squirrels and pine martens, moths, butterflies and many species of birds including woodcock.

It was James Hamilton, created Earl of Clanbrassil in 1756, who built the house (demolished) in 1730 and laid out the park in the naturalistic manner of William

Kent; he planted many trees, particularly larch and some rare and exotic species. The follies were built by the second Earl. The estate then passed to the Earls of Roden who sold it to the State in 1939 and 1941.

★**Silent Valley Reservoir** ⊘ – *Car park at the end of the drive.* The dam and reservoir (2.5mi/4km x 1.5mi/2.4km) were built between 1928 and 1933 to supply Belfast and Co Down with water (30 million gallons/136 million litres per day).

There is a pleasant walk *(2hr there and back on foot)* to the dam which provides a superb **view★** of the still waters of the re-servoir at the foot of the west face of Slieve Binnian (2 441ft/ 744m). The **Mourne Wall**, which encloses the catchment area of the dam, can be seen snaking its way up the slope. From

Christophe Boisvieux

Boley Fair, Hilltown

the east end of the dam the path continues north to **Ben Crom Reservoir** (3mi/4.8km). From the west end of the dam the path returns down the valley past **Sally Lough**, an attractive natural lake, through a grove of conifers and back over a wooden footbridge spanning the Kilkeel river.

★**Spelga Pass and Dam** – From the dam there is a superb **view** north over the foothills of the Mourne Mountains to the rolling hills of Co Down.

The still waters of the reservoir, which provides fine angling for brown trout,

Brontë Country

Among the rolling northern foothills of the Mourne Mountains stands the ruined cottage *(plaque)* where Patrick Brontë, the father of the famous literary sisters, Charlotte, Emily and Anne, was born in 1777. In 1802 he went to study theology at St John's College, Cambridge. He was ordained in 1811 and moved to Haworth in Yorkshire in 1820.

He seems to have changed his name from Brunty (O'Pronitaigh), which is a local one, to Brontë before leaving Ireland; three years earlier in 1799 Lord Nelson had been made Duke of Brontë, a place in Sicily, by Ferdinand, King of Naples, in recognition of Nelson's assistance in recapturing Naples from the French.

cover the Deer's Meadow, formerly summer pasture which was inundated in 1959.

★**Drumena Cashel and Souterrain** – The cashel consists of an oval area enclosed by a drystone wall containing the foundations of a house and a T-shaped underground tunnel, called a souterrain. It was a farmstead enclosure and dates from the early-Christian period.

Brontë Centre ⊙ – *1.5mi/2.5km north of Rathfriland, off B 25 in Drumballyroney (sign)*. The little white schoolhouse and church in this hamlet have been turned into an interpretative centre which makes the most of the area's connections with the Brontë family. The occasion of the first sermon preached by Patrick Brontë, father of the famous literary sisters, is recreated in the adjoining deconsecrated church. A **tour** *(signed 10mi/16km)* leads to other sites associated with the family.

Crocknafeola Forest – *Picnic areas.* The small coniferous forest stands beside the road which traverses the Mourne Mountains from north to south skirting the west face of Slieve Muck (2 198ft/670m).

ON THE COAST *East to west*

Bloody Bridge – In 1641 a group of prisoners, being conducted from Newry to Downpatrick to be exchanged for rebel prisoners, was murdered by the man in charge of them, an insurgent called Russell, who was afraid of being attacked.

Narrow Water Castle

Christopher Hill, Belfast

★Annalong Marine Park and Cornmill ⊘ – *From A 2 turn south by the Police Station towards the shore.* On the banks of a stream stands an early-19C corn mill (restored), driven by a back-shot breast-shot water-wheel. It is typical of some 20 mills which existed in the Kingdom of Mourne in the late 17C and 18C for grinding wheat and oats or scutching flax. The Exhibition Room describes the history of milling.

The tour starts in the kiln house where the grain was dried overnight on perforated metal plates; anthracite was used to avoid tainting. The grain was then collected in hoppers and hoisted to the top storey where it was fed into one of three mill wheels: one of French burr for wheat, two of Mourne granite for dehusking and grinding oats. The water-wheel drives all the machinery in the mill and the teeth of the gear wheels are made of wood for easy replacement.

Kilkeel – Population 6 024. Kilkeel is a small town, with stepped pavements and many changes of level, in an attractive setting at the mouth of the Kilkeel River.

The harbour is a lively place when the fishing fleet, the largest in Northern Ireland, is in port and the catch is being sold on the quay.

Greencastle ⊘ – The ruins of an Anglo-Norman stronghold, probably built in the mid 13C, are set on a low outcrop of rock extending into Carlingford Lough. The castle consisted of a large rectangular keep within a four-sided walled enclosure with D-shaped corner towers, which was surrounded by a moat cut in the rock. From the top of the keep there is a fine view *(south-*

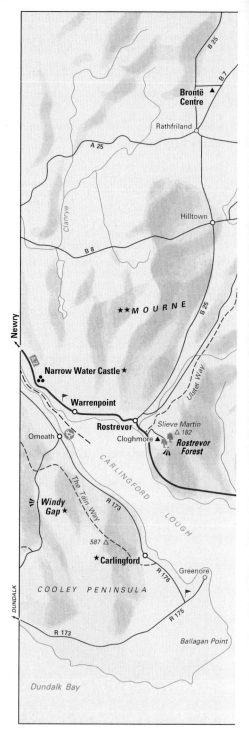

east) to Cranfield Bay with its sandy beach which is ideal for bathing, *(north)* to the Mourne Mountains, *(northwest)* up Carlingford Lough, and *(southwest)* across the straits to Greenore and the Cooley Peninsula in the Republic.

Rostrevor Forest Park – *Forest Drive to car park.* The pine forest covers the south bank of the Kilbroney River and the steep northwest slopes of Slieve Martin (597ft/182m) beside a mountain stream. There are several walks – to the **Clogh-**

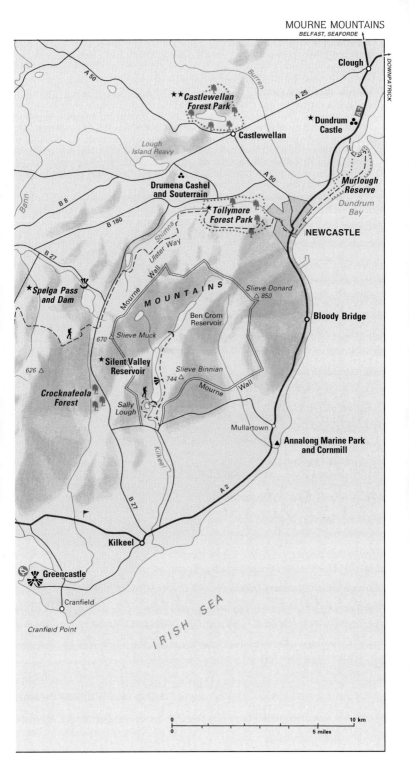

more, a great glacial boulder, and to the **viewpoint★** high above Rostrevor Bay; on the opposite shore of Carlingford Lough rise the mountains of the Cooley Peninsula in the Republic.

Rostrevor – Population 2 269. This is an attractive little town, which extends from the central square to the waterfront on Carlingford Lough. Even palm trees and mimosa thrive in its sheltered position at the foot of Slieve Martin.

Warrenpoint – *Ferry and cruises* ⊘. Population 5 408. The town is both a port, equipped to take container traffic, and a pleasant resort, with a vast central square, used for markets and festivals, and a promenade facing south down Carlingford Lough between the Mourne Mountains and the Cooley Peninsula.

★**Narrow Water Castle** ⊘ – *2mi/3.2km north of Warrenpoint on A 2.* The castle occupies an attractive and strategic site on a promontory commanding the narrows at the mouth of the Newry River where it enters Carlingford Lough. It was built in the 1650s as an English garrison at the cost of £361 4s 2d. Although restored, it is an excellent example of a **tower house**, complete with its **bawn**. The entrance to the three-storeyed tower was defended by a murder-hole immediately above the door. On the first floor the wickerwork support, used in recent restoration of the windows, has been left in place to illustrate this peculiarly Irish technique. From the narrow windows there is a view of the river.

For adjacent sights see DUNDALK, NEWCASTLE, NEWRY.

Lough NEAGH★

Co Antrim, Armagh, Tyrone and Londonderry
Michelin Atlas p 102 and Map 923 – M N 3 4

The largest lake in the British Isles (153sq mi/400km² and 40–50ft/12m–15m deep) is drained by the Lower Bann and fed by 10 rivers, which flow into it from the south, east and west.

The waters of Lough Neagh and its tributaries provide every kind of freshwater fish: rudd, roach, pike, eels as well as the rare dollaghan and pollan; giant pike in Lough Beg on the Lower Bann, bream in the Blackwater, trout and salmon in the Bann, Main, Six Mile Water, Blackwater, Ballinderry and Moyola rivers. At Toome, where the River Bann flows north out of the lake, there is an important eel fishery, which exports most of its catch.

Lough Neagh and its tiny northern neighbour, Lough Beg, are sites of international importance for wintering wildfowl; nature reserves have been established on many of the islands. Only in Antrim Bay is the shore lined with woodland; elsewhere it is low and marshy and sometimes infested with (non-biting) midges. As there is no shore road, the lake is best explored by boat.

Out and about on Lough Neagh

Lake Cruises ⊘ are available from **Kinnego Marina** on the south shore and from **Sixmile-water Marina** in Antrim. Occasionally there is also a **Bann cruise** between **Antrim** and **Castle-rock** *(35mi – 6/7hr).*

Fishing licences ⊘ for Lough Neagh are available from tackle shops and from the Fishery Conservancy Board in Portadown.

Fishing permits and gillie services for the Lower Bann are available from Bann Systems, Coleraine.

SIGHTS *In clockwise order starting from the southeast corner*

Lough Neagh Discovery Centre ⊘ – *South shore; Oxford Island; sign at Junction 10 on M 1.* This modern visitor centre, set among lakeside meadows and reached across a moat, is one of the best places to make the acquaintance of the lough. It presents an exhibition about the wildlife, history and management of the lake through audio-visual shows and touch-screen computers; there are five bird-watching hides and footpaths *(4mi/7km)* along the shoreline – reedbeds, wildflower meadows, woodland – and marina in Kinnego Bay.

Peatlands Park ⊘ – *South shore; sign at Junction 13 on M 1.* The park (618 acres/250ha), including Derryadd Lough, was used in the 19C for hunting and growing timber. About half the acreage has been designated a **National Nature Reserve** with restricted access to protect the natural flora and fauna. The public park includes a **bog garden**, two small lakes, an orchard and woodland; **demonstrations of turf cutting** by hand and machine are given at the outdoor turbary station. The **narrow-gauge railway** installed by the previous owners, the Irish Peat Development Company, provides a scenic tour in trains hauled by the original diesel engines. General information on bogs and peat extraction is displayed in the **Visitor Centre**.

Maghery – *South shore.* Country park from which Coney Island, a densely wooded island, can be visited by boat.

Ballyronan – *West shore.* Small marina and beach enhanced by pleasant walks.

Mountjoy Castle – *West shore.* A ruined early-17C castle with gun loops, built of stone and well-weathered brick.

Kinturk Cultural Centre ⊘ – *West shore*. A lavish new community centre contains a fascinating exhibition dealing comprehensively with the long-established Lough Neagh eel fishery.

★**Ardboe Cross** – *West shore, east of Cookstown by B 73*. The cross, which stands at the entrance to a graveyard round the ruins of a 17C church, is the finest in Ulster and extensively carved with biblical scenes: Old Testament on the east side and New Testament on the west. The cross probably dates from the 10C and marked the site of Ardboe Abbey, probably a 6C foundation, which was associated with St Colman.

From Ardboe Point there is an extensive **view**★ of Lough Neagh surrounded by mountains: Slieve Gallion and the Sperrin Mountains *(northwest)*, Slemish *(northeast)*, Divis Mountain *(east)*, the Mourne Mountains *(southeast)*.

Bellaghy Bawn ⊘ – *North shore; in Bellaghy, 4mi/7km north of A 6*. The 17C bawn (restored) in the village of Bellaghy was built by the Vintners' Company in 1619; its exhibits pay tribute to Seamus Heaney and his writing. As well as books and manuscripts, there is the opportunity to see a film introduced by Heaney and listen to recordings of his broadcasts.

Churchtown Point – *North shore*. A low promontory marked by a holy well and the ruins of Cranfield Church, which probably dates from the 13C and attracted many pilgrims in the past.

Shane's Castle Terrace – *North shore; see p 274*.

Seamus Heaney

The poet and Nobel Prize winner Seamus Heaney (b 1939) was born at his family's farm near Bellaghy. Much of his work, in particular his Lough Neagh cycle, reflects the influence of the landscapes and people of his youth. His feeling for the land of Ireland and his respect for those who, like his father, were bound to it by hard physical work, is carried over into his own physical act of writing:

> "Between my finger and my thumb
> The squat pen rests.
> I'll dig with it."
> *Digging* (1966)

For adjacent sights see ANTRIM, ARMAGH, BELFAST, LISBURN, SPERRIN MOUNTAINS.

NEWCASTLE

AN CAISLEÁN NUA – Co Down – Population 7 214
Michelin Atlas p 99 and Map 923 – O 5 – Local map see Mourne Mountains

The town "where the mountains of Mourne sweep down to the sea", immortalized in verse by Percy French, is one of Ireland's foremost resorts which began to develop in the early 19C when seaside holidays became fashionable. From the tiny harbour a long promenade of hotels, shops and amusement arcades extends northeast beside a long sandy beach overlooking Dundrum Bay. Beyond the red-brick bulk of the Slieve Donard Hotel, built by the railway company in 1898, lie the championship links of the Royal County Down Golf Club.

Our Lady of the Assumption ⊘ – The Roman Catholic church is a circular building (1967), decorated with bold and vivid stained-glass windows installed in 1969; the clerestory windows represent the 12 Apostles with their appropriate symbols; the windows in the side chapels bear a symbolic representation of the Birth, Life, Passion and Crucifixion of Jesus.

In and around Newcastle

Castle and Islands Park, *Town centre*, provides swings, slides, Slippery Dip, crazy golf, miniature golf, 9-hole pitch and putt course, tennis courts, boating lake.
Tropicana offers heated outdoor sea-water fun pools, giant water slides, bouncy castle, adventure playground, supervised crèche and kiddies' club.
Coco's Indoor Adventure Playground has snake slides, free fall, an assault course and a soft play activity area.
There are 13 **caravan parks** in and around Newcastle.

Donard Park – The park on the banks of the Glen River was once the grounds of Donard Lodge (demolished), which was built in the 1830s as a summer house by Earl Annesley of Castlewellan *(see below)*. There is a path which leads up from the Donard Bridge through Donard Wood to **Slieve Donard** *(2 796ft/850m)*. The highest peak in the Mourne Mountains, originally known as Slieve Slanga, was renamed in honour of Donard, a local chief, who is supposed to have been converted by St Patrick. After his death in 506, pilgrims used to make an annual pilgrimage on 25 July to St Donard's cairn on the summit.

EXCURSIONS

★★**Castlewellan Forest Park** ◷ – *4mi/6.4km north of Newcastle by A 50*. The park, which was sold to the Department of Agriculture in 1967, surrounds a lake providing excellent fishing. The **Sculpture Trail** *(3mi/5km)* along the lake shore presents pieces created since 1992 from natural materials, most of which were gathered in the park. There is an ice-house on the south shore and a pagan standing stone now covered with Christian symbols on the north bank. Higher up the hill behind the castle *(private)* are the **Annesley Gardens**, enclosed by a wall and embellished by two fountains; all the plants are labelled. The formal garden contains geometric beds and greenhouses; the informal **Arboretum** was planted between 1850 and 1900 and the surrounding parkland is thought to have been planted between 1740 and 1760. The rest of the estate, which rises to a central high point, Slievenaslat (896ft/273m), is covered in woodland.

The land at Castlewellan was purchased from the Magennises in 1742 by the Annesley family, originally of Breton origin, who moved to England during the Norman Conquest and thence to Ireland in the reign of Elizabeth I. They lived at The Grange, an 18C farm beside the car park, or at Castlewellan Cottage (demolished) on the north shore of the lake, before building the present castle which was designed in the Scottish baronial style by William Burn in 1856.

Castlewellan – *4mi/6.4km north of Newcastle by A 50*. Population 2 133. The elegant town was laid out in 1750 by the Earl of Annesley. The buildings are pleasantly arranged round two squares; the market house (1764) stands in the centre of the western square; the eastern square is lined with trees.

Castlewellan

Legananny Dolmen – *11mi/18km north of Newcastle by A 50 and side roads (signed) from north of Castlewellan*. The dolmen, which consists of a huge slanting capstone delicately balanced on three unusually-low supporting stones, is a prehistoric burial monument. From its site on the south slope of Slieve Croob (1 745ft/532m) there is a magnificent view of the Mourne Mountains.

Murlough National Nature Reserve ◷ – *2mi/3.2km east of Newcastle by A 2. Car park*. This reserve consists of a stretch of sand dunes, some at least 5 000 years old, between the Carrigs River and the northwest shore of Dundrum Bay. Many plants thrive on the soil, providing an environment attractive to a wide variety of birds. Archeologists have discovered evidence of early human habitation as well as a tripod **dolmen** (8ft/2.5m high), which is about 4 000 years old.

★**Dundrum Castle** ⊘ – *4mi/6.4km east of Newcastle by A 2; in Dundrum turn left uphill; car park.* The ruins of the castle stand on an attractive grassed and wooded site on a hilltop north of the town. It is also known as the Magennis Castle after the Irish family of that name who held it in the later Middle Ages. The Lower Ward (13C to 15C) contains the ruins of a once-grand house built by the Blundell family in the 17C.

The Upper Ward, the oldest part of the present ruins, was built on a previously occupied site, probably by John de Courcy c 1177 to defend the Lecale Peninsula. The natural defences have been supplemented by an impressively deep rock-cut ditch. The circular 13C keep was modified in the 15C; the original entrance at first-floor level was linked to the curtain wall by a bridge. In place of the usual well, a cistern, cut into the rock and fed by seepage, supplied the castle with water.

From the parapet of the keep there is a splendid **view** *(east)* of the Lecale Peninsula, and *(southeast)* of the Blackstaff estuary and the narrow channel leading into Dundrum Bay, which extends from the lighthouse on St John's Point *(east)* to Slieve Donard and the Mourne Mountains *(southwest).*

Clough – *6mi/10km east of Newcastle by A 2.* Population 269. North of the cross-roads stands a stone tower (13C with later medieval additions) surmounting an Anglo-Norman earthwork castle, which in the late 12C or early 13C was surrounded by a wooden palisade.

Seaforde Garden ⊘ – *7mi/12km east of Newcastle by A 2.* The old walled garden at Seaforde has been revived with a large hornbeam **maze.** Beyond is the Pheasantry, a deep dell dominated by great rhododendrons and exotic trees. Even more exotic is the **tropical butterfly house**, where brilliantly coloured specimens flutter among the vegetation and other creatures lurk in the lush undergrowth.

Loughinisland Churches – *10mi/16km northeast of Newcastle by A 2 and A 25; north of Seaforde turn right to Loughinisland; turn right onto Drumgooland Road; turn left onto a causeway.* Three ruined churches stand on what was originally an island overlooking the lake. The oldest church (13C) stands in the middle. The larger church dates from the 15C and was in use until 1720. The smaller church bears the date 1636 over the door but it may be earlier; the initials PMC stand for Phelim MacCartan, whose family held land in the district and probably used the graveyard for their burials.

For adjacent sights see DOWNPATRICK, MOURNE MOUNTAINS.

NEWRY

AN TIÚR – Co Armagh and Co Down – Population 22 975
Michelin Atlas p 98 and Map 923 – M N 5

Newry occupies a strategic position in the "Gap of the North", the Moyry Gap in the line of hills which separates Ulster from the plains of Meath.

The city has something of a split personality since it straddles the Clanrye River, which is the border between Co Down and Co Armagh, and the Town Hall (1893) is said to have been built over the river so that it should be in neither county. More recently a dual carriageway has separated the older east side of the city from the modern shopping centre.

16C Foundation – When Sir Nicholas Bagenal, Marshal of Ireland, came into possession of the lands of Newry in the 16C he took up residence in a former Cistercian Abbey, founded in 1157. He built a castle, which has not survived, and St Patrick's Church (1578), with his coat of arms in the porch, on the hill east of the

---

Newry Canal

Newry was once a port of some importance, as is evident from the warehouses by the canal. The inland canal, from Newry to the River Bann, was begun in 1731, opened in 1742 and closed in 1956. The town stretch, which is now obstructed by low bridges, is used for fishing. The Ship Canal, from Newry to Carlingford Lough, which operated from 1761 to 1974 when the shipping trade moved downstream to Warrenpoint, was re-opened in 1987 for leisure use.

---

city centre; it was the first Anglican church built in Ireland after the Reformation. He was succeeded by his son Henry who was killed at the Battle of Yellow Ford *(see p 311)* in 1598.

SIGHTS

Newry Cathedral ⊘ – *Town Centre.* Newry became the seat of the Roman Catholic diocese of Dromore in about 1750. The cathedral, which is dedicated to St Patrick and St Colman, was the first Roman Catholic cathedral to be built in Ireland at the time of the Act of Emancipation. Its Tudor-Gothic exterior was designed by Thomas Duff in 1825; the tower and transepts date from 1888. The interior decor of stained glass and mosaics was added later.

Newry Museum ⊘ – The museum is housed in the modern Arts Centre beside the Town Hall. Through its exhibits it traces the history of the area: the seal of the abbey – seated abbot flanked by yew trees – which has been adopted as the City seal; lace and linen from Bessbrook *(see below)*; a panelled room from the Old Coach House (early 18C) which stood in North Street; 18C Delft tiles from a Dutch house on the site of the abbey; photographs of old Newry and the canal.

EXCURSION

★**Slieve Gullion** *Round tour of 27mi/43.5km – 1 day*

From Newry take A 25 west; after 1.5mi/2.4km turn right onto B 133 to Bessbrook.

Bessbrook – Population 3 132. The village consists of granite terrace cottages ranged round three sides of two grass squares (bowling green and children's playground) on the north side of the road; opposite with its attendant ponds stood the flax mill where the inhabitants worked. The settlement, which included churches, schools, a community hall and shops but no public houses, was founded in 1845 by John Richardson, a Quaker linen manufacturer. One of the first industrial model villages, Bessbrook later inspired the Cadbury family to build Bournville near Birmingham.

From Bessbrook take B 112; turn right onto A 25. West of Camlough village turn left onto B 30.

Cam Lough – From the road there is a fine view of the narrow lake extending south along the west foot of Camlough Mountain (1 417ft/423m).

At the crossroads turn left onto a narrow road along the west side of Cam Lough.

Killevy Churches – An ancient graveyard, overhung with beech trees, surrounds the ruins of two churches, standing end to end. The eastern church is medieval and its east window dates from the 15C. The western building is earlier (12C) although the west wall, which is pierced by a doorway below a massive lintel, may be 10C or 11C. A granite slab in the northern half of the graveyard is said to be the grave of St Monenna (also known as Darerca and Bline) who founded an important early nunnery at Killevy in the 5C; later it became a convent of Augustinian nuns until it was suppressed in 1542. A path north of the graveyard leads to a holy well.

Continue south for 1.5mi/2.4km; turn right onto B 113.

★**Slieve Gullion Forest Park** ⊘ – *Car park and picnic area. 8mi/13km Scenic Drive; steep gradients and difficult bends.* The forest which consists of pines, larches, spruce and other conifers, covers the lower slopes of the southwest face of Slieve Gullion. The Visitor Centre, which contains an exhibition on forestry and a display of obsolete hand tools, is housed in old farm buildings adjoining a walled garden set out with lawns round a small pond.
After climbing through the wood, the Scenic Drive emerges on the open slopes of Slieve Gullion and runs northwest skirting the forest; on the left is an extensive view over the treetops; on the right is the path, waymarked in white, to the top of the south peak of Slieve Gullion (1 894ft/573m) where there is a cairn; another cairn crowns the lower north peak. The Drive swings left downhill and doubles back along the southwest slope, through the trees and rocks, to a **viewpoint**★ *(car park)* overlooking a section of the **Ring of Gullion**, a ring-dyke of smaller volcanic hills which encircle Slieve Gullion.

At the exit turn right onto B 113 and immediately turn left. After 1.5mi/2.4km turn right; after 1mi/1.6km park at the T-junction.

Kilnasaggart Stone – *6min there and back on foot across two fields and stiles.* In a hedged enclosure in the third field stands a tall granite pillar, which dates from about AD 700 and marks the site of an early-Christian cemetery. It bears 10 crosses on the northwest face and three on the southeast face, which also bears an inscription in Irish stating that the site was dedicated under the patronage of Peter the Apostle by the son of Ceran Bic, Ternohc, who died c 715.

Return to B 113; turn right towards Newry; after 5mi/8km turn left to Ballymacdermot Cairn (sign).

Ballymacdermot Cairn – Beside the road *(right)* on the south slope of Ballymacdermot Mountain are the remains of a Neolithic court grave, which consisted of two burial chambers preceded by an antechamber and a circular forecourt enclosed in a trapezoidal cairn. From the site there is a fine **view** southwest across the Meigh plain to Slieve Gullion and the Ring of Gullion.

Continue for 1mi/1.6km.

★★★ **Bernish Rock Viewpoint** – *Car park.* The view extends from Newry in the valley below to the Mourne Mountains on the horizon to the east.

Return downhill to Newry.

Cullyhanna

Cardinal O'Fiaich Centre – *Cullyhanna; 15mi/24km west of Newry by B30 and north by A 29 and a minor road (left).* The centre is devoted to the life story of Tomás O'Fiaich, a local boy, who became Cardinal-Primate of all Ireland. It reviews his career as student, priest, professor, scholar, using audio-visual presentations of interviews and conversations, personal memorabilia, panels depicting life and times, archeological models and artefacts.

For adjacent sights see ARMAGH, DUNDALK, MONAGHAN, MOURNE MOUNTAINS.

SPERRIN MOUNTAINS★

Co Tyrone and Co Londonderry
Michelin Atlas p 101–102 and Map 923 – J K L 3 – Local map below

The Sperrin Mountain range, a curved ridge of schists and gneisses including rare but minute deposits of gold, rises to its highest point in Sawel Mountain (2224ft/678m). The area was once covered in magnificent forests of Scots pines and other species. The extensive open moorland of the upper slopes, composed of blanket bog and purple heather, is used as sheep pasture; woodland and farmland alternate on the better-drained sand and gravel of the lower slopes and in the valleys, providing a suitable habitat for red grouse, pheasant and woodcock, and also the cloudberry which grows nowhere else in Ireland. The deep gorges created by the mountain streams are now thickly wooded. The land along the south shore of Lough Foyle (slob land) was reclaimed from the sea in the 19C and drained by pumps to grow flax but now produces good grain crops, and the mouth of the River Roe has been designated a nature reserve.

Plantation – In the 17C some of the area was granted to the London city livery companies – Drapers, Skinners, Grocers and Fishmongers – who brought in new settlers mainly from Scotland. Initially the land was let through local landlords on the rundale system *(see p 23)*; by the early 19C it was overpopulated. Traces remain of the direct management which was then adopted in some areas. Assisted emigration was introduced; the land was reallocated in holdings of 20–30 acres/8-12ha of neatly-hedged fields; model farms were established to promote modern methods; roads and bridges, churches, schools and dispensaries were built.

> ### Out and about in the Sperrin Mountains
>
> The many good angling streams drain southeast into Lough Neagh, or north and west down the River Roe and the Foyle tributaries into the Foyle estuary.
> The Owenkillew and the Glenelly are both good trout streams.

CENTRAL HEIGHTS

Sperrin Heritage Centre ⊘ – The Centre, which is built in the vernacular style to resemble three adjoining cottages, is set in the beautiful Glenelly Valley surrounded by the natural beauty of the Sperrin scenery. The symbol of the centre is the Hen Harrier, an indigenous bird of prey which still survives in the Sperrin uplands. Videos, computers and exhibitions enable visitors to explore the local flora and fauna, history and culture, and consider future management options.

Scenic Routes – The **Sawel Mountain Drive★**, a narrow unfenced road along the east face of Sawel Mountain (2229ft/678m), the highest peak, passes through the wild and austere beauty of the open moorland; the **views★★** are spectacular.
The **Oak Lough Scenic Road★** is a minor road which loops round a cluster of lakes, the delight of canoeists, and provides a fine **view** of Gortin (population 300) on the Owenkillew River.
The **Barnes Gap** carries the road through a narrow cleft in the hills between the valleys of the Owenkillew and Glenelly Rivers.

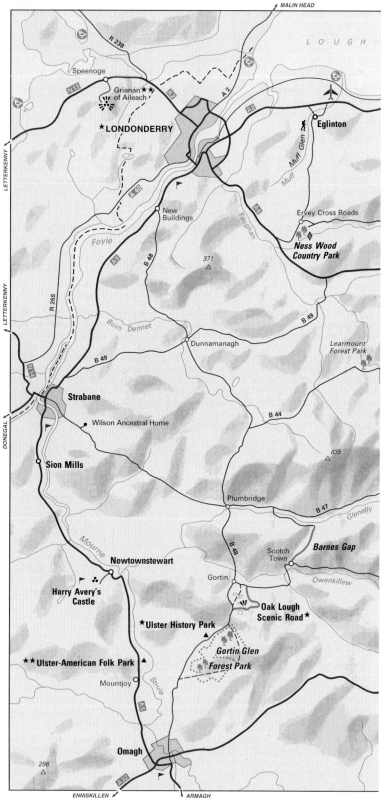

*The **Key** explains the abbreviations and symbols used in the text or on the maps.*

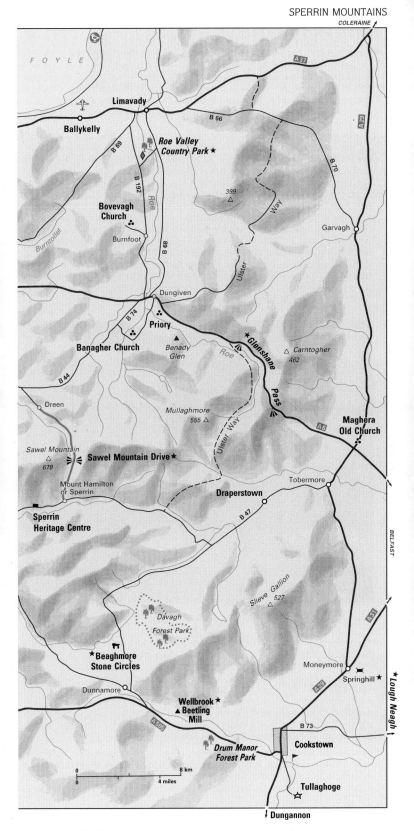

The towns and sights described in this guide are shown in black on the maps.

EASTERN FOOTHILLS

★**Springhill** ⊘ – This house was the family home of the Conynghams, who came to Ulster from Ayrshire early in the 17C. They were already extensive landowners when they acquired the Springhill estate (350 acres/141ha) for £200. The oldest part of the house seems to have been built c 1680 by William Conyngham for his bride Anne Upton of Templepatrick in Co Antrim. The property was altered by subsequent generations of Conynghams, who usually followed military careers, and was transferred to the National Trust in 1957.

The original 17C slate-roofed house was enlarged in the 18C by the addition of the bay window wings. There are family portraits throughout the house and much **fine 18C and 19C furniture** including a set of 18C "ladder-back" chairs, an oak press inscribed by its maker, an early-18C medicine chest, Wedgwood basalt ware, a Dutch rosewood cabinet, two Regency pieces – an inlaid card table and a rosewood stool – and three French pieces – the early-19C sofas, a Louis XV chair and the clock on the mantelpiece. The oak **stairs** have a yew handrail with two balusters, one spiral and one plain, to each shallow tread. In the Library are some **rare books**, mostly collected in the 18C by the third William Conyngham. The **Dining Room** is furnished with an 18C mahogany plate bucket, a hexagonal wine-cooler and a set of marquetry walnut fiddle-back chairs (late-17C); the mantelpiece is made of marble brought from Herculaneum by the Earl Bishop *(see p 307)*. The **Gun Room** contains a "cock-fighting" chair and a collection of weapons: four flintlocks used during the Siege of Derry and later converted to muzzle-loaders, and two pikes from the Battle of Vinegar Hill *(see p 171)*.

Gun Room, Springhill

The entrance court is flanked by low outbuildings which accommodated *(east)* the senior staff and *(west)* the junior staff, stables, laundry, brewhouse, slaughterhouse and turf-shed which was kept stocked by the tenants. They now house a **costume collection** consisting of about 150 articles of men's and women's dress from the 18C, 19C and 20C, which are displayed in rotation and include several rare 18C men's costumes and a court mantua of Spitalfields silk (1759). The **barn**, built of the same rough-hewn local oak for the timberwork as was used in the house, is surmounted by a bell which could be rung to warn of approaching danger; a circular **dovecot** stands between the house and the road.

★**Beaghmore Stone Circles** – The stone circles, seven in number, are formed of quite small stones set on, rather than in, the ground. Six of the circles are arranged in pairs, with a cairn and a row of stones near the point of intersection. The area enclosed in the seventh unattached circle is studded with close-set stones, known as "Dragons' Teeth".

Archeological investigations suggest that the circles date from the Bronze Age, between 1500 and 800 BC; they may have been used to calculate the rising and setting of the sun and moon.

Beaghmore Stone Circles

Slide File, Dublin

★**Wellbrook Beetling Mill** ⊘ *– 5mi/8km west by A 505; after 3mi/5km turn right (sign)*. Beetling is the last stage in the production of linen where the cloth is beaten to close up the weave and give it a smooth sheen. The first mill at Wellbrook came into operation in September 1767; eventually there were six and the present mill, known as no 6, dates from about 1830. It continued in operation until 1961 and is maintained in working order by the National Trust.

The **tour** starts with a display on the production of linen and the history of the Irish linen industry; it occupies the drying loft which was originally fitted with frames capable of holding 100 pieces of cloth (23yd/21m long).

On the lower floor are the seven **beetling machines** turned by an external wooden water-wheel, which is fed by water carried from the mill race in a wooden flume (restored). The amount of noise produced by two beetling engines operating for a few minutes explains why deafness was common among beetlers, who worked from early morning to nine at night.

Drum Manor Forest Park ⊘ *– 2.5mi/4km west by A 505*. The Forest Park, which was formerly a private estate, consists of open parkland and three walled gardens surrounded by woodland. The Visitor Centre contains an exhibition on butterflies and forest habitats.

The **butterfly garden**, which is perfectly sheltered in one of the old walled gardens, presents butterflies living naturally without restraint. The centre of the garden is laid out with paths and planted with flowers and shrubs, such as buddleia, sweet rocket, single Michaelmas daisies, lavender and aubrietia, which provide nectar for the butterflies; the corners are allowed to grow wild to provide grass, docks, nettles and other wild plants as food for the caterpillars.

A most attractive **flower garden** has been created in the ruins of the manor house which was built between 1829 and 1869. Steps descend from the terrace to the south lawn which slopes to the pond where ducks and other wildfowl congregate.

Draperstown – The town is a pleasant and busy market centre in the heart of Sperrin Mountain country. In the **Plantation of Ulster Museum** ⊘ visitors move through a series of different settings to watch videos of costumed actors relating the defeat and flight of the Earls of Ulster *(see p 135)*, and Tudor and Stuart plans to settle the area with English and Scottish planters. An exhibition follows, tracing the history of the Plantation from the 17C to the present day, with interesting displays on the Great Famine and emigration, and the influence of the Drapers' Company on the life and architecture of Draperstown itself.

Royal Charter

Cookstown takes its name from Dr Allen Cooke who c 1620 obtained a Royal Charter to establish a market town; it was destroyed in the Rebellion (1641–43). A second project, in which every house possessed a garden, as most still do, was implemented in the early 1700s by James and William Stewart; they laid out a broad avenue extending south from Dr Cooke's settlement to their own property at Killymoon Castle *(private)*, which was redesigned by John Nash in 1803; the grounds are now a golf course.

Cookstown – Population 9842. Once an important linen centre, Cookstown now serves a predominantly agricultural community processing pork and dairy products. Its most notable feature is the very broad main street which, under 10 different names, extends north from the River Ballinderry towards the silhouette of Slieve Gallion (1 732ft/528m). On the west side stands **Holy Trinity Church** (Roman Catholic) designed by JJ McCarthy in 1860. The neighbouring convent **chapel**, completed in 1965, is decorated with bronze panels and stained-glass windows. Opposite stands the 18C **courthouse**.

Tullaghoge Fort – *2mi/3.2km south by A 29 and B 520. Turn left on a blind corner into the car park; 10min there and back on foot.* This hillfort is unusual in that it is surrounded by a wide outer bank but no ditch; at the centre of the oval inner area is a shallow depression. It was the residence of the O'Hagans and the headquarters of the O'Neills, the kings of the *Cenél nEógain*; their stone inauguration chair, which stood on the hillside nearby *(southeast)*, was broken up by Lord Mountjoy in 1602.

The **view** from the tree-crowned earthworks is extensive: southwest to the circular walled graveyard at Donaghrisk where the O'Hagans, who were the guardians of the fort, were buried; east towards Lough Neagh; north to Slieve Gallion with the River Ballinderry in the foreground and Killymoon Castle in the trees by the river.

SOUTHERN UPLANDS

★★Ulster-American Folk Park ⊘ – The park is devoted to emigration from Ireland to America and has been developed with the generous assistance of the Mellon family of Pittsburg, Pennsylvania, round the ancestral cottage from which Thomas Mellon emigrated with his family at the age of five in 1818.

Ulster Scots – Scotch Irish

In the 18C and 19C some 250 000 Ulster Scots – known in the USA as Scotch Irish – emigrated to America. The heartland of Ulster settlement was in the Appalachian back country; the name hillbilly is derived from King William III. Many Ulstermen were involved in the War of Independence, in pushing the frontier westwards and building the American railways.

Visitor Centre – The exhibition traces the Ulster connection with America. On display is a **Conestoga wagon**, in which the pioneers trekked into the Wild West; this sort of covered wagon originated in the 18C in Lane County, Pennsylvania and was drawn by four to six horses.

The **Emigration Gallery** describes in detail the reasons for emigration at different times, the sort of people who left and how they travelled – initially by sailing ship and packhorse but later by steamship and rail – and their success or failure in the New World.

Outdoor Exhibition – In the **Old World** section a typical **18C Ulster village** has been created by erecting other buildings from the same period round the Mellon cottage. The **Ship and Dockside Gallery** contains a replica of part of an emigration ship; the voyage could take from 20 days to 12 weeks. The **New World** section of the park shows the way of life the emigrants adopted on arrival in America – log cabins.

In the workshops and cottages local people in **period costume** demonstrate the old crafts: cooking, spinning,

Conestoga Wagon, Ulster-American Folk Park

NITB, Belfast

weaving, basket weaving; making candles and soap; working in the forge and the carpenter's shop; turf fires burn on the hearths throughout the year filling the air with their sweet fragrance.

★Ulster History Park ⊘ – *Development in progress.* The theme of the park (35 acres/14ha) is the history of settlement in Ireland, from the arrival of Mesolithic hunters to the 17C Plantation. The indoor display and film explain the origins of the full-scale reconstructions in the open-air park – a Mesolithic encampment (c 7000–4000 BC) and two Neolithic houses (c 4000–2000 BC), a court tomb and a wedge tomb, a standing stone and a stone circle, an early-Christian rath *(see p 55)* containing several round thatched huts, a cooking pit where the water was heated with hot stones *(fulacht fiadh)*, a crannóg, an early-Christian complex of round tower and church, a Norman motte and bailey, and a 17C Plantation house and bawn with a water mill.

Gortin Glen Forest Park ⊘ – The park, which was opened in 1967, is part of the larger Gortin Forest, a coniferous woodland planted to produce timber for commercial purposes. The forest drive *(5mi/8km – one direction only)* offers a number of beautiful vistas over the Sperrin Mountains. Detailed information is supplied in the Nature Centre and on the forest trails. The deer enclosure provides a close-up view of the Sika deer, and the pond attracts wildfowl.

Strabane – Population 11 670. This small town has developed where the River Finn and the Mourne River flow into the Foyle, which forms the border between Co Londonderry and Co Donegal.

Behind the bowed Georgian shopfront of **Gray's Printery** ⊘ *(49 Main Street, Strabane)*, a 19C printing shop has been preserved with its 19C hand- and foot-operated presses.

In the 18C, **Strabane** was a lively publishing centre. Two local apprentices made their mark in the USA: John Dunlap (1747–1812), an apprentice in Gray's Printery, printed the American Declaration of Independence in his newspaper the *Pennsylvania Packet*; James Wilson became editor of a Philadelphia newspaper.

The **Wilson Ancestral Home** ⊘ is a whitewashed thatched cottage, where James Wilson, Woodrow Wilson's grandfather, lived until he left for America in 1807 at the age of 20. The house contains some of the original furniture: a cupboard bed by the kitchen fire and curtained beds in the main bedroom. The first-floor room is a later addition. Wilsons still live in the modern farmhouse behind the cottage.

Sion Mills – Population 1 676. Broad grass verges, beech and chestnut trees line the main street of this model village which was established by the three Herdman brothers, who in 1835 started a flax-spinning operation in an old flour mill on the Mourne. Twenty years later they built a bigger mill which is still working. The terraced cottages for the millworkers were built in the Gothic style. The black-and-white half-timbered buildings, in particular Sion House, were designed by James Herdman's son-in-law, William Unsworth, an English architect, who also designed the Church of the Good Shepherd in an Italianate Romanesque style, modelled on a church in Pistoia in Italy. St Teresa's Roman Catholic Church (1963) is a striking modern building by Patrick Haughey of Belfast; a slate mural of *The Last Supper* by Oisin Kelly adorns the façade.

Newtonstewart – The **Grange House Museum and Gateway Centre** is an eclectic and absorbing collection of antiques and memorabilia; the museum includes toys, cameras, Victorian knick-knacks, "Trench Art" made by First World War soldiers from debris on the Front, tongs for picking up hedgehogs, medical paraphernalia, women's travelling chamber-pots and much more. A viewpoint opposite the centre looks over the River Mourne and its valley. Self-catering apartments and a café make up the rest of the complex.

On a nearby hilltop stands **Harry Avery's Castle**, two D-shaped towers from a 14C Gaelic stone castle built by Henry Aimbreidh O'Neill who died in 1392. There is a clear view of the surrounding countryside.

Omagh – Population 17 280. Omagh is a quiet market town built on a steep slope overlooking the point where two rivers, the Camowen and the Drumragh, join to form the Strule. The main street divides in front of the Courthouse (1820).

NORTHERN UPLANDS

★**Glenshane Pass** – The pass between Mullaghmore (1 818ft/555m – south) and Carntogher (1 516ft/462m – north) carries the main road through the Sperrin Mountains. The northern approach through dramatic mountain scenery overlooks Benady Glen on the River Roe; the southern approach *(viewing point)* provides a **panoramic view**★★ across Lough Neagh in the mid-Ulster plain to Slemish *(see p 275)*.

★**Roe Valley Country Park** ⊘ – The country park extends along a stretch *(3mi/4.8km)* of the wild thickly-wooded valley where the peaty red River Roe tumbles over rocks and through gorges on its way north to the sea at Lough Foyle. As well as great natural beauty and scenes of the O'Cahans' legendary exploits, the park preserves evidence of early industrial activity: bleach greens, weirs and mill races, and 18C water-powered mills for sawing wood, scutching flax, weaving and beetling linen. An unusual feature is the stone-built **Power House**, built in 1896 and the site of early success in generating hydroelectric power. The **Visitor Centre** at the Dogleap Bridge provides information on the local flora and fauna, old industries and on the 17C Plantation.

Ness Wood Country Park – *From the car park walk through the picnic area into the wood. The waterfall (30ft/9m) is unfenced; children should be accompanied. Woodland walk along both sides of the stream meeting at a bridge about 600yd/548m from the car park.*

The spectacular waterfall (*an eas* in Irish) was created, together with a series of gorges, potholes and rapids, by the River Burntollet eroding a channel through the metamorphic schist rock since the end of the last Ice Age. The wood (46 acres/19ha) was mostly oak trees until the 17C but now many species flourish.

Eglinton – Population 1 658. This elegant little village with its **Courthouse** was developed by the Grocers' Company between 1823 and 1825 round a tree-shaded green beside the Muff River. Upstream the river tumbles through **Muff Glen**, a narrow tree-lined valley of pleasant walks.

Dungiven Priory ⊘ – The priory ruins stand on a natural strongpoint above the River Roe. A pre-Norman monastery, associated with St Nechtan, was replaced late in the 12C with a priory of Augustinian canons which flourished until the mid 16C. The **church** is an impressive example of medieval architecture. The nave, the oldest part of the church, probably dates from the early 12C and was originally shorter; two round-headed arches in the Romanesque style in the east wall are most likely the work of the Augustinians, who also added the chancel in the 13C. Against the south wall stands a magnificent **tomb** designed in the tradition of 15C western Scotland; beneath a traceried canopy lies an armed figure, said to be a chieftain of the O'Cahans, Cooey-na-Gal, who died in 1385; on the front of the tomb are six "gallowglasses", Scottish mercenaries in kilts.

In the 17C Sir Edward Doddington, who constructed the walls of Londonderry, built himself a house in the cloister; its foundations were excavated in 1982.

North of the path is a **bullaun**, a hollowed stone which was originally used for grinding grain but now collects rainwater; it is visited by people seeking cures for warts who tie rags on the overhanging tree.

Banagher Church – The ruined church dates from the late 11C or early 12C. In the graveyard stands a **mortuary house**, built of dressed stone early in the 12C, probably to house some relics disturbed by the addition of a chancel to the church. The panel on the west gable depicts a figure with a hand raised in blessing and bearing a crozier. According to tradition it is the tomb of St Muiredach O'Heney and sand from his tomb brings good luck.

Bovevagh Church – In the churchyard of a ruined medieval church stands a **mortuary house** similar to the one at Banagher *(see above)*; its ruined state reveals the cavity, which contained the body, and the hand hole in the east end through which the faithful could touch the relics.

Maghera Old Church ⊘ – *At the north end of the main street turn right into Bank Square, then left to the car park.* The nave of the ruined church probably dates from the 10C. The fine west door is probably mid-12C and similar in structure to the door of Banagher Church *(see above)*; the lintel bears a Crucifixion scene. The chancel was added c 1200 and the tower in the 17C. In the graveyard stands a rough pillar stone, carved with a ringed cross, which, according to tradition, is the grave of St Lurach who founded an important monastery on this site in the 6C.

Ballykelly – Population 2 140. The village was established early in the 17C by the Fishmongers' Company who built a model farm which still stands on the north side of the road; a two-storey block is linked to two one-storey pavilions by curtain walls enclosing a farmyard. Opposite is the Presbyterian Church (1827). The Anglican Church, which stands on a slight hill screened by beech trees on the east side of the village, was built in 1795 by the Earl Bishop of Derry.

Limavady – Population 10 350. The town takes its name from the Irish for Dogleap since the original settlement was two miles upstream by the 13C O'Cahan castle in the Roe Valley Country Park *(see above)*. It was re-founded as Newtown-Limavady in the 17C by Sir Thomas Phillips, Chief Agent of the City of London in Ulster. It is now a pleasant Georgian market town where the famous song *Danny Boy*, also known as *The Londonderry Air*, was noted down in 1851 by Jane Ross (1810–79) who lived at 51 Main Street *(plaque)*.

For adjacent sights see DUNGANNON, LONDONDERRY, Lough NEAGH.

STRANGFORD LOUGH ★
Co Down
Michelin Atlas p 99 and Map 923 – P 4 – Local map below

Strangford Lough is a landlocked sea-inlet (18mi/29km long with an 80mi/142km coastline). It is linked to the Irish Sea by a narrow channel through which 350 million tonnes of sea water races at about 10 knots when the tide changes. The Viking name Strangford (violent fjord) has prevailed over the old Irish name of Lough Cuan. The area invaded by the sea was composed of drumlins which now emerge from the water as smooth green hummocks, particularly along the sheltered western shore; those along the eastern shore have mostly been eroded by the prevailing westerly wind. By the water's edge are attractive lakeside villages.

The whole of the Lough is now a **Marine Nature Reserve**, the first to be designated in Northern Ireland. Some islands, stretches of the foreshore and neighbouring areas are protected as National Nature Reserves or as Areas of Special Scientific Interest. Most of the shore is managed by public bodies, the National Trust or the Royal Society for the Protection of Birds.

Out and about on Strangford Lough

The Tourist Information Centre in Portaferry presents an exhibition on things to see around Strangford Lough, flora and fauna, local history and a film about tower houses.

The many places where wild flowers, nesting birds, flocks of wildfowl, seals and other marine animals can be seen include bird hides at Castle Espie, Delamont, Quoile Countryside Centre, Castle Ward and Mount Stewart. The marine life of the Lough can be viewed at **Exploris**, an aquarium in Portaferry. **Strangford Narrows car ferry** ⊘ carries vehicles between Strangford and Portaferry. *The places of interest on the lake shore are described below.*

SIGHTS *Clockwise from Strangford*

★**Strangford** – Population 400. This charming little port, which dates from the Middle Ages, nestles on the west side of the Narrows. The **tower house** ⊘ was begun in the 15C but is chiefly 16C in style. An internal wooden stair climbs the three storeys to a very narrow roof walk which provides a fine **view** of the port, the Narrows, Portaferry and the southern end of the Ards Peninsula.

Kilclief Castle ⊘ – *2.5mi/4km south of Strangford by coast road (A 2).* The **tower house**, which is in the gatehouse style, with two projections to protect the entrance, was built, probably by the bishop of Down between 1413 and 1441, to guard the entrance to the Strangford Narrows.

★**Audley's Castle** – *Access via Castle Ward or by minor road west of Castle Ward estate. Drive through the gate to the car park.* The ruins of this 15C **tower house**, which was designed in the "gatehouse" style, stand on a spit of land projecting into Strangford Lough. It was built by the Audley family, who held land in the area in the 13C, and sold in 1646 to the Wards of Castle Ward. There is a fine view of the wooded shores. The hamlet of Audleystown was demolished in the 1850s and the inhabitants are thought to have emigrated to the USA.

Audleystown Cairn – *Walk across the fields.* The cairn, which is revetted with drystone walling, is a dual court tomb with a forecourt at each end opening into galleries. Excavations in 1952 discovered 34 partly-burned skeletons, Neolithic pottery and flint implements.

★**Quoile Countryside Centre** ⊘ – In 1957 a barrage was built at Hare Island excluding the sea from the Quoile estuary, which had formerly been tidal, and turning the last few miles of the river into a freshwater lake with sluice gates to control flooding. This area (494 acres/200ha) is now a Nature Reserve with woodland, rushy grassland and reedbeds, providing a habitat for many woodland and wetland birds and several species of waterfowl, as well as otters.

From **Quoile Quay**, which was built in 1717 by Edward Southwell and served as a port for Downpatrick until 1940, the road reaches **Quoile Castle**, a late-16C tower house inhabited by the West family until the mid 18C; the south corner collapsed in 1977 revealing two vaulted rooms with gun loops on the ground floor. The **Visitor Centre** gives details of the local and natural history. The road ends at the Steamboat Quay, which was built in 1837 by David Ker as part of an unsuccessful attempt to establish a paddle-steamer service to Liverpool.

★**Inch Abbey** ⊘ – *2mi/3.2km northwest of Downpatrick by A 7; after 1mi/1.6km turn left; car park.* The attractive site of the abbey ruins was originally an island in the marshes on the north bank of the Quoile River, approached by a causeway which carries the modern road; the stretch of greensward covers most of the monastic precinct. The abbey, which was a daughter house of the Cistercian abbey at Furness in Lancashire, was founded c 1180 by John de Courcy to atone for the destruction of Erenagh, south of Downpatrick. The 13C church consisted of a nave, side aisles, transepts and chancel; the last was lit by an eastern triple-lancet window flanked by pairs of lancets; in the south wall are a triple sedilia and a piscina. Each transept contained two side chapels but these and the western end of the nave were walled off and abandoned in the 15C. Only the foundations remain of the buildings which surrounded the cloisters south of the church: the vestry, chapter-house, parlour and day-room below the dormitory in the eastern range, the refectory and kitchen on the south side. The detached buildings near the river were probably an infirmary *(southeast)*, a bakehouse and well *(southwest)* and a guest-house.

Delamont Country Park ⊘ – *Spacious bird hide.* The park, which contains a walled garden laid out with formal beds of shrubs, extends to the shore of Strangford Lough. In spring the woodlands are bright with wildflowers, and young lambs gambol in the meadows. One can see foxes, stoats and badgers; by the water, otters and seals. The bird population includes herons, which nest and rear their young between February and midsummer, treecreepers, owls, wrens, finches, wildfowl, guillemots, curlews, oystercatchers and several sorts of terns.

Killyleagh – Population 2 221. Killyleagh is an attractive sailing centre on the west shore of Strangford Lough, dominated by its turreted **castle**, which was redesigned in 1850 by Charles Lanyon, and incorporates two circular towers

> Killyleagh was the birthplace of **Sir Hans Sloane**, whose collection of curios, books and manuscripts formed the nucleus of both the Natural History Museum and the British Museum in London.

dating from the 13C and 17C. The original castle, which was built by de Courcy, came into the possession of the O'Neills, was destroyed by General Monk in 1648 and then rebuilt by the Hamiltons, Earls of Clanbrassil *(see p 332)* and Viscounts Clandeboye.

Sketrick Castle – *Car park.* The four-storey tower house, which collapsed in a storm in 1896, was erected to command the approach to the island from the mainland, probably in the 15C before the causeway was built. The ground floor was divided into four rooms; the largest, which is vaulted, was probably the kitchen; the one in the centre may have been a boat bay. At the rear a tunnel leads to a spring covered by a corbelled vault.

★**Nendrum Monastery** ⊘ – *At the north end of Mahee Island; car park.* The causeway approach is commanded by the ruins *(dangerous)* of **Mahee Castle**, built in 1570 by Captain Browne, an English soldier.
The **Visitor Centre** presents the history of the site and of the missionaries of the early Celtic church. The early-Christian site, originally approached by boat or across fords, is composed of three concentric enclosures protected by drystone walls. The innermost enclosure contained the round tower and the church, which may date from the 10C or 11C at the west end, while the east end is 12C Benedictine; the surrounding area was the graveyard. The school stood on the west side of the intermediate enclosure, which also contained the monks' workshops. The outer enclosure was probably given over to the guesthouse, tenants' dwellings, gardens, orchards, pastures and arable fields. St Mochaoi (5C), from which Mahee is derived, appears to be connected with the monastery's origins but the written records and the archeological evidence date from the 7C. The monastery suffered during the Viking invasions, and in the 12C John de Courcy established a Benedictine house at Nendrum but it seems to have closed by the early 14C. The site was identified in 1844 and excavated in 1922–24.

★**Wildfowl and Wetlands Trust (Castle Espie Centre)** ⊘ – The centre occupies an attractive site on the west shore of Strangford Lough. Its freshwater lakes, formerly clay and limestone workings belonging to a brick, tile and pottery factory, make ideal breeding grounds and wintering habitats for both wild birds and endangered species bred in captivity. From the Lance Turtle hide, one can observe some of the wildfowl which migrate to Strangford Lough each winter from the Arctic. Among the ducks, geese and swans from all over the world are Bufflehead, King Eider and Cinnamon Teal; Hawaiian Geese will feed from the hand; many small birds are attracted to the feeding stations in the woodland walk.

Scrabo Country Park ⊘ – *Car park at the top of the hill; 5min on foot to the tower. Second car park in Killynether Wood.* The dominant features of the park are Scrabo Hill, formed by a layer of volcanic lava covering and protecting the underlying sandstone, and **Scrabo Tower**, which was erected in 1857 to commemorate the

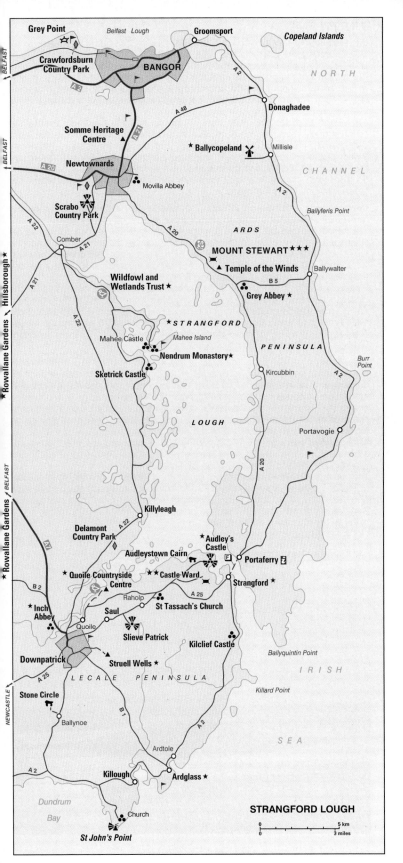

Grey Point

Belfast Lough

Groomsport

Copeland Islands

Crawfordsburn Country Park

BANGOR

NORTH

A 2

Donaghadee

A 48

BELFAST

A 21

Somme Heritage Centre

Millisle

★ **Ballycopeland**

CHANNEL

A 20

Newtownards

A 2

BELFAST

Scrabo Country Park

Movilla Abbey

Ballyferis Point

A 22

Comber

A 20

A 21

ARDS

MOUNT STEWART ★★★

▲ **Temple of the Winds**

Ballywalter

B 5

Wildfowl and Wetlands Trust ★

Grey Abbey ★

Hillsborough ★

★ **Rowallane Gardens**

A 21

A 22

★ *STRANGFORD*

Mahee Castle

Mahee Island

PENINSULA

Nendrum Monastery ★

Kircubbin

Burr Point

A 2

Sketrick Castle

LOUGH

Portavogie

A 20

Killyleagh

A 22

Delamont Country Park

★ **Audley's Castle**

Audleystown Cairn

🄴 **Portaferry** 🅸

BELFAST

Quoile Countryside Centre

★★ **Castle Ward**

Strangford ★

A 25

Raholp

Rowallane Gardens

★ **Inch Abbey**

B 2

Quoile

Saul

St Tassach's Church

Slieve Patrick

Kilclief Castle

Ballyquintin Point

NEWCASTLE

Downpatrick

▲ **Struell Wells ★**

A 25

LECALE PENINSULA

IRISH

Killard Point

Stone Circle

Ballynoe

B 1

A 2

Ardtole

A 2

SEA

Killough

Ardglass ★

Dundrum Bay

Church

STRANGFORD LOUGH

St John's Point

| 0 | | | | | 5 km |
| 0 | | | 3 miles | |

351

3rd Marquess of Londonderry (1778–1854) *(see p 330)* and his concern for his tenants during the Great Famine. The tower (135ft/41m high, walls 4ft/1.25m thick) was designed by Lanyon and Lynn and constructed of **Scrabo stone**, dark dolerite for the walls and light sandstone for the roof, quoins and dressings. It now houses an exhibition about the country park – geology, early settlers, flora and fauna – and *The Story of Strangford Lough*, an audio-visual presentation *(12min; every 30min)*.

The **view★★** from the top *(122 steps – viewing maps)* is panoramic: within the confines of the park are the North Quarry and Newtownards *(north)*, the South Quarry and Strangford Lough *(southeast)*, and the golf course and Killynether Wood, part-beech and part-mixed woodland planted in the 19C *(southwest)*; on the horizon are Belfast and its shipyards *(west)*, the Antrim Mountains and the Scottish coast *(north)*, the Ards Peninsula and the Isle of Man *(southeast)*, the Mourne Mountains *(southwest)*.

Newtownards – Population 23 869. The town is now a busy modern shopping centre half a mile inland from the north shore of Strangford Lough.

The handsome **town hall**, built as a market house in 1765 of local Scrabo stone, stands in the town centre on the north side of Conway Square where a market is held on Saturdays. At the east end of the High Street stands the **market cross** which was severely damaged in 1653. In Court Street on the south side of the town are the ruins of the church of **Newtownards Priory** which was founded in the 13C by Walter de Burgh; it was built of Scrabo stone and contains the burial vault of the Londonderry family *(see p 330)*; the tower dates from the 17C. A fine collection of 13C **cross slabs★** inscribed with foliate crosses is built into the north wall of the ruined church of **Movilla Abbey** *(2mi/3.2km northeast by A 48, B 172 and Old Movilla Road (right); entry through the graveyard)*; the abbey, one of the most important in Ulster, was founded c 540 by St Finian.

★**Grey Abbey** ⊘ – *Car park.* The ruins of the monastery stand in a quiet verdant hollow beside a stream. It was founded in 1193 by Affreca, the wife of John de Courcy, as a daughter house of Holm Cultram Abbey in Cumbria, a Cistercian foundation. Already in a poor state of repair at the Reformation, it was burned during the Elizabethan wars but then re-roofed and equipped with a bell turret and used as the parish church until 1778. The little visitor centre has displays on monastic life and on the building of the Abbey.

A magnificent **west door** (1220–30) with elaborate moulding and dog-tooth decoration leads into the aisleless nave. The high altar stood under the triple-lancet east window. Each transept contained two east chapels.

The monastic buildings are ranged round the cloisters according to the usual Cistercian practice: *(starting from the south transept)* vestry, chapter-house, slype or parlour, day room, stairs to the dormitory in the corner next to a passage, the warming room with its huge fireplace, the refectory with a reading pulpit and a hatch to the kitchen in the west wall.

Drumlins in Strangford Lough

The herb garden contains over 50 different medicinal plants and herbs of the kinds the Cistercian monks may have used in practising medicine.

Portaferry – Population 2 324. *Strangford Narrows car ferry*. A busy coastal town until the mid 19C, Portaferry is now a yachting and sea angling centre. The attractive long waterfront, facing Strangford across the narrow strait, includes two handsome Georgian houses, now the marine biology centre of Queen's University, Belfast. **Portaferry Castle**, a tower house with only one projection flanking the entrance, was probably built early in the 16C by the Savage family.

★**Exploris** ⊘ – Much more than just an aquarium, Exploris presents the marine life of Strangford Lough and the Irish Sea in all its richness and complexity, with convincing re-creations of many underwater and shoreline habitats. There are Touch Tanks, a Marine Discovery Lab, and an Open Sea Tank, one of the largest of its kind in the United Kingdom, which visitors can view from above or from the depths of an underwater cave.

For adjacent sights see BANGOR, CASTLE WARD, DOWNPATRICK, HILLSBOROUGH and MOUNT STEWART.

Jaunting Cars at Muckross

Practical
Information

Planning a trip

Climate – The best time of year to visit Ireland is in the summer; the sunniest months are May and June, the warmest are July and August. The southeast enjoys the most sun and the east coast is drier than the west.

Passport – Visitors entering Ireland must be in possession of a valid national passport (except British citizens). In case of loss or theft report to the embassy and the local police.

Visa – Visitors who require an **entry visa** should apply at least three weeks in advance to the Irish Embassy *(see below)*.
US citizens should obtain the booklet *Your Trip Abroad* ($1.50), which provides useful information on visa requirements, customs regulations, medical care etc for international travellers:

> **Superintendent of Documents**, PO Box 371954, Pittsburgh, PA 15250-7954, ☎ 202 512-1800.

Customs – Tax-free allowances for various commodities are governed by EU legislation. Details of these allowances are available at most ports of entry to Ireland and Great Britain, and from customs authorities. US citizens should obtain the booklet *Know before you go.*

> **Customs and Excise**, Custom House, Dublin 1, ☎ 01 873 4555.
> **HM Customs & Excise**, Eldon Court, 75 London Road, Reading, Berks, RG1 5BS, ☎ 0118 964 4355.
> **US Customs Service**, PO Box 7407, Washington DC 20044, ☎ 202 927 6724.

Irish Tourist Board (Bord Fáilte) – For information, brochures, maps and assistance in planning a trip to Ireland apply to the Irish Tourist Board (Bord Fáilte) and the Northern Ireland Tourist Board (NITB) *(addresses below)*.

Tourist Information Centres – The addresses and telephone numbers of the Tourist Information Centres to be found in most large towns and many tourist resorts in Ireland are printed in the Admission Times and Charges *(see p 374)*; some are open only during the summer months. The centres can supply town plans, timetables and information on sightseeing, local entertainment and sports facilities. Many have bureau de change facilities.

National Trust – Members of the National Trust in England and Wales and Scotland may use their membership cards to visit NT properties in Northern Ireland.

> Head Office, Rowallane House, Saintfield, Ballynahinch, Co Down BT24 7LH, ☎ 01238 510 721; Fax 01238 511 242.

Tourism for the Disabled – Some of the sights described in this guide are accessible to disabled people; *(see Admission times and charges p 374)*. The **Michelin Red Guide Great Britain and Ireland** indicates hotels with facilities suitable for disabled people. Information on tourism, accommodation, transport and activity centres is available from several organizations:

> **Irish Wheelchair Association**, Blackheath Drive, Clontarf, Dublin 3, ☎ 01 833 3884.
> **National Rehabilitation Board**, 25 Clyde Road, Dublin 4, ☎ 01 668 4181.
> **Northern Ireland Council on Disability**, 2 Annadale Avenue, Belfast BT7 3JH, ☎ 01232 491 011.

IRISH TOURIST BOARD

Australia – 5th Level, 36 Carrington Street, Sydney, NSW 2000. ☎ 02 9299 6177; Fax 02 9299 6323.

Belgium – Lers Nationaal Bureau voor Toerisme de Beaulieulaan 25, 1160 Brussels. ☎ 02 673 9940; Fax 02 672 1066.

Canada – Callers from Canada should telephone the New York office on ☎ 1800 223 6470.

Denmark – Klostergarden, Amagertorv 29.3, 1160 København K. ☎ 33 15 80 45; Fax 33 93 63 90.

Finland – Irlannin Matkailutoimisto, Embassy of Ireland, Erottajankatu 7A, PL33, 00130 Helsinki. ☎ 09 60 89 66; Fax 09 64 60 22.

France – 33 rue de Miromesnil, 75008 Paris. ☎ 01 53 43 12 12; Fax 01 47 42 01 64.

Germany – Untermainanlage 7, D-60329 Frankfurt/Main. ☎ 069 92 31 85 50; Fax 069 92 31 85 88.

Ireland – Baggot Street Bridge, Dublin 2. ☎ 01850 230 330; Fax 066 979 2035 (callers within Republic of Ireland only).

Japan – Ireland House 5F, 2-10-7 Kojimachi, Chiyodi-ku, Tokyo 102. ☎ 03 52 75 16 11; Fax 03 52 75 16 23.

Netherlands – Spuistraat 104, 1012 VA Amsterdam. ☎ 020 62 23 101; Fax 020 62 08 089.

Norway – Drammensveien 126A, PB 295 Skøyen, 0212 Oslo. ☎ 22 56 33 10; Fax 22 12 20 70.

Spain – Paseo de la Castellana 46.3, 28046 Madrid. ☎ 91 57 71 787; Fax 91 57 76 934.

Sweden – Sibyliegatan 49, PO Box5292, 10246 Stockholm. ☎ 08 66 28 510; Fax 08 66 17 595.

United Kingdom – 150 NewBond Street, London WIY 0AQ. ☎ 0171 493 3201; Fax 0171 493 9065. 53 Castle Street, Belfast BT1 1GH. ☎ 01232 327 888; Fax 01232 240 201. 44 Foyle Street, Londonderry. ☎/Fax 01504 369 501.

United States – 345 Park Avenue, New York, NY 10154. ☎ 212 418 0800; Fax 212 379 9052.

NORTHERN IRELAND TOURIST BOARD

Europe – Fur Fremdenverkehr, Westendstr 16-22, D-60325, Frankfurt, Germany. ☎ 069 23 45 04; Fax 069 23 34 80.

Ireland – 16 Nassau Street, Dublin 2. ☎ 01 679 1977.

North America – 551 5th Avenue, Suite 701, New York, NY 10176. ☎ 212 922-0101; Fax 212 922-099.

United Kingdom – St Anne Court, 59 North Street, Belfast BT1 1NB. ☎ 01232 231 221. 24 Haymarket, London SW1Y 4DG. ☎ 0171 766 9920; Fax 0171 766 9929.

REGIONAL TOURISM ORGANIZATIONS

Cork/Kerry Tourism – Grand Parade, Cork. ☎ 021 273 251; Fax 021 273 504.

Dublin Tourism – St Andrew's Church, Suffolk Street; Dublin Airport; B & I Terminal; Town Centre, Tallaght; Dun Laoghaire Tourist Office, New Ferry Terminal. ☎ 1850 230 330; Fax 066 979 2035 (within Republic of Ireland only).

Ireland West Tourism – Aras Fáilte, Victoria Place, Eyre Square, Galway. ☎ 091 563 081; Fax 091 565 201.

Midlands East Tourism – Dublin Road, Mullingar, Co Westmeath. ☎ 044 48761; Fax 044 40413.

North West Tourism – Aras Reddan, Temple Street, Sligo. ☎ 071 61201; Fax 071 60360.

South East Tourism – 41 TheQuay, Waterford. ☎ 051 875 788; Fax 051 877 388. Railway Square, Tramore. ☎ 051 381 572.

Shannon Development – Shannon Town Centre, Shannon, Co Clare. ☎ 061 361 555; Fax 061 361 903.

IRISH EMBASSY

Australia – 20 Arkana Street, Yarraluma, ACT 2600, Australia. ☎ 026 27 33 022; Fax 026 27 33 741.

Belgium – 89/93 RueFroissart, B-1040 Brussels. ☎ (02) 23 05 337; Fax (02) 23 05 360.

Canada – Suite 1105, 130 Albert Street, Ontario, Ottawa KIP SG4. ☎ 613 22 36 281; Fax 613 23 35 835.

Denmark – Østbanegade 21, 2100 Copenhagen. ☎ 031 42 32 33; Fax 035 43 18 58.

Finland – Erottajankatu 7A, PL33, 00130 Helsinki. ☎ (09) 64 60 06; Fax (09) 64 60 22.

France – 12 Avenue Foch, 75116 Paris. ☎ 01 44 17 67 00; Fax 01 44 17 67 60.

Germany – Godesberger Allee 119, 53175 Bonn. ☎ (0228) 95 92 90; Fax (0228) 37 35 00.

Japan – Ireland House 5F, 2-10-7 Kojimachi, Chiyoda-Ku, Tokyo 102. ☎ (03) 32 63 06 95; Fax (03) 32 65 22 75.

Netherlands – Dr Kuyperstraat 9, 2514 BA The Hague. ☎ (070) 36 30 993; Fax (070) 36 17 604.

Portugal – Rua da Imprensa, a Estrela 1-4, 1200 Lisbon. ☎ (01) 39 29 440; Fax (01) 39 77 363.

Spain – Ireland House, Paseo de la Castellana 46-4, 28046 Madrid. ☎ (091) 57 63 500; Fax (091) 43 51 677.

Sweden – Ostermalmsgatan 97, PO Box 10326, 100 55, Stockholm. ☎ 08 66 18 005; Fax 08 66 01 353.

United Kingdom – 17 Grosvenor Place, London SW1X 7HR. ☎ 0171 235 2171; Fax 0171 245 6961.

United States – 2234 Massachusetts Avenue NW, Washington DC 20008. ☎ 202 462 3939; Fax 202 232 5993.

Travelling to and in Ireland

By air – Many international airlines operate flights to the international airports in Ireland – Dublin, Shannon and Belfast. There are also flights from the UK to the regional airports and a shuttle service from Heathrow to Belfast. All airports are linked by bus to the neighbouring towns.

Information, brochures and timetables are available from the airlines and from travel agents. Fly-Drive schemes are operated by most airlines.

British Airways – Telephone the UK sales office on ☎ 0345 222 111 (within the UK) or 00 44 141 222 2345 (from outside the UK). Alternatively, Aer Lingus in Dublin act as a sales agent for British Airways.

Aer Lingus, 40-41 Upper O'Connell Street, Dublin 1; 13 St Stephen's Green, Dublin 2; 12 Upper George's Street, Dun Laoghaire; Jury's Hotel, Ballsbridge; Aer Lingus Ticket Desk, Departures Level, Terminal Building, Dublin Airport. ☎ 01 705 3333.

British Midland, ☎ 0345 554 554 (reservations); 00 44 1332 854 854 (from outside the UK).

By sea – Details of passenger ferry and car ferry services to Ireland from the United Kingdom and France can be obtained from travel agencies or from the main carriers.

Brittany Ferries, ☎ 0990 360 360 (callers within UK); Cork ☎ 021 277 801.

Irish Ferries, Ferryport, Alexandra Road, Dublin 1. ☎ 01 855 2222 (Head Office); 01 661 0511 (reservations, callers within Republic of Ireland); 0990 171 717 (reservations, callers within UK).

Stena Line, Charter House, Park Street, Ashford, Kent, TN 24 8EX.
☎ 0990 707 707, 01232 747 747 (Holyhead-Dun Laoghaire, Fishguard-Rosslaire, Stranraer-Belfast); 0990 980 777 (Cairnryan-Larne).

Seacat, ☎ 0990 523 523 (Stranraer-Larne).

Information about ferries to the offshore islands is given in the Admission times and charges *(see p 374)*.

By rail – Irish Rail Service (Iarnród Éireann), Northern Ireland Railways and British Rail operate train services between the major cities in Ireland and the United Kingdom. Special discount tickets available.

Irish Rover: valid for the whole of Ireland, **rail only**, for five days out of 15 consecutive days, IR£75, IR£37 (child).

Emerald Card: valid for the whole of Ireland, **rail and bus**, for eight days out of 15 consecutive days IR£105, IR£53 (child); for 15 days out of 30 consecutive days, IR£180, IR£90 (child).

Irish Explorer: valid for the Republic of Ireland, **rail and bus**, eight days out of 15 consecutive days, IR£90, IR£45 (child).

Irish Explorer: valid for the Republic of Ireland, **rail only**, for five days out of 15 consecutive days, IR£60, IR£30 (child).

Freedom of Northern Ireland: valid for Northern Ireland, **rail and bus**, seven consecutive days, £35, £17.50 (child).

Student Travelsave, enabling students with an International Student Card to obtain 50% reduction on Irish Rail and 30% reduction on Bus Éireann, available from USIT, 19–21 Aston Quay, Dublin, ☎ 01 679 8833.

Eurorail Pass, **Flexipass** and **Saver Pass** are options available in the US for travel in Europe and must be purchased in the US, ☎ 1-800-4EURAIL, 1-888-BRITRAIL and 1-888-EUROSTAR (automated lines for callers within the US only); www.raileurope.com/us/

Irish Rail, Travel Centre, 35 Lower Abbey Street, Dublin 1, ☎ 01 836 6222.

Irish Rail, Connolly Station, Dublin 1, ☎ 01 836 3333 (enquiries), Fax 01 836 4760.

Irish Rail, Heuston Station, Dublin 8, ☎ 01 677 1871 (enquiries), Fax 01 677 1350.

Irish Rail, Pearse Station, Westland Road, Dublin 2, ☎ 01 703 3634 (booking office).

Irish Rail, Talking timetables:
> 01 855 4400 Dublin to Cork;
> 01 855 4411 Dublin to Limerick;
> 01 855 4422 Dublin to Galway and Westport;
> 01 855 4433 Dublin to Waterford;
> 01 855 4455 Dublin to Sligo;
> 01 855 4466 Dublin to Killarney and Tralee;
> 01 855 4477 Dublin to Belfast;
> 01 855 4488 Dublin to Wexford and Rosslare.

Dublin Area Rapid Transit (DART), ☎ 01 836 6222, Fax 01 703 4690, operates a suburban electric rail service from Dublin north to Howth and south to Bray.

Northern Ireland Rail, Central Station, Belfast 1, ☎ 01232 899 411.

By coach – **Bus Éireann**, **Ulsterbus** and **National Express** operate a regular coach service via the car ferry ports at Rosslare, Dublin Ferryport and Larne between the major Irish towns and the major cities in the UK and on the Continent. Special discount tickets available – Emerald Card, Rambler Ticket and Freedom of Northern Ireland.

Emerald Card: *see above By Rail.*

Irish Explorer: *see above By Rail.*

Freedom of Northern Ireland: *see above By Rail.*

Student Travelsave: *see above By Rail.*

Irish Rambler: valid for the Republic of Ireland, **bus only**, three days out of eight consecutive days, IR£28, IR£14 (child); eight days out of 15 consecutive days, IR£68, IR£34 (child); 15 days out of 30 consecutive days, IR£98, IR£49 (child).

Irish Rover: valid for the whole of Ireland, **bus only**, three days out of eight consecutive days, IR£36, IR£18 (child); eight days out of 15 consecutive days, IR£85, IR£43 (child); 15 days out of 30 consecutive days, IR£130, IR£65 (child).

Bus Éireann	Store Street, Dublin 1. ☎ 01 836 6111. Fax 01 873 4534. Colbert Station, Limerick; Passenger Enquiries – ☎ 061 313 333.
Dublin Bus	59 Upper O'Connell Street, Dublin 1. Customer Services & Enquiries – ☎ 01 873 4222, Fax 01 703 3177. Ticket Sales – ☎ 01 703 3028.
Ulsterbus	Europa Bus Centre, Glengall Street, Belfast BT12 5AH. ☎ 01232 320 011.
Eurolines	52 Grosvenor Gardens, London SW1W 0AU. ☎ 0171 730 8235.

Motoring in Ireland

Documents – Nationals of EU countries require a valid national driving licence; nationals of non-EU countries require an **international driving licence**. This is obtainable in the US from the American Automobile Club for $US10; two passport photos are also required. Alternatively, the international driving licence is available from AAA for $12 (non-members), $6 (basic members), free (plus member). ☎ 800 222 4537).
For the vehicle it is necessary to have the **registration papers** (log-book) and a **nationality plate** of the approved size.

Insurance – Insurance cover is compulsory. Although no longer a legal requirement, the International Insurance Certificate (Green Card) is the most effective proof of insurance cover and is internationally recognized by the police and other authorities.
Certain motoring organizations in Ireland and the UK run accident insurance and breakdown service schemes for members. Members of the American Automobile Club should obtain the brochure *Offices to serve you abroad*.

Automobile Association (AA), Fanum House, Basing View, Basingstoke, Hants, RG21 2EA, ☎ 0990 448 866 (switchboard), 0800 444 999 (joining & membership renewal).

Automobile Association (AA), 23 Suffolk Street, Dublin 2, ☎ 01 283 3555.

Royal Automobile Club (RAC), RAC House, 1 Forest Road, Feltham, TW13 7RR, ☎ 0181 917 2500 (Head Office), ☎ 0990 722 722 (Customer Services).

Royal Automobile Club (RAC), New Mount House, 22–24 Lower Mount Street, Dublin 2, ☎ 01 676 0113.

Europ-Assistance, Sussex House, Perrymount Road, Haywards Heath, West Sussex, RH16 1DN, ☎ 01444 442 442 (Customer Services).

Highway Code – Traffic drives on the **left**. Traffic on main roads and on roundabouts has priority.

Seat belts – It is compulsory for the driver and front-seat passengers to wear **seat belts**. In the Republic children under the age of 12 may travel in the front seat provided they wear seat belts. In Northern Ireland rear-seat belts must be worn where they are fitted; children under 10 must travel in the rear seats.

Lights – Full or dipped headlights should be switched on in poor visibility and at night; use sidelights only when the vehicle is stationary in an area without street lighting.

Breakdown – It is obligatory to carry a red warning triangle or to have hazard warning lights to use in the case of a breakdown or accident.

Penalties – Drivers suspected of **speeding** or **driving while under the influence of alcohol** are liable to prosecution. Parking offences in the Republic may attract an on-the-spot fine.

Speed limits   – Republic of Ireland: 40kph (25mph) in built-up areas
                                        100kph (55mph) elsewhere
             – Northern Ireland: 30mph (48kph) in built-up areas
                                        60mph (96kph) on country roads
                                        70mph (113kph) on dual carriageways and motorways

Parking regulations – There are multi-storey car parks in towns, parking meters, disc systems and paying parking zones; in the last case, tickets must be obtained from the ticket machines (small change necessary) and displayed inside the windscreen; failure to display may result in a fine. In Northern Ireland city centre parking may be restricted.

Route Planning – Michelin Map 923 shows the major roads (N or A) and many of the minor roads (R/L or B) in Ireland.
The only toll roads are the Dublin East-Link (60p), which spans the Liffey estuary, and the West-Link (80p), which runs north–south on the western edge of the city. ☎ 01 668 2888 (East-Link); 01 820 2000 (West-Link).

Car Rental – There are car rental agencies at airports, railway stations and in all large towns throughout Ireland. European cars usually have manual transmission but automatic cars are available on request. An **international driving licence** is required for non-EU nationals.
Before crossing the border between the Republic and Northern Ireland it is important to check that the insurance cover extends to the other country. It is cheaper to return a hire car to its pick-up point than to leave it elsewhere.

Accommodation

The Touring Programmes Map on pp 7-9 indicates places to stay overnight and seaside resorts.
The **Michelin Red Guide Great Britain and Ireland** provides a selection of hotels, guesthouses and restaurants.
The Irish Tourist Board (Bord Fáilte) publishes several booklets:
    Be Our Guest Guide, which gives a comprehensive listing of all approved hotels and guesthouses in Ireland;
    Ireland's Blue Book of country houses and restaurants;
    The Hidden Ireland, listing accommodation in private heritage houses;
    Friendly Homes of Ireland, listing family homes and small hotels.
The Northern Irish Tourist Board (NITB) publishes *Where to stay* (£3.99).
An **accommodation booking service** is operated by Irish Regional Tourism Organizations and by Tourist Information Centres; a small fee is charged for the service and a proportion of the price is paid direct to the booking service and the balance to the proprietor. The following telephone numbers are for credit card reservations in Dublin:
    ☎ 00800 668 668 66 (from UK, Ireland, France, Germany, Italy, Sweden, Norway);
    ☎ 011 800 668 668 66 (from USA);
    ☎ 066 92082 (from other countries);
    e-mail reservations@dublintourism.ie (reservations).
Information on **self-catering holiday homes** to rent is available from Dublin Tourism and the NITB *(addresses above)*.
Information about **farmhouse** holidays is presented in one booklet:
    Irish Farm Holidays, 2 Michael Street, Co Limerick, ☎ 061 400 700, Fax 061 400 771.

Low-Budget Accommodation – There are 50 **youth hostels** in the Republic and six in Northern Ireland. Package holidays are available comprising youth hostel vouchers, rail and bus pass or hostel vouchers, return rail fare and cycle hire:
    An Oige, 61 Mountjoy Street, Dublin 7, ☎ 01 830 4555, Fax 01 830 5808.
    Hostelling International Northern Ireland, 22 Donegal Road, Belfast BT12 5JN, ☎ 01232 324 733, Fax 01232 439 699.
Simple accommodation is available in single, twin and 4/6-bedded rooms at the following addresses:
    Kinlay House, 2-12 Lord Edward Street, **Dublin 2**, ☎ 01 679 6644, Fax 01 679 7437;
    Kinlay House, Shandon, Bob & Joan Walk, **Cork**, ☎ 021 508 966, Fax 021 506 927;
    Kinlay House, Merchants Road, **Galway**, ☎ 091 565 244, Fax 091 565 245;
    Harding Hotel in Temple Bar in Dublin (Fishamble Street, Christchurch, **Dublin 2**, ☎ 01 679 6500, Fax 01 679 6504).
Accommodation in **universities** – single rooms and self-catering apartments – is available during the vacations:
    Usit Accommodation Centres, Merville Reception, c/o UCD Village, Belfield, Dublin 4, ☎ 01 706 1071, Fax 01 269 1129;

MUSA, c/o Accommodation Office, Trinity College, Dublin 2, ☎ 01 608 1177, Fax 01 671 1267.

Camping – Ireland has many officially-graded caravan and camping parks with modern facilities and a variety of additional sports facilities. A brochure (IR£2), which covers the whole country, is available:

Irish Caravan & Camping Council, PO Box 4443, Dublin 2; or request brochures by Fax 098 28237.

Where to Stay, published by the NITB (£3.99), lists camping and caravan parks in Northern Ireland only.

Horse-drawn Caravans, Co Kerry

Slide file, Dublin

General information

Time – In winter standard time throughout Ireland is Greenwich Mean Time (GMT). In summer (mid March to October) clocks are advanced by one hour to give British Summer Time (BST) which is the same as Central European Time.
Time may be expressed according to the 24-hour clock or the 12-hour clock:

12.00	12 noon	19.00	7pm
13.00	1pm	20.00	8pm
14.00	2pm	21.00	9pm
15.00	3pm	22.00	10pm
16.00	4pm	23.00	11pm
17.00	5pm	24.00	12 midnight
18.00	6pm		

Public holidays – For specific dates see Admission Times and Charges – *p 374*.
On public holidays shops, museums and other monuments may be closed or may vary their hours of admission. In the Republic national museums and art galleries are usually closed on Mondays. In addition to the usual school holidays at Christmas and in the spring and summer, there are mid-term breaks at Hallowe'en and round St Patrick's Day (17 March).

Medical treatment – Visitors from EU countries should apply to their own National Social Security Offices for **Form E111** (not obligatory for UK nationals; proof of identity only necessary) which entitles them to medical treatment under an EU Reciprocal Medical Treatment arrangement, provided treatment is sought from a doctor in Ireland whose name is on the Health Board Panel of Doctors (list available from the local health board).
Nationals of non-EU countries should take out comprehensive insurance. American Express offers a service, *Global Assist*, which makes funds available for any medical, legal or personal emergency – call collect from anywhere ☎ 312-935-3600.

Currency – The currency is the *punt* (IR£1 = 100 pence) in the Republic of Ireland and Sterling (£1 = 100 pence) in Northern Ireland.
There is no limit on the amount of currency visitors can import into the Republic of Ireland; as there is a limit on the amount that may be exported in Irish currency and in foreign bank notes, non-residents are advised to complete a currency declaration form on arrival.

Banking – Banks are open Mondays to Fridays (except public holidays), 10am-12.30pm and 1.30-3pm (3.30pm in Northern Ireland).
Exchange facilities outside these hours are available at Belfast, Dublin, Shannon, Connaught and Cork Airports, in some tourist information centres *(see p 374)*, travel agencies and hotels.
Some form of identification is necessary when cashing travellers cheques or Eurocheques in banks. Commission charges vary; hotels usually charge more than banks.

Credit Cards – The major credit cards – American Express, Visa/Barclaycard (Carte Bleue), Eurocard (Mastercard/Access) and Diners Club – are widely accepted in shops, hotels, restaurants and petrol stations.

Post – Irish postage stamps must be used in the Republic, British stamps in Northern Ireland; they are available from Post Offices and some shops (newsagents, tobacconists etc).

In the Republic post offices are open Mondays to Saturdays, 8am–5.30pm or 6pm; they are closed on Sundays and public holidays and for 1hr 15min at lunchtime; sub-post offices usually close at 1pm one day a week. In Northern Ireland post offices are open Mondays to Fridays, 9am–5.30pm, and Saturdays, 9am–12.30pm; sub-post offices close at 1pm on Wednesdays.

Telephone – In an **emergency** phone **999** – fire, police, ambulance, lifeboats, coastal, mountain and cave rescue.

Pre-paid callcards for internal and international calls from public phones are available from Post Offices and some shops (newsagents, tobacconists etc).

It is usually more expensive to make a long-distance telephone call from a hotel than from a telephone box.

353	International Code for the Republic of Ireland
44	International Code for Northern Ireland

The zero at the beginning of the area codes should be omitted when dialling from outside either country.

Electricity – The electric current is 230 volts AC (50 hertz); 3-pin flat or 2-pin round wall sockets are standard.

EMBASSIES

Australia	Fitzwilton House (2nd floor), Wilton Terrace, Dublin 2. ☎ 01 676 1517, Fax 01 678 5185.
Canada	Canada House, 65 St Stephen's Green, Dublin 2. ☎ 01 478 1988, Fax 01 478 1285.
UK	29 Merrion Road, Dublin 4. ☎ 01 269 5211, Fax 01 205 3885.
USA	42 Elgin Road, Ballsbridge, Dublin 4. ☎ 01 668 8777, Fax 01 668 9946.

Shopping and crafts

Opening times – Shops in the major cities are open Mondays to Saturdays, 9am–5.30pm (8pm Thursdays). Elsewhere there is all-day or early closing on Mondays or Wednesdays or Thursdays. Some shops may open later and may close for an hour at lunchtime.

Derek Robinson, Belfast

Belleek pottery

Craft shops – Shops selling souvenirs and craftwork are to be found in some tourist information centres, visitor centres and heritage centres and at many tourist sights.

Manufacturers of textiles, glass and porcelain usually offer a tour of the factory and showrooms and shops on the premises; their goods are often available in department stores or specialist shops in the major towns. The Tourist Information Centre in Banbridge organizes the *Linen Homelands Tour* which visits various linen manufacturers as well as the Lisburn Museum *(see p 325)*.

Many craft studios and craft villages (pottery, weaving, lace, jewellery) are open to visitors in summer.

Demonstrations of obsolete crafts take place in some Folk Museums and Folk Villages.

See also p 63.

Craft Shops	Craftworks, Bedford Street, **Belfast**, Co Antrim
	Coppermoon, Fisherwick Place, **Belfast**, Co Antrim
	The Wickerman, 14 Donegal Arcade, Castle Place, **Belfast**
	Shandon Crafts Centre, **Cork**, Co Cork
	Boland, **Kinsale**, Co Cork
	Whitethorn Crafts, **Ballyvaughan**, Co Clare
	Doolin Crafts Gallery, **Doolin**, Co Clare
	Kenny Woollen Mills, Main Street, **Lahinch**, Co Clare
	Lurgy Vale, **Kilmacrenan**, Co Donegal
	Crafts Council Retail Gallery, Powerscourt Centre, **Dublin 2**
	DESIGNyard, Temple Bar, **Dublin 2**
	Kilkenny Shop, Nassau Street, **Dublin 2**
	National Museum Shop, Kildare Street, **Dublin 2**
	National Museum Shop, Benburb Street, **Dublin 7**
	Cleo Ltd, 18 Kildare Street, **Dublin 2**
	Buttermarket, Down Street, **Enniskillen**, Co Fermanagh
	Caerdlann na Coille, **Dingle**, Co Kerry
	Muckross House, **Killarney**, Co Kerry
	Kilkenny Design Centre, **Kilkenny**, Co Kilkenny
	Londonderry Craft Village, **Londonderry**, Co Londonderry
	O'Reilly & Turpin, 1 Upper Bridge Street, **Westport**, Co Mayo
	The Cat & the Moon, 4 Castle Street, **Sligo**, Co Sligo
	Belvedere, **Mullingar**, Co Westmeath
Craft Villages	**Donegal Town**, Co Donegal
	Roundstone, Co Galway
	Blennerville, Tralee, Co Kerry
Demonstrations	Arthur Cottage, **Cullybackey**, Co Antrim
	Ulster Folk and Transport Museum, **Cultra**, Co Down
	Muckross House and Farms, **Killarney**, Co Kerry
	Ulster-American Folk Park, **Camphill**, Omagh, Co Tyrone
Basketry	Basket weaving, **Mount Nugent**, Co Cavan
Bookbinding	Muckross House, **Killarney**, Co Kerry
Carpets	**Killybegs**, Co Donegal
Ceramics	Stephen Pearse Pottery, **Midleton**, Co Cork
	Keane on Ceramics, Pier Road, **Kinsale**, Co Cork
	Donegal Parian China, **Ballyshannon**, Co Donegal
	Cavanacor House, **Ballindrait**, Lifford, Co Donegal
	Belleek Pottery, **Belleek**, Co Fermanagh
	Kylemore Abbey Craft Shop, **Kylemore Abbey**, Co Galway
	Muckross House, **Killarney**, Co Kerry
	Irish Dresden, **Dromcolliher**, Co Limerick
	Ardmore Pottery Shop, **Ardmore**, Co Waterford
Glass	Cavan Crystal, **Cavan**, Co Cavan
	Kerry Glass Studio, **Killarney**, Co Kerry
	Newgrange Crystal, **Newgrange**, Boyne Valley, Co Meath
	Sligo Crystal, **Grange**, Co Sligo
	Tipperary Crystal, **Clonmel**, Co Tipperary
	Tyrone Crystal, **Dungannon**, Co Tyrone
	Waterford Crystal, **Waterford**, Co Waterford
Jewellery	Angles, 10 Westbury Centre, Harry Street, **Dublin 2**
Lace	**Kenmare**, Co Kerry
	Limerick, Co Limerick
	Carrickmacross, Co Louth
	Clones, Co Monaghan
Linen	Wellbrook Beetling Mill, **Corkhill**, Cookstown, Co Tyrone
Metalwork	Mullingar Bronze and Pewter, **Mullingar**, Co Westmeath
Musical Instruments	Roundstone Musical Instruments, **Roundstone**, Co Galway
Tweed	Blarney Woollen Mills, **Blarney**, Co Cork
	Foxford Woollen Mills, **Foxford**, Co Mayo
	Kilcar, Co Donegal
	Ardara, Co Donegal
	Downies, Co Donegal
	Kerry Woollen Mills, **Killarney**, Co Kerry
	Avoca Weavers, **Avoca**, Wicklow Mountains, Co Wicklow
	Avoca Weavers, **Kilmacanogue**, Co Wicklow
	Avoca Weavers, **Bunratty**, Co Clare
	Avoca Weavers, **Moll's Gap**, Killarney, Co Kerry *(summer)*
	Avoca Weavers, **Kenmare**, Co Kerry *(summer)*
	Muckross House, **Killarney**, Co Kerry

Entertainment

Theatres – In Dublin modern and classic plays are performed at the **Abbey Theatre** (Abbey Street, ☎ 01 878 7222) and the **Gate Theatre** (Parnell Square East, ☎ 01 874 4045). The **Olympia Theatre** (72 Dame Street, ☎ 01 677 7744) offers more popular performances such as musicals.

The performances of the **National Folk Theatre of Ireland** (*Siamsa Tíre*, ☎ 066 23055, Fax 066 27276) in Tralee draw on the local Gaelic tradition to evoke the traditional seasonal festivals and rural way of life in music, song, dance and mime. The Irish Theatre (**Taibhearc na Gaillimhe**, ☎ 091 562 024) in Galway is a state-sponsored body. In Limerick the **Belltable Arts Centre**, ☎ 061 319 866, hosts various theatre productions, and the **Theatre Royal**, Upper Cecil Street, ☎ 061 414 224, is a popular venue for various forms of entertainment.

Music – In Dublin the **National Concert Hall** (Earlsfort Terrace) has a regular programme of classical and modern orchestral music. Smaller venues offering more specialized music, such as jazz, blues etc, are to be found in Temple Bar (Temple Bar Information Centre, Eustace Street, ☎ 01 671 5717).

In Belfast the **Waterfront Hall** offers a varied programme of events, ☎ 01232 334 455.

Wexford Festival Opera *(late October)* has an international reputation.

Castleward Opera *(June)* is an opera festival, details available from ☎ 01232 661 090 (Mrs H Logan).

Concerts of **chamber music** *(summer)* are given by Irish and international musicians in some of the great Irish houses; details available from Ms Judith Woodworth, ☎ 01 475 1666 (National Concert Hall).

Traditional Music – In recent years traditional music has grown in importance. This sort of music is played at sessions in pubs, at a gathering known as a *céile* and at the weekly and monthly sessions held in the local branches of the national **cultural organization** – Comhaltas Ceoltóirí Éireann, Cultúrlann na hÉireann, 32 Belgrave Square, Monkstown, Co Dublin, ☎ 01 280 0295. Information also available from Tourist Information Centres. For the formal festivals and competitions *(see p 370)*.

The most popular instruments are the violin – called the fiddle by traditional musicians – the flute, the goatskin drum *(bodhrán)* and the free-reed instruments such as the accordion, melodeon and concertina; and also more recently the guitar and banjo. The harp is now rarely played but there are two O'Carolan Harp Festivals in Keadew *(July–Aug)* and Nobber *(October)*.

Dancing – The most popular form of dance is "set dancing" which dates from the 18C and is, for the most part, an adaptation of military dances to existing tunes such as jigs, reels, hornpipes and polkas. Individual old-style *(sean-nós)* dancing is also a feature of Irish traditional music.

Traditional dancing - Group of three

Slide File, Dublin

Evening Entertainment – Evening entertainment in the form of various combinations of dinner and music is provided at several venues:

Medieval banquet and music – Knappogue Castle, ☎ 061 360 788 (Shannon Heritage and Banquets);

Medieval banquet and music – Bunratty Castle, ☎ 061 360 788 (Shannon Heritage and Banquets);

Medieval banquet accompanied by extracts from the writings of Synge, Yeats and Go-garty – Dunguaire Castle, ☎ 061 360 788 (Shannon Heritage and Banquets);

Feasting and music – Killarney Manor, Loreto Road, Killarney, Co Kerry, ☎ 064 31551, Fax 064 333 66.

Cultural Festivals – Ireland hosts a number of literary and musical festivals in honour of individual artists or groups of artists *(see p 370)*.

Tracing ancestors

The organizations listed below can assist in tracing Irish ancestors.

Republic of Ireland

Co Cavan	**Cavan Genealogical Centre**, Tourist Information Office, Farnham Street, Cavan, Co Cavan; ☎ 049 61094.
Co Clare	**Clare Heritage Centre**, Corrofin, Co Clare – ♿ Open mid Mar–Oct, daily, 10am–6pm; otherwise, Mon–Fri, 9am–5pm. £2. ☎ 065 37955. Parking. Tearoom. – Extensive genealogical records making it possible to trace people who emigrated from Clare in the last century; in the aftermath of the Great Famine between 1851 and 1871 at least 100 000 people left the region.
Co Cork	**Cork Archives Institute**, Cork, Co Cork – Copious material consisting of family and private papers, some of potential genealogical interest, and chiefly of historical records relating to business, local government and trade union activities.
Co Donegal	**Donegal Genealogical Centre**, Lifford Old Courthouse, Main Square, Lifford, Co Donegal.
	Rathmelton Family History Research Centre, Rathmelton, Co Donegal – Open all year, Mon–Fri, 9am–4.30pm, ☎ 074 38124 (Caretaker).
Co Dublin	**National Library of Ireland**, Kildare Street, Dublin 2; ☎ 01 661 8811 – No postal queries.
	General Register Office, Births, Deaths and Marriages, Joyce House, 8ñ11 Lombard Street East, Dublin 2; ☎ 01 671 1000.
	Hibernian Research Co Ltd, P O Box 3097, Dublin 6; ☎ 01 496 6522 (24hr), Fax 01 497 3011.
	National Archives, Bishop Street, Dublin 8; ☎ 01 478 3711.
Co Leitrim	**Leitrim Heritage Centre**, County Library, Ballinamore, Co Leitrim – Open Mon–Fri, 10am–1pm and 2–5pm. ☎ 078 44012; Fax 078 44425.
Co Limerick	**Irish Palatine Heritage Centre**, Rathkeale, Co Limerick – Genealogical service for tracing Palatine ancestors.
Co Monaghan	**Roslea Heritage Centre**, Monaghan Road, Roslea, Monaghan – Open Apr–Sept, Mon–Fri, 9am–5pm, weekends by appointment; Oct–Mar, Mon–Fri, 9am–5pm. £1, 50p (child), ☎ 013657 51750.
Co Offaly and Co Laois	**Offaly and Laois Historical and Archeological Society**, Tullamore, Co Offaly – Open Mon–Fri, 9am–1pm and 2–4pm. **Public Reading Room:** Open 10am–4pm.
Co Roscommon	**Roscommon County Heritage Centre**, Strokestown, Co Roscommon – Genealogical research service.
Co Tipperary	**Genealogical Service**, Old Gaol, Tipperary; Clans Office, James Street, Tipperary.
	Brú Ború Cultural Centre, Cashel, Co Tipperary – Genealogy and Celtic Studies Centre.
	North Tipperary Genealogical Service, Nenagh District Heritage Centre, Nenagh, Co Tipperary – Open daily except bank holidays, 10am–4pm; closed at lunchtime, ☎ 067 33850; Fax 067 33586.
	Roscrea Heritage Centre, Damer House, Roscrea, Co Tipperary – Computerized genealogical service.
Co Waterford	**Genealogy Office**, St Patrick's Church, Jenkin's Lane, Waterford.
Co Westmeath	**Dún na Sí** (Fairy Fort), Moate, Co Westmeath – Genealogy Research Centre for Co Westmeath.
Co Wicklow	**Genealogical Research Unit**, Wicklow County Heritage Centre, Wicklow, Co Wicklow.

365

Armagh   **Genealogical Research Centre**, St Patrick's Trian, Armagh.

Armagh Ancestry, 42 English Street, Armagh, BT61 7BA – Open all year, Mon–Sat, ☎ 01861 527 808; Fax 01861 528 329.

Clan Gatherings

There are 243 Irish clans which hold annual **clan gatherings** on ancestral sites; information available from Clans of Ireland, Dr Margaret Tierney, Grange Clare, Kilmeague, Neath, Co Kildare.

Co Tyrone **Genealogical Research Centre**, Heritage World, Main Street, Dungannon, Co Tyrone – Extensive computerized archives enabling people to discover the path to their Irish roots.

Recreation

Ireland is naturally well-endowed to provide many different physical environments for outdoor **sports and leisure activities**. The long and indented coastline provides facilities for deep-sea fishing, angling, sailing, wind-surfing, scuba-diving and bathing. The many inland lakes and waterways attract anglers and are good for cruising, canoeing and water-skiing. For golfers there are both inland and links courses. The magnificent mountain ranges which fringe the Atlantic coast from north to south provide exhilarating locations for walking, rambling, orienteering and mountaineering. Hunting and horse racing are concentrated in the flatter, agricultural counties of the south and midlands; pony trekking is country-wide.

Information on all the activities listed below is available from the Irish Tourist Board (Bord Fáilte) and the Northern Irish Tourist Board (NITB).

Crafts – *See Crafts and Shopping p 362.*

Cruising – *Cruising Ireland*, published by the Irish Tourist Board, provides information on hiring cruisers on rivers, lakes and canals, holiday cruises and short pleasure cruises on the Shannon, barge or waterbus cruises and cruising restaurants. It is recommended that boat operators be members of the Irish Boat Rental Association (IBRA).

The Inland Waterways Association publishes a guide to the *Grand Canal*. Canal boat trips in summer are available from Robertstown *(see p 192)*. Details of annual waterway rallies and festivals are also available from Tourist Information Centres. The main waterways for cruising are the River Shannon, the Shannon-Erne Waterway and Lough Erne; canal barges are more suited to the River Barrow, the Grand Canal and the River Shannon.

Skelan Lock, Shannon-Erne Waterway

Department of Arts, Culture & Gaeltacht, Ireland

Corraquill Cruising Holidays Ireland, Derrylin, Co Fermanagh, ☏ 013657 48712; Fax 013657 48493.

Riversdale Barge Holidays, Ballinamore, Co Leitrim, ☏ 078 44122; Fax 078 44813.

Canalways Ireland Barge Holidays, Spencer Bridge, Rathangan, Co Kildare, ☏ 045 52 46 46; Fax 52 40 19.

Celtic Canal Cruisers Ltd, Tullamore, Co Offaly, ☏ 0506 21861; Fax 0506 51266.

Cycling – *Cycling*, a brochure published by the Irish Tourist Board, suggests several routes. Airlines, ferry companies and the rail network will transport accompanied bicycles. Facilities for cycle hire throughout Ireland are provided by the firms listed below; a list of shops hiring cycles in Northern Ireland is available from the NITB.

Raleigh Rent-a-Bike Division, Raleigh Ireland Limited, PO Box 3520, Raleigh House, Kylemore Road, Dublin 10, ☏ 01 626 1333, Fax 01 626 1770;

The Bike Store, 58 Lower Gardiner Street, Dublin 1, ☏ 01 872 5399, Fax 01 874 4247;

Irish Cycle Hire Ltd, Mayoralty Street, Drogheda, Co Louth, ☏ 041 41067, ☏/Fax 041 35369.

Fishing – The Irish Tourist Board publishes three brochures on *Game Angling*, *Sea Angling* and *Coarse Fishing*, which provide information on the seasons, fisheries, price of licences and permits, dates of festivals and accommodation. Detailed information is available from the Fisheries Board:

Central Fisheries Board, Mobhi Boreen, Glasnevin, Dublin 9, ☏ 01 837 9206.

Game fishing permits and licences in Northern Ireland are available from local tackle shops and from the fishery authorities:

Fisheries Conservancy Board for Northern Ireland, 1 Mahon Road, Portadown, BT62 3EE, ☏ 01762 334 666;

Foyle Fisheries Commission, 8 Victoria Road, Londonderry, BT47 2AB, ☏ 01504 342 100.

Slide file, Dublin

Castleconnell, Co Limerick

Gliding – Paragliding and hang-gliding are both organized by the same body:

Irish Hang-Gliding Association, House of Sport, Long Mile Road, Dublin 12, ☏ 01 450 9845, Fax 01 450 2805.

Golf – The Irish Tourist Board publishes *Golfing*, a brochure identifying a selection of golf courses, both links and parkland, and *Land of Golf* for courses in Galway, Mayo and Roscommon. The NITB publishes a leaflet listing the 80 golf courses in Northern Ireland.

Horse-Drawn Caravans – This is a leisurely way of exploring the Irish country roads:

Slattery's Horse-drawn Caravans, 1 Russell Street, Tralee, Co Kerry, ☏ 066 26277, Fax 066 25981.

Horse Racing – Racecourses are common in almost every part of Ireland. The most well known in the Dublin area are The Curragh, Punchestown, Leopardstown and Fairyhouse.
The particularly popular festivals are **Fairyhouse** *(Easter)*, **Killarney** *(May)*, **Curragh** *(June)*, **Killarney** *(July)*, **Galway**, **Tramore** and **Tralee** *(August)*, **Galway** and **Listowel** *(September)* and **Leopardstown** and **Limerick** *(December)*.

Golf in Co Kerry

Hunting – *Equestrian Ireland*, published by the Irish Tourist Board, lists all the hunts (fox hunting, stag hunting and harriers) in the Republic of Ireland.

Mountaineering – Information on mountaineering, rock climbing and orienteering is available from the following organizations:

Tollymore Mountain Centre, Bryansford, Newcastle, ☎ 013967 22158.

Sports Council for Northern Ireland, House of Sport, 2A Upper Malone Road, Belfast BT9 5LA, ☎ 01232 381 222.

Nature Reserves – Ireland has four **national parks** in the Republic, numerous **nature reserves** (wildfowl sanctuaries, peat bogs and sand dunes) and many **forest parks** managed for public use and recreation:

Irish Peatland Conservation Council, Capel Chambers, 119 Capel Street, Dublin 1, ☎ 01 872 2397;

Birdwatch Ireland, Ruttledge House, 8 Longford Place, Monkstown, Co Dublin, ☎ 01 280 4322;

Royal Society for Protection of Birds, Belvoir Park Forest, Belfast BT8 4QT, ☎ 01232 491 547;

The Wildlife Service (Dúchas), 51 St Stephen's Green, Dublin 2, ☎ 01 661 3111;

Environment & Heritage Service, Natural Heritage, Commonwealth House, 35 Castle Street, Belfast BT1 1GH, ☎ 01232 251 477.

National Hunt Racing

Parachuting – Information is available from the major association and from two clubs:

Parachute Association of Ireland, AFAS, House of Sport, Longmile Road, Dublin 12, ☎ 01 450 9845;

Falcons Parachute Club, Kilrush Airfield, Nr Kilcullen, Co Kildare, ☎ 045 897 991;

Irish Parachute Club, Clonbullogue, Co Offaly, ☎ 0405 31608 (Fergus McDonnell, weekdays), 0405 30103 (weekends).

Rambling – *See Walking below.*

Riding and Pony Trekking – *Equestrian Ireland*, published by the Irish Tourist Board, provides information on trail riding, based trails, residential centres, horse riding holidays based on hotels.

Association of Irish Riding Establishments (AIRE), 11 Moore Park, Droichead Nua, Newbridge, Co Kildare, ☎ 045 431 584, Fax 045 435 103.

Sailing – There are sailing marinas all round the coast of Ireland and on the inland lakes. *Sailing Ireland*, published by the Irish Tourist Board, gives information on **yacht chartering** and **offshore racing** which attracts international teams. All yacht clubs are linked to the Irish Sailing Association:

Irish Sailing Association, 3 Park Road, Dun Laoghaire, Co Dublin, ☎ 01 280 0239.

Scenic Routes – A number of scenic routes *(Slí)* have been signposted by the local Tourist Boards.

Shooting – Permits and walk-up shooting are available on application to the Forest Conservation Officer in Northern Ireland:

Forest Environment Branch, Room 34, Dundonald House, Upper Newtownards Road, Belfast BT4 3SB, ☎ 01232 524 949, Fax 01232 524 570.

Surfing – The best conditions are to be found on the northwest and the mid-west coasts; good conditions prevail on the north, the southwest and the south coast; the east coast is reasonable only during a storm or strong southerly winds. Surfboards are available for hire.

Rossnowlagh Surf Club, Rossnowlagh, Co Donegal;

County Sligo Surf Club, Strandhill, Co Sligo;

Surf Centre, Easkey House, Easkey, Sligo, ☎ 096 49428, Fax 096 49020.

Walking – *Walking Ireland* gives details of the **national waymarked ways** in the Republic of Ireland; detailed information sheets for individual long-distance walks are available. Waymarked ways are for walking only and are unsuitable for horses and mountain bikes; large groups are also undesirable; dogs should not be brought on ways which cross farmland; any dog seen chasing domestic animals is likely to be shot.

Department of Tourism, Sport & Recreation, Frederick Buildings, South Frederick Street, Dublin, ☎ 01 662 1444, Fax 01 679 9285;

Sports Council for Northern Ireland, House of Sport, 2A Upper Malone Road, Belfast BT9 5LA, ☎ 01232 381 222;

East–West Mapping, Ballyredmond, Clonegal, Enniscorthy, Co Wexford, ☎/Fax 054 77835; e-mail eastwest@tinet.ie
www.homepage.tinet.ie/~eastwest

Water-Skiing – Information available from the Irish Water-Ski Federation:

President of Irish Water-Ski Federation, 59 Broadford Drive, Ballinteer, Dublin 16, ☎ 01 494 2449, e-mail C owen@hotmail.com

Windsurfing – Some of the most popular places for windsurfing/sailboarding/boardsailing are in northwest Ireland on the coast of Co Mayo at **Easky**, where the Tiki Cold Water Classic was held in 1997, and on the coast of Co Donegal at **Bundoran**, where the European championships attract many nationalities.

Oysterhaven Boardsailing Centre, Kinsale, Co Cork, ☎ 021 770 738;

Wind and Wave Windsurfing School, Monkstown, Co Dublin, ☎ 01 284 4177.

*The **Michelin Green Guide** Rome (French and English editions)*
proposes many walks in the Eternal City visiting:
  – the best-known sights
  – the districts steeped in 3 000 years of history
  – the art treasures in the museums and galleries

Calendar of events

Marching Band, Inishowen, Co Donegal

SLIDE FILE

Galway .... Oyster Festival – worldwide participation in competitions for opening oysters, held in the pubs

Mid–Late September

Listowel .... Horse Racing

September–October

Waterford..................................... Waterford International Festival of Light Opera

Early October

Kinsale .... Gourmet Festival

Ballinasloe 923 – H 8.................. Great October Fair – for buying and selling horses

Larne .... Mounthill Fair – horse fair dating from the 17C

October

Nobber .... O'Carolan Harp and Cultural Festival – harp and instrumental workshops and competitions, traditional Irish concerts, step and set dancing, traditional festival Mass in Irish *(see p 377)*

Mid–end October

Wexford .... Opera Festival

End October–November

Belfast .... Belfast Festival at Queen's – music from classical to folk and jazz, together with drama, ballet and cinema

November

Londonderry and Belfast .... Foyle Film Festival

Further reading

Titles which are out of print may be obtained through public libraries in the United Kingdom.

Art

The Architecture of Ireland from the Earliest Times to 1880 by Maurice Craig (Batsford 1982)

Irish Art and Architecture by Peter Harbison, Homan Potterton, Jeanne Sheehy (Thames & Hudson 1978)

The Irish Country House by Peter Somerville-Large (Sinclair-Stevenson 1995)

A Guide to Irish Country Houses by Mark Bence-Jones (1988)

The Painters of Ireland by Anne Crookshank and the Knight of Glin (1978/9)

Exploring the Book of Kells by George Otto Simms (1988)

History

Brendan the Navigator by George Otto Simms (O'Brien Press)

The Celts edited by Joseph Raftery (The Mercier Press, Dublin 1988)

An Introduction to Celtic Christianity by James P Mackey (T & T Clark, Ltd, Edinburgh 1989)

Ancient Ireland by Jacqueline O'Brien and Peter Harbison

Ireland in Early Medieval Europe edited by Dorothy Whitelock, Rosamund McKitterick, David Dumville (Cambridge University Press 1982)

The Peoples of Ireland by Liam de Paor (Hutchinson 1986)

Huguenot Settlements in Ireland by GI Lee(Longman Green & Co 1936)

The Oxford History of Ireland by RF Foster – ISBN 0-19-285271

The Making of Modern Ireland 1603–1923 by JC Beckett (Faber & Faber 1966)

Citizen Lord by Stella Tillyard (Chatto & Windus) – ISBN 0-7011-6538-3

The Great Hunger by Cecil Woodham-Smith (Penguin Books 1988)

The Identity of Ulster by Ian Adamson (Pretani Press 1982)

Twilight of the Ascendancy by Mark Bence-Jones (1987)

Geography

Geology and Scenery in Ireland by JB Whittow (Penguin Books 1974)

The Book of the Irish Countryside edited by Frank Mitchell (Blackstaff Press 1987)

Reading the Irish Landscape by Frank Mitchell

The Shannon Floodlands – A Natural History by Stephen Heeny, (Tir Eolas – Newtownlynch, Kinvara, Co Galway 1993) – ISBN 1-873821-026

Mythology

A Guide to Irish Mythology by Daragh Smyth (Irish Academic Press)

Fairy and Folk Tales of Ireland by WB Yeats (Colin Smythe 1973)

Novels

Castle Rackrent by Maria Edgeworth (1800)

The Macdermots of Ballycloran, The Kellys and the O'Kellys, Castle Richmond and *The Landleaguers* by Anthony Trollope (1847, 1848, 1860, 1883)

Experiences of an Irish RM by E Somerville and M Ross (1899)

The Playboy of the Western World by JM Synge (1907)

A Portrait of the Artist as a Young Man by James Joyce (1916, 1960)

Ulysses by James Joyce (1922)

The Last September by Elizabeth Bowen (1929)

Troubles by JG Farrell (Fontana 1970) – ISBN 0-000-654046-5

Good Behaviour by Molly Keane (1981, 1988)

Hungry Hill by Daphne du Maurier (1983)

Autobiography

Twenty Years A-Growing by Maurice O'Sullivan (1953, 1992)

Wheels within Wheels by Dervla Murphy (1981)

Woodbrook by David Thomson (1988)

Angela's Ashes by Frank McCourt (1997)

Recipes

Simply Delicious Recipes by Darina Allen (1989, 1992)

The Irish Food Guide by Sally and John McKenna (Anna Livia, Dublin)

Admission times and charges

As admission times and charges are liable to alteration, the information printed below – valid for 1998 – is for guidance only.

◷ – Every sight for which times and charges are listed below is indicated by the symbol ◷ after the title in the Sights section of the guide.

Order – The information is listed in the same order as in the Sights section of the guide.

Dates – Dates given are inclusive. The term holidays means bank and public holidays; the term Sat–Sun means Sat and Sun.

Last admission – Ticket offices usually shut 30min before closing time; only exceptions are mentioned below. Some places issue timed tickets owing to limited space and facilities.

Charge – The charge given is for an individual adult. Reductions may be available for families, children, students, senior citizens (old-age pensioners) and the unemployed. Large parties should apply in advance, as many places offer special rates for group bookings and some have special days for group visits.

Prices – Prices are given in Irish punts in the Republic of Ireland and in Sterling in Northern Ireland.

Foreign languages – English is also available where other languages are mentioned.

Abbreviations – Dúchas = Department of Arts, Heritage, Gaeltacht and the Islands (formerly OPW = Office of Public Works); HM = Historic Monuments Branch of the Department of the Environment in Northern Ireland; NT = National Trust. Dúchas issues a Heritage Card, valid for one year and available from most Dúchas sites, which provides free admission to all Dúchas sites; £15, £6 (child/student), £10 (senior citizen).

Facilities for the disabled – ♿ means full access for wheelchairs; (♿) means limited access for wheelchairs. As the range of possible facilities is great (for impaired mobility, sight and hearing), readers are advised to telephone in advance to check what is available.

Churches – Many Church of Ireland (Anglican) and Presbyterian churches are locked when not in use for services.

Tourist Information Centres – The addresses and telephone numbers are given for the local Tourist Information Centres, which provide information on local market days, early closing days etc.

Public and bank holidays – On public holidays shops, museums and other monuments may be closed or may vary their times of admission. In the Republic national museums and art galleries are usually closed on Mon. In addition to the usual school holidays at Christmas and in the spring and summer, there are mid-term breaks at Hallowe'en and around St Patrick's Day (17 Mar).

> 1 Jan
> 17 Mar (St Patrick's Day) (Republic only)
> Monday nearest 17 March (Northern Ireland only)
> Good Friday (Republic only)
> Easter Monday
> Monday nearest 1 May (Northern Ireland only)
> Last Monday in May (Northern Ireland only)
> First Monday in June (Republic only)
> 12 July (Northern Ireland only)
> First Monday in Aug (Republic only)
> Last Monday in Aug (Northern Ireland only)
> Last Monday in Oct (Republic only)
> 25 Dec
> 26 Dec (St Stephen's Day/Boxing Day)

REPUBLIC OF IRELAND

A

ACHILL
🅱 ☎ 098 45384 (June–Aug)

ADARE
🅱 Heritage Centre ☎ 061 396 255 (Mar–Dec)

Adare Heritage Centre – ♿ Open Mar–Nov, daily, 9am–6.30pm; opening times may vary according to demand. Exhibition £3, £6.50 (family 2A+4C), £2 (child/reduction). ☎ 061 396 666; Fax 061 396 932.

Excursions

Glin Castle – ♿ Guided tour (30min) May–June, daily, 10am–noon and 2–4pm, every 30min; otherwise by appointment. £3, £1 (reduction). Parking. ☎ 068 34173, 34112; Fax 068 34364; e-mail Knight@aol.ie

Glin Heritage Centre – Open Apr–Sept.

Castle Matrix – (♿) Open May–Sept, Sat–Thur, 11.30am–5pm (other times by appointment). £3, £1.50 (reduction). Guided tour (20min) available. Poetry and musical evenings by arrangement. Parking. Wheelchair access to ground floor only. ☎ 069 64284.

Irish Palatine – ♿ Open June–Sept, Mon–Sat, 10am–noon and 2–5pm, Sun, 2–6pm. £2, £5 (family 2A+2C), £1 (child). Parking. Tearoom. ☎ 069 64397; Fax 069 64220; e-mail ipass@tinet.ie

Croom Mills – Open all year, daily, 8am–6pm; extended opening times during summer, telephone for details. £3, £8 (family 2A+2C), £2 (child/senior citizen). Guided tour available. Parking. Mill Race Restaurant. Corn Loft Bistro. Craft shop. Gift shop. ☎ 061 397 130; Fax 061 397 199 (Mary Hayes).

Desmond Hall – (♿) Open mid June–mid Sept, daily, 9.30am-6.30pm (5.45pm last tour). £1.50, £5 (family 2A+2C), 60p (child). Guided tour 45min. ☎ 01 661 3111 (Dúchas Head Office).

Foynes Flying Boat Museum – ♿ Open end Mar–Oct, daily, 10am–6pm; otherwise by appointment. £3, £8 (family 2A+4C). Guided tour (45min; French, German, Italian). Film and brochure (French, German, Italian). Parking. Refreshments. ☎/Fax 069 65416.

Desmond Castle (Dúchas) – Open mid Apr–mid June, Tues–Sun, 10am–6pm. Closed Mon except bank holidays. £1.50, 60p (child/student), £4 (family), £1 (senior citizen). Parking. ☎ 021 774 855.

ARAN ISLANDS 🖪 ☎ 099 61263; Fax 099 61420 (mid Mar–early Oct)

Air Service – Operates daily, from **Connemara Airport, Inverin** (west of Galway) at 9.30am, 11am, 4pm, 5pm; from Inishmore at 9.45am, 11.15am, 4.15pm, 5.15pm; also lands on Inishmaan and Inisheer. Air taxi service with flight every hour in summer. ☎ 091 593 034, 593 054 (reservations); ☎ 099 61109; Fax 091 593 238 (Aer Arann); e-mail info@aerarann.ie

Ferry from Galway (1) – Operates June–Sept, daily, from Galway Docks at 10.30am. Departs from Aran at 5pm. Time 2 hr. ☎ 091 567 676, 567 670, 567 671; Fax 091 567 672 (O'Brien Shipping).

Ferry from Rossaveal (1) – Operates Apr–Nov, from Rossaveal at 10.30am, 1.30pm, 6.30pm, from Inishmore at 9am, noon, 5pm, 7.30pm; Nov to Apr, twice daily; also May–Sept, extra crossings. Time 35min. Return £15, £40 (family), £10 (reduction). Inter-Island ferry service also available. Reservation service for minibus, bike hire, walking tours, accommodation, lunch and dinner. Supervised parking at Rossaveal. Coach service from Galway city. ☎ 091 568 903, 561 767, 572 050, 572 273 (after hours); Fax 091 568 538 (Island Ferries Teo).

Ferry to Doolin (Co Clare) – Operates June–Aug (weather permitting), daily: to Inisheer (30min), 10am–5.30pm, (6 sailings; additional sailing Fri only at 6.30pm); to Inishmaan (45min), at 10am and 1pm; to Inishmore (60min), at 10am and 1pm; from Inisheer, at 9am, 12.30pm, 3pm, 4.30pm and 6pm; from Inishmaan, at 12.15pm and 4.30pm; from Inishmore, at 11.30am and 4pm; Reduced sailings, Easter–May and Sept, telephone for details. Return £15–£20. ☎ 065 74455; 065 71710 and 74189 (after office hours); Fax 065 74417 (Doolin Ferry Co).

Aran Heritage Centre – (♿) Open June–Aug, daily, 10am–7pm, Apr–May and Sept–Oct, daily, 11am–5pm. £2.50, £6 (family 2A+2C), £1.50 (child/senior citizen), £2 (student). Documentary film *Man of Aran* also showing daily. Café. Book & Craft Shop. Bureau de change. Wheelchair access to ground floor only. ☎ 099 61355; 091 563 081 (Galway Tourist Office); Fax 099 61454.

ARDMORE 🖪 Community Office ☎ 024 94444 (May–Sept)

ARKLOW see WICKLOW MOUNTAINS 🖪 ☎ 0402 32484 (June–Sept)

ATHLONE 🖪 Athlone Castle ☎ 0902 94630, 92856 (Apr–Oct)

Shannon Boat Trips – Operate from Jolly Mariner Marina, Coosan, June–Aug, daily at 11am and 2.30pm (times subject to change). Time 90min. £4, £2.50 (child). Taped commentary; bar. Parking. Coffee shop. ☎ 0902 72892, 72113; Fax 0902 74386 (Athlone Cruises).

Athlone Castle – **Visitor Centre**: Open Apr–Oct, daily, 10am–5.30pm. Audio-visual presentation (40min; French, German). **Museum**: Open Apr–early Oct, daily, 10am-5.30pm. Visitor Centre and Museum £2.60, £6 (family 2A+2C), 80p (child), £1.75 (senior citizen/student). Parking. ☎ 0902 92912 (Castle), 72107 (Urban District Council).

ATHY

Heritage Centre – Open all year, daily, 10am–6pm (last admission 5pm). £2, £5 (family 2A+2C), £1 (child), £1.50 (reduction). ☎ 0507 33075; Fax 0507 33076.

Emo Court (Dúchas) – **Gardens**: Open all year, daily; guided tour, July–Aug, Sun at 3pm. **House**: Guided tour (30min) mid June–mid Sept, daily, 10am–6pm (5.15pm last admission). £2, £5 (family 2A+2C). Parking. Music recitals in winter. ☎/Fax 0502 26573.

Coolbanagher Church – **Services**: First Sun of month at 9.30am (Matins), second Sun at 10.45am (family service), third Sun (Holy Communion) at noon and fourth Sun (Matins) at noon. ☎ 0502 24143 (Rector).

Quaker Meeting House Library – Open all year: winter, Tues–Fri, noon–5pm, Sat. 1–5pm; summer, Wed–Sat, 1–6pm, Sun, 2–6pm. ☎ 0507 23344.

Crookstown Mill and Heritage Centre – (&) Open Apr–Sept, daily, 10am–7pm; Oct–Mar, daily, 11am–4pm. Closed Good Friday and 25 Dec. £2.50, £6 (family 2A+2C), £1.20 (child), £1.25 (student). Parking. Tearoom. Gift shop. Wheelchair access to ground floor only. ☎ 0507 23222.

Irish Pewter Mill and Craft Centre – (&) Open all year, Mon–Fri, 9.30am–5pm; also open Sat–Sun during summer, 9.30am–5pm. Closed Good Friday and Easter Sunday, 25 Dec. No charge. Audio-visual presentation (10min). Brochure (French, German). Parking. Limited facilities for the disabled; ramp. ☎ 0507 24164.

Abbeyleix Heritage House – Open Mar–Oct, Mon–Sat, 10am–6pm, Sun and bank holidays, 1–6pm; Nov–Feb, Mon–Fri, 9am–5pm. £2, £5 (family 2A+2C), £1 (child), £1.50 (reduction). Coffee parlour. ☎ 0502 31653.

Abbey Sense Garden – Open all year, 9am–4pm. Donation. ☎ 0502 31636, 31325; Fax 0502 31386.

Heywood Gardens – Open all year. Guided tour July–Aug, Sun. ☎ 0502 33563.

Stradbally Steam Museum – & Closed temporarily. Telephone for details. **Narrow-gauge railway**: Operates bank holiday Sat–Sun and open days, otherwise by appointment with the Secretary, Irish Steam Preservation Society, Stradbally. **Annual Steam Rally at Stradbally Hall**: Aug Bank Holiday weekend. ☎ 0502 25114, 25444.

AUGHRIM see LOUGHREA   🛈 ☎ 0905 73939 (mid Apr–end Sept)

B

BALLINA see KILLALA   🛈 ☎ 096 70848 (Apr–Sept)

BALLINASLOE see LOUGHREA   🛈 ☎ 0905 42131 (July–Aug)

BANTRY BAY   🛈 Old Courthouse, Bantry ☎ 027 50229 (May–Oct)
🛈 Glengarriff ☎ 027 63084 (July–Aug)

Garinish Island Ferry (1) – Operates from Glengarriff, Mar and Oct, daily, 10am (1pm Sun)–4.30pm (5pm Sun); Apr–June and Sept, daily, 10am (1pm Sun)–6.30pm (7pm Sun); July–Aug, daily, 9.30am (11am Sun)–6.30pm (7pm Sun); last landing 1 hr before closing time. Time 10min usually including Seal Island. £2.50, £6 (family 2A+2C), £1 (child/student), £1.75 (senior citizen). ☎ 027 63333, 63555 (Blue Pool Ferry); Fax 027 63149.

Garinish Island Ferry (2) – Operates from Glengarriff Mar–Oct, daily. £5, half price (child). ☎ 027 63116 (Harbour Queen Ferry), 087 234 5861 (mobile); Fax 027 63298.

Ilnacullin (Garinish Island) Gardens (Dúchas) – & Open July–Aug, Mon–Sat, 9.30am–6.30pm, Sun, 11am–7pm; Apr–June and Sept, Mon–Sat, 10am–6.30pm, Sun, 1pm–7pm; Mar and Oct, Mon–Sat, 10am–4.30pm, Sun, 1pm–5pm; last landing 1 hr (summer), 30min (winter) before closing time. £2.50, £6 fam, £1 (child/student), £1.75 (senior citizen); ferry charge (see above). Self-guiding trails. Guide book (Irish, French, German, Italian, Spanish). ☎ 027 63040; Fax 027 63149.

Bantry House – (&) **House**: Restoration in progress. Open Mar–Oct, daily, 9am–6pm. £6, £4 (reduction), no charge (accompanied child). Admission charge includes entry to garden. Brochure (Dutch, French, German, Italian, Spanish). Parking. Tearoom. Accommodation. Wheelchair access to ground floor only. ☎ 027 50047; Fax 027 50795.

1776 Armada – Open Mar–Oct, daily, 10am–6pm. £3, £6 (family). ☎ 027 51796, 51996; Fax 027 51309.

Whiddy Island Ferry – Operates in summer, daily, every hour.

BEARA PENINSULA

Derreen Gardens, Lauragh – Open Apr–Sept, daily, 11am–6pm. Time approx 1 hr. £2.50; garden map 20p. Parking. ☎ 064 83103.

Dursey Island Cable-Car – & Open all year, Mon–Sat, 9am–10.30am, 2.30–4.30pm, Sun, 9am–10.15am, noon–1pm. Return trip daily at 7pm. Return £2.50, 50p (child). Parking (mainland terminal). ☎ 027 73017.

Bere Island Car Ferry – 🦽 Operates all year, daily (weather permitting), from **Castletownbere Pier**: Summer, at 9am, 11.30am, 1.30pm, 3.30pm, 5.30pm, 8.30pm; Winter, at 9am, 11.30am, 1.30pm, 4.30pm, 6.30pm, (8.30pm Fri only); from **Bere Island**: Summer, at 8.30am, 10.30am, 12.30pm, 2.30pm, 4.30pm, 6pm, 8pm; Winter, at 8.30am, 10.30am, 12.45pm, 3.30pm, 6pm, (8pm Fri only). Time 10min. 17 car capacity. Return £15 (car + 2 passengers), return £4 (pedestrian). Parking. Refreshments. Wheelchair access to ferries. ☎ 027 75009 (Bere Island Ferry); 027 75014 (Patrick Murphy, Laurence Cove, Bere Island).

BIRR
🅱 Rosse Row ☎ 0509 20110; Fax 0509 20660 (mid May–early Sept)

Birr Castle Demesne – (🦽) Open all year round, daily, 9am–6pm. Horse-drawn carriage tours of the grounds. **Exhibition Gallery**: Open May–Sept, daily, 9am–6pm (exhibitions change annually). £5, £11 (family 2A+2C), £2.50 (child), £3.20 (reduction). Brochure (French, German, Italian, Spanish). Demonstration of the working of the telescope, daily, at 2.30pm. **Concerts**: mid June and mid Aug. **Driving Championships**: end Aug. Parking. Coffee shop; picnic areas. Facilities for the disabled; access to garden but not gallery. ☎ 0509 20336; Fax 0509 21583; e-mail birr@iol.ie

Birr Heritage Centre – Open June–Sept, Mon–Sat, 10.30am–1pm and 2–5pm, Sun, 3–5pm. No charge.

Excursions

Slieve Bloom Display Centre – Open Apr–Sept, daily. ☎ 0509 20029.

Shannon Cruise – From Banagher, 1 hr 30min. ☎ 0509 51112.

Clonmacnoise and West Offaly Railway – 🦽 Operates Apr–Oct, daily, 10am–5pm, on the hour. Time 50min. £3.95, £8.95 (family 2A+2C), £2.50 (child), £2.95 (reduction). Machine Museum. Craft shop. Parking. Tearoom. ☎ 0905 74114, 74121; Fax 0905 74210.

Cloghan Castle – Open July–Aug, daily except Mon, 2–6pm. Also open bank holiday Monday; by appointment only at other times. £4, £10 (family 2A+2C), £3 (senior citizen). ☎ 0509 51650.

BLARNEY
🅱 ☎ 021 381 624

Blarney Castle and Grounds – 🦽 Open all year, Mon–Sat, 9am–7pm (6pm May and Sept; 5pm/dusk, Oct–Apr); Sun, 9.30am–5.30pm/dusk. Closed 24–25 Dec. Time 1 hr. £3.50, £6.50 (family 2A+2C), £1 (child), £2.50 (reduction). Brochure (French, German). Parking. Refreshments. ☎ 021 385 252; Fax 021 381 518.

Blarney Woollen Mills – Open all year, daily, 9am (noon 1 Jan)–6pm (8pm Fri in December). Closed 25–26 December. Restaurant. ☎ 021 385 280.

BOYLE
🅱 King House ☎ 079 62145 (end Apr–end Sept)

Boyle Abbey (Dúchas) – (🦽) Open June–Sept, daily, 9.30am–6.30pm; last admission 45min before closing. £1, £3 (family 2A+2C), 40p (child/student), 70p (senior citizen). Parking. ☎ 079 62604.

King House – Open Apr–Oct, Sat–Sun and bank holidays, 10am–6pm; May–Sept, daily, 10am–6pm. £3, £2 (child), £2.50 (reduction). Parking (footbridge over river from car park to house). Coffee shop. Craft shop. ☎ 079 63242; Fax 079 63243.

Frybrook House – Open June–Sept, daily except Mon, 2–6pm. £3, £7 (family 2A+2C), £2 (child), £2.50 (reduction). Parking. ☎ 079 63513.

Excursions

Sliabh an Iarainn Visitor Centre – Open Apr–Oct, daily, 10am (2pm Sun)–6pm. £1, 50p (child). Audio-visual presentation (30min) £1. ☎ 078 41522.

Lough Key Forest Park – Open all year, daily. Admission charge from Easter–30 Sept. **Moylurgh Tower**: Open all year, daily, 8am (11am Sat–Sun)–4pm (6pm Sat, 7pm Sun). Parking. Coffee shop. ☎ 079 62363 (Irish Forestry Board – Coillte Teoranta).

O'Carolan Harp and Traditional Music Festival, Keadew – End July–beginning Aug. Information from the Secretary, Keadew, Co Roscommon. ☎ 078 47204; Fax 078 47511.

O'Carolan Harp and Cultural Festival, Nobber – First Fri–Sun in Oct. Information from the Secretary, Keadew, Co Roscommon. ☎ 046 52115 or 52272.

Dr Douglas Hyde Centre – 🦽 Open May–Sept, Tues–Fri, 2–5pm; Sat–Sun, 2–6pm; opening times may extend to mornings, telephone for details. Donation. Parking. Picnic area. ☎ 0907 70016.

BOYNE VALLEY
🅱 Newgrange ☎ 041 80305

Brú na Bóinne Visitor Centre (Dúchas) – Access to graves via Visitor Centre only. Centre is on the south bank of the river and linked by a footbridge to the bus depot. Shuttle-bus service from the depot to the graves (3mi/5km) every 30min. In peak season it is advisable to arrive at the Visitor Centre early in the day as the guided tours are on a first-come-first-served basis; advance bookings for groups only.

Newgrange Passage Grave: (&) Guided tour (35min) all year round; Nov–Feb, 9.30am–5pm; Mar–Apr and Oct, 9.30am–5.30pm; May and mid–end Sept, 9am–6.30pm; June–mid Sept, 9am–7pm; last tour 45min before closing. Closed 25–26 Dec. £3, £7.50 (family), £1.25 (child/student), £2 (senior citizen). Parking. ☎ 041 24488; Fax 041 24798.

Knowth Passage Grave: Guided tour (30min; no access to interior of graves) May–Oct; May, 9am–6.30pm; June–mid Sept, 9am–7pm; mid–end Sept, 9am–6.30pm; Oct, 9.30am–5.30pm; last admission 45min before closing. £2, £5 (family 2A+2C), £1 (child/student), £1.50 (senior citizen); combined ticket for Newgrange, Knowth and Visitor Centre, £5, £12.50 (family), £2.25 (child), £3.50 (senior citizen). Parking. ☎ 041 24824; Fax 041 24488.

Mellifont Old Abbey (Dúchas) – Open mid June–mid Sept, daily, 9.30am–6.30pm; May–mid June and mid Sept–Oct, daily, 10am–5pm; last admission 45min before closing. £1.50, £4 (family 2A+2C), 60p (child/student), £1 (senior citizen). Parking. Access by stone steps. ☎ 041 26459; Fax 041 24488.

Termonfeckin Tower House (Dúchas) – Key available from the cottage opposite.

Slane Castle – Open Sat, from 11.30pm. ☎ 041 24207.

Ledwidge Cottage Museum – & Open all year, daily, 10am-1pm and 2–6pm. £2, 50p (child), £1 (reduction), £5 (family). Parking. ☎ 041 24285 and 24244.

BUNCRANA see INISHOWEN PENINSULA   🄸 Shore front ☎ 077 62600 (June–Aug)

BUNDORAN see DONEGAL   🄸 Main Street ☎ 072 41350 (June–Sept)

BUNRATTY

Bunratty Castle and Folk Park – & Open June–Aug, daily, 9am–6.30pm (5.30pm last admission); Sept–May, daily, 9.30am–5.30pm (4pm last admission). Closed Good Friday, 24–26 Dec. £5.25, £12.60 (family 2A+2C), £3 (child), £3.80 (student/senior citizen); Folk Park only £3.90, £2.20 (child). ☎ 061 361 511, 360 788; Fax 061 361 020. Tour (2hr; Dutch, French, German, Irish, Italian, Japanese, Spanish). Brochure (French, German, Italian). **Medieval banquets**: all year, daily at 5.30pm and 8.45pm; £32, £24.25 (child 10–12), £16.50 (child 6–9); ☎ 061 360 788 (Shannon Heritage). **Traditional Irish Night** (Shannon céile): May–Oct, daily at 5.30pm and 8.45pm; £27, £20.25 (child 10–12), £13.50 (child 6–9); Parking. Refreshments. ☎ 061 360 788 (Shannon Heritage); Fax 061 361 020.

BURREN   🄸 Cliffs of Moher ☎ 065 81171 (Apr–Oct)

Burren eXposure – & Open Apr–mid Oct, daily, 10am–5pm. £3.50, £1.50 (child). Parking. ☎ 065 77277; Fax 065 77278.

Newtown Castle and Trail – Open Easter–Sept, daily, 10am–6pm (7pm July–Aug); last admission 1 hr before closing. Castle and trail £3.50, castle or trail £2. Parking. No wheelchair access. ☎ 065 77200; Fax 065 77201.

Aillwee Cave – (&) Open mid Mar–Nov, daily, 10am–5.30pm (last tour); last admission 6.30pm in July–Aug. £4.25, £2.50 (child), £14 (family 2A+4C). Guided tour (35min; French, German). Brochure (French, German, Japanese, Spanish). Parking. Restaurant. Disabled by appointment only. ☎ 065 77036, 77067; Fax 065 77107.

Burren Perfumery – Open Easter-Oct, daily, 9am–5pm (7pm June–Sept); in winter by appointment. No charge. Parking. ☎ 065 89102; Fax 065 89200.

Leamaneh Castle – For permission to view ask at the modern house (left of the castle).

Burren Centre – & Open Mar–Oct, daily, 10am (9.30am June–Sept)–5pm (6pm June–Sept). £2.50. Guided tour (30min; French, German and others). Parking. Restaurant. Bookshop. Tourist information. Bureau de change. ☎ 065 88030; Fax 065 88102.

Poulnabrone, The Burren

Irish Picture Library

Cliffs of Moher – & **Site**: Open all year. **Visitor Centre**: Open June–Aug, daily, 9am–8pm; Sept–May, daily, 9.30am –5.30pm. Closed Good Friday, 24–26 Dec. **O'Brien's Tower**: (weather permitting) May–Sept, daily, 9.30am-5.30pm. O'Brien's Tower £1, 60p (child). No charge. Parking. Tearoom. ☎ 061 360 788 or 065 81565.

C

CAHER

☎ 052 41453 (Apr–Sept)

Caher Castle (Dúchas) – (♿) Open mid Mar–mid June and mid Sept–mid Oct, daily, 9.30am–5.30pm; mid June–mid Sept, daily, 9am–7.30pm; mid Oct–mid Mar, daily, 9.30am–4.30pm; last admission 45min before closing. Closed Good Friday, 25–26 Dec. £2, £5 (family), £1 (child/student), £1.50 (senior citizen). Audio-visual presentation (French, German, Italian). ☎ 052 41011; Fax 052 42324.

Swiss Cottage (Dúchas) – Guided tour (25min) mid Mar, Oct and Nov, Tues–Sun, 10am–4.30pm; Apr, Tues–Sun, 10am–5pm; May–Sept, daily, 10am–6pm. Last admission 45min before closing. Closed Mon except bank holiday Mondays, and 1–2pm, Mar–Apr and Oct–Nov. £2, £5 (family), £1 (child), £1.50 (senior citizen). Parking. Guide book (Irish, Italian, French, German). Access by stone steps. ☎ 052 41144.

Excursions

Mitchelstown Cave – Guided tour (35min; French, German) all year, daily, 10am–6pm. £3, £7 (family 2A+2C), £1 (child). Parking. ☎ 052 67246.

Ronald Reagan Centre – ♿ Open all year, daily, 10am–5pm (7pm Sat–Sun and public holidays). No charge. Guided tour (30min). Parking. Refreshments.

CAHERCIVEEN see IVERAGH PENINSULA 🅱 RIC Barracks ☎ 066 72589 (June–mid Sept)

CARLOW

🅱 Town Centre ☎ 0503 31554

Carlow Museum – Open all year, Tues–Sun, 10am (2pm Sat–Sun)–5.30pm. £1, 50p (child). Guided tour available. ☎ 0503 40730.

Excursions

Altamont Gardens – (♿) Open Apr–Oct, Sun and bank holidays, 2–6pm; at other times by request. £3, £8 (family), £1 (child), £2 (reduction). Unusual plant sales. Residential garden and painting courses. Parking. ☎/Fax 0503 59128; ☎ 0503 59444.

CARRICK-ON-SHANNON

🅱 The Marina ☎ 078 20170

Costello Chapel – Open daily, Mar–Oct. No charge. Brochure (French, German). ☎ 078 20251.

Excursions

Lough Rynn Demesne – Open May–Sept, daily, 10am–7pm. Guided tour of principal buildings at 11am, 11.30am, noon, 2.30pm, 3.30pm, 4pm, 4.30pm. Grounds £1.25, or £3.50 max per car. Guided tour £1, 70p (reduction). Restaurant. Craft shop. Plant sales. ☎ 078 31427; Fax 078 31518.

CASHEL

🅱 Main Street ☎ 062 61333 (Apr–Sept)

Cashel Heritage Tram – Leaves from The Rock every 30min for tour of town. Charge including entry to Cashel Heritage Centre.

Rock of Cashel (Dúchas) – (♿) Open mid June–mid Sept, daily, 9am–7.30pm; otherwise, daily, 9.30am–5.30pm (4.30pm mid Sept–mid Mar); last admission 45min before closing. Closed 25–26 Dec. £3, £7.50 (family), £1.25 (child/student), £2 (senior citizen). Audio-visual presentation (French, German, Italian). Parking 50p. Access for disabled visitors by prior arrangement. ☎ 062 61437; Fax 062 62988.

Brú Ború – ♿ Open May–Sept, daily, 9am–6pm. **Folk Theatre** (music, song and dance): Open June–Sept, Tues–Sat, at 9pm. **Craft shop:** Open all year. Theatre show £8; Theatre show and Banquet £25. Restaurant. ☎ 062 61122; Fax 062 62700.

Cashel Heritage Centre – Open Mar–Aug, daily, 9.30am–5.30pm (8pm July–Aug); Sept–Feb, Mon–Fri, 9.30am–5.30pm, Sat–Sun by appointment. £1, £3 (family 2A+2C), 50p (child). Commentary (10min; French, German, Italian, Spanish). ☎ 062 62511; Fax 062 62068.

Cashel Palace Gardens – Open all year, daily; Bishop's Walk closed Nov-Good Friday. Parking. Café. ☎ 062 62707.

GPA Bolton Library – Open May–Sept, Tues–Sun, 10am–6pm; otherwise by appointment. £1.50, 50p (reduction). Guided tour (30min) available. Can be visited as part of Cashel Tram Tour. Parking. ☎ 062 61944 (Library), 62511 (Cashel Heritage Centre).

Anglican Cathedral – Open May–Sept, daily, 9.30am–5.30pm. No charge. Parking. ☎ 062 61232.

Folk Village – ♿ Open mid Mar–mid Oct, daily, 9.30am–7.30pm (earlier out of season). £2, £5 (family), 50p (child). Brochure (Dutch, French, German, Irish, Italian, Spanish). Guided tour (1 hr) available, subject to demand. Parking. ☎ 062 62525.

Bothán Scoir – Open by appointment only. £1. ☎ 062 61360.

CASHEL

Excursions

Holy Cross Abbey Church – Open all year, daily, 10am–6pm. Guided tours, June–Sept. ☎ 0504 43241, 43118.

Lár na Páirce – Open Mar–Oct, daily, 10am–1pm and 2–5.15pm. £2.50, £1.50 (reduction). ☎ 0504 23579.

CASTLEBAR 🔃 Castlebar ☎ 094 21207 (May–mid Sept)

Excursions

Foxford Woollen Mills Visitor Centre – Guided tour (1 hr) daily, 10am (2pm Sundays)–6pm, every 20min. £3.50, £10 (family 2A+2C), £2.50 (senior citizen/student). Parking. Restaurant. Shop. Bureau de change. Jewellery craft centre. Guided tour (French, German, Italian, Spanish). Brochure (French, German, Italian, Spanish). ☎ 094 56756; Fax 094 56794; e-mail mconlon@foxford.iol.ie

Michael Davitt Memorial Museum – ♿ Open Mar–Oct, daily, 10am–6pm; at all other times by appointment. £1.50, 75p (child/student), £1 (senior citizen). Parking.

Ballintubber Abbey – Open all year, daily, 9am–midnight. Donation. Guided tour (30min) available. Video. Brochure (French, German). Parking. Refreshments. Shop. ☎ 094 30934; Fax 094 30018.

CAVAN 🔃 Farnham Street ☎ 049 31942 (June–Sept)

Life Force Mill – Open May–Sept, daily. Tour (1 hr) every hour. £4, £3.50 (child under 10). ☎ 049 62722; Fax 049 62923.

Cavan Crystal – ♿ Open all year, Mon–Fri, 9.30am–5.30pm; Sat–Sun and public holidays, 2pm (10am Sat)–5pm; guided factory tour (20min). No charge. Brochure (French, German). Parking. Coffee shop (summer). ☎ 049 31800.

Cavan County Museum – Open all year, Tues–Sat, 10am–5pm, Sun (June–Sept only), 2–6pm. £2, £1 (child/reduction). ☎ 049 44070; Fax 049 44332; e-mail ccmuseum@tinet.ie

Excursions

Carraig Craft Visitor Centre and Basketry Museum – Open all year, daily, 10am (2pm Sun)–6pm. Craft shop. Coffee shop. Tourist information. ☎ 049 40179.

Kilmore Cathedral – Open by appointment. Key available from the Deanery, Danesfort. No charge. Parking. ☎/Fax 049 31918; e-mail dean@kilmore.anglican.org

CLIFDEN see CONNEMARA 🔃 ☎ 095 21163 (Apr–Sept)

CLONAKILTY see KINSALE 🔃 Rossa Street ☎ 023 33226 (June–mid Sept)

CLONMACNOISE 🔃 ☎ 0905 74134 (Apr–Oct)

Clonmacnoise Site and Visitor Centre (Dúchas) – ♿ Open mid May–early Sept, daily, 9am–7pm; otherwise, daily, 10am–6pm (5.30pm Nov–mid Mar); last admission 45min before closing. Closed 25 Dec. £3, £7.50 (family 2A+2C), £1.25 (child/student), £2 (senior citizen). Audio-visual presentation (22min; French, German, Italian). Parking. ☎ 0905 74195; Fax 0905 74273.

Temple Connor – Open for Anglican services only, May–Aug, last Sun in the month.

CLONMEL 🔃 Community Office Town Centre ☎ 052 22960

County Museum – Open all year, Tues–Sat, 10am–5pm. Closed lunch hour and public holidays. ☎ 052 25399; Fax 052 24355.

St Mary's Church – Services: Sun, 10.45am. ☎ 052 26643 (Revd George Knowd), 087 284 2350 (mobile).

Museum of Transport – Open all year, Mon–Sat, 10am–6pm; also June–Sept, Sun, 2–6pm. ☎ 052 29727.

Excursions

Ormond Castle (Dúchas) – (♿) Open mid June–Sept, daily, 9.30am–6.30pm; last admission 45min before closing. £2, £5 (family), £1 (child/student), £1.50 (senior citizen). Public parking nearby. Restricted access for disabled visitors. ☎ 051 640 787.

Tipperary Crystal – (♿) Open all year, daily, 9am–6pm (10am–5.30pm Sat–Sun and Nov–Feb). Guided tour (30min) May–Sept. No charge. Parking. Refreshments. Facilities for the disabled (telephone in advance). ☎ 051 641 188; Fax 051 641 190; e-mail tippcrys@iol.ie

Fethard Museum – ♿ Open all year round. Sun and bank holiday Monday, 12.30–5pm. Open at all other times by appointment. Sunday admission: £1, 50p (child). Admission at other times: £2, £1 (child). Guided tour (30min). Brochure (French). **Collectors' market and car boot sale**: all year, Sun. Parking. Picnic area. Playground. ☎ 052 31516.

🚲 The Old Midleton Distillery, Midleton ☎ 021 613 702 (Apr–Oct)

Cork Harbour Car Ferry – **Carrigaloe/Glenbrook**: Operates all year, Mon–Fri, 7.15am–12.30am, Sat–Sun, 7.15am–12.30am. Time 5min. Capacity 28 cars. Return £3.50 (car), £1 (pedestrian), 30p (child); single £2.50 (car), 60p (pedestrian), 20p (child). ☎ 021 811 223; Fax 021 812 645.

Cork Harbour Cruises – Operate from **Kennedy Pier** (1 hr – harbour forts, Spike Island, Naval base and major harbour industries) June–Sept, daily, telephone for times; otherwise by appointment. £3.50, £1.75 (child). Parking (5–10min walk). Refreshments available ashore. ☎ 021 811 485 (Marine Transport Services Ltd).

St Colman's Cathedral – Open all year, daily, 7.30am–9pm (8pm winter). No charge. Brochure (French, German, Irish, Italian, Spanish). Parking. ☎ 021 813 222; Fax 021 813 488.

Cobh Heritage Centre: The Queenstown Story – ♿ Open daily, 10am–6pm (5pm last admission). £3.50, £10 (family 2A+3C), £2 (child). Audio-visual presentation (5min). Brochure (French, German, Italian, Spanish). Café; Blarney Woollen Mills shop. ☎ 021 813 591; Fax 021 813 595; e-mail cobhher@indigo.ie

Cobh Museum – Open Mon–Sat, daily, 11am–6pm (last admission 5.30pm); Sun, 3–6pm. Closed daily, 1–2pm. 50p, 20p (child). Brochure (French, German, Spanish). ☎ 021 814 240.

Rail service – Operates between Cobh and Cork via Fota Island Wildlife Park, daily. ☎ 021 506 766 (Cork Railway Station).

Excursions

Fota Wildlife Park – ♿ Open Apr–end Oct, daily, 10am (11am Sun)–6pm; last admission 5pm. Time 90min. £4. Tour train. Volunteer visitor information service. Parking. Coffee shop. ☎ 021 812 678, 812 736.

Fota Arboretum – (♿) Open Apr–Oct, daily, 10am–6pm; Nov–Mar, Mon–Fri, 10am–5pm. Parking £1. Guided tours by arrangement. ☎/Fax 021 812 728; ☎ 087 279 9508.

Fota House – Closed for restoration. ☎ 021 812 555 (Administrator), 021 273 251 (Cork Tourist Office).

🚲 ☎ 092 46542 (early Mar–end Sept)

Cong Abbey (Dúchas) – Open dawn-dusk; when closed key available from the caretaker, Mrs A Varley, Abbey Street, Cong, Co Mayo.

Ashford Castle Hotel Grounds – Open all year, daily, summer, 8am–6pm; winter, 10am–6pm. £3.50. Brochure (French, Italian, Spanish). ☎ 092 46003; Fax 092 46260; e-mail ashford@ashford.ie. **Tour of the grounds in a jaunting car or trap**: ☎ 092 46029. **Boat cruises on Lough Corrib** (including visit to Inchagoill island): ☎ 092 46029. Pony trekking. Parking. Refreshments.

🚲 Clifden ☎ 095 21163 (early Apr–Sept)

Inishbofin Ferry (1) – **Dun Aengus** operates Apr, May and Sept, daily, **from Cleggan**, at 11.30am and 6.45pm, from Inishbofin at 9.15am and 5pm; June–Aug, daily, **from Cleggan**, at 11.30am, 2pm and 6.45pm, from Inishbofin at 9.15am, 12.30pm and 5pm. Time 40min. Return £10. Brochure (French, German, Irish, Italian, Spanish). ☎ 095 45806 (Patrick O'Halloran).

Inishbofin Ferry (2) – Operates (weather permitting) July–Aug, **from Cleggan**, at 11.30am, 2pm and 6.45pm; **from Inishbofin**, at 9am, 1pm, 5pm; Apr–June and Sept–Oct, **from Cleggan**, at 11.30am and 6.45pm; **from Inishbofin**, at 9am, 5pm. ☎ 095 4642, 21520; Fax 095 44327 (Kings Ferries); e-mail conamara@indigo.ie www/failte.con/cleggan/

Connemara National Park (Dúchas) – ♿ Open all year. **Visitor Centre**: Open May–Sept, daily, 10am (9.30am July–Aug)-6.30pm (5.30pm May and Sept); last admission 45min before closing. £2, £5 (family), £1 (child/student), £1.50 (senior citizen). Audio-visual presentation (15min). Natural History talk, Wed, 8.30am. Guided nature walks, July-Aug (rainwear and boots required). Nature Mornings for children, Tues and Thur at 10.30am. Parking. Tearoom; indoor and outdoor picnic areas. ☎ 095 41054, 41066; Fax 095 41005.

CONNEMARA

Kylemore Abbey – (♿) **Visitor Centre**: Open mid Mar–Oct, daily, 9am–6pm; Nov–Mar, daily, 10am–4pm. Closed Good Friday and Christmas week. £3, £6 (family), £2 (reduction). **Castle**: Open as above. Audio-visual presentation (French, German, Italian). Leaflet (French, German, Italian, Spanish, Dutch). **Gothic Church**: Open all year, daily, 9.30am–6.30pm. Parking. Restaurant. Wheelchair access to Visitor Centre. ☎ 095 41146; Fax 095 41145; e-mail enquiries@kylemoreabbey.ie

Leenane Sheep and Wool Museum – Open Apr–Oct, daily, 10am–7pm; otherwise for groups only. £2, £5 (family), £1 (reduction). Audio-visual presentation (13min; French, German, Irish, Italian). Audio-guide (French, German, Irish, Italian). Brochure (French, German). Shop. Café. ☎ 095 42323, 42231; Fax 095 42337.

St MacDara's Island Ferry – No regular sailings. Passage offered (weather permitting) by local fishermen on Festival Day (16 July) and other days.

Patrick Pearse's Cottage (Dúchas) – (♿) Open mid June–mid Sept, daily, 9.30am–1.30pm and 2.30–6.30pm; last admission 45min before closing. £1, £3 (family), 40p (child/student), 70p (senior citizen). Parking. ☎ 091 574 292.

CORK

☐ Grand Parade ☎ 021 273 251; Fax 021 273 504
☐ Cork Airport Freephone at Airport Terminal

Cork Harbour Cruises – See COBH above.

Triskel Arts Centre – ♿ Open all year, Mon–Sat, 10am–5.30pm. Doors open at 7pm for evening performances. Gallery no charge. Café. Bar. ☎ 021 272 022; Fax 021 272 592; e-mail triskel@iol.ie

Crawford Art Gallery – ♿ Open all year, Mon–Sat, 10am–5pm. No charge. Guided tour by appointment. Restaurant. ☎ 021 273 377; Fax 021 275 680.

Cork Archives Institute – Open by appointment all year, Tues–Fri, 10am–1pm and 2.30–5pm. Closed public holidays. ☎ 021 277 809.

Cork Vision Centre – Open all year, Tues–Sat, 10am–5pm. £1, 50p (child). ☎ 021 279 925.

University College – Tours for groups only, by prior arrangement. £15 per group. ☎ 021 902 371; Fax 021 277 000. **Walking Tour**: Operates June–Sept, Mon–Fri, at 2.30pm. Starts from the main University gates on Western Road. ☎ 021 276 871.

Cork Public Museum – Open all year, Mon–Fri, 11am–1pm and 2.15–6pm (5pm Sept–May); Sun, 3–5pm. Closed public holidays. Time 30min. Sun 75p, £1 50 (family). Parking. ☎ 021 270 679; Fax 021 270 931.

St Fin Barre's Cathedral – ♿ Open all year, Mon–Sat, 10am–5.30pm (5pm Oct–Apr). **Services**: Sun, at 8am, 11.15am and 7pm. Closed public holidays. Donation (£1). Guided tour available. Leaflets (French, German, Italian, Spanish, Dutch, Japanese). Parking. ☎ 021 964 742, 963 387 (Revd Michael Jackson).

Cork Heritage Park – ♿ Open Easter–end Apr, Sun, noon–3.30pm; May–Sept, daily, 10.30am (noon Sat–Sun)–5.30pm. £3.50, £7 (family 2A+2C), £1.50 (senior citizen), £2 (student). Parking. Café, picnic areas. Bus routes 2 and 10 from Cork city centre. ☎ 021 357 730; Fax 021 359 395.

Shandon Bells – Open all year, Mon–Sat and public holidays, 10am–5pm (summer), 10am–4pm (winter); Sun, 9.45am–11.30am. £2. Parking. No wheelchair access. ☎ 021 505 906.

Cork City Gaol – Open Mar–Oct, daily, 9.30am–6pm; Nov–Feb, 10am–5pm. Last admission 1 hr before closing. £3.50, £2 (child), £2.50 (reduction), £9 (family 2A+3C). Audio-guide (French, German, Irish, Italian, Spanish). Brochure (French, German, Italian, Spanish). ☎ 021 305 022; Fax 021 307 230.

Excursions

Dunkathel House – Open May–mid Oct, Wed–Sun, 2–6pm. £2, £1 (child), £1.50 (senior citizen/student). Brochure (French, German, Italian). Guided tour (30min) available. Parking. ☎ 021 821 014; Fax 021 821 023.

Riverstown House – Open May–Sept, Wed–Sat, 2–6pm; otherwise by appointment. £3. Guided tour available. Parking. ☎ 021 821 205.

Ballincollig Gunpowder Mills – ♿ Guided tour (1 hr) Mar–Sept, daily, 10am–6pm. £3, £1.80 (child), £2.50 (reduction), £8 (family 2A+3C). Audio-visual presentation (15min). Guided tour (French, German). Guide books (French, German). Parking. Coffee shop. Craft shop. ☎ 021 874 430; Fax 021 874 836.

D

🄱 The Quay, Dingle ☎ 066 51188 (Mar–end Oct)

Craft Centre, Ceardlann na Coille – Open all year, daily, 9.30am–6pm. No charge. Parking. Wholefood café. ☎ 066 51778.

Presentation Convent Chapel – Open June–Aug, Mon–Fri, 10am–noon and 2–4pm.

Dingle Library – Open all year, Tues–Sat, 10.30am–1.30pm and 2.30–5pm. ☎ 066 51499.

Blasket Islands Heritage Centre (Ionad an Bhlascaoid Mhóir) (Dúchas) – ♿ Open Apr–Oct, daily, 10am–6pm (7pm July–Aug); last admission 45min before closing. Closed 25–26 Dec. £2.50, £6 (family), £1 (child/student), £1.75 (senior citizen). Audio-visual presentation (French, German, Irish, Italian). Parking. Restaurant. ☎ 066 56444, 5637.

Blasket Islands Ferry – An t-Oilernach and Oilerin na n-óg operate cruises and truos from Dunquin in calm weather. ☎ 066 56422, 56455.

Corca Dhuibhne Regional Museum – Open May–Sept, daily, 10am–5pm; otherwise by request. £1.50. Refreshments in summer. Bureau de Change. Bookshop. ☎ 066 56100, 56333; Fax 066 56348.

Magharee Islands Ferry – Operates from Kilshannig in calm weather (boats uninsured and unlicensed).

🄱 The Quay ☎ 073 21148; Fax 073 22762
🄱 Main Street, Bundoran ☎ 072 41350 (June–Sept)

Hand-loom Weaving Demonstration (Magee's Shop) – (♿) Open all year, Mon–Sat, 9am–6pm. Leaflet (French, German). ☎ 073 22660; Fax 073 23271; e-mail sales@mageeshop.com

Donegal Castle (Dúchas) – (♿) Open June–Sept, daily, 9.30am–6.30pm; last admission 45min before closing. £2, £1 (child/student), £1.50 (senior citizen), £5 (family). ☎ 073 22405.

Donegal Railway Heritage Centre – Open June–Sept, Mon–Sat, 10am–5.30pm, Sun 2–5pm. ☎ 073 22655.

Excursions

Waterworld – Open June–Aug, daily, 11am–7pm; Easter week, daily, 11am–7pm; Apr, May and Sept, Sat–Sun only, 11am–7pm. Restaurant. ☎ 072 41172/3; Fax 072 42168.

Assaroe Abbey Waterwheels – Open Easter week, May–Aug, daily, 10.30am–6.30pm; otherwise, Sun, 1.30pm–6.30pm. Audio-visual presentation; charge. Parking. Coffee shop. Craft shop. ☎ 072 51580.

🄱 Main Street, Dungloe ☎ 075 21297 (June–Aug)

Glencolumbkille Folk Village – ♿ Guided tour (20min) Apr–Sept, daily, 10am (noon Sun)–6pm, every hour; also every 30min in July and Aug. £2, £1 (child/reduction). Brochure (English only). Guided tour. Nature walks. Craft shop. Parking. Tea house. ☎ 073 30017, 39026; Fax 073 30334.

Ulster Cultural Institute – ♿ Open all year, Mon–Fri, 9.30am–5pm; also Sat–Sun in summer. No charge. Restaurant. ☎ 073 30248.

Aradara Heritage Centre – Open June–Sept, daily, 10am–6pm; shorter hours in winter. Audio-visual presentation (15min). Tearoom. ☎ 075 41704.

St Connall's Museum and Heritage Centre – Open Apr–late Sept, Mon–Fri, 10am–4.30pm. £2, 50p (child). Parking.

Arranmore Island Ferry – For operating times see table; fewer sailings out of season. Single £6, £3 (child), £3 (student), £9 (car and driver). ☎ 075 20532; Fax 075 20750.

From **Burtonport**				From **Arranmore**			
June		July–Aug		June		July–Aug	
Mon–Sat	Sun + church hols	Mon–Sat	Sun + church hols	Mon–Sat	Sun + church hols	Mon–Sat	Sun + church hols
8.30am		8.30am		9am		9am	
10am	noon	10am	noon	10.30am	10.30am	12.30pm	
noon	1pm	noon	1pm	1pm	12.30pm	1pm	1.30pm
2pm	2pm	2pm	2pm	2.30pm	1.30pm	2.30pm	2.30pm
3pm	4pm	3pm	3pm	3.30pm	2.30pm	3.30pm	3.30pm
5pm	6pm	5pm	4pm	7.30pm	6.30pm	5.30pm	4.30pm
7pm	7pm	7pm	6pm		7.30pm	7.30pm	6.30pm
	8pm	8pm				8.30pm	8.30pm

Tory Island Ferry – For operating times (weather permitting) see table. Return £14, £7 (child), £12 (reduction); 074 35502 and 074 35920 (accommodation on Tory Island).

Bunbeg – Tory – Bunbeg (1 hr 30min)

from Bunbeg			from Tory Island
June–Aug daily	Oct daily	Nov–May per week	June–Aug daily
9am	once	3 sailings	10.30am

Magheroarty – Tory – Magheroarty (45min)

from Magheroarty		from Tory Island	
June daily	July–Aug daily	June daily	July–Aug daily
11.30am	11.30am		12.30pm
	1.30pm		
	(except Wed)	4pm	4pm
5pm	5pm	6pm	6pm

Coastal Cruises from Bunbeg: Operate on request. ☎ 075 31991 (Bunbeg Pier Office); 31320 and 31340; Fax 075 31665 (Donegal Coastal Cruises [Turasmara Teo], Strand Road, Middletown, Derrybeg, Co Donegal).

Coastal Cruises from Magheroarty (Meenlaragh): Operate on request. 074 35061 (Magheroarty Pier Office).

Doe Castle (Dúchas) – Closed until 1999 for refurbishment. Parking. ☎ 074 38124 (Caretaker).

"Flight of the Earls" Exhibition – (&) Open Apr–June, Sat–Sun, noon–6pm; July–Sept, daily, 10am (noon Sat–Sun and public holidays)–6pm. Closed Good Friday. £1.50, 50p (reduction), £4 (family 2A+3C). Guided tour (45min) available. Parking. ☎ 074 58229.

Family History Research Centre – Closed for repair. ☎ 074 38124 (Caretaker).

DONEGAL GLENS   🖪 Derry Road, Letterkenny ☎ 074 21160; Fax 074 25180

Donegal County Museum – & Open all year, Mon–Fri, 10am–12.30pm and 1–4.30pm, Sat, 1–4.30pm. No charge. ☎ 074 24613; Fax 074 26522.

Newmills Corn and Flax Mills – Open mid June–mid Sept, daily, 10am–6.30pm; last admission 45min before closing. £2, £1 (child/student), £1.50 (senior citizen), £5 (family 2A+2C). Parking. ☎ 074 25115.

Black Pig Train (An Mhuc Dhubh) – & Operates May–Sept, daily, 11am–5pm. £2, £6 (family 2A+3C), £1 (child). Café. ☎ 075 46280.

Colmcille Heritage Centre – & Open Easter and mid May–early Oct, daily, 10.30am (1pm Sun)–6.30pm; otherwise by appointment. £1.50, £1 (child). Guided tour (15min; Irish, English) available. Audio-guide available. Brochure (French, German, Irish). Multi-lingual audio-visual presentation (Irish, German, French). Parking. Tearoom. ☎ 074 37306, 37044.

Glebe House and Gallery (Dúchas) – (&) Open Easter (Holy Saturday-Low Sunday) and late May-late Sept, daily except Fri, 11am–6.30pm; last admission 1 hr before closing. £2, £1 (child/student), £1.50 (senior citizen), £5 (family). Guided tour (35min) available. Parking. Tearoom (summer). Wheelchair access to ground floor and gallery only. ☎ 074 37071; Fax 074 37072.

Glenveagh National Park (Dúchas) – & **Park and Visitor Centre**: Open Easter weekend-early Nov, daily, 10am–6.30pm (7.30pm Sun, early June–early Sept); Oct–early Nov, daily except Fri, 10am–6.30pm; last admission 90min before closing. £2, £1 (child/student), £1.50 (senior citizen), £5 (family). **Castle**: Guided tour (45min), 10.30am–5.30pm (6.30pm summer). £2, £1 (child/student), £1.50 (senior citizen), £5 (family). Audio-visual presentation (French, German, Irish, Italian). Leaflet (French, German, Dutch, Irish, Italian, Spanish). Guide book (English only). Guided tours available. Parking. Minibus (no charge) between Visitor Centre and Castle and gardens. Restaurant, cafeteria. Tearoom in castle. Wheelchair access to Visitor Centre, gardens and ground floor of castle. ☎ 074 37088; Fax 074 37072.

Dunlewy Lakeside Centre – Open Easter-2nd week in Nov, Mon-Sat, 10.30am–6pm, Sun, 11am–7pm. No charge. Guided tour of cottage, £3. Boat trip with commentary, £3. Craft shop. Restaurant. ☎ 075 31699.

Lurgy Vale Thatched Cottage – Open Easter week and mid May–Sept, daily, 10am–6.30pm. £1. Guided tour (French) available. **Traditional music**: mid May–Sept, Thur, 9pm–midnight. Parking. Refreshments. ☎ 074 39024, 21160.

Raphoe Cathedral – Open all year, daily, 8.30am–7pm. **Services**: Sun, 8am, 12.15pm, 6pm; Wed, 10.30am; Saints' Days 8pm. ☎ 074 45226.

Seat of Power Visitor Centre – Open Easter-Oct, daily, 10am–6pm. £3, £1.50 (child), £2 (reduction), £8 (family). ☎ 074 41733; Fax 074 41228.

Cavanacor House – Open Easter–end Aug, Tues–Sun and bank holidays, noon (2pm Sun)–6pm. £2.50. Brochure (French, German, Italian, Russian). ☎/Fax 074 41143.

🅷 Donore Road ☎ 041 37070; Fax 041 45340

Drogheda Museum – (&) Open all year, Tues–Sat, 10am–6pm; Sun, 2.30–5.30pm. Last admission 1 hr before closing. £1.50, 75p (child). Guided tour (1 hr) available. Parking. ☎/Fax 041 33097.

St Peter's Roman Catholic Church – & Open all year, daily, 8.30am–7.30pm. **Services**: Sun at 8am, 11am, noon; Sat, 6.15pm. ☎/Fax 041 38537.

St Peter's Anglican Church – Open by arrangement. **Services**: Sun at 11.30am, 1st and 3rd Sun of the month at 8.30am.

Excursions

Whiteriver Mills – Open Apr–Sept, daily, 10am (2pm Sun)–6pm. £1.50, 75p (child). ☎ 041 51141.

DUBLIN

🅳 St Andrew's Church, Suffolk Street
🅳 Baggot Street Bridge
🅳 Dublin Airport
🅳 B & I Terminal (July–Aug)
🅳 Town Centre, Tallaght
🅳 Dun Laoghaire Tourist Office, New Ferry Terminal
☎ 1850 230 330 (from the Republic of Ireland); Fax 066 979 2035
☎ 0171 493 3201 (Irish Tourist Board, London, from the UK)
Ticket reservation ☎ 01 605 7769
e-mail reservations@dublintourism.ie (reservations)
e-mail information@dublintourism.ie (information)
www.visit.ie/dublin

Historical Walking Tour – For information ☎ 01 878 0227.

Dublin Bus City Tour – Operates May–Sept, daily, 9.30am–5pm, every 10min; 5–6.30pm, every 30min. No tour 17 Mar, 31 Oct, 25 Dec. Hop-on-hop-off circular tour (10 stops; min 1 hr 15min) starting from 59 Upper O'Connell Street. £6, £3 (child). ☎ 01 873 4222; Fax 01 703 3177 (Dublin Bus).

Gray Line Bus Old Dublin Tour – Operates Mar–Oct, daily, 10am–5pm every 15min. Hop-on-hop-off circular tour (9 stops; min 1 hr) starting from 14 Upper O'Connell Street and including Merrion Square, Fitzwilliam Square and Phoenix Park. £7, £2 (child); ticket valid all day. ☎ 01 605 7705, 458 0808 (Gray Line Tours).

Guide Friday Dublin Tour – Operates all year, daily; Mon–Fri, every 15min, Sat–Sun, every 10min. Hop-on hop-off circular tour (8 stops; min 1 hr 30min) starting from O'Connell Street. First bus at 9.30am; time of last bus varies according to time of year, telephone for details. £7, £6 (reduction), £3 (child); ticket valid all day. ☎ 01 676 5377 (Guide Friday [Ireland] Ltd).

Bicycle Tour – Details from ☎ 01 679 0899.

Sightseeing Tour by horse-drawn carriage – Departs from St Stephen's Green (top of Grafton Street), in summer, daily; otherwise, weekends only or by appointment. 4/5 people per carriage. Long tour (75 min) £40 per carriage; medium tour (35min) £20 per carriage; shorter ride £10 per carriage, shortest ride £5 per carriage. ☎ 01 453 4619. By appointment only; £40 per hour; ☎ 01 453 3333 (Francis McCabe).

Steam Train Excursions – Details from ☎/Fax 01 837 4533 or from the Railway Preservation Society of Ireland, PO Box6238, Whitehall, Dublin 9 *(send a stamped addressed envelope [SAE])*.

Dublin Castle (Dúchas) – (&) Guided tour (50min including **State Apartments** [unless closed for official use] and Undercroft) daily, 10am (2pm Sat–Sun and bank holidays) 5pm. Last admission 1 hr before closing. Closed Good Friday, 24–26 Dec. £3, £1 (child), £2 (reduction), £4.50 (family). Guided tour and Brochure (French, German, Italian, Spanish). **Church of the Holy Trinity**: Open as above. Entrance via Lower Yard. Restaurant. Wheelchair access (except Undercroft). ☎ 01 677 7129; Fax 01 679 7831. **Chester Beatty Library**: Closed temporarily pending relocation in Dublin Castle in summer 1999. Opening times available from ☎ 01 269 2386, 01 269 5187; Fax 01 283 0983.

Christchurch Cathedral – Open all year, daily, 10am–5pm. Closed 26 Dec. Donation (£2). Self-guided tour with numbered leaflet (10 languages). ☎ 01 677 8099; Fax 01 679 8991.

Dublinia – (&) Open Apr–Sept, daily, 10am–5pm; Oct–Mar, daily, 11am (10am Sun and bank holidays)–4pm (4.30pm Sun and bank holidays). £3.95, £2.90 (child), £2.90 (reduction), £10 (family 2A+2C). Audio-guide (5 languages). No disabled access to 17C tower or pedestrian bridge to cathedral (cathedral can be accessed instead by crossing street). ☎ 01 679 4611; Fax 01 679 7116.

St Patrick's Cathedral – & Open all year, Mon–Fri, 9am–6pm; Sat, 9am–5pm (4pm Nov–Mar); Sun, 10am–11am and 12.30pm–3pm; also July–Aug only, 4.15pm–5pm; public holidays, 9.30am–4pm. Closed 25–26 Dec(except for services). £2, £1.50 (reduction). Leaflet (Dutch, French, German, Italian, Japanese, Spanish, Swedish, Irish). Parking. ☎ 01 453 9472, 475 4817; Fax 01 454 6374.

Marsh's Library – (&) Open all year, Mon, Wed–Fri, 10am–12.45pm and 2–5pm; Sat, 10.30am–12.45pm. £1. Brochure (14 languages). Guided tour (30min) by appointment. Limited parking. Facilities for the disabled (researchers only); telephone in advance. ☎ 01 454 3511; Fax 01 454 3511; e-mail marshlib@iol.ie www.kst.dit.ie/marsh

Tailors' Hall – & Open by appointment only. Bookings for functions to be made through Dublin Castle Conference Centre, Dublin 2. ☎ 01 679 3713; Fax 01 679 7831.

Dublin City Hall – Closed for refurbishment until January 2000. For further information ☎ 01 677 5877 (Dublin City Archives).

St Werburgh's Church – Open all year, Mon–Fri, 10am–4pm (on request). **Services**: Sun, 10am. Key available from 8 Castle Street. ☎ 01 478 3710.

St Audoen's Church – Opening times under revision, telephone for details. **Services**: Sun, 10.15am. ☎ 01 454 2274 (John Crawford).

Temple Bar Information Centre – & Open all year, 9am–5.30pm. ☎ 01 671 5717; 01 671 5717 (24hr infoline). www.temple.bar.ie

Viking Adventure – & Open Mar–Oct, Tues–Sat, 10am–1pm and 2–4.30pm. £3.75, £10 (family 2A+2C), £1.75 (child), £2.95 (reduction). Book and craft shop. ☎ 01 679 6040; Fax 01 679 6033.

Trinity College – & **Old Library (Book of Kells)**: Open all year, Mon–Sat, 9.30am–5pm, Sun and public holidays, noon–4.30pm; Sun opening times also apply to 17 Mar, Good Friday, Easter Monday and Oct bank holiday. Closed 24 Dec–3 Jan. £4.50, no charge (child under 12), £4 (reduction), £9 (family 2A+4C). ☎ 01 608 2320. **Dublin Experience**:Open late May–Sept, daily, 10am–5pm (last show), every hour. Time 45min. £3, £6 (family); joint ticket with Old Library £5, £4 (reductions), £10 (family). Head sets (French, German, Italian). Refreshments. ☎ 01 608 1688. **College Tour** (including The Colonnades and the Book of Kells): late May–Sept, daily, 10am–4pm (last tour), every 15min from the Front Square. £4.50; joint ticket with the Dublin Experience £7.

Bank of Ireland – & Open all year, Mon–Fri, 10am–4pm. Closed public holidays. Guided tour (45min) of Old Building, Tues at 10.30am, 11.30am, 1.45pm. ☎ 01 661 59331.

Bewley's Café Museum – Opening times as for café, all year, daily, 7.30am–9pm. Guided tour available in summer. Refreshments. ☎ 01 677 6761.

Powerscourt Centre – Open all year, daily except Sun and bank holidays, 9am–6pm. No charge.

Civic Museum – Open all year, Tues–Sat, 10am–6pm, Sun, 11am–2pm. Closed Mon including bank holidays. No charge. Time 30min. ☎ 01 679 4260.

St Ann's Church – Open all year, Mon–Fri, 10am–4pm. **Services**: Sun at 8am, 10.45am, 6.30pm; Mon–Fri, daily at 12.45pm. Lunch-hour and evening concerts. Coffee Shop (noon–2.30pm). ☎ 01 676 7727.

National Museum (Kildare Street) – & Open all year, Tues–Sun, 10am (2pm Sun)–5pm. Closed Good Friday, 25 Dec. No charge. Leaflet (French, German, Italian, Spanish). Audio-guide (French, German). Guided tour by appointment only. Refreshments. ☎ 01 677 7444; Fax 01 677 7828.

National Gallery – & Open all year, Mon–Sat, 10am–5.30pm (8.30pm Thur); Sun, 2–5pm. Closed Good Friday, 24–26 Dec. No charge. Guided tour Sat at 3pm, Sun at 2.15pm, 3pm, 4pm. Brochure (Irish). Restaurant. Book shop. ☎ 01 661 5133; Fax 01 661 5372.

St Stephen's Church – Open June–Aug, 12.30–2pm. **Services**: Sun, at 11am, Wed, at 11.30am. ☎ 01 288 0663 (Vicarage).

St Stephen's Church – Open mid Apr–early Oct, Mon–Fri, 12.30–2pm. **Services**: Sun at 11am, Wed at 11.30am. ☎ 01 288 0663 (Vicarage).

Number Twenty Nine – Guided tour all year, daily except Mon, 10am (2pm Sun)–5pm. Closed Good Friday, 2 weeks prior to Christmas. £2.50, £1 (reduction). Audio-visual presentation (10min), followed by guided tour of exhibition. Brochure (French, German, Irish, Italian, Spanish). Tearoom. Gift shop. ☎ 01 702 6165; Fax 01 702 7796.

Natural History Museum – (&) Open all year, Tues–Sun, 10am (2pm Sun)–5pm. No charge. Wheelchair access to ground floor only. ☎ 01 677 7444; Fax 01 676 6116.

Heraldic Museum – & Open all year, Mon–Fri, 10am–4.30pm. Closed public holidays and 24 Dec–2 Jan. No charge. Guided tour (20min; French, Irish, Spanish) by appointment. ☎ 01 661 1626, 661 4877; Fax 01 662 1062.

Parliament – Public gallery: Open during parliamentary sessions (Tues–Thur and sometimes Fri, by appointment). Closed Jan, Easter (2 weeks), mid July–early Oct and at Christmas. **Cabinet Rooms**: Guided tour by appointment, July, Sat. ☎ 01 668 9333 (Prime Minister's Office). ☎ 01 618 3296 (Captain of the Guard).

Government Buildings – Guided tour (40min; Taoiseach's Office, Ceremonial Stairs, Cabinet Room) Saturdays, 10.30am–3.30pm; ticket available same day from National Museum, 7-9 Merrion Row.

St Stephen's Green (Dúchas) – Open daily, 8am (10am Sun and bank holidays)–dusk; 25 Dec, 10am–1pm. No charge. ☎ 01 475 7816.

Iveagh Gardens – Open all year, daily, 8.30am (10.15am Sun)-dusk (5.30pm summer). No charge. ☎ 01 475 7816.

Newman House – Open July–Aug, Tues–Sat, noon (2pm Sat)–4.30pm; Sun, 11am–2pm; at other times by appointment only. £2, £1 (reduction). Guided tour (40min) available. Leaflet (French, German, Italian, Spanish). ☎ 01 706 7422, 01 475 7255; Fax 01 706 7211.

University Church – ও Open all year, daily. **Services**: Sat, at 7pm; Sun at 10am and noon; other days at 10am, 1.05pm. Ramp for wheelchairs. ☎ 01 478 0616.

St Mary's Pro-Cathedral – Open 8.30am–6.30pm. **Services**: Sun, at 8am (St Kevin's Oratory), 10am, 11am (Latin mass with Palestrina choir), noon (Italian mass, St Kevin's Oratory), 12.30pm, 6.30pm, 7pm (Spanish Mass, St Kevin's Oratory, 1st Sun of month); Mon–Sat, at 8.30am, 10am, 11am, 12.45pm, 5.45pm. Sat only: Vigil Mass for Sunday, 6pm; Vigil Mass for Young Adults, St Kevin's Oratory, 8pm. Irish Mass, 1st Fri of month only, 8pm. Guide book. Leaflet. ☎ 01 874 5441; Fax 01 874 2406.

Custom House – Open mid Mar–Oct, daily, 10am (2pm Sat and Sun)–5pm; Nov–mid Mar, Wed–Fri, 10am–5–m, Sun, 2–5–m. £1, £3 (family 2A+2C). ☎ 01 878 7660.

Garden of Remembrance (Dúchas) – (ও) Open Jan–Feb, daily, 11am–4pm; Mar–Apr, daily, 11am–7pm; May–Sept, daily, 9.30am–8pm; Oct, daily, 11am–7pm; Nov–Dec, daily, 11am–4pm. No charge. ☎ 01 661 3111.

Hugh Lane Municipal Gallery of Modern Art – ও Open all year, daily except Mon, 9.30am (11am Sun)–6pm (5pm Fri–Sun; 8pm, Thurs, July–Aug). Closed Good Friday and at Christmas. No charge. Guided tour (40min) available, £10 charge. Restaurant. Bookshop. Facilities for the disabled; wheelchair access; ramp. ☎ 01 874 1903, 878 8761; Fax 01 872 2182.

Dublin Writers Museum – Open all year, daily, 10am (11am Sun and public holidays)–5pm (6pm Sun and public holidays; also 6pm, Mon–Fri, July–Aug). £3, £1.40 (child), £2.55 (reduction), £8.25 (family 2A+4C); combined ticket with James Joyce Tower or George Bernard Shaw Birthplace available. Audio-guide (French, German, Italian, Japanese, Spanish). Guided tour by appointment. Brochure (Dutch, French, German, Italian, Spanish, Japanese). Children's salon (Seomra na Nog). Restaurant; coffee shop. Bookshop. ☎ 01 872 2077; Fax 01 872 2231.

Rotunda Hospital Chapel – To visit apply in advance to the Matron. Open 9am-1pm and 2pm–4pm. Leaflet available.

James Joyce Centre – Open daily, 9.30am (12.30pm Sun)–5pm. £2.75, 75p (child), £2 (reduction). Library. Café. ☎ 01 878 8547; Fax 01 878 8488.

National Wax Museum – Open all year, daily, 10am (noon Sun)–5.30pm. £3, £2 (child), £2.50 (student). Coffee shop. ☎ 01 872 6340.

St Michan's Church – (ও) Open mid Mar–Oct, Mon–Fri, 10am–1pm and 2–4.45pm, Sat, 10am–1pm; Nov–mid Mar, 12.30–3.30pm. £2, 50p (child), £1.50 (reduction). Guided tour (30–40min). Brochure (Danish, Dutch, French, German, Irish/Gaelic, Italian, Japanese, Spanish, Swedish). Parking. Gift shop. Wheelchair access to church not vaults. ☎ 01 872 4154; Fax 01 878 2615.

Old Jameson Distillery – ও Guided tour (75min; French, German, Italian, Japanese, Spanish), all year, 9am–5.30pm (last tour). £3.50, £1.50 (child). ☎ 01 807 2355.

St Mary's Abbey (Dúchas) – Open mid June–mid Sept, Wed and Sun, 10am–5pm; last admission 45min before closing. £1, 40p (child/student), 70p (senior citizen), £3 (family). Guided tour available. Access by stairs only. ☎ 01 872 1490.

Western Suburbs

National Museum (**Collins Barracks**) – Open all year, daily, 10am (Sun 2pm)–5pm. Guided tour (40min): daily at frequent intervals; £1. ☎ 01 677 7444; Fax 01 677 7828.

Phoenix Park Visitor Centre (Dúchas) – ও Open mid-end Mar and Oct, daily, 9.30am–5pm; Apr–May, daily, 9.30am–5.30pm; June–Sept, daily, 10am–6pm; Nov–mid Mar, Sat–Sun, 9.30am–4.30pm; last admission 45min before closing. Closed 25–26 Dec. £2, £1 (child/student), £1.50 (senior citizen), £5 (family). Audio-visual presentation (20min). Nature Trails. Parking. Tearoom. ☎ 01 677 0095.

President's Residence – Guided tour (1 hr) all year, Sat, 9.40am–4.20pm. Ticket available on the day from Phoenix Park Visitor Centre. ☎ 01 670 9155.

Dublin Zoological Gardens – Open all year, daily, 9.30am (10.30am Sun)-6pm/dusk. £5.90, £15.90 (family 2A+2C), £18 (family 2A+4C). Refreshments. Shop. ☎ 01 677 1425; Fax 01 677 1660; e-mail info@dublinzoo.ie
www.dublinzoo.ie

Guinness Hopstore – ♿ Open all year, Mon–Sat, 9.30am–5pm (4pm Oct–Mar), Sun and bank holidays, 10.30am (noon Oct–Mar)–4.30pm (4pm Oct–Mar). Closed Good Friday, 25–26 Dec. Time 1 hr. £4, £1 (child), £3 (reduction). ☎ 01 408 4800; Fax 01 408 4965
www.guinness.ie

Irish Museum of Modern Art – ♿ Open all year, Tues–Sun, 10am (noon Sun and public holidays)–5.30pm. Closed 17 Mar, Good Friday, 24–26 Dec. No charge. Guided tour Wed and Fri at 2.30pm, Sat at 11.30am. Leaflets on the history of the building (French, German, Irish, Italian, Spanish). Parking. Refreshments. Bookshop. ☎ 01 671 8666; Fax 01 671 8695. **Guided tour of the North Range**: By appointment only (functions permitting). Time 45min. No charge. ☎ 01 612 9900.

Kilmainham Gaol Museum – (♿) Guided tour Apr–Sept, daily, 9.30am–6pm; Oct–Mar, Mon–Fri, 9.30am–5pm, Sun, 10am–6pm; last admission 1 hr 15min before closing. Closed Sat, Oct–Mar; 24–26 Dec. £3.20, £1.25 (child/student), £2 (senior citizen), £7.50 (family). Audio-visual presentation (25min; French, German, Irish, Italian, Spanish). Parking. Ground floor of prison and exhibition accessible to wheelchairs. ☎ 01 453 5984; Fax 01 453 2037.

Drimnagh Castle – (♿) Guided tour Apr–end Sept, Wed, Sat and Sun, noon-5pm; Oct-Mar, Sun, noon-5pm; last tour 4.30pm; £1.50, 50p (child), £1 (senior citizen/student). Brochure (French, German, Italian). ☎ 01 450 2530; Fax 01 450 5401.

Southern Suburbs

Waterways Visitor Centre (Dúchas) – (♿) Open June–Sept, daily, 9.30am–6.30pm; Oct–May, Wed–Sun, 12.30–5pm; last admission 45min before closing. Closed 25–26 Dec. £2, £1 (child/student), £1.50 (senior citizen), £5 (family). Disabled access to ground floor only. ☎ 01 677 7510; Fax 01 677 7514.

Museum of Childhood – (♿) Telephone for opening times. Parking. Wheelchair access to ground floor only. ☎ 01 497 3223, 497 8696.

Shaw Birthplace – Open May–Oct, daily, 10am–1pm and 2pm (11am Sun and public holidays)–5pm. £2.60, £2.10 (reduction), £1.30 (child), £7.75 (family 2A+4C); combined ticket with Dublin Writers Museum available. Audio-guide (30min; Dutch, French, German, Italian, Spanish). Brochure (Dutch, French, German, Italian, Spanish). Bookshop. ☎ 01 475 0854; Fax 01 872 2231.

Jewish Museum – Open May–Sept, Sun, Tues and Thur, 11am–3.30pm; Oct–Apr, Sun, 10.30am–2.30pm or by appointment. Time 1 hr. Donation. ☎ 01 676 0737, 497 4252 (answerphone).

Rathfarnham Castle (Dúchas) – ♿ Guided tour Easter weekend, Sat–Mon, 10am–5pm; mid–end Apr, Sun, 10am–5pm; May, daily, 10am–5pm; June–Sept, daily, 10am–6pm; Oct, daily, 10am–5pm. Last tour 1 hr before closing; otherwise ☎ 01 661 3111. £1.50, 60p (child/student), £1 (senior citizen), £4 (family). Tearoom (10am–5pm). Leaflet (English only). ☎ 01 493 9461.

Pearse Museum (Dúchas) – (♿) **Park**: Open all year, daily, 10am–8pm (7pm Apr and Sept–Oct; 5.30pm Feb–Mar; 4.30pm Nov–Jan). **House**: Open all year, daily, 10am–1pm and 2–5.30pm (5pm Feb–Apr and Sept–Oct; 4pm Nov–Jan); last admission 45min before closing. Closed 25–26 Dec. No charge. Audio-visual presentation (20min). Open-air concerts (summer). Parking. Tearoom (summer). Wheelchair access to ground floor only. ☎ 01 493 4208; Fax 01 493 6120.

Northern Suburbs

National Botanic Gardens (Dúchas) – **Gardens**: Open summer, daily, 9am (11am Sun)-6pm; winter, daily, 10am (11am Sun)–4.30pm. **Glasshouses**: Open summer, Mon–Sat, 9am–12.45pm and 2–5.15pm (3.15pm Thurs, 5.45pm Sat), Sun, 2–5.45pm; winter, Mon–Sat, 10am–12.45pm and 2–4.15pm, Sun, 2–4.15pm. No charge. Guided tour (1 hr) by arrangement. Parking. Facilities for the disabled; wheelchair available; full access (some steep gradients) for wheelchairs. ☎ 01 837 7596, 4388; Fax 01 836 0080.

GAA Museum – Open May–Sept, daily, 10am–5pm; Oct–Apr, daily except Mon, 2–5pm. £3, £1.25 (child), £6 (family 2A+2C).

Marino Casino (Dúchas) – Guided tour Feb–Apr and Nov, Sun and Wed, noon–4pm; May, daily, 10am–5pm; June–Sept, daily, 9.30am–6.30pm; Oct, daily, 10am–5pm; last admission 45min before closing. Closed 25–26 Dec. £2, £1 (child/student), £1.50 (senior citizen), £5 (family). Parking. ☎ 01 833 1618.

Marino Casino, Dublin

North Bull Island Interpretive Centre – Open all year, daily, 10.15am–1pm and 1.30–4pm (2.30pm Fri). Audio-guide (French). Brochure (German, Spanish). Parking. ☎ 01 833 8341.

DUNDALK
🄸 Jocelyn Street ☎ 042 35484; Fax 042 38070

Historical Walking Tour of Dundalk – Thurs. at 7pm. ☎ 042 28061 (H Smith, TIC).

Louth County Museum – Open Tues–Sat, 10.30am–5.30pm, Sun and bank holidays, 2-6pm. £2, 60p (child), £5 (family 2A+2C). ☎ 042 27056/7.

Excursions

Carlingford Heritage Centre – Open Mar–Oct. £l, 50p (child). ☎ 042 937 3454.

Carlingford Lough Passenger Ferry (cross-border Omeath/Warrenpoint) – Operates May–Sept, 1–6pm every 20min. Return £2, £1 (child). ☎ 016937 73070, 72682, 72598.

Carrickmacross Lace Gallery – Open mid Apr–Oct, Mon, Tues, Thur and Fri, 9.30am–12.30pm and 1.30pm–5pm, Wed, 9.30am–12.30pm, Sat, 10am–noon. ☎ 042 62506, 62088.

Inniskeen Folk Museum – Open May–Sept, Sun, 2–6pm; otherwise by appointment. Donation £1. ☎ 042 78109.

DUNGARVAN
🄸 The Square ☎ 058 41741

Dungarvan Museum – Open all year, Mon–Fri, 11am–1pm and 2–5pm. No charge. ☎ 058 41231 (Dungarvan Library; ask for Museum).

DUN LAOGHAIRE
🄸 New Ferry Terminal (Walk–in service)

National Maritime Museum – (&) Open May–Sept, Tues–Sun; Oct, Sat–Sun, 2.30–5.30pm. £1.50, 80p (child), £4 (family). Wheelchair access to ground floor. ☎ 01 280 0969 (24hr).

James Joyce Museum – Open Apr–Oct, daily, 10am–1pm and 2–5pm (6pm Sun and public holidays); Nov–Mar by arrangement. £2.60, £2.10 (reduction), £1.30 (child), £7.75 (family 2A+4C); combined ticket with Dublin Writers Museum available. Brochure (Danish, Dutch, French, German, Italian, Japanese, Spanish). ☎ 01 280 9265, 872 2077; Fax 01 280 9265.

Dalkey Heritage Centre – Open Apr–Oct, Tues–Fri, 9.30am –5pm, Sat, Sun and public holidays, 11am–5pm; Nov–Dec, Sat, Sun and public holidays, 11am–5pm. £2.50, £8 (family 2A+2C), £1.50 (child). ☎ 01 285 8366.

DUNGLOE see DONEGAL COAST

E

ENNIS

🛈 Clare Road ☎ 065 28366

Ennis Friary (Dúchas) – (♿) Open late May–late Sept, daily, 9.30am–6.30pm (5.45pm last admission). £1, 40p (child/student), 70p (senior citizen), £3 (family). Guided tour on request. Parking. ☎ 065 29100.

De Valera Library – ♿ Closed temporarily. ☎ 065 21616 ext 352, 353; Fax 065 42462.

Excursions

Dromore Wood National Nature Reserve (Dúchas) – **Forest Park**: Open all year. **Information Centre**: Open mid June–mid Sept, daily, 10am–6pm. No charge. Guidebook to two trails (20min and 40min) £1. ☎ 065 37166.

Dysert O'Dea Archeology Centre – Open May–Sept, daily, 10am–6pm. £2.50, £1 (child), £6 (family). Brochure (English only). Parking. Refreshments. ☎ 065 37401; 065 42292 (evenings and off season). Audio-visual presentation (English, German).

Clare Heritage Centre – ♿ Open daily, 10am–6pm. Guided tour (30min) available. Brochure (French, German). Parking. Tearoom. ☎ 065 37955.

Quin Franciscan Friary (Dúchas) – Open dawn–dusk. If closed, key available from the house nearest to the bridge.

Knappogue Castle – (♿) Open Apr–Oct, daily, 9.30am–5.30pm (4.30pm last admission). £2.75, £6.80 (family 2A+2C), £1.65 (child), £1.90 (student/senior citizen). ☎ 061 360 788 (Shannon Heritage); Fax 061 361 020. **Medieval banquets**: Apr–Oct, daily at 5.30pm and 8.45pm; £32, £24.25 (child 10–12), £16.50 (child 6–9); Parking. Wheelchair access to ground floor only. ☎ 061 360 788 (Shannon Heritage).

Craggaunowen Centre – ♿ Open Good Friday–Oct, daily, 10am (9am mid May–Aug)–6pm (5pm last admission). £4.20, £11 (family 2A+2C), £2.60 (child), £3.30 (student/senior citizen). Guided tour available. Brochure (French, German). Parking. Refreshments. ☎ 061 360 788 (Shannon Heritage), 061 367 146, 367 178.

ENNISCORTHY

🛈 Town Centre ☎ 054 34699 (mid June–end Aug)
🛈 Gorey Town Centre ☎ 055 21248

Enniscorthy Tour – Guided tour (30min or 1 hr; French, Italian; starting from opposite the castle) June–Sept, daily at 11am, 12.30pm, 3pm, 4.30pm, Sat–Sun by booking only. £2, £1 (child). ☎ 054 36800; Fax 054 36628.

Enniscorthy Castle – Keys available from Mr Jim Gellings, 36 Castle Way.

County Museum – (♿) Open June–Sept, Mon–Sat, 10am–1pm and 2–6pm, Sun, 2–5.30pm; Oct–Nov and Feb–Mar, daily, 2–5.30pm; Dec–Jan, Sun 2–5.30pm. £3, 50p (child), £2 (reduction). Guided tour (1 hr) available. Wheelchair access to ground floor only. ☎ 054 35926; e-mail wexmus@iol.ie

Carley's Bridge Potteries – Open all year, Mon–Fri, 8.30am–12.45pm and 2–5.30pm; also summer, Sat, 10am–4.30pm, Sun, 2–4.30pm; bank holidays, variable hours; check in advance. No charge. Guided tour (1 hr) available. Parking. ☎ 054 33512, 33080; Fax 054 34360.

FINGAL

St Mary's Abbey – Key from Mrs O'Rourke, 3 Church Street, Howth.

Ireland's Eye Ferry – Operates daily on demand (only in calm weather, Apr–Oct), noon–6pm, from East Pier, Howth Harbour. Not suitable for disabled. Return £4. ☎ 01 831 4200.

National Transport Museum – (♿) Open Oct–May, Sat–Sun and bank holidays, 2–5.30pm; 26 Dec–1 Jan, daily, 2–5.30pm; June–Sept, daily, 10am (2pm Sat)–5.30pm. £1.50, 50p (child/senior citizen), £3 (family 2A+5C). Parking. ☎ 01 848 0831.

Howth Castle Rhododendron Gardens – Open only to patrons of the Deer Park Hotel and golf courses all year, daily, dawn–dusk. Closed 25 Dec. No charge. ☎ 01 832 2624; Fax 01 839 2405.

Malahide Castle – Open Apr–Oct, Mon–Sat, 10am–12.45pm and 2–5pm, Sun and public holidays, 11am–12.45pm and 2–6pm; Nov–Mar, Mon–Fri, 10am–12.45pm and 2–5pm, Sat–Sun and public holidays, 2–5pm. £3.10, £1.70 (child), £2.60 (reduction), £8.50 (family 2A+4C); combined ticket with Fry Model Railway Museum or Newbridge House available. Audio-guide (Dutch, French, German, Italian, Japanese, Spanish). Brochure (French, German, Italian, Japanese, Spanish). Parking. Restaurant, coffee shop; banquets on request. Craft shop. ☎ 01 846 2184, 846 2516; Fax 01 846 2537.

Howth ferry to Ireland's Eye

Fry Model Railway Museum – Open Apr–Sept, Mon–Thur and Sat, 10am–1pm and 2–5pm; Sun and public holidays, 2–6pm; Oct–Mar, Sat–Sun and public holidays, 2–5pm. £2.85, £1.65 (child), £2.15 (reduction), £7.75 (family 2A+4C); combined ticket with Malahide Castle or Newbridge House available. Audio-guide (French, Italian, Spanish). Parking. ☎ 01 846 3779; Fax 01 846 2537.

Newbridge – House: Guided tour (45min) Apr–Sept, Tues–Sat, 10am–1pm and 2–5pm; Sun and public holidays, 2–6pm; Oct–Mar, Sat–Sun and public holidays, 2–5pm. **Courtyard and Farm:** Open as above. House and farm £3.85, £3.30 (reduction), £9.50 (family); house only £2.85, £1.55 (child), £2.50 (reduction), £7.75 (family 2A+4C); farm only £1, 80p (reduction), £2 (family 2A+4C); combined ticket with Malahide Castle £4.75, £11.95 (family 2A+4C). Parking. Coffee shop. Craft shop. ☎ 01 843 6534; Fax 01 846 2537.

Ardgillan Castle – Open Apr–Sept, Tues–Sun and public holidays, 11am–6pm (open daily, July–Aug); Oct–Mar, Tues–Sun and public holidays, 11am–4.30pm. Closed 23 Dec–1 Jan. £2.75, £1.75 (reduction), £6.50 (family). ☎ 01 849 2212; Fax 01 849 2786. ☎ 01 412 178 (Balbriggan Information Office).

Swords Castle – ♿ Open all year, Mon, Wed, Thurs and Fri, 10am–noon and 2–4pm (3pm Fri). No charge. ☎ 01 840 0891.

Lusk Heritage Centre (Dúchas) – Open mid June–mid Sept, Fri, 10am–5pm. Last admission 45min before closing. £1, 40p (child), 70p (senior citizen), £3 (family). ☎ 01 843 7683.

G

GALWAY

🛈 Victoria Place, Eyre Square ☎ 091 563 081; Fax 091 565 201
🛈 Galway Railway Station ☎ 091 567 555 (June–Aug)
🛈 Salthill ☎ 091 563 081 (mid May–mid Sept)
🛈 Oughterard ☎ 091 552 808; Fax 091 552 2811

Druid Theatre – ☎ 091 568 617.

Irish Theatre (An Taibhdhearc na Gaillimhe) – Open summer. ☎ 091 562 024 (office), 757 479; Fax 091 62195.

St Nicholas' Church – Open 9am–4.30pm. Brochure (Dutch, French, German, Italian, Japanese, Spanish). ☎ 091 564 648, 521 914, 522 998, 524 557.

Galway City Museum – Open Apr–Oct, daily, 10am–5.15pm, Oct–Apr, Mon, Wed, Fri, noon–4pm. £1, 50p (child/student). Guided tour (20min) by appointment. ☎ 091 567 641.

GALWAY

Nora Barnacle House Museum – Open mid May–mid Sept, Mon–Sat, 10am–1pm and 2–5pm. £1. ☎ 091 564 743.

Bank of Ireland – Open all year, Mon–Fri, 10am–4pm. Closed public holidays.

Excursions

Lough Corrib Cruise – ♿ Operates from **Wood Quay**, end Apr–Oct, daily at 2.30pm, 4.30pm. Time 90min. £5, £12 (family 2A+2C). Commentary (various languages). Bar. ☎ 091 592 447 (Corrib Tours).

Aughnanure Castle (Dúchas) – (♿) Open mid June–mid Sept, daily, 9.30am–6.30pm; last admission 45min before closing. £2, £1 (child/student), £1.50 (senior citizen), £5 (family). Guided tour available. Parking. No wheelchair access to roof of Tower House. ☎ 091 552 214.

GLENDALOUGH   🏛 ☎ 0404 45581 (June–Sept)

Glendalough (Dúchas) – ♿ **Site**: Open all year, daily. **Visitor Centre**: Open mid Mar–mid Oct, daily, 9.30am–6pm; late Oct–mid Mar, daily, 9.30am–5pm; last admission 45min before closing. Closed 25–26 Dec. £2, £1 (child), £1.50 (senior citizen), £5 (family). Audio-visual presentation (French, German, Italian, if booked in advance). Guided tour (French, German, Spanish, Swedish if booked in advance). Parking. Picnic area. ☎ 0404 45325, 45352.

GLENGARRIFF see BANTRY BAY   🏛 ☎ 027 63084

GOREY see ENNISCORTHY   🏛 Town Centre ☎ 055 21248

H

HOOK HEAD PENINSULA

Dunbrody Abbey – Open Apr–Sept, daily, 10am–6pm (7pm July–Aug). Abbey £1.50, £1 (child); Maze £1.50, £1 (child). ☎ 051 388 603 or 051 389 104.

Tintern Abbey – ♿ Re-opening after restoration June 1998. £1.50, £4 (family 2A+2C), 60p (child). Guided tour available on request. ☎ 01 661 3111 (Head Office).

Ballyhack Castle (Dúchas) – Open June–Sept, daily, 10am–6pm. Closed Mon–Fri, 1–2pm. Last admission 45min before closing. £1, 50p (child/student), £3 (family). Public parking nearby. Guided tours available on request. Access by stone steps. ☎ 051 338 9468.

Kilmokea Gardens – Open daily, 10am–5pm. £4, no charge (accompanied child). Guided tour available. Plants for sale. Teas in Georgian conservatory. ☎ 051 388 109; Fax 051 388 776; e-mail: kilmokea@indigo.ie

Duncannon Fort – (♿) Open June–mid Sept, daily, 10am–5.30pm. £1.50, 50p (child), £1 (senior citizen). Craft shop. Café. Guided tours available. ☎ 051 389 188; ☎/Fax 051 389 454.

I

INISHOWEN   🏛 Shore Front, Buncrana ☎ 077 62600 (June–Aug)

Dunree Fort – Open June–Sept, daily, 10.30am (12.30pm Sun)–6pm. £1.50, 75p (reduction). Guided tour (30min) available. Parking. Refreshments. ☎ 077 61817.

Buncrana Vintage Car Museum – ♿ Open June–Sept, daily, 10am–8pm or later; Oct–May, Sun and public holidays, noon–8pm; at other times by appointment. £2, 50p (child). Guided tour (30min) available. Parking. ☎ 077 61130.

Grianán Ailigh – Open daily, 10am (noon in winter)–6pm. £2, £5 (family 2A+2C), £1.10 (reduction). Restaurant (open daily 10am (noon in winter)–10pm). ☎ 077 68512; Fax 077 68530.

IVERAGH PENINSULA   🏛 Heritage Centre, Kenmare ☎ 064 41233 (Apr–Oct)
🏛 RIC Barracks, Caherciveen ☎ 066 72589 (June–mid Sept)

Puck Fair Exhibition – Open daily, noon–9pm. ☎ 066 61353 (Patrick Houlihan).

Valencia Island–Renard Point Car Ferry – Operates a shuttle service (5min) Apr–Sept, daily, 8.15am (9am Sun)–10pm. Car + passengers £3 (single), £4 (return); pedestrian £1 each way; cyclist £2 (single), £3 (return). ☎ 066 76141; Fax 066 76377.

392

Skellig Experience Visitor Centre – ♿ Open Easter–Oct, daily, 10am–6.30pm. Exhibition £3, £1.50 (child), £2.70 (reduction), £7 (family 2A+4C). Audio-visual presentation. Audio-guide (French, German). **Skellig Islands Cruise**: Discontinued until further notice. Parking. Refreshments. ☎ 066 76306.

Skellig Islands Ferry – ☎ 066 77101 (Portmagee Post Office); 066 76306 (Skellig Experience Centre) for details about boats which (weather permitting) will put people ashore on the islands. On Great Skellig, only very experienced climbers should continue above the monastery ruins to the cross carved near the summit.

Derrynane National Historic Park (Dúchas) – (♿) Open Apr and Oct, Tues–Sun, 1pm–5pm; May–Sept, Mon–Sat, 9am–6pm, Sun, 11am–7pm; Nov–Mar, Sat–Sun, 1pm–5pm; last admission 45min before closing. £2, £1 (child/student), £1.50 (senior citizen), £5 (family). Audio-visual presentation (25min). Parking. Tearoom (summer). Facilities for the disabled; wheelchair access to ground floor only. ☎ 066 75113.

Sneem Church – Key available from café opposite. **Services**: Sun, at 10am. ☎/Fax 064 41121.

Kenmare Heritage and Lace and Design Centre – Open mid June–Aug, daily, 9.30am–5.30pm. No charge. **Lace-making demonstrations**: Good Friday-mid June and Sept–early Oct, 10.15am–5.30pm; in winter on request. £2, £5 (family 2A+4C). Audio-guide (French, German). ☎ 064 41233, 31633, 41688 (Heritage Centre); ☎/Fax 064 41491 (Lace and Design Centre).

K

KELLS

St Columba's Anglican Church – Open 10am–1pm and 2–5pm.

Excursions

St Kilian's Heritage Centre – Open Easter–Oct, daily except Mon, 10am (12.30pm Sun)–6pm; also open bank holiday Monday. £3, £1 (child), £1.50 (reduction). Video (15min). Parking. Restaurant. Craft shop. ☎/Fax 046 42433.

Loughcrew Passage Graves (Dúchas) – Guided tour (1 hr including 20min up and 20min down) mid June–Sept, daily, 10am–6pm; last admission 45min before closing time. £1. Out of season, key available (£5 deposit) from the house on the corner at the bottom of the lane on the south side of the hill ☎ 049 41256 (Mrs Balse).

KENMARE see IVERAGH PENINSULA ▪ Heritage Centre ☎ 064 41233 (Apr–Oct)

KILDARE ▪ Town Centre ☎ 045 522 696 (mid May–Sept)

Kildare Cathedral – Open Mon–Sat, 10am–1pm and 2–5pm, Sun, 2–5pm. **Services**: Sun, noon (HC). ☎ 045 441 654.

Excursions

Irish National Stud and Japanese Gardens – ♿ Open mid Feb–mid Nov, daily, 9.30am–6pm. £6, £14 (family 2A+4C), £3 (child), £4.50 (reduction). Brochure (Dutch, French, German, Italian, Spanish). Parking. Refreshments. Gift/craft shop. ☎ 045 521 617, 522 963; Fax 045 522 964.

Bord Fáilte, Dublin

Irish National Stud

Peatland World – Open all year, Mon–Fri, 9.30am–5pm, Sat–Sun, 2–6pm. £3, £2.50 (reduction), £6 (family). Guided tour (90min) available on request for groups. Parking. Refreshments. ☎ 045 860 133; Fax 045 860 481.

Robertstown – **Old Canal Hotel**: Open Mon–Sat, 9am–5pm; Sun and public holidays, 2–6pm. **Canal barge cruises**: Operate Apr–Sept, Mon–Fri, by arrangement; Sun and public holidays, 2–6pm. Time 1 hr (3 hr cruise also available). £3, £1.50 (child), £7 (family 2A+2C). Parking. Restaurant. Shop ☎ 045 870 005 or 860 260.

KILKEE see KILRUSH ▪ ☎ 065 56112 (end May–early Sept)

🏛 Shee Alms House, Rose Inn Street 🕾 056 51500; Fax 056 63955

Medieval Kilkenny Walking Tour – Operates from Kilkenny Tourist Office in Rose Inn Street Mar–Oct, Mon–Sat at 9.15am, 10.30am, 12.15pm, 1.30pm, 3pm, 4.30pm, Sun at 11am, 12.15pm, 3pm; Nov–Feb, Tues–Sat at 10.30am, 12.15pm, 3pm. £3, £1 (child). 🕾 056 65929, 087 265 1745 (mobile); Fax 056 63955 (Tynan Tours).

Kilkenny Castle (Dúchas) – (♿) **Park**: Guided tour all year, daily, 10am–8.30pm (4pm in winter). **Castle**: Guided tour (French, Irish) June–Sept, daily, 10am–7pm; Apr–May, daily, 10.30am–5pm; Oct–Mar, daily except Mon, 10.30am (11am Sun)–12.45pm and 2–5pm; last admission 1 hr before closing. Closed Good Friday, 25–26 Dec. £3, £1.25 (child/student), £2 (senior citizen), £7.50 (family). 🕾 056 21450; Fax 056 63488. Audio-visual presentation. **Butler Gallery of Contemporary Art** (basement): Open as above. No charge. Tearoom (May–Sept). Wheelchair access to ground floor only. 🕾 056 61106.

Kilkenny Design Centre – Open all year, daily, 9am–6pm. Closed Jan–Mar, Sun and bank holidays. Restaurant (not suitable for disabled visitors, steep stairs). 🕾 056 22118; Fax 056 65905.

St Canice's Cathedral – ♿ Open all year, daily: Easter–Sept, Mon–Sat, 9am–1pm and 2–6pm, Sun, 2–6pm; Oct–Easter, Mon–Sat, 10am–1pm and 2–6pm, Sun 2–4pm. Closed Wed and Holy Days, 10–11am; Good Friday, 25 Dec–1 Jan. £1 donation per adult. Guided tours available. Leaflet (French, German, Spanish, Italian, Dutch, Japanese, Irish). Guide book (English only). Gift shop. 🕾 056 21516 (the Dean), 64971 (Cathedral). Guided tour (30min; French sometimes). Leaflet (French, German, Italian, Spanish) 20p. **Round Tower**: Open (weather permitting) Easter–mid Sept; £1, 50p (child).

Shee Alms House – Open Nov–Mar, Mon–Fri, 9am–5pm; Apr–Sept, Mon–Sat, 9am–6pm (8pm July–Aug); Oct, Mon–Sat, 9am–5pm; also open May–Sept, Sun, 11am–5pm. 🕾 056 51500; Fax 056 63955.

Black Abbey – ♿ Open all year, daily, 7.30am (8.30am Sat–Sun)–7pm. No visiting during services. Donation. Brochure (English only). 🕾 056 21279.

Rothe House – Open all year, daily, 10.30am (1.30pm Sun)–5.30pm. Closed Good Friday. £2, £1 (child), £1.50 (senior citizen/student). Audio-visual presentation. Guided tour (45min) available. Leaflet (French, German). 🕾 056 22893.

Tholsel – Open all year, Mon–Fri, 9am–1pm and 2–5pm. No charge. 🕾 056 21076.

Excursions

Ladywell Water Garden – Open Tues–Sat, 10am–5pm; also open Sun, June–Oct, noon–5.30pm and Sun in Dec, 2–5.30pm. Closed Mon. **Garden centre and coffee shop**: Open all year except Christmas and New Year. 🕾 056 24690.

Mount Juliet – Advance booking for sporting facilities. 🕾 056 73000; Fax 056 73019; e-mail info@mountjuliet.ie
www.mountjuliet.ie

Kilfane Glen and Waterfall – Open May–mid Sept, Tues–Sun, 2–6pm; at other times by appointment. £3, £2 (child), £2.50 (reduction), £9 (family). 🕾 056 24558; Fax 056 27491.

Jerpoint Abbey (Dúchas) – (♿) Open June–late Sept, daily, 9.30am–6.30pm; late Sept–mid Oct, daily, 10am–5pm; Apr–June, daily, 10am–5pm; last admission 45min before closing. £2, £1 (child/student), £1.50 (senior citizen), £5 (family). Exhibition in Visitor Centre. Guided tour available. Brochure (French, German, Spanish, Italian, Irish). Parking. 🕾 056 24623.

Edmund Rice Centre – ♿ Open all year, daily, 10am–1pm and 2–6pm (5pm Oct–Apr). Closed Good Friday, 25 Dec. No charge. Admission by application to the adjoining monastery. Guided tour (1 hr) available. Parking. 🕾 056 25141.

Bród Tullaroan – Open Easter–May and Oct–Nov, Sun, 2–5pm; June–Sept, Mon–Fri, 10am–5.30pm, Sun, 2–6pm. £3, no charge (accompanied child), £2 (senior citizen), £6 (family 2A+2C). 🕾 056 69107.

Dunmore Cave (Dúchas) – Guided tour (30min) mid June–Oct, daily, 10am–7pm (5pm mid Sept–Oct); mid Mar–mid June, daily, 10am–7pm; otherwise, Sat–Sun and public holidays, 10am–5pm; last admission 45min before closing. Closed 25–26 Dec. £2, £1 (child/student), £1.50 (senior citizen), £5 (family). Parking. No wheelchair access. 🕾 056 67726.

🏛 Ballina 🕾 096 70848 (early Apr–Sept)

Céide Fields Visitor Centre (Dúchas) – Open mid Mar–May and Oct–Nov, daily, 10am–5pm (4.30pm Nov); June–Sept, daily, 9.30am–6.30pm. Last admission 1 hr before closing. Closed 25–26 Dec. For winter opening hours 🕾 01 661 3111. £2.50, £1 (child/student), £1.75 (senior citizen), £6 (family). Audio-visual presentation (20min). Guided tour of site available. Exhibition text (French, German, Italian). Parking. Tearoom. 🕾 096 43325; Fax 096 43261.

Belderrig Prehistoric Farm ⊘ – (🚻) Open June–Sept, 9.30am–6.30pm; mid Mar–May and Oct–Nov, 10am–5pm (4.30pm Nov). £2.50, £6 (family 2A+2C), £1 (child/student), £1.75 (senior citizen). Audio–visual (20min) presentation. Guide book and leaflets (French, German, Italian). Tearoom. Wheelchair access to Visitor Centre only.

KILLALOE

🛈 Heritage centre ☎ 061 376 866 (May–Sept)

St Flannan's Cathedral – Open all year, daily, during daylight hours; guided visit to tower, only when shop is open, usually Easter to Sept, 11am–4.30pm. Cathedral, donation; tower and bells, £1. ☎/Fax 061 376 687.

Killaloe Heritage Centre – Open May–Sept, daily, 10am–6pm (5pm last admission). £1.60, £4.10 (family), 80p (child), £1.10 (student, senior citizen). ☎ 061 360 788 (Shannon Heritage).

Excursions

East Clare Heritage Centre – Open June–Oct, daily. Audio–visual presentation (10min). Guided tour (French, German) available on request. ☎ 061 921 351 (also information on boat trips from Mountshannon).

Holy Island Ferry – Operates from Mountshannon June–mid Sept (weather permitting). £3 per person. ☎ 061 921 351.

KILLARNEY

🛈 Beech Road ☎ 064 31633; Fax 064 34506
🛈 Kerry County Airport, Farranfore ☎ Freephone at Airport Terminal

St Mary's Cathedral – 🚻 Open all year, daily, 9am–9pm. If locked, apply to the Cathedral Office. No charge. Parking. ☎ 064 31014.

Museum of Irish Transport – Open Apr–Oct, daily, 10am–6pm. Time 1 hr. £3, £1 (child), £1.50 (student), £7 (family 2A+2C). Parking. ☎ 064 34677; Fax 064 31582.

St Mary's Church – Open all year, daily, 9.30am–5pm.

Excursions

Killarney National Park – Open all year, daily, 9am–5.30pm (7pm July–Aug). No charge. **Muckross Information Centre**: Open as for Muckross House (see below). Audio-visual presentation (20min). ☎ 064 31440. **Torc Information Office**: Open end June–mid Sept, daily, 9.30am–6.30pm.

Knockreer Demesne – Open all year, daily. Tearoom. ☎ 064 31246.

Ross Castle (Dúchas) – (🚻) Open Easter and Apr, daily, 11am–6pm; May, daily, 10am–6pm; June–Aug, daily, 9am–6.30pm; Sept, daily, 10am–6pm; Oct, daily, 10am–5pm. Closed 31 Oct–Easter. Access by guided tour only; last admission 45min before closing. Closed 25–26 Dec. £2.50, £1 (child/student), £1.75 (senior citizen), £6 (family). Parking. Wheelchair access to ground floor only by prior arrangement. ☎ 064 35851, 35852.

Lough Leane Boat Trips – Operate from Ross Castle all year, daily (weather permitting): *Pride of the Lakes* at 11am, 12.30pm, 2.30pm, 4pm, 5.15pm (☎/Fax 064 32638 Destination Killarney); *Lily of Killarney* at 10.30am, noon, 1.45pm, 3.15pm, 4.30pm, 5.45pm (☎ 064 31068, 064 31251, 31567; Fax 064 34077 (Dero's Tours). ☎ 064 31068; Fax 064 35001 (Killarney Boating and Tour Centre). Time 1 hr. £5, £2.50 (child). Bus shuttle between Scott's Gardens and Ross Castle.

Andy Williams

KILLARNEY

Muckross Abbey (Dúchas) – Open mid June–early Sept, daily, 10am–5pm. Last admission 45min before closing. No charge. Time 30min. Guided tours available on request. ☎ 064 31440; Fax 064 33926.

Muckross House and Farms (Dúchas) – ♿ **House**: Open all year, daily: Nov–mid Mar, 9am–5.30pm; mid Mar–June, 9am–6pm; July–Aug, 9am–7pm; Sept–Oct, 9am–6pm. Closed one week at Christmas. **Farms**: Open mid Mar–Apr and Oct, Sat–Sun and bank holidays, 2–6pm; May, daily, 1–6pm; June–Sept, daily, 10am–7pm. Last admission 45min before closing. House or farms £3.80, £1.60 (child/student), £2.70 (senior citizen), £9 (family); house and farms £5.50, £2.75 (child/student) £4 (senior citizen), £14 (family). Leaflet (French, German, Italian, Spanish, Dutch). Parking. Licensed restaurant; picnic areas. Craft shop. ☎ 064 31440; Fax 064 33926; e-mail mucros@iol.ie

Muckross Jaunting Car Trips – Operate from Muckross House round the lake (1 hr). £6.

Gap of Dunloe Excursion – Operates Apr–Oct, daily (weather permitting), 10.30am–5pm (round tour (6–7 hr) from Killarney by bus to Kate Kearney's Cottage, by pony or pony trap or on foot through the Gap to Lord Brandon's Cottage, by boat across the three lakes, by bus to Killarney). Bus and boat £13; pony £12; pony trap £10. ☎ 064 31633; Fax 064 34506 (Tourist Office); ☎ 064 32496, 31115; Fax 064 35088 (Castlelough Tours); ☎ 064 31052 (O'Connor); 064 31251, 31567; Fax 34077 (Deros Tours); ☎ 064 43151; Fax 36555 (Corcoran's).

Kate Kearney's Cottage – ♿ Open all year, daily, 9am–11.30pm (11pm Dec–Apr). No charge. **Irish dancing**: summer months, Sun, Wed and Fri. Parking. Bar food; dinner (6.30pm–9pm). ☎ 064 44146; Fax 064 44641.

Dunloe Castle Hotel Gardens – Open May–end Sept, by appointment. Catalogue £1. ☎ 064 44111; Fax 064 44583.

Kerry Woollen Mills – ♿ **Shop**: Open Apr–Oct, daily except Sun, 9am–5pm; Nov–Mar, Mon–Fri, 9am–5pm. **Guided tour of factory**: May–Sept except for 2 weeks in Aug, booking advisable. £2, £5 (family 2A+2C). Parking. Tearoom. ☎ 064 44122; Fax 064 44556.

KILMALLOCK

Excursions

Lough Gur Interpretive Centre – ♿ Open May–Sept, daily, 10am–6pm (5.30pm last admission). £2.10, £5.75 (family 2A+2C), £1.20 (child), £1.60 (student/senior citizen). Audio-guide. Parking. Refreshments. ☎ 061 360 788 (Shannon Heritage).

Irish Dresden – **Showroom**: Open all year, Mon–Fri, 9am–1pm and 2–5pm. **Factory**: Guided tour (20min) all year, Mon–Fri, 11.15am–noon and 3pm–4pm, by appointment only. ☎ 063 83030 (Irish Dresden Ltd, Dromcolliher, Co Limerick).

De Valera Museum and Bruree Heritage Centre – ♿ Open all year, Tues–Fri, 10am–5pm; Sat–Sun, 2–5pm; otherwise by appointment. £3, £1 (child over 12), £5 (family 2A+3C). Audio-visual presentation (20min). Parking. Picnic area. ☎ 063 91300; 063 90900.

KILRUSH

🛈 Town Hall, Kilrush ☎ 065 51577 (end May–early Sept)
🛈 Kilkee ☎ 065 56112 (end May–early Sept)
🛈 Shannon Airport ☎ 061 471 664

Dolphin Watching on the Shannon – Operates from Kilrush Creek Marina (subject to demand and weather conditions) May–Sept. Time 2–3 hr. £9, £5 (child). ☎ 065 51327 (Griffins); e-mail shannondolphins@tinet.ie

Dolphin Watching Cruise – Operates from Carrigaholt daily; booking essential. £10, £6 (child); unsuitable for children under 5. Brochure (partial French, German). Accommodation available. ☎ 065 58156 (July–Aug), 088 584 711 (May, June and Sept); Fax 065 58334.

Shannon Ferry – Operates from **Killimer** (north bank), hourly on the hour: Apr–Sept, daily, 7am (9am Sun)–9pm; Oct–Mar, daily 7am (10am Sun)–7pm; from **Tarbert** (south bank) hourly on the half hour: Apr–Sept, daily, 7.30am (9.30am Sun)–9.30pm; Oct–Mar, daily, 7.30am (10.30am Sun)–7.30pm. Closed 25 Dec. Time 20min. Capacity 44–52 vehicles. Car £8 (single), £12 (return); pedestrian £2 (single), £3 (return). ☎ 065 53124; Fax 065 53125 (Shannon Ferry Ltd). **Visitor Centre**: Open daily, 9am–9pm (7pm Oct–Mar). Parking. Bureau de Change.

Kilrush Heritage Centre – Open May–Sept, Mon–Sat and public holidays, 10am–5pm; Sun, noon–3pm. £2, £1 (child), £5 (fam4ily 2A+4C). ☎ 065 51577, 51047.

Kilrush Forest Park – Parking. Picnic sites.

Scattery Island Visitor Centre (Dúchas) – ♿ Open mid June–mid Sept, daily, 9.30am–6.30pm (5.45pm last admission). Closed 25–26 Dec. No charge. Parking. ☎ 065 52139, 52144.

Scattery Island – Boat (15–20min) from Kilrush Creek Marina (subject to tide and weather) operates Apr–Oct, daily; confirm timetable. 1–2 hr on the island. Return £4.50, £2.50 (child). ☎/Fax 065 51327 (Griffins); e-mail shannondolphins@tinet.ie

West Clare Railway – Open in summer. ☎ 065 52787 (Clancy's Bar).

🛈 Pier Road ☎ 021 772 234; Fax 021 774 438 (Mar–Nov)
🛈 Rossa Street, Clonakilty ☎ 023 33226 (June–mid Sept)

St Multose Church – Open Easter–Sept when possible, Mon–Sat, 10am–noon and 2–4pm. Donation. Guidebook. **Services**: Sun at 8am, 11.30am, Wed at noon (Eucharist). ☎ 021 772 220 (Rectory).

Kinsale Regional Museum – Open all year; summer: Mon–Sat, 11am–1pm; winter: daily, 2pm (3pm Sun and public holidays)–5.30pm. Closed 25 Dec. £1. Guided tour (20min). Historical tour. Brochure (French, German, Japanese, Spanish, Swedish). ☎ 021 772 044.

Desmond Castle (Dúchas) – Open mid Apr–mid June, Tues–Sun, 10am–6pm; mid June–early Oct, daily, 10am–6pm. Last admission 45min before closing. Guided tour available on request. £1.50, 60p (child/student), £1 (senior citizen), £4 (family). Brochure. Leaflet. Access by stone stairway. ☎ 021 774 855.

Charles Fort (Dúchas) – (♿) Open mid Apr–Oct, daily, 10am–6pm. Last admission 45min before closing. £2, £1 (child/student), £1.50 (senior citizen), £5 (family). Guided tour (1 hr) available. Guide book (Irish, German, French, Spanish, Italian, Dutch). Parking. Facilities for the disabled; wheelchair access limited. ☎ 021 772 263.

Excursions

Timoleague Castle Gardens – Open June–Aug, daily, 11am (2pm Sun)–5.30pm. £2.50, £1 (child), £2 (senior citizen/student). Guided tour (30min) by appointment only. ☎ 023 46116; Fax 023 46523.

Lios na gCon – Open summer, daily, 10am (11am Sat–Sun)–5pm. £3, £1.50 (child). Parking. Guided tours. Brochure. Leaflet. ☎ 023 33302 (9.15am–5pm), 023 33279 (after 6pm); Fax 023 34449.

West Cork Heritage Centre – Open May–Oct, daily, 10.30am (2.30pm Sun and public holidays)–5.30pm; otherwise, Sun, 3pm–5pm. £1.50. Guided tour by appointment. Parking. ☎ 023 33224.

West Cork Model Railway Village – Open daily, 11am (1pm Sat–Sun in winter)–5pm. £3, £1.25 (child 5–12), £2 (student/senior citizen), £7.50 (family 2A+3C). Parking. Tearoom. ☎/Fax 023 33224 (Clonakilty Enterprise Board Ltd, Town Hall, Kent Street, Clonakilty, Co Cork); Fax 023 34843.

St Fachtna's Cathedral – (♿) Open daily. **Services**: Sun at 8am, 11.30am, Saints' Days and Holy Days at 11am. Leaflet (French, German). Bookshop (open Sat, 2pm–5pm). Wheelchair access available on request. ☎ 023 48166.

🛈 Knock ☎ 094 88193 (end Apr–Sept)
🛈 Connaught Airport, Knock ☎ 094 67247 (June–Sept)

Knock Folk Museum – ♿ Open May–Oct, daily, 10am–6pm (7pm July–Aug). £2, £1.25 (child/senior citizen), £7 (family). Demonstrations of traditional crafts in Aug. Guided tour (30min) by appointment. Brochure (English only). Guide Book (French). Parking. ☎ 094 88100; Fax 094 88295; e-mail info@knock-shrine.ie

L

🛈 Derry Road ☎ 074 21160; Fax 074 25180

🛈 Arthur's Quay ☎ 061 317 522; Fax 061 317 939

Historical Walking Tours – Daily at 11am and 2.30pm from St Mary's Action Centre, 44 Nicholas Street. ☎/Fax 061 318 106; e-mail smidp@iol.ie

St Mary's Cathedral – Open summer, daily, 9.30am–12.45pm and 2.15–5pm; otherwise by appointment. Donation £1. Brief written guide (French, German, Italian). ☎ 061 416 238, 310 293; Fax 061 315 721.

Limerick Museum – ♿ Open all year, Tues–Sat, 10am–1pm and 2.15–5pm. Closed public holidays. Time 30min. No charge. Parking. ☎ 061 417 826.

LIMERICK

King John's Castle – (♿) Open June–Aug, daily, 9am–6pm (5pm last admission); Apr–May and Sept–Oct, daily, 9.30am–5.30pm (4.30pm last admission). £4.20, £11 (family 2A+2C), £2.60 (child), £3.30 (student/senior citizen). Audio-visual presentation (20min). Audio-guide and brochure (French, German, Irish, Italian). Parking. Coffee shop. Wheelchair access to ground floor only. ☎ 061 360 788 (Shannon Heritage); Fax 061 361 020.

Old Bishops' Palace – Open all year, Mon–Fri, office hours. ☎ 061 313 399; Fax 061 315 513.

Hunt Museum – ♿ Open all year, Tues–Sat, 10am–5pm, Sun, 2–5pm; also open Mon, May–Oct. £3.90, £2.50 (child/senior citizen), £9 (family 2A+6C). Shop. Restaurant. ☎ 061 312 833; Fax 061 312 834.

Georgian House – Open all year, Mon–Fri, 10am–5pm; at other times for groups by special request. Admission charge unknown. ☎ 061 314 130 (Limerick Civic Trust).

St John's Cathedral – ♿ Open all year, daily, 9am–6pm (8pm Sat–Sun). No charge. Brochure (French, German, Irish, Italian, Spanish). Guided tour available. Parking. ☎ 061 414 624; Fax 061 316 570.

Limerick City Gallery of Art – Housed in the City Hall until February 1999. Open daily, 10am–6pm (1pm Sat, 7pm Thu). Closed 1 Jan and at Christmas. ☎ 061 310 633.

Franciscan Church – Open all year, daily, 7.50am (6.30am Sun)–6.45pm (12.45pm Sun). Mass: Sun, at 7am, 10.30am and noon; weekdays at 11am and 1.05pm; Sat (Vigil Mass) at 8pm. ☎ 061 413 911; Fax 061 310 939.

St Saviour's Dominican Church – Open daily, 7.30am–8.15pm (2.45pm Sun).

Excursions

Cratloe Woods House – (♿) Open June–mid Sept, Mon–Sat, 2–6pm; otherwise by arrangement. Guided tour. £2.50, £1.50 (child), £2 (senior citizen/student). Tearoom. ☎ 061 327 028; Fax 327 031.

Glenstal Abbey Church – Open all year, daily, 6.30am–1pm and 2–9pm. ☎ 061 386 103; Fax 061 386 328.

LISMORE   🅱 ☎ 058 54975 (Apr–Oct)

Lismore Castle Gardens – Open early Apr–end Sept, daily, 1.45–4.45pm. Time 45min. £3, £1.50 (child). Brochure (French). ☎ 058 54424; Fax 058 54896.

St Carthage's Cathedral (Anglican) – Open Apr–Sept, 9am–6pm (4pm Oct–Mar). No charge. Information board bearing the history of the Cathedral plus other details (Dutch, French, German, Irish, Spanish, Swedish). Time 20min. Parking. ☎ 058 54137.

St Carthach's Church – Open all year, daily, 9.30am–8pm (5pm winter). ☎ 058 54246.

Lismore Heritage Centre – Open Mar–Oct, daily, 9.30am–6pm; Nov–Feb, Mon–Sat, 9.30am–5.30pm. £3. Audio-visual presentation (30min) and brochure (French, German, Italian). ☎ 058 54975; Fax 058 53009.

Lismore Castle Gardens

Excursions

Mount Melleray Abbey Church – Open 7.15am–8.30pm.

LISTOWEL see TRALEE   🏛 St John's Church ☎ 068 22590 (June–Sept)

LONGFORD   🏛 Main Street ☎ 043 46566 (June–Sept)

St Mel's Cathedral – 👤 Open all year, daily, 7.45am–8pm (9pm Sat, 6pm Sun). No charge. Parking. ☎ 043 46465.

St Mel's Diocesan Museum – Open June–Sept, Tue–Wed, 11am–1pm, Sat, noon–2pm, Sun, 1.45–3.45pm. 50p. Guided tour (2 hr) available. ☎ 043 46465.

St John's Church (Anglican) – Open all year, Sun at 12.15pm, Saints' Days at 10.30am (as announced).

Excursions

Carrigglas Manor – 👤 **Garden Museum**: Open May and Sept, Mon and Fri, 10.30am–3pm; June–Aug, Mon, Tues, Fri, 10.30am–5pm, Sun, 2–6pm. **House**: Open same days as museum. Guided tour of house (45min; French, German, Italian): May and Sept at 11am, noon and 2pm; June–Aug, Mon, Tues and Fri at 11am, noon, 2pm and 3pm, Sun at 2pm, 3pm, 4pm and 5pm. Gardens and museum £2.50, £1.50 (reduction); house £2.50 extra. Parking. Tearoom. Gift shop. ☎ 043 45165; Fax 043 41026; e-mail greenrock@tinet.ie

Ardagh Heritage Centre – Open all year, daily, 9am–9pm. £2, £5 (family 2A+3C), £1 (reduction). Video (15min). Restaurant. Craft shop. ☎ 043 75277; Fax 043 75278.

Corlea Trackway Visitor Centre – Guided tour Apr–May, daily, 10am–5pm; June–Sept, daily, 9.30am–6.30pm; last admission 45min before closing. £2.50, £1 (child/student), £1.75 (senior citizen), £6 (family 2A+2C). Audio–visual presentation (20min), displays. Parking. Tearoom; picnic area. ☎ 043 22386; 01 661 3111 ext 2386 (Head Office for winter hours).

LOUGHREA   🏛 Aughrim ☎ 0905 73939 (mid Apr–end Sept)
                                  🏛 Ballinasloe ☎ 0905 42131 (July–Aug)
                                  🏛 Thoor Ballylee ☎ 091 631 436 (Mar–Sept)

St Brendan's Cathedral – Open all year, daily, 9.30am–9.30pm. No charge. Leaflet, books available. ☎ 091 841 212; Fax 091 847 367. **Diocesan Museum**: apply to the Presbytery. Guided tour by arrangement. Parking. ☎ 091 841 212.

Excursions

Thoor Ballylee – (👤) Open Apr–Sept, daily, 10am–6pm. £3, family rate available, 75p (child), £2.50 (senior citizen/student). Audio–visual presentation (17min). Audio–guide (Dutch, French, German, Irish, Italian, Spanish). Guided tour (30min) available. Parking. Tearoom. ☎ 091 631 436 (Easter–Sept), 091 563 081 (Oct–Easter); Fax 091 565201.

Coole Park Visitor Centre (Dúchas) – 👤 Open mid Apr–mid June, Tues–Sun, 10am–5pm; mid June–end Aug, daily, 9.30am–6.30pm; Sept, daily, 10am–5pm. Last admission 45min before closing. £2, £1 (child/student), £1.50 (senior citizen), £5 (family). Audio–visual presentation. Nature trails. Parking. Tearoom. ☎ 091 631 804; Fax 091 631 653.

Dunguaire Castle – Open mid Apr–Oct, daily, 9.30am–5.30pm (4.30pm last admission). £2.75, £6.80 (family 2A+2C), £1.65 (child), £1.90 (student/senior citizen). ☎ 091 37108 or 061 361 511 (Shannon Heritage); Fax 061 361 020. **Medieval banquets** (songs, poems and extracts from Irish writers): daily at 5.45pm and 8.45pm; £30, £22.75 (child 10–12), £15.50 (child 6–9). Parking. Souvenir shop. ☎ 061 360 788 (Shannon Heritage).

Athenry Castle (Dúchas) – (👤) Open mid June–mid Sept, daily, 9.30am–6.30pm; last admission 45min before closing. £2, £1 (child/student), £1.50 (senior citizen), £5 (family). Audio-visual presentation. Parking. Ground-floor access for wheelchair users. ☎ 091 844 797.

Athenry Dominican Friary (Dúchas) – Key available from Mrs Sheehan in Church Street (£5 deposit).

Battle of Aughrim Centre – Open Easter–early Oct, daily, 10am–6pm; otherwise by appointment. £3, £1 (child), £2 (reduction), £6 (family 2A+3C). Parking. Refreshments. ☎/Fax 0905 73939.

LOUISBURGH see WESTPORT

M

MALLOW

St James' Church – Open to visitors by appointment. **Services**: Sun at 11.30am (except for 5th Sun in month, when service is at 11am). ☎ 022 21473 (Rector).

Excursions

Doneraile Wildlife Park (Dúchas) – (♿) Open mid Apr–Oct, Mon–Sat, 8am (10am Sat)–8.30pm, Sun and public holidays, 11am–7pm; Nov–mid Apr, daily, 8am (10am Sat–Sun and public holidays)–4.30pm. Closed 25–26 Dec. £1, 40p (child/student), 70p (senior citizen), £3 (family). Parking. Picnic areas. Pathways accessible to disabled people. ☎ 022 24244.

Annes Grove Gardens – Open mid Mar–Sept, daily, 10am (1pm Sun)–5pm (6pm Sun); otherwise by appointment. Time 45min. £3, £1 (child), £2 (senior citizen/student). Leaflet (French, German). Guided tour (French). Parking. Picnic area. ☎/Fax 022 26145.

MAYNOOTH

Maynooth College Visitor Centre – Open May–Sept, Mon–Fri, 11am–5pm, Sat–Sun, 2–6pm. ☎ 01 708 3576; Fax 01 628 9063.

Excursions

Castletown House (Dúchas) – (♿) Restoration in progress; reopening during 1999. Check times in advance. Guided tour Apr–Sept, daily, 10am (11am Sat, 2pm Sun and public holidays)–6pm; Oct, daily except Sat, 10am (2pm Sun and public holidays)–5pm; Nov–Mar, times available by telephone; last admission 1 hr before closing. Closed Good Friday, Christmas/New Year. £2.50, £1 (child/student), £1.75 (senior citizen), £6 (family). Leaflet (French, German, Italian). No photography. Parking. Te room. Access by stone steps. ☎ 01 628 8252; Fax 01 627 1811.

Steam Museum – (♿) Open Apr–May, Sun and bank holidays, 2.30–5.30pm; June–Aug, Tues–Sun and bank holidays, 2–6pm; Sept, Sun and bank holidays, 2.30–5.30pm £3, £2 (child/senior citizen), £10 (family 2A+2C). Parking. Teahouse. Steam and Garden shop. ☎ 01 627 3155; Fax 01 627 3477.

Wonderful Barn, Castletown

Slide File, Dublin

Coolcarrigan Gardens – Open by appointment only, Apr–Aug. £3. ☎ 045 863 512, 01 834 1141.

MIDLETON

Old Midleton Distillery – ♿ Guided tour (60min) daily, 9am–6pm (4.30pm last tour); otherwise by appointment. £3.95, £1.50 (child), £9.50 (family). Audio-visual presentation (15min). Whiskey tasting in the bar. Audio-guide, guided tour and brochure (French, German, Italian, Spanish). Parking. Restaurant (summer). Gift shop. ☎ 021 613 594; Fax 021 613 642.

Excursions

Cloyne Cathedral – ♿ Open May–Sept, daily, 10am–6pm; otherwise key available at the cottage. Donation welcome; ascent of tower £1. Guided tour by appointment. **Service**: Sun, noon. Parking.

Stephen Pearce Pottery – ♿ **Workshop**: Open all year, Mon–Thurs, 8am–5pm; Fri, 8am–4.15pm. Closed on Good Friday and for two weeks over Christmas. **Pottery shop**: Open all year, daily, 8am (10am Sat, noon Sun)–5pm (4.15pm Fri, 6pm Sat–Sun). **Emporium**: Open all year, daily, 10am–6pm. All closed 25–26 Dec. Parking. ☎ 021 646 807; Fax 021 646 706; e-mail spearce@indigo.ie

Barryscourt Castle (Dúchas) – Open all year except first two weeks in Jan and Thur in winter, daily, 10am–5pm; last admission 45min before closing. £1.50, 60p (child/student), £1 (senior citizen), £4 (family). Parking. Teashop. Craft shop. ☎ 021 883 864.

MONAGHAN

🄸 Market House ☎ 047 81122
🄸 Ulster Canal Stores, Clones ☎ 047 52125, 51718; Fax 047 52039

St Macartan's Cathedral – ♿ Open all year, daily, 9am–6pm. No charge. Parking. ☎ 047 82300.

County Museum – (♿) Open all year, Tues–Sat, 11am–1pm and 2–5pm. Closed public holidays. Time 1 hr. No charge. Facilities for the disabled; partial access for wheelchairs. ☎ 047 82928; Fax 047 71189; e-mail moncomuseum@tinet.ie

St Louis Heritage Centre – Open Mon, Tues, Thur and Fri, 10am–noon and 2.30–4.30pm, Sat–Sun, 2.30pm–4.30pm. Closed Wed. £1. ☎ 047 83529.

Excursions

Rossmore Forest Park – Gates open at all times. Jan–Dec. Parking (£2). Picnic area. ☎ 047 81968.

Ulster Canal Stores – Open June–Sept, daily, 10am (2pm Sun)–6pm. £1.50, 50p (child). Tourist Information Centre. Cycle hire. ☎ 047 52125, 51718 (Development Office); Fax 047 52039.

Castle Leslie – Guided historical tour (50min) 6 June–10 Sept, Mon–Thur, 2–5pm every hour; minimum of 4 people per tour. £3.50, £2 (child/senior citizen), £8 (family). Parking. Open for accommodation and dinner Easter to Hallowe'en. ☎ 047 88109; Fax 047 88256; e-mail ultan@castle-leslie.ie
www.castle-leslie.ie

MULLINGAR

🄸 Dublin Road ☎ 044 48650; Fax 044 40413

Cathedral of Christ the King – (♿) Open all year, daily, 7.30am–9pm. No charge. **Ecclesiastical Museum**: May–Sept, Thur, Sat and Sun, 3–4pm. £1. Parking. Wheelchair access to Cathedral only. ☎ 044 48338.

Excursions

Tullynally – **Gardens**: Open May–Sept, daily, 2–6pm. **Castle**: Guided tour June–end July, daily, 2–6pm. Garden only £2.50; castle and gardens £4. ☎ 044 61159 or 61289; Fax 044 61856.

Mullingar Bronze and Pewter – Open all year round, daily except Sun, 9.30am (10am Sat)–6pm. Last tour Fri, 12.30pm. Parking. ☎ 044 44948, 43078, 48791.

Belvedere House and Gardens – Open all year, Mon–Fri, 8am–4pm, Sat–Sun, noon–6pm. £1, 50p (child/senior citizen). Parking. ☎ 044 40861.

N

NENAGH

🄸 Conolly Street ☎ 067 31610; Fax 067 33418 (mid May–early Sept)

Nenagh District Heritage Centre – Open May–Sept, daily except Sat, 10am (2.30pm Sun)–5pm. £2, £1 (reduction), £4 (family). Guided tour (90min) by appointment. Brochure (French, German). ☎ 067 32633; Fax 067 33586. **Tipperary North Genealogical Centre**: Open daily except bank holidays, 10am–4pm; closed at lunchtime. ☎ 067 33850; Fax 067 33586.

NEW ROSS

🄸 The Quay ☎ 051 421 857 (mid June–end Aug)

St Mary's Church – **Services**: Sun, at 11.45am. ☎051 425 004.

Tholsel – Open all year, Mon–Fri, 9am–4pm.

Excursions

Duiske Abbey – Open all year, daily, 8.30am–7pm (later in summer). **Mass**: Mon–Fri at 8am, 10am (July–Aug), Sat at 11am, Sun at 8.30am, 11am and 7pm (Vigil). ☎ 0503 24238. **Abbey Centre**: Open Mon–Fri, 10am–5pm; Sat–Sun (summer only), 11am–1pm and 2–5pm.

Kennedy Arboretum (Dúchas) – ♿ Open all year, daily, 10am–8pm (6.30pm Apr and Sept; 5pm Oct–Mar); last admission 45min before closing. Closed Good Friday, 25 Dec. £2, £1 (child/student), £1.50 (senior citizen), £5 (family). Audio–visual presentation. Guided tour. Self-guiding trails. Parking. Tearoom in summer (051 388 195); picnic area. Facilities for the disabled; wheelchair access. ☎ 051 388 171; Fax 051 388 172.

Kennedy Homestead – Open on request dawn–dusk. No charge.

O – P

 🛈 ☎ 091 552 808; Fax 091 552 2811

PORTLAOISE

🛈 James Fintan Lawlor Avenue ☎ 0502 21178

PORTUMNA

Portumna Castle (Dúchas) – (♿) Open mid June–mid Sept, daily, 9.30am–6.30pm; last admission 45min before closing. £1.50, £4 (family), 60p (child/student), £1 (senior citizen). Parking. Limited access for disabled people to gardens and Gate House. ☎ 0509 41658.

Excursions

Clonfert Cathedral – Open summer, daily, 9am–9pm. If locked, key available at the lodge. ☎/Fax 0509 51269; e-mail clonfert@clonfert.anglican.org

Shannon Bridge (Dúchas) – Closed to road vehicles for 10–15min early Apr–late Sept, Mon–Fri at 9.45am, 11am, 12.30pm, 3pm, 5.30pm, 7.30pm, Sun at 11am, 12.30pm, 3pm, 5.30pm; late Sept to early Nov, Mon–Fri at 9.45am, 11am, 12.30pm, 1pm, 5pm, 6.30pm, Sun at 11am, 12.30pm, 2.30pm, 4pm; mid Mar to early Apr, Mon–Fri at 9.45am, 11am, 12.30pm, 2.30pm, 4.30pm, 5.30pm, Sun at 11am, 12.30pm, 2.30pm, 4pm; early Nov to mid Mar, Mon–Fri at 9.45am, 11am, noon, Sun at 11am, noon.

POWERSCOURT

Powerscourt Gardens – (♿) Open all year, daily, 9.30am–5.30pm. Closed 25–26 Dec. Gardens £3.50, £2 (child), £3.20 (reduction). Brochure (French, German, Italian, Japanese, Spanish). **House exhibition**: £1.50, £1 (child), £1.30 (reduction). Tree trail. Parking. Terrace café. Speciality shops. Garden Centre. Play area. Gardens partially suitable for wheelchair access. ☎ 01 204 6000; Fax 01 286 3561.

Powerscourt Waterfall – (♿) Open all year: summer, daily, 9.30am–7pm; winter, 10.30am–dusk. £1.50, 80p (child). Nature trail; play area for children. Parking. Refreshments. ☎ 01 286 7676; Fax 01 286 3561.

R

🛈 ☎ 0903 26342 (mid May–mid Sept)

Excursion

Clonalis House – (♿) Guided tour (45min) June–mid Sept, daily except Mon, 11am–5pm. £3.50, £1.50 (child), £2.50 (senior citizen/student). Parking. Refreshments. Wheelchair access to ground floor only. ☎/Fax 0907 20014.

ROSCREA

Roscrea Castle, Heritage Centre and Damer House (Dúchas) – Open June–Sept, daily, 9.30am–6pm; otherwise check times. £2.50, £1 (child/student), £1.75 (senior citizen), £6 (family). Guided tour on request. Public parking nearby. Access to house by stone steps. ☎ 0505 21850.

ROSSLARE see WEXFORD

🛈 Rosslare Terminal ☎ 053 33232; Fax 053 33421
🛈 ☎ 053 33622 (May–Sept)

RUSSBOROUGH

Russborough House – Guided tour (including 5min film) Apr and Oct, Sun and bank holidays, 10.30am–5.30pm; May and Sept, Mon–Sat, 10.30am–2.30pm, Sun and bank holidays, 10.30am–5.30pm; June–Aug, daily, 10.30am–5.30pm. Booklet (French, German, Spanish). Main rooms £4, £2 (child), £3 (senior citizen/student); bedrooms £2.50. Restaurant. Shop. Craft workshops. Children's playground. ☎ 045 865 239; Fax 045 865 054.

To plan a special itinerary:
– consult the Map of Touring Programmes which indicates the recommended routes, the tourist regions, the principal towns and main sights;
– read the descriptions in the Sights section which include Excursions from the main tourist centres.
Michelin Map no923 shows scenic routes, interesting sights, viewpoints, rivers, forests...

S

SALTHILL see GALWAY   🛈 ☎ 091 520 500 (mid May–mid Sept)

SHANNON AIRPORT see KILRUSH   🛈 ☎ 061 471 664

SKIBBEREEN   🛈 North Street ☎ 028 21766; Fax 028 21353

West Cork Arts Centre – Open all year, Mon–Sat, 10am–6pm. ☎ 028 22090.

Excursions

Creagh Gardens – ♿ Open Mar–Oct, daily, 10am–6pm; otherwise by appointment. Time 1–2 hr. £3, £2 (child). No dogs. Parking. ☎/Fax 028 22121.

Liss Ard Experience – (♿) Open May–Sept by appointment. £5 (including garden tour), £2 (child), £3 (reduction). No dogs. Parking. ☎ 028 22368; Fax 028 22905; e-mail lissardfoundation@tinet.ie
www.lissard.com

St Barrahane's Church – Open to visitors all year, daily. **Services**: in summer, Sun at 9.45am; in winter, first Sun of the month at 9am.

Sherkin Island Passenger Ferry – Operates June–Sept, daily, from Baltimore Pier at 9am (except Sun), 10.30am, noon, 2pm, 4pm, 5.30pm, 7pm, 8.30pm; otherwise, daily, from Baltimore Pier at 10.30am, 2pm, 5.30pm; from Sherkin Island, 15min after above times. Time 15min. Return £4. ☎ 028 20125.

Cape Clear Island Ferry – From **Baltimore**: Operates July–Aug, daily (weather permitting) at 11am (noon Sun), 2.15pm, 7pm; June and Sept, daily at 2.15pm, 7pm; May, Mon–Fri, daily at 11am, 5.30pm, Sat at 2.15pm, Sun at 5pm; Oct–Apr, daily. Return £9, £5 (child), £22 (family 2A+2C). ☎ 028 39135 (Capt O'Driscoll), 028 39159 (office); 028 20114; Fax 028 20442 (Booking Office); also 028 39119; Fax 028 39150 (Coiste Naomh Ciaran); e-mail ccteo@iol.ie. From **Skull**: Operates (1 hr) July and Aug, daily (weather permitting) at 10am, 2.30pm, 4.30pm; June, daily at 2.30pm. Return £9. ☎ 028 28138 (Kieran Molloy, Pier Road, Skull).

Baltimore-Skull Ferry – Operates June–Aug, daily: from Baltimore to Hare Island (15min) to Skull (35min) at 10am, 1.45pm and 4.40pm; from Skull to Hare Island (35min) to Baltimore (15min) at 11.30am, 3pm and 5.30pm. £6, £9 (return), £20 family return. Bord Fáilte and Department of Marine approved. ☎ 028 39153, 087 268 0760 (mobile); Fax 028 39164 (Ciaran O'Driscoll, North Harbour, Cape Clear Island).

Schull Planetarium – (♿) Open Apr–May, Sun, 3–5pm (Starshow at 4pm); June, Tues, Thurs and Sat, 3–5pm (Starshow at 4pm); July–Aug, Tues–Sat, 2–5pm, Mon and Thurs, 7–9pm (Starshows Wed and Sat at 4pm, Mon and Thurs at 8pm). Star–show £3, £2 (child), £7 (family 2A+2C). Parking. ☎ 028 28552; Fax 028 28467.

Skull Harbour

Slide File, Dublin

The Ewe, Goleen – (&) Open Apr–Oct, daily, 10am–6pm. £1. Parking. ☎ 028 35492.

Mizen Vision – Open mid Mar–May and Oct, daily, 10.30am–5pm; June–Sept, daily, 10am–6pm; Nov–mid Mar, Sat–Sun, 11am–4pm. £2.50, £1.25 (child), £1.75 (reduction), £7 (family 2A+3C). **Audio-visual presentations**: Lighthouse-keeping (30min); Irish Lights (50min), Royal National Lifeboat Institution (RNLI) (35min). Parking. ☎ 028 35115 (enquiries in summer only); otherwise ☎ 028 35591 or 35253; Fax 028 35603; e-mail mizenvision@tinet.ie
www.westcorkweb.ie

SLIGO
🛈 Temple Street ☎ 071 61201; Fax 071 60360

Waterbus Trips – Operate daily from Doorly Park and Parke's Castle. ☎ 071 64266; Mobile 088-598869.

Sligo Abbey (Dúchas) – Open mid June–mid Sept, daily, 9.30am–6.30pm; last admission 45min before closing; when closed, key available at 6 Charlotte Street. £1.50, 60p (child/student), £1 (senior citizen), £4 (family). Public parking nearby. Access by stone steps. ☎ 01 661 3111 (Head Office in Dublin).

County Museum and the Niland Gallery – **Museum**: Open June–Sept, Tues–Sat, 10am–noon and 2–4.50pm; Oct–May, 2–4.50pm. Closed Mon. No charge. **Niland Gallery**: Open June–Sept, Tues–Sat, 10am–noon and 2–4.50pm; Oct–May, 2–4.50pm. No charge. Time 1 hr. ☎ 071 47190; Fax 071 46798; e-mail sligolib@iol.ie

St John's Cathedral – Open all year, Sun, 8am–noon; Mon–Sat, 10am–6pm (4pm winter) by prior arrangement. Apply to the Dean, The Rectory, Strandhill Road, Sligo.

Cathedral of the Immaculate Conception – & Open all year, daily, 7am–9pm. No charge. Parking. ☎ 071 62670.

Excursions

Lough Gill Cruises – Operate from Parke's Castle daily, at 12.30pm, 1.30pm, at 3.30pm (to Innisfree; 1 hr) at 4.30pm (to Sligo and back), at 6.30pm (to Innisfree; 1 hr); from Doorly Park at 2.30pm (to The Garavogue and Lough Gill stopping at Parke's Castle; 3 hr), at 5.30pm (to Parke's Castle); Fri, from Parke's Castle at 9pm (Irish music, bar). Innisfree £5; Garavogue and Lough Gill £6. Refreshments. ☎ 071 64266; 087 598 8869 (mobile).

Carrowmore Megalithic Cemetery (Dúchas) – (&) **Site**: Open all year. **Visitor Centre**: Open May–Oct, daily, 9.30am–6.30pm (6pm Oct). £1.50, 60p (child/student), £1 (senior citizen), £4 (family). Slide show (15min). Guided tour available May–Sept. Parking. ☎ 071 61534.

Innisfree Ferry – Operates on request (weather permitting). Return £3 per head. ☎ 071 64079.

Parke's Castle (Dúchas) – (&) Open June–Sept, daily, 9.30am–6.30pm; weekend of 17 Marand early Apr–end May, daily (closed Mon except bank holidays), 10am–5pm; Oct, daily, 10am–5pm. £2, £1 (child/student), £1.50 (senior citizen), £5 (family). Audio-visual presentation (French, German, Italian). Leaflet (French, German, Italian, Spanish, Irish). Tearoom. Facilities for the disabled; ground access for wheelchair users. ☎ 071 64149.

Lissadell House – Guided tour (40min) June–Sept, daily except Sun, 10.30am–1pm and 2–5pm; last admission 45min before closing. £3, £1 (child). Parking. ☎ 071 63150; Fax 071 66906.

Inishmurray – Boat trips (minimum 15 passengers) from Mullaghmore ☎ 071 66124 and Rosses Point ☎ 071 42391.

STROKESTOWN

Strokestown Park – (&) **Famine Museum**: Open Apr–Oct, daily, 11am–5.30pm. **House**: Guided tour (40min) Apr–Oct, daily, 11am–5.30pm. House and museum £7.50; house or museum only £3. Restaurant. Leaflet (French, German). Wheelchair access to museum and ground floor of house. ☎ 078 33013; Fax 078 33712; e-mail info@strokestownpark.ie
www.strokestownpark.ie.

County Roscommon Heritage Centre – & Open May–Sept, Mon–Fri, 2.30–4.30pm. Closed Sat–Sun and bank holidays. Donation. Parking. ☎ 078 33380.

The length of time given in this guide
  – for touring allows time to enjoy the views and the scenery;
  – for sightseeing is the average time required for a visit.

T

TARA

Tara (Dúchas) – (♿) **Site**: Open all year. **Visitor Centre**: Open mid June–mid Sept, daily, 9.30am–6.30pm; May–mid June and mid Sept–Oct, daily, 10am–5pm; last admission 45min before closing. For winter opening times (groups only) ☎ 041 24488. £1.50, 60p (child/student), £1 (senior citizen), £4 (family). Audio-visual presentation (20min; French, German, Italian). Guided tour on request. Parking. ☎/Fax 046 25903.

THOOR BALLYLEE see LOUGHREA

🛈 ☎ 091 631 436 (early Mar–end Sept)

TIPPERARY

🛈 James Street, Tipperary ☎ 062 51457 (May–Oct)

Old IRA Exhibition – Open all year, daily, 10am–10pm (7pm in winter). Parking.

TRALEE

🛈 Ashe Hall ☎ 066 712 1288
🛈 St John's Church, Listowel ☎ 068 22590 (June–Sept)

National Folk Theatre (Siamsa Tíre) – ♿ Opening times vary according to performances, telephone for details. Closed Good Friday, 25–26 Dec. Theatre productions £11, £10 (reduction); gallery no charge. Refreshments. Facilities for the disabled; wheelchair access; audio loop. ☎ 066 712 3055; Fax 066 712 7276.

Aqua Dome – Open mid May–early Sept, daily, 10am–10pm; Easter week, Mon–Fri, 10am–10pm, Sat–Sun, 11am–8pm; mid Apr–mid May, Mon–Fri, noon–10pm, Sat–Sun, 11am–8pm. £5, £3 (child); July–Aug: £6, £4 (child). Parking. ☎ 066 28899 (Reception), 066 712 8755 (Administration), 066 712 9150 (24hr information); Fax 066 712 9130.

Kerry The Kingdom – ♿ Open mid Mar–Dec, daily, 10am–6pm (7pm Aug); Closed 24–27 Dec. £5.50, £3 (child), £4.75 (reduction), £17 (family 2A+3C). Audio-guide (French, German). Commentary (Dutch, French, German, Irish, Italian, Japanese, Spanish). Museum brochure (Dutch, French, German, Italian, Spanish). Guided tour available. Parking. Café. ☎ 066 712 7777; Fax 066 712 7444.

Tralee-Blennerville Light Railway – ♿ Operates Apr–Sept, daily, 11am (noon Sun, Apr, May and Sept)–5.30pm, on the hour from **Ballyard Station** in Tralee, on the half-hour from **Blennerville**. Closed second Mon of the month for maintenance work. £2.75, £1.50 (child), £7 (family 2A+3C); reductions for entrance to the Windmill (see below). Audio-guide and brochure (French, German, Italian). Parking. Restaurant at Blennerville. ☎ 066 712 8888.

Excursions

Blennerville Windmill – ♿ Open Apr–Oct, daily, 10am–6pm. £2.75, £1.50 (child), £2.25 (reduction), £7 (family 2A+3C); reductions for train passengers (see above). Audio-visual presentation (15min; French, German, Italian). Audio-guide and brochure (French, German, Italian). Guided tour (1 hr) available. Parking. Restaurant. Craft centre. ☎ 066 712 1064.

Crag Cave – ♿ Guided tour (30min; French, German) Mar–Nov, daily, 10am–6pm (7pm June–Aug); last tour 30min before closing. £3, £8 (family), £1.50 (child). Brochure (French, German, Italian). Parking. Refreshments. Shop. ☎ 066 714 1244; Fax 066 714 2352.

Ardfert Cathedral (Dúchas) – Open May–Sept, daily, 9.30am–6.30pm; also open Easter weekend and Oct bank holiday weekend. Last admission 45min before closing. £1.50, 60p (child/student), £1 (senior citizen), £4 (family). Parking. Access for disabled people to exhibition area and viewing point. ☎ 066 713 4711.

Fenit Sea World – ♿ Open Easter–end Sept, daily, 10am–6pm (9pm July–Aug). £4, £1.50 (child), £12 (family 2A+5C). Parking. Access for disabled people to exhibition area and viewing point. ☎/Fax 066 713 6544.

Rattoo-North Kerry Museum and Interpretive Centre – ♿ Open Apr–Sept, daily, 10am (2pm Sun)–6pm. £2, £1 (child), no charge (disabled). Guided tour available. ☎/Fax 066 713 1000.

St John's Art and Heritage Centre – ♿ Open June–Sept, Mon–Sat, 10am–6pm, Sun, 11am–3pm; otherwise, Mon–Fri, 10am–6pm, Sat, 2–5pm. Closed Good Friday. Monthly programme of theatre, music, dance, films, exhibitions and youth performance workshops. Parking. Refreshments. Facilities for the disabled; full wheelchair access. ☎ 068 22566; Fax 068 23485.

Tarbert Bridewell – Open Apr–Oct, daily, 10am–6pm. £3, £1.50 (child/senior citizen), £2 (student), £7 (family). Guide books (French, German, Italian, Spanish). ☎ 068 36500; Fax 068 36500.

Tarbert House – Open mid May–mid Aug, 10am–noon and 2–4pm. £2.50. ☎ 068 36106, 36500.

Shannon Ferry – See KILRUSH.

🚉 Railway Square ☎ 051 381 572 (mid June–end Aug)

TRIM

🚉 ☎ 046 37111 (May–Sept)

Trim Castle – Closed for restoration until 2000. View of site from observation platform only.

TUAM

🚉 ☎ 093 24463, 25486 (June–Aug)

St Mary's Cathedral – (♿) Open to visitors all year, daily, 10am–4pm. **Services**: Sun, Festivals and Holy Days at noon (Holy Communion). Guided tour available in July and Aug. Ramp for wheelchairs on request. ☎ 093 25598 (Office), 092 46017 (Dean's residence), 093 24141 (Caretaker).

Cathedral of the Assumption – (♿) Open to visitors all year, daily, 8.30am–9.30pm. **Mass**: Sun at 8.30am, 10am, 11.15am, 12.30pm, weekdays at 9am, 10am, 7.30pm; additional mass Sat at 7.30pm. Ramp at the entrance. ☎ 093 24388.

Mill Museum – ♿ Open June–Sept, daily, 10am–6pm. Audio–visual presentation. Guided tour available in July and Aug. Parking. ☎ 093 24463, 24141.

TULLAMORE

🚉 ☎ 0506 52617 (mid June–mid Sept)
Open Mon–Sat, 9.30am–1pm and 2–5.30pm

Charleville Forest Castle (IHP) – Guided tour (40min) by appointment at all times. £2.50, £1 (child), £2 (reduction), family ticket available. Licensed restaurant. ☎ 0506 21279; Fax 0506 23039.

Excursion

Locke's Distillery Museum – (♿) Open Apr–Oct, daily, 9am–6pm; otherwise, daily, 10am–4pm. Closed 23–30 Dec. Time 40min–1 hr. £3. Guided tour (French, German in summer). Brochure (French, German, Italian, Spanish). Parking. Refreshments. Very limited wheelchair access. ☎/Fax 0506 32134.

W

WATERFORD

🚉 41 TheQuay ☎ 051 875 788; Fax 051 877 388
🚉 Railway Square, Tramore; ☎ 051 381 572 (mid June–end Aug)

Garter Lane Arts Centre – ♿ Open all year, Mon–Sat, 10am–6pm. No charge. Facilities for the disabled; wheelchair access. ☎ 0151 855 038; Fax 0151 871 570; e-mail admin@garterlane.iol.ie

Waterford Town Walks – Tour departs from Granville Hotel on the Quay, Mar–Oct, daily, noon and 2pm. £3. ☎ 051 873 711; Fax 051 850 645 (Jack Burtchaell).

Waterford Harbour Car Ferry (Passage East/Ballyhack) – Operates all year, daily, 7am (9.30am Sun and public holidays)–10pm (8pm Oct–Mar). Closed 25–26 Dec. Capacity 30 cars. £6, (return journey, car), £4 (single journey, car), £1 (pedestrian return), 80p (pedestrian single). ☎ 051 382 480, 382 488; Fax 051 382 598 (Passage East Ferry Co Ltd).

Waterford Crystal – ♿ **Visitor Centre**: Open Apr–Oct, daily, 8.30am–6pm; Nov–Mar, Mon–Sat, 9am–5pm. **Factory**: Guided tour (2 hr) Apr–Oct, daily, 8.30am–4pm; Nov–Mar, Mon–Fri, 9am–3.15pm. **Showrooms**: Mar–Oct, daily, 8.30am–6pm; Nov–Mar, daily, 9am–5pm; Jan–Feb, Mon–Fri, 9am–5pm. Admission charge. Brochure (major European languages). Audio–visual presentation. Parking. Restaurant. ☎ 051 373 311; Fax 051 378 539.

City Hall and Theatre Royal – Open all year, Mon–Fri, 10am–5pm. Opening times may vary – telephone for details. No charge. Guided tour (20min) by appointment. ☎ 051 873 501.

Reginald's Tower Museum – Open June–Aug, Mon–Sat, 8.30am–8.30pm (5pm Sat); Sept, daily, 10am–1pm and 2–5pm; Oct, Mon–Fri, 10am–1pm and 2–5pm. £1.50, 50p (child). Public parking nearby. ☎ 051 871 227.

Waterford Treasures – ♿ Open June–Aug, Mon–Sat, 9am–8pm (5pm Sat); Sept, daily, 10am–1pm and 2–5pm; Oct, Mon–Fri, 10am–1pm and 2–5pm. £2.50, £10 (family). Public parking nearby. ☎ 051 871 227.

French Church (Dúchas) – Open all year, daily. If closed, key available opposite 5 Greyfriars Street (Mrs M White).

Christ Church Cathedral – Audio performances: Apr, May, Sept and Oct, Mon–Fri, at 10.30am, 2.15pm and 4pm; June–Aug, Mon–Sat, at 10.30am, 2.15pm, 3.30pm and 4pm, Sun, at 2.30pm and 4pm. **Services**: Wed, at 10.30am, Sun, at 8am and 10am. £2, £1.50 (reduction), 50p (child), £5 (family). ☎/Fax 051 858 958. ☎ 086 818 3165 (mobile).

Municipal Library – ♿ Open all year, Tues, Thur and Sat, 11am–1pm and 2.30–5.30pm; Wed, Fri, 2–8pm. No charge. Guided tour (30min; Irish). Local history and genealogy service (no charge). Parking. Facilities for the disabled; large print; audio books. ☎ 051 873 501.

Chamber of Commerce – Open all year, Mon–Fri, 9am–5pm. Literature (French). ☎ 051 872 639; Fax 051 876 002.

WESTPORT

ℭ The Mall ☎ 098 25711; Fax 098 26709

Westport House – Open July–late Aug, daily, 10.30am (2pm Sun)–6pm; June and late Aug–mid Sept, daily, 2–6pm (5pm Sept). **Zoo**: June–Aug, same hours as above. **Antique shop**: June–mid Sept, same hours as above. House and zoo £6.50, £3.25 (child), £4 (senior citizen/student), £18.50 (family), £45 (family season ticket); house only £6, £3 (child), £3.50 (senior citizen/student). Brochure (French, German). Parking. Refreshments. ☎ 098 25141, 25430; Fax 098 25206. The property is very popular with families during the school holidays.

Slide File, Dublin

Holy Trinity Church – Open July–Aug, daily. If locked, ask at the Rectory.

Clew Bay Heritage Centre – Open Apr–Oct, Mon–Fri, 9am–4pm, Sun, 3–5pm. £1. Parking.

Excursions

Louisburgh Folk and Heritage Centre – Open June–Sept, daily, 10am–6pm; otherwise by appointment. £2.50, £6 (family). Parking. Refreshments. ☎ 098 66341.

Clare Island Ferry (1) – Operates (20min) May–Sept, daily; from **Roonagh Quay**: May, at 11am, 2.15pm and 6pm; June and Sept, at 10.15am, 11am, 2.15pm and 6pm; July–Aug, at 10.15am, 11am, 11.30am, 12.30pm, 1.15pm, 2.15pm, 6pm and 8pm; from **Clare Island**: May, at 10am, 1.15pm and 5pm; June and Sept, at 9am, 10am, 1.15pm and 5pm; July–Aug, at 9am, 10am, 10.30am, 11.30am, 12.15pm, 1.15pm, 5pm and 7.15pm; otherwise by appointment. Return £10, £25 (family 2A+2C). ☎ 087 241 4653 (mobile), ☎ 098 26307, 26307 (Chris O'Grady, Clare Island).

Clare Island Ferry (2) – The Pirate Queen: Operates **from Westport Quay** (90min), July–Aug, daily. Return £10–£12. Capacity 96 passengers; sundeck; bar; video and commentary. ☎/Fax 098 28288; Mobile 087 414 653 (Clare Island Ferry and Clew Bay Cruises Ltd).

WEXFORD

ℭ Crescent Quay ☎ 053 23111; Fax 053 41743
ℭ Rosslare Terminal ☎ 053 33622; Fax 053 33421
ℭ Kilrane, Rosslare Harbour ☎ 053 33232; Fax 053 33421

Theatre Royal – (♿) **Opera Festival**: Operates mid Oct–early Nov. ☎ 053 22400 (Festival Office), 053 22144 (Box Office); Fax 053 24289; e-mail info@wex-opera@iol.ie

Wexford Arts Centre – ♿ Open all year, daily, 10am–6pm. Closed public holidays. No charge for exhibitions. Guided tour (15min) available. Restaurant. ☎ 053 23764; Fax 053 24544.

Wexford Tour – Depart from Crescent Quay at various times. Telephone for timetable. ☎ 053 21053 (Viking Tours), 053 23111 (TIC).

Franciscan Friary – (♿) Open all year, Mon–Fri, 8am–7pm; Sat, 9am–8pm; Sun, 8am–6pm. Disabled parking; access to church and friary for disabled. ☎ 053 22758; Fax 053 21499.

St Iberius' Church – Open daily, Mon–Sat, 10am–5pm (3pm winter). Donation £1. When closed, key available from The Rectory. Brochure (Dutch, French, German, Italian, Japanese, Spanish, Swedish). ☎ 053 43013; Fax 053 43013.

Westgate Heritage Centre – Open all year, Mon–Sat, 9.30am–5.30pm; also during Festival Week, Sun, 2–6pm. Audio-visual presentation (30min) £1.50, £1 (reduction). ☎ 053 46506.

Excursions

Wexford Wildfowl Reserve Visitor Centre (Dúchas) – (♿) Open mid Apr–Sept, daily, 9am–6pm; otherwise, daily, 10am–5pm. Closed 25 Dec. Last admission 45min before closing. No charge. Audio-visual presentation. Lectures. Guided tour on request. Bird watching. Resident warden. Parking. Picnic area. ☎ 053 23129; Fax 053 24785.

Tacumshane Windmill (Dúchas) – Key available from Michael Meyler (store/pub next door).

Irish Agricultural Museum (Johnstown Castle) – (♿) Open Apr–May and Sept–early Nov, Mon–Fri, 9am–12.30pm and 1.30–5pm, Sat–Sun and bank holidays, 2–5pm; June–Aug, Mon–Fri, 9am–5pm, Sat–Sun and bank holidays, 2–5pm; early Nov–Mar, Mon–Fri, 9am–12.30pm and 1.30–5pm. £2.50, £1.25 (child), £6 (family). Parking. Refreshments (summer). Parking and facilities for the disabled; wheelchair access to ground floor only. ☎ 053 42888 (weekdays); Fax 053 42213.

Kilmore Quay Maritime Museum – Open June–Sept, daily, noon–6pm; otherwise by appointment. £2, £1 (reduction), £5 (family). Audio-guide (French, German). Guided tour available on request. Access by gangplank. ☎ 053 29655, 29832.

Boat trips from Kilmore Quay – Operate Apr–Oct; groups only (max 12). Reef and wreck fishing. Environmental and sightseeing trips around Saltees Islands. ☎ 053 29704, 087 254 9111 (Dick Hayes).

Irish National Heritage Park – ♿ Open Apr–Nov, daily, 9.30am–6.30pm (5pm last admission). Time 1 hr. £4.50, £2.50 (child 4–12), £3 (child 12–16), £4 (reduction), £11.50 (family). Guided tour (French, German). Audio-visual presentation (French, German, Spanish, Italian). Parking. Craft shop. Restaurant. ☎ 053 20733; Fax 053 20911; e-mail inhp@iol.ie
www.wexford.ie

WICKLOW   🅱 Fitzwilliam Street ☎ 0404 69117; Fax 0404 69118

Anglican Church – Open all year, daily, 9.30am–dusk. Printed history of the church fixed to back internal wall of the church.

Wicklow Historic Gaol – Open mid Mar–Oct, daily, 10am–5pm (4pm Mar and Oct). £3.75. ☎ 0404 61599.

WICKLOW MOUNTAINS   🅱 Arklow ☎ 0402 32484 (June–Sept)
see also WICKLOW

Wicklow Mountains National Park (Dúchas) – ♿ **Information Point at Upper Lake, Glendalough:** Open May–Aug, daily, 10am–6pm; Apr and Sept, Sat–Sun, 10am–6pm. No charge. Weekly guided walks – telephone for details. ☎ 0404 45425, 45338 (winter); Fax 0404 45306 (Sean Casey).

Poulaphouca Reservoir Waterbus – **Sailings:** Mon–Fri at 4pm; Sat–Sun at 1pm, 3pm and 5pm, from Blessington Lakes Leisure Centre. Time 1 hr. Capacity 78 seats. £6, £3 (child), £18 (family 2A+2C). Advance booking advisable. Leaflet (Italian, French, Spanish). ☎ 045 865 092; Fax 045 865 024.

Killruddery – (♿) **House:** Open May, June and Sept, daily, 1–5pm. **Gardens:** Open Apr–Sept, daily, 1–5pm. House and garden £4, £2.50 (reduction); garden £2, £1.50 (reduction). Guided tour of garden for groups, by appointment only, extra charge. Parking. ☎ 01 286 3405; ☎/Fax 01 286 2777.

Avoca Handweavers – ♿ **Kilmacanogue:** Open all year, daily, 9.30am–6pm (5.30pm winter). Parking. Restaurant. Café and Garden Terrace. ☎ 01 286 7466, 01 286 7482; Fax 01 286 2367. **Avoca Mill:** Open all year, daily, 9.30am–6pm (5.30pm winter). No charge. Guided tour of the weaving process. Parking. Tearoom. ☎ 0402 35105, 35284; Fax 0402 35446.

Mount Usher Gardens – ♿ Open mid Mar–end Oct, daily, 10.30am–6pm. £3.50, £2.50 (reduction). Guided tour (1 hr) by appointment. Brochure (German). Parking. Tearoom. Craftshops. ☎ 0404 40116; ☎/Fax 0404 40205.

Clara Lara Fun Park – (♿) Open May–Aug, daily, 10.30am–6pm. £4. Parking. Refreshments. ☎ 0404 46161.

Avondale Estate – (&) **Park**: Open all year, daily. **House**: Open all year, daily, May–Sept, 11am–6pm; Oct–Apr, 11am–5pm; last admission 1 hr before closing. Closed Good Friday and over Christmas. Grounds only £2 per car; House (extra) £3, £6 (family 2A+1C; £1.50 each additional child), £2 (reduction). Audio-visual presentation (25min). Leaflet (French, Italian, Dutch, German, Japanese). Guided tour available. Parking. Tearoom, coffee shop, picnic areas. ☎ 0404 46111; Fax 0404 46111.

Bray Heritage Centre – Open all year, daily, 10am–4pm (later in summer). Exhibitions change each month – telephone for further details ☎01 286 6796.

National Sea-Life Centre – & Open Apr–Sept, daily, 10am–5pm; less frequently in winter. £4.95, £15 (family 2A+3C), £3.50 (child), £4.50 (senior citizen), special rates for the disabled (no charge for carers). ☎ 01 286 6939.

Arklow Maritime Museum – Open May–Sept, Mon–Sat, 10am–1pm and 2–5pm; Oct–Apr, Mon–Fri, 10am–1pm and 2–5pm. £2.50, no charge (accompanied child), £1 (senior citizen). Parking. ☎ 0402 32868; Fax 0402 32868.

Y

YOUGHAL
🛈 Heritage Centre ☎ 024 92390 (May–end Sept)

St Mary's Collegiate Church – Open mid May–mid Sept, daily, 9.30am–6.30pm. Brochure (Dutch, French, German, Italian). ☎ 024 92390; e-mail youghal@tinet.ie

Youghal Heritage Centre – Open Mon–Sat, 9.30am (10am Sat)–1pm and 2–6pm. £1. **Guided walking tour** (90min; French): June–Aug, Mon–Sat at 11am and 3pm. £2.50, £1 (child). Brochure. ☎ 024 92390, 92447; Fax 024 92447; e-mail youghal@tinet.ie

NORTHERN IRELAND

A

ANTRIM

🅱 16 High Street; ☎ 01849 465 156
Open all year, Mon–Sat, 9.30am–6pm. ♿
🅱 Council offices, The Steeple; ☎ 01849 463 113 (Seasonal opening)
🅱 Antrim Lough Shore Park (Seasonal opening)

Pogue's Entry – ♿ Open May–Sept, Thurs and Fri, 2–5pm, Sat, 11am–5pm. No charge. Guided tour (15min). ☎ 01849 428 000; Fax 01849 460 360 (Clotworthy Arts Centre).

Antrim Castle Gardens – Open all year, Mon–Sat, 9.30am–4.30pm (1pm Sat), Sun, 2–5pm. No charge. ☎ 01849 428 000; Fax 01849 460 360.

Shane's Castle Grounds – Closed until 1999. ☎ 01849 428 216; Fax 01849 468 457.

Excursions

Patterson's Spade Mill (NT) – ♿ Open June–Aug, daily except Tues, 2–6pm; Apr, May and Sept, Sat–Sun and holiday Mon, 2–6pm; Good Friday–Easter Tuesday, 2–6pm. £2.50, £1.25 (child). Facilities for the disabled; ramps; wheelchairs available. ☎ 01849 433 619.

Ballance House – (♿) Open Apr–Sept, Tues–Sun and bank holiday Monday, 11am (2pm Sat–Sun)–5pm. £2. Parking. Lunches and refreshments. Ground floor only accessible to wheelchairs. ☎ 01846 648 492; Fax 01846 648 098.

Templetown Mausoleum (NT) – Open all year, daily, during daylight hours. No charge. ☎ 01238 510 721 (Regional Office).

Arthur Cottage – ♿ Open May–Sept, Mon–Sat, 10.30am–5pm (4pm Sat). £1, 50p (child). Guided tour (30min). Parking. ☎ 01266 880 781 (in season), 01266 660 300; Fax 01266 660 400.

ANTRIM GLENS

🅱 Narrow Gauge Road, Larne; ☎ 01574 260 088
Open July–Aug, Mon–Wed and Sat, 9am–5pm, Thur–Fri 9am–6.30pm;
Easter–June and Sept, Mon–Sat 9am–5pm; otherwise Mon–Fri 9am–5pm.
Bureau de change. ♿
🅱 Carnfunnock Country Park, Coast Road, Larne; ☎ 01574 270 541
🅱 Community Hall, 2 The Bridge, Glenarm; ☎ 01574 841 087
🅱 McKillops, Harbour Road, Carnlough; ☎ 01574 885 236
🅱 Sheskburn House, 7 Mary Street, Ballycastle; ☎ 012657 62 024
Open July–Aug, Mon–Fri 9.30am–7pm, Sat 10am–6pm, Sun, 2–6pm;
Easter–June and Sept, Mon–Fri 9.30am–5pm, Sat 10am–4pm;
otherwise Mon–Fri 9.30am–5pm. ♿

Larne Lough Ferry (Larne/Island Magee) – Operates all year (weather permitting), daily, 7.30am–5.30pm (5pm Sat–Sun), every hour; more frequently early mornings and late afternoons. Single 60p, 30p (child). ☎ 01574 274 085.

Glenariff Falls, Co Antrim

Christopher Hill, Belfast

Carnfunnock Country Park – Open Easter–Sept, daily, 10am–6pm (8pm July–Aug). Maze, no charge in July and Aug; target ball £1, 50p (child); crazy ball £1, 50p (child); putting £1, 50p (child); combined ticket £2, £1 (child); 9–hole golf course £3.50, £1.75 (child); club hire £4 (£5 deposit). Parking (£2). Miniature railway. ☎ 01574 270 541; ☎/Fax 01574 260 088 (Larne TIC).

Glenariff Forest Park – ♿ Open all year, daily, 8am–dusk. Car £3; coach £17.50; pedestrians £1.50, 50p (child). Educational tours (2 hr) by appointment. Parking. Restaurant; picnic area. ☎ 01266 758 232; Fax 01266 758 828.

☑ Old Bank Building, 40 English Street; ☎ 01861 521 800
Open July–Aug, Mon–Sat 9am–5pm, Sun 1–5.30pm;
otherwise, Mon–Sat 9am–5pm, Sun 2–5pm. ♿

Armagh Anglican Cathedral – ♿ Open all year, daily, 9.30am–5pm (4pm Sun and winter). No charge. Guided tour (20min) available. Leaflet (French, German etc). Parking. St Patrick's Day (17 Mar) pilgrimage to Hill of Patrick. ☎ 01861 523 142; Fax 01861 524 177.

Armagh Roman Catholic Cathedral – Open all year, daily, 10am–5pm (NB services on Sunday mornings). No charge. Guided tour by appointment, contact the sacristan: ☎ 01861 522638. Parking.

Armagh County Museum – ♿ Open all year, Mon–Fri, 10am–5pm, Sat, 10am–1pm and 2–5pm. Closed 12–13 July, 25–26 Dec. No charge. ☎ 01861 523 070; Fax 01861 522 631.

Regimental Museum of the Royal Irish Fusiliers – Open all year including bank holidays, Mon–Fri, 10am–12.30pm and 1.30–4pm. £1.50, £1 (reduction). Guided tour (30min). ☎ 01861 522 911.

Palace Stables Heritage Centre and Primate's Chapel – ♿ Open all year: Sept–June, Mon–Sat, 10am–5pm, Sun, 2–5pm; July–Aug, Mon–Sat, 10am–5.30pm, Sun, 1–6pm. Closed over Christmas. Guided tour (90min). £3.50, £2 (child), £2.50 (senior citizen), £9 (family 2A+4C). Sensory gardens. Adventure playground. Parking. Restaurant. Facilities and parking for the disabled; full wheelchair access. ☎ 01861 529 629; Fax 01861 529 630; e-mail acdc@iol.ie
www.armagh.gov.uk

St Patrick's Trian – Open all year, Mon–Sat 10am–5pm, Sun 2–5pm. Allow 1 hr 15min. Closed 25–26 Dec. £3.30, £8.60 (family 2A+4C). ☎ 01861 521 801; Fax 01861 510 180.

Planetarium – ♿ Open all year, daily (except Sun, Sept–Mar), 10am (1.15pm Sat–Sun)–4.45pm. Closed Good Friday, 12 July, 24–27 Dec. £3.75, £2.75 (child under 16/senior citizen), £11 (family 2A+3C); exhibition only £1. Show (45min) at 2pm, 3pm. Exhibition (1 hr). ☎ 01861 523 689; Fax 01861 526 187.
www.armagh-planetarium.co.uk

Observatory Grounds: Open as for Planetarium. Astropark (20min); no charge. Brochure (French, German, Spanish). Parking. Café.
www.star.arm.ac.uk

Slide File, Dublin

Armagh (Robinson) Public Library – Open all year, Mon–Fri, 10am–1pm and 2–4pm. Closed public holidays. No charge. Guided tour (15min, small charge). Parking. ☎ 01861 523 142; Fax 01861 524 177.

Excursions

The Argory (NT) – (♿) Open June–Aug, daily except Tues, 2pm (1pm public holidays)–6pm; Apr–May and Sept, Sat–Sun and public holidays, 2pm (1pm public holidays)–6pm; Good Friday–Easter Tuesday, 2–6pm; last admission 45min before closing. £2.50, £1.25 (child). Guided tour (50min). Parking £1.50. Tearoom; picnic area. Wheelchair available; wheelchair access to ground floor, walks, tearoom. ☎ 01868 784 753; Fax 01868 789 598.

Ardress (NT) – (♿) **House**: Open June–Aug, daily except Tues, 2–6pm; May and Sept, Sat–Sun and public holidays, 2–6pm; Apr, Sat–Sun, 2–6pm; Good Friday–Easter Tuesday, 2–6pm. **Farmyard**: Open as above. £2.40, £1.20 (child), £6 (family). Guided tour (30min). Parking. Picnic area. Wheelchair access to ground floor, part of farmyard and picnic area. ☎/Fax 01762 851 236.

Orange Order Museum – Open Mon–Sat 10.30am–5.30pm, Sun 2–5.30pm. Apply to the caretaker's house next door (right). ☎ 01762 851 344.

Tayto Potato Crisp Factory – Guided tour by appointment only (1 hr 30min; max 60 people) all year, Mon–Thur, at 10.30am and 1.30pm, Fri at 10.30am. Closed Easter, 12–13 July and Christmas week. No charge. Brochure (French, German). Parking. ☎ 01762 840 249, ext 256/248; Fax 01762 840 085.

Gosford Forest Park – & Open all year, daily, 10am–dusk. £1.50, 50p (child); £3 (car). Guided tour (2 hr) by prior arrangement. Parking. Café, barbecue area. Pony trekking. ☎ 01861 552 169 (Forest Ranger), 01861 551 277.

Navan Fort – & **Site**: Open all year, daily. **Visitor Centre**: Open all year, daily except 25 Dec; July–Aug 10am (noon Sun)–7pm; Apr–June and Sept, 10am (noon Sun)–6pm; winter season 10am (noon Sun)–5pm. Last tour leaves 1 hr 15min before closing. £3.95, £2.10 (child), family ticket and reductions available. Guided tour. Brochure in various languages. Film *The Dawning* 10min; film about Navan myths 25min. Parking. Restaurant. ☎ 01861 525 550; Fax 01861 522 323.

B

BANBRIDGE

🛈 Gateway Tourist Information Centre, 200 Newry Road;
☎ 018206 23 322
Open July–Aug, Mon–Sat 9am–7pm, Sun 2–6pm;
otherwise, Mon–Sat 10am–5pm, plus Easter–Oct Sun 2–6pm. Bureau de change. &

BANGOR

🛈 34 Quay Street; ☎ 01247 270 069
Open July–Aug, Mon–Fri 9am–7pm, Sat 10am–7pm, Sun noon–6pm;
June and Sept, Mon–Fri 9am–5pm, Sat 10.30am–4.30pm, Sun 1–5pm;
Jan–May and Oct–Dec, Mon–Fri 9am–5pm, Sat 10am–4pm. Bureau de change. &

Bangor–Ballywalter Open-top Bus – Operates (weather permitting) July–Aug, Tues–Sat: from Bangor bus station at 10.10am, 12.10pm, 2.15pm, 4.15pm; from Ballywalter at 10.55am, 12.55pm, 3.15pm, 5.10pm. Journey can be broken. Return £3.20; single £1.60. ☎ 01247 271 143; Fax 01247 465 594.

Bangor Bay Cruise – Operates from Bangor seafront July–Aug, daily, 2pm; May–June and Sept–Oct, Sat–Sun, 2pm. Time 30min. Also bird watching, angling and longer pleasure cruises. £2, £1 (child). ☎ 01247 455 321 (Bangor Harbour Boats).

Bangor Abbey – Open all year, Mon, Wed and Fri, 10am–noon; otherwise by appointment. ☎ 01247 451 087.

North Down Heritage Centre – & Open all year, Tues–Sun and bank holiday Monday, 10.30am (2pm Sun)–5.30pm (4.30pm Sept–June). No charge. Guided tour (45min) by appointment. Leaflet (French, German, Spanish) Parking. Refreshments. ☎ 01247 271 200; Fax 01247 271 370.

Excursions

Crawfordsburn Country Park – & Open all year, daily, 9am–8pm (4.45pm Oct–Easter). **Visitor Centre**: Open all year, daily, 10am–6pm (5pm Oct–Easter). Closed one week at Christmas (23–31 Dec). **Grey Point Fort**: Open Easter–Oct, daily except Tues, 2–5pm; Oct–Easter, Sun only, 2–5pm. No charge for admission to park, visitor centre and fort. Parking. Restaurant. Leaflet available in audiotape format and Braille. ☎ 01247 853 621; Fax 01247 852 580.

Ulster Folk and Transport Museum – & Open July–Aug, daily, 10.30am (noon Sun)–6pm; Apr–June and Sept, Mon–Fri, 9.30am–5pm, Sat, 10.30am–6pm, Sun, noon–6pm; Oct–Mar, Mon–Fri, 9.30am–4pm, Sat–Sun, 12.30–4.30pm. Time 4–5 hr. £4, £2.50 (child), £9 (family 2A+4C). Brochure (French, German, Italian, Japanese, Spanish). Parking. Refreshments. ☎ 01232 428 428; Fax 01232 428 728.

Somme Heritage Centre – Open Jul–Aug, daily, 10am (noon Sat–Sun)–5pm; Apr–Jun and Sept, daily except Fri, 10am (noon Sat–Sun)–4pm; Oct–Mar, Mon–Thu, 10am–4pm. Closed 25 Dec–mid Jan. £3.50, £2.50 (child under 15/reductions). Parking. Restaurant. ☎ 01247 823 202.

Belfast Lough Cruises – Operates from Donaghadee (weather permitting) June–Sept, daily. Time 2–3 hr. Colour video. Ship–to–shore radio. Radar. ☎ 01247 883 403 (Nelson's Boats), 0378 893 920.

Copeland Islands Ferry – **From Donaghadee**: Operates May–Oct (July–Aug, daily) ☎ 01247 883 403 (Quinton Nelson, Nelson's Boats). **From Bangor**: Operates June–Aug, only on specified dates. £4.50, £2.50 (child). ☎ 01247 455 321.

Ballycopeland Windmill (HM) – Open Apr–Sept, Tues–Sun and bank holiday Monday, 10am (2pm Sun)–7pm. 75p, 40p (child/senior citizen). ☎ 01232 235 000.

i St Anne's Court, 59 North Street; ☎ 01232 246 609
Open July–Aug, Mon–Fri 9am–7pm, Sat 9am–5.15pm, Sun noon–4pm
otherwise, Mon–Sat, 9am–5.15pm. Bureau de change. ♿
i City Hall; ☎ 01232 320 202
i Belfast City Airport, Sydenham Bypass; ☎ 01232 457 745
Open daily, Mon–Fri 5.30am–10pm, Sat 5.30am–9pm, Sun 5.30am–10pm. ♿
i Belfast International Airport; ☎ 01849 422 888
Open all year, daily, 24 hr. ♿

Citybus Tours – Operate from Castle Place, early June–early Sept: **Belfast City Tour** (shipyards, Belfast Castle, City Hall; 40mi/65km; 3 hr 30min) Wed and Sat at 1pm; **Belfast Living History tour** (scenes of historical significance) Thur and Sun at 1pm; **North Down History and Scenic Tour** (50mi/80km southeast of Belfast stopping at Bangor Heritage Park) Mon at 1pm; **North Shore Drive** (north of Belfast stopping (45min) in Carnfunnock Country Park) Fri at 1pm (Castle Place) and 1.15pm (Glengormley). £6.50, £4.50 (reduction). Commentary. Refreshments. ☎ 01232 458 484, 246 485 (enquiries); Fax 01232 743 442.

Ulster Museum – ♿ Open all year, Mon–Fri 10am–4.50pm, Sat 1–4.50pm, Sun 2–4.50pm. Closed New Year, 12 July, Christmas. No charge. Café. Shop. Parking for the disabled; audio loop; lifts. ☎ 01232 383 000.

Botanic Gardens – Open all year, daily, 7.30am–dusk. **Palm House and Tropical Ravine**: Open all year, daily, 10am–noon and 1–4pm (5pm Apr–Sept). No charge. Guided tour by appointment for a fee (contact Reg Maxwell, ☎ 01232 320 202). Parking. ☎ 01232 324 902.

Belfast City Hall – ♿ Guided tour (1 hr) June–Sept, Mon–Fri at 10.30am, 11.30am and 2.30pm, Sat at 2.30pm; Oct–May, Mon–Tue and Thur–Sat at 2.30pm, Wed at 10.30am. No charge. Brochure (French, German). Closed 1 Jan, 17 Mar, Easter, 12–13 July, 30 Aug. No charge. ☎ 01232 270 456, 01232 320 202 ext 2346.

Linen Hall Library – Open all year, Mon–Sat, 9.30am–5.30pm (4pm Sat). Closed public holidays. No charge. Guided tour (20min) on request. Refreshments. ☎ 01232 321 707.

St Anne's Cathedral – (♿) Open all year, Mon–Sat, 9am–5pm; Sun, 9.30am–4.30pm. No charge. Guided tour available, 10am–4pm. Leaflet (French, German, Italian, Spanish). **Choral Services**: Sun at 11am and 3.30pm, Tues at 5.15pm. ☎ 01232 328 332; Fax 01232 238 855; e-mail belfast.cathedral@dial.pipex.com

Crown Liquor Saloon (NT) – ♿ Open all year, Mon–Sat, 11.30am–midnight, Sun, 12.30–10pm. Closed 12–13 July, 25–26 Dec. No charge. Full bar and snack lunches. ☎ 01232 249 476.

Sinclair Seamen's Church – Open all year, Sun, 11am–1pm and 6.30–8.30pm; also Mar–Oct, Wed, 2–5pm. Otherwise contact Mrs Carole Davis ☎ 01232 772 429.

St Malachy's Church – Open all year, daily, 8am (Mass)–6pm (or until after Evening Mass); otherwise by appointment. ☎ 01232 321 713, 233 241 (caretaker).

Oval Church – (♿) Open all year, Sun and Wed, 10.30am–12.30pm; otherwise by appointment. **Musical recital**: July–Aug, Wed at 1.15pm. ☎ 01232 843 592, 422 639; Fax 01232 594 070.

Lagan Lookout – ♿ Open Apr–Sept, daily, 11am (noon Sat, 2pm Sun)–5pm; Oct–Mar, daily except Mon, 11am (1pm Sat, 2pm Sun)–3.30pm (4.30pm Sat–Sun). £1.50, 75p (child), £4 (family). ☎ 01232 315 444; Fax 01232 311 955.

Presbyterian Historical Society Museum (Church House) – ♿ Guided tour all year, Mon–Tue and Thur–Fri, 10am–12.30pm, Wed, 2–4pm. Closed public holidays. No charge. ☎ 01232 322 284.

Royal Ulster Rifles Museum – Open all year, Mon–Fri, 10am–4pm (3pm Fri). Closed public holidays. Guided tour (30min). ☎ 01232 232 086.

Excursions

Belfast Zoological Gardens – ♿ Open all year, daily, 10am–5pm (3.30pm Oct–Mar; 2.30pm Fri). Closed 25 Dec. Time 2–3 hr. £5, £14 (family 2A+2C), £2.50 (child); reductions in winter. Leaflet (French, German, Italian, Spanish). Parking. Café. ☎ 01232 776 277; Fax 01232 370 578.

Belfast Castle – ♿ Open all year, Mon–Sat 9am–10pm, Sun 9am–6pm. During functions, parts of the castle may not be accessed. Closed 25–26 Dec. Lift. No charge. ☎ 01232 776 925.

Stormont – **Grounds**: Open daily during daylight hours.

Glencairn People's Museum – ♿ Open all year, daily, 10am (1pm Sun)–4pm. No charge. Restaurant. ☎ 01232 715 599.

413

C

🖪 Heritage Plaza, Antrim Street; ☏ 01960 366 455
Open all year, Mon–Fri 9am–5pm;
Apr–Sept, Mon–Fri 9am–6pm, Sat 10am–6pm; July–Aug, Sun noon–6pm.
Bureau de change. &

Carrickfergus Castle (HM) – & Open all year, daily. Apr–Oct, Mon–Sat, 10am–6pm, Sun, 2–6pm (11am–8pm June–Aug); Nov–Mar, Mon–Sat, 10am–4pm, Sun, 2–4pm. Last admission 30min before closing. Closed 25–26 Dec. £2.70, £1.35 (child/senior citizen), £7.30 (family 2A+2C); joint ticket with Knight Ride £4.85, £2.40 (child), £13.15 (family 2A+2C). Guided tour if booked in advance. Brochure (French, German, Italian, Spanish). Parking. Access for the disabled; chairlift to first floor of keep. ☏ 01960 351 273; Fax 01960 365 190.

St Nicholas' Church – Ring the Revd McMaster, ☏ 01960 363 244.

Knight Ride – & Open all year, daily, 10am (noon Sun)–6pm (5pm Oct–Mar). Time 30min. £2.70, £1.35 (child), £7.30 (family 2A+2C); joint ticket with Carrickfergus Castle £4.85, £2.40 (child), £13.15 (family 2A+2C). Leaflet (French, German, Spanish, Italian). Restaurant. ☏ 01960 366 455; Fax 01960 350 350.

Excursions

Andrew Jackson Centre – Open Apr–May and Oct, Mon–Fri 10am–1pm and 2–4pm, Sat–Sun 2–4pm; June–Sept, Mon–Fri 10am–1pm and 2–6pm, Sat–Sun 2–6pm. £1.20, 60p (reduction). Parking. ☏ 01960 366 455 (TIC).

Railway Preservation Collection – **Steam trains and historic carriages**: Open all year, Sat–Sun, 10am–5pm; mid June–end Aug, Sun afternoon only. **Steam train excursions throughout Ireland:** mainly spring–autumn. Advance booking recommended. For details of times and fares ☏/Fax 01960 353 567 (recorded message when unattended) or send sae to Railway Preservation Society of Ireland, c/o 22 Town Lane, Islandmagee BT40 3SZ. Parking.

Larne Lough Ferry (**Island Magee/Larne**) – See ANTRIM GLENS above.

Castle Coole (NT) – (&) **House**: Open May–Aug, daily except Thur, 1–6pm; Apr and Sept, Sat–Sun and public holidays, 1–6pm; Good Friday–Easter Tues, 2–6pm; last admission 45min before closing. **Grounds**: Open to pedestrians during daylight hours. £2.80, £1.40 (child); grounds £2 (per car). Guided tour (45min). Parking. Tearoom; picnic area. Facilities for the disabled; wheelchair access to ground floor, sympathetic hearing scheme. ☏ 01365 322 690; Fax 01365 325 665.

Castle Ward (NT) – & **House**: Guided tour (1 hr) June–Aug, daily except Thur, 1–6pm; Apr (from Easter), May, Sept and Oct, Sat–Sun, 1–6pm; Good Friday–Low Sunday, 1–6pm. £2.60, £1.30 (child). **Estate and Grounds**: Open all year, daily, during daylight hours. £3.50 per car; £1.75 per car (out of season). **Strangford Lough Wildlife Centre**: Open as house, 2pm–6pm, except only Sat–Sun and public holidays in May and June, 2pm–6pm. Parking. Tearoom. Adventure playground. ☏ 01396 881 204.

🖪 Railway Road, Coleraine; ☏ 01265 44 723
Open all year, Mon–Sat 9am–5pm; July–Aug, Mon–Sat 9am–6pm. &
🖪 Dunluce Centre, Sandhill Drive, Portrush; ☏ 01265 823 333
Open March, Sat–Sun noon–5pm; Apr–mid June, Mon–Fri 9am–5pm, Sat–Sun noon–5pm;
mid June–Sept, daily 9am–8pm; Oct, Sat–Sun noon–5pm. Bureau de change. &
🖪 Town Hall, The Crescent, Portstewart; ☏ 01265 832 286
🖪 Benone Tourist Complex, 52 Benone Avenue, Seacoast Road, Magilligan;
☏ 015047 50 555

Causeway Coast Open-top Bus – Passengers are advised to consult the North Region Bus Timetable (available from Ulster bus depots and TICs) under Service 177. Details for 1998: operates (weather permitting, otherwise normal single-decker bus is used) July–Aug, Mon–Sun (check at bus depot for 12–13 July); from Coleraine, at 9.10am, 11.30am, 1.50pm, 4pm, 6.15pm; from Giant's Causeway, at 10.20am, 12.40pm, 2.55pm, 5.10pm, 6.55pm. Journey may be broken at Portstewart, Portrush, Portballintrae, Bushmills. Return £4.20; single £2.30. ☏ 01265 43334.

Holy Trinity Church, Ballycastle – Open all year, daily, 9am (8.30am Sun)–dusk. If closed, try the Sexton's house next door. ☏ 012657 62024 (Ballycastle TIC).

Rathlin Island Ferry – Operates (weather permitting) June–Sept, daily, from Ballycastle at 9.30am, 11.30am, 4pm, 6pm; from Rathlin at 8.30am, 10.30am, 3pm, 5pm. For sailings at other times telephone for details. Time 40min. Return £7.60, £3.80 (child 5–16), £5.60 (senior citizen). ☏ 01265 769 299 (bookings), 763 915. Be prepared to stay overnight at Rathlin Guesthouse ☏ 01265 763 917; accommodation also available at The Manor House, Rathlin Island ☏ 01265 763 964.

Rathlin Island mini-bus tour – Operates approximately Apr–Aug, daily from the harbour. West Lighthouse bird sanctuary return £4, £2 (child); Rue Point return £2.50, £1 (child). ☎ 01265 763 909; Fax 01265 763 988 (Augin McCurdy).

Carrick-a-Rede Rope Bridge (NT) – Open (except in high winds) mid Mar–mid Sept, daily 10am–6pm (8pm July–Aug). Guided tour by appointment. **Information Centre**: Open Easter–mid Sept, daily, 11am–6pm. Parking £2. ☎ 01265 31582 (Visitor Services Manager); Fax 01265 732 963.

Bushmills Distillery – (&) Guided tour (1 hr) Apr–Oct, Mon–Sat, 9.30am–5.30pm, Sun, noon–5.30pm; Nov–Mar, Mon–Fri, at 10.30am, 11.30am, 1.30pm, 2.30pm and 3.30pm. £3, £1.50 (child), £2.50 (senior citizen), £8 (family). Parking. Visitor Centre and shops accessible to the disabled. ☎ 01265 731 521; Fax 01265 731 339. www.irish-whiskey-trail.com

Larrybann, Co Antrim

Dunluce Castle (HM) – Open Apr–Oct, Mon–Sat 10am–7pm, Sun 2–7pm (11am–8pm July–Aug); Nov–Mar, Mon–Sat 10am–4pm, Sun 2–4pm. Last admission 30min before closing. £1.50, 75p (child/senior citizen). Audio-guide in various languages £1. Parking. ☎ 01265 731 938.

Dunluce Centre – (&) Open Mar–June and Sept, daily, noon–5pm (6pm Sat–Sun; 10am–8pm during Easter); July–Aug, daily, 10.30am–7.30pm; Oct, Sat–Sun, noon–5pm. £5, £15 (family 2A+2C). Parking, Café. ☎ 01265 824 444; Fax 01265 822 256.

Countryside Centre – Open July–Aug, daily except Tues, noon–8pm; June and Sept, telephone for opening times. No charge. Parking. ☎ 01265 823 600.

Benvarden ⊘ – Open June–Aug, daily except Mon, 2–6pm. No dogs. ☎ 012657 41331.

Leslie Hill Open Farm – & **Farm Park**: Open Easter–end May, Sun and bank holidays, 2–6pm; June, Sat–Sun, 2–6pm; July–Aug, Mon–Sat, 11am–6pm; Sept, Sun, 2–6pm. £2.50, £1.70 (child/senior citizen). Tearoom. Shop. ☎ 01265 666 803.

Hezlett House (NT) – & Guided tour (40min; max 15 people) June–Aug, daily except Tues, 1–5pm; Apr–May and Sept, Sat–Sun and public holidays, 1–5pm; Good Friday–Easter Tuesday, daily, 1–5pm. Last tour 30min before closing. Charge (telephone for details). Parking. Wheelchair access to ground floor only. ☎/Fax 01265 848 567.

Downhill (NT) – **Mussenden Temple**: Open July–Aug, daily, noon–6pm; Apr–June and Sept, Sat–Sun and public holidays, noon–6pm; Good Friday–Easter Tuesday, noon–6pm. **Grounds**: Open all year, during daylight hours. No charge. Parking. Picnics welcome. ☎ 01265 848 728.

The star ratings are allocated for various categories:
– regions of scenic beauty with dramatic natural features
– cities with a cultural heritage
– elegant resorts and charming villages
– ancient monuments and fine architecture, museums and picture galleries.

D

🛈 74 Market Street; ☎ 01396 612 233
Open all year, Mon–Sat 9am–5pm, closed Sat only 1–2pm;
mid June–Sept, Mon–Sat 9am–6pm, Sun, 2–6pm. Bank/public holidays 11am–6pm.
Bureau de change. ♿

Down Cathedral – ♿ Open all year, Mon–Fri and public holidays, 9.15am–1pm and 2–5pm; Sat–Sun, 2–5pm. Closed Good Friday, 25–26 Dec. No charge. Guided tour available. Brochure (French, German). Parking. Bookshop. ☎ 01396 614922.

Down County Museum – (♿) Open June–Aug, daily, 11am (2pm Sat–Sun)–5pm; Sept–May, Tues–Sat, 11am (2pm Sat–Sun)–5pm. No charge. Guided tour (1 hr) by prior arrangement. Brochure (French, German, Japanese, Spanish). ☎ 01396 615 218.

Excursions

St Patrick's Memorial Church – Open all year, daily, 8am–dusk. **Service**: Sun at 10am. ☎ 01396 613 101.

Jordan's Castle (HM) – Open July–Aug, Mon–Fri 10am–7pm, Sun 2–7pm. (1996 prices) 75p, 40p (child/senior citizen).

🛈 Council Offices, Circular Road; ☎ 01868 725 311
🛈 Killymaddy Tourist Information Centre, Ballygawley Road, Dungannon (off A 4);
☎ 01868 767 259. Open all year, Mon–Fri 9am–5pm;
Apr–June and Sept, Sat–Sun 10am–4pm;
July–Aug, Mon–Thur and Sat 9am–6pm, Fri 9am–7pm. ♿

Tyrone Crystal – ♿ Guided tour (45min) all year round, Mon–Fri, 9.30am–3.30pm; last tour Fri at noon; other days at 3.30pm. £2, no charge (senior citizen/child under 12). **Factory Shop**: Open all year, Mon–Sat, 9am–5pm. Brochure (French, German). Parking. Coffee shop (open as for Factory Shop). Facilities for the disabled; wheelchair available. ☎ 01868 725 335; Fax 01868 726 260.

Heritage World Genealogy Centre – ♿ Open all year, Mon–Thur, 9am–1pm and 2–5pm, Fri, 9am–1pm. Genealogical consultation fee £15 minimum. Facilities for the disabled; ramp. ☎ 01868 724 187; Fax 01868 752 141.

Excursions

Cornmill Heritage Centre – ♿ Open all year, Mon–Fri 10am–4pm, weekends by appointment only; last admission 1 hr before closing time. £1.50, 80p (child), £1.20 (senior citizen/student). Parking. Lift. ☎ 01868 748 532; Fax 01868 748 695.

Donaghmore Heritage Centre – Open all year, Mon–Fri, 9am–5pm, also June–Aug, Sat, 11am–4pm. ☎ 018687 67039.

Parkanaur Forest Park – ♿ Open all year, daily, 8am–dusk. £2 (per car). Deer enclosure. Wildfowl pond. Guided tour (1 hr) by appointment. Parking. ☎ 01868 759 311.

Simpson Grant Homestead – ♿ Open Easter–end Sept, Mon–Sat, noon–5pm, Sun, 2–6pm. Time 1 hr. £1, 50p (reduction). Guided tour on request. Parking. Refreshments. ☎ 01662 557 133.

Clogher Cathedral – Open by prior arrangement only. Guided tour on request. Contact: Mr Jack Johnston, Ratory, Clogher, ☎ 016625 48288; Very Revd TR Moore MA, The Deanery, Augher Road, Clogher, ☎ 016625 48235; Mrs M Fannin, 75 Main Street, Clogher, ☎ 016625 48287; Mr W Taggart, 35 Main Street, Clogher, ☎ 016625 48946.

E

🛈 Fermanagh TIC, Wellington Road; ☎ 01365 323 110
Open all year, Mon–Fri 9am–5.30pm; July–Aug, 9am–6.30pm
Easter–Sept, also Sat 10am–6pm, Sun 11am–5pm. Bureau de change. ♿

Enniskillen Castle – (♿) Open July–Aug, Tues–Fri and bank holiday Monday, 10am–5pm, other Mon and Sat–Sun, 2–5pm; May, June and Sept, Tues–Fri and bank holiday Monday, 10am–5pm, other Mon and Sat, 2–5pm; Oct–Apr, Tues–Fri and bank holiday Monday, 10am–5pm, other Mon, 2–5pm. Subject to variation at New Year and Christmas. Guide and information (French, German, Spanish, Italian). £2, £1 (child), £5 (family 2A+2C). Parking. Refreshments. Facilities for the disabled; lift. ☎ 01365 325 000; Fax 01365 327 342. **Museum of the Royal Inniskilling Fusiliers**: Open as above. Wheelchair access to ground floor only. ☎ 01365 323 142.

Cole's Monument – Open mid May–mid Sept, daily, 11am–1pm and 2–6pm. 70p, 30p (child). Brochure (French, German).

Lough Erne Waterbus Cruises – Operates from Round "O" Jetty (Brook Park, Belleek Road (A 46), Enniskillen) July–Aug, daily at 10.30am, 2.15pm, 4.15pm, also Tues, Thur and Sun at 7.15pm evening cruise to Bellanaleck; May–June, Sun and public holidays at 2.30pm; Sept, Tues, Sat and Sun at 2.30pm. Time 1 hr 45min (stopping for 30min at Devenish Island). £5, £2.50 (child under 14). MV Kestrel, all weather vessel (covered deck); capacity 56; refreshments, bar. ☎ 01365 322 882 (Erne Tours Ltd); Fax 01365 387 954.

Upper Lough Erne Cruises – For times and prices contact Share Holiday Village. ☎ 01365 722 122; Fax 01365 721 893.

Day Boats – Enniskillen ☎ 26257 (P Bailey); Killadeas ☎ 013656 21561; Kesh ☎ 013656 31091, 31527 (JE Bromstone); 013656 31668 (RA Graham); Belleek ☎ 0136565 8181 (Carlton Cottages); Garrison ☎ 0136565 380 (M Gilroy); Bellanaleck ☎ 0136582 267 (Erne Marine).

Devenish Island (HM) – Open Apr–Sept, Tues–Sun and bank holiday Monday, 10am (2pm Sun)–7pm. Access by ferry (capacity 12) from Trory Point. £2.25, £1.20 (child/senior citizen); 75p (excluding ferry). Guided tour (90min) available. Parking. ☎ 01232 235 000.

Castle Archdale Country Park – Open all year, daily. **Visitor Centre**: Open July–Aug, daily except Mon, 11am–7pm; otherwise by arrangement. No charge. Parking. ☎ 01365 621 588; Fax 01365 21375.

White Island (HM) – Ferry (capacity 10) operates from Castle Archdale Marina (weather permitting) Easter–Aug: Apr–Jun Sun only 2–6pm; July–Aug daily 11am–6pm; every hour on the hour; check with the Marina at Castle Archdale. £3, £2 (child/senior citizen). Guided tour available. Parking. ☎ 01365 621 333.

Janus Figure, Co Fermanagh

Christophe Boisvieux

Castle Caldwell Forest Park – ♿ Open all year, daily. No charge. Parking. Café (summer).

Belleek Pottery – **Pottery**: Guided tour (30min), Mon–Fri, every 30min; last tour on Fri at 3.30pm. £2. Audio-guide (French, German, Italian). Brochure (French, German, Italian). **Visitor Centre**: Open July–Aug, daily, 9am (10am Sat, 11am Sun)–8pm (6pm Sat); Mar–June and Sept–Oct, daily, 9am (10am Sat, 2pm Sun)–6pm (5.30pm Mon–Sat in Oct); Nov–Feb, Mon–Fri, 9am–5.30pm. Museum. Showroom. Parking. Restaurant. ☎ 01365 658 501; Fax 01365 658 625.

ExplorErne – ♿ Open mid Mar–end Oct, daily, 10am–6pm; otherwise to groups by appointment. Exhibitions £1, 50p (child/senior citizen), £2.50 (family 2A+2C). Parking. ☎ 01365 658 866; Fax 01365 658 833.

Tully Castle (HM) – Open Apr–Sept, Tues–Sun and bank holiday Monday, 10am (2pm Sun)–7pm. £1, 50p (child/senior citizen). ☎ 01232 235 000.

Lough Navar Forest Park – Open all year, dawn-dusk. £2.50 (car), £1.50 (motorcycle), £5 (minibus). Parking. picnic area; fishing. ☎ 01365 641 256.

Crom Estate (NT) – ♿ **Visitor Centre**: Open Apr–Sept, daily, 10am (noon Sun)–6pm. £3 by car or boat. Guided walks by arrangement. Visitor guide (French, German). Guide book (English only). Parking. Tearoom. Gift shop. ☎ 01365 738 38174; ☎/Fax 01365 738 118.

F

FLORENCE COURT

Florence Court (NT) – **Grounds**: Open all year, daily, 10am–7pm/dusk. Closed 25 Dec. Parking £2. **House**: (♿) Guided tour (45min) Apr and Sept, Sat–Sun and bank holidays, 1–6pm; Good Friday–Easter Tuesday, daily, 1–6pm; May–Aug, daily except Tues, 1–6pm. Last tour 45min before closing. Closed 25 Dec. £2.80, £1.40 (child), £7 (family). Pony rides. Parking. Tearoom; picnic area. Facilities for the disabled; wheelchair access to ground floor and garden. ☎ 01365 348 249; Fax 01365 348 873.

Florence Court Forest Park – Open all year, daily except 25 Dec, Apr–Sept 10am–7pm; Oct–Mar 10am–4pm (these times apply to cars because the gates close; walkers can get in any time). £2 (per car). Parking. ☎ 01365 348 497.

Excursions

Marble Arch – **Forest Nature Reserve**: Open all year, daily. **Caves**: Guided tour (1 hr 30min) Easter–Sept, Mon–Sun from 10am; last tour 4.30pm (5pm July–Aug). £5, £2 (child), £3 (reduction), £12 (family 2A+4C). Audio-visual presentation (20min). Guided tour for groups in foreign languages (French, German) by prior arrangement only. Tour translations in French, German, Spanish and Italian. Advance booking recommended. Tour may be curtailed by heavy rain. Stout shoes and warm clothes advisable. Parking. Refreshments. Caves not suitable for wheelchairs. ☎ 01365 348 855; Fax 01365 348 928.

G

GIANT'S CAUSEWAY

🄸 Visitor Centre, 44 Causeway Road, Bushmills; ☎ 012657 31 855
Open summer Mon–Sun 10am–7pm; spring/autumn Mon–Sun 10am–6pm; winter Mon–Fri 10am–4.30pm, Sat–Sun 10am–5pm. Bureau de change. ♿

Giant's Causeway (NT) – Open all year, daily. Parking £3 including NT members. Guided tour by appointment. ☎ 01265 731 582; Fax 01265 732 963 (Visitor Services Manager).

Visitor Centre – ♿ Open July–Aug, daily, 10am–7pm; June, daily, 10am–6pm; May, daily, 10am–5.30pm; Sept–Oct, Mon–Fri 10am–5.30pm, Sat–Sun 10am–5.30pm; Mar–Apr, Mon–Fri 10am–5pm, Sat–Sun 10am–5.30pm; Nov–Feb, Mon–Sun 10am–4.30pm. £1 return bus fare to causeway (0.75mi/1.2km). Audio-visual presentation. Guided tour of Causeway by prior arrangement. Brochure in various languages. Parking £3. Tearoom. Bureau de change. Craft and souvenir shops. Tourist information. ☎ 01265 731 855.

Mini Bus Shuttle to Causeway (Translink/NT) – Operates during the season. Small charge. Time 15min. Minibus with hoist. ☎ 01265 731 582 (Visitor Services Manager).

Causeway Coast Open-top Bus – See CAUSEWAY COAST above.

H – L

HILLSBOROUGH

🄸 Council Offices, The Square; ☎ 01846 682 477

Hillsborough Fort (HM) – Open Apr–Sept, Tues–Sat 10am–7pm, Sun 2–7pm; Oct–Mar, Tues–Sat, 10am–4pm, Sun 2–4pm. For bank holiday Mondays, telephone to check as the fort may be open on the holiday and closed another day that week. No charge. Parking. ☎ 01846 683 285.

Hillsborough Court House – Open May–Sept, Mon–Sat, 9.30am–6pm, Sun, 2–5.30pm; Oct–Apr, Tues–Sat, 11am–3.30pm. No charge. ☎ 01232 543 037.

Excursion

Rowallane Gardens (NT) – ♿ Open Apr–Oct, daily. 10.30am (2pm Sat–Sun)–6pm; Nov–end Mar, Mon–Fri, 10.30am–5pm. Closed 1 Jan, 25–26 Dec. Time 2 hr. £2.50, £1.25 (child); winter £1.40, 70p (child). Parking. Tearoom. Wheelchair available. ☎ 01238 510 131.

LISBURN

🄸 Irish Linen Centre and Lisburn Museum, Market Square; ☎ 01846 660 038. Open all year Mon–Sat 9.30am–5pm; Apr–Sept Mon–Sat 9.30am–5.30pm, Sun 2–5.30pm. Bureau de change. ♿

Irish Linen Centre and Lisburn Museum – ♿ Open all year, Mon–Sat, 9.30am–5.30pm. Last admission 1 hr before closing. Time 2 hr. Coffee shop. Speciality linen and crafts shop. Tourist Information Centre. Facilities for the disabled; adapted toilet, loop system. Audio exhibition commentary available on request. Leaflet (French, German, Italian). ☎ 01846 663 377; Fax 01846 672 624.

Linen Homelands Tour – Operates May–Sept (except for last 3 weeks in July), Wed (all day), 9.45am to 4pm; Sat, 1pm–4pm. Full day £10, £8 (reduction); half day £7, £5.50 (reduction). By bus from Banbridge TIC. Full–day tour includes McConvilles in Dromore, a traditional flax frame and water–powered scutching mill (demonstration of scutching), the Linen Centre in Lisburn *(lunch)*; one of four local factories (Thomas Fergusson in Banbridge, Ewart Lidell, Blacker's Mill in Portadown, or Dunmurray Print). Half-day tour excludes the visit to a local factory.

Christchurch Cathedral – **Services**: Sun at 11am and 6.30pm; also first and third Sun in the month at 9.30am. Usually locked; key available from the Sexton's House in the church grounds. ☎ 01846 602 400 (office), 662 865 (Rectory).

Excursions

Hilden Brewery Visitor Centre – Open daily, 10am–5pm. Guided tour of brewery (40min), daily, at 11.30am and 2.30pm. £2. Tap Room restaurant. Parking. ☎ 01846 663 863.

Drumbeg Church – Open all year, daily, 8am–5pm.

Malone House – ♿ Open all year, Mon–Sat, 10am–4.30pm. Closed 25 Dec. No charge. Parking. Restaurant. Wheelchair access to ground floor only. ☎ 01232 681 246; Fax 01232 682 197.

LONDONDERRY

🛈 44 Foyle Street; ☎ 01504 267 284
Open all year, Mon–Thur 9am–5.15pm, Fri 9am–5pm;
Easter–June, Mon–Thur 9am–5.15pm, Fri–Sat 9am–5pm;
July–Sept, Mon–Sat 9am–8pm, Sun 10am–6pm. Bureau de change. ♿

City Walls – (♿) Accessible to the general public all year, daily. Information panels. No charge. Guided walking tours available. Walls are accessible for wheelchairs with the exception of the Bishop's Gate. ☎ 01504 267 284.

St Columb's Cathedral – Open summer, Mon–Sat, 9am–5pm; winter, 9am–1pm and 2–5pm. Donation £1. Audio-visual presentation: *The History and Role of the Cathedral*; *The Siege of Derry in 1689*. Brochure (French, German, Italian, Spanish). ☎ 01504 267 313.

Tower Museum – Open July–Aug, daily, 10am (2pm Sun)–5pm; Sept, Mon–Sat, 10am–5pm; Oct–June, Tues–Sat, 10am–5pm; also open bank holiday Monday. Last admission 4.30pm throughout the year. £3.50, £1.20 (reduction), £7 (family). ☎ 01504 372 411.

Fifth Province – ♿ Show runs all year, Mon–Fri at 11.30am and 2.30pm. £3, £1 (children and reductions). Public parking. ☎ 01504 373 177.

Long Tower Church – Open all year, Mon–Sat, 7.30am–9pm; Sun, 8am–6.30pm.

Guildhall – ♿ Open all year, Mon–Fri, 9am–5pm, except bank holiday Monday. No charge. Guided tour (30min) July–Aug. ☎ 01504 377 335; Fax 01504 377 964.

Harbour Museum – Open all year, Mon–Fri, 10am–1pm and 2–4.30pm. No charge. ☎ 01504 377 331; Fax 01504 377 633.

St Eugene's Cathedral – Open all year, Mon–Sat, 7.30am (8.30am Sat)–9pm; Sun, 6.30am–6.30pm. ☎ 01504 262 894, 365 712; Fax 01504 377 494.

Foyle Valley Railway Centre – ♿ Open Apr–Sept, Tues–Sat, 10am (11.30am Sat)–4.30pm. Special opening times at Christmas and Easter. Train excursion £2.50, £1.25 (child), £7 (family). Parking. Refreshments. ☎ 01504 265 234.

Workhouse Museum – Open Tues–Sat, 10am–5pm. No charge. ☎ 01504 342 963.

Michelin Green Guide France:
Designed to enhance your travels in France,
it leads to the discovery of extraordinary
natural and man-made wonders.
Remember to take the **Green Guides** *for the regions you will visit.*

MOUNT STEWART

Mount Stewart (NT) – ♿ **House:** Open May–Sept, daily except Tues, 1–6pm; Apr and Oct, Sat–Sun, 1–6pm; Good Friday–Low Sunday, 1–6pm. Guided tour (45min). **Gardens:** Open Apr–Sept, daily, 11am–6pm; Oct, Sat–Sun, 11am–6pm; Mar, Sun, 2–5pm. **Temple of the winds:** Open as house, 2–5pm. Guided tour (15min) available. House, gardens and temple £3.50, £1.75 (child); temple £1, 50p (child). Parking. Tearoom. Shop. Facilities for the disabled: wheelchairs and powered buggy, sympathetic hearing scheme. ☎ 01247 788 387, 88487; Fax 01247 788 569.

Christophe Boisvieux

MOURNE MOUNTAINS

🏢 6 Newcastle Street, Kilkeel; ☎ 016937 62 525
Open all year, Mon–Sat, 9am–5.30pm. Bureau de change. ♿

Mourne Countryside Centre – 91 Central Promenade. Open June–Sept, Sat–Sun, 9am–5pm. The centre is staffed from Mourne Heritage Trust's adjoining offices from Mon–Fri, 9am–5pm. Brochure. Leaflet. Programme of hill walks in summer months. ☎ 01396 724 059; Fax 01396 726 493.

Mourne Rambler – Bus tour Newcastle/Silent Valley Reservoir, July–Aug, daily, at 9.30am and 3pm, from Newcastle bus station. £2.50, £1.75p (child/senior citizen). ☎ 01396 722 296.

Tollymore Forest Park – ♿ Open all year, daily, 10am–dusk. £1.50, 50p (child), £3.50 (car). Guided tour by appointment. Parking. Café; picnic areas. Fishing. ☎ 01396 722 428.

Silent Valley Reservoir – ♿ Open daily, 10am–6.30pm (4pm Oct–Apr). £3 (car). **Information Centre:** Open as above. No charge. ☎ 0345 440 088. **Bus Shuttle between car park and Ben Crom Reservoir:** July–Aug, daily; May–June and Sept, Sat–Sun; £1.20, 90p (reduction). Parking. Refreshments (summer).

Brontë Centre – (♿) Open Mar–Oct, Tues–Fri, 11am–5pm, Sat and Sun, 2–6pm. £1, 50p (child/senior citizen). Parking. Picnic sites. Disabled access to church and school. Guide book (French, German). ☎ 018206 31152.

Annalong Marine Park and Cornmill – (♿) Guided tour (30min) June–Sept, daily, 2–6pm; Easter–May and Oct, Sat–Sun, 2–6pm. £1.20, 60p (child/senior citizen), £2.40 (family). Parking. Wheelchair access to Marine Park only. ☎ 01396 768 736.

Greencastle (HM) – Open July–Aug, Tues–Sun and bank holiday Monday, 10am (2pm Sun)–7pm. 75p, 40p (child/senior citizen). Parking. ☎ 01232 235 000.

Narrow Water Castle (HM) – Open July–Aug, Tues–Sun and bank holiday Monday, 10am (2pm Sun)–7pm. 75p, 40p (child/senior citizen). Parking. ☎ 01232 235 000.

M Guillot

N

🏛 Lough Neagh Discovery Centre, Oxford Island; ☎ 01762 322 205

Lough Neagh Boat Trip – Operates (weather permitting) Sat–Sun, every 30min; Mon–Fri from **Kinnego Marina** (south shore) to Lough Neagh Discovery Centre (30min). Fares from £4, £2 (child). Capacity 12; refreshments. ☎ 01762 327 573 (Oxford Island Marina).

Lough Neagh Cruises – Operate June–Sept, daily, from **Sixmilewater Marina** in Antrim. £3, £1.80 (reduction). ☎ 01849 463 113 for timetable. **Bann cruises** July and Aug, certain weekends, from Antrim to Castlerock (6/7 hr; 35mi/56km). **Maid of Antrim:** capacity 100 passengers; covered deck; bar, refreshments. All cruises subject to weather and demand. ☎ 01849 465 961 (24 hr info), 01849 428 331; Fax 01849 487 844 (Antrim Tourist Information Centre).

Fishing licences for Lough Neagh – Available from Fishery Conservancy Board, 1 Mahon Road, Portadown; Open all year, Mon–Fri, 9am–1pm and 2pm–5pm. Licence for game and coarse fishing £20.50 per annum, £10 for 8 days, £4 for 1 day. Licence for coarse fishing (rod and line) £8 per annum, £4 for 8 days, less for 3 days. ☎ 01762 334 666.

Fishing licences for the Lower Bann – Available from Bann Systems, Coleraine. Max fee £50 per day. ☎ 01265 44796.

Lough Neagh Discovery Centre – ♿ Open Apr–Sept, daily, 10am–7pm; Oct–Mar, Wed–Sun, 10am–5pm. £3, £6.70 (family), reductions available. Bird-watching hides. Exhibition guide sheet (French, German, Spanish). TIC. Parking. Café. ☎ 01762 322 205.

Peatlands Park – ♿ Open all year, daily, 9am–9pm/dusk. Closed 25 Dec. No charge. Guided tour by appointment. Parking. Picnic area. Tearoom. ☎ 01762 851 102; Fax 01762 851 821. **Visitor Centre:** Open June–Aug, daily, 2pm–6pm; also Easter–Sept, Sat–Sun and public holidays, 2pm–6pm. **Narrow–gauge railway:** Open as for Visitor Centre. ☎ 01589 410 554.

Kinturk Cultural Centre – ♿ Open June–Sept, Mon–Fri, 10am–8pm, Sat–Sun, 11am–6pm; Oct–May, daily except Sat, 11am (12.30pm Sun)–6pm. £1.50, 75p (children). Audio-visual presentation. Lough Neagh Exhibition. Guided walks and boat trips. Parking. Licensed restaurant. ☎ 01648 736 512.

Bellaghy Bawn – Open all year, Tues–Sat, 10am–6pm (5pm Oct–Mar). ☎ 01648 386 812.

🏛 Newcastle Centre, 10–14 Central Promenade; ☎ 013967 22 222
Open all year, Mon–Sat 10am–5pm, Sun 2–6pm;
longer hours in summer. Bureau de change. ♿

Mourne Rambler – See MOURNE MOUNTAINS above.

Our Lady of the Assumption – Open all year, daily, 8am–8pm.

Excursions

Castlewellan Forest Park – ♿ Open all year, daily, 10am–dusk. £3.50 (car). Guided tour by appointment. Parking. Café; barbecue site. Fishing. ☎ 013967 78664; Fax 013967 71762.

Murlough National Nature Reserve (NT) – Open all year, dawn–dusk. **Information Centre**: Open (weather permitting) July–Aug and first weekend of Sept, daily, 10am–5pm. Parking £2 (car). ☎ 013967 51467, 24362; Fax 013967 51467.

Dundrum Castle (HM) – Open Apr–Sept, Tues–Sun and bank holiday Monday, 10am (2pm Sun)–7pm. 75p, 40p (child/senior citizen). Guided tour (30min). Parking. ☎ 01232 235 000.

Seaforde Garden – Open Easter–Sept, Mon–Sat, 10am–5pm, Sun, 1–6pm. Admission charge. Parking. ☎ 013968 11225.

NEWRY

🛈 Town Hall; ☎ 01693 68877
🛈 Carlingford Lough (Cruise Booking Office), The Marina, Warrenpoint; ☎ 01693 772 950

Newry Cathedral – Open all year, daily, 8am–6pm. ☎ 01693 62586; Fax 01693 67505.

Newry Museum – (♿) Open all year, Mon–Fri, 11.30am–4.30pm. No charge. Café. ☎ 01693 66232.

Excursions

Slieve Gullion Forest Park – Open Easter–Sept, daily, from 8am. £2.50 (car). ☎ 016937 38284, 016938 48226; Fax 016937 39413.

Cardinal O'Fiaich Centre – Open Mon–Fri, 10am–5pm, Sun 2–6pm, bank holidays, 11am–6pm. £1.50, £1 (student/senior citizen), no charge (child under 11). Restaurant. Souvenir shop. ☎ 01693 868 757.

S

SPERRIN MOUNTAINS

🛈 48 Molesworth Street, Cookstown; ☎ 016487 66727
Open Easter–June and Sept, Mon–Fri 9am–5pm, Sat 10am–4pm;
July–Aug, Mon–Sat 9am–5pm (6pm Tues and Thur); Oct, Mon–Fri 9am–5pm. ♿
🛈 Sperrin Heritage Centre, 274 Glenelly Road, Cranagh; ☎ 016626 48 142
🛈 Council Offices, 7 Connell Street, Limavady; ☎ 015047 22 226
Open all year, Mon to Fri 9am–5pm; Easter–Sept, Sat 9.30am–5.30pm;
July–Aug, Mon–Fri 9am–5.45pm, Sat 9.30am–5.30pm. Bureau de change. ♿
🛈 1 Market Street, Omagh; ☎ 01662 247 831, 240 774 (after hours)
Open all year, Mon–Fri 9am–5pm; Easter to Sept, Sat 9am–5pm;
July–Aug, Mon–Fri 9am–5.30pm, Sat 9am–1pm and 1.30–5pm. ♿
🛈 151 Melmount Road, Sion Mills; ☎ 016626 58027
🛈 Abercorn Square, Strabane; ☎ 01504 883 735
Open Apr–Oct, Mon–Thur 9am–5pm, Fri–Sat 9am–4.30pm. ♿
🛈 Council Offices, 47 Derry Road, Strabane; ☎ 01504 382 204

Sperrin Heritage Centre – Open Apr–Oct, Mon–Sat, 11am (11.30am Sat)–6pm, Sun 2–7pm; last admission 45min before closing. Time 1 hr. £2, £1.10 (child/senior citizen), £6.25 (family). Audio-guide (French, German). Parking. Refreshments. ☎ 016626 48142.

Springhill (NT) – (♿) **House**: Open June–Aug, daily except Thur, 2–6pm; Apr–May and Sept, Sat–Sun and public holidays, 2–6pm; Good Friday–Easter Tuesday, daily, 2–6pm. £2.50, £1.25 (child). Parking. Refreshments. Wheelchair access to ground floor only; sympathetic hearing scheme. ☎ 01648 748 210.

Wellbrook Beetling Mill (NT) – Open July–Aug, daily except Tues, 2–6pm; Apr–June and Sept, Sat–Sun and public holidays, 2–6pm; Good Friday–Easter Tuesday, daily, 2–6pm. £1.80, 90p (child), £4.50 (family). Guided tour (30min). Leaflet (French, German). Parking. ☎ 01648 751 735, 51715; Fax 016487 51735.

Drum Manor Forest Park – ♿ Open all year, daily, 8am–10pm (4.30pm winter). £1, £2.50 (car). Guided tour by appointment. Parking. Refreshments. Caravan and camping site. ☎ 01868 759 311.

Plantation of Ulster Museum – Open –Sept, daily, 11am–5pm. ☎ 01648 27800; Fax 01648 27732; e-mail info@workspace.org.uk
www.workspace.org.ik/plantation/

Ulster-American Folk Park and Visitor Centre – ♿ Open Easter-late Sept, Mon–Sat, 11am–6.30pm, Sun and public holidays, 11.30am–7pm; Oct–Easter, Mon–Fri, 10.30am–5pm; last admission 90min before closing. £3.50, £10 (family 2A+3C), £1.70 (child/senior citizen). Brochure (French, German). Parking. Café; picnic area. ☎ 01662 243 292; Fax 01662 242 241; e-mail uafp@iol.ie
www.folkpark.com

Ulster History Park – ♿ Open Apr–Sept, daily, 10.30am (11.30am Sun)–6.30pm (7pm Sun and public holidays); Oct–Mar, Mon–Fri, 10.30am–5pm. £3. Guided tour (2 hr). Brochure (French, German). Parking. Refreshments; picnic area; cafeteria. ☎ 01662 648 188; Fax 016626 48011.

Gortin Glen Forest Park – Open all year, daily, 10am–dusk. £3 (car). Guided tour (1 hr) by appointment. Parking. Café; picnic areas; barbecue by arrangement. Campsite £1.70 per person/night. Play area for children. ☎ 01662 648 217; Fax 016626 48070.

Gray's Printing Press (NT) – ♿ Open Apr–Sept, Tues–Sat, 2–5pm. £1.50, 75p (child), £3.50 (family). Audio-visual presentation. Guided tour (1 hr) by arrangement. ☎ 01504 884 094.

Wilson Ancestral Home – Open all year, daily, 1–6pm; ring the bell and wait.

Gateway Centre – ♿ Open Easter–Oct, Tues–Sat, 11am–4pm, Sun, 2–5pm. ☎ 01662 661 877.

Roe Valley Country Park – Open all year, daily. **Visitor Centre**: Open summer, daily, 10am–8pm; winter, Mon–Fri, 10am–5pm. Guided tours organized by the environmental educator (☎ 01504 67532). ☎ 01504 722 074.

Dungiven Priory (HM) – Open all year. No charge. ☎ 01232 235 000.

Maghera Old Church (HM) – Key from the Recreation Centre (reception) in St Lurach's Road, east of Bank Square. ☎ 01232 235 000.

National Trust Photographic Library

STRANGFORD LOUGH

🛈 The Stables, Castle Street, Portaferry; ☎ 012477 29 882. Open Easter–Sept, Mon–Sat 10am–5pm (5.30pm Jul–Aug), Sun 2–6pm. Hotel bookings. Bureau de change. ♿
🛈 31 Regent Street, Newtownards; ☎ 01247 826 846. Open all year, Mon–Fri 9.15am–5pm, Sat 9.30am–5pm; July–Aug, Mon–Thur 9am–5.15pm, Fri–Sat 9am–5.30pm. Bureau de change. ♿

Strangford Narrows Ferry – Operates all year, daily (except 25 Dec), every 30min: from **Strangford** (on the hour and half–hour) Mon–Fri, 7.30am–10.30pm, Sat, 8am–11pm, Sun, 9.30am–10.30pm; from **Portaferry** (15min past and 15min to the hour) Mon–Fri, 7.45am–10.45pm, Sat, 8.15am–11.15pm, Sun, 9.45am–10.45pm. Car £4; passenger 80p, 40p (child); motorcycle £2.50. ☎ 01396 881 637.

Strangford Tower House (HM) – Key from the house opposite. ☎ 01232 235 000.

Kilclief Castle (HM) – Open July–Aug, Tues–Sun and bank holiday Monday, 10am (2pm Sun)–7pm. 75p, 40p (child/senior citizen). ☎ 01232 235 000.

Quoile Countryside Centre – ♿ Open Apr–Sept, daily, 11am–5pm; otherwise, Sat–Sun, 1–5pm. Closed 1 Jan, 25–26 Dec. No charge. Guided tour (British sign language) by arrangement. Parking. Facilities for the disabled, wheelchair access to new bird–hide. ☎ 01396 615 520; Fax 01396 613 280.

Inch Abbey (HM) – Open Apr–Sept, Tues–Sun and bank holiday Monday, 10am (2pm Sun)–7pm; otherwise, Sat–Sun, 10am (2pm Sun)–4pm. 75p, 40p (child/senior citizen). Parking. ☎ 01232 235 000.

Delamont Country Park – Open all year, daily, 9am–dusk (5pm in winter). Playground for children. Look–out tower. Orienteering. Pony trekking. Parking. Tearoom; picnic area. Gift shop. Plant sales. Boat trips. ☎/Fax 01396 828 333 (Park Warden).

Nendrum Monastery (HM) – Open Apr–Sept, Tues–Sun and bank holiday Monday, 10am (2pm Sun)–7pm; Oct–Mar, Sat–Sun, 10am (2pm Sun)–4pm. 75p, 40p (child/senior citizen). Parking. ☎ 01232 235 000.

Wildfowl and Wetlands Trust (Castle Espie) – ♿ Open Mar–Oct, Mon–Sat 10.30am–5pm, Sun 11.30am–6pm; Nov–Feb, Mon–Fri 11.30am–4.15pm, Sat 11.30am–4.30pm, Sun 11.30am–5pm. Closed 24–25 Dec. £3.25, £2 (child), £2.70 (reduction), £8.50 (family 2A+3C). Bird–hides. Education centre. Parking. Coffee room. ☎ 01247 874 146.

Scrabo Country Park – ♿ Open all year. **Scrabo Tower**: Open Easter and June–Sept, daily except Fri, 11am–6.30pm. Time 30min. No charge. Parking. ☎ 01247 811 491; Fax 01247 820 695 (Warden).

Grey Abbey (HM) – Open Apr–Sept, Tues–Sun and bank holiday Monday, 10am (2pm Sun)–7pm. £1, 50p (child/senior citizen). Guided tour (30min). Parking. ☎ 01247 788 585 (Supervisor), 01232 235 000 (HQ in Belfast).

Exploris – ♿ Open daily, 10am (11am Sat, 1pm Sun)–6pm (5pm Sept–Feb). £3.75, £2.60 (reduction), £11.75 (family 2A+4C). Brochure. Leaflet. Visitor map and guide (French, German, Spanish). Parking. Café. Gift shop. Facilities for the disabled; ramp; lifts. ☎ 012477 28062; Fax 28396.

Index

Y – Z

Notes

Manufacture Française des Pneumatiques Michelin
Société en commandite par actions au capital de 2 000 000 000 de francs
Place des Carmes-Déchaux – 63000 Clermont-Ferrand (France)
R.C.S. Clermont-Fd B 855 200 507

© *Michelin et Cie, Propriétaires-éditeurs 1999*
Dépôt légal mars 1999 – ISBN 2-06-153503-8 – ISSN 0763-1383

Printed in the EU 02-99/4

Cover illustration by Arthur PHILIPPS

Michelin Green Guide Collection

France

- *Alsace, Lorraine, Champagne*
- *Atlantic Coast*
- *Auvergne, Rhône Valley*
- *Brittany*
- *Burgundy, Jura*
- *Châteaux of the Loire*
- *Dordogne, Berry, Limousin*
- *French Alps*
- *French Riviera*
- *Normandy*
- *Northern France and the Paris Region*
- *Paris*
- *Provence*
- *Pyrenees, Languedoc, Tarn Gorges*

World

- *Austria*
- *Belgium, Luxembourg*
- *Berlin*
- *Brussels*
- *California*
- *Canada*
- *Chicago*
- *Europe*
- *Florida*
- *France*
- *Germany*
- *Great Britain*
- *Greece*
- *Ireland*
- *Italy*
- *London*
- *Mexico, Guatemala, Belize*
- *Netherlands*
- *New England*
- *New York, New Jersey, Pennsylvania*
- *New York City*
- *Portugal*
- *Quebec*
- *Rome*
- *San Francisco*
- *Scandinavia, Finland*
- *Scotland*
- *Sicily*
- *Spain*
- *Switzerland*
- *Tuscany*
- *Venice*
- *Vienna*
- *Wales*
- *Washington DC*
- *The West Country of England*